ghton
in
ourt

CALIFORNIA

Printed in the U.S.A.

ISBN 978-0-544-20411-9

2 3 4 5 6 7 8 9 10 0877 22 21 20 19 18 17 16 15 14 13

4500431140 A B C D E F G

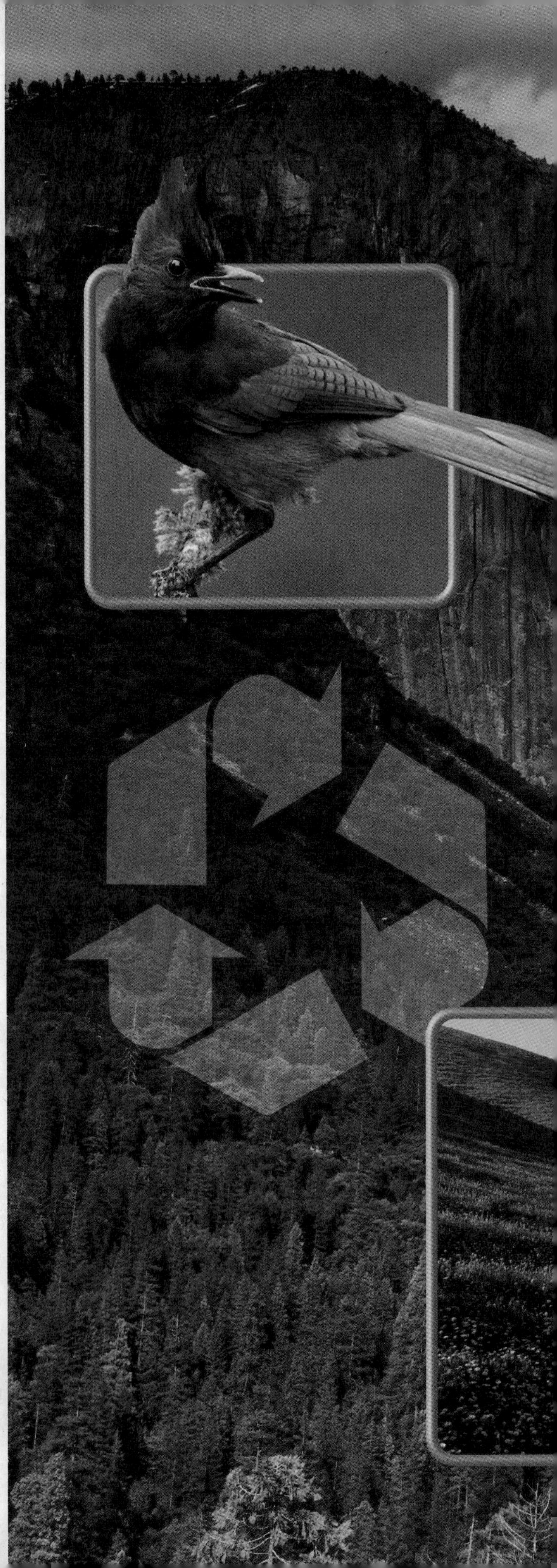

Dear Students and Families,

Welcome to **California Go Math!**, Grade 6! In this exciting mathematics program, there are hands-on activities to do and real-world problems to solve. Best of all, you will write your ideas and answers right in your book. In **California Go Math!**, writing and drawing on the pages helps you think deeply about what you are learning, and you will really understand math!

By the way, all of the pages in your **California Go Math!** book are made using recycled paper. We wanted you to know that you can Go Green with **California Go Math!**

Sincerely,

The Authors

Made in the United States
Text printed on 100% recycled paper

GO MATH!

Authors

Juli K. Dixon, Ph.D.
Professor, Mathematics Education
University of Central Florida
Orlando, Florida

Matthew R. Larson, Ph.D.
K-12 Curriculum Specialist for Mathematics
Lincoln Public Schools
Lincoln, Nebraska

Edward B. Burger, Ph.D.
President, Southwestern University
Georgetown, Texas

Martha E. Sandoval-Martinez
Math Instructor
El Camino College
Torrance, California

Steven J. Leinwand
Principal Research Analyst
American Institutes for Research (AIR)
Washington, D.C.

English Learners Consultant

Elizabeth Jiménez
CEO, GEMAS Consulting
Professional Expert on English Learner Education
Bilingual Education and Dual Language
Pomona, California

The Number System

Critical Area Completing understanding of division of fractions and extending the notion of number to the system of rational numbers, which includes negative numbers

Critical Area

GO DIGITAL

Go online! Your math lessons are interactive. Use iTools, Animated Math Models, the Multimedia eGlossary, and more.

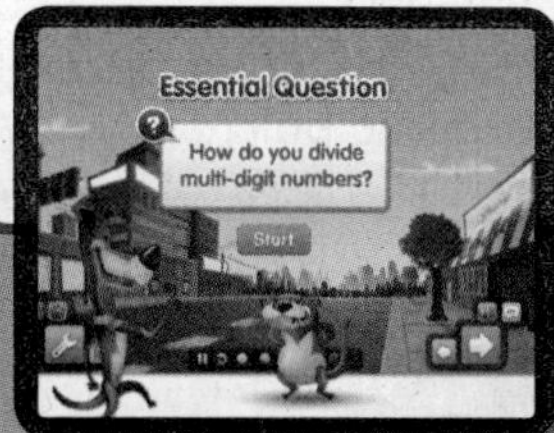

Chapter 1 Overview

In this chapter, you will explore and discover answers to the following **Essential Questions**:

- How do you solve real-world problems involving whole numbers and decimals?
- How does estimation help you solve problems involving decimals and whole numbers?
- How can you use the GCF and the LCM to solve problems?

Chapter 2 Overview

In this chapter, you will explore and discover answers to the following **Essential Questions**:

- How can you use the relationship between multiplication and division to divide fractions?
- What is a mixed number?
- How can you estimate products and quotients of fractions and mixed numbers?

Chapter 3 Overview

In this chapter, you will explore and discover answers to the following **Essential Questions**:

- How do you write, interpret, and use rational numbers?
- How do you calculate the absolute value of a number?
- How do you graph an ordered pair?

Ratios and Rates

Critical Area Connecting ratio and rate to whole number multiplication and division and using concepts of ratio and rate to solve problems

4 Ratios and Rates 151

Domain Ratios and Proportional Reasoning

CALIFORNIA COMMON CORE STANDARDS 6.RP.1, 6.RP.2, 6.RP.3a, 6.RP.3b

5 Percents 193

Domain Ratios and Proportional Reasoning

CALIFORNIA COMMON CORE STANDARDS 6.RP.3c

Critical Area

GO DIGITAL

Go online! Your math lessons are interactive. Use iTools, Animated Math Models, the Multimedia eGlossary, and more.

Chapter 4 Overview

In this chapter, you will explore and discover answers to the following **Essential Questions**:

- How can you use ratios to express relationships and solve problems?
- How can you write a ratio?
- What are equivalent ratios?
- How are rates related to ratios?

Chapter 5 Overview

In this chapter, you will explore and discover answers to the following **Essential Questions**:

- How can you use ratio reasoning to solve percent problems?
- How can you write a percent as a fraction?
- How can you use a ratio to find a percent of a number?

Chapter 6 Overview

In this chapter, you will explore and discover answers to the following **Essential Questions**:

- How can you use measurements to help you describe and compare objects?
- Why do you need to convert between units of measure?
- How can you use a ratio to convert units?
- How do you transform units to solve problems?

6 Units of Measure 227

Domain Ratios and Proportional Reasoning

CALIFORNIA COMMON CORE STANDARDS 6.RP.3d

Expressions and Equations

Critical Area Writing, interpreting, and using expressions and equations

7 Algebra: Expressions 259

Domain Expressions and Equations

CALIFORNIA COMMON CORE STANDARDS 6.EE.1, 6.EE.2a, 6.EE.2b, 6.EE.2c, 6.EE.3, 6.EE.4, 6.EE.6

Critical Area

GO DIGITAL

Go online! Your math lessons are interactive. Use iTools, Animated Math Models, the Multimedia eGlossary, and more.

Chapter 7 Overview

In this chapter, you will explore and discover answers to the following **Essential Questions**:

- How do you write, interpret, and use algebraic expressions?
- How can you use expressions to represent real-world situations?
- How do you use the order of operations to evaluate expressions?
- How can you tell whether two expressions are equivalent?

Chapter 8 Overview

In this chapter, you will explore and discover answers to the following **Essential Questions**:

- How can you use equations and inequalities to represent situations and solve problems?
- How can you use Properties of Equality to solve equations?
- How do inequalities differ from equations?
- Why is it useful to describe situations by using algebra?

8 Algebra: Equations and Inequalities 305

Domain Expressions and Equations

CALIFORNIA COMMON CORE STANDARDS 6.EE.5, 6.EE.7, 6.EE.8

Chapter 9 Overview

In this chapter, you will explore and discover answers to the following **Essential Questions**:

- How can you show relationships between variables?
- How can you determine the equation that gives the relationship between two variables?
- How can you use tables and graphs to visualize the relationship between two variables?

9 Algebra: Relationships Between Variables 355

Domain Expressions and Equations

CALIFORNIA COMMON CORE STANDARDS 6.EE.9

Geometry and Statistics

COMMON CORE **Critical Area** Solve real-world and mathematical problems involving area, surface area, and volume; and developing understanding of statistical thinking

10 Area 387

Domain Geometry

CALIFORNIA COMMON CORE STANDARDS 6.G.1, 6.G.3

11 Surface Area and Volume 433

Domain Geometry

CALIFORNIA COMMON CORE STANDARDS 6.G.2, 6.G.4

Critical Area

GO DIGITAL

Go online! Your math lessons are interactive. Use iTools, Animated Math Models, the Multimedia eGlossary, and more.

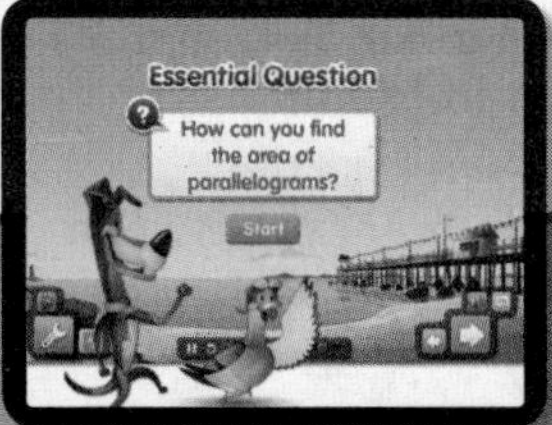

Chapter 10 Overview

In this chapter, you will explore and discover answers to the following **Essential Questions**:

- How can you use measurements to describe two-dimensional figures?
- What does area represent?
- How are the areas of rectangles and parallelograms related?
- How are the areas of triangles and trapezoids related?

Chapter 11 Overview

In this chapter, you will explore and discover answers to the following **Essential Questions**:

- How can you use measurements to describe three-dimensional figures?
- How can you use a net to find the surface area of a three-dimensional figure?
- How can you find the volume of a rectangular prism?

Chapter 12 Overview

In this chapter, you will explore and discover answers to the following **Essential Questions**:

- How can you display data and analyze measures of center?
- When does it make sense to display data in a dot plot? in a histogram?
- What are the differences between the three measures of center?

12 Data Displays and Measures of Center 471

Domain Statistics and Probability

CALIFORNIA COMMON CORE STANDARDS 6.SP.1, 6.SP.4, 6.SP.5a, 6.SP.5b, 6.SP.5c, 6.SP.5d

Chapter 13 Overview

In this chapter, you will explore and discover answers to the following **Essential Questions**:

- How can you describe the shape of a data set using graphs, measures of center, and measures of variability?
- How do you calculate the different measures of center?
- How do you calculate the different measures of variability?

13 Variability and Data Distributions 513

Domain Statistics and Probability

CALIFORNIA COMMON CORE STANDARDS 6.SP.2, 6.SP.3, 6.SP.4, 6.SP.5c, 6.SP.5d

Critical Area

The Number System

CRITICAL AREA Completing understanding of division of fractions and extending the notion of number to the system of rational numbers, which includes negative numbers

California is one of the nation's largest growers of apples.

Project

Sweet Success

Businesses that sell food products need to combine ingredients in the correct amounts. They also need to determine what price to charge for the products they sell.

Get Started

A company sells Apple Cherry Mix. They make large batches of the mix that can be used to fill 250 bags each. Determine how many pounds of each ingredient should be used to make one batch of Apple Cherry Mix. Then decide how much the company should charge for each bag of Apple Cherry Mix, and explain how you made your decision.

Important Facts

Ingredients in Apple Cherry Mix (1 bag)

- $\frac{3}{4}$ pound of dried apples
- $\frac{1}{2}$ pound of dried cherries
- $\frac{1}{4}$ pound of walnuts

Cost of Ingredients

- dried apples: $2.80 per pound
- dried cherries: $4.48 per pound
- walnuts: $3.96 per pound

Completed by ______________________

Chapter 1

Whole Numbers and Decimals

Show What You Know

Check your understanding of important skills.

Name ______________________

Factors **Find all of the factors of the number.**

1. 16 ______________
2. 27 ______________
3. 30 ______________
4. 45 ______________

Round Decimals **Round to the place of the underlined digit.**

5. 0.3<u>2</u>3 → 0.3̲23
6. 4̲.096
7. 10̲.67
8. 5.27̲8

Multiply 3-Digit and 4-Digit Numbers **Multiply.**

9. $2{,}143 \times 6$
10. 375×8
11. $3{,}762 \times 7$
12. 603×9

Math Detective

Maxwell saved $18 to buy a fingerprinting kit that costs $99. He spent 0.25 of his savings to buy a magnifying glass. Be a Math Detective and help Maxwell find out how much more he needs to save to buy the fingerprinting kit.

Personal Math Trainer
Online Assessment and Intervention

Vocabulary Builder

▶ Visualize It

Complete the Flow Map using the words with a ✓.

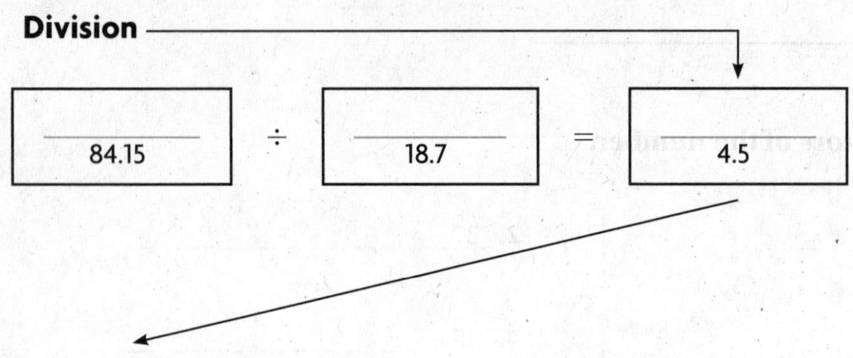

Review Words

✓ compatible numbers
decimal
✓ dividend
divisible
✓ divisor
factor
prime number
✓ quotient
thousandth

Preview Words

common factor
greatest common factor
least common multiple
prime factorization

▶ Understand Vocabulary

Complete the sentences using the preview words.

1. The least number that is a common multiple of two or more numbers is the ______________________.

2. The greatest factor that two or more numbers have in common is the ______________________.

3. A number that is a factor of two or more numbers is a ______________________.

4. A number written as the product of its prime factors is the ______________________ of the number.

GO DIGITAL
• Interactive Student Edition
• Multimedia eGlossary

Name ____________________

Divide Multi-Digit Numbers

Essential Question How do you divide multi-digit numbers?

The Number System—6.NS.2

MATHEMATICAL PRACTICES
MP.1, MP.2

Unlock the Problem 

When you watch a cartoon, the frames of film seem to blend together to form a moving image. A cartoon lasting just 92 seconds requires 2,208 frames. How many frames do you see each second when you watch a cartoon?

 **Divide** 2,208 ÷ 92.

Estimate using compatible numbers. _____ ÷ _____ = _____

```
       2□
 92)2,208    Divide the tens.
   -1 84↓
      368    Divide the ones.
    -  □
       □
```

Compare your estimate with the quotient. Since the estimate, _____, is close to _____, the answer is reasonable.

So, you see _____ frames each second when you watch a cartoon.

Example 1 Divide 12,749 ÷ 18.

Estimate using compatible numbers. _____ ÷ _____ = _____

STEP 1 Divide.

```
        70□ r5
 18)12,749
   -12 6↓ |
       14 |
     -  0 ↓
       149
     -  □
        □
```

STEP 2 Check your answer.

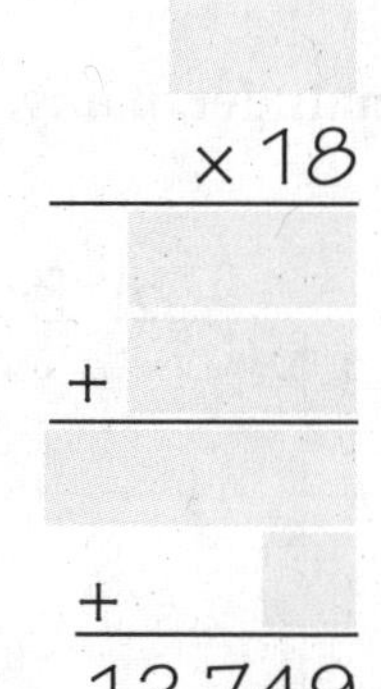

```
     □
   × 18      Multiply the whole number part of the quotient by the divisor.
     □
   + □
     □
   + □       Add the remainder.
   12,749
```

So, 12,749 ÷ 18 = __________.

Math Idea

You can write a remainder with an r, as a fractional part of the divisor, or as a decimal. For 131 ÷ 5, the quotient can be written as 26 r1, $26\frac{1}{5}$, or 26.2.

Example 2

Divide 59,990 ÷ 280. **Write the remainder as a fraction.**

Estimate using compatible numbers. ______ ÷ ______ = ______

STEP 1 Divide.

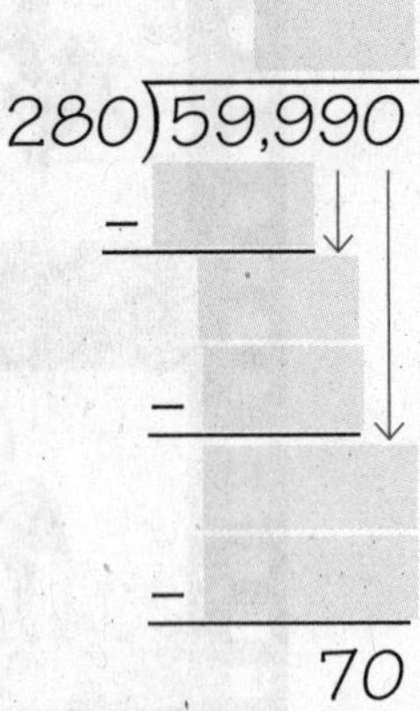

STEP 2 Write the remainder as a fraction.

$\frac{\text{remainder}}{\text{divisor}} = \frac{\square}{280}$ Write the remainder over the divisor.

$\frac{70 \div \square}{280 \div \square} = \frac{\square}{\square}$ Simplify.

Compare your estimate with the quotient. Since the estimate, ______ is close to ______, the answer is reasonable.

So, 59,990 ÷ 280 = ______.

MATHEMATICAL PRACTICE 1 Describe two ways to check your answer in Example 2.

______

______

______

Share and Show

Estimate. Then find the quotient. Write the remainder, if any, with an r.

1. $29\overline{)986}$ **Think:** 30 × 3 = 90

______

2. $37\overline{)3,786}$

______

Name ____________________

Share and Show

Estimate. Then find the quotient. Write the remainder, if any, as a fraction.

3. 6,114 ÷ 63

4. 11,050 ÷ 26

Mathematical Practices

Explain why you can use multiplication to check a division problem.

On Your Own

Estimate. Then find the quotient. Write the remainder, if any, as a fraction.

5. 3,150 ÷ 9

6. 2,115 ÷ 72

7. 20,835 ÷ 180

Find the least whole number that can replace ■ to make the statement true.

8. ■ ÷ 9 > 700

9. ■ ÷ 19 > 89

10. 110 < ■ ÷ 47

11. MATHEMATICAL PRACTICE 2 **Use Reasoning** Name two whole numbers that can replace ■ to make both statements true.

2 × ■ < 1,800 ÷ 12   ■ > 3,744 ÷ 52

12. GO DEEPER A factory produces 30,480 bolts in 12 hours. If the same number of bolts are produced each hour, how many bolts does the factory produce in 5 hours?

Problem Solving • Applications Real World

Use the table for 13–16.

13. A Boeing 747-400 jet carried 6,045 passengers last week, and all of its flights were full. How many flights did the jet make last week?

14. GO DEEPER Last month an airline made 6,322 reservations for flights from Newark, New Jersey, to Frankfurt, Germany. If there were 21 full flights and 64 reservations were cancelled, which airplane made the flights?

15. THINK SMARTER An airline carries about 750 passengers from Houston to Chicago each day. How many McDonnell Douglas MD-90 jets would be needed to carry this many passengers, and how many empty seats would there be?

Airplane Passenger Seats

Type of Plane	Seats
Airbus A330-300	298
Boeing 747-400	403
McDonnell Douglas MD-90	160
Embraer 170	70

WRITE Math • Show Your Work

16. THINK SMARTER **Pose a Problem** Refer back to Problem 13. Use the information in the table to write a similar problem involving airplane passenger seats.

17. THINK SMARTER For numbers 17a–17d, choose Yes or No to indicate whether the equation is correct.

17a. 1,350 ÷ 5 = 270 ○ Yes ○ No

17b. 3,732 ÷ 4 = 933 ○ Yes ○ No

17c. 4,200 ÷ 35 = 12 ○ Yes ○ No

17d. 1,586 ÷ 13 = 122 ○ Yes ○ No

FOR MORE PRACTICE: Standards Practice Book

Name ____________________________________

Prime Factorization

Essential Question How do you write the prime factorization of a number?

The Number System—6.NS.4

MATHEMATICAL PRACTICES
MP.1, MP.7, MP.8

Unlock the Problem

Secret codes are often used to send information over the Internet. Many of these codes are based on very large numbers. For some codes, a computer must determine the prime factorization of these numbers to decode the information.

The **prime factorization** of a number is the number written as a product of all of its prime factors.

One Way Use a factor tree.

The key for a code is based on the prime factorization of 180. Find the prime factorization of 180.

Remember

A prime number is a whole number greater than 1 that has exactly two factors: itself and 1.

Choose any two factors whose product is 180. Continue finding factors until only prime factors are left.

A Use a basic fact.

Think: 10 times what number is equal to 180?

10 × ________ = 180

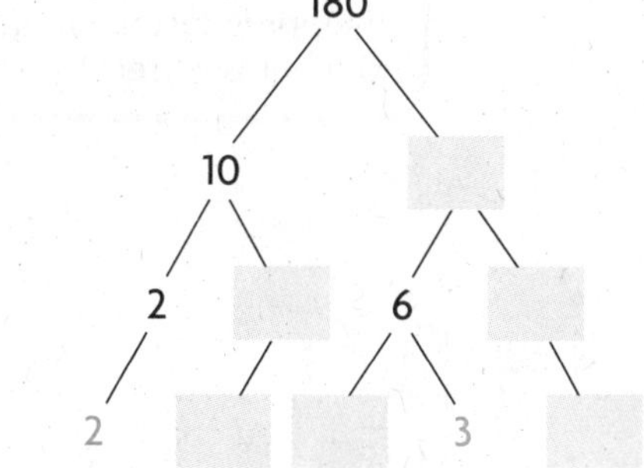

B Use a divisibility rule.

Think: 180 is even, so it is divisible by 2.

2 × ________ = 180

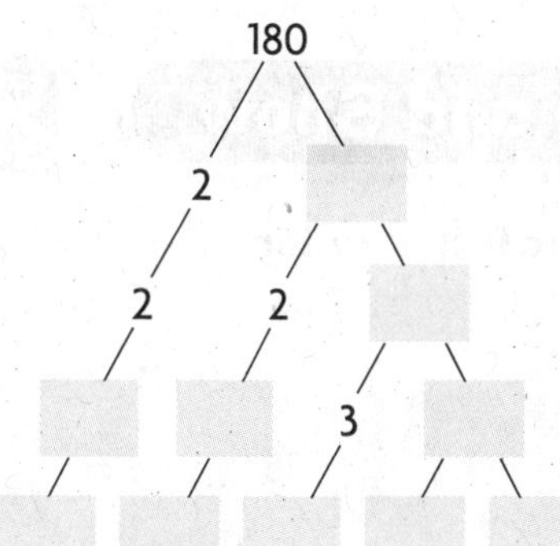

180 = ________ × ________ × ________ × ________ × ________ List the prime factors from least to greatest.

So, the prime factorization of 180 is ________ × ________ × ________ × ________ × ________.

Math Talk Mathematical Practices

Explain how you know whether a number is divisible by another number.

Another Way Use a ladder diagram.

The key for a code is based on the prime factorization of 140. Find the prime factorization of 140.

Choose a prime factor of 140. Continue dividing by prime factors until the quotient is 1.

A Use the divisibility rule for 2.

Think: 140 is even, so 140 is divisible by 2.

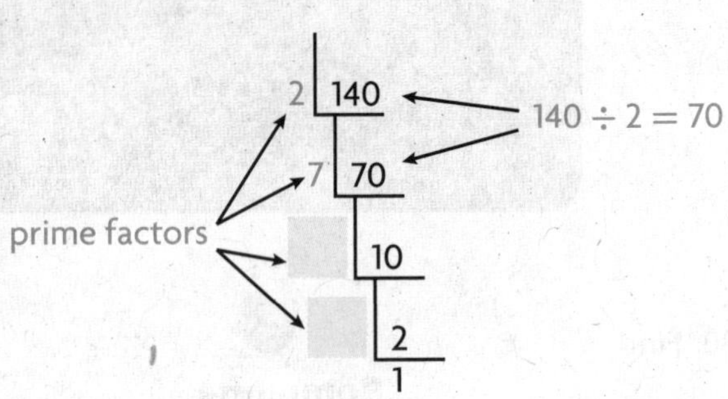

140 = ______ × ______ × ______ × ______

B Use the divisibility rule for 5.

Think: The last digit is 0, so 140 is divisible by 5.

5 | 140
2 |
14
2

List the prime factors from least to greatest.

So, the prime factorization of 140 is ______ × ______ × ______ × ______.

Math Talk **Mathematical Practices**

How can you check whether the prime factorization of a number is correct?

Share and Show

Find the prime factorization.

1. 18

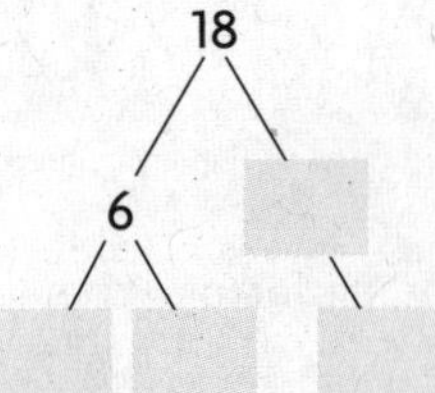

18 = ______ × ______ × ______

2. 42

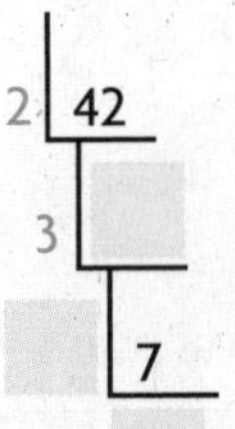

42 = ______ × ______ × ______

Name ______________________

Share and Show

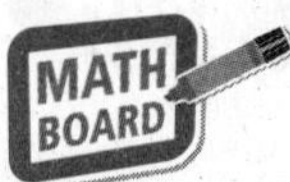

Find the prime factorization.

3. 75

✓ 4. 12

✓ 5. 65

Mathematical Practices

Explain why a prime number cannot be written as a product of prime factors.

On Your Own

Write the number whose prime factorization is given.

6. $2 \times 2 \times 2 \times 7$

7. $2 \times 2 \times 5 \times 5$

8. $2 \times 2 \times 2 \times 2 \times 3 \times 3$

Practice: Copy and Solve **Find the prime factorization.**

9. 45

10. 50

11. 32

12. 76

13. 108

14. 126

15. The area of a rectangle is the product of its length and width. A rectangular poster has an area of 260 square inches. The width of the poster is greater than 10 inches and is a prime number. What is the width of the poster?

16. MATHEMATICAL PRACTICE 7 **Look for Structure** Dani says she is thinking of a secret number. As a clue, she says the number is the least whole number that has three different prime factors. What is Dani's secret number? What is its prime factorization?

Problem Solving • Applications Real World

Use the table for 17–19. Agent Sanchez must enter a code on a keypad to unlock the door to her office.

17. In August, the digits of the code number are the prime factors of 150. What is the code number for the office door in August?

18. GO DEEPER In September, the fourth digit of the code number is 2 more than the fourth digit of the code number based on the prime factors of 225. The prime factors of what number were used for the code in September?

Code Number Rules
1. The code is a 4-digit number.
2. Each digit is a prime number.
3. The prime numbers are entered from least to greatest.
4. The code number is changed at the beginning of each month.

19. THINK SMARTER One day in October, Agent Sanchez enters the code 3477. How do you know that this code is incorrect and will not open the door?

WRITE Math • Show Your Work

20. THINK SMARTER Use the numbers to complete the factor tree. You may use a number more than once.

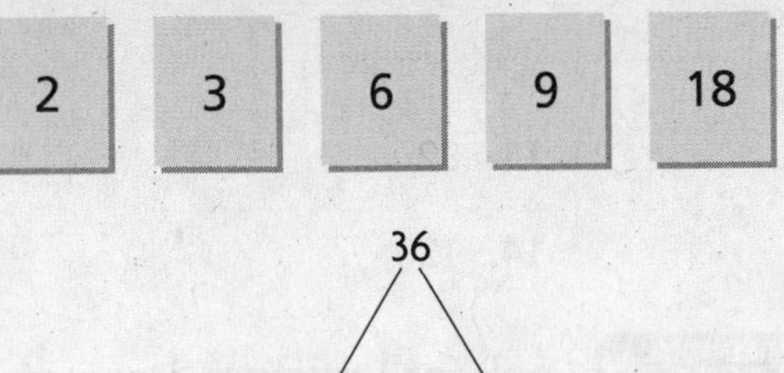

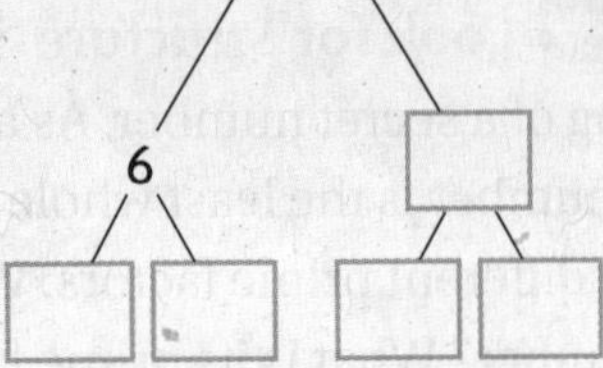

Write the prime factorization of 36.

FOR MORE PRACTICE:
Standards Practice Book

Name ______________________________

Least Common Multiple

Essential Question How can you find the least common multiple of two whole numbers?

The Number System—6.NS.4
MATHEMATICAL PRACTICES
MP.4, MP.6

Unlock the Problem

In an experiment, each flowerpot will get one seed. If the flowerpots are in packages of 6 and the seeds are in packets of 8, what is the least number of plants that can be grown without any seeds or pots left over?

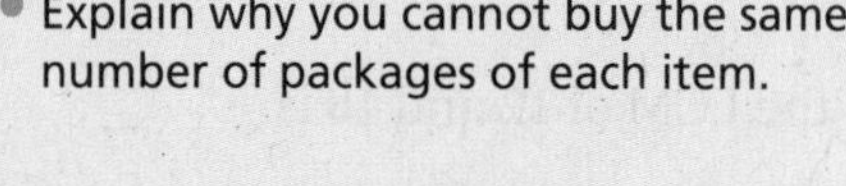

- Explain why you cannot buy the same number of packages of each item.

____

____

____

The **least common multiple**, or **LCM**, is the least number that is a common multiple of two or more numbers.

One Way Use a list.

Make a list of the first eight nonzero multiples of 6 and 8. Circle the common multiples. Then find the least common multiple.

Multiples of 6: 6, 12, 18, ______, ______, ______, ______, ______

Multiples of 8: 8, 16, 24, ______, ______, ______, ______, ______

The least common multiple, or LCM, is ______.

Another Way Use prime factorization and a Venn diagram.

Write the prime factorization of each number.

$6 = 2 \times$ ______

$8 = 2 \times$ ______ $\times$ ______

List the common prime factors of the numbers, if any.

6 and 8 have one prime factor of ______ in common.

Place the prime factors of the numbers in the appropriate parts of the Venn diagram.

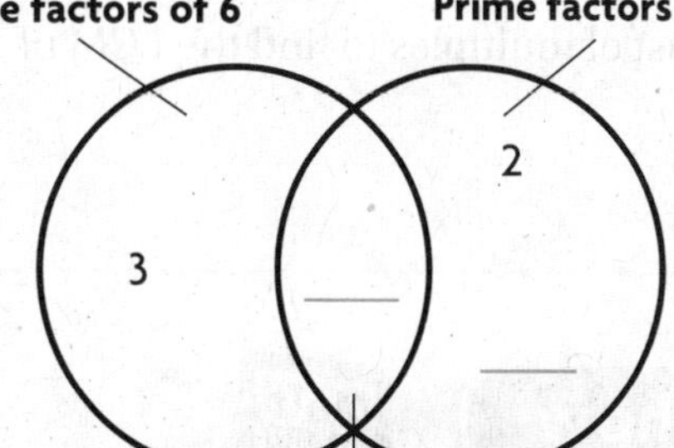

To find the LCM, find the product of all of the prime factors in the Venn diagram.

$3 \times 2 \times 2 \times 2 =$ ______

The LCM is ______.

So, the least number of plants is ______.

Math Talk Mathematical Practices

Explain how the diagram shows the prime factorization of 6 and 8.

Example Use prime factorization to find the LCM of 12 and 18.

Write the prime factorization of each number.

$12 = 2 \times 2 \times$ ____

Line up the common factors.

$18 = 2 \quad \times \quad 3 \quad \times$ ____

Multiply one number from each column.

$2 \times 2 \times \quad 3 \quad \times \quad 3 = 36$

Math Idea

The factors in the prime factorization of a number are usually listed in order from least to greatest.

So, the LCM of 12 and 18 is ____.

Try This! **Find the LCM.**

A 10, 15, and 25

Use prime factorization.

10 = ____

15 = ____

25 = ____

____

The LCM is ____.

B 3 and 12

Use a list.

Multiples of 3: ____

Multiples of 12: ____

The LCM is ____.

1. How can you tell whether the LCM of a pair of numbers is one of the numbers? Give an example.

____

____

2. MATHEMATICAL PRACTICE 6 **Explain** one reason why you might use prime factorization instead of making a list of multiples to find the LCM of 10, 15, and 25.

____

____

Share and Show

1. List the first six nonzero multiples of 6 and 9. Circle the common multiples. Then find the LCM.

Multiples of 6: ____

Multiples of 9: ____

The LCM of 6 and 9 is ____.

Name ____________________

Share and Show

Find the LCM.

2. 3, 5 ______

3. 3, 9 ______

4. 9, 15 ______

Math Talk — Mathematical Practices

Explain what the LCM of two numbers represents.

On Your Own

Find the LCM.

5. 5, 10 ______

6. 3, 8 ______

7. 9, 12 ______

MATHEMATICAL PRACTICE 2 Use Reasoning **Algebra** **Write the unknown number for the ■.**

8. 5, 8 LCM: ■

■ = ______

9. 5, ■ LCM: 15

■ = ______

10. ■, 6 LCM: 42

■ = ______

11. MATHEMATICAL PRACTICE 3 Verify the Reasoning of Others Mr. Haigwood is shopping for a school picnic. Veggie burgers come in packages of 15, and buns come in packages of 6. He wants to serve veggie burgers on buns and wants to have no items left over. Mr. Haigwood says that he will have to buy at least 90 of each item, since $6 \times 15 = 90$. Do you agree with his reasoning? Explain.

______

______

12. GO DEEPER A deli has a special one-day event to celebrate its anniversary. On the day of the event, every eighth customer receives a free drink. Every twelfth customer receives a free sandwich. If 200 customers show up for the event, how many of the customers will receive both a free drink and a free sandwich?

______

Unlock the Problem Real World

13. Katie is making hair clips to sell at the craft fair. To make each hair clip, she uses 1 barrette and 1 precut ribbon. The barrettes are sold in packs of 12, and the precut ribbons are sold in packs of 9. How many packs of each item does she need to buy to make the least number of hair clips with no supplies left over?

a. What information are you given? ______

______

______

b. What problem are you being asked to solve? ______

______

______

c. Show the steps you use to solve the problem.

d. Complete the sentences.

The least common multiple of 12 and 9 is ______.

Katie can make ______ hair clips with no supplies left over.

To get 36 barrettes and 36 ribbons, she needs to buy ______ packs of barrettes and ______ packs of precut ribbons.

14. THINK SMARTER Reptile stickers come in sheets of 6 and fish stickers come in sheets of 9. Antonio buys the same number of both types of stickers and he buys at least 100 of each type. What is the least number of sheets of each type he might buy?

______

______

15. THINK SMARTER For numbers 15a–15d, choose Yes or No to indicate whether the LCM of the two numbers is 16.

15a. 2, 8 ○ Yes ○ No

15b. 2, 16 ○ Yes ○ No

15c. 4, 8 ○ Yes ○ No

15d. 8, 16 ○ Yes ○ No

FOR MORE PRACTICE: Standards Practice Book

Name ______________________________

Greatest Common Factor

Essential Question How can you find the greatest common factor of two whole numbers?

The Number System—6.NS.4

MATHEMATICAL PRACTICES
MP.2, MP.4

A **common factor** is a number that is a factor of two or more numbers. The numbers 16 and 20 have 1, 2, and 4 as common factors.

Factors of 16: (1), (2), (4), 8, 16

Factors of 20: (1), (2), (4), 5, 10, 20

The **greatest common factor**, or **GCF**, is the greatest factor that two or more numbers have in common. The greatest common factor of 16 and 20 is 4.

Remember

A number that is multiplied by another number to find a product is a factor.

Factors of 6: 1, 2, 3, 6

Factors of 9: 1, 3, 9

Every number has 1 as a factor.

Unlock the Problem

Jim is cutting two strips of wood to make picture frames. The wood strips measure 12 inches and 18 inches. He wants to cut the strips into equal lengths that are as long as possible. Into what lengths should he cut the wood?

12 inches

18 inches

Find the greatest common factor, or GCF, of 12 and 18.

One Way Use a list.

Factors of 12: 1, 2, ______, ______, ______, 12

Factors of 18: 1, ______, ______, ______, ______, ______

The greatest common factor, or GCF, is ______.

Mathematical Practices

Into what other lengths could Jim cut the wood to obtain equal lengths?

Write the prime factorization of each number.

$12 = 2 \times$ ______ $\times 3$

$18 =$ ______ $\times 3 \times$ ______

Place the prime factors of the numbers in the appropriate parts of the Venn diagram.

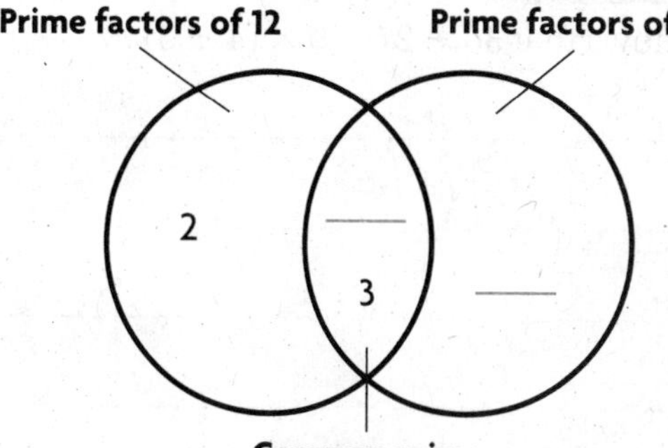

To find the GCF, find the product of the common prime factors.

$2 \times 3 =$ ______ The GCF is ______.

So, Jim should cut the wood into ______-inch lengths.

Distributive Property

Multiplying a sum by a number is the same as multiplying each addend by the number and then adding the products.	$5 \times (8 + 6) = (5 \times 8) + (5 \times 6)$

You can use the Distributive Property to express the sum of two whole numbers as a product if the numbers have a common factor.

Example Use the GCF and the Distributive Property to express 36 + 27 as a product.

Find the GCF of 36 and 27. GCF: ______

Write each number as the product of the GCF and another factor.

$36 + 27$

$(9 \times \_\_\_\_) + (9 \times \_\_\_\_)$

Use the Distributive Property to write 36 + 27 as a product. $9 \times (4 + \_\_\_\_)$

Check your answer. $36 + 27 = \_\_\_\_$

$9 \times (4 + \_\_\_\_) = 9 \times \_\_\_\_ = \_\_\_\_$

So, $36 + 27 = \_\_\_\_ \times (\_\_\_\_ + \_\_\_\_)$.

1. Explain two ways to find the GCF of 36 and 27.

______

______

2. MATHEMATICAL PRACTICE 4 **Use Diagrams** Describe how the figure at the right shows that $36 + 27 = 9 \times (4 + 3)$.

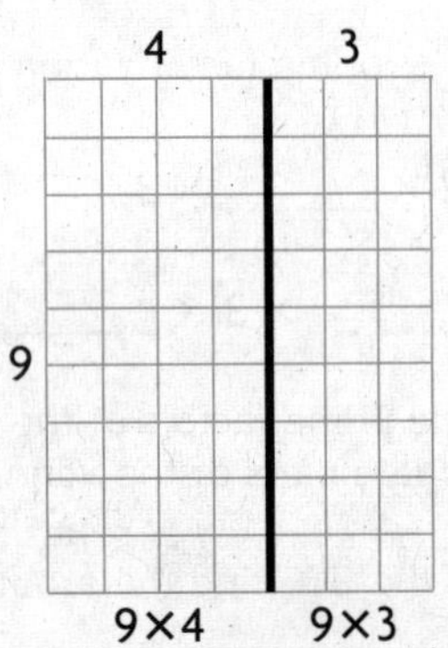

______

______

______

______

______

______

Name ______________________

Share and Show

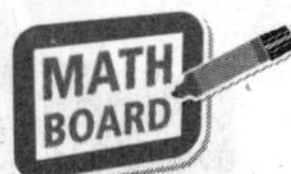

1. List the factors of 12 and 20. Circle the GCF.

Factors of 12: ______________

Factors of 20: ______________

Find the GCF.

2. 16, 18

3. 25, 40

✓4. 24, 40

5. 14, 35

Use the GCF and the Distributive Property to express the sum as a product.

6. 21 + 28

✓7. 15 + 27

8. 40 + 15

9. 32 + 20

Math Talk — **Mathematical Practices**

Explain how to use the prime factorization of two numbers to find their GCF.

On Your Own

Find the GCF.

10. 8, 25

11. 31, 32

12. 56, 64

13. 150, 275

Use the GCF and the Distributive Property to express the sum as a product.

14. 24 + 30

15. 49 + 14

16. 63 + 81

17. 60 + 12

18. MATHEMATICAL PRACTICE 1 **Describe** the difference between the LCM and the GCF of two numbers.

____

Problem Solving • Applications Real World

Use the table for 19–22. Teachers at the Scott School of Music teach only one instrument in each class.

19. Francisco teaches group lessons to all of the violin and viola students at the Scott School of Music. All of his classes have the same number of students. What is the greatest number of students he can have in each class?

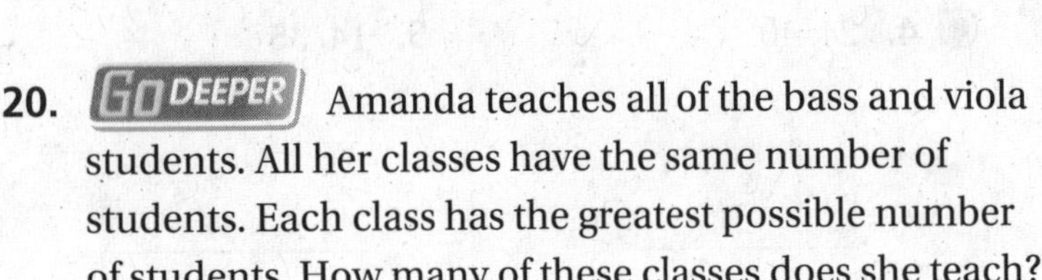

____

20. GO DEEPER Amanda teaches all of the bass and viola students. All her classes have the same number of students. Each class has the greatest possible number of students. How many of these classes does she teach?

____

Scott School of Music	
Instrument	Number of Students
Bass	20
Cello	27
Viola	30
Violin	36

21. THINK SMARTER Mia teaches jazz classes. She has 9 students in each class, and she teaches all the students who play two instruments. How many students does she have, and which two instruments does she teach?

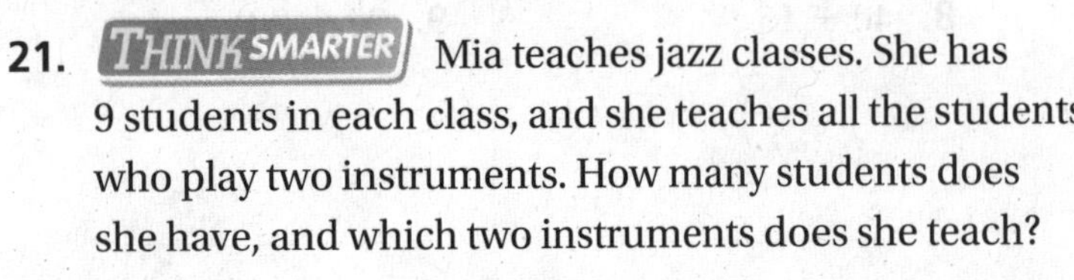

____

22. WRITE ▸*Math* Explain how you could use the GCF and the Distributive Property to express the sum of the number of bass students and the number of violin students as a product.

____

____

____

____

23. THINK SMARTER The prime factorization of each number is shown.

$6 = 2 \times 3$

$12 = 2 \times 2 \times 3$

Using the prime factorization, complete the Venn diagram and write the GCF of 6 and 12.

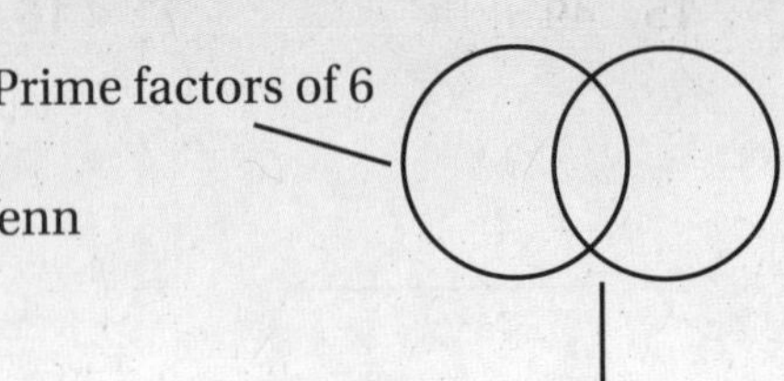

GCF = ______________________

FOR MORE PRACTICE:
Standards Practice Book

Name ____________________

Problem Solving • Apply the Greatest Common Factor

Essential Question How can you use the strategy *draw a diagram* to help you solve problems involving the GCF and the Distributive Property?

The Number System—6.NS.4

MATHEMATICAL PRACTICES
MP.1, MP.4, MP.5, MP.6

Unlock the Problem (Real World)

A trophy case at Riverside Middle School holds 18 baseball trophies and 24 soccer trophies. All shelves hold the same number of trophies. Only one sport is represented on each shelf. What is the greatest number of trophies that can be on each shelf? How many shelves are there for each sport?

Use the graphic organizer to help you solve the problem.

Read the Problem

What do I need to find?

I need to find ____________________

____

____

What information do I need to use?

I need to use ____________________

____

How will I use the information?

I can find the GCF of __________ and use it to draw a diagram representing

the __________ of the trophy case.

Solve the Problem

Total trophies = baseball + soccer

18 + 24

Find the GCF of 18 and 24. GCF: ______

Write each number as the product of the GCF and another factor.

18 + 24

(6 × ______) + (6 × ______)

Use the Distributive Property to write 18 + 24 as a product.

6 × (______ + ______)

Use the product to draw a diagram of the trophy case. Use B's to represent baseball trophies. Use S's to represent soccer trophies.

B B B B B B

S S S S S S

So, there are ______ trophies on each shelf. There are ______ shelves of baseball trophies and ______ shelves of soccer trophies.

Math Talk — **Mathematical Practices**

Explain how the Distributive Property helped you solve the problem.

Try Another Problem

Delia is bagging 24 onion bagels and 16 plain bagels for her bakery customers. Each bag will hold only one type of bagel. Each bag will hold the same number of bagels. What is the greatest number of bagels she can put in each bag? How many bags of each type of bagel will there be?

Use the graphic organizer to help you solve the problem.

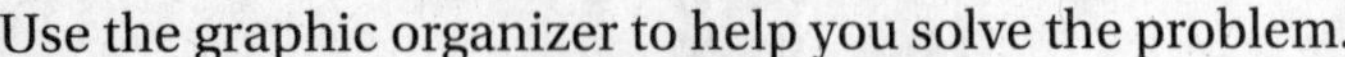

Read the Problem	Solve the Problem
What do I need to find?	
What information do I need to use?	
How will I use the information?	

So, there will be ______ bagels in each bag. There will be ______ bags of onion bagels and ______ bags of plain bagels.

- MATHEMATICAL PRACTICE 6 **Explain** how knowing that the GCF of 24 and 16 is 8 helped you solve the bagel problem.

____

____

Name ______________________________

Share and Show

1. Toby is packaging 21 baseball cards and 12 football cards to sell at a swap meet. Each packet will have the same number of cards. Each packet will have cards for only one sport. What is the greatest number of cards he can place in each packet? How many packets will there be for each sport?

First, find the GCF of 21 and 12.

____

Next, use the Distributive Property to write 21 + 12 as a product, with the GCF as one of the factors.

____

So, there will be ______ packets of baseball cards and ______ packets of football cards. Each packet will contain ______ cards.

2. THINK SMARTER **What if** Toby had decided to keep one baseball card for himself and sell the rest? How would your answers to the previous problem have changed?

____

____

____

____

3. Melissa bought 42 pine seedlings and 30 juniper seedlings to plant in rows on her tree farm. She wants each row to have the same number of seedlings. She wants only one type of seedling in each row. What is the greatest number of seedlings she can plant in each row? How many rows of each type of tree will there be?

____

____

____

Unlock the Problem

- ✓ Circle important facts.
- ✓ Check to make sure you answered the question.
- ✓ Check your answer.

WRITE ▸ Math
Show Your Work

On Your Own

4. MATHEMATICAL PRACTICE 1 **Make Sense of Problems** A drum and bugle marching band has 45 members who play bugles and 27 members who play drums. When they march, each row has the same number of players. Each row has only bugle players or only drummers. What is the greatest number of players there can be in each row? How many rows of each type of player can there be?

WRITE Math • Show Your Work

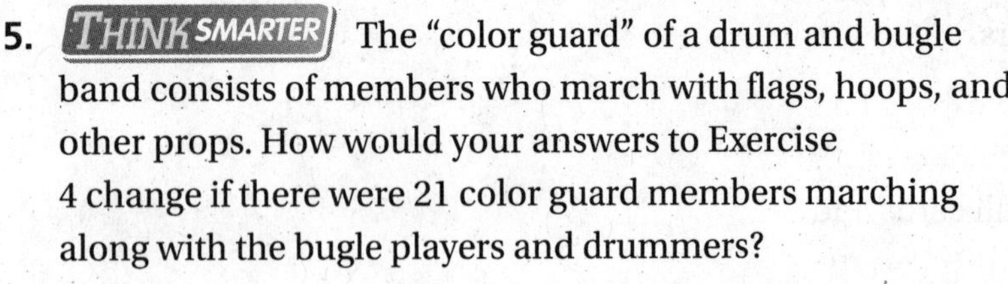

5. THINK SMARTER The "color guard" of a drum and bugle band consists of members who march with flags, hoops, and other props. How would your answers to Exercise 4 change if there were 21 color guard members marching along with the bugle players and drummers?

6. GO DEEPER If you continue the pattern below so that you write all of the numbers in the pattern less than 500, how many even numbers will you write?

4, 9, 14, 19, 24, 29...

Personal Math Trainer

7. THINK SMARTER + Mr. Yaw's bookcase holds 20 nonfiction books and 15 fiction books. Each shelf holds the same number of books and contains only one type of book. How many books will be on each shelf if each shelf has the **greatest** possible number of books? Show your work.

FOR MORE PRACTICE:
Standards Practice Book

Name ___________________________________

Mid-Chapter Checkpoint

Vocabulary

Choose the best term from the box to complete the sentence.

Vocabulary
greatest common factor
least common multiple
prime number

1. The ______________________ of two numbers is greater than or equal to the numbers. (p.13)

2. The ______________________ of two numbers is less than or equal to the numbers. (p.17)

Concepts and Skills

Estimate. Then find the quotient. Write the remainder, if any, with an r. (6.NS.2)

3. 2,800 ÷ 25

4. 19,129 ÷ 37

5. 32,111 ÷ 181

Find the prime factorization. (6.NS.4)

6. 44

7. 36

8. 90

Find the LCM. (6.NS.4)

9. 8, 10

10. 4, 14

11. 6, 9

Find the GCF. (6.NS.4)

12. 16, 20

13. 8, 52

14. 36, 54

15. A zookeeper divided 2,440 pounds of food equally among 8 elephants. How many pounds of food did each elephant receive? (6.NS.2)

16. DVD cases are sold in packages of 20. Padded mailing envelopes are sold in packets of 12. What is the least number of cases and envelopes you could buy so that there is one case for each envelope with none left over? (6.NS.4)

17. Max bought two deli sandwich rolls measuring 18 inches and 30 inches. He wants them to be cut into equal sections that are as long as possible. Into what lengths should the rolls be cut? (6.NS.4)

18. Susan is buying supplies for a party. If spoons only come in bags of 8 and forks only come in bags of 6, what is the least number of spoons and the least number of forks she can buy so that she has the same number of each? (6.NS.4)

19. Tina is placing 30 roses and 42 tulips in vases for table decorations in her restaurant. Each vase will hold the same number of flowers. Each vase will have only one type of flower. What is the greatest number of flowers she can place in each vase? (6.NS.4)

Name ______________________________

Add and Subtract Decimals

Essential Question How do you add and subtract multi-digit decimals?

The Number System—6.NS.3

MATHEMATICAL PRACTICES
MP.2, MP.6, MP.7

CONNECT The place value of a digit in a number shows the value of the digit. The number 2.358 shows 2 ones, 3 tenths, 5 hundredths, and 8 thousandths.

Place Value						
Thousands	Hundreds	Tens	Ones	Tenths	Hundredths	Thousandths
			2 .	3	5	8

Unlock the Problem

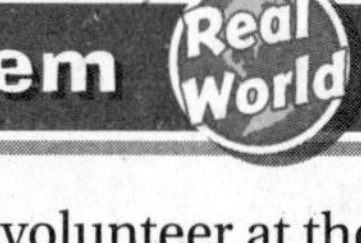

Amanda and three of her friends volunteer at the local animal shelter. One of their jobs is to weigh the puppies and kittens and chart their growth. Amanda's favorite puppy weighed 2.358 lb last month. If it gained 1.08 lb, how much does it weigh this month?

- How do you know whether to add or subtract the weights given in the problem?

____

____

Add 2.358 + 1.08.

Estimate the sum. ______ + ______ = ______

Add the thousandths first.

Then add the hundredths, tenths, and ones.

Regroup as needed.

$$\begin{array}{r} 2.358 \\ +\ 1.08 \\ \hline \end{array}$$

Compare your estimate with the sum. Since the estimate,

________, is close to ______________, the answer is reasonable.

So, the puppy weighs ______________ lb this month.

1. MATHEMATICAL PRACTICE 7 **Look for Structure** Is it necessary to add a zero after 1.08 to find the sum? Explain.

____

2. Explain how place value can help you add decimals.

____

Example 1

Remember

You can place zeros to the right of a decimal without changing its value.

4.91 = 4.910 = 4.9100

A bee hummingbird, the world's smallest bird, has a mass of 1.836 grams. A new United States nickel has a mass of 5 grams. What is the difference in grams between the mass of a nickel and the mass of a bee hummingbird?

Subtract 5 − 1.836.

Estimate the difference. ______ − ______ = ______

Think: 5 = 5.__________

Subtract the thousandths first.

Then subtract the hundredths, tenths, and ones.

Regroup as needed.

$$\begin{array}{r} 5.\square \\ -1.836 \\ \hline \square \end{array}$$

Bee hummingbird

U.S. Nickel

Compare your estimate with the difference. Since the estimate,

______, is close to __________, the answer is reasonable.

So, the mass of a new nickel is __________ grams more than the mass of a bee hummingbird.

Math Talk — **Mathematical Practices**

Explain how to use inverse operations to check your answer to 5 − 1.836.

Example 2 **Evaluate (6.5 − 1.97) + 3.461 using the order of operations.**

Write the expression. $(6.5 - 1.97) + 3.461$

Perform operations in parentheses.

$$\begin{array}{r} 6.50 \\ -1.97 \\ \hline \square \end{array}$$

Add.

$$\begin{array}{r} \square \\ +3.461 \\ \hline \square \end{array}$$

So, the value of the expression is __________.

Math Talk — **Mathematical Practices**

Describe how adding and subtracting decimals is like adding and subtracting whole numbers.

Name ______________________

Share and Show

1. Find 3.42 − 1.9.

Estimate. ______ − ______ = ______

Subtract the ____________________ first.

$$\begin{array}{r} 3.42 \\ -1.90 \\ \hline \end{array}$$

Estimate. Then find the sum or difference.

2. 2.3 + 5.68 + 21.047

3. 33.25 − 21.463

4. Evaluate (8.54 + 3.46) − 6.749.

Math Talk — **Mathematical Practices**

Explain why it is important to align the decimal points when you add or subtract decimals.

On Your Own

Estimate. Then find the sum or difference.

5. 57.08 + 34.71

6. 20.11 − 13.27

7. 62 − 9.817

8. 35.1 + 4.89

Practice: Copy and Solve Evaluate using the order of operations.

9. 8.01 − (2.2 + 4.67)

10. 54 + (9.2 − 1.413)

11. (3.26 + 1.51) + 4.77

12. (2.4 + 13.913) − 0.92

13. 21.3 − (19.1 − 3.22)

14. 23.7 + (96.5 + 9.25)

15. MATHEMATICAL PRACTICE 3 **Make Arguments** A student evaluated 19.1 + (4.32 + 6.9) and got 69.2. How can you use estimation to convince the student that this answer is not reasonable?

16. THINK SMARTER For numbers 16a–16d, select True or False for each equation.

16a. $3.76 + 2.7 = 6.46$ ○ True ○ False

16b. $4.14 + 1.8 = 4.32$ ○ True ○ False

16c. $2.01 - 1.33 = 0.68$ ○ True ○ False

16d. $51 - 49.2 = 1.8$ ○ True ○ False

Connect to Science

Comparing Eggs

Different types of birds lay eggs of different sizes. Small birds lay eggs that are smaller than those that are laid by larger birds. The table shows the average lengths and widths of five different birds' eggs.

Average Dimensions of Bird Eggs

Bird	Length (m)	Width (m)
Canada Goose	0.086	0.058
Hummingbird	0.013	0.013
Raven	0.049	0.033
Robin	0.019	0.015
Turtledove	0.031	0.023

Canada Goose

Use the table for 17–19.

17. What is the difference in average length between the longest egg and the shortest egg?

18. GO DEEPER Which egg has a width that is eight thousandths of a meter shorter than its length?

19. THINK SMARTER How many robin eggs, laid end to end, would be about equal in length to two raven eggs? Justify your answer.

FOR MORE PRACTICE: Standards Practice Book

Name ______________________

Multiply Decimals

Essential Question How do you multiply multi-digit decimals?

The Number System—6.NS.3

MATHEMATICAL PRACTICES
MP.2, MP.3, MP.6, MP.8,

Unlock the Problem Real World

Last summer Rachel worked 38.5 hours per week at a grocery store. She earned $9.70 per hour. How much did she earn in a week?

- How can you estimate the product?

____

____

Multiply $9.70 × 38.5.

First estimate the product. $10 × 40 = ________

You can use the estimate to place the decimal in a product.

$9.70
× 38.5

Multiply as you would with whole numbers.

\+
$

The estimate is about $ ________,

so the decimal point should be

placed after $________.

Since the estimate, ________, is close to ________, the answer is reasonable.

So, Rachel earned ________ per week.

1. Explain how your estimate helped you know where to place the decimal in the product.

____

____

Try This! What if Rachel gets a raise of $1.50 per hour? How much will she earn when she works 38.5 hours?

Counting Decimal Places Another way to place the decimal in a product is to add the numbers of decimal places in the factors.

Example 1 Multiply 0.084 × 0.096.

0.084 ______ decimal places

× 0.096 ______ decimal places

Multiply as you would with whole numbers.

+

______ + ______, or ______ decimal places

Example 2 Evaluate 0.35 × (0.48 + 1.24) using the order of operations.

Write the expression. 0.35 × (0.48 + 1.24)

Perform operations in parentheses. 0.35 × ______

Multiply. 0.35 ______ decimal places

× ______ decimal places

+

______ + ______, or ______ decimal places

So, the value of the expression is ______.

Math Talk **Mathematical Practices**

Is the product of 0.5 and 3.052 greater than or less than 3.052? **Explain.**

2. MATHEMATICAL PRACTICE 8 **Use Repeated Reasoning** Look for a pattern. Explain.

0.645 × 1 = 0.645

0.645 × 10 = 6.45 The decimal point moves ______ place to the right.

0.645 × 100 = ______ The decimal point moves ______ places to the right.

0.645 × 1,000 = ______ The decimal point moves ______ places to the right.

____

____

Name ______________________________

Share and Show

Estimate. Then find the product.

1. 12.42 × 28.6

_____ × _____ = _____

$$\begin{array}{r} 12.42 \\ \times\ 28.6 \\ \hline \end{array}$$

Estimate.

Think: The estimate is about _______, so the decimal point should be placed after _______.

2. 32.5 × 7.4

MATHEMATICAL PRACTICE 6 Attend to Precision **Algebra** **Evaluate using the order of operations.**

3. 0.24 × (7.3 + 2.1)

4. 0.075 × (9.2 − 0.8)

5. 2.83 + (0.3 × 2.16)

On Your Own

Estimate. Then find the product.

6. 29.14 × 5.2

7. 6.95 × 12

8. 0.055 × 1.82

MATHEMATICAL PRACTICE 6 Attend to Precision **Algebra** **Evaluate using the order of operations.**

9. (3.62 × 2.1) − 0.749

10. 5.8 − (0.25 × 1.5)

11. (0.83 + 1.27) × 6.4

12. 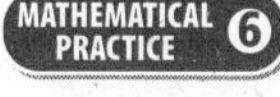 Jamal is buying ingredients to make a large batch of granola to sell at a school fair. He buys 3.2 pounds of walnuts for \$4.40 per pound and 2.4 pounds of cashews for \$6.25 per pound. How much change will he receive if he pays with two \$20 bills?

Unlock the Problem

The table shows some currency exchange rates for 2009.

Major Currency Exchange Rates in 2009				
Currency	**U.S. Dollar**	**Japanese Yen**	**European Euro**	**Canadian Dollar**
U.S. Dollar	1	88.353	0.676	1.052
Japanese Yen	0.011	1	0.008	0.012
European Euro	1.479	130.692	1	1.556
Canadian Dollar	0.951	83.995	0.643	1

Different denominations of Euro

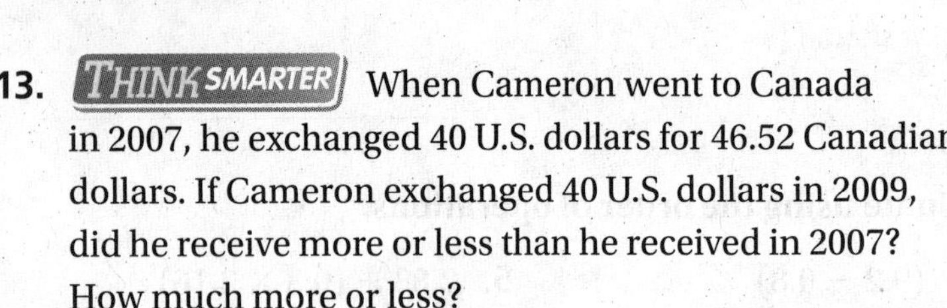

13. THINK SMARTER When Cameron went to Canada in 2007, he exchanged 40 U.S. dollars for 46.52 Canadian dollars. If Cameron exchanged 40 U.S. dollars in 2009, did he receive more or less than he received in 2007? How much more or less?

a. What do you need to find?

____

____

b. How will you use the table to solve the problem?

____

____

____

____

c. Complete the sentences.

40 U.S. dollars were worth __________ Canadian dollars in 2009.

So, Cameron would receive __________ __________ Canadian dollars in 2009.

Personal Math Trainer

14. THINK SMARTER + At a convenience store, the Jensen family puts 12.4 gallons of gasoline in their van at a cost of \$3.80 per gallon. They also buy 4 water bottles for \$1.99 each, and 2 snacks for \$1.55 each. Complete the table to find the cost for each item.

Item	Calculation	Cost
Gasoline	12.4 × \$3.80	
Water bottles	4 × \$1.99	
Snacks	2 × \$1.55	

Mrs. Jensen says the total cost for everything before tax is \$56.66. Do you agree with her? Explain why or why not.

____

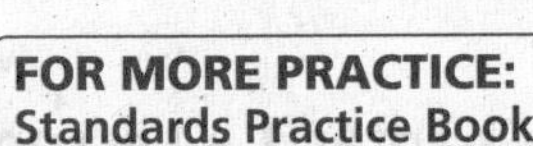

FOR MORE PRACTICE: Standards Practice Book

Name ____________________

Divide Decimals by Whole Numbers

Essential Question How do you divide decimals by whole numbers?

The Number System—6.NS.3
MATHEMATICAL PRACTICES
MP.1, MP.2, MP.6

Dan opened a savings account at a bank to save for a new snowboard. He earned $3.48 interest on his savings account over a 3-month period. What was the average amount of interest Dan earned per month on his savings account?

Divide $3.48 ÷ 3.

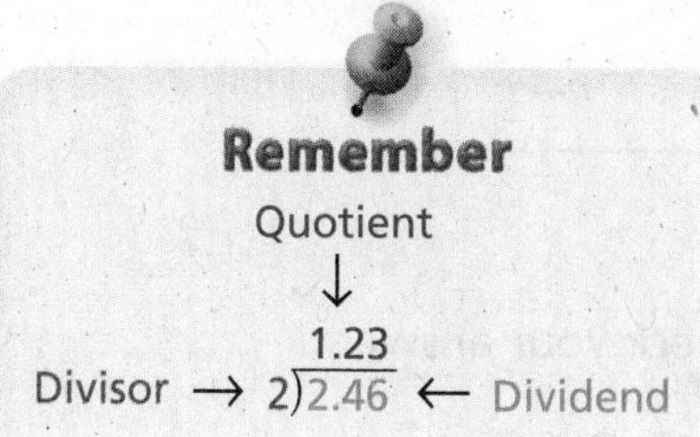

First estimate. 3 ÷ 3 = ______

```
     1.__
  3)3.48
   -3
    04
   - 3
     18
   - 18
      0
```

Think: 3.48 is shared among 3 groups.

Divide the ones. Place a decimal point after the ones place in the quotient.

Divide the tenths and then the hundredths. When the remainder is zero and there are no more digits in the dividend, the division is complete.

Check your answer.

```
   $____
  ×    3
   $3.48
```

Multiply the quotient by the divisor to check your answer.

So, Dan earned an average of ________ in interest per month.

Mathematical Practices

Explain how you know your answer is reasonable.

1. MATHEMATICAL PRACTICE 1 **Analyze Relationships** What if the same amount of interest was gained over 4 months? Explain how you would solve the problem.

____

Example Divide 42.133 ÷ 7.

First estimate. 42 ÷ 7 = ______

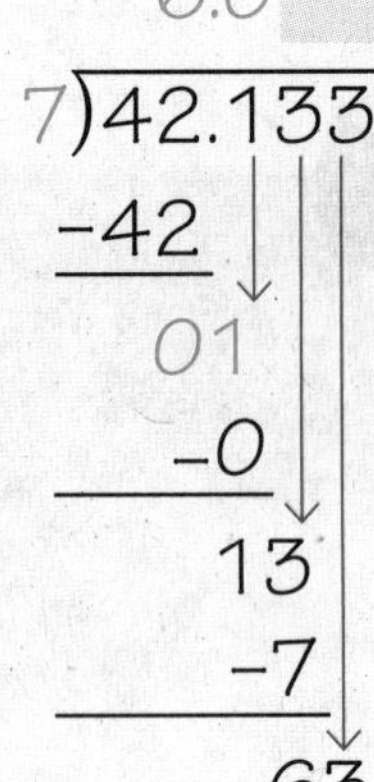

Think: 42.133 is shared among 7 groups.

Divide the ones. Place a decimal point after the ones place in the quotient.

Divide the tenths. Since 1 tenth cannot be shared among 7 groups, write a zero in the quotient. Regroup the 1 tenth as 10 hundredths. Now you have 13 hundredths.

Continue to divide until the remainder is zero and there are no more digits in the dividend.

Check your answer.

6.019
× 7

Multiply the quotient by the divisor to check your answer.

So, 42.133 ÷ 7 = ______.

2. Explain how you know which numbers to multiply when checking your answer.

______

______

Share and Show

MATH BOARD

1. Estimate 24.186 ÷ 6. Then find the quotient. Check your answer.

Estimate. ______ ÷ ______ = ______

Think: Place a decimal point after the ones place in the quotient.

6)24.186

× 6

Name ____________________

Share and Show

Estimate. Then find the quotient.

2. $7\overline{)\$17.15}$

✓ 3. $4\overline{)1.068}$

4. $12\overline{)60.84}$

✓ 5. $18.042 \div 6$

Math Talk — Mathematical Practices

Explain how you know where to place the decimal point in the quotient when dividing a decimal by a whole number.

On Your Own

Estimate. Then find the quotient.

6. $\$21.24 \div 6$

7. $28.63 \div 7$

8. $1.505 \div 35$

9. $0.108 \div 18$

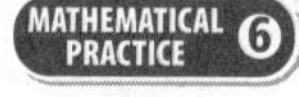

Attend to Precision **Algebra** **Evaluate using the order of operations.**

10. $(3.11 + 4.0) \div 9$

11. $(6.18 - 1.32) \div 3$

12. $(18 - 5.76) \div 6$

13. MATHEMATICAL PRACTICE 5 **Use Appropriate Tools** Find the length of a dollar bill to the nearest tenth of a centimeter. Then show how to use division to find the length of the bill when it is folded in half along the portrait of George Washington.

14. GO DEEPER Emilio bought 5.65 pounds of green grapes and 3.07 pounds of red grapes. He divided the grapes equally into 16 bags. If each bag of grapes has the same weight, how much does each bag weigh?

Problem Solving • Applications Real World

Pose a Problem

15. THINK SMARTER This table shows the average height in inches for girls and boys at ages 8, 10, 12, and 14 years.

Average Height (in.)				
	Age 8	Age 10	Age 12	Age
Girls	50.75	55.50	60.50	62.5
Boys	51.00	55.25	59.00	65.2

To find the average growth per year for girls from age 8 to age 12, Emma knew she had to find the amount of growth between age 8 and age 12, then divide that number by the number of years between age 8 and age 12.

Emma used this expression: $(60.50 - 50.75) \div 4$

She evaluated the expression using the order of operations.

Write the expression.	$(60.50 - 50.75) \div 4$
Perform operations in parentheses.	$9.75 \div 4$
Divide.	2.4375

So, the average annual growth for girls ages 8–12 is 2.4375 inches.

Write a new problem using the information in the table for the average height for boys. Use division in your problem.

Pose a Problem

Solve Your Problem

16. THINK SMARTER The table shows the number of books each of three friends bought and the cost. On average, which friend spent the most per book? Use numbers and words to explain your answer.

Friend	Number of books Purchased	Total Cost (in dollars)	Average Cost (in dollars)
Joyce	1	$10.95	
Nabil	2	$40.50	
Kenneth	3	$51.15	

FOR MORE PRACTICE: Standards Practice Book

Name ______________________________

Divide with Decimals

Essential Question How do you divide whole numbers and decimals by decimals?

The Number System—6.NS.3

MATHEMATICAL PRACTICES MP.1, MP.2, MP.8

CONNECT Find each quotient to discover a pattern.

$4 \div 2 =$ ______

$40 \div 20 =$ ______

$400 \div 200 =$ ______

When you multiply both the dividend and the divisor by the same power of ______, the quotient is the __________. You can use this fact to help you divide decimals.

Unlock the Problem — Real World

Tami is training for a triathlon. In a triathlon, athletes compete in three events: swimming, cycling, and running. She cycled 66.5 miles in 3.5 hours. If she cycled at a constant speed, how far did she cycle in 1 hour?

Remember

Compatible numbers are pairs of numbers that are easy to compute mentally.

Divide 66.5 ÷ 3.5.

Estimate using compatible numbers.

$60 \div 3 =$ ______

STEP 1

Make the divisor a whole number by multiplying the divisor and dividend by 10.

$3.5\overline{)66.5}$

Think: $3.5 \times 10 = 35$ $66.5 \times 10 = 665$

STEP 2

Divide.

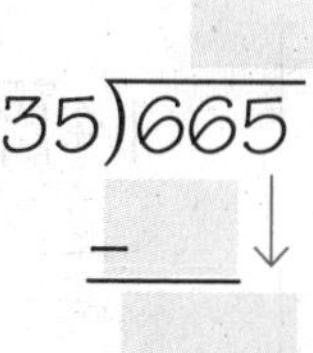

$35\overline{)665}$

So, Tami cycled __________ in 1 hour.

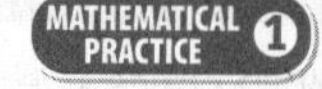

• MATHEMATICAL PRACTICE 1 **Evaluate Reasonableness** Explain whether your answer is reasonable.

Example 1 Divide 17.25 ÷ 5.75. Check.

STEP 1

Make the divisor a whole number by multiplying the divisor and dividend by ______.

5.75 × ______ = ______

17.25 × ______ = ______

$5.75\overline{)17.25}$

STEP 2

Divide.

$575\overline{)1,725}$

−

STEP 3

Check.

×

So, 17.25 ÷ 5.75 = ______.

Example 2 Divide 37.8 ÷ 0.14.

STEP 1

Make the divisor a whole number by multiplying the divisor and dividend by ______.

______ × ______ = ______

______ × ______ = ______

$0.14\overline{)37.80}$

Think: Add a zero to the right of the dividend so that you can move the decimal point.

ERROR Alert

Be careful to move the decimal point in the dividend the same number of places that you moved the decimal point in the divisor.

STEP 2

Divide.

$14\overline{)3,780}$

−

−

−

So, 37.8 ÷ 0.14 = ______.

Math Talk **Mathematical Practices**

Explain how to check the quotient.

Name ________________________________

Share and Show

MATH BOARD

1. Find the quotient.

$14.8\overline{)99.456}$

Think: Make the divisor a whole number by

multiplying the divisor and dividend by ______.

Estimate. Then find the quotient.

2. $10.80 ÷ $1.35

3. 26.4 ÷ 1.76

4. $8.7\overline{)53.07}$

Math Talk — Mathematical Practices

Explain how you know how many places to move the decimal point in the divisor and the dividend.

On Your Own

Estimate. Then find the quotient.

5. 75 ÷ 12.5

6. 544.6 ÷ 1.75

7. $2.7\overline{)22.41}$

Practice: Copy and Solve **Find the quotient.**

8. 2.64 ÷ 0.2

9. 1.43 ÷ 1.1

10. $0.3\overline{)3.15}$

11. $0.78\overline{)0.234}$

MATHEMATICAL PRACTICE 6 Attend to Precision **Algebra** **Evaluate using the order of operations.**

12. $36.4 + (9.2 - 4.9 \div 7)$

13. $16 \div 2.5 - 3.2 \times 0.043$

14. $142 \div (42 - 6.5) \times 3.9$

15. THINK SMARTER The table shows the earnings and the number of hours worked for three employees. Complete the table by finding the missing values. Which employee earned the least per hour? Explain.

Employee	Total Earned (in dollars)	Number of Hours Worked	Earnings per Hour (in dollars)
1	$34.02		$9.72
2	$42.75	4.5	
3	$52.65		$9.75

Connect to Science

Amoebas

Amoebas are tiny one-celled organisms. Amoebas can range in size from 0.01 mm to 5 mm in length. You can study amoebas by using a microscope or by studying photographic enlargements of them.

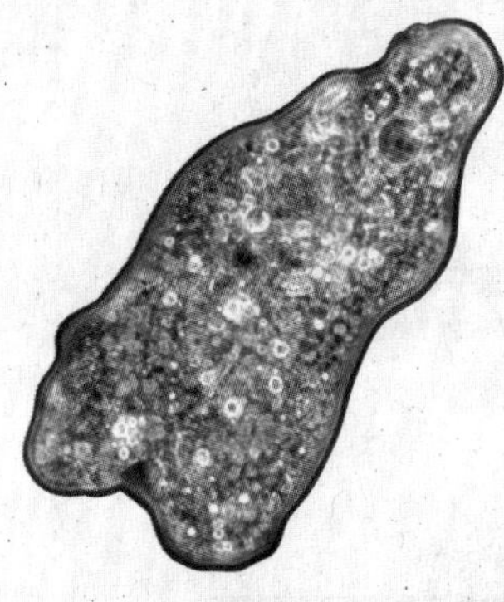

Jacob has a photograph of an amoeba that has been enlarged 1,000 times. The length of the amoeba in the photo is 60 mm. What is the actual length of the amoeba?

Divide 60 ÷ 1,000 by looking for a pattern.

60 ÷ 1 = 60

60 ÷ 10 = 6.0 The decimal point moves _____ place to the left.

60 ÷ 100 = _______ The decimal point moves _____ places to the left.

60 ÷ 1,000 = _______ The decimal point moves _____ places to the left.

So, the actual length of the amoeba is ___________ mm.

16.  Explain the pattern.

17. GO DEEPER *Pelomyxa palustris* is an amoeba with a length of 4.9 mm. *Amoeba proteus* has a length of 0.7 mm. How many *Amoeba proteus* would you have to line up side by side to equal the length of three *Pelomyxa palustris* that are side by side? Explain.

FOR MORE PRACTICE: Standards Practice Book

Name ________________________________

Chapter 1 Review/Test

1. Use the numbers to complete the factor tree. You may use a number more than once.

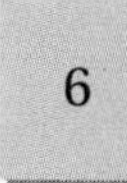

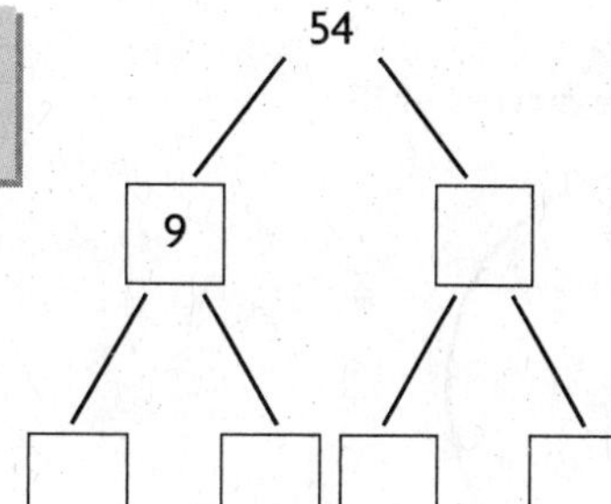

Write the prime factorization of 54.

____

2. For numbers 2a–2d, choose Yes or No to indicate whether the LCM of the two numbers is 15.

2a. 5, 3 ○ Yes ○ No

2b. 5, 10 ○ Yes ○ No

2c. 5, 15 ○ Yes ○ No

2d. 5, 20 ○ Yes ○ No

3. Select two numbers that have 9 as their greatest common factor. Mark all that apply.

(A) 3, 9

(B) 3, 18

(C) 9, 18

(D) 9, 36

(E) 18, 27

GO DIGITAL Assessment Options Chapter Test

4. The prime factorization of each number is shown.

$$15 = 3 \times 5$$
$$18 = 2 \times 3 \times 3$$

Part A

Using the prime factorization, complete the Venn diagram.

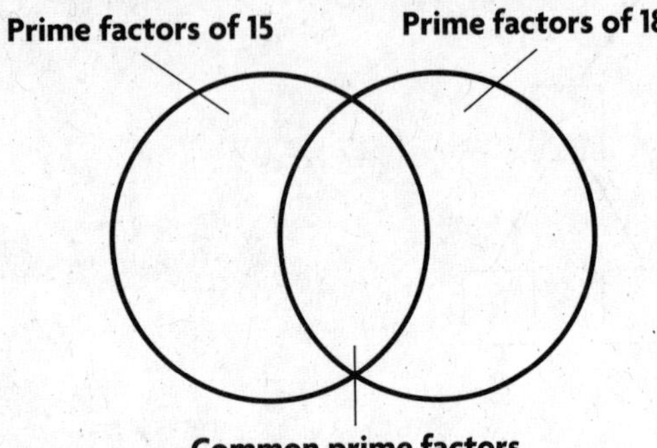

Part B

Find the GCF of 15 and 18.

____

5. For numbers 5a–5d, choose Yes or No to indicate whether each equation is correct.

5a. $222.2 \div 11 = 22.2$ ○ Yes ○ No

5b. $400 \div 50 = 8$ ○ Yes ○ No

5c. $1{,}440 \div 36 = 40$ ○ Yes ○ No

5d. $7{,}236 \div 9 = 804$ ○ Yes ○ No

Name ___________________________

6. For numbers 6a–6d, select True or False for each equation.

6a. $1.7 + 4.03 = 6$ ○ True ○ False

6b. $2.58 + 3.5 = 6.08$ ○ True ○ False

6c. $3.21 - 0.98 = 2.23$ ○ True ○ False

6d. $14 - 1.3 = 0.01$ ○ True ○ False

7. Four friends went shopping at a music store. The table shows the number of CDs each friend bought and the total cost. Complete the table to show the average cost of the CDs each friend bought.

Friend	Number of CDs Purchased	Total Cost (in dollars)	Average Cost (in dollars)
Lana	4	$36.72	
Troy	5	$40.50	
Juanita	5	$47.15	
Alex	6	$54.36	

8. The table shows the earnings and the number of hours worked for five employees. Complete the table by finding the missing values.

Employee	Total Money Earned (in dollars)	Number of Hours Worked	Earnings per Hour (in dollars)
1	$23.75		$9.50
2	$28.38	3.3	
3	$38.50		$8.75
4	$55.00	5.5	
5	$60.00	2.5	

9. The distance around the outside of Cedar Park is 0.8 mile. Joanie ran 0.25 of the distance during her lunch break. How far did she run? Show your work.

10. A one-celled organism measures 32 millimeters in length in a photograph. If the photo has been enlarged by a factor of 100, what is the actual length of the organism? Show your work.

11. You can buy 5 T-shirts at Baxter's for the same price that you can buy 4 T-shirts at Bixby's. If one T-shirt costs $11.80 at Bixby's, how much does one T-shirt cost at Baxter's? Use numbers and words to explain your answer.

Name ______________________________

12. Crackers come in packages of 24. Cheese slices come in packages of 18. Andy wants one cheese slice for each cracker. Patrick made the statement shown.

> If Andy doesn't want any crackers or cheese slices left over, he needs to buy at least 432 of each.

Is Patrick's statement correct? Use numbers and words to explain why or why not. If Patrick's statement is incorrect, what should he do to correct it?

13. There are 16 sixth graders and 20 seventh graders in the Robotics Club. For the first project, the club sponsor wants to organize the club members into equal-size groups. Each group will have only sixth graders or only seventh graders.

Part A

How many students will be in each group if each group has the greatest possible number of club members? Show your work.

Part B

If each group has the greatest possible number of club members, how many groups of sixth graders and how many groups of seventh graders will there be? Use numbers and words to explain your answer.

14. The Hernandez family is going to the beach. They buy sun block for \$9.99, 5 snacks for \$1.89 each, and 3 beach toys for \$1.49 each. Before they leave, they fill up the car with 13.1 gallons of gasoline at a cost of \$3.70 per gallon.

Part A

Complete the table by calculating the total cost for each item.

Item	Calculation	Total Cost
Gasoline	13.1 × \$3.70	
Snacks	5 × \$1.89	
Beach toys	3 × \$1.49	
Sun block	1 × \$9.99	

Part B

What is the total cost for everything before tax? Show your work.

Part C

Mr. Hernandez calculates the total cost for everything before tax using this equation.

Total cost = 13.1 + 3.70 × 5 + 1.89 × 3 + 1.49 × 9.99

Do you agree with his equation? Use numbers and words to explain why or why not. If the equation is not correct, write a correct equation.

Chapter 2

Fractions

Show What You Know

Check your understanding of important skills.

Name ______________________

Compare and Order Whole Numbers **Compare. Write <, >, or = for the ◯.**

1. 289 ◯ 291
2. 476,225 ◯ 476,225
3. 5,823 ◯ 5,286
4. 30,189 ◯ 30,201

Benchmark Fractions **Write whether the fraction is closest to 0, $\frac{1}{2}$ or 1.**

5. $\frac{3}{5}$ ________
6. $\frac{6}{7}$ ________
7. $\frac{1}{6}$ ________
8. $\frac{1}{3}$ ________

Multiply Fractions and Whole Numbers **Find the product. Write it in simplest form.**

9. $\frac{2}{3} \times 21$ ________
10. $\frac{1}{4} \times 10$ ________
11. $6 \times \frac{2}{9}$ ________
12. $\frac{3}{4} \times 14$ ________
13. $35 \times \frac{2}{5}$ ________
14. $\frac{3}{8} \times 12$ ________

Math Detective

Cyndi bought an extra large pizza, cut into 12 pieces, for today's meeting of the Mystery Club. She ate $\frac{1}{6}$ of the pizza yesterday afternoon. Her brother ate $\frac{1}{5}$ of what was left last night. Cyndi knows that she needs 8 pieces of pizza for the club meeting. Be a Math Detective and help Cyndi figure out if she has enough pizza left for the meeting.

Personal Math Trainer
Online Assessment and Intervention

Vocabulary Builder

▶ Visualize It

Complete the Bubble Map using review words that are related to fractions.

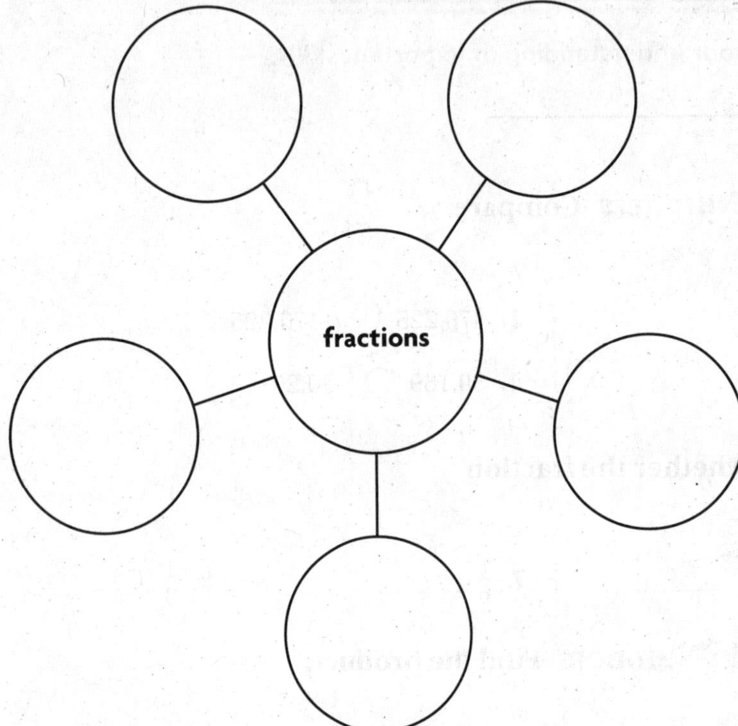

Review Words

✓ benchmark
✓ compatible numbers
denominator
✓ equivalent fractions
fractions
mixed numbers
numerator
✓ simplest form

Preview Words

✓ multiplicative inverse
✓ reciprocal

▶ Understand Vocabulary

Complete the sentences using the checked words.

1. ________________ are numbers that are easy to compute with mentally.

2. One of two numbers whose product is 1 is a ________________ or a ________________.

3. A ________________ is a reference point that is used for estimating fractions.

4. When the numerator and denominator of a fraction have only 1 as a common factor, the fraction is in ________________.

5. Fractions that name the same amount are ________________.

GO DIGITAL
• Interactive Student Edition
• Multimedia eGlossary

Name ______________________________

Fractions and Decimals

Essential Question How can you convert between fractions and decimals?

The Number System—6.NS.6c

MATHEMATICAL PRACTICES
MP.2, MP.4

CONNECT You can use place value to write a decimal as a fraction or a mixed number.

Place Value			
Ones	Tenths	Hundredths	Thousandths
1 .	2	3	4

Unlock the Problem

The African pygmy hedgehog is a popular pet in North America. The average African pygmy hedgehog weighs between 0.5 lb and 1.25 lb. How can these weights be written as fractions or mixed numbers?

- How do you know if a fraction is in simplest form?

____

____

____

Write 0.5 as a fraction and 1.25 as a mixed number in simplest form.

0.5

0.5 is five ________.

$0.5 = \frac{5}{\square}$

Simplify using the GCF.

The GCF of 5 and 10 is ________.

$\frac{5}{\square} = \frac{5 \div \square}{\square \div \square} = \frac{\square}{\square}$

Divide the numerator and the denominator by ________.

1.25

1.25 is one and ________.

$1.25 = 1\frac{\square}{\square}$

Simplify using the GCF.

The GCF of 25 and 100 is ________.

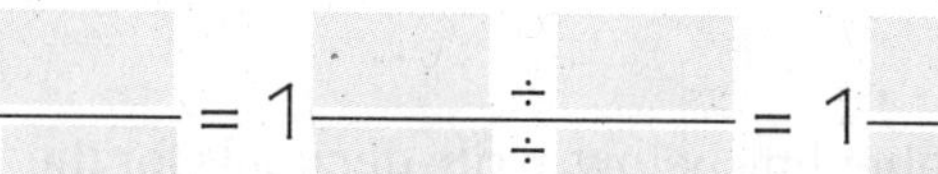

$1\frac{\square}{\square} = 1\frac{\square \div \square}{\square \div \square} = 1\frac{\square}{\square}$

Divide the numerator and the denominator by ________.

So, the average African pygmy hedgehog weighs between ________ lb and ________ lb.

Math Talk **Mathematical Practices**

Explain how you can use place value to write 0.05 and 0.005 as fractions. Then write the fractions in simplest form.

You can use division to write a fraction or a mixed number as a decimal.

Example Write $6\frac{3}{8}$ as a decimal.

STEP 1

Use division to rename the fraction part as a decimal.

The quotient has ______ decimal places.

____

$8\overline{)3.000}$

STEP 2

Add the whole number to the decimal.

6 + ______ = ______

So, $6\frac{3}{8}$ = ______.

Math Talk **Mathematical Practices**

Explain why zeros were placed after the decimal point in the dividend.

1. MATHEMATICAL PRACTICE 4 **Use Graphs** Sometimes you can use a number line to convert between fractions and decimals. Can you use this number line to write a decimal for $3\frac{3}{5}$? Explain.

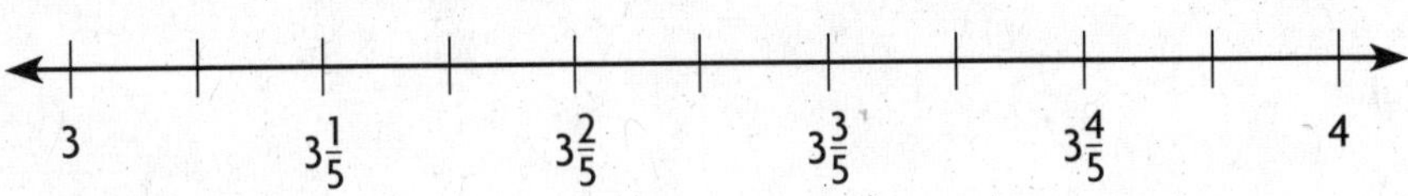

2. THINK SMARTER On the number line below, write decimals for the fractions $\frac{1}{50}$ and $\frac{2}{25}$.

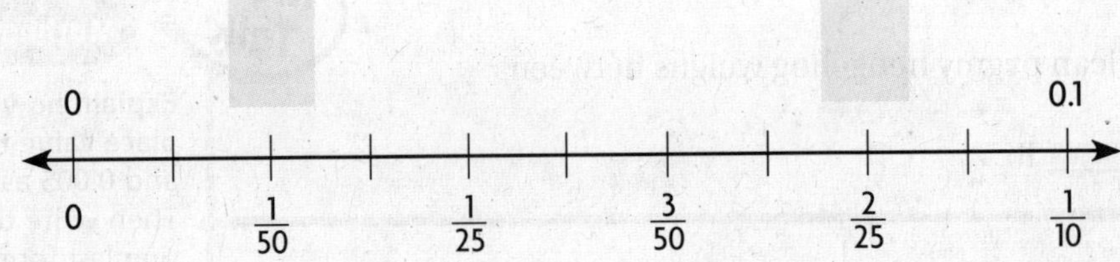

Name ______________________________

Share and Show

Write as a fraction or as a mixed number in simplest form.

1. $95.5 = 95\frac{5}{\square} = \square$

2. 0.6

3. 5.75

Write as a decimal.

4. $\frac{7}{8}$

5. $\frac{13}{20}$

6. $\frac{3}{25}$

Mathematical Practices

Explain how you can find the decimal that is equivalent to $\frac{7}{8}$.

On Your Own

Write as a fraction or as a mixed number in simplest form.

7. 0.27

8. 0.055

9. 2.45

Write as a decimal.

10. $\frac{3}{8}$

11. $3\frac{1}{5}$

12. $2\frac{11}{20}$

Identify a decimal and a fraction in simplest form for the point.

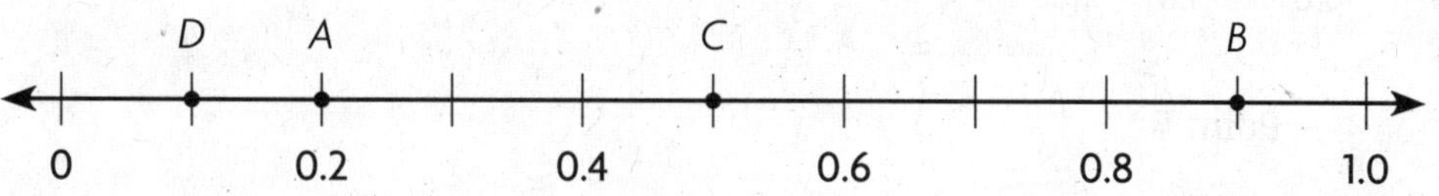

13. Point A

14. Point B

15. Point C

16. Point D

Problem Solving • Applications

Use the table for 17 and 18.

Ozark Trail Hiking Club

Hiker	June	July
Maria	2.95	$2\frac{5}{8}$
Devin	3.25	$3\frac{1}{8}$
Kelsey	3.15	$2\frac{7}{8}$
Zoey	2.85	$3\frac{3}{8}$

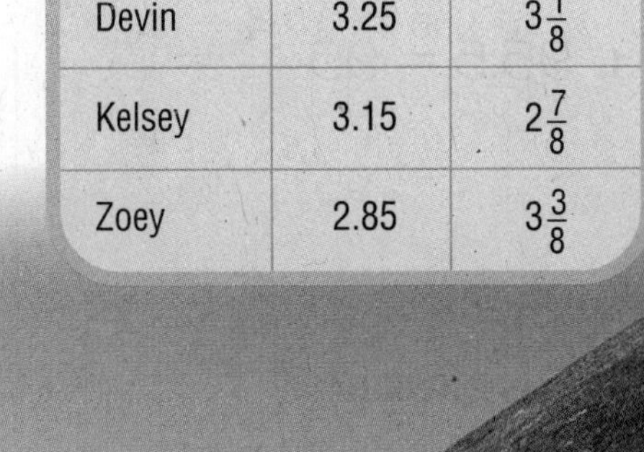

17. Members of the Ozark Trail Hiking Club hiked a steep section of the trail in June and July. The table shows the distances club members hiked in miles. Write Maria's July distance as a decimal.

____

18. GO DEEPER How much farther did Zoey hike in June and July than Maria hiked in June and July? Explain how you found your answer.

____

____

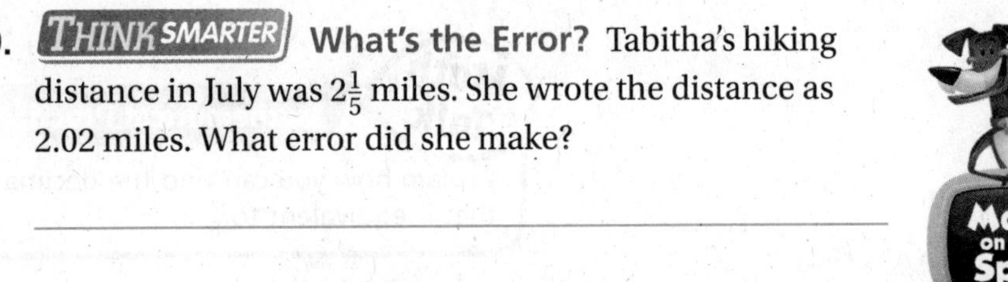

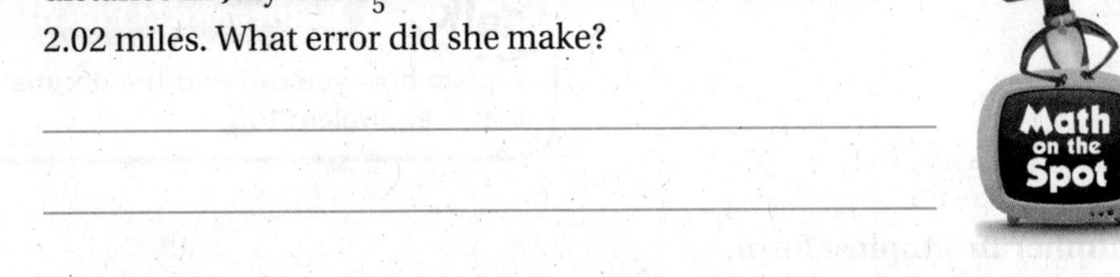

19. THINK SMARTER **What's the Error?** Tabitha's hiking distance in July was $2\frac{1}{5}$ miles. She wrote the distance as 2.02 miles. What error did she make?

____

____

____

20. MATHEMATICAL PRACTICE 5 **Use Patterns** Write $\frac{3}{8}$, $\frac{4}{8}$, and $\frac{5}{8}$ as decimals. What pattern do you see? Use the pattern to predict the decimal form of $\frac{6}{8}$ and $\frac{7}{8}$.

____

____

21. THINK SMARTER Identify a decimal and a fraction in simplest form for the point.

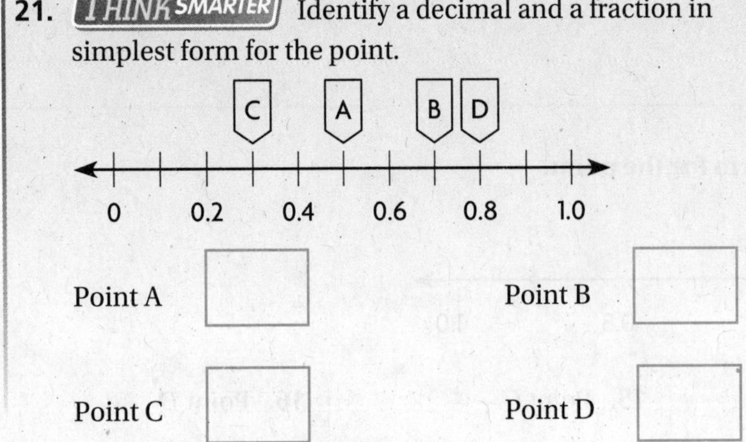

Point A ☐ Point B ☐

Point C ☐ Point D ☐

FOR MORE PRACTICE: Standards Practice Book

Name ________________

Compare and Order Fractions and Decimals

The Number System—6.NS.6c

MATHEMATICAL PRACTICES MP.4, MP.5

Essential Question How can you compare and order fractions and decimals?

To compare fractions with the same denominators, compare the numerators. To compare fractions with the same numerators, compare the denominators.

Same Denominators

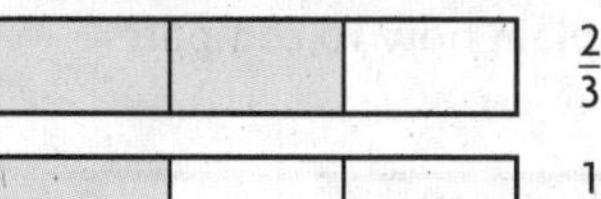

$\frac{2}{3}$

$\frac{1}{3}$

Two of three equal parts is greater than one of three equal parts.

So, $\frac{2}{3} > \frac{1}{3}$.

Same Numerators

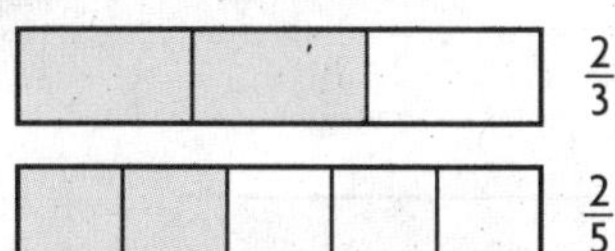

$\frac{2}{3}$

$\frac{2}{5}$

Two of three equal parts is greater than two of five equal parts.

So, $\frac{2}{3} > \frac{2}{5}$.

Unlock the Problem

Three new flowering dogwood trees were planted in a park in Springfield, Missouri. The trees were $6\frac{1}{2}$ ft, $5\frac{2}{3}$ ft, and $5\frac{5}{8}$ ft tall. Order the plant heights from least to greatest.

To compare and order fractions with unlike denominators, write equivalent fractions with common denominators.

Remember

- Equivalent fractions are fractions that name the same amount or part.
- A common denominator is a denominator that is the same in two or more fractions.

One Way Order $6\frac{1}{2}$, $5\frac{2}{3}$, and $5\frac{5}{8}$ from least to greatest.

STEP 1

Compare the whole numbers first.

$6\frac{1}{2}$ $5\frac{2}{3}$ $5\frac{5}{8}$ 5 ◯ 6

STEP 2

If the whole numbers are the same, compare the fractions.

Use common denominators to write equivalent fractions.

Think: ______ is a multiple of 3 and 8,

so ______ is a common denominator.

$5\frac{2 \times 8}{3 \times 8} = 5\frac{\square}{\square}$ $5\frac{5 \times \square}{8 \times \square} = 5\frac{\square}{\square}$

STEP 3

Compare the numerators.

Order the fractions from least to greatest.

$5\frac{\square}{\square} < 5\frac{\square}{\square} < 6\frac{1}{2}$

So, from least to greatest, the order is ______ ft, ______ ft, ______ ft.

Mathematical Practices

Explain how you could compare $3\frac{3}{4}$ and $3\frac{3}{7}$.

Fractions and Decimals You can compare fractions and decimals.

One Way Compare to $\frac{1}{2}$.

Compare 0.92 and $\frac{2}{7}$. Write <, >, or =.

STEP 1 Compare 0.92 to $\frac{1}{2}$.

0.92 ◯ $\frac{1}{2}$

STEP 2 Compare $\frac{2}{7}$ to $\frac{1}{2}$.

$\frac{2}{7}$ ◯ $\frac{1}{2}$

So, 0.92 ◯ $\frac{2}{7}$.

Math Talk **Mathematical Practices**

Explain how to compare $\frac{2}{7}$ to $\frac{1}{2}$.

Another Way Rewrite the fraction as a decimal.

Compare 0.8 and $\frac{3}{4}$. Write <, >, or =.

STEP 1 Write $\frac{3}{4}$ as a decimal.

4)3.00

−

−

0

$\frac{3}{4}$ = ____

STEP 2 Use <, >, or = to compare the decimals.

0.80 ◯ ____

So, 0.8 ◯ $\frac{3}{4}$.

You can use a number line to order fractions and decimals.

Example Use a number line to order 0.95, $\frac{3}{10}$, $\frac{1}{4}$, and 0.45 from least to greatest.

STEP 1 Write each fraction as a decimal.

$\frac{3}{10}$ → 10)3.00 $\frac{1}{4}$ → 4)1.00

Math Idea

- Numbers read from left to right on a number line are in order from least to greatest.
- Numbers read from right to left are in order from greatest to least.

STEP 2 Locate each decimal on a number line.

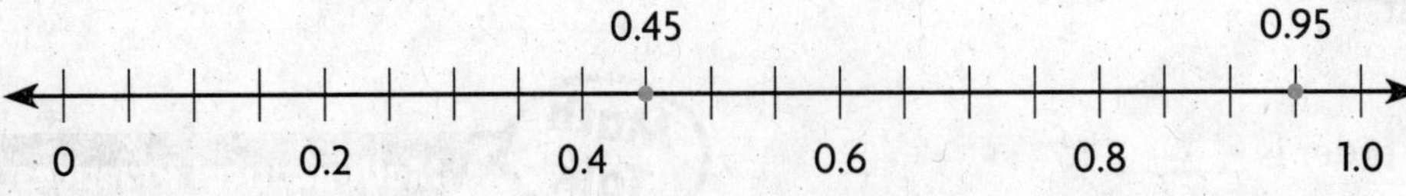

So, from least to greatest, the order is ____, ____, ____, ____.

Name ______________________

Share and Show

Order from least to greatest.

1. $3\frac{3}{6}, 3\frac{5}{8}, 2\frac{9}{10}$

Think: Compare the whole numbers first.

$3\frac{3\times}{6\times} = 3$ ____ $3\frac{5\times}{8\times} = 3$ ____ ____, ____, ____

Write <, >, or =.

2. $0.8 \bigcirc \frac{4}{12}$

3. $0.22 \bigcirc \frac{1}{4}$

4. $\frac{1}{20} \bigcirc 0.06$

Use a number line to order from least to greatest.

5. $1\frac{4}{5}, 1.25, 1\frac{1}{10}$

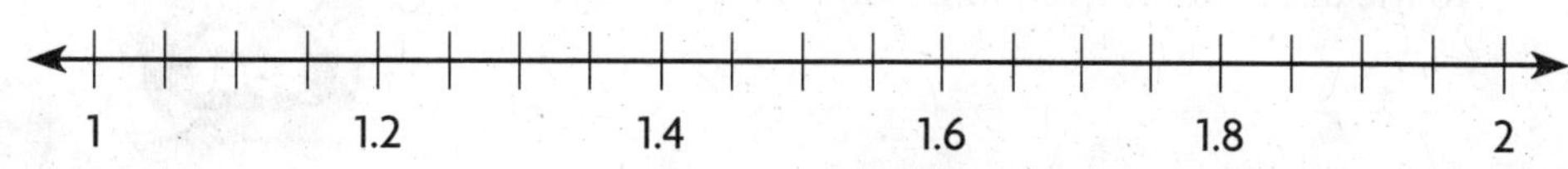

____

Math Talk Mathematical Practices

Explain how to compare $\frac{3}{5}$ and 0.37 by comparing to $\frac{1}{2}$.

On Your Own

Order from least to greatest.

6. $1\frac{3}{4}, \frac{5}{7}, 1\frac{3}{5}$

7. $0.6, \frac{4}{5}, 0.75$

8. $\frac{1}{2}, \frac{2}{5}, \frac{7}{15}$

Write <, >, or =.

9. $\frac{7}{15} \bigcirc \frac{7}{10}$

10. $\frac{1}{8} \bigcirc 0.125$

11. $7\frac{1}{3} \bigcirc 6\frac{2}{3}$

Order from greatest to least.

12. $5\frac{1}{2}, 5.05, 5\frac{5}{9}$

13. $\frac{37}{10}, 3\frac{2}{5}, 3\frac{1}{4}$

14. $\frac{5}{7}, \frac{5}{6}, \frac{5}{12}$

Problem Solving • Applications

Use the table for 15–18.

Day	Altoona	Bethlehem
Monday	$2\frac{1}{4}$	2.6
Tuesday	$3\frac{1}{4}$	3.2
Wednesday	$2\frac{5}{8}$	2.5
Thursday	$4\frac{3}{5}$	4.8
Friday	$4\frac{3}{4}$	2.7

Altoona and Bethlehem Snowfall (inches)

15. GO DEEPER In one week, Altoona, PA, and Bethlehem, PA, received snowfall every day, Monday through Friday. On which days did Altoona receive over 0.1 inch more snow than Bethlehem?

____

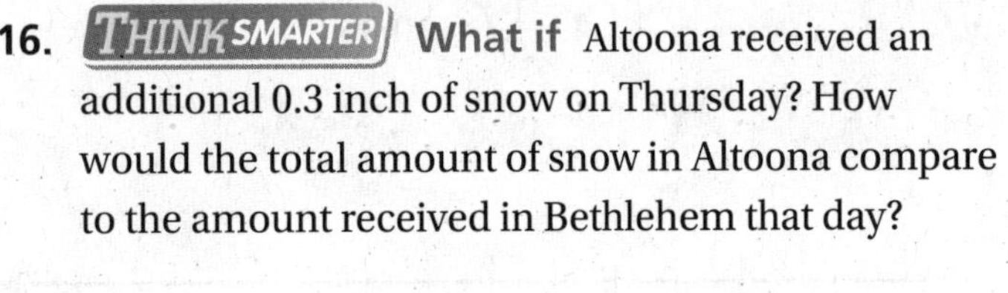

16. THINK SMARTER **What if** Altoona received an additional 0.3 inch of snow on Thursday? How would the total amount of snow in Altoona compare to the amount received in Bethlehem that day?

____

____

17. MATHEMATICAL PRACTICE 6 **Explain** two ways you could compare the snowfall amounts in Altoona and Bethlehem on Monday.

____

____

____

____

18. WRITE ▸ *Math* Explain how you could compare the snowfall amounts in Altoona on Thursday and Friday.

____

____

____

19. THINK SMARTER Write the values in order from least to greatest.

$\frac{1}{3}$	0.45	0.39	$\frac{2}{5}$

_______ _______ _______ _______

FOR MORE PRACTICE:
Standards Practice Book

Name ________________________________

Multiply Fractions

Essential Question How do you multiply fractions?

The Number System—6.NS.4

MATHEMATICAL PRACTICES
MP.2, MP.6

Unlock the Problem

Sasha still has $\frac{4}{5}$ of a scarf left to knit. If she finishes $\frac{1}{2}$ of the remaining part of the scarf today, how much of the scarf will Sasha knit today?

Multiply $\frac{1}{2} \times \frac{4}{5}$. Write the product in simplest form.

Multiply the numerators.
Multiply the denominators.

$$\frac{1}{2} \times \frac{4}{5} = \frac{1 \times \square}{2 \times \square} = \frac{\square}{\square}$$

Simplify using the GCF.

The GCF of 4 and 10 is ______.

Divide the numerator and the denominator by ______.

$$= \frac{\square \div \square}{10 \div \square} = \frac{\square}{\square}$$

$\frac{1}{2} \times \frac{4}{5} =$ ______, so Sasha will knit ______ of the scarf today.

Remember

You can find the product of two fractions by multiplying the numerators and multiplying the denominators.

$$\frac{1}{3} \times \frac{2}{5} \times \frac{1 \times 2}{3 \times 5} \times \frac{2}{15}$$

Example 1

Multiply $1\frac{1}{4} \times 1\frac{2}{3}$. Write the product in simplest form.

Estimate. $1 \times$ ______ $=$ ______

Write the mixed numbers as fractions greater than 1.

$$1\frac{1}{4} \times 1\frac{2}{3} = \frac{5}{4} \times \frac{\square}{3}$$

Multiply the fractions.

Write the product as a fraction or mixed number in simplest form.

$$= \frac{5 \times \square}{4 \times 3} = \frac{\square}{\square}, \text{ or } \_\_\_\_\_\_$$

Since the estimate is ______, the answer is reasonable.

So, $1\frac{1}{4} \times 1\frac{2}{3} =$ ______, or ______.

Mathematical Practices

Explain whether the product $\frac{1}{3} \times \frac{3}{4}$ will be less than or greater than $\frac{3}{4}$.

Example 2

Evaluate $\frac{4}{5} + \left(6 \times \frac{3}{8}\right)$ using the order of operations.

Remember

A benchmark is a reference point, such as 0, $\frac{1}{2}$, or 1, that is used for estimating fractions.

STEP 1

Estimate using benchmarks.

$$\square + \left(6 \times \frac{1}{2}\right) = \square + 3 = \square$$

STEP 2

Perform operations in parentheses.

$$\frac{4}{5} + \left(6 \times \frac{3}{8}\right) = \frac{4}{5} + \left(\frac{6 \times 3}{\square \times 8}\right)$$

$$= \frac{4}{5} + \frac{\square}{\square}$$

STEP 3

Write equivalent fractions using a common denominator.

Then add.

$$= \frac{4 \times 8}{5 \times 8} + \frac{\square \times 5}{\square \times 5}$$

$$= \frac{32}{40} + \frac{\square}{\square} = \frac{\square}{\square}$$

STEP 4

Simplify using the GCF.

$$= \frac{122 \div \square}{40 \div \square}$$

$$= \frac{\square}{\square}, \text{ or } \underline{\qquad}$$

Since the estimate is ______, the answer is reasonable.

So, $\frac{4}{5} + \left(6 \times \frac{3}{8}\right) =$ ______, or ______.

1. **MATHEMATICAL PRACTICE 2 Use Reasoning** What if you did not follow the order of operations and instead worked from left to right? How would that affect your answer?

____

____

2. **MATHEMATICAL PRACTICE 6 Explain** how you used benchmarks to estimate the answer.

____

____

Name ___________________________

Share and Show

Find the product. Write it in simplest form.

1. $6 \times \frac{3}{8}$

$\frac{6}{1} \times \frac{3}{8} = \frac{\square}{\square}$

$\frac{\square \div \square}{8 \div \square} = \frac{\square}{\square}$

or ______

2. $\frac{3}{8} \times \frac{8}{9}$

______

3. Sam and his friends ate $3\frac{3}{4}$ bags of fruit snacks. If each bag contained $2\frac{1}{2}$ ounces, how many ounces of fruit snacks did Sam and his friends eat?

______

MATHEMATICAL PRACTICE 6 Attend to Precision **Algebra** **Evaluate using the order of operations. Write the answer in simplest form.**

4. $\left(\frac{3}{4} - \frac{1}{2}\right) \times \frac{3}{5}$ ______

5. $\frac{1}{3} + \frac{4}{9} \times 12$ ______

6. $\frac{5}{8} \times \frac{7}{10} - \frac{1}{4}$ ______

7. $3 \times \left(\frac{5}{18} + \frac{1}{6}\right) + \frac{2}{5}$ ______

Math Talk Mathematical Practices

Explain why the product of two fractions has the same value before and after dividing the numerator and denominator by the GCF.

On Your Own

Practice: Copy and Solve **Find the product. Write it in simplest form.**

8. $1\frac{2}{3} \times 2\frac{5}{8}$

9. $\frac{4}{9} \times \frac{4}{5}$

10. $\frac{1}{6} \times \frac{2}{3}$

11. $4\frac{1}{7} \times 3\frac{1}{9}$

12. $\frac{5}{6}$ of the pets in the pet show are cats. $\frac{4}{5}$ of the cats are calico cats. What fraction of the pets are calico cats?

______

13. Five cats each ate $\frac{1}{4}$ cup of cat food. How much food did the five cats eat?

______

MATHEMATICAL PRACTICE 6 Attend to Precision **Algebra** **Evaluate using the order of operations. Write the answer in simplest form.**

14. $\frac{1}{4} \times \left(\frac{3}{9} + 5\right)$ ______

15. $\frac{9}{10} - \frac{3}{5} \times \frac{1}{2}$ ______

16. $\frac{4}{5} + \left(\frac{1}{2} - \frac{3}{7}\right) \times 2$ ______

17. $15 \times \frac{3}{10} + \frac{7}{8}$ ______

18. *THINK SMARTER* Write and solve a word problem for the expression $\frac{1}{4} \times \frac{2}{3}$. Show your work.

Connect to Health

Changing Recipes

You can make a lot of recipes more healthful by reducing the amounts of fat, sugar, and salt.

Kelly has a recipe for muffins that asks for $1\frac{1}{2}$ cups of sugar. She wants to use $\frac{1}{2}$ that amount of sugar and more cinnamon and vanilla. How much sugar will she use?

Find $\frac{1}{2}$ of $1\frac{1}{2}$ cups to find what part of the original amount of sugar to use.

Write the mixed number as a fraction greater than 1.

$$\frac{1}{2} \times 1\frac{1}{2} = \frac{1}{2} \times \frac{\square}{2}$$

Multiply.

$$= \frac{\square}{\square}$$

So, Kelly will use ______ cup of sugar.

19. *GO DEEPER* Michelle has a recipe that asks for $2\frac{1}{2}$ cups of vegetable oil. She wants to use $\frac{2}{3}$ that amount of oil and use applesauce to replace the rest. How much applesauce will she use?

20. *THINK SMARTER* Cara's muffin recipe asks for $1\frac{1}{2}$ cups of flour for the muffins and $\frac{1}{4}$ cup of flour for the topping. If she makes $\frac{1}{2}$ of the original recipe, how much flour will she use for the muffins and topping?

FOR MORE PRACTICE:
Standards Practice Book

Name ______________________________

Simplify Factors

Essential Question How do you simplify fractional factors by using the greatest common factor?

The Number System—6.NS.4

MATHEMATICAL PRACTICES
MP.3, MP.6

Unlock the Problem

Some of the corn grown in the United States is used for making fuel. Suppose $\frac{7}{10}$ of a farmer's total crop is corn. He sells $\frac{2}{5}$ of the corn for fuel production. What fraction of the farmer's total crop does he sell for fuel production?

Multiply $\frac{2}{5} \times \frac{7}{10}$.

One Way Simplify the product.

Multiply the numerators.
Multiply the denominators.

$$\frac{2}{5} \times \frac{7}{10} = \frac{2 \times 7}{5 \times 10} = \frac{\square}{\square}$$

Write the product as a fraction in simplest form.

$$= \frac{\square \div 2}{50 \div \square} = \frac{\square}{\square}$$

So, $\frac{2}{5} \times \frac{7}{10} =$ ______.

Another Way Simplify before multiplying.

Write the problem as a single fraction.

$$\frac{2}{5} \times \frac{7}{10} = \frac{2 \times 7}{5 \times 10}$$

Think: Do any numbers in the numerator have common factors with numbers in the denominator?

2 in the numerator and ______ in the denominator have a common factor other than 1.

Divide the numerator and the denominator by the GCF.

The GCF of 2 and 10 is ______.

$2 \div 2 =$ ______ $10 \div 2 =$ ______

$$\frac{\overset{1}{\cancel{2}} \times 7}{5 \times \cancel{10}}$$

Multiply the numerators.
Multiply the denominators.

$$\frac{1 \times 7}{5 \times \square} = \frac{\square}{\square}$$

$\frac{2}{5} \times \frac{7}{10} =$ ______, so the farmer sells ______ of his crop for fuel production.

Math Talk **Mathematical Practices**

When you multiply two fractions, will the product be the same whether you multiply first or simplify first? **Explain.**

Example

Find $\frac{5}{8} \times \frac{14}{15}$. Simplify before multiplying.

Divide a numerator and a denominator by their GCF.

The GCF of 5 and 15 is ______.

$$\frac{\overset{1}{\cancel{5}}}{8} \times \frac{14}{\cancel{15}}$$

The GCF of 8 and 14 is ______.

$$\frac{\overset{1}{\cancel{5}}}{\cancel{8}} \times \frac{\cancel{14}}{\underset{3}{\cancel{15}}}$$

Multiply the numerators.
Multiply the denominators.

$$\frac{1}{\square} \times \frac{\square}{3} = \frac{\square}{\square}$$

So, $\frac{5}{8} \times \frac{14}{15} =$ ______.

ERROR Alert

Be sure to divide both a numerator and a denominator by a common factor to write a fraction in simplest form.

Try This! **Find the product. Simplify before multiplying.**

A $\frac{3}{8} \times \frac{2}{9}$

The GCF of 3 and 9 is ______.

The GCF of 2 and 8 is ______.

$$\frac{\cancel{3}}{\cancel{8}} \times \frac{\cancel{2}}{\cancel{9}} = \frac{\square}{\square}$$

B $\frac{4}{7} \times \frac{7}{12}$

The GCF of 4 and 12 is ______.

The GCF of 7 and 7 is ______.

$$\frac{\cancel{4}}{\cancel{7}} \times \frac{\cancel{7}}{\cancel{12}} = \frac{\square}{\square}$$

1. MATHEMATICAL PRACTICE 6 **Explain** why you cannot simplify before multiplying when finding $\frac{3}{5} \times \frac{6}{7}$.

____

____

2. MATHEMATICAL PRACTICE 3 **Compare Strategies** What if you divided by a common factor other than the GCF before you multiplied? How would that affect your answer?

____

____

Name ______________________

Share and Show

Find the product. Simplify before multiplying.

1. $\frac{5}{6} \times \frac{3}{10}$

$\frac{\not{5}}{\not{6}} \times \frac{\not{3}}{\not{10}} = \underline{\quad}$

2. $\frac{3}{4} \times \frac{5}{9}$

3. $\frac{2}{3} \times \frac{9}{10}$

4. After a picnic, $\frac{5}{12}$ of the cornbread is left over. Val eats $\frac{3}{5}$ of the leftover cornbread. What fraction of the cornbread does Val eat?

5. The reptile house at the zoo has an iguana that is $\frac{5}{6}$ yd long. It has a Gila monster that is $\frac{4}{5}$ of the length of the iguana. How long is the Gila monster?

Math Talk Mathematical Practices

Explain two ways to find the product $\frac{1}{6} \times \frac{2}{3}$ in simplest form.

On Your Own

Find the product. Simplify before multiplying.

6. $\frac{3}{4} \times \frac{1}{6}$

7. $\frac{7}{10} \times \frac{2}{3}$

8. $\frac{5}{8} \times \frac{2}{5}$

9. $\frac{9}{10} \times \frac{5}{6}$

10. $\frac{11}{12} \times \frac{3}{7}$

11. Shelley's basketball team won $\frac{3}{4}$ of their games last season. In $\frac{1}{6}$ of the games they won, they outscored their opponents by more than 10 points. What fraction of their games did Shelley's team win by more than 10 points?

12. GO DEEPER Mr. Ortiz has $\frac{3}{4}$ pound of oatmeal. He uses $\frac{2}{3}$ of the oatmeal to bake muffins. How much oatmeal does Mr. Ortiz have left?

13. MATHEMATICAL PRACTICE 3 **Compare Strategies** To find $\frac{16}{27} \times \frac{3}{4}$, you can multiply the fractions and then simplify the product or you can simplify the fractions and then multiply. Which method do you prefer? Explain.

Problem Solving • Applications Real World

14. Three students each popped $\frac{3}{4}$ cup of popcorn kernels. The table shows the fraction of each student's kernels that did not pop. Which student had $\frac{1}{16}$ cup unpopped kernels?

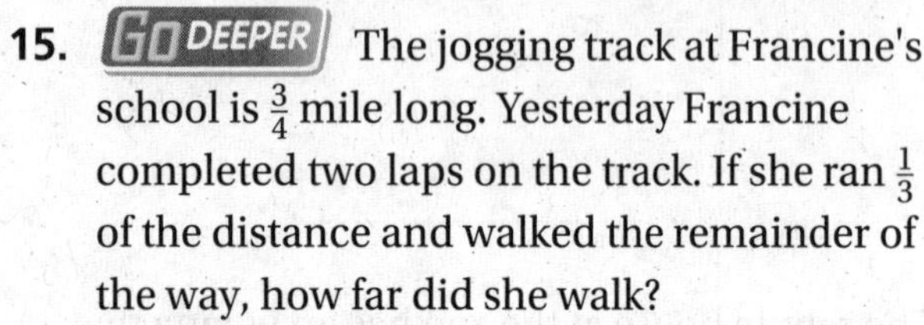

Popcorn Popping	
Student	**Fraction of Kernels not Popped**
Katie	$\frac{1}{10}$
Mirza	$\frac{1}{12}$
Jawan	$\frac{1}{9}$

____

15. GO DEEPER The jogging track at Francine's school is $\frac{3}{4}$ mile long. Yesterday Francine completed two laps on the track. If she ran $\frac{1}{3}$ of the distance and walked the remainder of the way, how far did she walk?

____

16. THINK SMARTER At a snack store, $\frac{7}{12}$ of the customers bought pretzels and $\frac{3}{10}$ of those customers bought low-salt pretzels. Bill states that $\frac{7}{30}$ of the customers bought low-salt pretzels. Does Bill's statement make sense? Explain.

____

____

____

WRITE Math • Show Your Work

17. THINK SMARTER The table shows Tonya's homework assignment. Tonya's teacher instructed the class to simplify each expression by dividing the numerator and denominator by the GCF. Complete the table by simplifying each expression and then finding the value.

Problem	Expression	Simplified Expression	Value
a	$\frac{2}{7} \times \frac{3}{4}$		
b	$\frac{3}{7} \times \frac{7}{9}$		
c	$\frac{5}{7} \times \frac{2}{3}$		
d	$\frac{4}{15} \times \frac{3}{8}$		

FOR MORE PRACTICE:
Standards Practice Book

Name ______________________________

Mid-Chapter Checkpoint

Vocabulary

Choose the best term from the box to complete the sentence.

Vocabulary
common denominator
equivalent fractions
mixed number

1. The fractions $\frac{1}{2}$ and $\frac{5}{10}$ are ____________________. (p. 55)

2. A ____________________ is a denominator that is the same in two or more fractions. (p. 55)

Concepts and Skills

Write as a decimal. (6.NS.6c)

3. $\frac{7}{20}$ ________

4. $8\frac{39}{40}$ ________

5. $1\frac{5}{8}$ ________

6. $\frac{19}{25}$ ________

Order from least to greatest. (6.NS.6c)

7. $\frac{4}{5}$, $\frac{3}{4}$, 0.88 ________

8. 0.65, 0.59, $\frac{3}{5}$ ________

9. $1\frac{1}{4}$, $1\frac{2}{3}$, $\frac{11}{12}$ ________

10. 0.9, $\frac{7}{8}$, 0.86 ________

Find the product. Write it in simplest form. (6.NS.4)

11. $\frac{2}{3} \times \frac{1}{8}$ ________

12. $\frac{4}{5} \times \frac{2}{5}$ ________

13. $12 \times \frac{3}{4}$ ________

14. Mia climbs $\frac{5}{8}$ of the height of the rock wall. Lee climbs $\frac{4}{5}$ of Mia's distance. What fraction of the wall does Lee climb?

____

15. In Zoe's class, $\frac{4}{5}$ of the students have pets. Of the students who have pets, $\frac{1}{8}$ have rodents. What fraction of the students in Zoe's class have rodents? (6.NS.4)

____

16. A recipe calls for $2\frac{2}{3}$ cups of flour. Terell wants to make $\frac{3}{4}$ of the recipe. How much flour should he use? (6.NS.4)

____

17. Following the Baltimore Running Festival in 2009, volunteers collected and recycled 3.75 tons of trash. Write 3.75 as a mixed number in simplest form. (6.NS.6c)

____

18. Four students took an exam. The fraction of the total possible points that each received is given. Which student had the highest score? (6.NS.6c)

Student	Score
Monica	$\frac{22}{25}$
Lily	$\frac{17}{20}$
Nikki	$\frac{4}{5}$
Sydney	$\frac{3}{4}$

____

Name ______________________________

Model Fraction Division

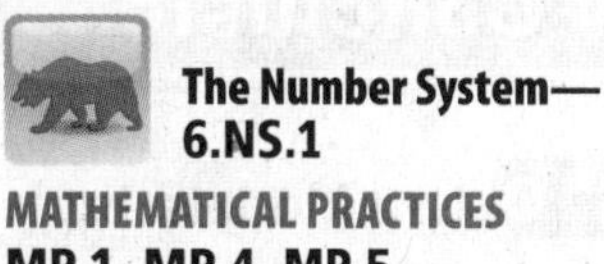

MATHEMATICAL PRACTICES
MP.1, MP.4, MP.5

Essential Question How can you use a model to show division of fractions?

CONNECT There are two types of division problems. In one type you find how many or how much in each group, and in the other you find how many groups.

Investigate

Materials ■ fraction strips

A class is working on a community project to clear a path near the lake. They are working in teams on sections of the path.

A. Four students clear a section that is $\frac{2}{3}$ mi long. If each student clears an equal part, what fraction of a mile will each clear?

Divide $\frac{2}{3} \div 4$.

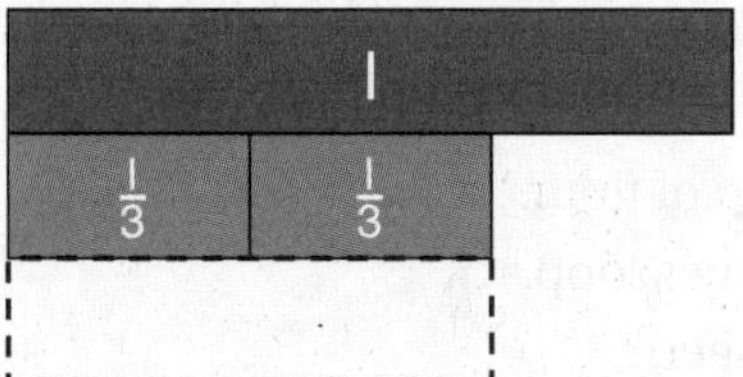
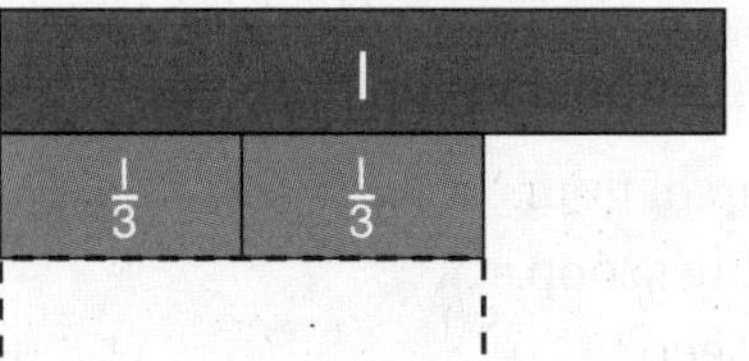

- Use fraction strips to model the division. Draw your model.

- What are you trying to find?

____

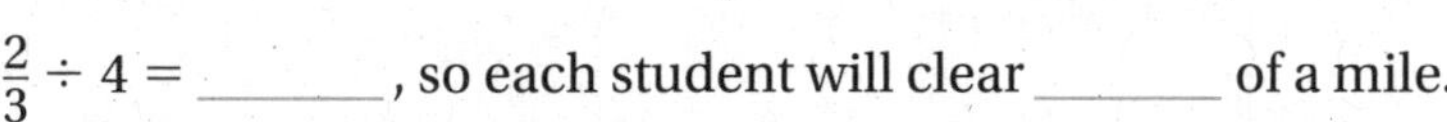

____

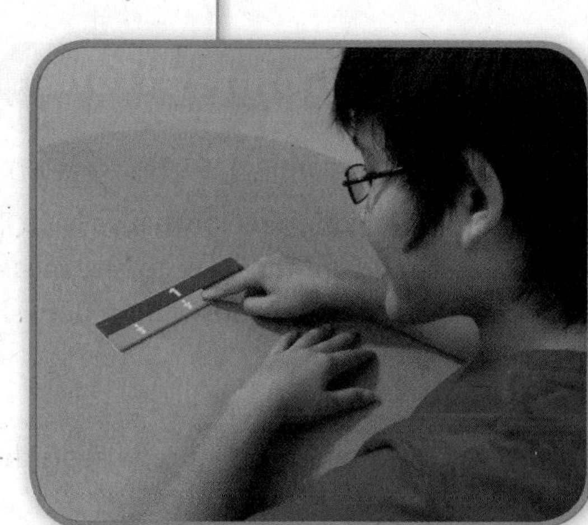

$\frac{2}{3} \div 4 =$ ______, so each student will clear ______ of a mile.

B. Another team clears a section of the path that is $\frac{3}{4}$ mi long. If each student clears $\frac{1}{8}$ of a mile, how many students are on the team?

Divide $\frac{3}{4} \div \frac{1}{8}$.

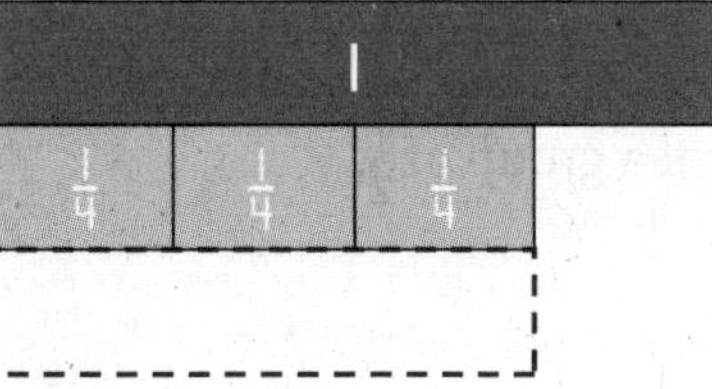

- Use fraction strips to model the division. Draw your model.

- What are you trying to find?

____

$\frac{3}{4} \div \frac{1}{8} =$ ______, so there are ______ students on the team.

Draw Conclusions

1. MATHEMATICAL PRACTICE 4 **Use Models** Explain how the model in problem A shows a related multiplication fact.

____

2. MATHEMATICAL PRACTICE 1 **Analyze** Suppose a whole number is divided by a fraction between 0 and 1. Is the quotient greater than or less than the dividend? Explain and give an example.

____

____

____

Make Connections

You can draw a model to help you solve a fraction division problem.

Jessica is making a recipe that calls for $\frac{3}{4}$ cup of flour. Suppose she only has a $\frac{1}{2}$ cup-size measuring scoop. How many $\frac{1}{2}$ cup scoops of flour does she need?

Divide $\frac{3}{4} \div \frac{1}{2}$.

STEP 1 Draw a model that represents the total amount of flour.

Think: Divide a whole into ________.

Jessica needs ________ cup.

STEP 2 Draw fraction parts that represent the scoops of flour.

Think: What are you trying to find?

____

There is ______ full group of $\frac{1}{2}$ and ______ of a group of $\frac{1}{2}$.

So, there are ______ groups of $\frac{1}{2}$ in $\frac{3}{4}$.

$\frac{3}{4} \div \frac{1}{2} =$ ______, so Jessica will need ______ scoops of flour.

Math Talk **Mathematical Practices**

Explain how you used the model to determine the number of groups of $\frac{1}{2}$ in $\frac{3}{4}$.

- **What if** Jessica's recipe calls for $\frac{1}{4}$ cup flour? How many $\frac{1}{2}$ cup scoops of flour does she need?

____

Name ______________________________

Share and Show

Use the model to find the quotient.

1. $\frac{1}{2} \div 3 =$ ______

Think: $\frac{1}{2}$ is shared among 3 groups.

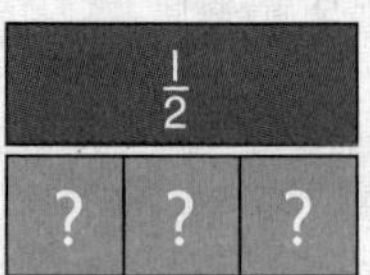

2. $\frac{3}{4} \div \frac{3}{8} =$ ______

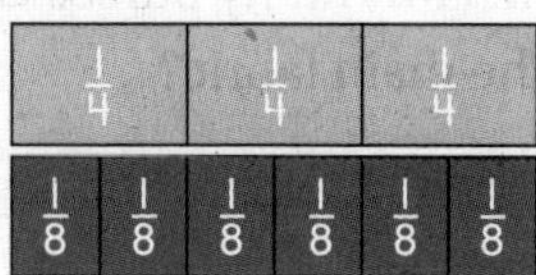

Use fraction strips to find the quotient. Then draw the model.

3. $\frac{1}{3} \div 4 =$ ______

4. $\frac{3}{5} \div \frac{3}{10} =$ ______

Draw a model to solve.

5. How many $\frac{1}{4}$ cup servings of raisins are in $\frac{3}{8}$ cup of raisins?

______

6. How many $\frac{1}{3}$ lb bags of trail mix can Josh make from $\frac{5}{6}$ lb of trail mix?

______

7. WRITE ▸Math **Pose a Problem** Write and solve a problem for $\frac{3}{4} \div 3$ that represents how much in each of 3 groups.

______

______

Problem Solving • Applications Real World

The table shows the amount of each material that students in a sewing class need for one purse.

Use the table for 8–10. Use models to solve.

Purse Materials (yd)	
Ribbon	$\frac{1}{4}$
Main fabric	$\frac{1}{6}$
Trim fabric	$\frac{1}{12}$

8. GO DEEPER Mrs. Brown has $\frac{1}{3}$ yd of blue denim and $\frac{1}{2}$ yd of black denim. How many purses can be made using denim as the main fabric?

9. THINK SMARTER One student brings $\frac{1}{2}$ yd of ribbon. If 3 students receive an equal length of the ribbon, how much ribbon will each student receive? Will each of them have enough ribbon for a purse? Explain.

10. MATHEMATICAL PRACTICE 3 **Make Arguments** There was $\frac{1}{2}$ yd of purple and pink striped fabric. Jessie said she could only make $\frac{1}{24}$ of a purse using that fabric as the trim. Is she correct? Use what you know about the meanings of multiplication and division to defend your answer.

WRITE Math • Show Your Work

11. THINK SMARTER Draw a model to find the quotient.

$\frac{1}{2} \div 4 = \square$

FOR MORE PRACTICE:
Standards Practice Book

Name ______________________________

Estimate Quotients

Essential Question How can you use compatible numbers to estimate quotients of fractions and mixed numbers?

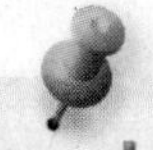

The Number System—6.NS.1

MATHEMATICAL PRACTICES
MP.1, MP.2, MP.3, MP.6

CONNECT You have used compatible numbers to estimate quotients of whole numbers and decimals. You can also use compatible numbers to estimate quotients of fractions and mixed numbers.

Remember

Compatible numbers are pairs of numbers that are easy to compute mentally.

Unlock the Problem Real World

Humpback whales have "songs" that they repeat continuously over periods of several hours. Eric is using an underwater microphone to record a $3\frac{5}{6}$ minute humpback song. He has $15\frac{3}{4}$ minutes of battery power left. About how many times will he be able to record the song?

- Which operation should you use to solve the problem? Why?

____

____

- How do you know that the problem calls for an estimate?

____

One Way Estimate $15\frac{3}{4} \div 3\frac{5}{6}$ using compatible numbers.

Think: What whole numbers close to $15\frac{3}{4}$ and $3\frac{5}{6}$ are easy to divide mentally?

$15\frac{3}{4}$ is close to ______.

$3\frac{5}{6}$ is close to ______.

Rewrite the problem using compatible numbers.

$15\frac{3}{4} \div 3\frac{5}{6}$

$\downarrow \quad \downarrow$

Divide.

$16 \div 4 =$ ______

So, Eric will be able to record the complete whale song about ______ times.

1. MATHEMATICAL PRACTICE 3 **Compare Strategies** To estimate $15\frac{3}{4} \div 3\frac{5}{6}$, Martin used 15 and 3 as compatible numbers. Tina used 15 and 4. Were their choices good ones? Explain why or why not.

____

____

____

Example Estimate using compatible numbers.

A $5\frac{2}{3} \div \frac{5}{8}$

Rewrite the problem using compatible numbers.

$$5\frac{2}{3} \div \frac{5}{8}$$
$$\downarrow \qquad \downarrow$$
$$\_\_\_\_\_ \div \_\_\_\_\_$$

Think: How many halves are there in 6? $6 \div \frac{1}{2} = \_\_\_\_\_$

So, $5\frac{2}{3} \div \frac{5}{8}$ is about ______.

B $\frac{7}{8} \div \frac{1}{4}$

Rewrite the problem using compatible numbers.

$$\frac{7}{8} \div \frac{1}{4}$$
$$\downarrow \qquad \downarrow$$
$$\_\_\_\_\_ \div \frac{1}{4}$$

Think: How many fourths are there in 1? $1 \div \frac{1}{4} = \_\_\_\_\_$

So, $\frac{7}{8} \div \frac{1}{4}$ is about ______.

2. MATHEMATICAL PRACTICE 2 **Use Reasoning** Will the actual quotient $5\frac{2}{3} \div \frac{5}{8}$ be greater than or less than the estimated quotient? Explain.

3. Will the actual quotient $\frac{7}{8} \div \frac{1}{4}$ be greater than or less than the estimated quotient? Explain.

4. MATHEMATICAL PRACTICE 6 **Explain** how you would estimate the quotient $14\frac{3}{4} \div 3\frac{9}{10}$ using compatible numbers.

Name ______________________

Share and Show

Estimate using compatible numbers.

1. $22\frac{4}{5} \div 6\frac{1}{4}$
   ↓ ↓
   ______ ÷ ______ = ______

2. $12 \div 3\frac{3}{4}$ ______

3. $33\frac{7}{8} \div 5\frac{1}{3}$ ______

4. $3\frac{7}{8} \div \frac{5}{9}$ ______

5. $34\frac{7}{12} \div 7\frac{3}{8}$ ______

6. $1\frac{2}{9} \div \frac{1}{6}$ ______

Mathematical Practices

Explain how using compatible numbers is different than rounding to estimate $35\frac{1}{2} \div 6\frac{5}{6}$.

On Your Own

Estimate using compatible numbers.

7. $44\frac{1}{4} \div 11\frac{7}{9}$ ______

8. $71\frac{11}{12} \div 8\frac{3}{4}$ ______

9. $1\frac{1}{6} \div \frac{1}{8}$ ______

THINK SMARTER **Estimate to compare. Write <, >, or =.**

10. $21\frac{3}{10} \div 2\frac{5}{6}$ ◯ $35\frac{7}{9} \div 3\frac{2}{3}$

11. $29\frac{4}{5} \div 5\frac{1}{6}$ ◯ $27\frac{8}{9} \div 6\frac{5}{8}$

12. $55\frac{5}{6} \div 6\frac{7}{10}$ ◯ $11\frac{5}{7} \div \frac{5}{8}$

13. Marion is making school flags. Each flag uses $2\frac{3}{4}$ yards of felt. Marion has $24\frac{1}{8}$ yards of felt. About how many flags can he make?

____

14. GO DEEPER A garden snail travels about $2\frac{3}{5}$ feet in 1 minute. At that speed, about how many hours would it take the snail to travel 350 feet?

____

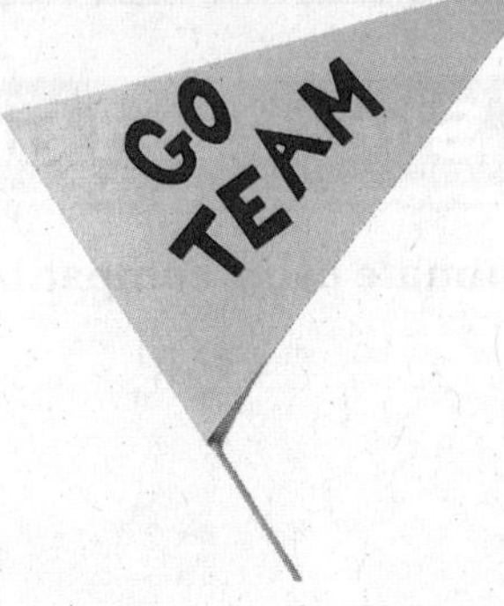

What's the Error?

15. Megan is making pennants from a piece of butcher paper that is $10\frac{3}{8}$ yards long. Each pennant requires $\frac{3}{8}$ yard of paper. To estimate the number of pennants she could make, Megan estimated the quotient $10\frac{3}{8} \div \frac{3}{8}$.

Look at how Megan solved the problem. Find her error.

Estimate:

$10\frac{3}{8} \div \frac{3}{8}$

$\downarrow \quad \downarrow$

$10 \div \frac{1}{2} = 5$

Correct the error. Estimate the quotient.

So, Megan can make about ______ pennants.

- MATHEMATICAL PRACTICE 1 **Describe** the error that Megan made.

- MATHEMATICAL PRACTICE 6 **Explain** Tell which compatible numbers you used to estimate $10\frac{3}{8} \div \frac{3}{8}$. Explain why you chose those numbers.

16. THINK SMARTER For numbers 16a–16c, estimate to compare. Choose <, >, or =.

16a. $18\frac{3}{10} \div 2\frac{5}{6}$ [< / > / =] $30\frac{7}{9} \div 3\frac{1}{3}$

16b. $17\frac{4}{5} \div 6\frac{1}{6}$ [< / > / =] $19\frac{8}{9} \div 4\frac{5}{8}$

16c. $35\frac{5}{6} \div 6\frac{1}{4}$ [< / > / =] $11\frac{5}{7} \div 2\frac{3}{4}$

FOR MORE PRACTICE: Standards Practice Book

Name ____________________

Lesson 2.7

Divide Fractions

Essential Question How do you divide fractions?

The Number System—6.NS.1

MATHEMATICAL PRACTICES
MP.1, MP.7, MP.8

Unlock the Problem (Real World)

Toby and his dad are building a doghouse. They need to cut a board that is $\frac{2}{3}$ yard long into $\frac{1}{6}$ yard pieces. How many $\frac{1}{6}$ yard pieces can they cut?

One Way Divide $\frac{2}{3} \div \frac{1}{6}$ by using a number line.

STEP 1 Draw a number line, and shade it to represent the total length of the board.

Think: Divide a whole into thirds.

Toby and his dad have $\frac{2}{3}$ yard, so shade $\frac{2}{3}$.

STEP 2 Show fraction parts that represent the pieces of board.

Think: Find the number of groups of $\frac{1}{6}$ in $\frac{2}{3}$.

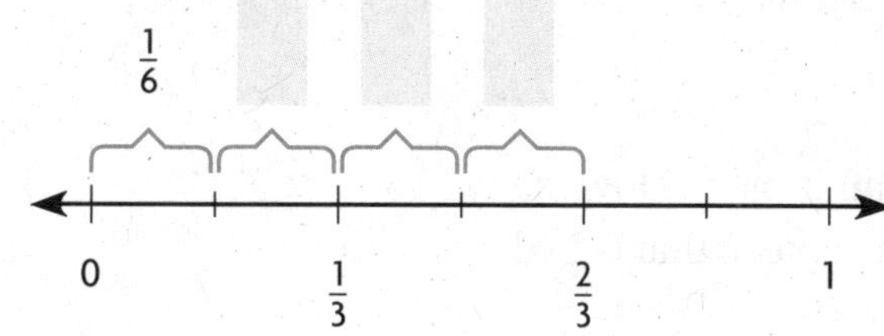

So, there are ______ $\frac{1}{6}$ yard pieces in $\frac{2}{3}$ yard.

Another Way Divide $\frac{2}{3} \div \frac{1}{6}$ by using a common denominator.

STEP 1 Write equivalent fractions using a common denominator.

Think: ______ is a multiple of 3 and 6,

so ______ is a common denominator.

$$\frac{2}{3} \div \frac{1}{6} = \frac{2 \times \square}{3 \times \square} \div \frac{1}{6} = \frac{\square}{6} \div \frac{1}{6}$$

STEP 2 Divide.

Think: There are ______ groups of $\frac{1}{6}$ in $\frac{4}{6}$.

$$\frac{4}{6} \div \frac{1}{6} = \_\_\_\_$$

So, $\frac{2}{3} \div \frac{1}{6} =$ ______. Toby and his dad can cut ______ $\frac{1}{6}$ yard pieces.

Math Talk **Mathematical Practices**

Explain how to find the quotient $\frac{2}{3} \div \frac{2}{9}$ by using a common denominator.

You can use reciprocals and inverse operations to divide fractions.

Two numbers whose product is 1 are **reciprocals** or **multiplicative inverses**.

$\frac{2}{3} \times \frac{3}{2} = 1$ $\frac{2}{3}$ and $\frac{3}{2}$ are reciprocals.

Activity Find a pattern.

- Complete the table by finding the products.
- How are each pair of division and multiplication problems the same, and how are they different?

______

______

______

Division	Multiplication
$\frac{4}{7} \div \frac{2}{7} = 2$	$\frac{4}{7} \times \frac{7}{2} =$
$\frac{5}{6} \div \frac{4}{6} = \frac{5}{4}$	$\frac{5}{6} \times \frac{6}{4} =$
$\frac{1}{3} \div \frac{5}{9} = \frac{3}{5}$	$\frac{1}{3} \times \frac{9}{5} =$

- How could you use the pattern in the table to rewrite a division problem involving fractions as a multiplication problem?

______

______

Example

Winnie needs pieces of string for a craft project. How many $\frac{1}{12}$ yd pieces of string can she cut from a piece that is $\frac{3}{4}$ yd long?

Divide $\frac{3}{4} \div \frac{1}{12}$.

Estimate. ______ $\div \frac{1}{12} =$ ______

Use the reciprocal of the divisor to write a multiplication problem. $\frac{3}{4} \div \frac{1}{12} = \frac{3}{4} \times$ ______

Simplify the factors. $= \frac{3}{4} \times \frac{12}{1}$

Multiply. $=$ ______

Check your answer. $\frac{1}{12} \times$ ______ $=$ ______ $=$ ______

Since the estimate is ______, the answer is reasonable.

So, Winnie can cut ______ $\frac{1}{12}$ yd pieces of string.

Mathematical Practices

Explain how you used multiplication to check your answer.

Name ______________________________

Share and Show

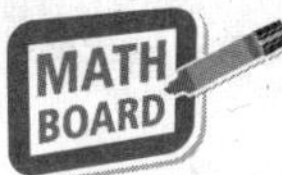

Estimate. Then find the quotient.

1. $\frac{5}{6} \div 3$

Estimate. ______ $\div 3 =$ ______

Write the whole number as a fraction.

$\frac{5}{6} \div \frac{3}{\square}$

Use the reciprocal of the divisor to write a multiplication problem.

$\frac{5}{6} \times \frac{\square}{\square} = \frac{\square}{\square}$

Use a number line to find the quotient.

2. $\frac{3}{4} \div \frac{1}{8} =$ ______

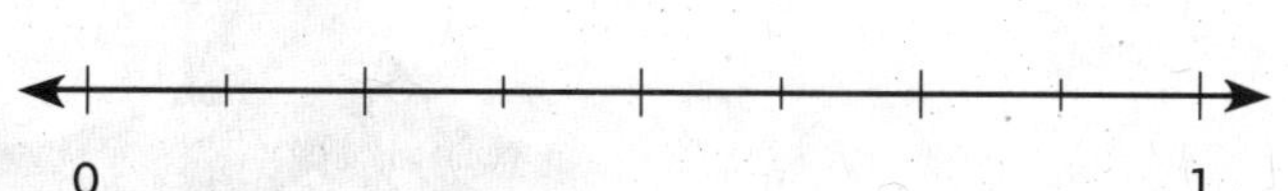

3. $\frac{3}{5} \div \frac{3}{10} =$ ______

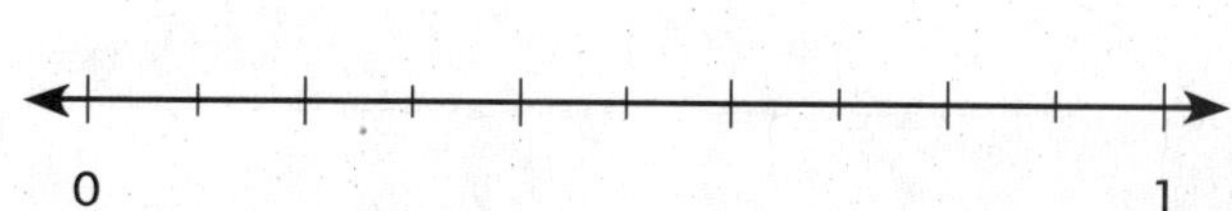

Estimate. Then write the quotient in simplest form.

4. $\frac{3}{4} \div \frac{5}{6}$ ______

5. $3 \div \frac{3}{4}$ ______

6. $\frac{1}{2} \div \frac{3}{4}$ ______

7. $\frac{5}{12} \div 3$ ______

Mathematical Practices

Explain how to find a reasonable estimate for $\frac{11}{12} \div \frac{1}{4}$.

On Your Own

Practice: Copy and Solve **Estimate. Then write the quotient in simplest form.**

8. $2 \div \frac{1}{8}$

9. $\frac{3}{4} \div \frac{3}{5}$

10. $\frac{2}{5} \div 5$

11. $4 \div \frac{1}{7}$

Practice: Copy and Solve **Evaluate using the order of operations. Write the answer in simplest form.**

12. $\left(\frac{3}{5} + \frac{1}{10}\right) \div 2$

13. $\frac{3}{5} + \frac{1}{10} \div 2$

14. $\frac{3}{5} + 2 \div \frac{1}{10}$

15. MATHEMATICAL PRACTICE 8 **Generalize** Suppose the divisor and the dividend of a division problem are both fractions between 0 and 1, and the divisor is greater than the dividend. Is the quotient less than, equal to, or greater than 1?

____

Problem Solving • Applications

Use the table for 16–19.

Tree House Measurements	
Item	Board Length
Ladder rung	$\frac{3}{4}$ ft
"Keep Out" sign	$\frac{5}{8}$ yd
Windowsill	$\frac{1}{2}$ yd

16. Kristen wants to cut ladder rungs from a 6 ft board. How many ladder rungs can she cut?

______

17. THINK SMARTER **Pose a Problem** Look back at Problem 16. Write and solve a new problem by changing the length of the board Kristen is cutting for ladder rungs.

______

______

______

______

18. Dan paints a design that has 8 equal parts along the entire length of the windowsill. How long is each part of the design?

______

19. GO DEEPER Dan has a board that is $\frac{15}{16}$ yd. How many "Keep Out" signs can he make if the length of the sign is changed to half of the original length?

______

WRITE ▸ Math • Show Your Work

Personal Math Trainer

20. THINK SMARTER + Lauren has $\frac{3}{4}$ cup of dried fruit. She puts the dried fruit into bags, each holding $\frac{1}{8}$ cup. How many bags will Lauren use? Explain your answer using words and numbers.

______

______

______

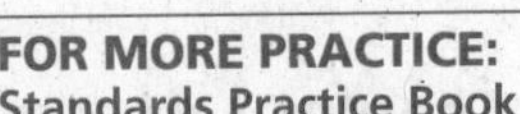

FOR MORE PRACTICE:
Standards Practice Book

Name ______________________________

Model Mixed Number Division

Essential Question How can you use a model to show division of mixed numbers?

The Number System—6.NS.1

MATHEMATICAL PRACTICES
MP.2, MP.4, MP.5

Investigate

Materials ■ pattern blocks

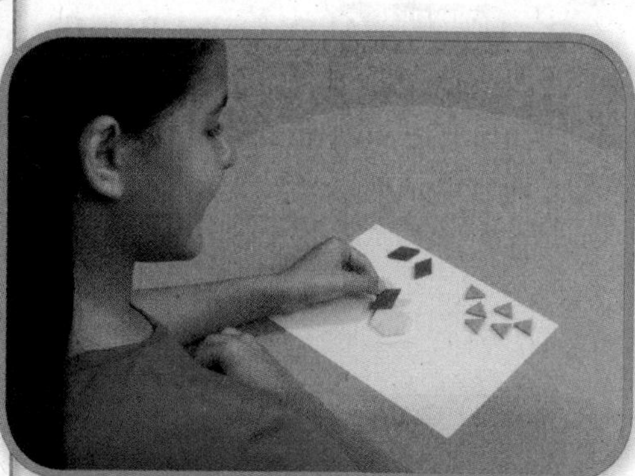

A science teacher has $1\frac{2}{3}$ cups of baking soda. She performs an experiment for her students by mixing $\frac{1}{6}$ cup of baking soda with vinegar. If the teacher uses the same amount of baking soda for each experiment, how many times can she perform the experiment?

A. Which operation should you use to find the answer? Why?

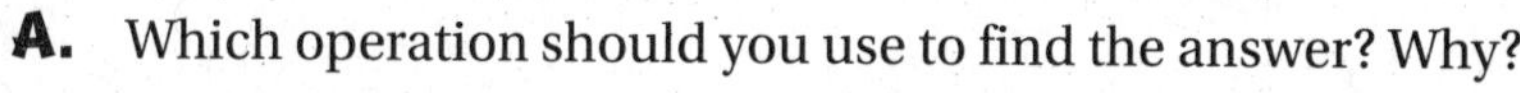

____

____

B. Use pattern blocks to show $1\frac{2}{3}$.

Draw your model.

Think: A hexagon block is one whole, and a rhombus is

_______ of a whole.

- What type and number of blocks did you use to model $1\frac{2}{3}$?

____

C. Cover $1\frac{2}{3}$ with blocks that represent $\frac{1}{6}$ to show dividing by $\frac{1}{6}$. Draw your model.

Think: One ____________ block represents _______ of a whole.

_______ triangle blocks cover $1\frac{2}{3}$.

$1\frac{2}{3} \div \frac{1}{6} =$ _______

So, the teacher can perform the experiment _______ times.

Math Talk **Mathematical Practices**

Explain how you could check that your answer is reasonable.

Draw Conclusions

1. MATHEMATICAL PRACTICE 4 **Communicate** Tell how your model shows a related multiplication problem.

2. MATHEMATICAL PRACTICE 4 **Describe Relationships** Suppose a mixed number is divided by a fraction between 0 and 1. Is the quotient greater than or less than the dividend? Explain and give an example.

Make Connections

You can use a model to divide a mixed number by a whole number.

Naomi has $2\frac{1}{4}$ quarts of lemonade. She wants to divide the lemonade equally between 2 pitchers. How many quarts of lemonade should she pour into each pitcher?

Divide $2\frac{1}{4} \div 2$.

STEP 1 Draw a model that represents the total amount of lemonade.

Think: Divide 3 wholes into ______.

Shade ______.

STEP 2 Draw parts that represent the amount in each pitcher.

Think: What are you trying to find?

______

Think: In each of the two equal groups there is ______ whole and ______ of $\frac{1}{4}$.

$\frac{1}{2}$ of $\frac{1}{4}$ is ______.

So, $2\frac{1}{4} \div 2 =$ ______. Naomi should pour ______ quarts of lemonade into each pitcher.

Math Talk — **Mathematical Practices**

Explain how the quotient compares to the dividend when dividing a mixed number by a whole number greater than 1.

Name ___________________________

Share and Show

Use the model to find the quotient.

1. $3\frac{1}{3} \div \frac{1}{3} =$ ______

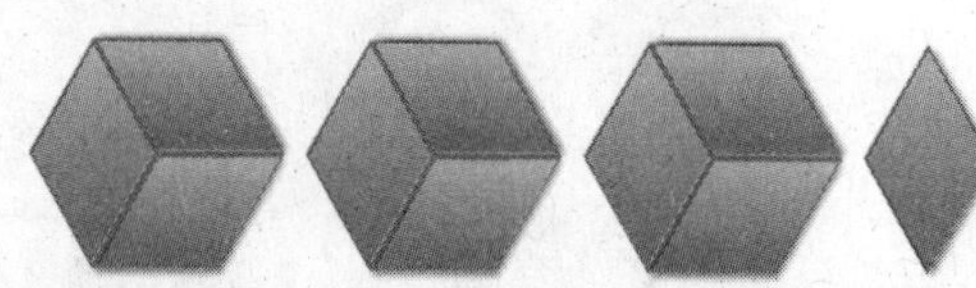

2. $2\frac{1}{2} \div \frac{1}{6} =$ ______

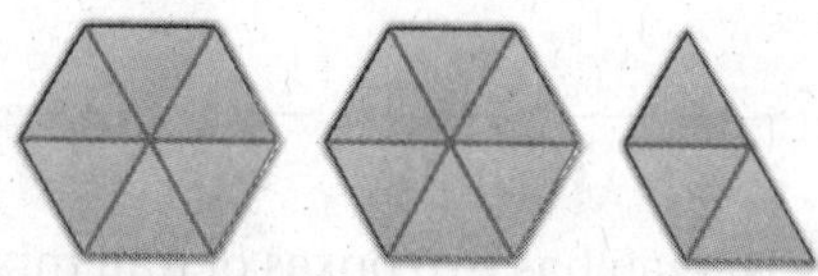

Use pattern blocks to find the quotient. Then draw the model.

3. $2\frac{2}{3} \div \frac{1}{6} =$ ______

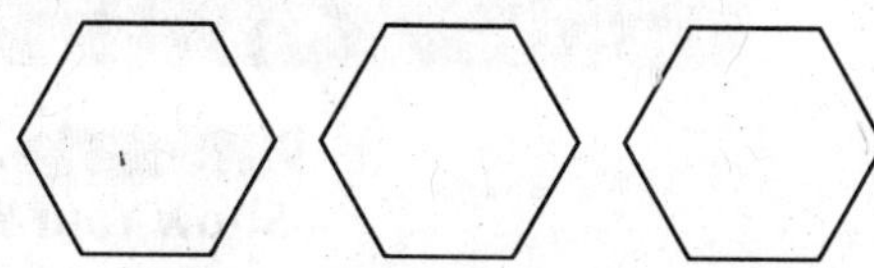

4. $3\frac{1}{2} \div \frac{1}{2} =$ ______

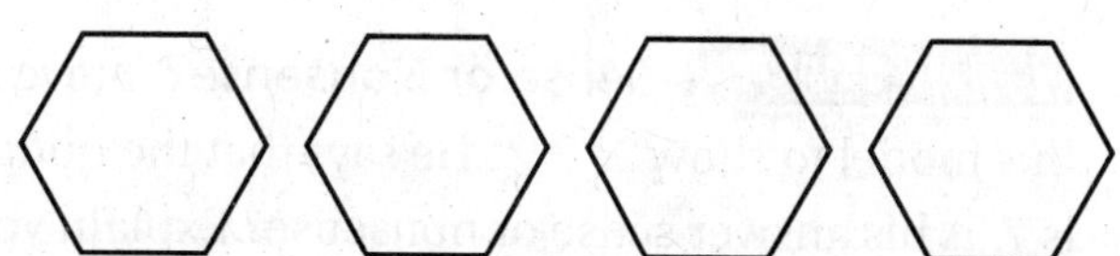

Draw a model to find the quotient.

5. $3\frac{1}{2} \div 3 =$ ______

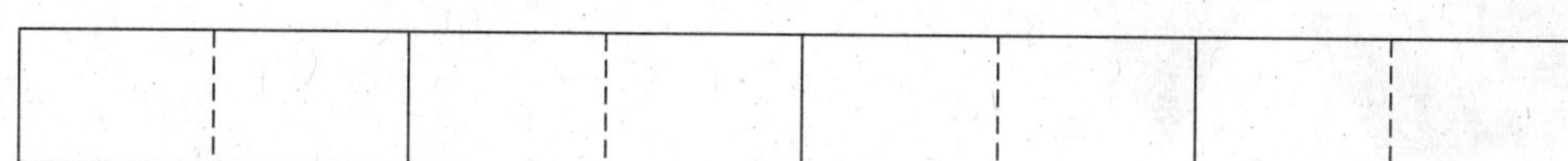

6. $1\frac{1}{4} \div 2 =$ ______

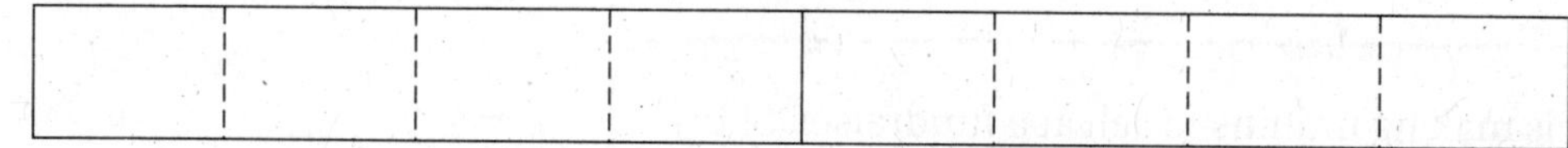

7. MATHEMATICAL PRACTICE 5 **Use Appropriate Tools** Explain how models can be used to divide mixed numbers by fractions or whole numbers.

____

____

____

____

Problem Solving • Applications

Use a model to solve.

8. MATHEMATICAL PRACTICE 4 **Use Models** Eliza opens a box of bead kits. The box weighs $2\frac{2}{3}$ lb. Each bead kit weighs $\frac{1}{6}$ lb. How many kits are in the box?

______

9. GO DEEPER Hassan has two boxes of trail mix. Each box holds $1\frac{2}{3}$ lb of trail mix. He eats $\frac{1}{3}$ lb of trail mix each day. How many days can Hassan eat trail mix before he runs out?

______

10. THINK SMARTER **Sense or Nonsense?** Steve made this model to show $2\frac{1}{3} \div \frac{1}{6}$. He says that the quotient is 7. Is his answer sense or nonsense? Explain your reasoning.

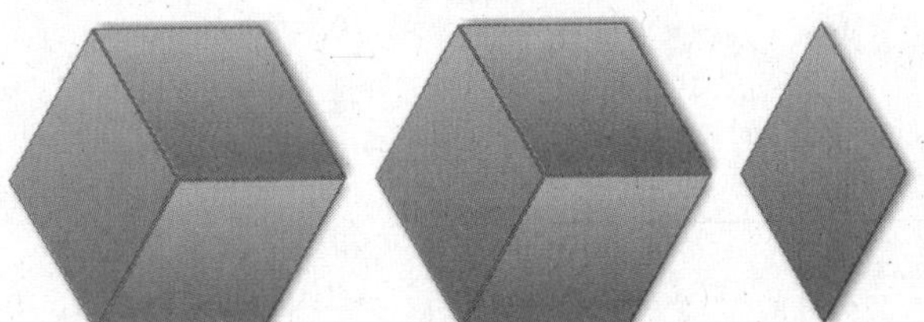

______

______

______

WRITE Math
Show Your Work

11. THINK SMARTER Eva is making muffins to sell at a fundraiser. She has $2\frac{1}{4}$ cups of flour, and the recipe calls for $\frac{3}{4}$ cup of flour for each batch of muffins. Explain how to use a model to find the number of batches of muffins Eva can make.

______

______

______

______

______

FOR MORE PRACTICE:
Standards Practice Book

Name ______________________

Divide Mixed Numbers

Essential Question How do you divide mixed numbers?

The Number System—6.NS.1
MATHEMATICAL PRACTICES MP.1, MP.6

Unlock the Problem

A box weighing $9\frac{1}{3}$ lb contains robot kits weighing $1\frac{1}{6}$ lb apiece. How many robot kits are in the box?

- Underline the sentence that tells you what you are trying to find.
- Circle the numbers you need to use to solve the problem.

Divide $9\frac{1}{3} \div 1\frac{1}{6}$.

Estimate the quotient. _______ ÷ _______ = _______

Write the mixed numbers as fractions. $9\frac{1}{3} \div 1\frac{1}{6} = \frac{\square}{3} \div \frac{\square}{6}$

Use the reciprocal of the divisor to write a multiplication problem. $= \frac{28}{3} \times \frac{\square}{\square}$

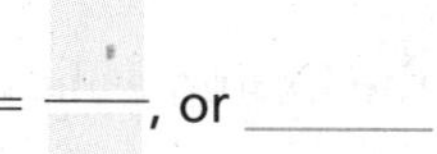

Simplify. $= \frac{\overset{\square}{\cancel{28}}}{\underset{\square}{\cancel{3}}} \times \frac{\overset{\square}{\cancel{6}}}{\underset{\square}{\cancel{7}}}$

Multiply. $= \frac{\square}{\square}$, or _______

Compare your estimate with the quotient. Since the estimate, _______,

is close to _______, the answer is reasonable.

So, there are _______ robot kits in the box.

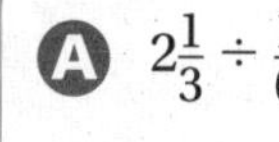

Try This! Estimate. Then write the quotient in simplest form.

Think: Write the mixed numbers as fractions.

A $2\frac{1}{3} \div \frac{1}{6}$

____

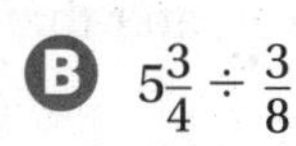

B $5\frac{3}{4} \div \frac{3}{8}$

____

Example

Four hikers shared $3\frac{1}{3}$ qt of water equally. How much did each hiker receive?

Divide $3\frac{1}{3} \div 4$. Check.

Estimate. ______ $\div 4 = 1$

Write the mixed number and the whole number as fractions. $3\frac{1}{3} \div 4 = \frac{\square}{3} \div \frac{\square}{\square}$

Use the reciprocal of the divisor to write a multiplication problem. $= \frac{10}{3} \times \frac{\square}{\square}$

Simplify. $= \frac{10}{3} \times \frac{1}{4}$

Multiply. $=$ ______

Check your answer. $4 \times$ ______ $= \frac{\square}{\square} =$ ______

So, each hiker received ______ qt.

Math Talk **Mathematical Practices**

Explain why your answer is reasonable using the information in the problem.

1. Describe what you are trying to find in the Example above.

______

2. MATHEMATICAL PRACTICE 6 **Compare** Explain how dividing mixed numbers is similar to multiplying mixed numbers. How are they different?

______

______

______

______

3. THINK SMARTER The divisor in a division problem is between 0 and 1 and the dividend is greater than 0. Will the quotient be greater than or less than the dividend? Explain.

______

______

Name ______________________________

Share and Show

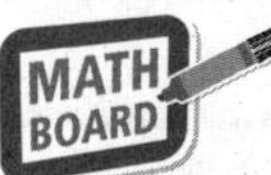

Estimate. Then write the quotient in simplest form.

1. $4\frac{1}{3} \div \frac{3}{4} = \frac{\square}{3} \div \frac{3}{4}$

$= \frac{13}{3} \times \frac{\square}{\square}$

$= \frac{\square}{\square}$, or $5\frac{\square}{9}$

2. Six hikers shared $4\frac{1}{2}$ lb of trail mix. How much trail mix did each hiker receive?

3. $5\frac{2}{3} \div 3$

4. $7\frac{1}{2} \div 2\frac{1}{2}$

Math Talk **Mathematical Practices**

Explain why you write a mixed number as a fraction before using it as a dividend or divisor.

On Your Own

Estimate. Then write the quotient in simplest form.

5. How many $3\frac{1}{3}$ yd pieces can Amanda get from a $13\frac{1}{3}$ yd ribbon?

6. Samantha cut $6\frac{3}{4}$ yd of yarn into 3 equal pieces. How long was each piece?

7. $5\frac{3}{4} \div 4\frac{1}{2}$

8. $5 \div 1\frac{1}{3}$

9. $6\frac{3}{4} \div 2$

10. $2\frac{2}{9} \div 1\frac{3}{7}$

MATHEMATICAL PRACTICE 1 Evaluate **Algebra** **Evaluate using the order of operations. Write the answer in simplest form.**

11. $1\frac{1}{2} \times 2 \div 1\frac{1}{3}$

12. $1\frac{2}{5} \div 1\frac{13}{15} + \frac{5}{8}$

13. $3\frac{1}{2} - 1\frac{5}{6} \div 1\frac{2}{9}$

14. MATHEMATICAL PRACTICE 7 Look for a Pattern Find these quotients: $20 \div 4\frac{4}{5}$, $10 \div 4\frac{4}{5}$, $5 \div 4\frac{4}{5}$. Describe a pattern you see.

Unlock the Problem

15. GO DEEPER Dina hikes $\frac{1}{2}$ of the easy trail and stops for a break every $3\frac{1}{4}$ miles. How many breaks will she take?

Hiking Trails			
Park	**Trail**	**Length (mi)**	**Difficulty**
Cuyahoga Valley National Park, Ohio	Ohio and Erie Canal Towpath	$19\frac{1}{2}$	easy
	Brandywine Gorge	$1\frac{1}{4}$	moderate
	Buckeye Trail (Jaite to Boston)	$5\frac{3}{5}$	difficult

a. What problem are you asked to solve?

b. How will you use the information in the table to solve the problem?

c. How can you find the distance Dina hikes? How far does she hike?

d. What operation will you use to find how many breaks Dina takes?

e. How many breaks will Dina take?

16. THINK SMARTER Carlo packs $15\frac{3}{4}$ lb of books in 2 boxes. Each book weighs $1\frac{1}{8}$ lb. There are 4 more books in Box A than in Box B. How many books are in Box A? Explain your work.

17. THINK SMARTER Rex's goal is to run $13\frac{3}{4}$ miles over 5 days. He wants to run the same distance each day. Jordan said that Rex would have to run $3\frac{3}{4}$ miles each day to reach his goal. Do you agree with Jordan? Explain your answer using words and numbers.

FOR MORE PRACTICE:
Standards Practice Book

Name ____________________

Problem Solving • Fraction Operations

Essential Question How can you use the strategy *use a model* to help you solve a division problem?

The Number System—6.NS.1

MATHEMATICAL PRACTICES
MP.1, MP.2, MP.4, MP.6

Unlock the Problem (Real World)

Sam had $\frac{3}{4}$ lb of granola. Each day he took $\frac{1}{8}$ lb to school for a snack. If he had $\frac{1}{4}$ lb left over, how many days did Sam take granola to school?

Use the graphic organizer below to help you solve the problem.

Read the Problem

What do I need to find?

I need to find ____________________

____

____________________.

What information do I need to use?

Sam started with ______ lb of granola and took ______ lb each day. He had ______ lb left over.

How will I use the information?

I will draw a bar model to find how much ____________________

____

____________________.

Solve the Problem

$\frac{3}{4}$ lb

$\frac{1}{8}$		
used		left

The model shows that Sam used ______ lb of granola.

______ groups of $\frac{1}{8}$ are equivalent to $\frac{1}{2}$

so $\frac{1}{2} \div \frac{1}{8} =$ ______.

So, Sam took granola to school for ______ days.

Math Talk — **Mathematical Practices**

Explain how you can justify your answer by solving the problem a different way.

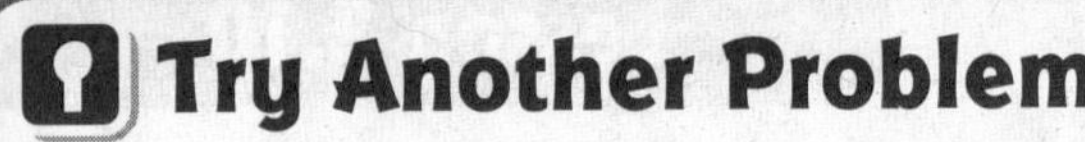

Try Another Problem

For a science experiment, Mr. Barrows divides $\frac{2}{3}$ cup of salt into small jars, each containing $\frac{1}{12}$ cup. If he has $\frac{1}{6}$ cup of salt left over, how many jars does he fill?

Read the Problem

What do I need to find?	What information do I need to use?	How will I use the information?

Solve the Problem

So, Mr. Barrows fills _______ jars.

1. MATHEMATICAL PRACTICE 4 **Write an Expression** you could use to solve the problem.

2. MATHEMATICAL PRACTICE 6 **Explain a Method** Suppose that Mr. Barrows starts with $1\frac{2}{3}$ cups of salt. Explain how you could find how many jars he fills.

Name ______________________________

Share and Show

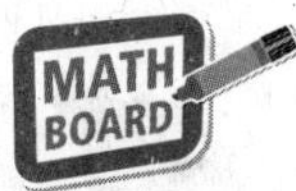

1. There is $\frac{4}{5}$ lb of sand in the class science supplies. If one scoop of sand weighs $\frac{1}{20}$ lb, how many scoops of sand can Maria get from the class supplies and still leave $\frac{1}{2}$ lb in the supplies?

First, draw a bar model.

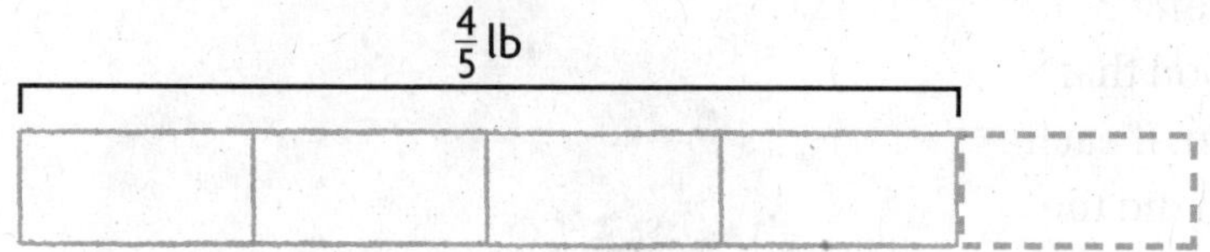

Next, find how much sand Maria gets.

Maria will get $\frac{\square}{10}$ lb of sand.

Finally, find the number of scoops.

_____ groups of $\frac{1}{20}$ are equivalent to $\frac{\square}{10}$

so $\frac{\square}{10} \div \frac{1}{20} =$ _____.

So, Maria will get _____ scoops of sand.

2. THINKSMARTER What if Maria leaves $\frac{2}{5}$ lb of sand in the supplies? How many scoops of sand can she get?

____

3. There are 6 gallons of distilled water in the science supplies. If 10 students each use an equal amount of the distilled water and there is 1 gal left in the supplies, how much will each student get?

____

Unlock the Problem

- Underline the question.
- Circle important information.
- Check to make sure you answered the question.

WRITE Math • Show Your Work

On Your Own

4. THINK SMARTER The total weight of the fish in a tank of tropical fish at Fish 'n' Fur was $\frac{7}{8}$ lb. Each fish weighed $\frac{1}{64}$ lb. After Eric bought some fish, the total weight of the fish remaining in the tank was $\frac{1}{2}$ lb. How many fish did Eric buy?

____

5. GO DEEPER Fish 'n' Fur had a bin containing $2\frac{1}{2}$ lb of gerbil food. After selling bags of gerbil food that each held $\frac{3}{4}$ lb, $\frac{1}{4}$ lb of food was left in the bin. If each bag of gerbil food sold for \$3.25, how much did the store earn?

____

6. MATHEMATICAL PRACTICE 1 **Describe** Niko bought 2 lb of dog treats. He gave his dog $\frac{3}{5}$ lb of treats one week and $\frac{7}{10}$ lb of treats the next week. Describe how Niko can find how much is left.

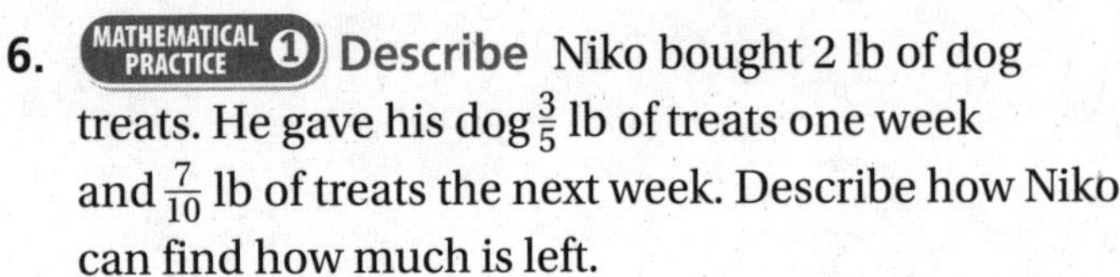

____

____

____

____

WRITE Math • Show Your W

Personal Math Trainer

7. THINK SMARTER + There were $14\frac{1}{4}$ cups of apple juice in a container. Each day, Elise drank $1\frac{1}{2}$ cups of apple juice. Today, there is $\frac{3}{4}$ cup of apple juice left.

Derek said that Elise drank apple juice on nine days. Do you agree with Derek? Use words and numbers to explain your answer.

____

____

____

____

FOR MORE PRACTICE: Standards Practice Book

Name ________________________________

Chapter 2 Review/Test

1. Write the values in order from least to greatest.

0.45	$\frac{3}{4}$	$\frac{5}{8}$	0.5

__________ __________ __________ __________

2. For numbers 2a–2d, compare. Choose <, >, or =.

2a. 0.75 [< | > | =] $\frac{3}{4}$

2b. $\frac{4}{5}$ [< | > | =] 0.325

2c. $1\frac{3}{5}$ [< | > | =] 1.9

2d. 7.4 [< | > | =] $7\frac{2}{5}$

3. The table lists the heights of 4 trees.

Type of Tree	Height (feet)
Sycamore	$15\frac{2}{3}$
Oak	$14\frac{3}{4}$
Maple	$15\frac{3}{4}$
Birch	15.72

For numbers 3a–3d, select True or False for each statement.

3a. The oak tree is the shortest. ○ True ○ False

3b. The birch tree is the tallest. ○ True ○ False

3c. Two of the trees are the same height. ○ True ○ False

3d. The sycamore tree is taller than the maple tree. ○ True ○ False

GO DIGITAL Assessment Options Chapter Test

4. For numbers 4a–4d, choose Yes or No to indicate whether the statement is correct.

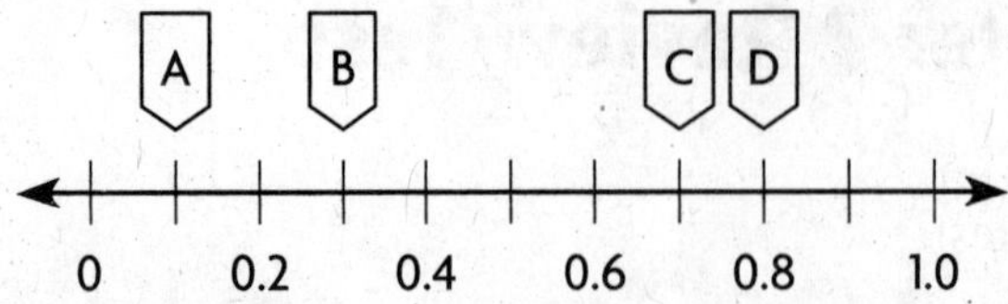

4a. Point *A* represents 1.0. ○ Yes ○ No

4b. Point *B* represents $\frac{3}{10}$. ○ Yes ○ No

4c. Point *C* represents 6.5. ○ Yes ○ No

4d. Point *D* represents $\frac{4}{5}$. ○ Yes ○ No

5. Select the values that are equivalent to one twenty-fifth. Mark all that apply.

Ⓐ $\frac{1}{25}$

Ⓑ 25

Ⓒ 0.04

Ⓓ 0.025

6. The table shows Lily's homework assignment. Lily's teacher instructed the class to simplify each expression by dividing the numerator and denominator by the GCF. Complete the table by simplifying each expression and then finding the product.

Problem	Expression	Simplified Expression	Product
a	$\frac{2}{5} \times \frac{1}{4}$		
b	$\frac{4}{5} \times \frac{5}{8}$		
c	$\frac{3}{7} \times \frac{5}{8}$		
d	$\frac{4}{9} \times \frac{3}{16}$		

Name ________________________________

7. Two-fifths of the fish in Gary's fish tank are guppies. One-fourth of the guppies are red. What fraction of the fish in Gary's tank are red guppies? Show your work.

8. One-third of the students at Finley High School play sports. Two-fifths of the students who play sports are girls. What fraction of all students are girls who play sports? Use numbers and words to explain your answer.

9. Draw a model to find the quotient.

$\frac{3}{4} \div 2 =$ ☐

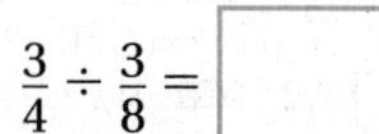

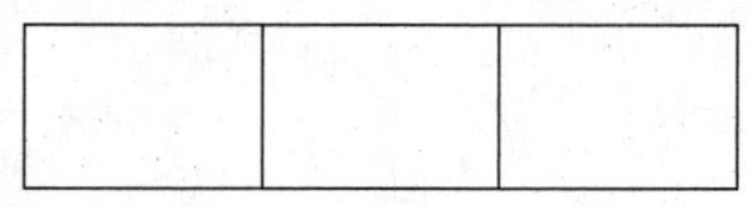

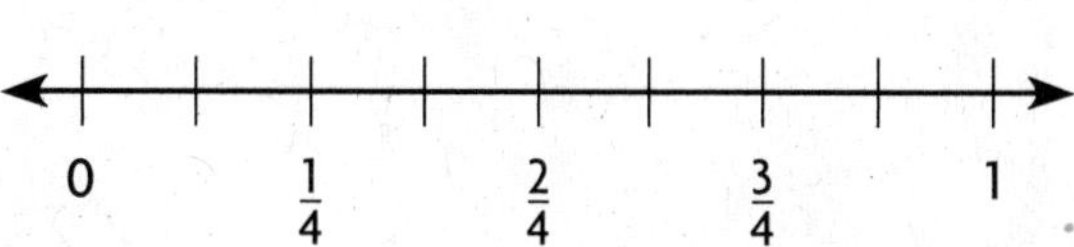

How are your models alike? How are they different?

10. Explain how to use a model to find the quotient.

$2\frac{1}{2} \div 2 =$ ☐

Divide. Show your work.

11. $\frac{7}{8} \div \frac{3}{5} =$ ☐

12. $2\frac{1}{10} \div 1\frac{1}{5} =$ ☐

13. Sophie has $\frac{3}{4}$ quart of lemonade. If she divides the lemonade into glasses that hold $\frac{1}{16}$ quart, how many glasses can Sophie fill? Show your work.

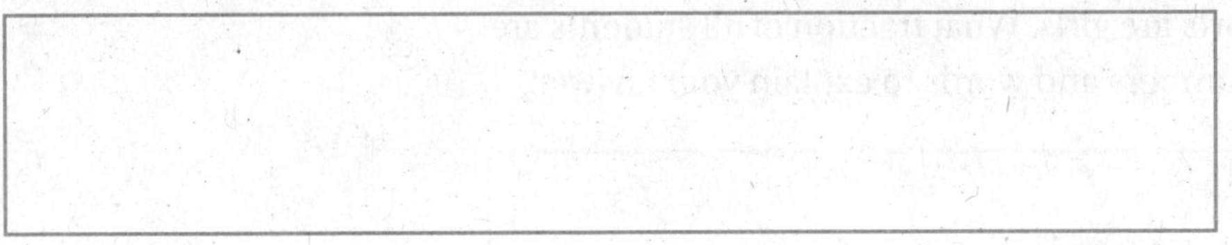

14. Ink cartridges weigh $\frac{1}{8}$ pound. The total weight of the cartridges in a box is $4\frac{1}{2}$ pounds. How many cartridges does the box contain? Show your work and explain why you chose the operation you did.

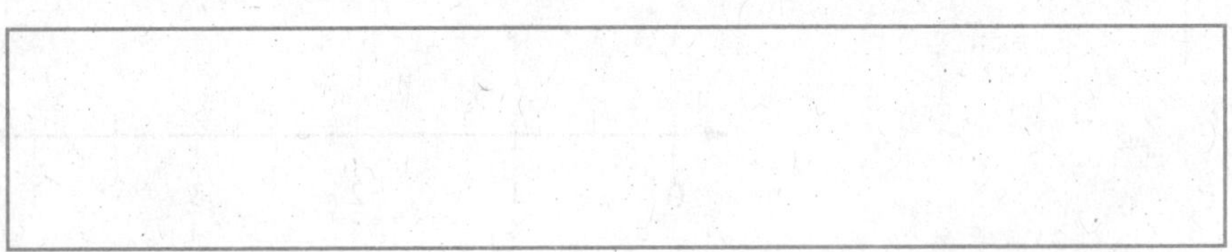

15. Beth had 1 yard of ribbon. She used $\frac{1}{3}$ yard for a project. She wants to divide the rest of the ribbon into pieces $\frac{1}{6}$ yard long. How many $\frac{1}{6}$ yard pieces of ribbon can she make? Explain your solution.

Name ______________________________

16. Complete the table by finding the products. Then answer the questions in Part A and Part B.

Division	Multiplication
$\frac{1}{5} \div \frac{3}{4} = \frac{4}{15}$	$\frac{1}{5} \times \frac{4}{3} =$
$\frac{2}{13} \div \frac{1}{5} = \frac{10}{13}$	$\frac{2}{13} \times \frac{5}{1} =$
$\frac{4}{5} \div \frac{3}{5} = \frac{4}{3}$	$\frac{4}{5} \times \frac{5}{3} =$

Part A

Explain how each pair of division and multiplication problems are the same, and how they are different.

Part B

Explain how to use the pattern in the table to rewrite a division problem involving fractions as a multiplication problem.

17. Margie hiked a $17\frac{7}{8}$ mile trail. She stopped every $3\frac{2}{5}$ miles to take a picture. Martin and Tina estimated how many times Margie stopped.

Martin's Estimate	Tina's Estimate
$17\frac{7}{8} \div 3\frac{2}{5}$ $\downarrow \quad \downarrow$ $16 \div 4 = 4$	$17\frac{7}{8} \div 3\frac{2}{5}$ $\downarrow \quad \downarrow$ $18 \div 3 = 6$

Who made the better estimate? Use numbers and words to explain your answer.

18. Brad and Wes are building a tree house. They cut a $12\frac{1}{2}$ foot piece of wood into 5 of the same length pieces. How long is each piece of wood? Show your work.

Chapter 3

Rational Numbers

Show What You Know

Check your understanding of important skills.

Name ______________________________

Compare Fractions Compare. Write <, >, or =.

1. $\frac{3}{5}$ ◯ $\frac{1}{3}$
2. $\frac{3}{7}$ ◯ $\frac{1}{2}$
3. $\frac{3}{3}$ ◯ $\frac{5}{5}$
4. $\frac{6}{8}$ ◯ $\frac{2}{4}$

Equivalent Fractions Write an equivalent fraction.

5. $\frac{3}{8}$ ______
6. $\frac{2}{5}$ ______
7. $\frac{10}{12}$ ______
8. $\frac{6}{9}$ ______

Compare Decimals Compare. Write <, >, or =.

9. 0.3 ◯ 0.30
10. 4 ◯ 3.8
11. 0.4 ◯ 0.51
12. \$2.61 ◯ \$6.21

Angie finds a treasure map. Be a Math Detective and use the clues to find the location of the treasure. Write the location as an ordered pair.

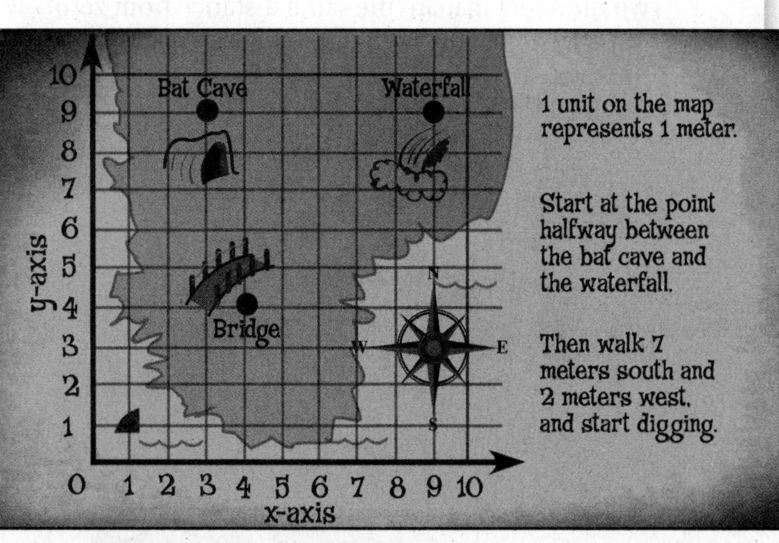

Personal Math Trainer
Online Assessment and Intervention

Vocabulary Builder

▶ Visualize It

Use the checked words to complete the flow map.

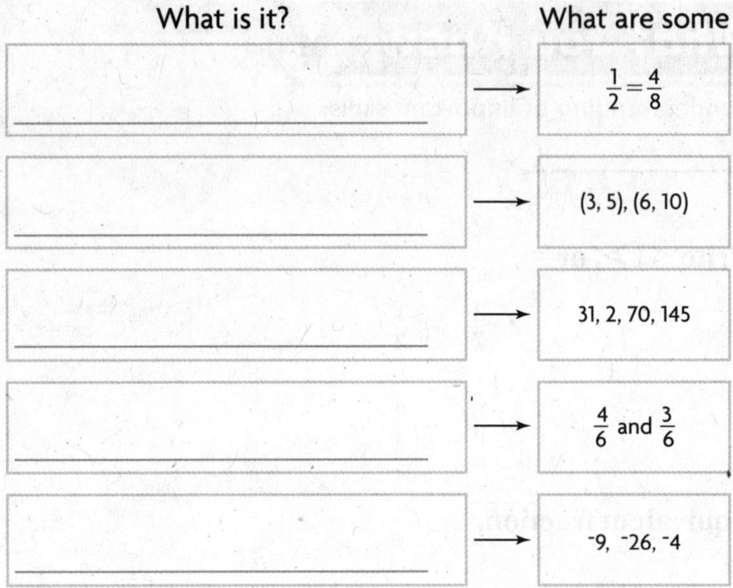

Review Words

- compare
- ✓common denominator
- ✓equivalent fractions
- order
- ✓whole numbers

Preview Words

- absolute value
- coordinate plane
- integers
- ✓negative number
- opposite
- ✓ordered pair
- origin
- positive number
- quadrants
- rational number

▶ Understand Vocabulary

Complete the sentences using the preview words.

1. The ______________________ are the set of whole numbers and their opposites.
2. The distance of a number from 0 on a number line is the number's ______________________.
3. Two numbers that are the same distance from zero on the number line, but on different sides of zero, are called ______________________.
4. A ______________________ is any number that can be written as $\frac{a}{b}$, where a and b are integers and $b \neq 0$.
5. The four regions of the coordinate plane that are separated by the x- and y-axes are called ______________________.

GO DIGITAL
- Interactive Student Edition
- Multimedia eGlossary

Name ______________________________

Understand Positive and Negative Numbers

Essential Question How can you use positive and negative numbers to represent real-world quantities?

The Number System—6.NS.5, 6.NS.6a

MATHEMATICAL PRACTICES
MP.5, MP.6, MP.7

Integers are the set of all whole numbers and their opposites. Two numbers are **opposites** if they are the same distance from 0 on the number line, but on different sides of 0. For example, the integers $^+3$ and $^-3$ are opposites. Zero is its own opposite.

Math Idea

You do not need to write the + symbol for positive integers, so $^+3$ can also be written as 3.

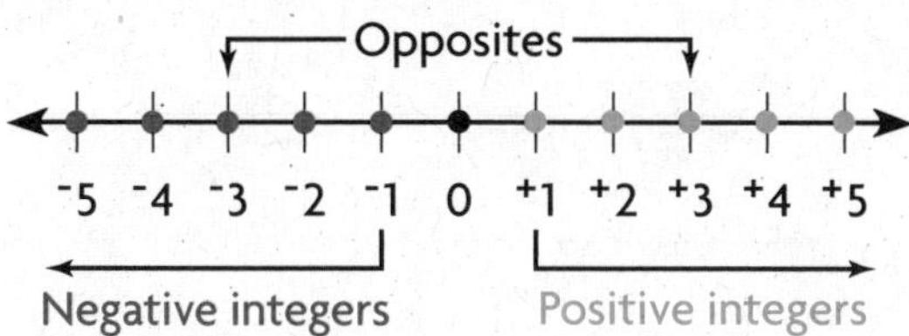

Positive numbers are located to the right of 0 on the number line, and negative numbers are located to the left of 0.

Unlock the Problem

The temperature at the start of a 2009 Major League Baseball playoff game between the Colorado Rockies and the Philadelphia Phillies was 2°C. The temperature at the end of the game was $^-4$°C. What is the opposite of each temperature?

- What are you asked to find?

____

- Where can you find the opposite of a number on the number line?

____

____

Graph each integer and its opposite on a number line.

A 2

The integer 2 is on the _______ side of 0.

Graph the opposite of 2 at _______.

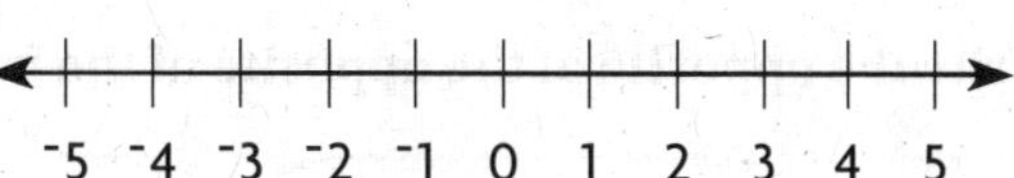

So, the opposite of 2°C is _______.

B $^-4$

The integer $^-4$ is on the _______ side of 0.

Graph the opposite of $^-4$ at _______.

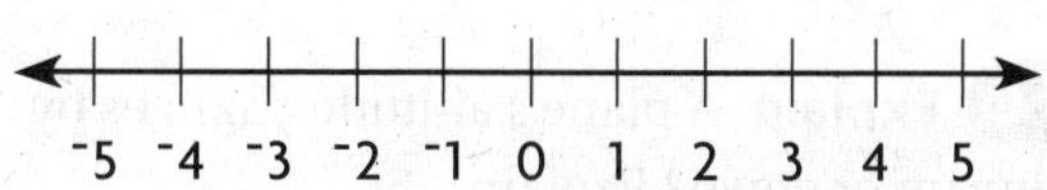

So, the opposite of $^-4$°C is _______.

Mathematical Practices

Explain how to find the opposite of $^-8$ on a number line.

Example 1 Name the integer that represents the situation, and tell what 0 represents in that situation.

Situation	Integer	What Does 0 Represent?
A team loses 10 yards on a football play.	$^{-}10$	the team neither gains nor loses yardage
A point in Yuma, Arizona, is 70 feet above sea level.		
A temperature of 40 degrees below zero was recorded in Missouri.		
Larry withdraws $30 from his bank account.		
Tricia's golf score was 7 strokes below par.		

Example 2 Use a number line to find $^{-}(^{-}3)$, the opposite of the opposite of 3.

STEP 1

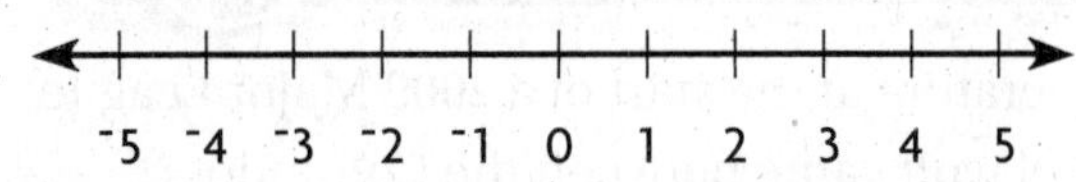

Graph 3 on the number line.

STEP 2

Use the number line to graph the opposite of 3.

STEP 3

Use the number line to graph the opposite of the number you graphed in Step 2.

So, $^{-}(^{-}3)$, or the opposite of the opposite of 3, equals ______.

Try This! **Write the opposite of the opposite of the integer.**

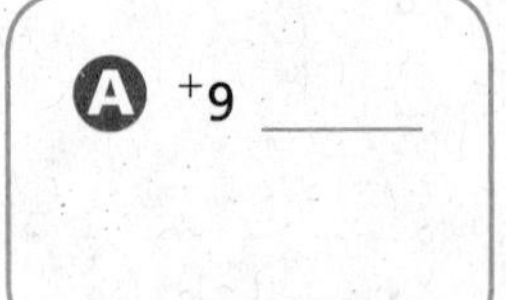
A $^{+}9$ ______

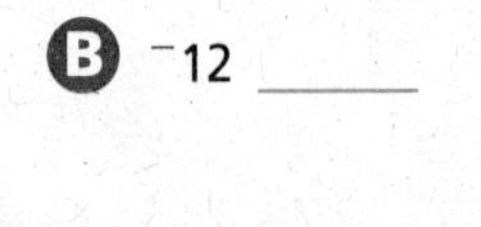
B $^{-}12$ ______

C 0 ______

Math Talk **Mathematical Practices**

Describe the pattern you see when finding the opposite of the opposite of a number.

- MATHEMATICAL PRACTICE 6 **Explain** A plane's altitude changes by $^{-}1{,}000$ feet. Is the plane going up or down? Explain.

Name ________________________

Share and Show

Graph the integer and its opposite on a number line.

1. $^{-}7$ opposite: ______

$^{-}10$ $^{-}8$ $^{-}6$ $^{-}4$ $^{-}2$ 0 2 4 6 8 10

2. 9 opposite: ______

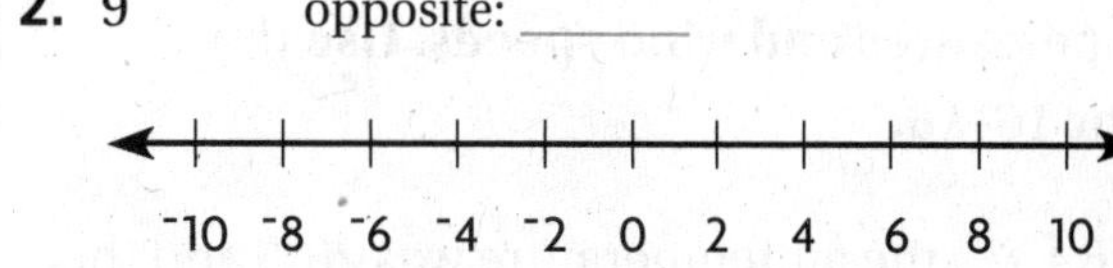

Name the integer that represents the situation, and tell what 0 represents in that situation.

Situation	Integer	What Does 0 Represent?
3. Kerri gained 24 points during a round of a game show.		
4. Ben lost 5 pounds during the summer.		
5. Marcy deposited $35 in her savings account.		

Math Talk — **Mathematical Practices**

Identify a real-world situation involving an integer and its opposite.

On Your Own

Write the opposite of the integer.

6. $^{-}98$ ______

7. 0 ______

8. $^{-}53$ ______

Name the integer that represents the situation, and tell what 0 represents in that situation.

Situation	Integer	What Does 0 Represent?
9. Desmond made $850 at his summer job.		
10. Miguel withdraws $300 from his checking account.		
11. Renee lost 18 points during her turn in the board game.		

Write the opposite of the opposite of the integer.

12. $^{-}23$ ______

13. 17 ______

14. $^{-}125$ ______

15. MATHEMATICAL PRACTICE 6 **Explain** Suppose you know the distance from zero of a certain number on the number line. Explain how you could find the number's distance from its opposite.

____

Problem Solving • Applications Real World

Wind makes the air temperature seem colder. The chart gives the wind chill temperature (what the temperature *seems* like) at several air temperatures and wind speeds. Use the chart for 16–18.

Wind Chill Chart

	Air Temperature (°F)			
Wind (mi/hr)	30	25	20	15
25	16	9	3	$^-4$
35	14	7	0	$^-7$
45	12	5	$^-2$	$^-9$
55	11	3	$^-4$	$^-11$

16. At 6 A.M., the air temperature was 20°F and the wind speed was 55 mi/hr. What was the wind chill temperature at 6 A.M.?

17. GO DEEPER At noon, the air temperature was 15°F and the wind speed was 45 mi/hr. At what air temperature and wind speed would the wind chill temperature be the opposite of what it was at noon?

18. THINK SMARTER The wind was blowing 35 mi/hr in both Ashton and Fenton. The wind chill temperatures in the two towns were opposites. If the air temperature in Ashton was 25°F, what was the air temperature in Fenton?

19. **Sense or Nonsense?** Claudia states that the opposite of any integer is always a different number than the integer. Is Claudia's statement sense or nonsense? Explain.

20. THINK SMARTER For numbers 20a–20d, choose Yes or No to indicate whether the situation can be represented by a negative number.

20a. Death Valley is located 282 feet below sea level. ○ Yes ○ No

20b. Austin's golf score was 3 strokes below par. ○ Yes ○ No

20c. The average temperature in Santa Monica in August is 75°F. ○ Yes ○ No

20d. Janai withdraws $20 from her bank account. ○ Yes ○ No

FOR MORE PRACTICE:
Standards Practice Book

Name ________________________

Compare and Order Integers

Essential Question How can you compare and order integers?

The Number System—6.NS.7a, 6.NS.7b

MATHEMATICAL PRACTICES
MP.5, MP.8

You can use a number line to compare integers.

Unlock the Problem

On one play of a football game, the ball changed position by $^-7$ yards. On the next play, the ball changed position by $^-4$ yards. Compare $^-7$ and $^-4$.

Use a number line to compare the numbers.

STEP 1 Graph $^-7$ and $^-4$ on the number line.

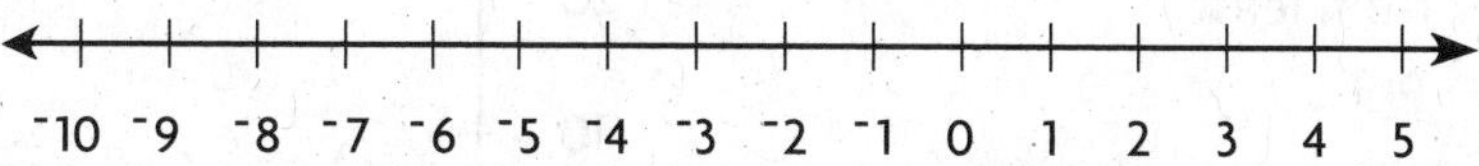

STEP 2 Note the locations of the numbers.

$^-7$ is to the ______________ of $^-4$ on the number line, so $^-7$ is ______________ $^-4$.

Math Idea

As you move to the right on a horizontal number line, the values become greater. As you move to the left, values become less.

Try This! **Use the number line to compare the numbers.**

A 5 and $^-9$

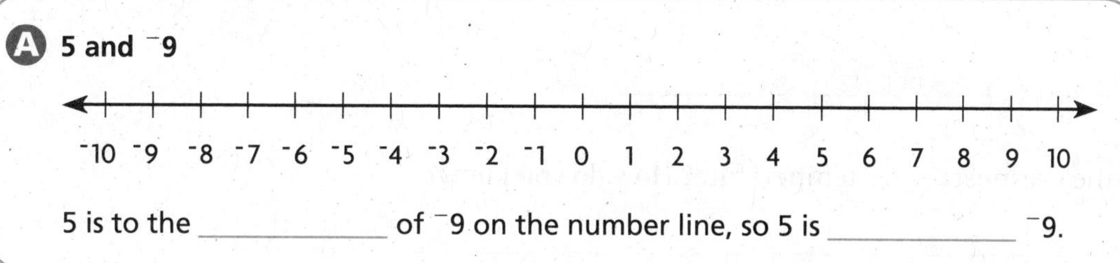

5 is to the ______________ of $^-9$ on the number line, so 5 is ______________ $^-9$.

B $^-2$ and 0

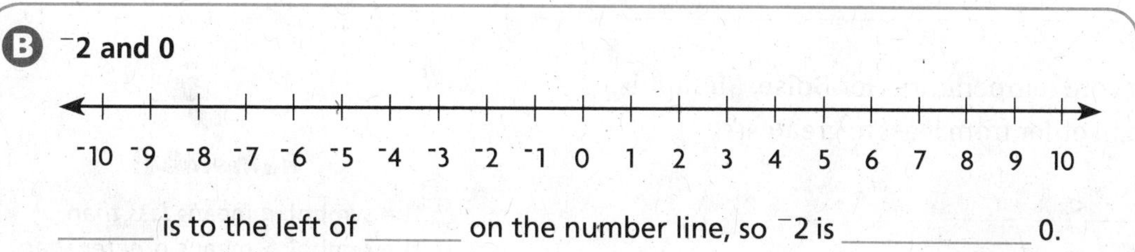

______ is to the left of ______ on the number line, so $^-2$ is ______________ 0.

Math Talk — **Mathematical Practices**

Explain how you know that $^-3$ is less than 0 without using a number line.

You can also use a vertical number line to order integers.

Example

The table gives the coldest temperatures recorded in seven cities in 2007.

Record Coldest Temperatures for 2007 (°F)					
Anchorage, AK $^{-}17$	Boise, ID 7	Duluth, MN $^{-}25$	Los Angeles, CA 35	Memphis, TN 18	Pittsburgh, PA $^{-}5$

A Order the temperatures from least to greatest.

STEP 1 Draw a dot on the number line to represent the record temperature of each city. Write the first letter of the city beside the dot.

Record Coldest Temperatures (°F) for 2007

40
30
20
10
0
$^{-}10$
$^{-}20$
$^{-}30$
$^{-}40$

STEP 2 Write the record temperatures in order from least to greatest. Explain how you determined the order.

B Use the table and the number line to answer each question.

- Which city had the colder record temperature, Memphis or Pittsburgh? How do you know?

- Which city had the warmest record temperature? How do you know?

- What are the record temperatures for Boise, Memphis, and Pittsburgh in order from least to greatest?

  _____ < _____ < _____

- What are the record temperatures for Anchorage, Duluth, and Los Angeles in order from greatest to least?

  _____ > _____ > _____

Remember

The symbol < means *less than*.
The symbol > means *greater than*.

Math Talk **Mathematical Practices**

Generalize What rule can you use to compare numbers on a vertical number line?

Name ____________________

Share and Show

Compare the numbers. Write < or >.

1. $^{-}8$ ◯ 6 Think: $^{-}8$ is to the ________ of 6 on the number line, so $^{-}8$ is ____________ 6.

2. 1 ◯ $^{-}8$

3. $^{-}4$ ◯ 0

4. 3 ◯ $^{-}7$

Order the numbers from least to greatest.

5. 4, $^{-}3$, $^{-}7$

____ < ____ < ____

6. 0, $^{-}1$, 3

____ < ____ < ____

7. $^{-}5$, $^{-}3$, $^{-}9$

____ < ____ < ____

Order the numbers from greatest to least.

8. $^{-}1$, $^{-}4$, 2

____ > ____ > ____

9. 5, 0, 10

____ > ____ > ____

10. $^{-}5$, $^{-}4$, $^{-}3$

____ > ____ > ____

Math Talk Mathematical Practices

Explain how you can use a number line to compare numbers.

On Your Own

Order the numbers from least to greatest.

11. 2, 1, $^{-}1$

____ < ____ < ____

12. $^{-}6$, $^{-}12$, 30

____ < ____ < ____

13. 15, $^{-}9$, $^{-}20$

____ < ____ < ____

Order the numbers from greatest to least.

14. $^{-}13$, 14, $^{-}14$

____ > ____ > ____

15. $^{-}20$, $^{-}30$, $^{-}40$

____ > ____ > ____

16. 9, $^{-}37$, 0

____ > ____ > ____

17. GO DEEPER Saturday's low temperature was $^{-}6$°F. Sunday's low temperature was 3°F. Monday's low temperature was $^{-}2$°F. Tuesday's low temperature was 5°F. Which day's low temperature was closest to 0°?

____

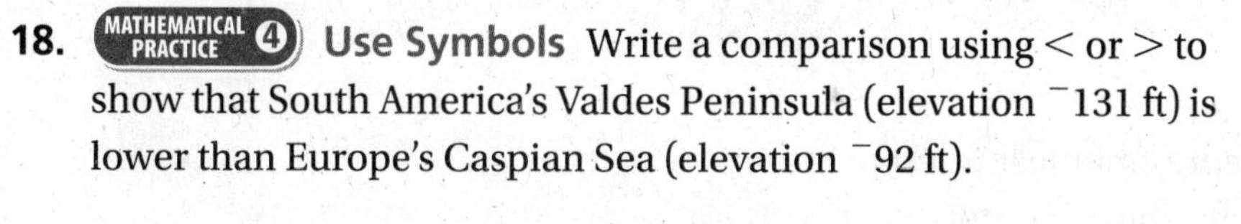

18. MATHEMATICAL PRACTICE 4 **Use Symbols** Write a comparison using < or > to show that South America's Valdes Peninsula (elevation $^{-}131$ ft) is lower than Europe's Caspian Sea (elevation $^{-}92$ ft).

____

Problem Solving • Applications

THINK SMARTER What's the Error?

19. In the game of golf, the player with the lowest score wins. Raheem, Erin, and Blake played a game of miniature golf. The table shows their scores compared to par.

Raheem	Erin	Blake
0	$^{-}5$	$^{-}1$

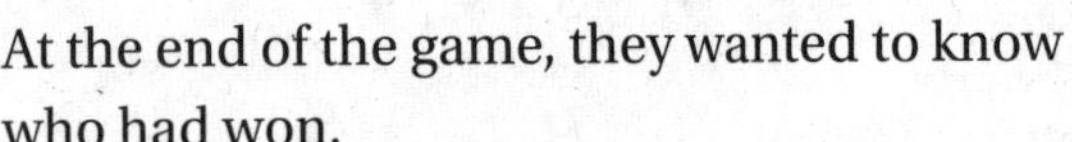

At the end of the game, they wanted to know who had won.

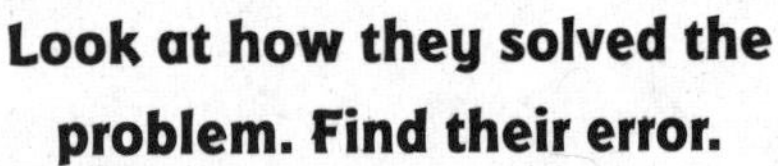

Look at how they solved the problem. Find their error.

STEP 1: 0 is greater than both $^{-}1$ and $^{-}5$. Since Raheem had the highest score, he did not win.

STEP 2: $^{-}1$ is less than $^{-}5$, so Blake's score was less than Erin's score. Since Blake had the lowest score, he won the game.

Correct the error by ordering the scores from least to greatest.

So, ______________ won. ______________ came in second. ______________ came in third.

- Describe the error that the players made.

____

20. THINK SMARTER Jasmine recorded the low temperatures for 3 cities.

City	Temperature (°F)
A	6
B	−4
C	2

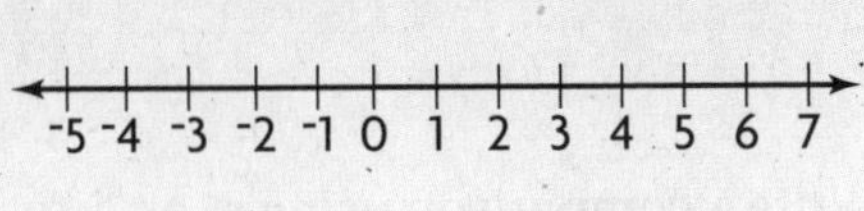

Draw a dot on the number line to represent the low temperature of each city. Write the letter of the city above the dot.

FOR MORE PRACTICE:
Standards Practice Book

Name ________________________________

Rational Numbers and the Number Line

The Number System—6.NS.6a, 6.NS.6c

MATHEMATICAL PRACTICES
MP.2, MP.4, MP.7

Essential Question How can you plot rational numbers on a number line?

CONNECT A **rational number** is any number that can be written as $\frac{a}{b}$, where a and b are integers and $b \neq 0$. Decimals, fractions, and integers are all rational numbers.

Unlock the Problem

The freezing point of a liquid is the temperature at which the liquid turns into a solid when it is cooled. The table shows the approximate freezing points of various liquids. Graph each temperature on a number line.

Liquid Freezing Points

Liquid	Freezing Point (°C)
Carbonated water	$^-0.3$
Fizzy lemonade	$^-0.5$
Hydrazine	1.4

Graph the values in the table.

STEP 1 Locate each number in relation to the nearest integers.

Think: $^-0.3$ is the opposite of ______.

0.3 is between the integers ______ and ______.
So, $^-0.3$ is between the opposites of these integers. $^-0.3$ is between ______ and ______.

$^-0.5$ is between ______ and ______. 1.4 is between ______ and ______.

STEP 2 Graph each temperature.

Think: $^-0.3$ is 3 tenths below 0 on the number line.

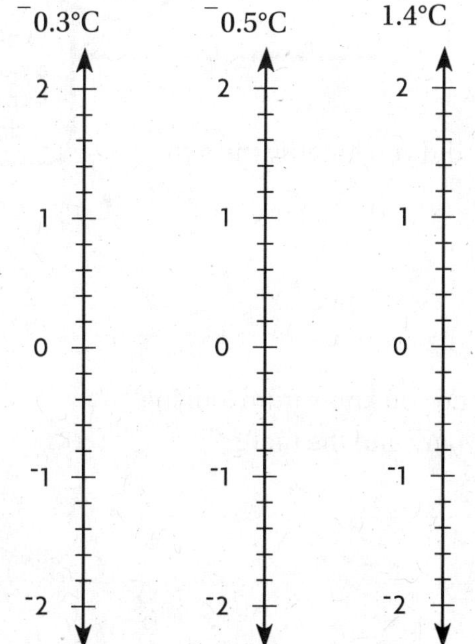

Math Talk **Mathematical Practices**

How can you tell which number $^-0.3$ is closer to, 0 or $^-1$? Explain.

Example

Points of Interest	
Name	**Location**
City Park	$-\frac{3}{8}$
Fountain	$-1\frac{1}{2}$
Library	$1\frac{1}{4}$
Mall	$\frac{3}{4}$

City Hall is located at point 0 on a map of Maple Avenue. Other points of interest on Maple Avenue are indicated by their distances, in miles, to the right of City Hall (positive numbers) or to the left of City Hall (negative numbers). Graph each location on a number line.

STEP 1 Locate the numbers in relation to the nearest integers.

$-\frac{3}{8}$ is between ______ and ______. $-1\frac{1}{2}$ is between ______ and ______.

$1\frac{1}{4}$ is between ______ and ______. $\frac{3}{4}$ is between ______ and ______.

STEP 2 Graph each location on the number line.

City Park: $-\frac{3}{8}$ **Think:** $-\frac{3}{8}$ is three eighths to the left of 0 on the number line.

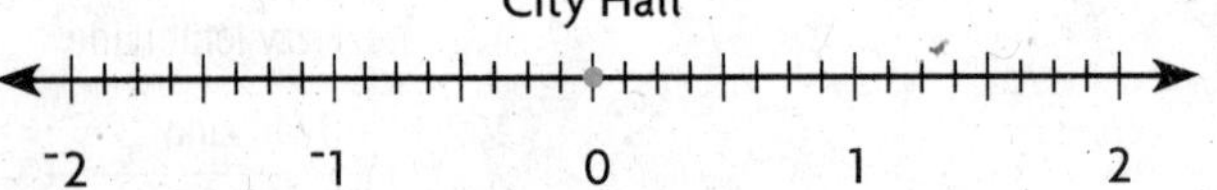

Fountain: $-1\frac{1}{2}$

City Hall

-2 -1 0 1 2

Library: $1\frac{1}{4}$

City Hall

-2 -1 0 1 2

Mall: $\frac{3}{4}$

City Hall

-2 -1 0 1 2

Math Talk **Mathematical Practices**

Explain how you can use a horizontal or vertical number line to graph a rational number.

1. MATHEMATICAL PRACTICE 2 **Reason Quantitatively** How did you identify the two integers that $-1\frac{1}{2}$ is between?

2. MATHEMATICAL PRACTICE 7 **Identify Relationships** How do you know from looking at the table that City Hall is between the city park and the mall?

Name ____________________

Share and Show

Graph the number on the horizontal number line.

1. $^{-}2\frac{1}{4}$

(number line from $^{-}3$ to 3)

The number is between the integers ______ and ______.

It is closer to the integer ______.

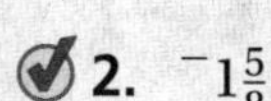 2. $^{-}1\frac{5}{8}$

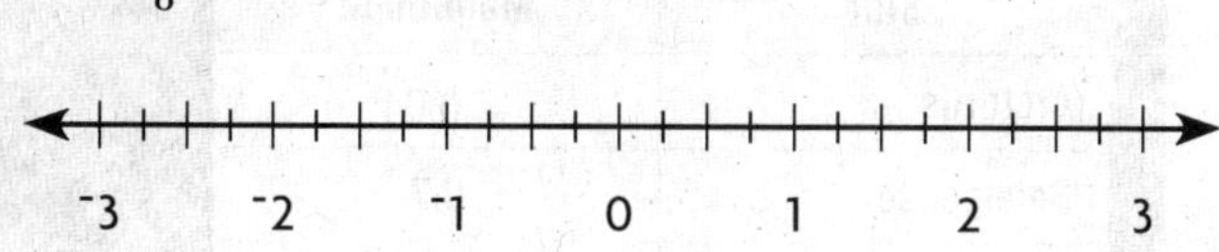

3. $\frac{1}{2}$

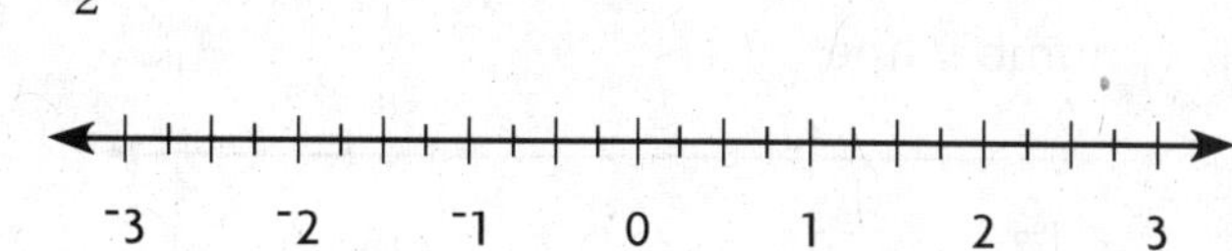

Math Talk — **Mathematical Practices**

Two numbers are opposites. Zero is not one of the numbers. Are the numbers on the same side or opposite sides of zero on a number line? **Explain.**

On Your Own

Practice: Copy and Solve **Graph the number on a vertical number line.**

4. 0.6
5. $^{-}1.25$
6. $^{-}1.5$
7. 0.3
8. $^{-}0.7$
9. 1.4
10. $^{-}0.5$
11. $^{-}0.25$

State whether the numbers are on the same or opposite sides of zero.

12. $^{-}1.38$ and 2.9 ______
13. $^{-}3\frac{9}{10}$ and $^{-}0.99$ ______
14. $\frac{5}{6}$ and $^{-}4.713$ ______

15. **GO DEEPER** The roots of 6 corn plants had depths of -3.54 feet, $-2\frac{4}{5}$ feet, -3.86 feet, $-4\frac{1}{8}$ feet, -4.25 feet, and $-3\frac{2}{5}$ feet. How many corn plants had roots between 3 and 4 feet deep?

____

Problem Solving • Applications Real World

A star's *magnitude* is a number that measures the star's brightness. Use the table of star magnitudes for 16–18.

16. Between what two integers is the magnitude of Canopus?

____

17. MATHEMATICAL PRACTICE 4 **Model Mathematics** Graph the magnitude of Betelgeuse on the number line.

−1 −0.5 0 0.5 1

Magnitudes of Stars

Star	Magnitude
Arcturus	−0.04
Betelgeuse	0.7
Canopus	−0.72
Deneb	1.25
Rigel Kentaurus A	−0.01
Sirius	−1.46

18. THINK SMARTER **What's the Error?** Jacob graphed the magnitude of Sirius on the number line. Explain his error. Then graph the magnitude correctly.

−2 −1 0

____

____

____

Personal Math Trainer

19. THINK SMARTER + The flag pole is located at point 0 on a map of Orange Avenue. Other points of interest on Orange Avenue are indicated by their distances, in miles to the right of the flag pole (positive numbers) or to the left of the flag pole (negative numbers). Graph and label each location on the number line.

Name	Location
School	0.4
Post Office	1.8
Library	−1
Fire Station	−1.3

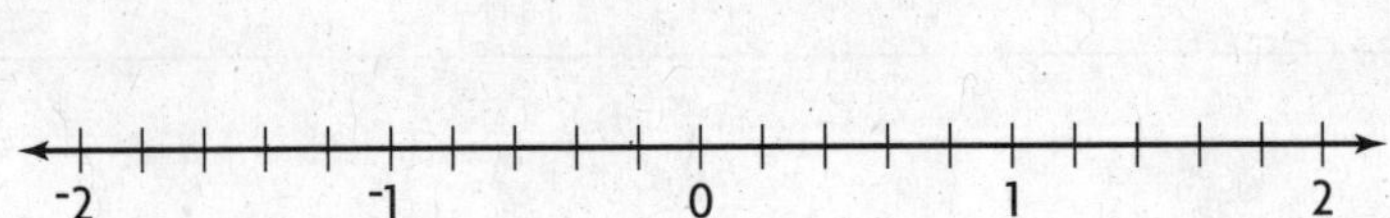

FOR MORE PRACTICE: Standards Practice Book

Name ________________________________

Compare and Order Rational Numbers

Essential Question How can you compare and order rational numbers?

The Number System—6.NS.7a, 6.NS.7b

MATHEMATICAL PRACTICES
MP.1, MP.5

CONNECT You have used a number line to compare and order integers. You can also use a number line to compare other rational numbers, including decimals and fractions.

Unlock the Problem

The table shows the average December temperatures in five U.S. cities. Which city has the greater average December temperature, Indianapolis or Boise?

Average December Temperatures	
City	**Temperature (°C)**
Boise, ID	$^{-}1$
Boston, MA	0.9
Indianapolis, IN	$^{-}0.6$
Philadelphia, PA	2.1
Syracuse, NY	$^{-}2$

One Way Use a number line.

Graph the temperatures for Indianapolis and Boise.

$^{-}3$ $^{-}2$ $^{-}1$ 0 1 2 3

Think: As you move to the ________ on a horizontal number line, the numbers become greater.

$^{-}0.6$ is to the ________ of $^{-}1$.

So, the city whose temperature is farther to the right is ____________.

Another Way Use place value to compare the decimals.

STEP 1 Write the temperatures with their decimal points lined up.

Indianapolis: ______

Boise: ______

STEP 2 Compare the digits in the ones place. If the number is negative, include a negative sign with the digit.

Think: 0 is ____________ than $^{-}1$.

$^{-}0.6$ is ____________ than $^{-}1$.

$^{-}0.6$°C is ____________ than $^{-}1$°C, so ____________ has a greater average December temperature than ____________.

Math Talk **Mathematical Practices**

Explain how you can order the average December temperatures of Boston, Philadelphia, and Syracuse from greatest to least.

Example 1

The elevations of objects found at a dig site are recorded in the table. Which object was found at a lower elevation, the fossil of the shell or the fossil of the fish?

Fossils	
Object	**Elevation (ft)**
shell	$^{-}3\frac{1}{2}$
fern	$\frac{1}{4}$
fish	$^{-}3\frac{1}{4}$

One Way **Use a number line.**

Graph the elevations for the fossil of the shell and the fossil of the fish.

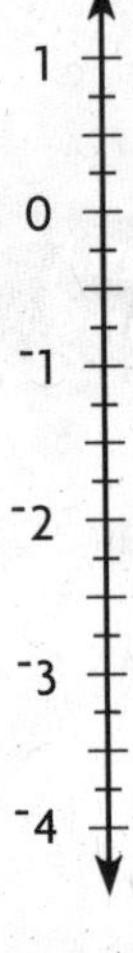

Think: As you move ____________ on a vertical number line, the numbers become less.

$^{-}3\frac{1}{2}$ is ____________ $^{-}3\frac{1}{4}$ on the number line.

Another Way **Use common denominators to compare fractions.**

STEP 1 Write the elevations with a common denominator.

$^{-}3\frac{1}{2} = {}^{-}3\frac{\square}{\square}$ $\qquad$ $^{-}3\frac{1}{4} = {}^{-}3\frac{\square}{\square}$

STEP 2 Since the whole numbers are the same, you only need to compare the fractions. If the number is negative, include a negative sign with the fraction.

$^{-}\frac{2}{4}$ is ____________ than $^{-}\frac{1}{4}$, so $^{-}3\frac{1}{2}$ is ____________ than $^{-}3\frac{1}{4}$

So, the fossil of the ____________ was found at a lower elevation than the fossil of the ____________.

Example 2 **Compare $^{-}0.1$ and $^{-}\frac{4}{5}$.**

Convert to all fractions or all decimals.

fractions $^{-}0.1 = \frac{^{-}\square}{10}$ $\quad$ $\frac{^{-}4}{5} = \frac{^{-}\square}{10}$

$^{-}8$ is ________ than $^{-}1$, so $^{-}\frac{4}{5}$ is less than $^{-}0.1$.

decimals $^{-}0.1 = {}^{-}0.1$ $\quad$ $^{-}\frac{4}{5} = {}^{-}0.\square$

$^{-}0.8$ is ________ than $^{-}0.1$, so $^{-}\frac{4}{5}$ is less than $^{-}0.1$.

Use a number line to check your answer.

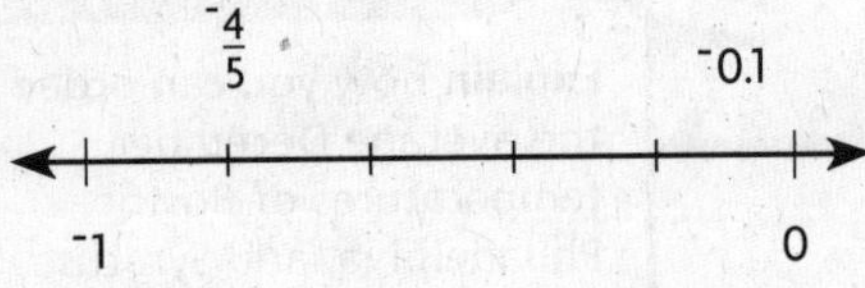

Mathematical Practices

Explain how you could use number sense to compare $^{-}0.1$ and $^{-}\frac{4}{5}$.

Name ______________________________

Share and Show

Compare the numbers. Write $<$ or $>$.

1. $^{-}0.3 \bigcirc 0.2$ Think: $^{-}0.3$ is to the ________ of 0.2 on the number line, so $^{-}0.3$ is ________ than 0.2.

2. $\frac{1}{3} \bigcirc \frac{-2}{5}$

3. $^{-}0.8 \bigcirc ^{-}0.5$

✔4. $\frac{-3}{4} \bigcirc ^{-}0.7$

Order the numbers from least to greatest.

5. $3.6, ^{-}7.1, ^{-}5.9$

______ < ______ < ______

6. $\frac{-6}{7}, \frac{1}{9}, \frac{-2}{3}$

______ < ______ < ______

✔7. $^{-}5\frac{1}{4}, ^{-}6.5, ^{-}5.3$

______ < ______ < ______

Math Talk — Mathematical Practices

Tell what the statement $\frac{-1}{3} > \frac{-1}{2}$ means. **Explain** how you know that the statement is true.

On Your Own

Compare the numbers. Write $<$ or $>$.

8. $\frac{-1}{2} \bigcirc \frac{-3}{7}$

9. $^{-}23.7 \bigcirc ^{-}18.8$

10. $^{-}3\frac{1}{4} \bigcirc ^{-}4.3$

Order the numbers from greatest to least.

11. $^{-}2.4, 1.9, ^{-}7.6$

______ > ______ > ______

12. $\frac{-2}{5}, \frac{-3}{4}, \frac{-1}{2}$

______ > ______ > ______

13. $3, ^{-}6\frac{4}{5}, ^{-}3\frac{2}{3}$

______ > ______ > ______

14. GO DEEPER Last week, Wednesday's low temperature was -4.5°F, Thursday's low temperature was -1.2°F, Friday's low temperature was -2.7°F, and Saturday's low temperature was 0.5°F. The average low temperature for the week was -1.5°F. How many of these days had low temperatures less than the average low temperature for the week?

____

15. MATHEMATICAL PRACTICE 4 **Use Symbols** Write a comparison using $<$ or $>$ to show the relationship between an elevation of $^{-}12\frac{1}{2}$ ft and an elevation of $^{-}16\frac{5}{8}$ ft.

____

Problem Solving • Applications

Elevations, in miles, are given for the lowest points below sea level for 4 bodies of water. Use the table for 16–19.

Lowest Points	
Location	**Elevation (mi)**
Arctic Ocean	$^{-}0.8$
Lake Superior	$^{-}\frac{1}{4}$
Lake Tanganyika	$^{-}0.9$
Red Sea	$^{-}\frac{1}{3}$

16. The lowest point of which has the greater elevation, the Arctic Ocean or Lake Tanganyika?

17. Which has a lower elevation, the lowest point of Lake Superior or a point at an elevation of $^{-}\frac{2}{5}$ mi?

18. List the elevations in order from least to greatest.

19. THINK SMARTER A shipwreck is found at an elevation of −0.75 miles. In which bodies of water could the shipwreck have been found?

WRITE ▸Math • Show Your Work •

20. THINK SMARTER Circle <, >, or =.

20a. $^{-}\frac{3}{5}$ [< / > / =] $^{-}\frac{4}{5}$

20b. $^{-}\frac{2}{5}$ [< / > / =] $^{-}\frac{3}{4}$

20c. $^{-}6.5$ [< / > / =] $^{-}4.2$

20d. $^{-}2.4$ [< / > / =] $^{-}3.7$

FOR MORE PRACTICE:
Standards Practice Book

Name ______________________________________

Mid-Chapter Checkpoint

Vocabulary

Vocabulary
integers
opposites
rational number

Choose the best term from the box to complete the sentence.

1. Any number that can be written as $\frac{a}{b}$, where a and b are integers and $b \neq 0$ is called a(n) ____________________. (p. 109)

2. The set of whole numbers and their opposites is the set of ____________________. (p. 101)

Concepts and Skills

Write the opposite of the integer. (6.NS.6a)

3. $^{-}72$ ______

4. 0 ______

5. $^{-}31$ ______

6. 27 ______

Name the integer that represents the situation, and tell what 0 represents in that situation. (6.NS.5)

Situation	Integer	What Does 0 Represent?
7. Greg scored 278 points during his turn in the video game.		
8. The temperature was 8 degrees below zero.		

Compare the numbers. Write $<$ or $>$. (6.NS.7a)

9. 3 ◯ $^{-}4$

10. $^{-}6$ ◯ $^{-}5$

11. 5 ◯ $^{-}6$

12. $\frac{1}{3}$ ◯ $-\frac{1}{2}$

13. $^{-}3.1$ ◯ $^{-}4.3$

14. $1\frac{3}{4}$ ◯ $^{-}2\frac{1}{2}$

Order the numbers. (6.NS.7a)

15. 5, $^{-}2$, $^{-}8$

_____ $<$ _____ $<$ _____

16. 0, $^{-}3$, 1

_____ $<$ _____ $<$ _____

17. $^{-}7$, $^{-}6$, $^{-}11$

_____ $>$ _____ $>$ _____

18. 2.5, $^{-}1.7$, $^{-}4.3$

_____ $<$ _____ $<$ _____

19. $\frac{2}{3}$, $^{-}\frac{1}{4}$, $\frac{5}{12}$

_____ $<$ _____ $<$ _____

20. $^{-}5.2$, $^{-}3.8$, $^{-}9.4$

_____ $>$ _____ $>$ _____

21. Judy is scuba diving at $^{-}7$ meters, Nelda is scuba diving at $^{-}9$ meters, and Rod is scuba diving at $^{-}3$ meters. List the divers in order from the deepest diver to the diver who is closest to the surface. (6.NS.7b)

22. A football team gains 8 yards on their first play. They lose 12 yards on the next play. What two integers represent the two plays? (6.NS.5)

23. The player who scores the closest to 0 points wins the game. The scores of four players are given in the table. Who won the game? (6.NS.7b)

Game Scores

Player	Points
Myra	-1.93
Amari	$-1\frac{2}{3}$
Justine	-1.8
Donovan	$-1\frac{1}{2}$

24. Which point on the graph represents $-3\frac{3}{4}$? (6.NS.6c)

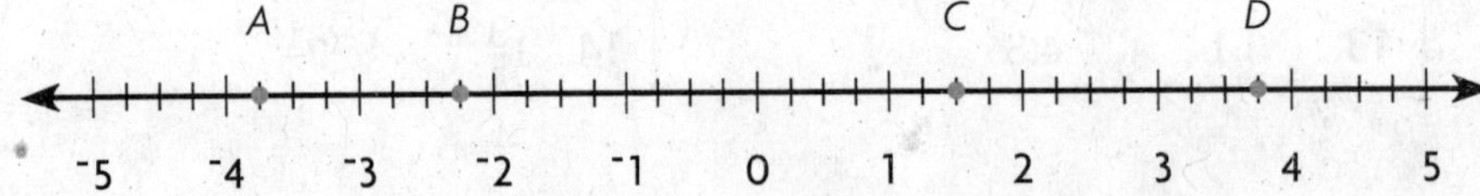

Name ________________________________

Absolute Value

Essential Question How can you find and interpret the absolute value of rational numbers?

The Number System—6.NS.7c

MATHEMATICAL PRACTICES
MP.2, MP.3, MP.4, MP.8

The **absolute value** of a number is the number's distance from 0 on a number line. The absolute value of $^-3$ is 3.

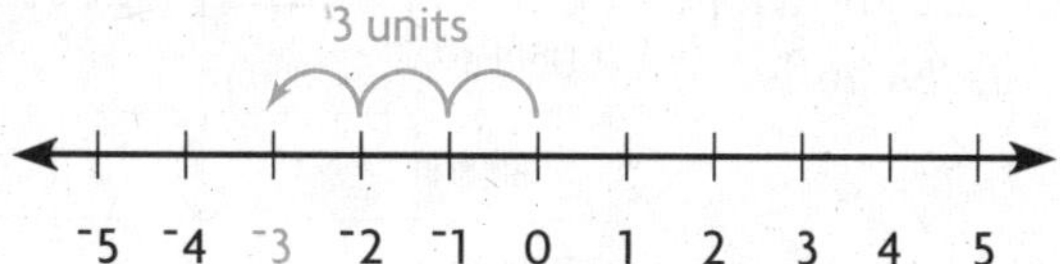

The absolute value of $^-3$ is written symbolically as $|^-3|$.

Unlock the Problem

In 1934, a cargo ship called the *Mohican* sank off the coast of Florida. Divers today can visit the ship at an elevation of $^-32$ feet. Use a number line to find $|^-32|$.

Graph $^-32$. Then find its absolute value.

Graph $^-32$ on the number line.

10, 0, $^-10$, $^-20$, $^-30$, $^-40$, $^-50$

Think: The distance from 0 to the point I graphed is _______ units.

So, $|^-32|$ = _______.

Math Idea

Since distance can never be negative, the absolute value of a number can never be negative.

Math Talk — **Mathematical Practices**

Compare the absolute values of two numbers that are opposites. Explain your reasoning.

1. The depth of a diver is her distance below sea level. Because depth represents a distance, it is never negative. Find the depth of a diver visiting the *Mohican*, and explain how her depth is related to the ship's elevation of $^-32$ ft.

____

____

2. Explain how the expression $|^-32|$ relates to the diver's depth.

____

____

____

You can find the absolute values of decimals, fractions, and other rational numbers just as you found the absolute values of integers.

Example 1

A food scientist tested a new dog food on five dogs. Each dog's weight was monitored during the course of the test. The results are shown in the table. Positive values indicate weight gains in pounds. Negative values indicate weight losses in pounds.

Food Test Results	
Name	**Weight Change (lb)**
Buck	$\frac{3}{4}$
Goldie	$\frac{-5}{8}$
Mackerel	$^{-}1\frac{7}{16}$
Paloma	$2\frac{1}{8}$
Spike	$\frac{-3}{8}$

Graph the weight changes on the number line. Then find their absolute values.

$^{-}3$ $^{-}2$ $^{-}1$ 0 1 2 3

Think: The distance from 0 to the point I graphed is $\frac{3}{4}$. $\left|\frac{3}{4}\right| = \frac{3}{4}$

$\left|\frac{-5}{8}\right| =$ ______ $\left|^{-}1\frac{7}{16}\right| =$ ______ $\left|2\frac{1}{8}\right| =$ ______ $\left|\frac{-3}{8}\right| =$ ______

3. **MATHEMATICAL PRACTICE 4** **Interpret a Result** Explain how the absolute values of the positive and negative weight changes relate to the starting weights of the dogs.

______

______

______

Example 2 Find all integers with an absolute value of 7.

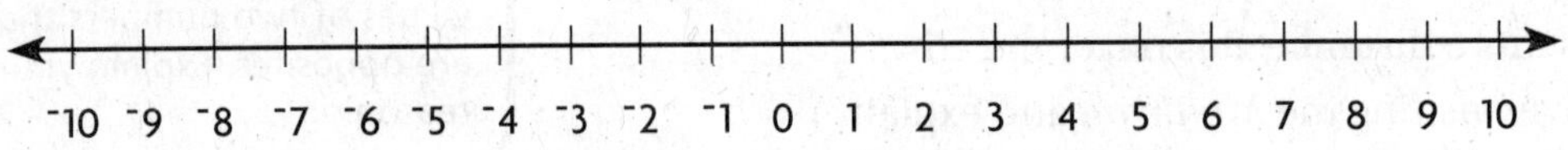

Think: The distance from 0 to integers with an absolute value of 7 is ______ units.

Graph integers located 7 units from 0 on the number line.

|______| = 7 and |______| = 7

So, both ______ and ______ have an absolute value of 7.

4. **MATHEMATICAL PRACTICE 3** **Use Counterexamples** Paula says that there are always two numbers that have a given absolute value. Is she correct? Explain.

______

Name ____________________

Share and Show

Find the absolute value.

1. $|^-2|$ Graph $^-2$ on the number line.

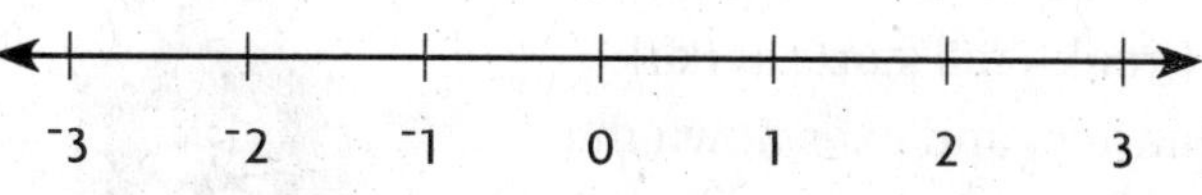

$^-2$ is ______ units from 0.

$|^-2| =$ ______

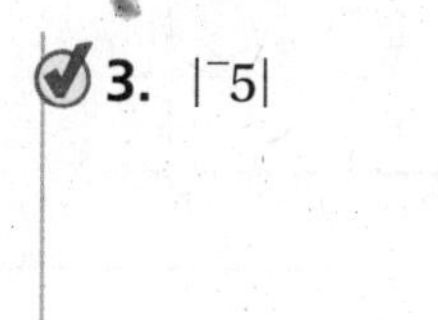

2. $|6|$ ______

3. $|^-5|$ ______

4. $|^-11|$ ______

5. $|9|$ ______

6. $|^-15|$ ______

Math Talk **Mathematical Practices**

Can a number have a negative absolute value? Explain.

On Your Own

Find the absolute value.

7. $|^-37|$ ______

8. $|1.8|$ ______

9. $\left|\frac{-2}{3}\right|$ ______

10. $|^-6.39|$ ______

11. $\left|^-5\frac{7}{8}\right|$ ______

Find all numbers with the given absolute value.

12. 13 ______

13. $\frac{5}{6}$ ______

14. 14.03 ______

15. 0.59 ______

16. $3\frac{1}{7}$ ______

MATHEMATICAL PRACTICE 2 Use Reasoning **Algebra** **Find the missing number or numbers to make the statement true.**

17. $|\blacksquare| = 10$ ______

18. $|\blacksquare| = 1.78$ ______

19. $|\blacksquare| = 0$ ______

20. $|\blacksquare| = \frac{15}{16}$ ______

21. GO DEEPER Find all of the integers whose absolute value is less than $|^-4|$.

____

Unlock the Problem

22. The Blue Ridge Trail starts at Park Headquarters in Big Bear Park and goes up the mountain. The Green Creek Trail starts at Park Headquarters and goes down the mountain. The table gives elevations of various points of interest in relation to Park Headquarters. How many points of interest are less than 1 kilometer above or below Park Headquarters?

Point of Interest	Elevation Compared to Park Headquarters (km)
A	1.9
B	1.1
C	0.7
D	0.3
E	$^-0.2$
F	$^-0.5$
G	$^-0.9$
H	$^-1.6$

a. How can you find how far above or below Park Headquarters a given point of interest is located?

____

____

b. How can you find the number of points of interest that are less than 1 km above or below Park Headquarters?

____

____

____

c. Find how far above or below Park Headquarters each point of interest is located.

____

____

____

____

d. How many points of interest are less than 1 kilometer above or below Park Headquarters?

____

23. MATHEMATICAL PRACTICE 2 **Use Reasoning** Name a rational number that can replace ■ to make both statements true.

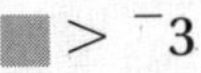

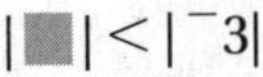

____

24. THINK SMARTER Laila said $|4|$ equals $|^-4|$. Is Laila correct? Use the number line and words to support your answer.

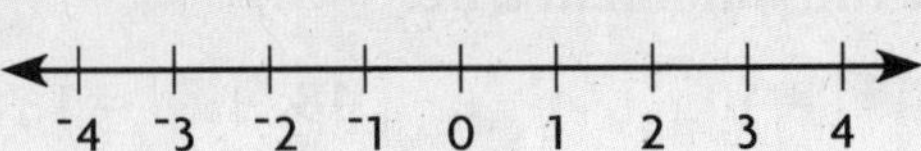

____

____

____

FOR MORE PRACTICE:
Standards Practice Book

Name ______________________________

Compare Absolute Values

Essential Question How can you interpret comparisons involving absolute values?

The Number System—6.NS.7d

MATHEMATICAL PRACTICES
MP. 1, MP.2

Unlock the Problem

Carmen is taking a one-day scuba diving class. Completion of the class will allow her to explore the ocean at elevations of less than $^{-}25$ feet. Use absolute value to describe the depths to which Carmen will be able to dive after taking the class.

- Graph an elevation of $^{-}25$ feet on the number line.
- List three elevations less than $^{-}25$ feet. Then graph these elevations.

  ____

- Elevations less than $^{-}25$ feet are found ____________ $^{-}25$ feet.
- Because depth represents a distance below sea level, it is never negative. In this situation, $|^{-}25|$ ft represents a depth of ______ feet.
- Write each elevation as a depth.

Elevation (ft)	Depth (ft)
$^{-}30$	
$^{-}35$	
$^{-}40$	

Elevation (feet)

30
20
10
0
$^{-}10$
$^{-}20$
$^{-}30$
$^{-}40$
$^{-}50$

- An elevation of less than $|^{-}25|$ feet is a depth ____________ than 25 feet.

So, Carmen will be able to dive to depths ____________ than 25 feet after taking the class.

1. Compare a $^{-}175$-foot elevation and a 175-foot depth. Explain your reasoning.

____

____

Example Cole has an online account for buying video games.

His account balance has always been greater than ⁻$16. Use absolute value to describe Cole's account balance as a debt.

STEP 1 Graph an account balance of ⁻$16 on the number line.

Account balance ($)

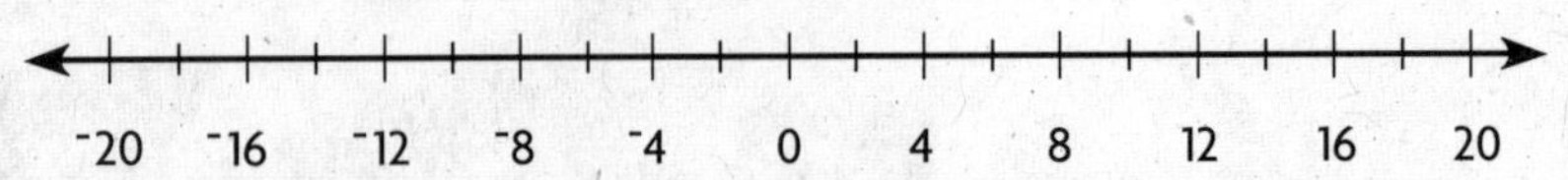

STEP 2 List three account balances greater than ⁻$16. Then graph these account balances on the number line above.

____

Balances greater than ⁻$16 are found to the ___________ of ⁻$16.

STEP 3 Express an account balance of ⁻$16 as a debt.

In this situation |⁻$16| represents a debt of ______.

STEP 4 Complete the table.

Balances Greater Than ⁻$16	Debt
⁻$15	
⁻$14	
	$13

Each debt in the table is ___________ than $16.

Cole's account balance is always greater than ⁻$16, so his debt on the account is always ___________ than $16.

Math Talk **Mathematical Practices**

The temperature at the North Pole was ⁻35°F at noon. **Explain** how you can use absolute value to express a temperature of ⁻35°F.

2. Explain how you can describe a debt as an absolute value.

____

____

3. MATHEMATICAL PRACTICE 1 **Describe** List three numbers greater than |⁻28|. Describe how you determined your answer.

____

____

Name ______________________

Share and Show

1. On Monday, Allie's bank account balance was $^-\$24$. On Tuesday, her account balance was less than it was on Monday. Use absolute value to describe Allie's balance on Tuesday as a debt.

   In this situation $|^-\$24|$ represents a debt of ______.

   On Tuesday, Allie had a debt of ______ than \$24.

2. Matthew scored $^-36$ points in his turn at a video game. In Genevieve's turn, she scored fewer points than Matthew. Use absolute value to describe Genevieve's score as a loss.

   Genevieve lost ______ than 36 points.

Mathematical Practices

Compare a negative bank balance and the amount of the debt owed to the bank. Explain.

On Your Own

3. GO DEEPER One of the cats shown in the table is a tabby. The tabby had a decrease in weight of more than 3.3 ounces. Which cat is the tabby?

____

Cat	Weight Change (ounces)
Missy	3.8
Angel	$^-3.2$
Frankie	$^-2.6$
Spot	$^-3.4$

Compare. Write <, >, or =.

4. $^-8$ ◯ $|^-8|$

5. 13 ◯ $|^-13|$

6. $|^-23|$ ◯ $|^-24|$

7. 15 ◯ $|^-14|$

8. 34 ◯ $|^-36|$

9. $^-5$ ◯ $|^-6|$

10. THINK SMARTER Write the values in order from least to greatest.

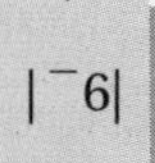

$|^-6|$ $|1|$

____

Connect to Reading

Compare and Contrast

When you *compare and contrast*, you look for ways that two or more subjects are alike (compare) and ways they are different (contrast). This helps you to discover information about each subject that you might not have known otherwise. As you read the following passage, think about how the main topics are alike and how they are different.

Trevor mows lawns after school to raise money for a new mountain bike. Last week, it rained every day, and he couldn't work. While waiting for better weather, he spent some of his savings on lawnmower repairs. As a result, his savings balance changed by $^{-}$\$45. This week, the weather was better, and Trevor returned to work. His savings balance changed by $^{+}$\$45 this week.

11. The passage has two main parts. Describe them.

12. Describe the two changes in Trevor's savings balance.

13. MATHEMATICAL PRACTICE 2 **Reason Quantitatively** Compare the two changes in Trevor's savings balance. How are they alike?

14. THINK SMARTER Contrast the two changes in Trevor's savings balance. How are they different?

FOR MORE PRACTICE:
Standards Practice Book

Name ____________________

Rational Numbers and the Coordinate Plane

Essential Question How do you plot ordered pairs of rational numbers on a coordinate plane?

The Number System—6.NS.6c

MATHEMATICAL PRACTICES
MP.6, MP.8

A **coordinate plane** is a plane formed by a horizontal number line called the ***x*-axis** that intersects a vertical number line called the ***y*-axis**. The axes intersect at 0 on both number lines. The point where the axes intersect is the **origin**.

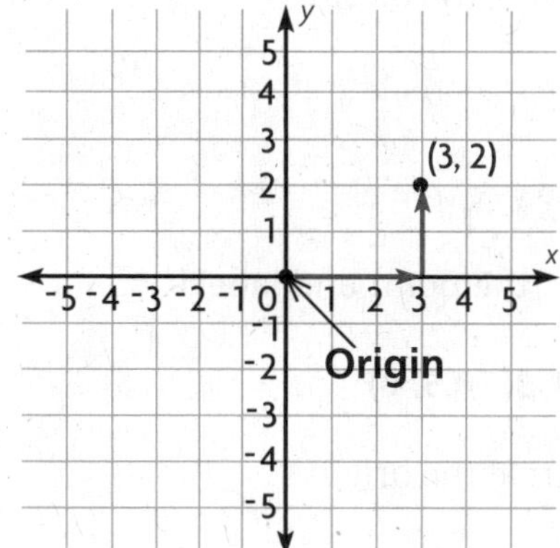

An **ordered pair** is a pair of numbers, such as (3, 2), that can be used to locate a point on the coordinate plane. The first number is the ***x*-coordinate**; it tells the distance to move left or right from the origin. The second number is the ***y*-coordinate**; it tells the distance to move up or down from the origin. The ordered pair for the origin is (0, 0).

Unlock the Problem

A screen in a video game shows a coordinate plane. The points *P*, *Q*, *R*, and *S* represent treasure chests. Write the ordered pair for each treasure chest's location.

- If a point is to the left of the *y*-axis, is its *x*-coordinate positive or negative?

____

Find the coordinates of each point.

To find the coordinates of point *P*, start at the origin.

To find the *x*-coordinate, move right (positive) or left (negative).	Move 2 units to the ______.
To find the *y*-coordinate, move up (positive) or down (negative).	Move ______ units up.

Point *P* is located at ($^-2$, ______).

Point *Q* is located at (______, ______).

Point *R* is located at (______, ______).

Point *S* is located at (______, ______).

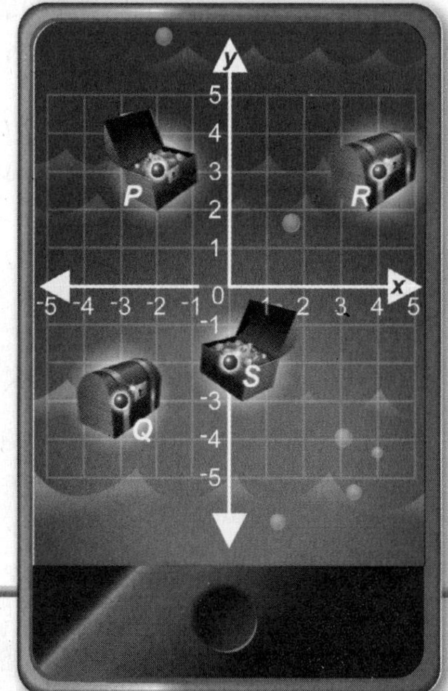

1. **MATHEMATICAL PRACTICE 8 Draw Conclusions** Make a conjecture about the *x*-coordinate of any point that lies on the *y*-axis.

____

2. Explain why (2, 4) represents a different location than (4, 2).

____

Example Graph and label the point on the coordinate plane.

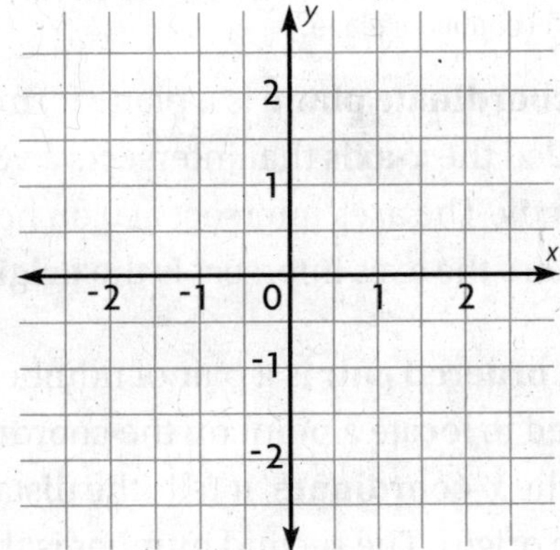

A $A(2, {}^{-}\frac{1}{2})$

Start at the origin.

The x-coordinate is positive. Move ______ units to the right.

The y-coordinate is negative. Move $\frac{1}{2}$ unit ______.

Plot the point and label it A.

B $B({}^{-}0.5, 0)$

Start at the origin.

The x-coordinate is ______. Move ______ unit to the ______.

The y-coordinate is 0. The point lies on the ______-axis.

Plot the point and label it B.

C $C(2\frac{1}{2}, \frac{3}{4})$

Start at the origin.

Move ______ units to the ______.

Move ______ unit ______.

Plot the point and label it C.

D $D({}^{-}1.25, {}^{-}1.75)$

Start at the origin.

Move ______ units to the ______.

Move ______ units ______.

Plot the point and label it D.

Math Talk **Mathematical Practices**

Describe the location of a point that has a positive x-coordinate and a negative y-coordinate.

Share and Show

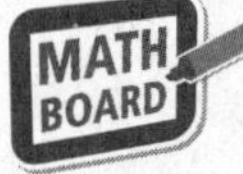

1. Write the ordered pair for point J.

Start at the origin. Move ______ units to the ______

and ______ units ______.

The ordered pair is ______.

Write the ordered pair for the point.

2. K ______

3. L ______

4. M ______

Name ______________________

Graph and label the point on the coordinate plane.

5. $P(^{-}2.5, 2)$ **6.** $Q(^{-}2, \frac{1}{4})$ **7.** $R(0, 1.5)$

8. $S(^{-}1, ^{-}\frac{1}{2})$ ✓ **9.** $T(1\frac{1}{2}, ^{-}2)$ **10.** $U(0.75, 1.25)$

11. $V(^{-}0.5, 0)$ **12.** $W(2, 0)$ **13.** $X(0, ^{-}2)$

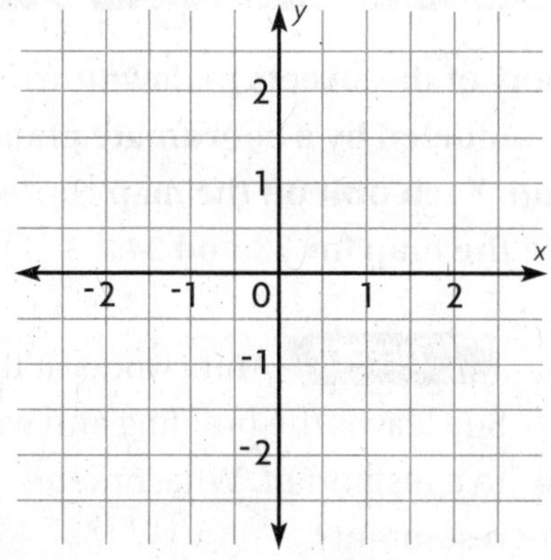

On Your Own

Math Talk **Mathematical Practices**

Explain how graphing (3, 2) is similar to and different from graphing $(3, ^{-}2)$.

Write the ordered pair for the point. Give approximate coordinates when necessary.

14. *A* ______ **15.** *B* ______ **16.** *C* ______

17. *D* ______ **18.** *E* ______ **19.** *F* ______

20. *G* ______ **21.** *H* ______ **22.** *J* ______

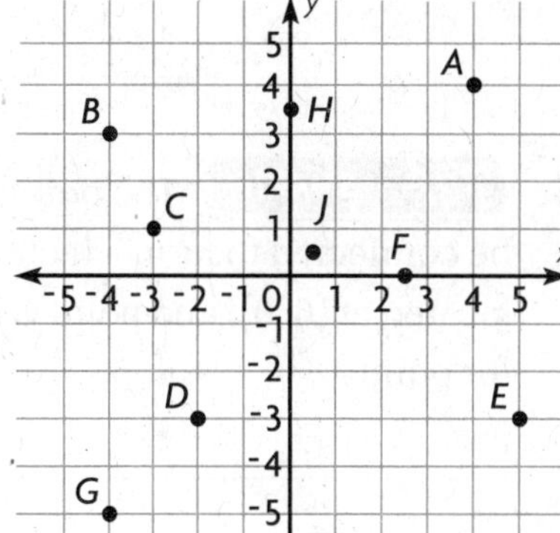

Graph and label the point on the coordinate plane.

23. $M(^{-}4, 0)$ **24.** $N(2, 2)$ **25.** $P(^{-}3, 3)$

26. $Q\left(0, 2\frac{1}{2}\right)$ **27.** $R(0.5, 0.5)$ **28.** $S\left(^{-}5, \frac{1}{2}\right)$

29. $T(0, 0)$ **30.** $U\left(3\frac{1}{2}, 0\right)$ **31.** $V(^{-}2, ^{-}4)$

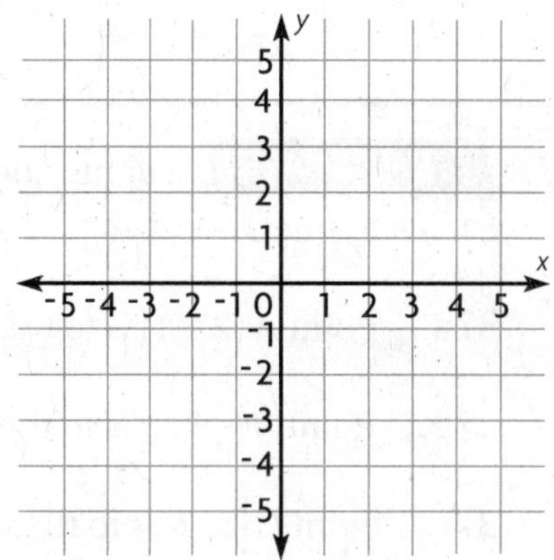

32. MATHEMATICAL PRACTICE 7 **Look for Structure** A point lies to the left of the *y*-axis and below the *x*-axis. What can you conclude about the coordinates of the point?

____

Problem Solving • Applications

Many of the streets in downtown Philadelphia can be modeled by a coordinate plane, as shown on the map. Each unit on the map represents one block. Use the map for 33 and 34.

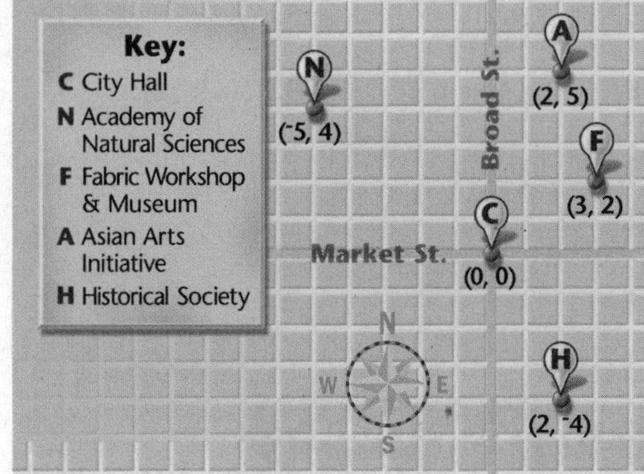

33. GO DEEPER Anita works at the Historical Society. She leaves the building and walks 3 blocks north to a restaurant. What ordered pair represents the restaurant?

____

34. THINK SMARTER **Pose a Problem** Write and solve a new problem that uses a location on the map.

____

____

____

35. THINK SMARTER The points *A*, *B*, *C*, and *D* on a coordinate plane can be connected to form a rectangle. Point *A* is located at (2, 0), point *B* is located at (6, 0), and point *C* is located at (6, 2.5). Write the ordered pair for point *D*.

____

36. MATHEMATICAL PRACTICE 7 **Identify Relationships** Explain how you can tell that the line segment connecting two points is vertical without graphing the points.

____

____

37. THINK SMARTER For numbers 37a–37d, select True or False for each statement.

37a. Point *A* (2, −1) is to the right of the *y*-axis and below the *x*-axis. ○ True ○ False

37b. Point *B* (−5, 2) is to the left of the *y*-axis and below the *x*-axis. ○ True ○ False

37c. Point *C* (3, 2) is to the right of the *y*-axis and above the *x*-axis. ○ True ○ False

37d. Point *D* (−2, −1) is to the left of the *y*-axis and below the *x*-axis. ○ True ○ False

FOR MORE PRACTICE:
Standards Practice Book

Name ______________________________

Ordered Pair Relationships

Essential Question How can you identify the relationship between points on a coordinate plane?

The Number System—6.NS.6b

MATHEMATICAL PRACTICES MP.4, MP.7

The four regions of the coordinate plane that are separated by the *x*- and *y*-axes are called **quadrants**. Quadrants are numbered with the Roman numerals I, II, III, and IV. If you know the signs of the coordinates of a point, you can determine the quadrant where the point is located.

Quadrant II (−, +)
Quadrant I (+, +)
Quadrant III (−, −)
Quadrant IV (+, −)

Unlock the Problem — Real World

The point ($^-3$, 4) represents the location of a bookstore on a map of a shopping mall. Identify the quadrant where the point is located.

- What is the *x*-coordinate of the point? ______
- What is the *y*-coordinate of the point? ______

Find the quadrant that contains ($^-3$, 4).

STEP 1 Examine the *x*-coordinate.

Think: The *x*-coordinate is ______, so the point is ______ units to the ______ of the origin.

Since the point is to the left of the origin, it must be located in either Quadrant ______ or Quadrant ______.

STEP 2 Examine the *y*-coordinate.

Think: The *y*-coordinate is ______, so the point is ______ units ______ from the origin.

Since the point is above the origin, it must be located in Quadrant ______.

Check by graphing the point ($^-3$, 4) on the coordinate plane.

So, the point representing the bookstore is located in Quadrant ______.

- MATHEMATICAL PRACTICE 7 **Look for Structure** Look at the signs of the coordinates of points in Quadrants I and II. What do they have in common? How are they different?

____

____

A figure has **line symmetry** if it can be folded about a line so that its two parts match exactly. If you cut out the isosceles triangle at the right and fold it along the dashed line, the two parts would match. A line that divides a figure into two halves that are reflections of each other is called a **line of symmetry**.

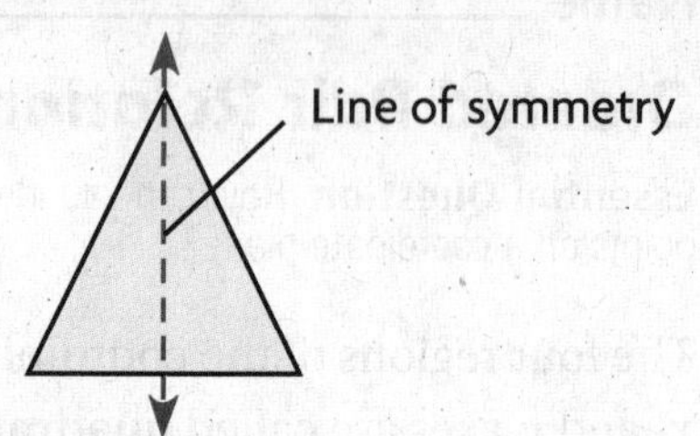

You can use the idea of line symmetry to analyze the relationship between points such as $(5, {}^{-}1)$ and $({}^{-}5, {}^{-}1)$ whose coordinates differ only in their signs.

Activity

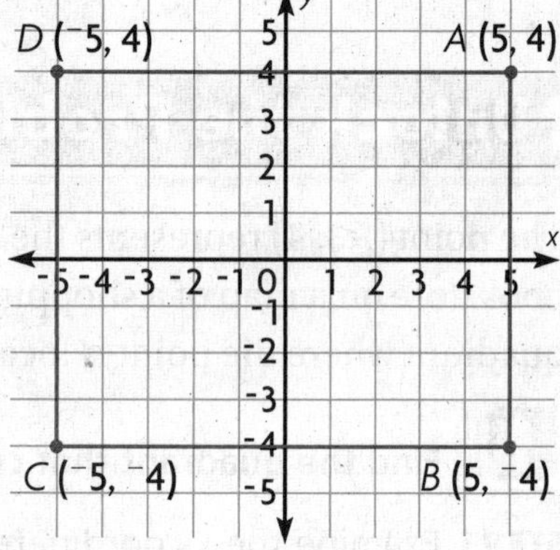

- Identify the lines of symmetry in the rectangle.

  The ______ -axis is a horizontal line of symmetry, and the ______ -axis is a vertical line of symmetry.

- Look at points *A* and *B*. What do you notice about the *x*-coordinates? What do you notice about the *y*-coordinates?

  ____

  ____

- Point *B* is a reflection of point *A* across which axis? How do you know?

  ____

  ____

- Look at points *A* and *D*. What do you notice about the *x*-coordinates? What do you notice about the *y*-coordinates?

  ____

- Point *D* is a reflection of point *A* across which axis? How do you know?

  ____

  ____

- Which point is a reflection of point *B* across the *x*-axis and then the *y*-axis?

  ____

- Compare the coordinates of point *B* with the coordinates of point *D*.

  ____

  ____

Math Talk — **Mathematical Practices**

Describe how the coordinates of a point change if it is reflected across the *x*-axis.

Name ______________________________

Share and Show

Identify the quadrant where the point is located.

1. (2, ⁻5)

To graph the point, first move to the _____ from the origin.

Then move _____.

Quadrant: _____

2. (4, 1)

Quadrant: _____

3. (⁻6, ⁻2)

Quadrant: _____

4. (⁻7, 3)

Quadrant: _____

5. (8, 8)

Quadrant: _____

6. (1, ⁻1)

Quadrant: _____

The two points are reflections of each other across the *x*- or *y*-axis. Identify the axis.

7. (⁻1, 3) and (1, 3)

axis: _____

8. (4, 4) and (4, ⁻4)

axis: _____

9. (2, ⁻9) and (2, 9)

axis: _____

10. (8, 1) and (⁻8, 1)

axis: _____

Math Talk **Mathematical Practices**

Explain how you can identify the quadrant where a given point is located.

On Your Own

Identify the quadrant where the point is located.

11. (⁻8, ⁻9)

Quadrant: _____

12. (12, 1)

Quadrant: _____

13. (⁻13, 10)

Quadrant: _____

14. (5, ⁻20)

Quadrant: _____

The two points are reflections of each other across the *x*- or *y*-axis. Identify the axis.

15. (⁻9, ⁻10) and (⁻9, 10)

axis: _____

16. (21, ⁻31) and (21, 31)

axis: _____

17. (15, ⁻20) and (⁻15, ⁻20)

axis: _____

Give the reflection of the point across the given axis.

18. (⁻7, ⁻7), *y*-axis

____

19. (⁻15, 18), *x*-axis

____

20. (11, 9), *x*-axis

____

Problem Solving • Applications

Use the map of Gridville for 21–23.

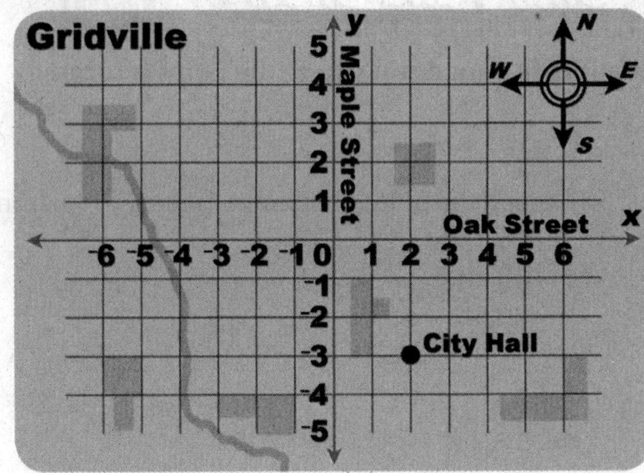

21. GO DEEPER The library's location has the same *y*-coordinate as City Hall but the opposite *x*-coordinate. Across which street could you reflect City Hall's location to find the library's location?

____

22. THINK SMARTER Each unit on the map represents 1 mile. Gregory leaves his house at $(^-5, 4)$, cycles 4 miles east, 6 miles south, and 1 mile west. In which quadrant of the city is he now?

____

23. The bus station has the same *x*-coordinate as City Hall but the opposite *y*-coordinate. In which quadrant of the city is the bus station located?

____

24. MATHEMATICAL PRACTICE 1 **Describe Relationships** Describe the relationship between the location of the points $(2, 5)$ and $(2, ^-5)$ on the coordinate plane.

____

____

25. THINK SMARTER Identify the quadrant where each point is located. Write each point in the correct box.

$(^-1, 3)$ $(4, ^-2)$ $(^-3, ^-2)$

$(1, ^-3)$ $(^-1, 2)$ $(3, 4)$

Quadrant I	Quadrant II	Quadrant III	Quadrant IV

FOR MORE PRACTICE:
Standards Practice Book

Name ______________________________

Distance on the Coordinate Plane

Essential Question How can you find the distance between two points that lie on a horizontal or vertical line on a coordinate plane?

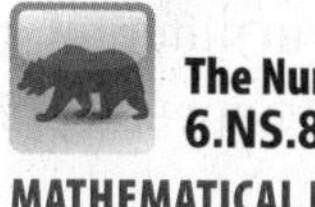

The Number System—6.NS.8

MATHEMATICAL PRACTICES
MP.1, MP.5, MP.6

Unlock the Problem

The map of Foggy Mountain Park is marked on a coordinate grid in units of 1 mile. There are two campgrounds in the park. Camp 1 is located at ($^-4$, 3). Camp 2 is located at (5, 3). How far is it from Camp 1 to Camp 2?

Foggy Mountain Park

Eagle Nest

Find the distance from Camp 1 to Camp 2.

STEP 1 Graph the points.

Think: The points have the same ______ -coordinate, so they are located on a horizontal line.

STEP 2 Find the horizontal distance from Camp 1 to the y-axis.

Find the distance between the x-coordinates of the point (______, 3) and the point (0, 3).

The distance of a number from 0 is the ______________ of the number.

$|^-4| = 4$

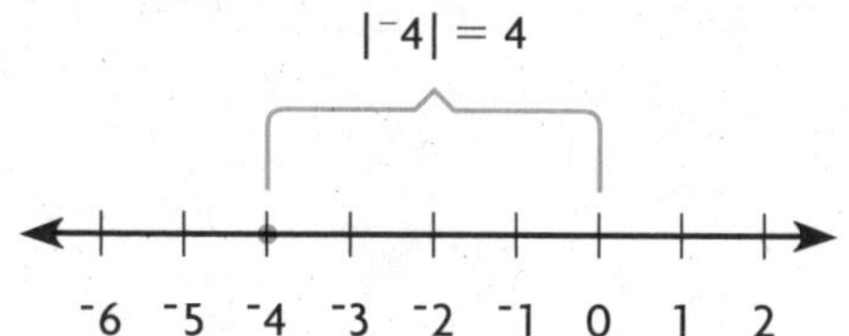

The distance from ($^-4$, 3) to (0, 3) is $|^-4|$ = ______ miles.

ERROR Alert

Remember that distance is never negative. You can find the distance between a negative number and 0 by using absolute value.

STEP 3 Find the horizontal distance from Camp 2 to the y-axis.

Find the distance between the x-coordinates of (______, 3) and (______, 3).

The distance from (5, 3) to (0, 3) is |______| = ______ miles.

Math Talk **Mathematical Practices**

Explain how you could check that you found the distance correctly.

STEP 4 Add to find the total distance: ______ + ______ = ______ miles.

So, the distance from Camp 1 to Camp 2 is ______ miles.

1. MATHEMATICAL PRACTICE 6 **Explain** how you could use absolute value to find the distance from Camp 2 to the Eagle Nest. What is the distance?

____

____

In the problem on the previous page, you used absolute value to find the distance between points in different quadrants. You can also use absolute value to find the distance between points in the same quadrant.

Example **Find the distance between the pair of points on the coordinate grid.**

C (8, 10)
D (8, 3)
A ($^-9$, $^-6$)
B ($^-4$, $^-6$)

A points *A* and *B*

STEP 1 Look at the coordinates of the points.

The ______ -coordinates of the points are the same, so the points lie on a horizontal line.

Think of the horizontal line passing through *A* and *B* as a number line.

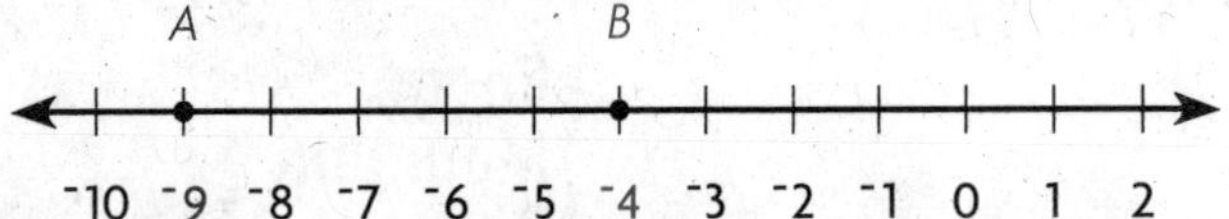

STEP 2 Find the distances of *A* and *B* from 0.

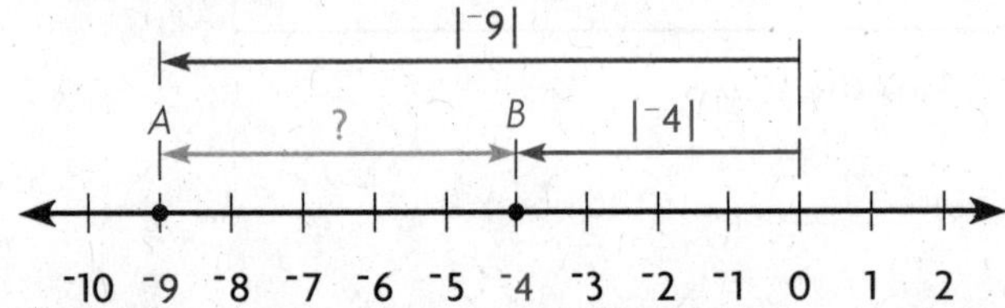

Distance of *A* from 0:

$|^-9|$ = ______ units

Distance of *B* from 0:

| ______ | = ______ units

STEP 3 Subtract to find the distance from *A* to *B*: ______ − ______ = ______ units.

So, the distance from *A* to *B* is ______ units.

B points *C* and *D*

STEP 1 Look at the coordinates of the points.

The ______ -coordinates of the points are the same, so the points lie on a vertical line.

Think of the vertical line passing through *C* and *D* as a number line.

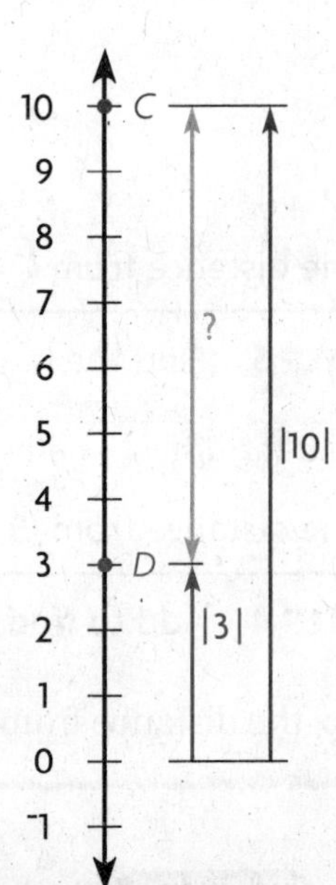

STEP 2 Find the distances of *C* and *D* from 0 on the vertical number line.

Distance of *C* from 0: | 10 | = ______ units

Distance of *D* from 0: | ______ | = ______ units

STEP 3 Subtract to find the distance from *C* to *D*:

______ − ______ = ______ units.

So, the distance between *C* and *D* is ______ units.

Math Talk **Mathematical Practices**

Explain how to find the distance from *M*(−5, 1) to *N*(−5, 7).

Name ___________________________

Share and Show

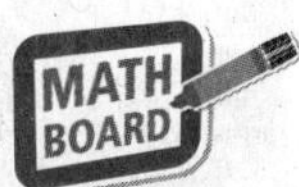

Find the distance between the pair of points.

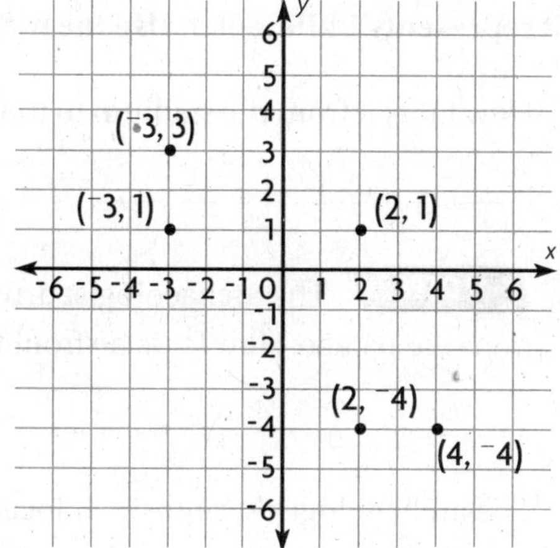

1. (⁻3, 1) and (2, 1)

Horizontal distance from (⁻3, 1) to *y*-axis:

|______| = ______

Horizontal distance from (2, 1) to *y*-axis: |______| = ______

Distance from (⁻3, 1) to (2, 1): ______________

2. (2, 1) and (2, ⁻4)

____

3. (2, ⁻4) and (4, ⁻4)

____

4. (⁻3, 3) and (⁻3, 1)

____

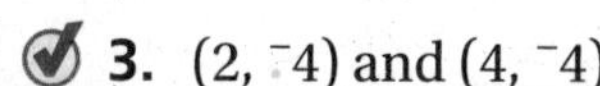

Math Talk **Mathematical Practices**

Explain how you can find the distance between two points that have the same *y*-coordinate.

On Your Own

Practice: Copy and Solve **Graph the pair of points. Then find the distance between them.**

5. (0, 5) and (0, ⁻5)

____

6. (1, 1) and (1, ⁻3)

____

7. (⁻2, ⁻5) and (⁻2, ⁻1)

____

8. (⁻7, 3) and (5, 3)

____

9. (3, ⁻6) and (3, ⁻10)

____

10. (8, 0) and (8, ⁻8)

____

MATHEMATICAL PRACTICE 2 **Use Reasoning** **Algebra** **Write the coordinates of a point that is the given distance from the given point.**

11. 4 units from (3, 5)

(3, ▢)

12. 6 units from (2, 1)

(▢, 1)

13. 7 units from (⁻4, ⁻1)

(⁻4, ▢)

Problem Solving • Applications Real World

An archaeologist is digging at an ancient city. The map shows the locations of several important finds. Each unit represents 1 kilometer. Use the map for 14–18.

Archaeological Site

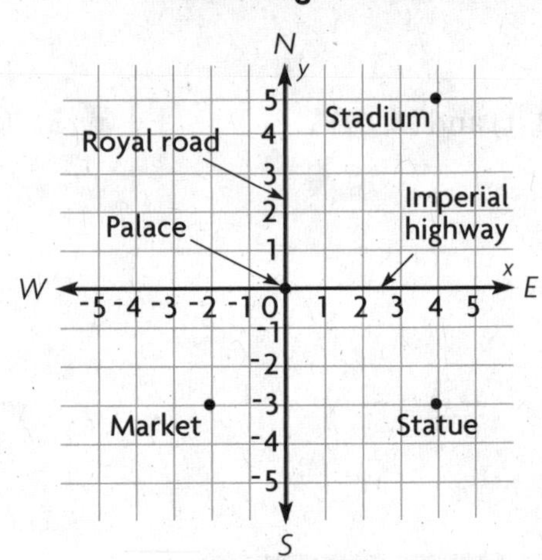

14. How far is it from the stadium to the statue?

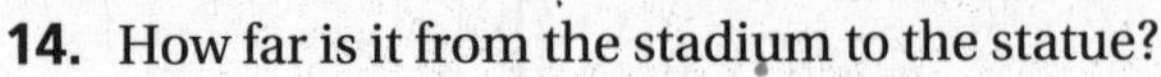

15. GO DEEPER The archaeologist drives 3 km south from the palace. How far is he from the market?

16. The archaeologist's campsite is located at $(^-9, {^-3})$. How far is it from the campsite to the market?

17. THINK SMARTER The archaeologist rode east on a donkey from the Great Gate, at $(^-11, 4)$, to the Royal Road. Then he rode south to the palace. How far did the archaeologist ride?

18. MATHEMATICAL PRACTICE 8 **Generalize** Explain how you could find the distance from the palace to any point on the Imperial Highway.

WRITE ▸ Math • Show Your Work

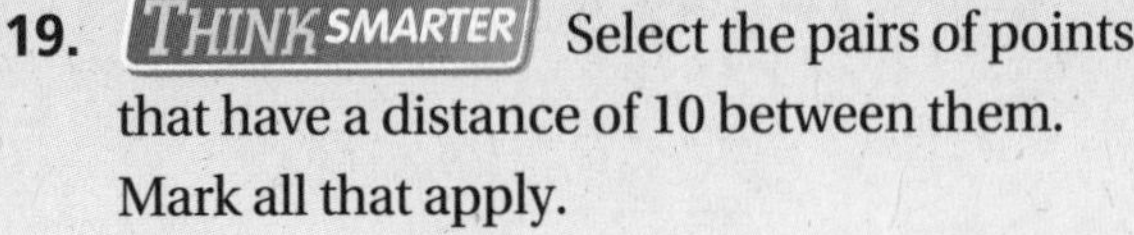

19. THINK SMARTER Select the pairs of points that have a distance of 10 between them. Mark all that apply.

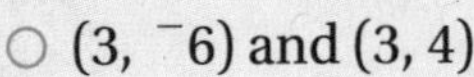

○ $(3, {^-6})$ and $(3, 4)$

○ $(^-3, 8)$ and $(7, 8)$

○ $(4, 5)$ and $(6, 5)$

○ $(4, 1)$ and $(4, 11)$

FOR MORE PRACTICE: Standards Practice Book

Name ___________________________

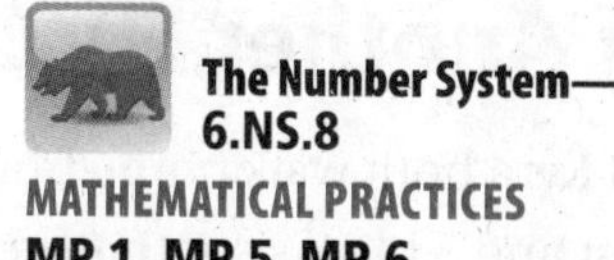

Problem Solving • The Coordinate Plane

Essential Question How can you use the strategy *draw a diagram* to help you solve a problem on the coordinate plane?

The Number System—6.NS.8
MATHEMATICAL PRACTICES
MP.1, MP.5, MP.6

Unlock the Problem (Real World)

An artist is using an illustration program. The program uses a coordinate plane, with the origin (0, 0) located at the center of the computer screen. The artist draws a dinosaur centered on the point (4, 6). Then she moves it 10 units to the left and 12 units down. What ordered pair represents the dinosaur's new location?

Use the graphic organizer to help you solve the problem.

Read the Problem

What do I need to find?	What information do I need to use?	How will I use the information?
I need to find the ______________ for the dinosaur's new location.	The dinosaur started at the point ________. Then the artist moved it ________ to the left and ________ down.	I can draw a diagram to graph the information on a ______________.

Solve the Problem

- Start by graphing and labeling the point ________.
- From this point, count ________ to the left.
- Then count ________ down.
- Graph and label the point at this location, and write its coordinates: ________.

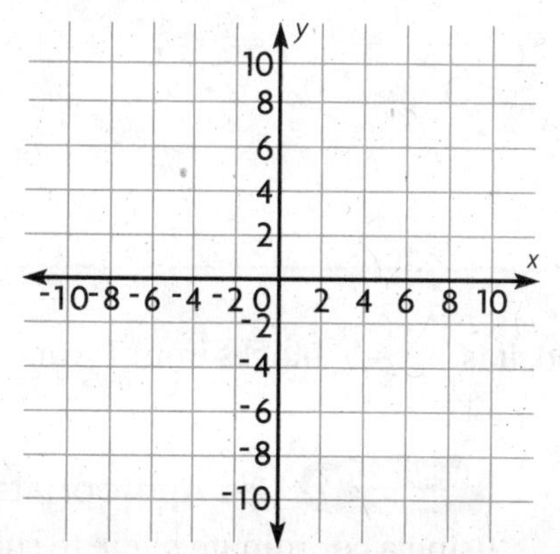

So, the dinosaur's new location is ________.

Math Talk Mathematical Practices

Explain how you could check that your answer is correct.

Try Another Problem

Tyrone and Kyra both walk home from school. Kyra walks 4 blocks east and 3 blocks south to get home. Tyrone lives 3 blocks west and 3 blocks south of the school. How far apart are Tyrone's and Kyra's homes?

Use the graphic organizer to help you solve the problem.

Read the Problem

What do I need to find?

What information do I need to use?

How will I use the information?

Solve the Problem

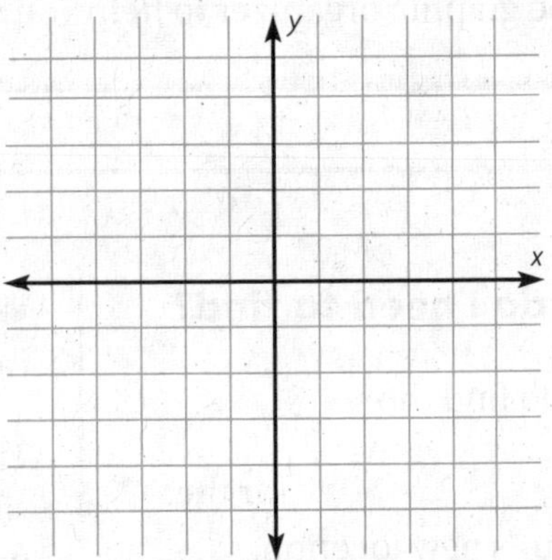

So, it is ______ blocks from Tyrone's house to Kyra's house.

Math Talk — **Mathematical Practices**

Explain how you know that your answer is reasonable.

- MATHEMATICAL PRACTICE 5 **Use Appropriate Tools** Describe the advantages of using a coordinate plane to solve a problem like the one above.

Name ___

Share and Show

1.  Busby County is rectangular. A map of the county on a coordinate plane shows the vertices of the county at $(^-5, 8)$, $(8, 8)$, $(8, ^-10)$, and $(^-5, ^-10)$. Each unit on the map represents 1 mile. What is the county's perimeter?

First, draw a diagram of Busby County.

Busby County

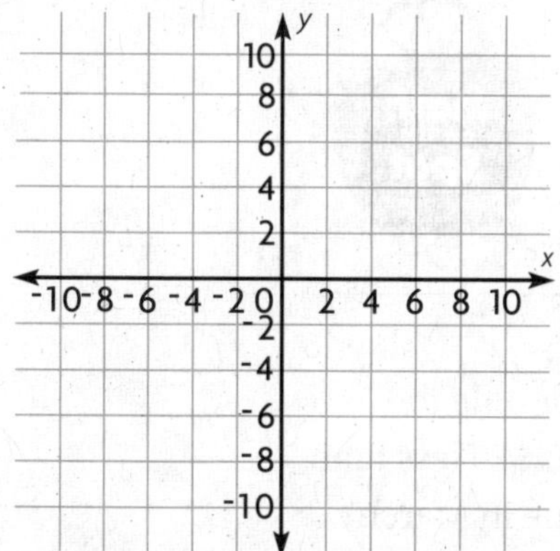

Next, use the diagram to find the length of each side of the rectangle. Then add.

___

So, the perimeter of Busby County is ___.

2. THINK SMARTER What if the vertices of the county were $(^-5, 8)$, $(8, 8)$, $(8, ^-6)$, and $(^-5, ^-6)$? What would the perimeter of the county be?

___

3. On a coordinate map of Melville, a restaurant is located at $(^-9, ^-5)$. A laundry business is located 3 units to the left of the restaurant on the map. What are the map coordinates of the laundry business?

___

4. GO DEEPER The library is 4 blocks north and 9 blocks east of the school. The museum is 9 blocks east and 11 blocks south of the school. How far is it from the library to the museum?

___

Unlock the Problem

- √ Draw a diagram of the situation.
- √ Use absolute value to find distance.

WRITE Math • Show Your Work

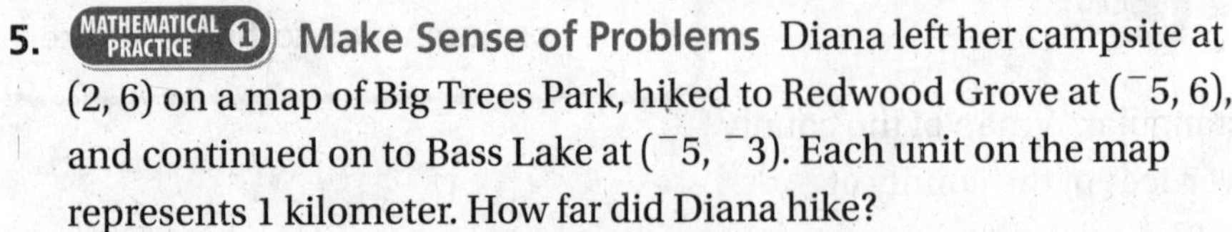

5. MATHEMATICAL PRACTICE 1 **Make Sense of Problems** Diana left her campsite at (2, 6) on a map of Big Trees Park, hiked to Redwood Grove at ($^-5$, 6), and continued on to Bass Lake at ($^-5$, $^-3$). Each unit on the map represents 1 kilometer. How far did Diana hike?

____

6. THINK SMARTER Hector left his house at ($^-6$, 13) on a map of Coleville and walked to the zoo at ($^-6$, 2). From there he walked east to his friend's house. He walked a total distance of 25 blocks. If each unit on the map represents one block, what are the coordinates of Hector's friend's house?

____

7. GO DEEPER In November, the price of a cell phone was double the price in March. In December, the price was \$57, which was \$29 less than the price in November. What was the price of the cell phone in March?

____

Personal Math Trainer

8. THINK SMARTER + A map of the city holding the Olympics is placed on a coordinate plane. Olympic Stadium is located at the origin of the map. Each unit on the map represents 2 miles.

Building	Location
Olympic Village	(−8, 4)
Aquatics Center	(8, 4)
Media Center	(4, −5)
Basketball Arena	(−8, −5)

Graph the locations of four other Olympic buildings.

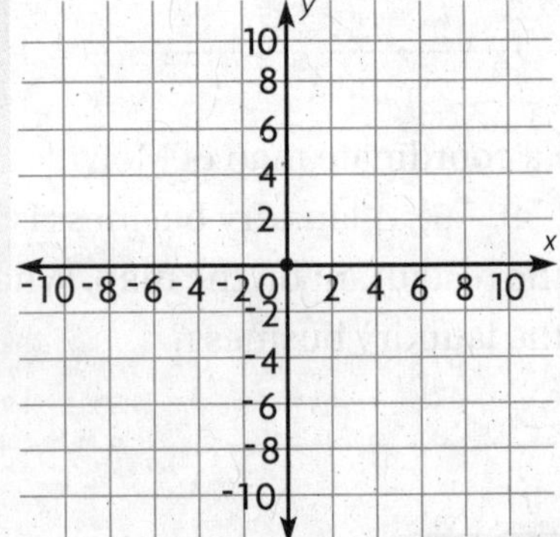

Max said the distance between the Aquatics Center and the Olympic Village is greater than the distance between the Media Center and the Basketball Arena. Do you agree with Max? Use words and numbers to support your answer.

____

____

____

____

____

FOR MORE PRACTICE:
Standards Practice Book

Name ___________________________________

Chapter 3 Review/Test

1. For numbers 1a–1d, choose Yes or No to indicate whether the situation can be represented by a negative number.

1a. Sherri lost 100 points answering a question wrong. ○ Yes ○ No

1b. The peak of a mountain is 2,000 feet above sea level. ○ Yes ○ No

1c. Yong paid $25 for a parking ticket. ○ Yes ○ No

1d. A puppy gained 3 pounds. ○ Yes ○ No

2. The low weekday temperatures for a city are shown.

Low Temperatures	
Day	**Low Temperature (°F)**
Monday	⁻5
Tuesday	⁻3
Wednesday	2
Thursday	⁻7
Friday	3

Part A

Using the information in the table, order the temperatures from lowest to highest.

____

Part B

Explain how to use a vertical number line to determine the order.

GO DIGITAL Assessment Options Chapter Test

3. For numbers 3a–3e, choose Yes or No to indicate whether the number is between $^{-}1$ and $^{-}2$.

3a. $\frac{^{-}4}{5}$ ○ Yes ○ No

3b. $1\frac{2}{3}$ ○ Yes ○ No

3c. $^{-}1.3$ ○ Yes ○ No

3d. $^{-}1\frac{1}{4}$ ○ Yes ○ No

3e. $^{-}2\frac{1}{10}$ ○ Yes ○ No

4. Compare $\frac{^{-}1}{5}$ and $^{-}0.9$. Use numbers and words to explain your answer.

5. Jeandre said $|3|$ equals $|^{-}3|$. Is Jeandre correct? Use the number line and words to support your answer.

6. Write the values in order from least to greatest.

$\|^{-}4\|$	$\|2\|$	$\|^{-}12\|$	$\|8\|$

________ ________ ________ ________

7. For numbers 7a–7d, select True or False for each statement.

7a. The *x*-coordinate of any point on the *y*-axis is 0. ○ True ○ False

7b. Point $D(^{-}2, 1)$ is to the left of the *y*-axis and below the *x*-axis. ○ True ○ False

7c. The point where the axes intersect is the origin. ○ True ○ False

7d. If both the *x*- and *y*- coordinates are positive, the point is to the right of the *y*-axis and below the *x*-axis. ○ True ○ False

Name ___________________________________

8. Mia's house is located at point (3, 4) on a coordinate plane. The location of Keisha's house is the reflection of Mia's house across the *y*-axis. In what quadrant is Keisha's house in?

____

9. Points *A*(3, 8) and *B*($^{-}$4, 8) are located on a coordinate plane. Graph the pair of points. Then find the distance between them. Use numbers and words to explain your answer.

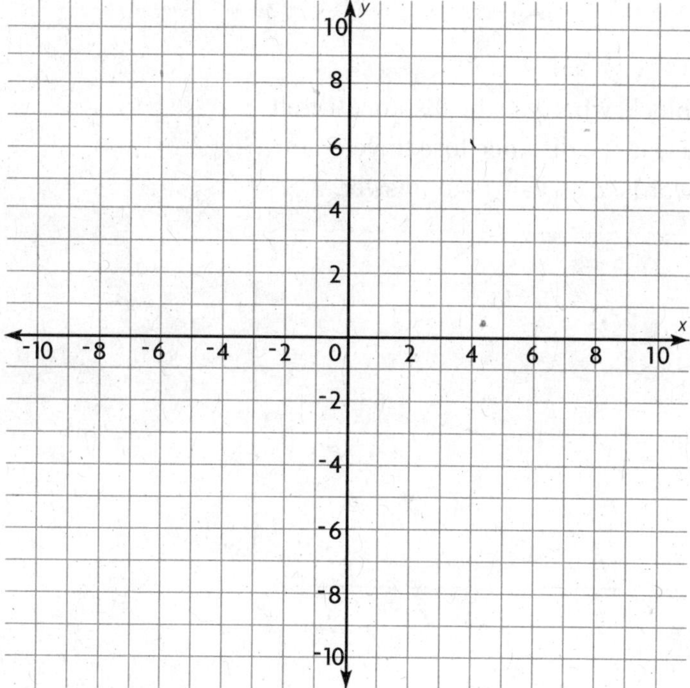

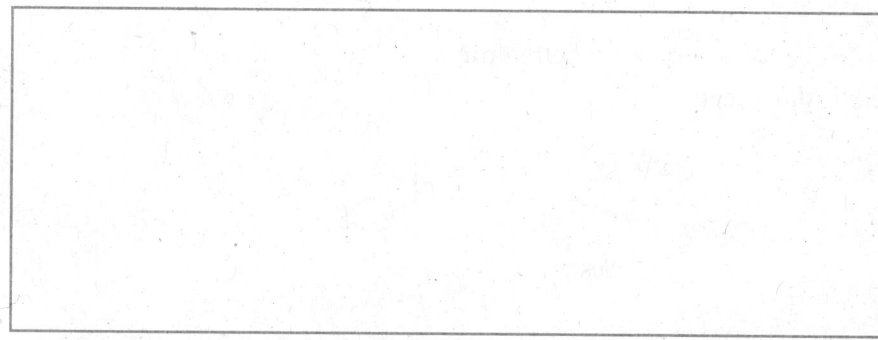

10. The map shows the location J of Jose's house and the location F of the football field. Jose is going to go to Tyrell's house and then the two of them are going to go to the football field for practice.

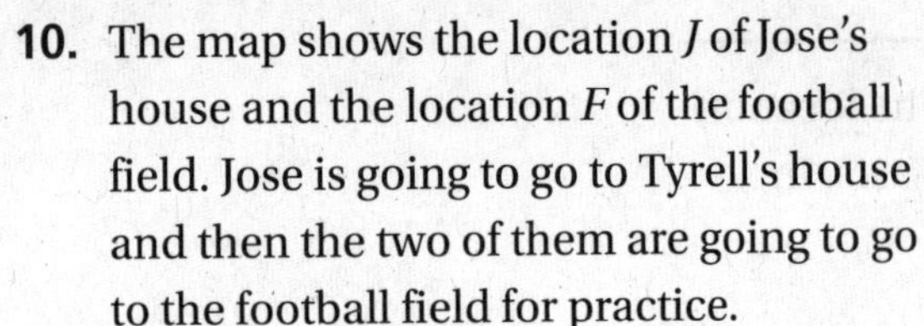

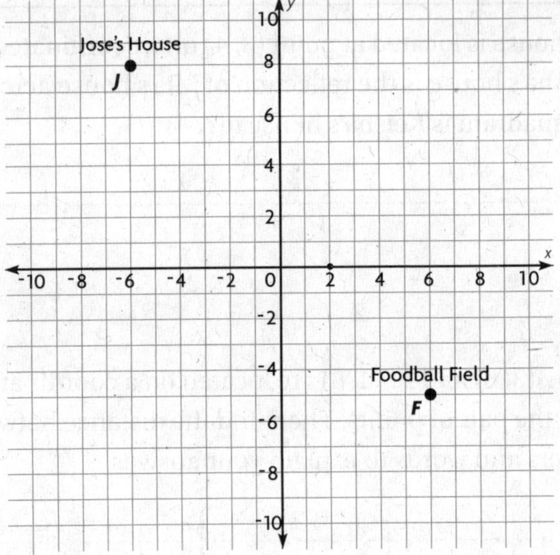

Part A

Tyrell's house is located at point T, the reflection of point J across the y-axis. What are the coordinates of points T, J, and F?

____

Part B

If each unit on the map represents 1 block, what was the distance Tyrell traveled to the football field and what was the distance Jose traveled to the football field? Use numbers and words to explain your answer.

11. For numbers 11a–11d, choose Yes or No to indicate whether the situation could be represented by the integer $^{+}3$.

11a. A football team gains 3 yards on a play. ○ Yes ○ No

11b. A golfer's score is 3 over par. ○ Yes ○ No

11c. A student answers a 3-point question correctly. ○ Yes ○ No

11d. A cat loses 3 pounds. ○ Yes ○ No

Name ________________________________

12. Jason used a map to record the elevations of five locations.

Elevations	
Location	**Elevation (feet)**
Nob Hill	5
Bear Creek	$^{-}18$
Po Valley	$^{-}20$
Fox Hill	8
Jax River	$^{-}3$

Jason wrote the elevations in order from lowest to highest. Is Jason correct? Use words and numbers to explain why or why not. If Jason is incorrect, what is the correct order?

$^{-}3, 5, 8, ^{-}18, ^{-}20$

13. For numbers 13a–13d, select True or False for each statement.

13a. $\frac{1}{5}$ is between 0 and 1. ○ True ○ False

13b. $^{-}2\frac{2}{3}$ is between $^{-}1$ and $^{-}2$. ○ True ○ False

13c. $^{-}3\frac{5}{8}$ is between $^{-}3$ and $^{-}4$. ○ True ○ False

13d. $4\frac{3}{4}$ is between 3 and 4. ○ True ○ False

14. Choose $<$, $>$, or $=$.

14a. 0.25 [$<$ / $>$ / $=$] $\frac{3}{4}$

14b. $\frac{1}{3}$ [$<$ / $>$ / $=$] 0.325

14c. $2\frac{7}{8}$ [$<$ / $>$ / $=$] 2.875

14d. $\frac{-3}{4}$ [$<$ / $>$ / $=$] $\frac{-1}{2}$

15. Graph 4 and -4 on the number line.

$^-4$ $^-3$ $^-2$ $^-1$ 0 1 2 3 4

Tyler says both 4 and -4 have an absolute value of 4. Is Tyler correct? Use the number line and words to explain why or why not.

16. Lindsay and Will have online accounts for buying music. Lindsay's account balance is $-\$20$ and Will's account balance is $-\$15$. Express each account balance as a debt and explain whose debt is greater.

17. Explain how to graph points $A(^-3, 0)$, $B(0, 0)$, and $C(0, -3)$ on the coordinate plane. Then, explain how to graph point D, so that $ABCD$ is a square.

18. Point $A(2, ^-3)$ is reflected across the x-axis to point B. Point B is reflected across the y-axis to point C. What are the coordinates of point C? Use words and numbers to explain your answer.

Critical Area

Ratios and Rates

CRITICAL AREA Connecting ratio and rate to whole number multiplication and division and using concepts of ratio and rate to solve problems

The St. Louis Cardinals, based in St. Louis, Missouri, were founded in 1882.

Project

Meet Me in St. Louis

Baseball teams, like the St. Louis Cardinals, record information about each player on the team. These statistics are used to describe a player's performance.

Get Started

A batting average is calculated from the ratio of a player's hits to the number of at bats. Batting averages are usually recorded as a decimal to the thousandths place. The table shows the batting results of three baseball players who received the Most Valuable Player award while playing for the St. Louis Cardinals. Write each batting ratio as a fraction. Then write the fraction as a decimal to the thousandths place and as a percent.

Important Facts

Player Name	Batting Results
Albert Pujols (2008)	187 hits in 524 at bats
Stan Musial (1948)	230 hits in 611 at bats
Rogers Hornsby (1925)	203 hits in 504 at bats

The players on a baseball team take their turns batting in the same order or sequence throughout a game. The manager sets the batting order. Suppose you are the manager of a team that includes Pujols, Musial, and Hornsby. What batting order would you use for those three players? Explain your answer.

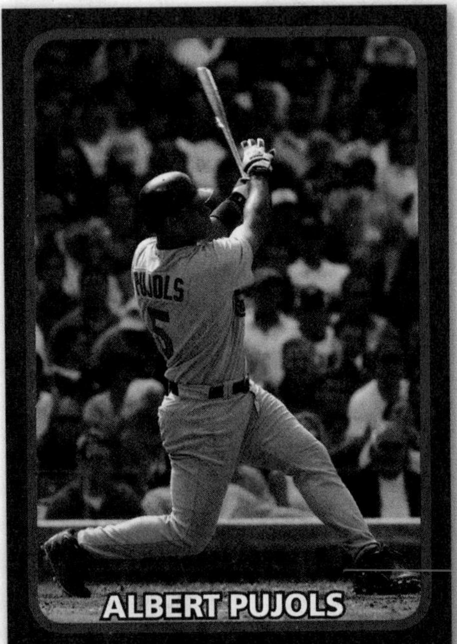

Completed by ______________________

Chapter 4

Ratios and Rates

Show What You Know 

Check your understanding of important skills.

Name ____________________

▶ **Multiply or Divide to Find Equivalent Fractions** **Multiply or divide to find two equivalent fractions for the given fraction.**

1. $\frac{1}{2}$ ____________

2. $\frac{5}{6}$ ____________

3. $\frac{12}{18}$ ____________

▶ **Extend Patterns** **Write a description of the pattern. Then find the missing numbers.**

4. 3, ______, 48, 192, 768, ______

____

5. 625, 575, 525, ______, ______, 375

____

▶ **Multiply by 2-Digit Numbers** **Find the product.**

6. $\begin{array}{r} 52 \\ \times\ 19 \\ \hline \end{array}$

7. $\begin{array}{r} 14 \\ \times\ 88 \\ \hline \end{array}$

8. $\begin{array}{r} 37 \\ \times\ 21 \\ \hline \end{array}$

9. $\begin{array}{r} 45 \\ \times\ 62 \\ \hline \end{array}$

The student council should have 1 representative for every 25 students. Be a Math Detective and determine which of these situations fits the description. Explain your answer.

a. 5 representatives for 100 students

b. 10 representatives for 250 students

c. 15 representatives for 300 students

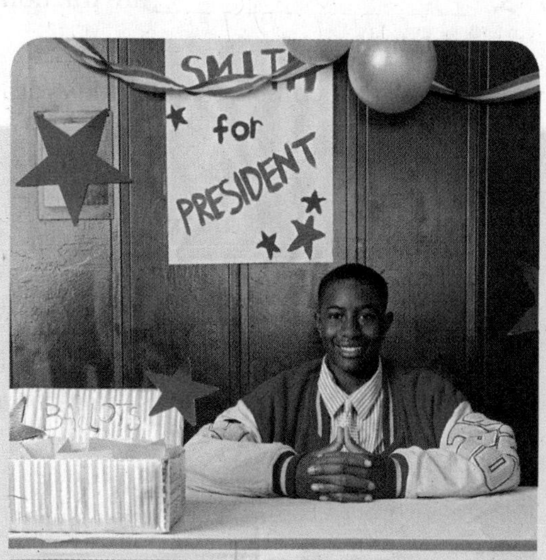

Personal Math Trainer
Online Assessment and Intervention

Vocabulary Builder

▶ Visualize It

Complete the bubble map with review words that are related to fractions.

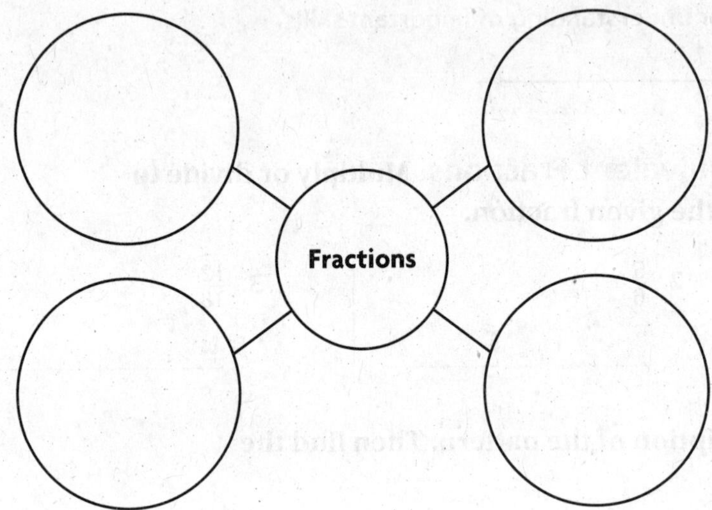

Review Words

- coordinate plane
- denominator
- ✓ equivalent fractions
- numerator
- ✓ ordered pair
- pattern
- simplify
- *x*-coordinate
- *y*-coordinate

Preview Words

- ✓ equivalent ratios
- ✓ rate
- ✓ ratio
- ✓ unit rate

▶ Understand Vocabulary

Complete the sentences using the checked words.

1. A comparison of one number to another by division is a

____________________.

2. ____________________ are ratios that name the same comparison.

3. ____________________ are fractions that name the same amount or part.

4. A ratio that compares quantities with different units is a

____________________.

5. A ____________________ is a rate that compares a quantity to 1 unit.

6. In an ____________________ the first number is the *x*-coordinate and the second number is the *y*-coordinate.

GO DIGITAL
- Interactive Student Edition
- Multimedia eGlossary

Name ______________________________

Model Ratios

Essential Question How can you model ratios?

Ratios and Proportional Relationships—6.RP.1

MATHEMATICAL PRACTICES
MP.5, MP.7

The drawing shows 5 blue squares and 1 red square. You can compare the number of blue squares to the number of red squares by using a ratio. A **ratio** is a comparison of two quantities by division.

The ratio that compares blue squares to red squares is 5 to 1.
The ratio 5 to 1 can also be written as 5:1.

Investigate

Hands On

Materials ■ two-color counters

Julie makes 3 bracelets for every 1 bracelet Beth makes. Use ratios to compare the number of bracelets Julie makes to the number Beth makes.

A. Use red and yellow counters to model the ratio that compares the number of bracelets Julie makes to the number of bracelets Beth makes.

Think: Julie makes _______ bracelets when Beth makes 1 bracelet.

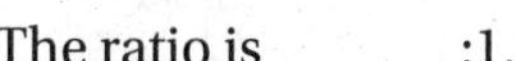

The ratio is _______:1.

B. Model the ratio that shows the number of bracelets Julie makes when Beth makes 2 bracelets. Write the ratio and explain how you modeled it.

____

____

C. How could you change the model from Part B to show the number of bracelets Julie makes when Beth makes 3 bracelets? Write the ratio.

____

____

Math Talk **Mathematical Practices**

For each ratio, divide the number of bracelets Julie makes by the number of bracelets Beth makes. **Describe** a pattern you notice in the quotients.

Draw Conclusions

1. Explain how you used counters to compare the number of bracelets Julie makes to the number of bracelets Beth makes.

2. MATHEMATICAL PRACTICE 8 **Generalize** Describe a rule that you can use to find the number of bracelets Julie makes when you know the number of bracelets Beth makes.

3. THINK SMARTER How can you use counters to find how many bracelets Beth makes if you know the number Julie makes? Explain and give an example.

Make Connections

You can use a table to compare quantities and write ratios.

A bakery uses 1 packing box for every 4 muffins. Draw a model and make a table to show the ratio of boxes to muffins.

STEP 1 Draw a model to show the ratio that compares boxes to muffins.

Think: There is ______ box for every ______ muffins.

The ratio is ______ : ______.

STEP 2 Complete the table to show the ratio of boxes to muffins.

Think: Each time the number of boxes increases by 1,

the number of muffins increases by ______.

Number of Boxes	1	2	3	4
Number of Muffins	4			

+1

+

What is the ratio of boxes to muffins when there are 2 boxes? ______

Write another ratio shown by the table. Explain what the ratio represents.

Math Talk **Mathematical Practices**

Describe the pattern you see in the table comparing the number of boxes to the number of muffins.

Name ____________________

Share and Show

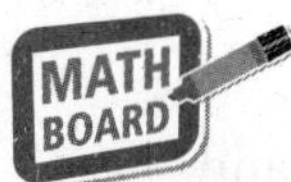

Write the ratio of yellow counters to red counters.

1.

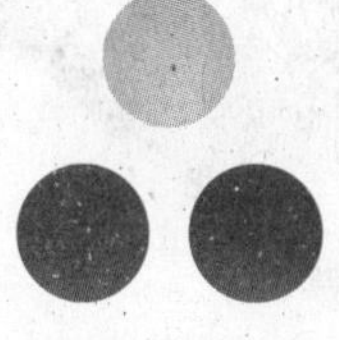

_____ : _____

2.

Draw a model of the ratio.

3. 3:2

4. 1:5

Use the ratio to complete the table.

5. Wen is arranging flowers in vases. For every 1 rose she uses, she uses 6 tulips. Complete the table to show the ratio of roses to tulips.

Roses	1	2	3	4
Tulips	6			

6. On the sixth-grade field trip, there are 8 students for every 1 adult. Complete the table to show the ratio of students to adults.

Students	8		24	
Adults	1	2		4

7. THINK SMARTER Zena adds 4 cups flour for every 3 cups of sugar in her recipe. Draw a model that compares cups of flour to cups of sugar.

Connect to Reading

Draw Conclusions

The reading skill *draw conclusions* can help you analyze and make sense of information.

Hikers take trail mix as a snack on long hikes because it is tasty, nutritious, and easy to carry. There are many different recipes for trail mix, but it is usually made from different combinations of dried fruit, raisins, seeds, and nuts. Tanner and his dad make trail mix that has 1 cup of raisins for every 3 cups of sunflower seeds.

8. MATHEMATICAL PRACTICE 4 **Model Mathematics** Explain how you could model the ratio that compares cups of raisins to cups of sunflower seeds when Tanner uses 2 cups of raisins.

The table shows the ratio of cups of raisins to cups of sunflower seeds for different amounts of trail mix. Model each ratio as you complete the table.

Trail Mix

Raisins (cups)	1	2	3	4	5
Sunflower Seeds (cups)	3				

9. THINK SMARTER Describe the pattern you see in the table.

10. MATHEMATICAL PRACTICE 8 **Draw Conclusions** What conclusion can Tanner draw from this pattern?

11. GO DEEPER What is the ratio of cups of sunflower seeds to cups of trail mix when Tanner uses 4 cups of raisins?

FOR MORE PRACTICE: Standards Practice Book

Name ____________________________

Ratios and Rates

Essential Question How do you write ratios and rates?

Ratios and Proportional Relationships—6.RP.1 *Also 6.RP.2*

MATHEMATICAL PRACTICES
MP.1, MP.2, MP.5

Unlock the Problem

A bird rescue group is caring for 3 eagles, 2 hawks, and 5 owls in their rescue center.

You can compare the numbers of different types of birds using ratios. There are three ways to write the ratio of owls to eagles in the rescue center.

Using words	As a fraction	With a colon
5 to 3	$\frac{5}{3}$	5:3

Ratios can be written to compare a part to a part, a part to a whole, or a whole to a part.

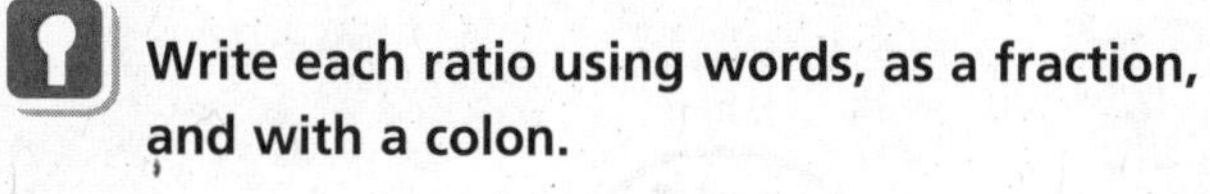

A Owls to hawks

______ to ______	$\frac{\square}{\square}$	______:______	Part to part

B Eagles to total birds in the rescue center

______ to ______	$\frac{\square}{\square}$	______:______	Part to whole

C Total birds in the rescue center to hawks

______ to ______	$\frac{\square}{\square}$	______:______	Whole to part

1. The ratio of owls to total number of birds is 5:10. Explain what this ratio means.

____

Example A restaurant sells veggie burgers at the rate of $4 for 1 burger. What rate gives the cost of 5 veggie burgers? Write the rate for 5 burgers using words, as a fraction, and with a colon.

A **rate** is a ratio that compares two quantities that have different units of measure.

A **unit rate** is a rate that makes a comparison to 1 unit. The unit rate for cost per veggie burger is $4 to 1 burger or $\frac{\$4}{1\text{ burger}}$.

Complete the table to find the rate that gives the cost of 5 veggie burgers.

Think: 1 veggie burger costs $4, so 2 veggie burgers cost $4 + ______, or 2 × ______.

	Unit Rate	2 • $4 ↓	3 • $4 ↓	___ • $4 ↓	___ • $4 ↓
Cost	$4	$8			
Veggie Burgers	1	2	3	4	
		↑ 2 • 1	↑ ___ • 1	↑ 4 • 1	↑ ___ • 1

The table shows that 5 veggie burgers cost ______.

So, the rate that gives the cost for 5 veggie burgers is

$______ to ______ burgers, $\frac{\$\_\_\_}{\_\_\_\text{ burgers}}$, or $______ : ______ burgers.

Math Talk **Mathematical Practices**

Describe two other ways to say "$4 per burger".

Try This! Write the rate in three different ways.

A The rate that gives the cost of 3 veggie burgers

____

B The rate that gives the cost of 4 veggie burgers

____

2. Explain why the ratio $\frac{\$4}{1\text{ burger}}$ is a unit rate.

____

3. MATHEMATICAL PRACTICE 5 **Use Patterns** Explain the pattern you see in the table in the Example.

____

____

Name ______________________________

Share and Show

1. Write the ratio of the number of red bars to blue stars.

Write the ratio in two different ways.

2. 8 to 16

3. $\frac{4}{24}$

4. 1:3

5. 7 to 9

6. Marilyn saves $15 per week. Complete the table to find the rate that gives the amount saved in 4 weeks. Write the rate in three different ways.

Savings		$30	$45		$75
Weeks	1	2	3	4	5

Math Talk — Mathematical Practices

Explain whether the ratios 5:2 and 2:5 are t same or different.

On Your Own

Write the ratio in two different ways.

7. $\frac{16}{40}$

8. 8:12

9. 4 to 11

10. 2:13

11. There are 24 baseball cards in 4 packs. Complete the table to find the rate that gives the number of cards in 2 packs. Write this rate in three different ways.

Cards			18	24
Packs	1	2	3	4

12. MATHEMATICAL PRACTICE 6 **Make Connections** Explain how the statement "There are 6 apples per bag" represents a rate.

Problem Solving • Applications

Use the diagram of a birdhouse for 13–15.

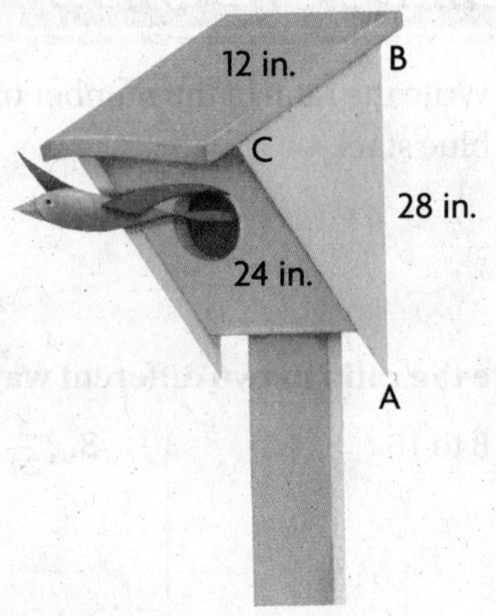

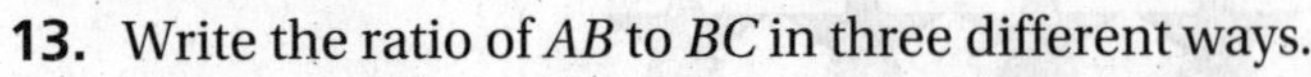

13. Write the ratio of *AB* to *BC* in three different ways.

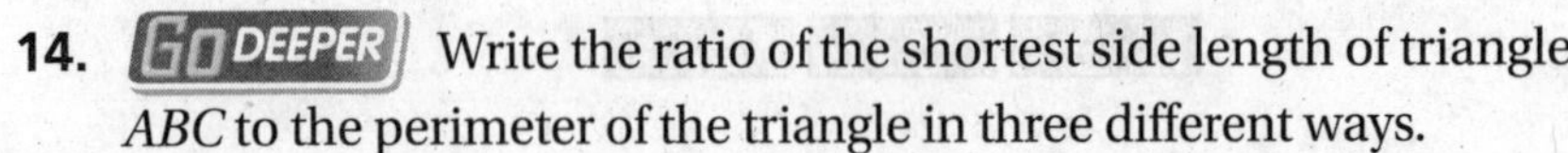

14. GO DEEPER Write the ratio of the shortest side length of triangle *ABC* to the perimeter of the triangle in three different ways.

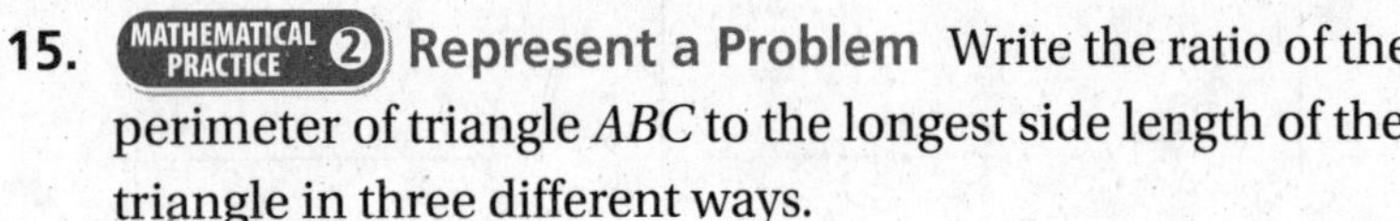

15. MATHEMATICAL PRACTICE 2 **Represent a Problem** Write the ratio of the perimeter of triangle *ABC* to the longest side length of the triangle in three different ways.

WRITE ▸Math • **Show Your Work**

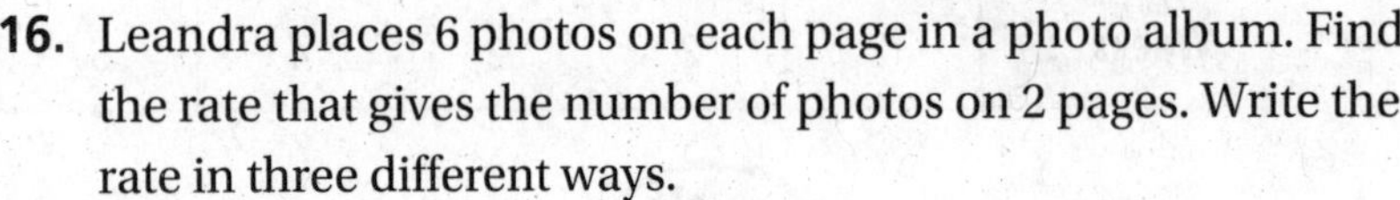

16. Leandra places 6 photos on each page in a photo album. Find the rate that gives the number of photos on 2 pages. Write the rate in three different ways.

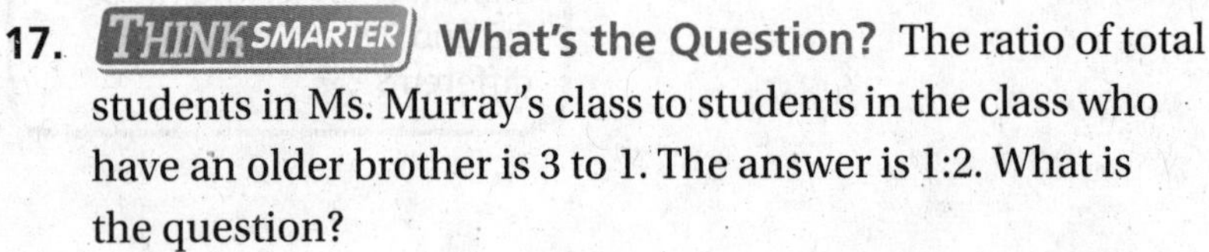

17. THINK SMARTER **What's the Question?** The ratio of total students in Ms. Murray's class to students in the class who have an older brother is 3 to 1. The answer is 1:2. What is the question?

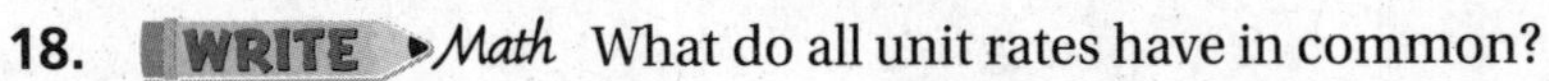

18. WRITE ▸Math What do all unit rates have in common?

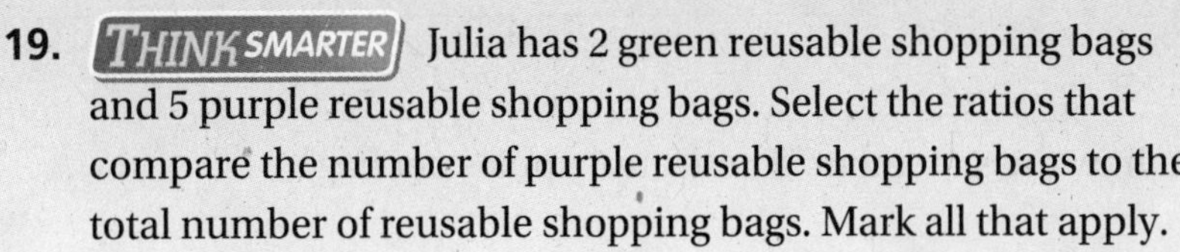

19. THINK SMARTER Julia has 2 green reusable shopping bags and 5 purple reusable shopping bags. Select the ratios that compare the number of purple reusable shopping bags to the total number of reusable shopping bags. Mark all that apply.

○ 5 to 7 ○ 5 : 2 ○ 2 to 7

○ 5 : 7 ○ $\frac{2}{5}$ ○ $\frac{5}{7}$

FOR MORE PRACTICE: Standards Practice Book

Name ______________________

Equivalent Ratios and Multiplication Tables

Essential Question How can you use a multiplication table to find equivalent ratios?

Ratios and Proportional Relationships—6.RP.3a

MATHEMATICAL PRACTICES
MP.1, MP.4, MP.6

The table below shows two rows from the multiplication table: the row for 1 and the row for 6. The ratios shown in each column of the table are equivalent to the original ratio. Ratios that name the same comparison are **equivalent ratios**.

	Original ratio	2 • 1 ↓	3 • 1 ↓	4 • 1 ↓	5 • 1 ↓
Bags	1	2	3	4	5
Apples	6	12	18	24	30
		↑ 2 • 6	↑ 3 • 6	↑ 4 • 6	↑ 5 • 6

×	1	2	3	4	5
1	1	2	3	4	5
2	2	4	6	8	10
3	3	6	9	12	15
4	4	8	12	16	20
5	5	10	15	20	25
6	6	12	18	24	30

You can use a multiplication table to find equivalent ratios.

Unlock the Problem Real World

The ratio of adults to students on a field trip is $\frac{3}{8}$.

Write two ratios that are equivalent to $\frac{3}{8}$.

×	1	2	3	4	5	6	7	8	9
1	1	2	3	4	5	6	7	8	9
2	2	4	6	8	10	12	14	16	18
3	3	6	9	12	15	18	21	24	27
4	4	8	12	16	20	24	28	32	36
5	5	10	15	20	25	30	35	40	45
6	6	12	18	24	30	36	42	48	54
7	7	14	21	28	35	42	49	56	63
8	8	16	24	32	40	48	56	64	72
9	9	18	27	36	45	54	63	72	81

Use the multiplication table.

STEP 1 Shade the rows that show the original ratio.

Think: The original ratio is . Shade the row for ______ and the row for ______ on the multiplication table.

STEP 2 Circle the column that shows the original ratio.

Think: There is one group of 3 adults for every group of 8 students.

STEP 3 Circle two columns that show equivalent ratios.

The column for 2 shows there are 2 • 3, or ______ adults when there are 2 • 8, or ______ students.

The column for 3 shows there are 3 • 3, or ______ adults when there are 3 • 8, or ______ students.

So, ______ and ______ are equivalent to $\frac{3}{8}$.

Math Talk **Mathematical Practices**

Explain whether the multiplication table shown represents all of the ratios that are equivalent to 3:8.

CONNECT You can find equivalent ratios by using a table or by multiplying or dividing by a form of one.

One Way Use a table.

Jessa made fruit punch by mixing 2 pints of orange juice with 5 pints of pineapple juice. To make more punch, she needs to mix orange juice and pineapple juice in the same ratio. Write three equivalent ratios for $\frac{2}{5}$.

Think: Use rows from the multiplication table to help you complete a table of equivalent ratios.

×	1	2	3	4	5
1	1	2	3	4	5
2	2	4	6	8	10
3	3	6	9	12	15
4	4	8	12	16	20
5	5	10	15	20	25

→

	Original ratio	2 • 2 ↓	3 • 2 ↓	 • 2 ↓
Orange juice (pints)	2			8
Pineapple juice (pints)	5		15	
		↑ 2 • 5	↑ ☐ • 5	↑ 4 • 5

So, $\frac{2}{5}$, ______, ______, and ______ are equivalent ratios.

Another Way Multiply or divide by a form of one.

Write two equivalent ratios for $\frac{6}{8}$.

Ⓐ Multiply by a form of one.

Multiply the numerator and denominator by the same number.

$$\frac{6 \cdot \square}{8 \cdot \square} = \frac{\square}{\square}$$

ERROR Alert

Be sure to multiply or divide the numerator and the denominator by the same number.

Ⓑ Divide by a form of one.

Divide the numerator and denominator by the same number.

$$\frac{6 \div \square}{8 \div \square} = \frac{\square}{\square}$$

So, $\frac{6}{8}$, ______, and ______ are equivalent ratios.

- MATHEMATICAL PRACTICE 6 **Compare** Explain how ratios are similar to fractions. Explain how they are different.

____

____

Name ______________________________

Share and Show

Write two equivalent ratios.

1. Use a multiplication table to write two ratios that are equivalent to $\frac{4}{7}$.

   Find the rows that show $\frac{4}{7}$.

   Find columns that show equivalent ratios. $\frac{4}{7} = \_\_\_\_ = \_\_\_\_$

2.

3		
7		

3.

5		
2		

4.

	2	
	10	

5. $\frac{4}{5}$ ______

6. $\frac{12}{30}$ ______

7. $\frac{2}{9}$ ______

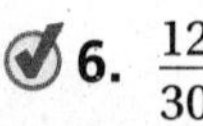

Math Talk — **Mathematical Practices**

Explain how the multiplication table helps you find equivalent ratios.

On Your Own

Write two equivalent ratios.

8.

9		
8		

9.

5		
4		

10.

	6	
	9	

11. $\frac{8}{7}$ ______

12. $\frac{2}{6}$ ______

13. $\frac{4}{11}$ ______

Determine whether the ratios are equivalent.

14. $\frac{2}{3}$ and $\frac{8}{12}$ ______

15. $\frac{8}{10}$ and $\frac{6}{10}$ ______

16. $\frac{16}{60}$ and $\frac{4}{15}$ ______

17. $\frac{3}{14}$ and $\frac{8}{28}$ ______

Problem Solving • Applications

×	1	2	3	4	5	6	7	8	9
1	1	2	3	4	5	6	7	8	9
2	2	4	6	8	10	12	14	16	18
3	3	6	9	12	15	18	21	24	27
4	4	8	12	16	20	24	28	32	36
5	5	10	15	20	25	30	35	40	45
6	6	12	18	24	30	36	42	48	54
7	7	14	21	28	35	42	49	56	63
8	8	16	24	32	40	48	56	64	72
9	9	18	27	36	45	54	63	72	81

Use the multiplication table for 18 and 19.

18. In Keith's baseball games this year, the ratio of times he has gotten on base to the times he has been at bat is $\frac{4}{14}$. Write two ratios that are equivalent to $\frac{4}{14}$.

____

19. THINK SMARTER **Pose a Problem** Use the multiplication table to write a new problem involving equivalent ratios. Then solve the problem.

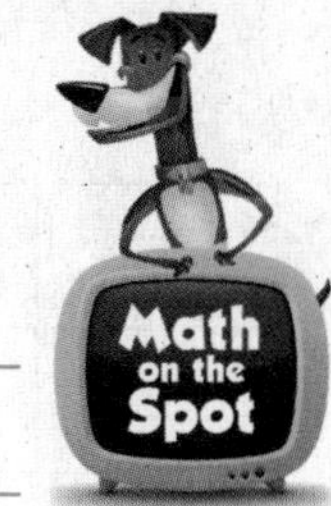

____

____

____

20. MATHEMATICAL PRACTICE 1 **Describe** how to write an equivalent ratio for $\frac{9}{27}$ without using a multiplication table.

____

____

____

21. GO DEEPER Write a ratio that is equivalent to $\frac{6}{9}$ and $\frac{16}{24}$.

____

22. THINK SMARTER Determine whether each ratio is equivalent to $\frac{1}{3}$, $\frac{5}{10}$, or $\frac{3}{5}$. Write the ratio in the correct box.

$\frac{2}{4}$ $\frac{3}{9}$ $\frac{7}{21}$ $\frac{18}{30}$ $\frac{10}{30}$ $\frac{6}{10}$ $\frac{1}{2}$ $\frac{8}{16}$

$\frac{1}{3}$	$\frac{5}{10}$	$\frac{3}{5}$

FOR MORE PRACTICE: Standards Practice Book

Name ______________________________

Problem Solving • Use Tables to Compare Ratios

Essential Question How can you use the strategy *find a pattern* to help you compare ratios?

Ratios and Proportional Relationships—6.RP.3a
MATHEMATICAL PRACTICES
MP.1, MP.5, MP.7

Unlock the Problem

A paint store makes rose-pink paint by mixing 3 parts red paint to 8 parts white paint. A clerk mixes 4 parts red paint to 7 parts white paint. Did the clerk mix the paint correctly to make rose-pink paint? Use tables of equivalent ratios to support your answer.

Use the graphic organizer to help you solve the problem.

Read the Problem

What do I need to find?

I need to find whether the ratio used by the clerk is ____________ to the ratio for rose-pink paint.

What information do I need to use?

I need to use the rose-pink paint ratio and the ratio used by the clerk.

How will I use the information?

I will make tables of equivalent ratios to compare the ratios ______ to ______ and ______ to ______.

Solve the Problem

Rose-Pink Paint				
Parts Red	3	6	9	12
Parts White	8			

Clerk's Paint Mixture				
Parts Red	4			
Parts White	7	14	21	28

Look for a pattern to determine whether the ratios in the first table are equivalent to the ratios in the second table.

Think: The number 12 appears in the first row of both tables.

$\frac{12}{\_\_}$ is/is not equivalent to $\frac{12}{\_\_}$.

The ratios have the same numerator and ____________ denominators.

So, the clerk ____________ mix the paint correctly.

Math Talk — **Mathematical Practices**

Explain how you can check that your answer is correct.

Try Another Problem

In Amy's art class, the ratio of brushes to students is 6 to 4. In Traci's art class, the ratio of brushes to students is 9 to 6. Is the ratio of brushes to students in Amy's class equivalent to the ratio of brushes to students in Traci's class? Use tables of equivalent ratios to support your answer.

Read the Problem

What do I need to find?	What information do I need to use?	How will I use the information?

Solve the Problem

So, the ratio of brushes to students in Amy's class is/is not equivalent to the ratio of brushes to students in Traci's class.

1. MATHEMATICAL PRACTICE 5 **Use Patterns** Explain how you used a pattern to determine whether the ratios in the two tables are equivalent.

2. Tell how writing the ratios in simplest form can help you justify your answer.

Name ______________________________

Share and Show

1. In Jawan's school, 4 out of 10 students chose basketball as a sport they like to watch, and 3 out of 5 students chose football. Is the ratio of students who chose basketball (4 to 10) equivalent to the ratio of students who chose football (3 to 5)?

First, make tables to show the ratios.

Basketball				

Football				

Next, compare the ratios in the tables. Find a ratio in the first table that has the same numerator as a ratio in the second table.

$\frac{12}{\square}$ ____________ equivalent to $\frac{12}{\square}$.

So, the ratios ____________ equivalent.

2. THINK SMARTER What if 20 out of 50 students chose baseball as a sport they like to watch? Is this ratio equivalent to the ratio for either basketball or football? Explain.

____

____

____

Unlock the Problem

- ✓ Circle the question.
- ✓ Underline important facts.
- ✓ Check to make sure you answered the question.

3. MATHEMATICAL PRACTICE 7 **Look for Structure** The table shows the results of the quizzes Hannah took in one week. Did Hannah get the same score on her math and science quizzes? Explain.

____

____

Hannah's Quiz Results	
Subject	**Questions Correct**
Social Studies	4 out of 5
Math	8 out of 10
Science	3 out of 4
English	10 out of 12

4. Did Hannah get the same score on the quizzes in any of her classes? Explain.

____

____

On Your Own

5. GO DEEPER For every $10 that Julie makes, she saves $3. For every $15 Liam makes, he saves $6. Is Julie's ratio of money saved to money earned equivalent to Liam's ratio of money saved to money earned?

6. THINK SMARTER A florist offers three different bouquets of tulips and irises. The list shows the ratios of tulips to irises in each bouquet. Determine the bouquets that have equivalent ratios.

Bouquet Ratios

Spring Mix
4 tulips to 6 irises

Morning Melody
9 tulips to 12 irises

Splash of Sun
10 tulips to 15 irises

7. The ratio of boys to girls in a school's soccer club is 3 to 5. The ratio of boys to girls in the school's chess club is 13 to 15. Is the ratio of boys to girls in the soccer club equivalent to the ratio of boys to girls in the chess club? Explain.

WRITE Math
Show Your Work

8. MATHEMATICAL PRACTICE 1 **Analyze** Thad, Joey, and Mia ran in a race. The finishing times were 4.56 minutes, 3.33 minutes, and 4.75 minutes. Thad did not finish last. Mia had the fastest time. What was each runner's time?

9. THINK SMARTER Fernando donates $2 to a local charity organization for every $15 he earns. Cleo donates $4 for every $17 she earns. Is Fernando's ratio of money donated to money earned equivalent to Cleo's ratio of money donated to money earned? Explain.

FOR MORE PRACTICE:
Standards Practice Book

Name ______________________________

Use Equivalent Ratios

Essential Question How can you use tables to solve problems involving equivalent ratios?

Ratios and Proportional Relationships—6.RP.3a

MATHEMATICAL PRACTICES
MP.4, MP.8

Unlock the Problem

In warm weather, the Anderson family likes to spend time on the family's boat. The boat uses 2 gallons of gas to travel 12 miles on the lake. How much gas would the boat use to travel 48 miles?

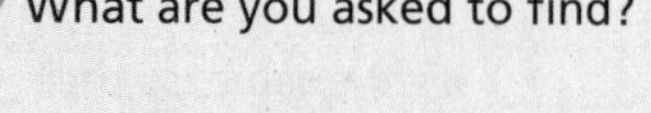

- What are you asked to find?

____

____

Solve by finding equivalent ratios.

Let ■ represent the unknown number of gallons.

$$\frac{\text{gallons}}{\text{miles}} \rightarrow \frac{2}{12} = \frac{■}{48} \leftarrow \frac{\text{gallons}}{\text{miles}}$$

Make a table of equivalent ratios.

	Original ratio	2 · 2 ↓	■ · 2 ↓	■ · 2 ↓
Gas used (gallons)	2		6	
Distance (miles)	12	24		48
		↑ ■ · 12	↑ 3 · 12	↑ ■ · 12

The ratios $\frac{2}{12}$ and ______ are equivalent ratios,

so $\frac{2}{12} = \frac{■}{48}$.

So, the boat will use ______ gallons of gas to travel 48 miles.

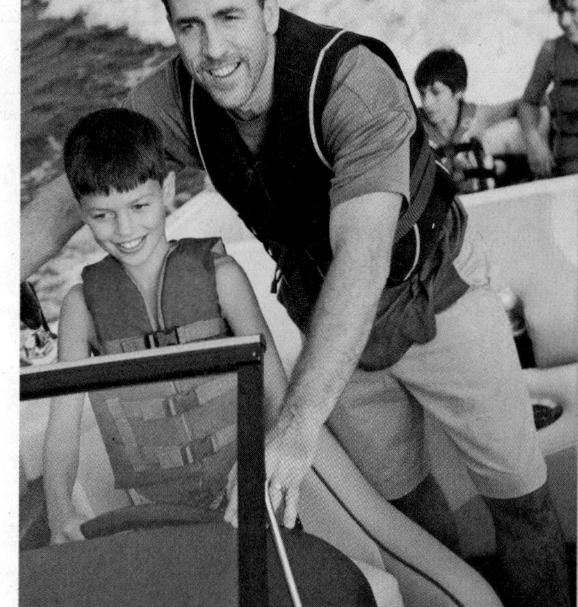

- What if the boat uses 14 gallons of gas? Explain how you can use equivalent ratios to find the number of miles the boat travels when it uses 14 gallons of gas.

____

____

____

Example Use equivalent ratios to find the unknown value.

A $\frac{3}{4} = \frac{■}{20}$

Use common denominators to write equivalent ratios.

_______ is a multiple of 4, so _______ is a common denominator.

Multiply the _______________ and denominator by _______ to write the ratios using a common denominator.

The _______________ are the same, so the _______________ are equal to each other.

So, the unknown value is _______ and $\frac{3}{4} = \frac{■}{20}$.

$$\frac{3}{4} = \frac{■}{20}$$

$$\frac{3 \times ■}{4 \times ■} = \frac{■}{20}$$

$$\frac{■}{20} = \frac{■}{20}$$

Check your answer by making a table of equivalent ratios.

Original ratio ■ ·3 ■ ·3 ■ ·3 ■ ·3

3	6			
4	8			

■ ·4 ■ ·4 ■ ·4 ■ ·4

B $\frac{56}{42} = \frac{8}{■}$

Write an equivalent ratio with 8 in the numerator.

Think: Divide 56 by _______ to get 8.

So, divide the denominator by _______ as well.

The _______________ are the same, so the _______________ are equal to each other.

So, the unknown value is _______ and $\frac{56}{42} = \frac{8}{■}$.

$$\frac{56}{42} = \frac{8}{■}$$

$$\frac{56 \div ■}{42 \div ■} = \frac{8}{■}$$

$$\frac{8}{■} = \frac{8}{■}$$

Math Talk — **Mathematical Practices**

Give an example of two equivalent ratios. **Explain** how you know that they are equivalent.

Check your answer by making a table of equivalent ratios.

Original ratio ■ ·8 ■ ·8 ■ ·8 ■ ·8 ■ ·8 ■ ·8

8	16					
6	12					

■ ·6 ■ ·6 ■ ·6 ■ ·6 ■ ·6 ■ ·6

Name ______________________

Share and Show

Use equivalent ratios to find the unknown value.

1. $\frac{\blacksquare}{10} = \frac{4}{5}$

$\frac{\blacksquare}{10} = \frac{4 \cdot \square}{5 \cdot \square}$

$\frac{\blacksquare}{10} = \frac{\square}{10}$

So, the unknown value is ______.

2. $\frac{18}{24} = \frac{6}{\blacksquare}$

$\frac{18 \div \square}{24 \div \square} = \frac{6}{\blacksquare}$

$\frac{6}{\square} = \frac{6}{\blacksquare}$

So, the unknown value is ______.

3. $\frac{3}{6} = \frac{15}{\blacksquare}$ ______

4. $\frac{\blacksquare}{5} = \frac{8}{10}$ ______

✓5. $\frac{7}{4} = \frac{\blacksquare}{12}$ ______

✓6. $\frac{10}{\blacksquare} = \frac{40}{12}$ ______

Math Talk — **Mathematical Practices**

Explain whether you can always find an equivalent ratio by subtracting the same number from the numerator and denominator. Give an example to support your answer.

On Your Own

Use equivalent ratios to find the unknown value.

7. $\frac{2}{6} = \frac{\blacksquare}{30}$ ______

8. $\frac{5}{\blacksquare} = \frac{55}{110}$ ______

9. $\frac{3}{9} = \frac{9}{\blacksquare}$ ______

10. $\frac{\blacksquare}{6} = \frac{16}{24}$ ______

11. MATHEMATICAL PRACTICE ② **Use Reasoning** Is the unknown value in $\frac{2}{3} = \frac{\blacksquare}{18}$ the same as the unknown value in $\frac{3}{2} = \frac{18}{\blacksquare}$? Explain.

____

____

Problem Solving • Applications

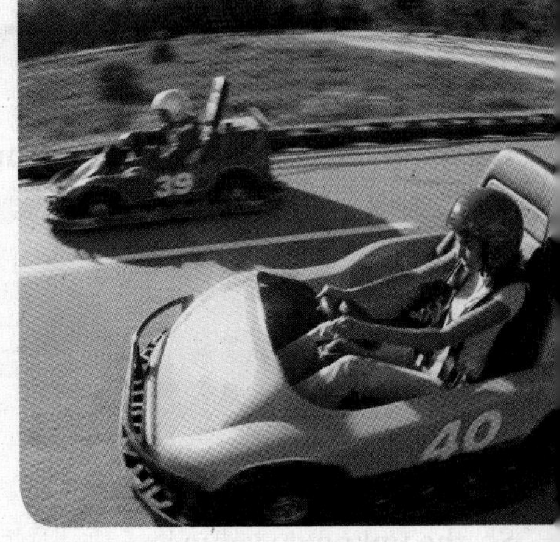

Solve by finding an equivalent ratio.

12. It takes 8 minutes for Sue to make 2 laps around the go-kart track. How many laps can Sue complete in 24 minutes?

____

13. GO DEEPER The width of Jay's original photo is 8 inches. The length of the original photo is 10 inches. He prints a smaller version that has an equivalent ratio of width to length. The width of the smaller version is 4 inches less than the width of the original. What is the length of the smaller version?

____

14. Ariel bought 3 raffle tickets for $5. How many tickets could Ariel buy for $15?

____

15. THINK SMARTER **What's the Error?** Greg used the steps shown to find the unknown value. Describe his error and give the correct solution.

$$\frac{2}{6} = \frac{■}{12}$$

$$\frac{2+6}{6+6} = \frac{■}{12}$$

$$\frac{8}{12} = \frac{■}{12}$$

The unknown value is 8.

____

____

____

16. THINK SMARTER Courtney bought 3 maps for $10. Use the table of equivalent ratios to find how many maps she can buy for $30.

3	6	
10	20	30

 FOR MORE PRACTICE: Standards Practice Book

Name ____________________

Mid-Chapter Checkpoint

Vocabulary

Choose the best term from the box to complete the sentence.

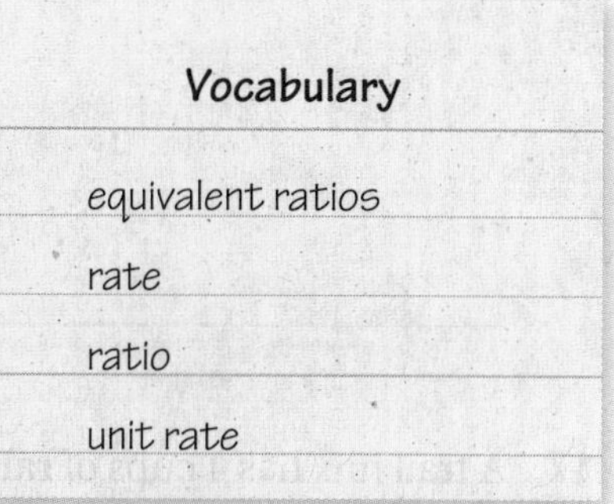

1. A ____________ is a rate that makes a comparison to 1 unit. (p. 158)

2. Two ratios that name the same comparison are ____________. (p. 161)

Concepts and Skills

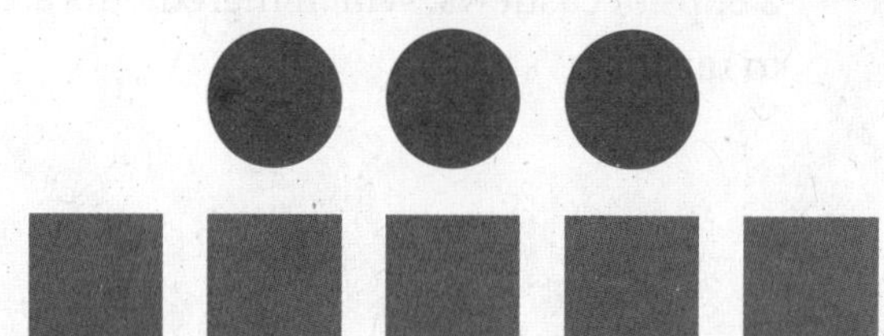

3. Write the ratio of red circles to blue squares. (6.RP.1)

____

Write the ratio in two different ways. (6.RP.1)

4. 8 to 12

5. 7:2

6. $\frac{5}{9}$

7. 11 to 3

Write two equivalent ratios. (6.RP.3a)

8. $\frac{2}{7}$

9. $\frac{6}{5}$

10. $\frac{9}{12}$

11. $\frac{18}{6}$

Find the unknown value. (6.RP.3a)

12. $\frac{15}{■} = \frac{5}{10}$

13. $\frac{■}{9} = \frac{12}{3}$

14. $\frac{48}{16} = \frac{■}{8}$

15. $\frac{9}{36} = \frac{3}{■}$

16. There are 36 students in the chess club, 40 students in the drama club, and 24 students in the film club. What is the ratio of students in the drama club to students in the film club? (6.RP.3a)

____

17. A trail mix has 4 cups of raisins, 3 cups of dates, 6 cups of peanuts, and 2 cups of cashews. Which ingredients are in the same ratio as cashews to raisins? (6.RP.3a)

____

18. There are 32 adults and 20 children at a school play. What is the ratio of children to people at the school play? (6.RP.3a)

____

19. Sonya got 8 out of 10 questions right on a quiz. She got the same score on a quiz that had 20 questions. How many questions did Sonya get right on the second quiz? (6.RP.3a)

____

Name ______________________________

Find Unit Rates

Essential Question How can you use unit rates to make comparisons?

Ratios and Proportional Relationships—6.RP.2 *Also 6.RP.3b*

MATHEMATICAL PRACTICES
MP.2, MP.3, MP.6

Unlock the Problem (Real World)

The star fruit, or carambola, is the fruit of a tree that is native to Indonesia, India, and Sri Lanka. Slices of the fruit are in the shape of a five-pointed star. Lara paid $9.60 for 16 ounces of star fruit. Find the price of 1 ounce of star fruit.

- Underline the sentence that tells you what you are trying to find.
- Circle the numbers you need to use to solve the problem.

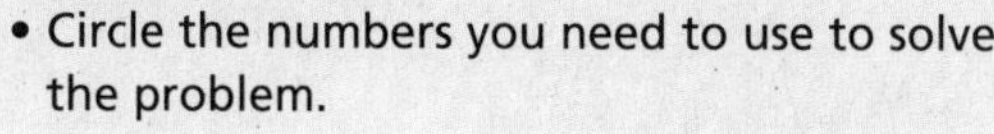

Recall that a unit rate makes a comparison to 1 unit. You can find a unit rate by dividing the numerator and denominator by the number in the denominator.

Write the unit rate for the price of star fruit.

Write a ratio that compares __________ to __________. $\frac{\text{price}}{\text{weight}} \rightarrow \frac{\$\_\_\_}{\_\_\_ \text{ oz}}$

Divide the numerator and denominator by the number in the __________. $\frac{\$9.60 \div \_\_\_}{16 \text{ oz} \div \_\_\_}$

$\frac{\$\_\_\_}{1 \text{ oz}}$

So, the unit rate is __________. The price is __________ per ounce.

Math Talk — **Mathematical Practices**
Explain the difference between a ratio and a rate.

1. MATHEMATICAL PRACTICE 6 **Explain** why the unit rate is equivalent to the original rate.

2. MATHEMATICAL PRACTICE 3 **Make Arguments** Explain a way to convince others that you found the unit rate correctly.

Example

A **During migration, a hummingbird can fly 210 miles in 7 hours, and a goose can fly 165 miles in 3 hours. Which bird flies at a faster rate?**

Write the rate for each bird. Hummingbird: $\frac{\square \text{ miles}}{7 \text{ hours}}$ Goose: $\frac{165 \text{ miles}}{\square \text{ hours}}$

Write the unit rates. $\frac{210 \text{ mi} \div \square}{7 \text{ hr} \div \square}$ $\frac{165 \text{ mi} \div \square}{3 \text{ hr} \div \square}$

$\frac{\square \text{ mi}}{1 \text{ hr}}$ $\frac{\square \text{ mi}}{1 \text{ hr}}$

Compare the unit rates. ______ miles per hour is faster than ______ miles per hour.

So, the ____________ flies at a faster rate.

B **A 64-ounce bottle of apple juice costs $5.76. A 15-ounce bottle of apple juice costs $1.80. Which item costs less per ounce?**

Write the rate for each bottle. 64-ounce bottle: $\frac{\square}{64 \text{ ounces}}$ 15-ounce bottle: $\frac{\square}{\square \text{ ounces}}$

Write the unit rates. $\frac{\square \div \square}{64 \text{ oz} \div \square}$ $\frac{\$1.80 \div \square}{\square \text{ oz} \div \square}$

$\frac{\square}{1 \text{ oz}}$ $\frac{\square}{1 \text{ oz}}$

Compare the unit rates. ______ per ounce is less expensive than ______ per ounce.

So, the ______ -ounce bottle costs less per ounce.

Try This! **At one grocery store, a dozen eggs cost $1.20. At another store, $1\frac{1}{2}$ dozen eggs cost $2.16. Which is the better buy?**

Store 1: Store 2:

The unit price is lower at Store ______, so a dozen eggs for ____________ is the better buy.

Name ________________________________

Share and Show

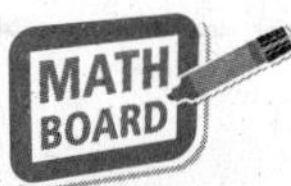

Write the rate as a fraction. Then find the unit rate.

1. Sara drove 72 miles on 4 gallons of gas.

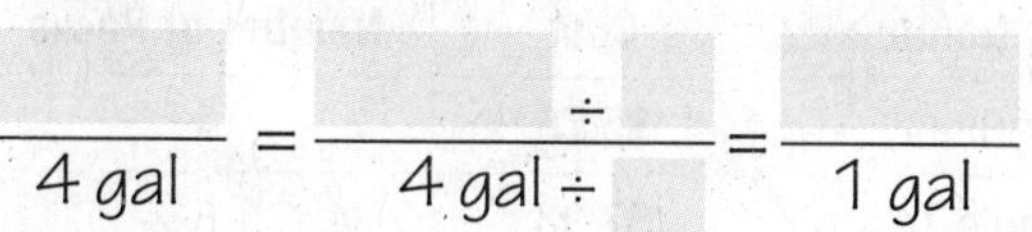

2. Dean paid $27.00 for 4 movie tickets.

3. Amy and Mai have to read *Bud, Not Buddy* for a class. Amy reads 20 pages in 2 days. Mai reads 35 pages in 3 days. Who reads at a faster rate?

4. An online music store offers 5 downloads for $6.25. Another online music store offers 12 downloads for $17.40. Which store offers the better deal?

Math Talk — Mathematical Practices

Explain how to find a unit rate.

On Your Own

Write the rate as a fraction. Then find the unit rate.

5. A company packed 108 items in 12 boxes.

6. There are 112 students for 14 teachers.

7. GO DEEPER Geoff charges $27 for 3 hours of swimming lessons. Anne charges $31 for 4 hours. How much more does Geoff charge per hour than Anne?

8. MATHEMATICAL PRACTICE 6 **Compare** One florist made 16 bouquets in 5 hours. A second florist made 40 bouquets in 12 hours. Which florist makes bouquets at a faster rate?

Tell which rate is faster by comparing unit rates.

9. $\frac{160 \text{ mi}}{2 \text{ hr}}$ and $\frac{210 \text{ mi}}{3 \text{ hr}}$

10. $\frac{270 \text{ ft}}{9 \text{ min}}$ and $\frac{180 \text{ ft}}{9 \text{ min}}$

11. $\frac{250 \text{ m}}{10 \text{ s}}$ and $\frac{120 \text{ m}}{4 \text{ s}}$

Unlock the Problem

12. THINK SMARTER Ryan wants to buy treats for his puppy. If Ryan wants to buy the treats that cost the least per pack, which treat should he buy? Explain.

Cost of Dog Treats		
Name	Cost	Number of Packs
Pup Bites	$5.76	4
Doggie Treats	$7.38	6
Pupster Snacks	$7.86	6
Nutri-Biscuits	$9.44	8

a. What do you need to find?

____

____

b. Find the price per pack for each treat.

____

____

____

____

____

____

____

____

c. Complete the sentences.

The treat with the highest price per pack is _______________.

The treat with the lowest price per pack is _______________.

Ryan should buy _______________

because _______________

____

_______________.

13. MATHEMATICAL PRACTICE 2 **Reason Abstractly** What information do you need to consider in order to decide whether one product is a better deal than another? When might the lower unit rate not be the best choice? Explain.

____

____

____

____

____

14. THINK SMARTER Select the cars that get a higher mileage per gallon of gas than a car that gets 25 miles per gallon. Mark all that apply.

- ○ Car A: 22 miles per 1 gallon
- ○ Car B: 56 miles per 2 gallons
- ○ Car C: 81 miles per 3 gallons
- ○ Car D: 51 miles per 3 gallons

FOR MORE PRACTICE: Standards Practice Book

Name ___________________________

ALGEBRA
Lesson 4.7

Use Unit Rates

Essential Question How can you solve problems using unit rates?

Ratios and Proportional Relationships—6.RP.3b

MATHEMATICAL PRACTICES
MP1, MP.3, MP.5

Unlock the Problem

The Champie family is traveling from Arizona to Texas. On the first part of the trip, they drove 500 miles in 10 hours. If they continue driving at the same rate, how many hours will it take them to drive 750 miles?

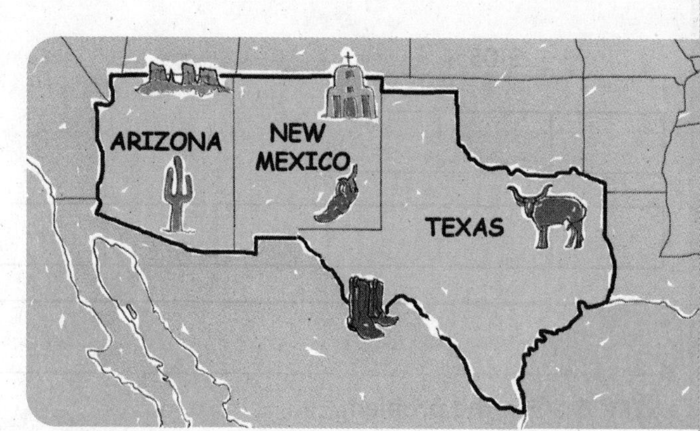

You can use equivalent ratios to find the number of hours it will take the Champie family to drive 750 miles. You may need to find a unit rate before you can write equivalent ratios.

Find equivalent ratios by using a unit rate.

Write ratios that compare miles to hours.

$$\frac{\text{miles}}{\text{hours}} \rightarrow \frac{500}{10} = \frac{750}{\blacksquare} \leftarrow \frac{\text{miles}}{\text{hours}}$$

750 is not a multiple of 500.

Write the known ratio as a unit rate.

$$\frac{500 \div \square}{10 \div 10} = \frac{750}{\blacksquare}$$

$$\frac{\square}{1} = \frac{750}{\blacksquare}$$

Write an equivalent rate by multiplying the ______________ and ______________ by the same value.

$$\frac{50 \cdot \square}{1 \cdot \square} = \frac{750}{\blacksquare}$$

Think: Multiply 50 by ________ to get 750.

So, multiply the denominator by ________ also.

The ______________ are the same, so the ______________ are equal to each other.

$$\frac{\square}{15} = \frac{750}{\blacksquare}$$

The unknown value is ______.

So, it will take the family ______ hours to drive 750 miles.

Mathematical Practices

Explain why you needed to find a unit rate first.

Example

Kenyon earns $105 for mowing 3 yards. How much would Kenyon earn for mowing 10 yards?

STEP 1 Draw a bar model to represent the situation:

$105

$?

STEP 2 Solve the problem.

The model shows that 3 units represent $105.

You need to find the value represented by ______ units.

Write a unit rate:

$$\frac{\$105}{3} = \frac{\$105 \div \square}{3 \div \square} = \frac{\$\square}{1}$$

1 unit represents $________.

10 units are equal to 10 times 1 unit,

so 10 units = 10 × $________.

10 × $________ = $________________

So, Kenyon will earn $______________ for mowing 10 yards.

Try This!

Last summer, Kenyon earned $210 for mowing 7 yards. How much did he earn for mowing 5 yards last summer?

STEP 1 Draw a bar model to represent the situation.

STEP 2 Solve the problem.

Name ____________________

Share and Show

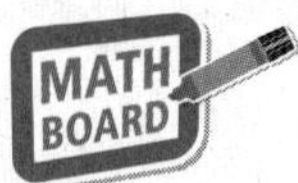

Use a unit rate to find the unknown value.

1. $\frac{10}{■} = \frac{6}{3}$

$\frac{10}{■} = \frac{6 \div \square}{3 \div 3}$

$\frac{10}{■} = \frac{\square}{1}$

$\frac{10}{■} = \frac{2 \cdot \square}{1 \cdot \square}$

$\frac{10}{■} = \frac{10}{\square}$

■ = ______

✓ 2. $\frac{6}{8} = \frac{■}{20}$

$\frac{6 \div \square}{8 \div 8} = \frac{■}{20}$

$\frac{\square}{1} = \frac{■}{20}$

$\frac{0.75 \cdot 20}{1 \cdot \square} = \frac{■}{20}$

$\frac{\square}{20} = \frac{■}{20}$

■ = ______

On Your Own

Use a unit rate to find the unknown value.

3. $\frac{40}{8} = \frac{45}{■}$ ______

4. $\frac{42}{14} = \frac{■}{5}$ ______

✓ 5. $\frac{■}{2} = \frac{56}{8}$ ______

6. $\frac{■}{4} = \frac{26}{13}$ ______

Practice: Copy and Solve **Draw a bar model to find the unknown value.**

7. $\frac{4}{32} = \frac{9}{■}$

8. $\frac{9}{3} = \frac{■}{4}$

9. $\frac{■}{14} = \frac{9}{8}$

10. $\frac{3}{■} = \frac{2}{1.25}$

11. MATHEMATICAL PRACTICE 5 **Communicate** Explain how to find an unknown value in a ratio by using a unit rate.

______

______

______

12. GO DEEPER Savannah is tiling her kitchen floor. She bought 8 cases of tile for $192. She realizes she bought too much tile and returns 2 unopened cases to the store. What was her final cost for tile?

______

Problem Solving • Applications Real World

Pose a Problem

13. THINKSMARTER Josie runs a T-shirt printing company. The table shows the length and width of four sizes of T-shirts. The measurements of each size T-shirt form equivalent ratios.

Adult T-Shirt Sizes		
Size	**Length (inches)**	**Width (inches)**
Small	27	18
Medium	30	20
Large	?	22
X-large	?	24

What is the length of an extra-large T-shirt?

Write two equivalent ratios and find the unknown value:

$$\frac{\text{Length of medium}}{\text{Width of medium}} \rightarrow \frac{30}{20} = \frac{\blacksquare}{24} \leftarrow \frac{\text{Length of X-large}}{\text{Width of X-large}}$$

$$\frac{30 \div 20}{20 \div 20} = \frac{\blacksquare}{24} \rightarrow \frac{1.5}{1} = \frac{\blacksquare}{24} \rightarrow \frac{1.5 \cdot 24}{1 \cdot 24} = \frac{\blacksquare}{24} \rightarrow \frac{36}{24} = \frac{\blacksquare}{24}$$

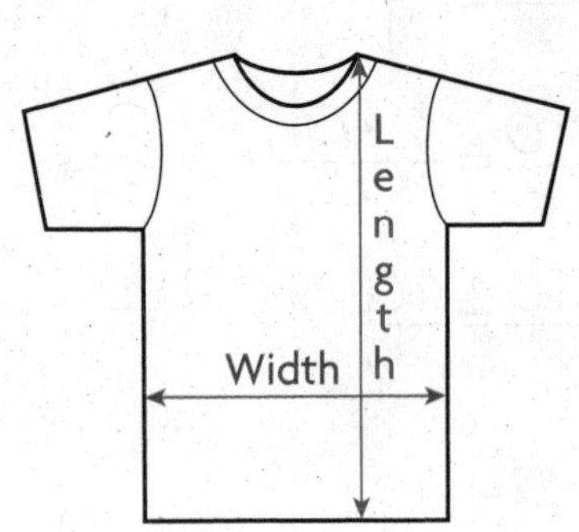

The length of an extra-large T-shirt is 36 inches.

Write a problem that can be solved by using the information in the table and could be solved by using equivalent ratios.

Pose a Problem

Solve Your Problem

Personal Math Trainer

14. THINKSMARTER + Peri earned \$27 for walking her neighbor's dog 3 times. If Peri earned \$36, how many times did she walk her neighbor's dog? Use a unit rate to find the unknown value.

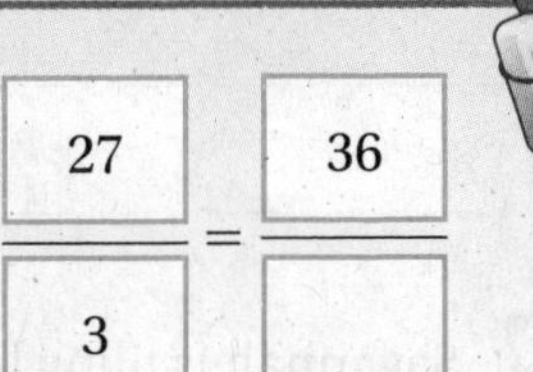

FOR MORE PRACTICE:
Standards Practice Book

Name ____

Equivalent Ratios and Graphs

Essential Question How can you use a graph to represent equivalent ratios?

Ratios and Proportional Relationships—6.RP.3a

MATHEMATICAL PRACTICES
MP.4, MP.5, MP.7

Unlock the Problem

A car travels at a rate of 50 miles per hour. Use equivalent ratios to graph the distance the car travels over time. Graph time on the x-axis and distance on the y-axis.

- What words in the problem tell the unit rate?

____

Write and graph equivalent ratios.

STEP 1 Use the unit rate to write equivalent ratios.

Write the unit rate. $\frac{\square \text{ miles}}{1 \text{ hour}}$

Write an equivalent ratio. $\frac{\square \text{ mi} \times 2}{1 \text{ hr} \times 2}$

$= \frac{\square \text{ mi}}{\square \text{ hr}}$

Complete the table of equivalent ratios.

Distance (mi)			150	200	
Time (hr)	1	2			5

STEP 2 Use an ordered pair to represent each ratio in the table.

Let the x-coordinate represent time in hours and the y-coordinate represent distance in miles.

$\frac{50 \text{ mi}}{1 \text{ hr}} \rightarrow (1, 50)$

(1, ______)

(2, ______)

(______, 150)

(______, 200)

(5, ______)

Remember

The first number in an ordered pair is the x-coordinate, and the second number is the y-coordinate.

STEP 3 Use the ordered pairs to graph the car's distance over time.

Think: The graph represents the same relationship as the unit rate.

For every 1 hour the car travels, the distance increases by

______ miles.

Car Travel

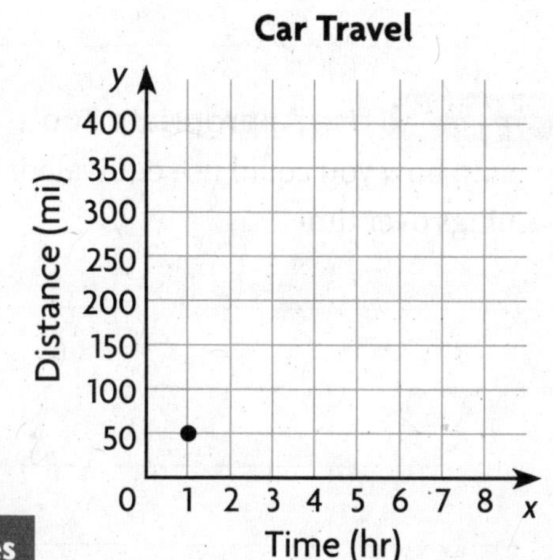

Math Talk **Mathematical Practices**

Identify a pattern in the graph.

Example

During a heavy rainstorm, the waters of the Blue River rose at a steady rate for 8 hours. The graph shows the river's increase in height over time. Use the graph to complete the table of equivalent ratios. How many inches did the river rise in 8 hours?

Think: On the graph, *x*-coordinates represent

time in ______________, and *y*-coordinates represent

the river's increase in height in ______________.

The ordered pair (1, ________) means that after ________

hour, the river rose ________ inches.

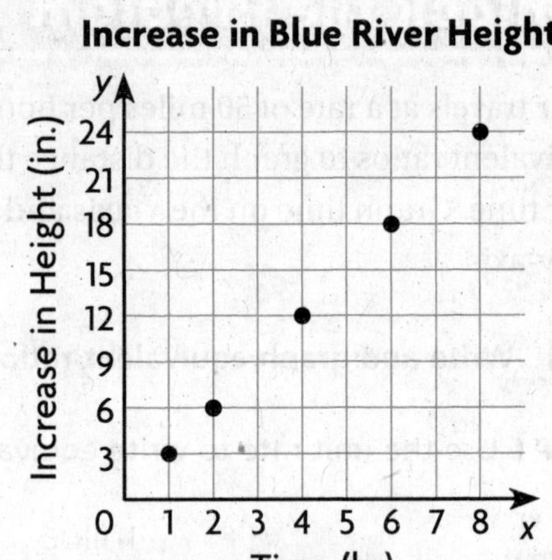

Increase in height (in.)	3				
Time (hr)	1	2	4	6	8

So, the river rose ________ inches in 8 hours.

1. MATHEMATICAL PRACTICE 7 **Look for a Pattern** Describe the pattern you see in the graph and the table.

____

____

2. Explain how you know that the ratios in the table are equivalent.

____

____

3. MATHEMATICAL PRACTICE 5 **Use Appropriate Tools** Matt earns $12 per hour. Explain how you could use equivalent ratios to draw a graph of his earnings over time.

____

____

____

____

Name ___________________________

Share and Show

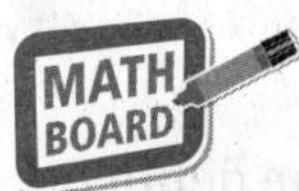

A redwood tree grew at a rate of 4 feet per year. Use this information for 1–3.

1. Complete the table of equivalent ratios for the first 5 years.

Height (ft)					
Time (yr)	1	2			

2. Write ordered pairs, letting the x-coordinate represent time in years and the y-coordinate represent height in feet.

(1, ______), (2, ______), (______, ______)

(______, ______), (______, ______)

3. Use the ordered pairs to graph the tree's growth over time.

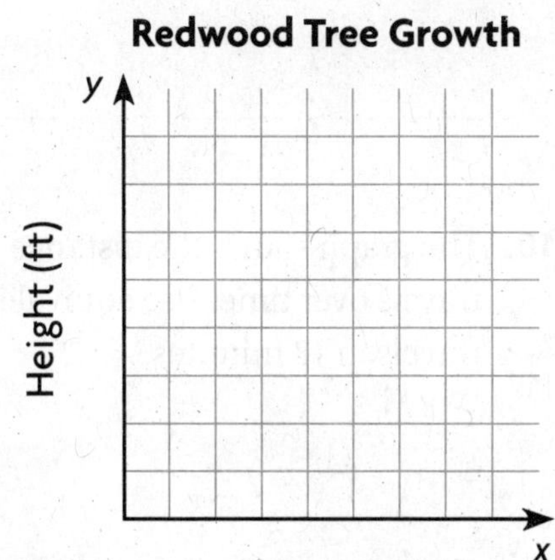

Math Talk — Mathematical Practices

Explain what the point (1, 4) represents on the graph of the redwood tree's growth.

On Your Own

The graph shows the rate at which Luis's car uses gas, in miles per gallon. Use the graph for 4–8.

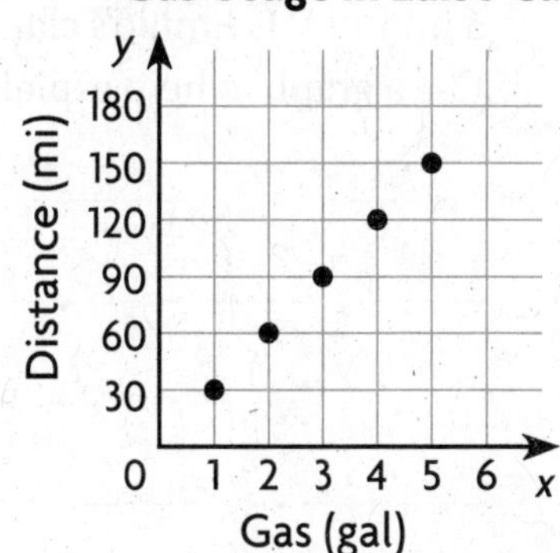

4. Complete the table of equivalent ratios.

Distance (mi)	30				
Gas (gal)	1	2	3	4	5

5. Find the car's unit rate of gas usage. $\frac{\square \text{ miles}}{\square \text{ gallon}}$

6. How far can the car go on 5 gallons of gas? ______

7. Estimate the amount of gas needed to travel 50 miles.

____

8. GO DEEPER Ellen's car averages 35 miles per gallon of gas. If you used equivalent ratios to graph her car's gas usage, how would the graph differ from the graph of Luis's car's gas usage?

____

____

Problem Solving • Applications

9. MATHEMATICAL PRACTICE 7 **Look for Structure** The graph shows the depth of a submarine over time. Use equivalent ratios to find the number of minutes it will take the submarine to descend 1,600 feet.

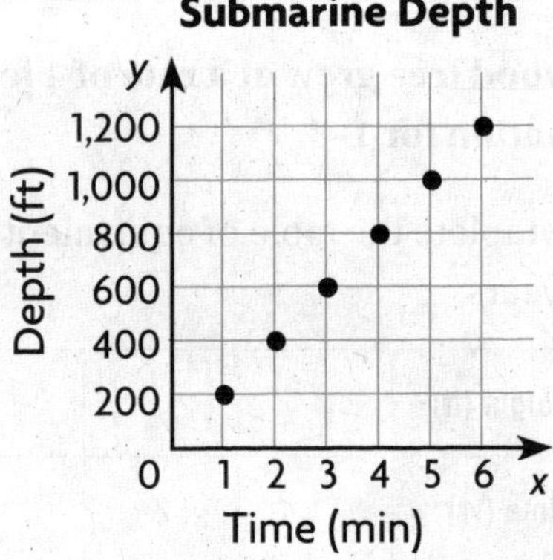

10. The graph shows the distance that a plane flying at a steady rate travels over time. Use equivalent ratios to find how far the plane travels in 13 minutes.

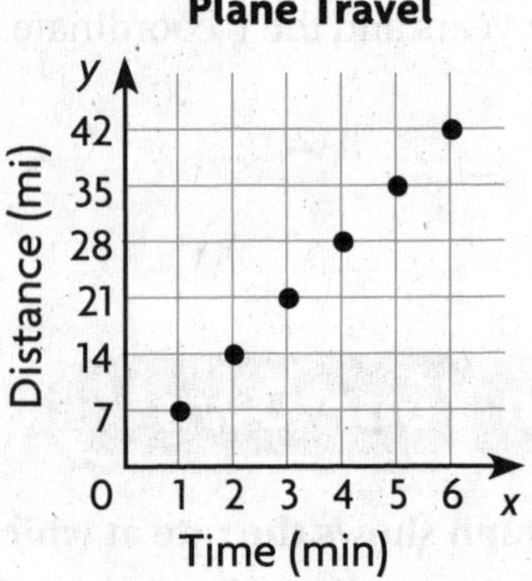

11. THINK SMARTER **Sense or Nonsense?** Emilio types at a rate of 84 words per minute. He claims that he can type a 500-word essay in 5 minutes. Is Emilio's claim sense or nonsense? Use a graph to help explain your answer.

Emilio's Typing Rate

y

Number of Words

x

Time (min)

Personal Math Trainer

12. THINK SMARTER + The Tuckers drive at a rate of 20 miles per hour through the mountains. Use the ordered pairs to graph the distance traveled over time.

Distance (miles)	20	40	60	80	100
Time (hours)	1	2	3	4	5

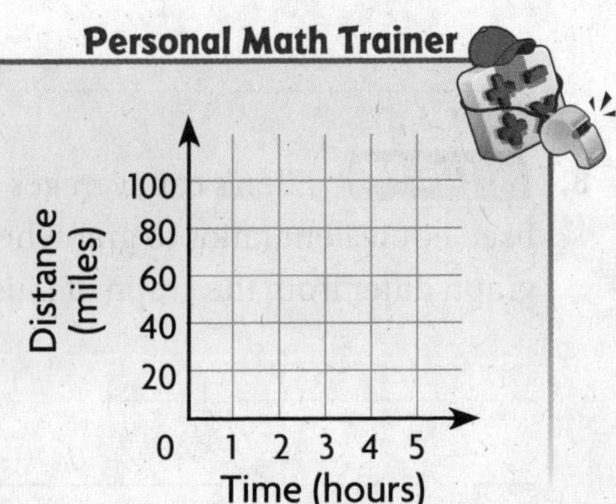

Name ______________________________

Chapter 4 Review/Test

1. Kendra has 4 necklaces, 7 bracelets, and 5 rings. Draw a model to show the ratio that compares rings to bracelets.

2. There are 3 girls and 2 boys taking swimming lessons. Write the ratio that compares the girls taking swimming lessons to the total number of students taking swimming lessons.

____

3. Luis adds 3 strawberries for every 2 blueberries in his fruit smoothie. Draw a model to show the ratio that compares strawberries to blueberries.

4. Write the ratio 3 to 10 in two different ways.

____

5. Alex takes 3 steps every 5 feet he walks. As Alex continues walking, he takes more steps and walks a longer distance. Complete the table by writing two equivalent ratios.

Steps	3		
Distance (feet)	5		

GO DIGITAL Assessment Options Chapter Test

6. Sam has 3 green apples and 4 red apples. Select the ratios that compare the number of red apples to the total number of apples. Mark all that apply.

- ○ 4 to 7
- ○ 3 to 7
- ○ 4 : 7
- ○ 4 : 3
- ○ $\frac{3}{7}$
- ○ $\frac{4}{7}$

7. Jeff ran 2 miles in 12 minutes. Ju Chan ran 3 miles in 18 minutes. Did Jeff and Ju Chan run the same number of miles per minute? Complete the tables of equivalent ratios to support your answer.

Jeff				
Distance (miles)	2			
Time (minutes)	12			

Ju Chan				
Distance (miles)	3			
Time (minutes)	18			

8. Jen bought 2 notebooks for $10. Write the rate as a fraction. Then find the unit rate.

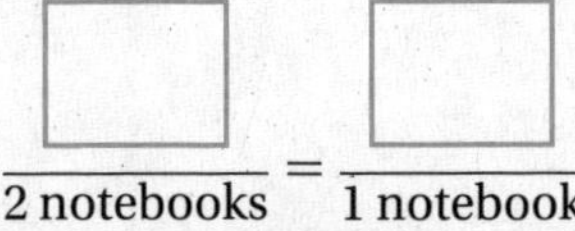

$\frac{\square}{\text{2 notebooks}} = \frac{\square}{\text{1 notebook}}$

Name ____________________

9. Determine whether each ratio is equivalent to $\frac{1}{2}$, $\frac{2}{3}$, or $\frac{4}{7}$. Write the ratio in the correct box.

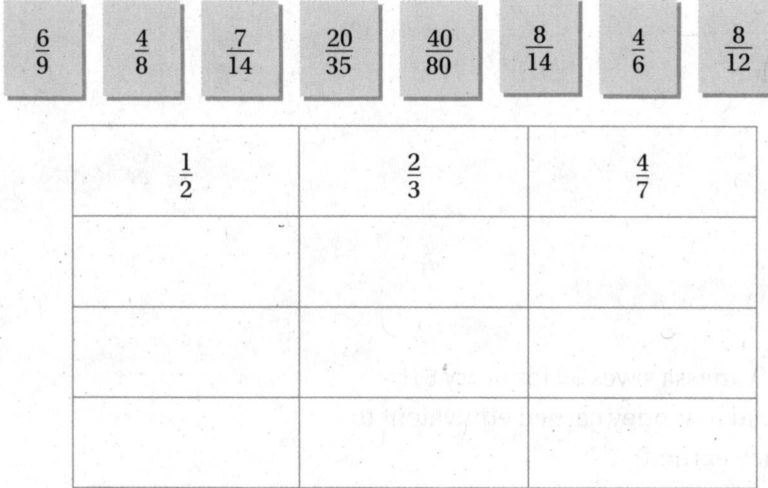

$\frac{6}{9}$ $\frac{4}{8}$ $\frac{7}{14}$ $\frac{20}{35}$ $\frac{40}{80}$ $\frac{8}{14}$ $\frac{4}{6}$ $\frac{8}{12}$

$\frac{1}{2}$	$\frac{2}{3}$	$\frac{4}{7}$

10. Amos bought 5 cantaloupes for $8. How many cantaloupes can he buy for $24? Show your work.

11. Camille said $\frac{4}{5}$ is equivalent to $\frac{24}{30}$. Check her work by making a table of equivalent ratios.

4					
5					

12. A box of oat cereal costs $3.90 for 15 ounces. A box of rice cereal costs $3.30 for 11 ounces. Which box of cereal costs less per ounce? Use numbers and words to explain your answer.

13. Scotty earns $35 for babysitting for 5 hours. If Scotty charges at the same rate, how many hours will it take him to earn $42?

_______ hours

14. Use a unit rate to find the unknown value.

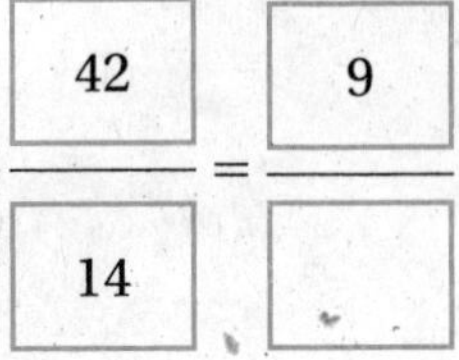

15. Jenna saves $3 for every $13 she earns. Vanessa saves $6 for every $16 she earns. Is Jenna's ratio of money saved to money earned equivalent to Vanessa's ratio of money saved to money earned?

____

16. The Henderson's are on their way to a national park. They are traveling at a rate of 40 miles per hour. Use the ordered pairs to graph the distance traveled over time.

Distance (miles)	40	80	120	160	200
Time (minutes)	1	2	3	4	5

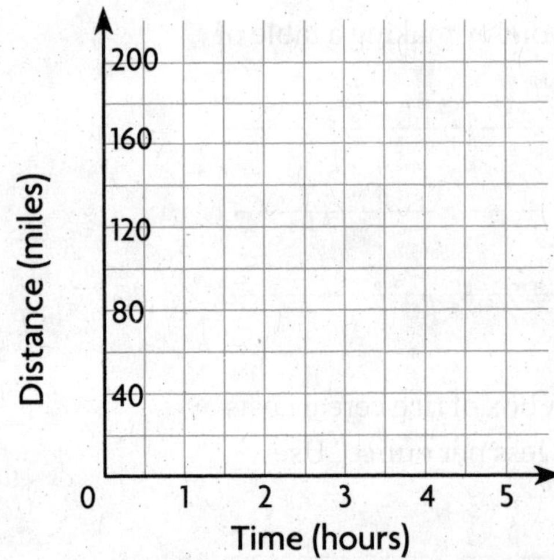

Name ______________________________

17. Abby goes to the pool to swim laps. The graph shows how far Abby swam over time. Use equivalent ratios to find how far Abby swam in 7 minutes.

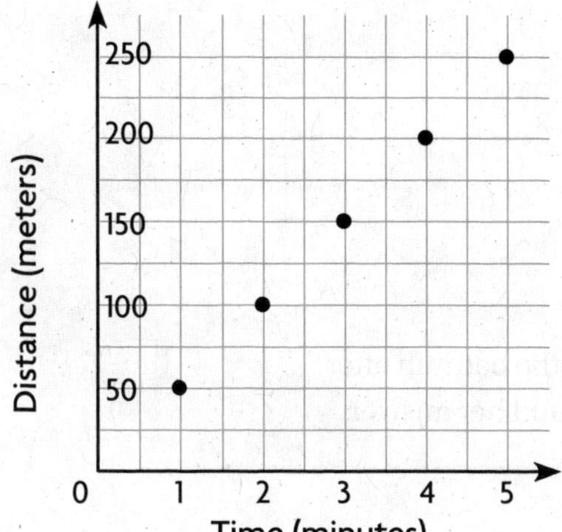

______ meters

18. A rabbit runs 35 miles per hour. Select the animals who run at a faster unit rate per hour than the rabbit. Mark all that apply.

○ Reindeer: 100 miles in 2 hours

○ Ostrich: 80 miles in 2 hours

○ Zebra: 90 miles in 3 hours

○ Squirrel: 36 miles in 3 hours

19. Caleb bought 6 packs of pencils for $12.

Part A

How much will he pay for 9 packs of pencils? Use numbers and words to explain your answer.

Part B

Describe how to use a bar model to solve the problem.

20. Water is filling a bathtub at a rate of 3 gallons per minute.

Part A

Complete the table of equivalent ratios for the first five minutes of the bathtub filling up.

Amount of Water (gallons)	3				
Time (minutes)	1				

Part B

Emily said there will be 36 gallons of water in the bathtub after 12 minutes. Explain how Emily could have found her answer.

Chapter 5

Percents

Show What You Know

Check your understanding of important skills.

Name ______________________

▶ Decimal Models Shade the model to show the decimal.

1. 0.31

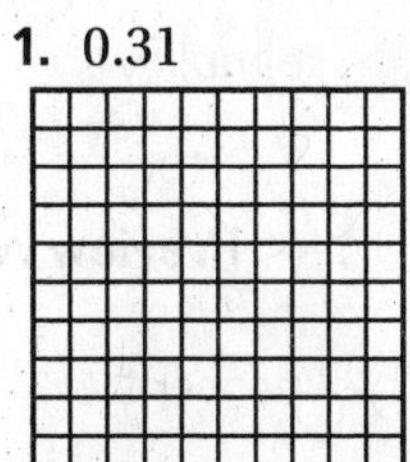

2. 0.7

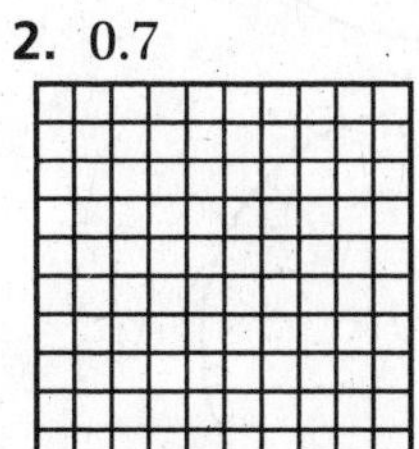

3. 1.7

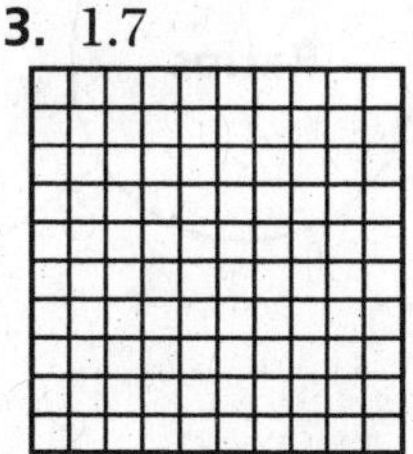

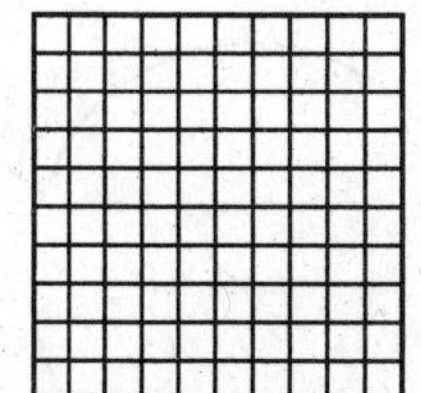

▶ Division Find the quotient.

4. 2,002 ÷ 91 ______

5. $98\overline{)3{,}038}$ ______

6. 24,487 ÷ 47 ______

7. $22\overline{)2{,}332}$ ______

▶ Multiply Whole Numbers by Decimals Find the product.

8. 2.38×4 ______

9. 32.06×7 ______

10. 4.60×18 ______

11. 7.04×32 ______

Esmeralda likes to listen to music while she works out. She had a playlist on her MP3 player that lasted 40 minutes, but she accidentally deleted 25% of the music. Be a Math Detective and figure out if Esmeralda has enough music left on her playlist for a 30-minute workout. Explain your answer.

Personal Math Trainer
Online Assessment and Intervention

Vocabulary Builder

▶ Visualize It

Complete the bubble map with review and preview words that are related to ratios.

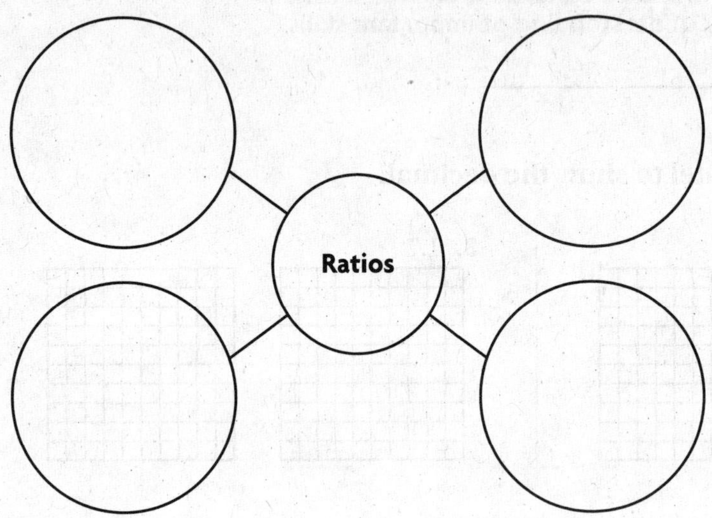

Review Words
decimal
equivalent ratios
factor
quotient
rate
ratio
simplify

Preview Word
percent

▶ Understand Vocabulary

Complete the sentences using review and preview words.

1. A comparison of one number to another by division is a ____________________.

2. ____________________ name the same comparison.

3. A ratio that compares quantities with different units is a ____________________.

4. A ____________________ is a ratio, or rate, that compares a number to 100.

5. ____________________ a fraction or a ratio by dividing the numerator and denominator by a common factor.

GO DIGITAL

- Interactive Student Edition
- Multimedia *e*Glossary

Name ______________________

Model Percents

Essential Question How can you use a model to show a percent?

Ratios and Proportional Relationships—6.RP.3c

MATHEMATICAL PRACTICES
MP.3, MP.5

Investigate

Materials ■ 10-by-10 grids

Not many people drive electric cars today. But one expert estimates that by 2025, 35 percent of all cars will be powered by electricity.

A **percent** is a ratio, or rate, that compares a number to 100. Percent means "per hundred." The symbol for percent is %.

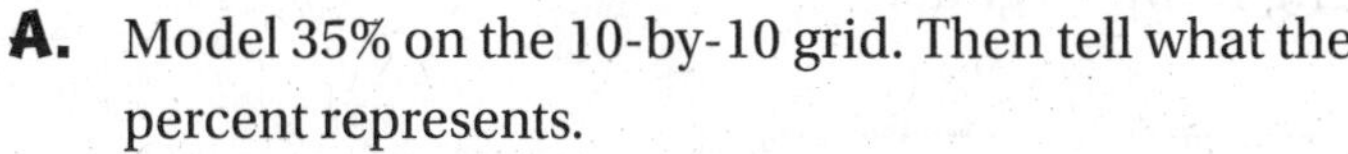

A. Model 35% on the 10-by-10 grid. Then tell what the percent represents.

The large square represents the whole, or 100%. Each small square represents 1%.

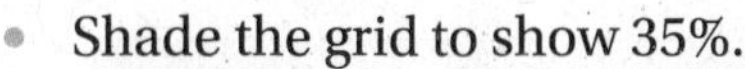

- Shade the grid to show 35%.

  Think: 35% is ______ out of 100.

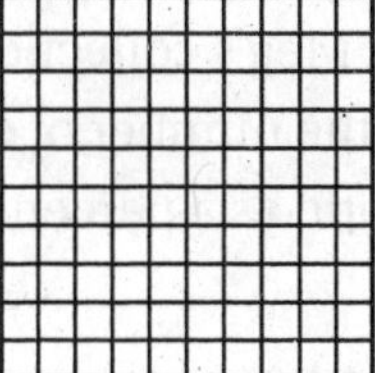

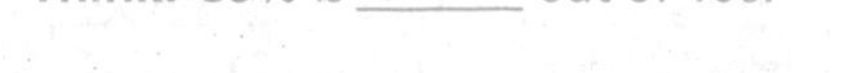

- Write 35% as a ratio comparing 35 to 100.

  Think: 35 out of 100 squares is $\frac{\_\_\_}{100}$.

- 35% = $\frac{\_\_\_}{\_\_\_}$

So, by 2025, ______ out of ______ cars may be powered by electricity.

B. Model 52% on a 10-by-10 grid.

- ______ out of ______ squares is $\frac{\_\_\_}{100}$.
- 52% = $\frac{\_\_\_}{100}$

C. Model 18% on a 10-by-10 grid.

- ______ out of ______ squares is $\frac{\_\_\_}{100}$.
- 18% = $\frac{\_\_\_}{100}$

Draw Conclusions

1. Explain how you would use a 10-by-10 grid to model 7%.

2. Model $\frac{1}{4}$ on a 10-by-10 grid. What percent is shaded? Explain.

3. MATHEMATICAL PRACTICE 5 **Use a Concrete Model** Explain how you could model 0.5% on a 10-by-10 grid.

4. THINKSMARTER How would you model 181% using 10-by-10 grids?

Make Connections

The table shows the types of meteorites in Meg's collection. Shade a grid to show the ratio comparing the number of each type to the total number. Then write the ratio as a percent.

Meg's Meteorite Collection	
Type	**Number**
Iron	21
Stone	76
Stony-iron	3

Think: A percent is a ratio that compares a number to ______.

Iron

______ out of ______ meteorites are iron.

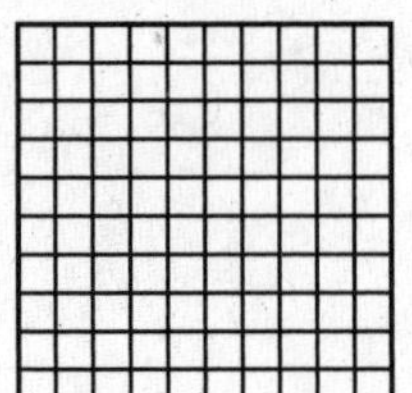

$\frac{\quad}{100}$ = ______ %

Stone

______ out of ______ meteorites are stone.

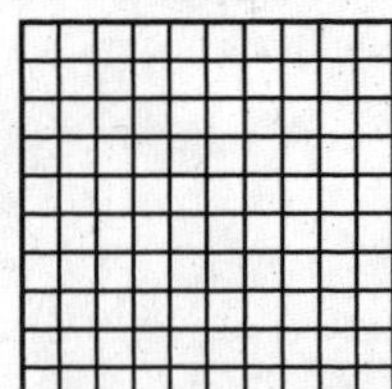

$\frac{\quad}{\quad}$ = ______ %

Stony-iron

______ out of ______ meteorites are stony-iron.

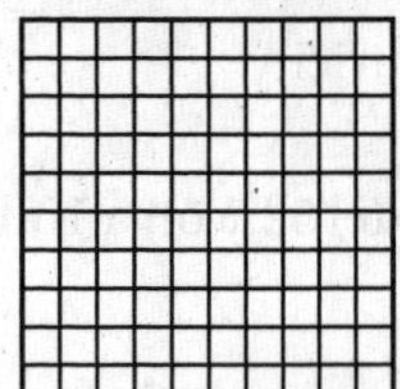

$\frac{\quad}{\quad}$ = ______ %

Math Talk Mathematical Practices

Explain what this statement means: 13% of the students at Harding Middle School are left-handed.

Name ______________________

Share and Show

Write a ratio and a percent to represent the shaded part.

1. 

ratio: ______ percent: ______

2. 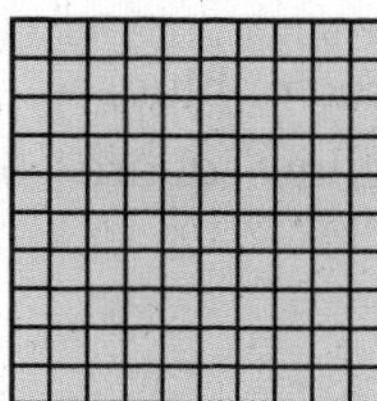

ratio: ______ percent: ______

3. 

ratio: ______ percent: ______

Model the percent and write it as a ratio.

4. 30%

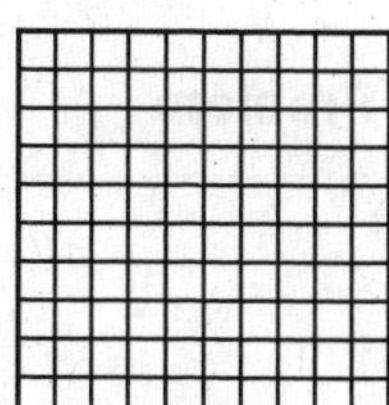

ratio: ______

5. 5%

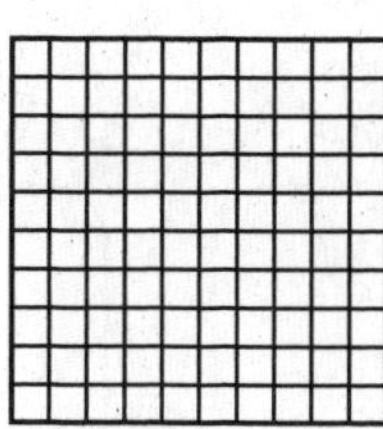

ratio: ______

6. 75%

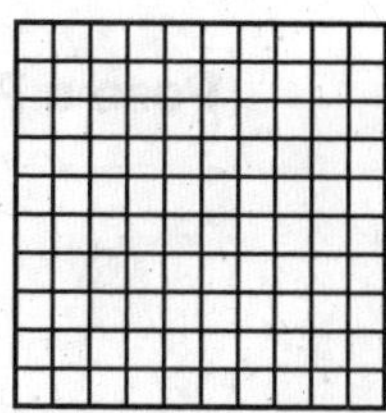

ratio: ______

Problem Solving • Applications

7. MATHEMATICAL PRACTICE 5 **Use a Concrete Model** Explain how to model 32% on a 10-by-10 grid. How does the model represent the ratio of 32 to 100?

____

____

____

8. GO DEEPER A floor has 100 tiles. There are 24 black tiles and 35 brown tiles. The rest of the tiles are white. What percent of the tiles are white?

____

Pose a Problem

9. THINK SMARTER Javier designed a mosaic wall mural using 100 tiles in 3 different colors: yellow, blue, and red. If 64 of the tiles are yellow, what percent of the tiles are either red or blue?

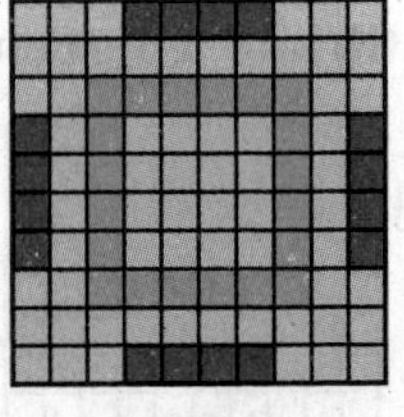

To find the number of tiles that are either red or blue, count the red and blue squares. Or subtract the number of yellow squares, 64, from the total number of squares, 100.

36 out of 100 tiles are red or blue.

The ratio of red or blue tiles to all tiles is $\frac{36}{100}$.

So, the percent of the tiles that are either red or blue is 36%.

Write another problem involving a percent that can be solved by using the mosaic wall mural.

Pose a Problem

Solve Your Problem

10. THINK SMARTER Select the 10-by-10 grids that model 45%. Mark all that apply.

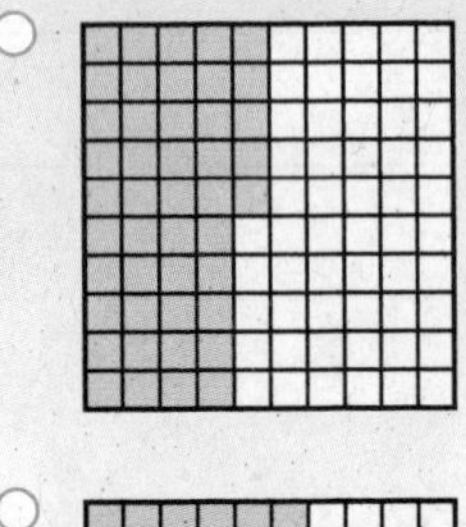
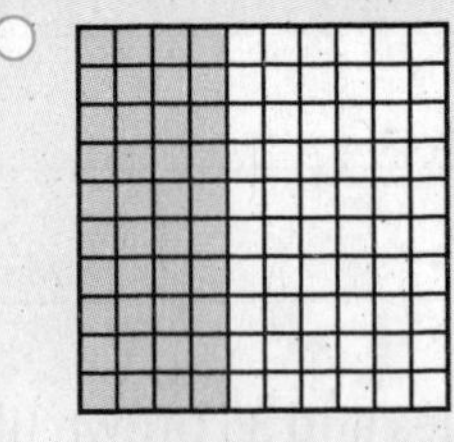
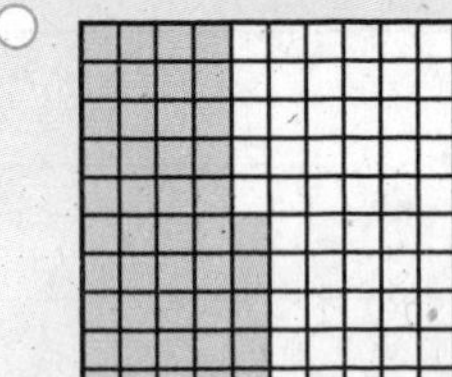
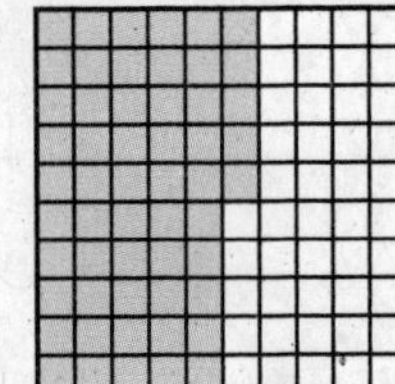
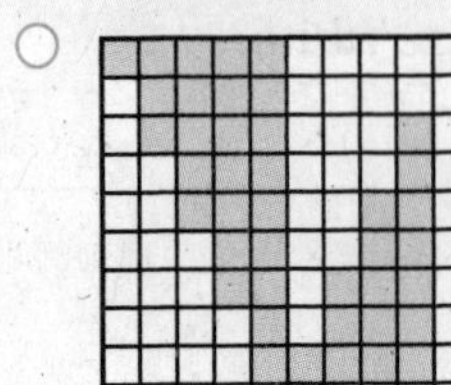
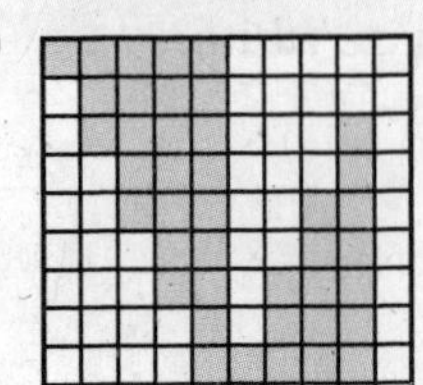

FOR MORE PRACTICE:
Standards Practice Book

Name ______________________

Write Percents as Fractions and Decimals

Essential Question How can you write percents as fractions and decimals?

Ratios and Proportional Relationships—6.RP.3c

MATHEMATICAL PRACTICES
MP.2, MP.5, MP.7, MP.8

To write a percent as a fraction or a decimal, first write the percent as a ratio that compares a number to 100. For example, $37\% = \frac{37}{100}$.

Unlock the Problem (Real World)

Carlos eats a banana, an orange, and a blueberry muffin for breakfast. What fraction of the daily value of vitamin C does each item contain?

Vitamin C Content	
Item	**Percent of Daily Value**
Banana	15%
Orange	113%
Blueberry Muffin	0.5%

Write each percent as a fraction.

A **Write 15% as a fraction.**

$15\% = \frac{\square}{100} = \frac{\square}{\square}$

15% is 15 out of 100.

Write the fraction in simplest form.

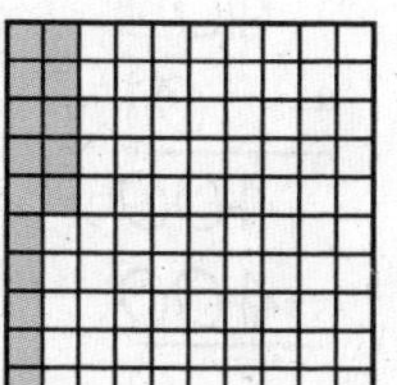

So, 15% = ______.

B **Write 113% as a fraction.**

$113\% = \frac{\square}{100} + \frac{13}{100}$

113% is 100 out of 100 plus 13 out of 100.

$= \_\_\_\_ + \frac{13}{100}$

$\frac{100}{100} = 1$

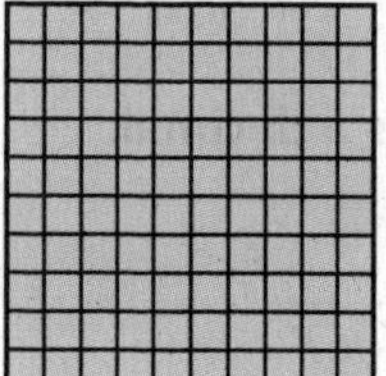

So, 113% = ______.

Write the sum as a mixed number.

C **Write 0.5% as a fraction.**

$0.5\% = \frac{\square}{100}$

0.5% is 0.5 out of 100.

$= \frac{0.5 \cdot 10}{100 \cdot 10} = \frac{\square}{1{,}000}$

Multiply the numerator and denominator by 10 to get a whole number in the numerator.

$= \frac{1}{\square}$

Write the fraction in simplest form.

So, 0.5% = ______.

- MATHEMATICAL PRACTICE 2 **Reason Quantitatively** Explain why two 10-by-10 grids were used to show 113%.

____

____

Example

A **Write 72% as a decimal.**

$72\% = \frac{\square}{100}$ 72% is 72 out of 100.

= ______ Use place value to write 72 hundredths as a decimal.

So, 72% = ______.

B **Write 4% as a decimal.**

$4\% = \frac{\square}{100}$ 4% is 4 out of 100.

Use division to write 4% as a decimal.

$$\begin{array}{r} \square \\ 100\overline{)4.00} \\ -0\downarrow \\ 40 \\ -\ \ 0\downarrow \\ 400 \\ -400 \\ 0 \end{array}$$

Divide the ones. Since 4 ones cannot be shared among 100 groups, write a zero in the quotient.

Place a decimal point after the ones place in the quotient.

Remember

When you divide decimal numbers by powers of 10, you move the decimal point one place to the left for each factor of 10.

So, 4% = ______.

C **Write 25.81% as a decimal.**

$25.81\% = \frac{\square}{100}$ 25.81% is 25.81 out of 100.

= ______ To divide by 100, move the decimal point 2 places to the left: 0.2581

So, 25.81% = ______.

Share and Show

Write the percent as a fraction.

1. 80%

$80\% = \frac{\square}{100} = \frac{\square}{\square}$

2. 150%

______

3. 0.2%

______

Write the percent as a decimal.

4. 58%

______

5. 9%

______

Math Talk **Mathematical Practices**

Explain how to use estimation to check that your answer is reasonable when you write a percent as a fraction or decimal.

Name ______________________________

On Your Own

Write the percent as a fraction or mixed number.

6. 17%

7. 20%

8. 125%

9. 355%

10. 0.1%

11. 2.5%

Write the percent as a decimal.

12. 89%

13. 30%

14. 2%

15. 122%

16. 3.5%

17. 6.33%

18. MATHEMATICAL PRACTICE 2 **Use Reasoning** Write <, >, or =.

21.6% ◯ $\frac{1}{5}$

19. GO DEEPER Georgianne completed 60% of her homework assignment. Write the portion of her homework that she still needs to complete as a fraction.

Problem Solving • Applications Real World

Use the table for 20 and 21.

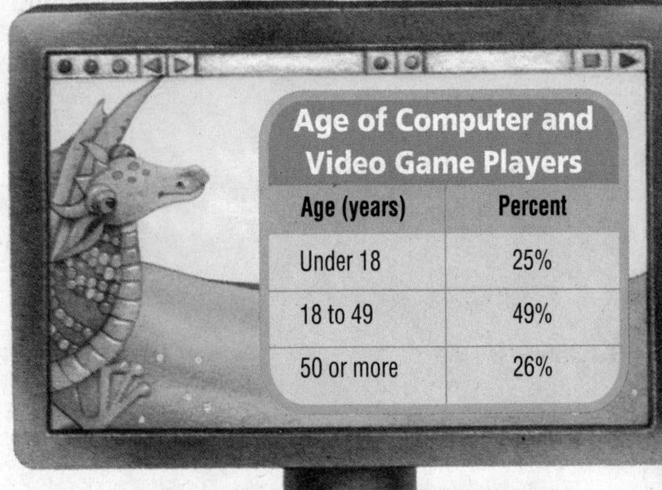

Age of Computer and Video Game Players	
Age (years)	**Percent**
Under 18	25%
18 to 49	49%
50 or more	26%

20. What fraction of computer and video game players are 50 years old or more?

____

21. What fraction of computer and video game players are 18 years old or more?

____

22. THINK SMARTER Box A and Box B each contain black tiles and white tiles. They have the same total number of tiles. In Box A, 45% of the tiles are black. In Box B, $\frac{11}{20}$ of the tiles are white. Compare the number of black tiles in the boxes. Explain your reasoning.

____

____

____

____

23. THINK SMARTER Mr. Truong is organizing a summer program for 6th grade students. He surveyed students to find the percentage of students interested in each activity. Complete the table by writing each percent as a fraction or decimal.

Activity	Percent	Fraction	Decimal
Sports	48%	$\frac{12}{25}$	
Cooking	23%		0.23
Music	20%		0.2
Art	9%	$\frac{9}{100}$	

FOR MORE PRACTICE: Standards Practice Book

Name ______________________________

Write Fractions and Decimals as Percents

Essential Question How can you write fractions and decimals as percents?

Ratios and Proportional Relationships—6.RP.3c

MATHEMATICAL PRACTICES
MP.5, MP.8

Unlock the Problem

During the 2008–2009 season of the National Basketball Association (NBA), the Phoenix Suns won about $\frac{11}{20}$ of their games. The Miami Heat won about 0.524 of their games. Which team was more successful during the season?

- Underline the sentence that tells you what you are trying to find.
- Circle the numbers you need to use.

To compare the season performances of the Suns and the Heat, it is helpful to write the fraction and the decimal as a percent.

Write the fraction or decimal as a percent.

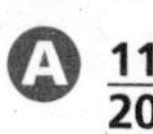

A $\frac{11}{20}$

Multiply the __________ and __________ by the same value to write an equivalent fraction with a denominator of 100.

$\frac{11}{20} = \frac{11 \times \square}{20 \times \square}$

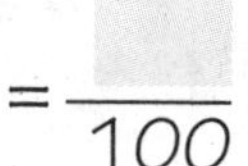

$= \frac{\square}{100}$

A percent is a ratio comparing a number to __________. Write the ratio as a __________.

$=$ ______

So, the percent of games won by the Phoenix Suns is ______.

B 0.524

To write a percent as a decimal, divide by ______.

To write a decimal as a percent, __________ by 100.

$0.524 \times 100 = 52.4$

To multiply by 100, move the decimal point 2 places to the __________.

$0.524 =$ ______ %

So, the percent of games won by the Miami Heat is ______.

Because they won a greater percentage of their games, the __________ were more successful during the 2008–2009 season.

CONNECT You can use what you know about fractions, decimals, and percents to write numbers in different forms.

Example

A Write 0.7 as a fraction and as a percent.

0.7 means 7 ______. Write 0.7 as a fraction.

$0.7 = \frac{7}{\square}$

To write as a percent, first write an equivalent fraction with a denominator of ______.

$= \frac{7 \times \square}{10 \times \square}$

Write the ratio of ______ to ______ as a percent.

$= \frac{\square}{100}$

$=$ ______

So, 0.7 written as a fraction is ______, and 0.7 written as a percent is ______.

ERROR Alert

If you want to write 0.7 as a percent without first writing it as a fraction, be sure to place a zero in the hundredths place when you move the decimal point 2 places to the right.

0.7 = 0.70 = 70%

B Write $\frac{3}{40}$ as a decimal and as a percent.

Since 40 is not a factor of 100, it is more difficult to find an equivalent fraction with a denominator of 100.

Use division to write $\frac{3}{40}$ as a decimal.

Divide 3 by 40.

$$\begin{array}{r} \square \\ 40\overline{)3.000} \\ -0 \\ \hline 30 \\ -0 \\ \hline 300 \\ -280 \\ \hline 200 \\ -200 \\ \hline 0 \end{array}$$

$\frac{3}{40} = 0.075$

To write a decimal as a percent, ______ by 100.

Move the decimal point 2 places to the ______.

0.075 = ______

So, $\frac{3}{40}$ written as a decimal is ______, and $\frac{3}{40}$ written as a percent is ______.

Math Talk Mathematical Practices

Explain why it makes sense that $\frac{3}{40}$ is less than 10%.

Name ______________________________

Share and Show

Write the fraction or decimal as a percent.

1. $\frac{3}{25}$

$$\frac{3 \times \square}{25 \times \square} = \frac{\square}{100}$$

______

2. $\frac{3}{10}$

______

3. 0.717

______

4. 0.02

______

On Your Own

Write the number in two other forms (fraction, decimal, or percent).

5. 0.01

______

6. $\frac{13}{40}$

______

7. $\frac{6}{5}$

______

8. 0.008

______

The table shows the portion of Kim's class that participates in each sport. Use the table for 9–10.

Participation in Sports	
Sport	**Part of Class**
Baseball	23%
Soccer	$\frac{1}{5}$
Swimming	0.09

9. GO DEEPER Do more students take part in soccer or in swimming? Explain your reasoning.

____

10. MATHEMATICAL PRACTICE 6 **Explain** What percent of Kim's class participates in one of the sports listed? Explain how you found your answer.

____

____

11. THINK SMARTER For their reading project, students chose to either complete a character study, or write a book review. $\frac{1}{5}$ of the students completed a character study, and 0.8 of the students wrote a book review. Joia said that more students wrote a book review than completed a character study. Do you agree with Joia? Use numbers and words to support your answer.

____

____

Connect to Art

Sand Sculptures

Every year, dozens of teams compete in the U.S. Open Sandcastle Competition. Recent winners have included complex sculptures in the shape of flowers, elephants, and racing cars.

Teams that participate in the contest build their sculptures using a mixture of sand and water. Finding the correct ratios of these ingredients is essential for creating a stable sculpture.

The table shows the recipes that three teams used. Which team used the greatest percent of sand in their recipe?

Sand Sculpture Recipes		
Team	Sand	Water
A	30 cups	10 cups
B	$\frac{19}{20}$	$\frac{1}{20}$
C	0.84	0.16

Convert to percents. Then order from least to greatest.

Team A	$\frac{30}{30+10} = \frac{30}{40} = 0.75 = \_\_\_\%$
Team B	$\frac{19}{20} = \frac{19 \times \_\_}{20 \times \_\_} = \frac{\_\_}{100} = \_\_\_\%$
Team C	$0.84 = \_\_\_\%$

From least to greatest, the percents are ______________.

So, Team ______________ used the greatest percent of sand.

Solve.

12. Which team used the greatest percent of water in their recipe?

____

13. Some people say that the ideal recipe for sand sculptures contains 88.9% sand. Which team's recipe is closest to the ideal recipe?

____

14. THINK SMARTER Team D used a recipe that consists of 20 cups of sand, 2 cups of flour, and 3 cups of water. How does the percent of sand in Team D's recipe compare to that of the other teams?

____

____

FOR MORE PRACTICE:
Standards Practice Book

Name ______________________________

Mid-Chapter Checkpoint

Vocabulary

Vocabulary
percent
rate

Choose the best term from the box to complete the sentence.

1. A __________ is a ratio that compares a quantity to 100. (p. 195)

Concepts and Skills

Write a ratio and a percent to represent the shaded part. (6.RP.3c)

2.

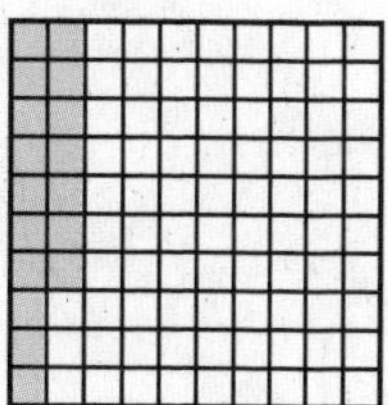

3.

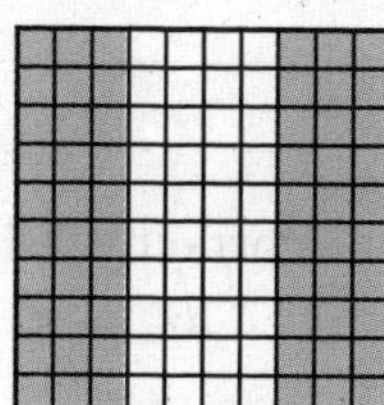

4.

5.

6.

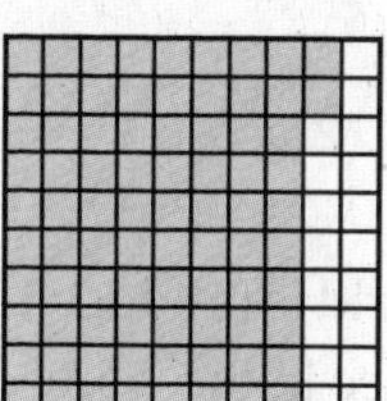

7.

Write the number in two other forms (fraction, decimal, or percent). (6.RP.3c)

8. 0.04

9. 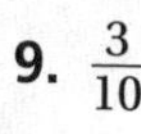 $\frac{3}{10}$

10. 1%

11. $1\frac{1}{5}$

12. 0.9

13. 0.5%

14. $\frac{7}{8}$

15. 355%

16. About $\frac{9}{10}$ of the avocados grown in the United States are grown in California. About what percent of the avocados grown in the United States are grown in California? (6.RP.3c)

____

17. Morton made 36 out of 48 free throws last season. What percent of his free throws did Morton make? (6.RP.3c)

____

18. Sarah answered 85% of the trivia questions correctly. What fraction describes this percent? (6.RP.3c)

____

19. About $\frac{4}{5}$ of all the orange juice in the world is produced in Brazil. About what percent of all the orange juice in the world is produced in Brazil? (6.RP.3c)

____

20. If you eat 4 medium strawberries, you get 48% of your daily recommended amount of vitamin C. What fraction of your daily amount of vitamin C do you still need? (6.RP.3c)

____

Name ______________________________

Percent of a Quantity

Essential Question How do you find a percent of a quantity?

Ratios and Proportional Relationships—6.RP.3c

MATHEMATICAL PRACTICES
MP.1, MP.2, MP.5

Unlock the Problem (Real World)

A typical family of four uses about 400 gallons of water each day, and 30% of this water is for outdoor activities, such as gardening. How many gallons of water does a typical family of four use each day for outdoor activities?

- Will the number of gallons of water for outdoor activities be greater than or less than 200 gallons? Explain.

____

____

One Way Use ratio reasoning.

Draw a bar model.

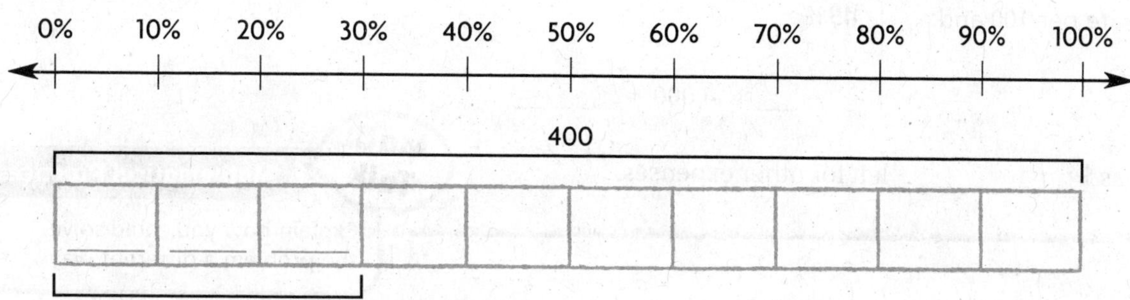

The model shows that 100% represents 400 gallons.

Think: 30% is 3 groups of 10%, so divide the model into 10 equal groups.

Find the value of 10% of 400. $10\% \text{ of } 400 = \frac{1}{10} \times 400 = \frac{400}{\square} = \_\_\_\_$

Find the value of 30% of 400. $30\% \text{ of } 400 = 3 \times \_\_\_\_ = \_\_\_\_$

Another Way Multiply.

You can find 30% of 400 by multiplying.

Write the percent as a rate per 100. $30\% = \frac{30}{100}$

Multiply to find $\frac{30}{100}$ of 400. $\frac{30}{100} \times 400 = \_\_\_\_$

So, 30% of 400 gallons is ______ gallons.

Math Talk **Mathematical Practices**

How can you find the number of gallons of water used for indoor activities?

Try This! **Find 65% of 300.**

65% = ______

______ × 300 = ______

Example

Charla earns $4,000 per month. She spends 40% of her salary on rent and 15% of her salary on groceries. How much money does Charla have left for other expenses?

STEP 1 Add to find the total percent of Charla's salary that is used for rent and groceries.	40% + ______ % = ______ %
STEP 2 Subtract the total percent from 100% to find the percent that is left for other expenses.	100% − ______ % = 45%
STEP 3 Write the percent from Step 2 as a rate per 100 and multiply.	45% = ______ ______ × 4,000 = ______

So, Charla has $ ______ left for other expenses.

Mathematical Practices

Explain how you could solve the problem a different way.

Share and Show

Find the percent of the quantity.

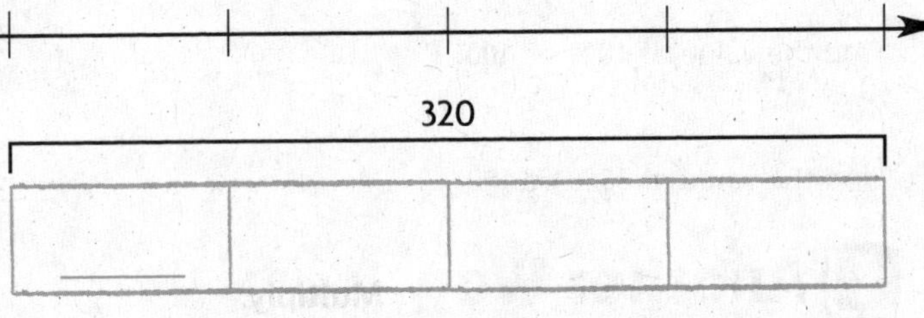

1. 25% of 320

   $25\% = \frac{1}{4}$, so use ______ equal groups.

   $\frac{1}{4} \times 320 = \frac{320}{} =$ ______

2. 80% of 50 ______

3. 175% of 24 ______

4. 60% of 210 ______

5. A jar contains 125 marbles. Given that 4% of the marbles are green, 60% of the marbles are blue, and the rest are red, how many red marbles are in the jar?

   ______

6. There are 32 students in Mr. Moreno's class and 62.5% of the students are girls. How many boys are in the class?

   ______

Math Talk

Mathematical Practices

Explain how you could estimate 49.3% of 3,000.

Name ______________________________

On Your Own

Find the percent of the quantity.

7. 60% of 90

8. 25% of 32.4

9. 110% of 300

10. 0.2% of 6,500

11. A baker made 60 muffins for a cafe. By noon, 45% of the muffins were sold. How many muffins were sold by noon?

12. There are 30 treasures hidden in a castle in a video game. LaToya found 80% of them. How many of the treasures did LaToya find?

13. A school library has 260 DVDs in its collection. Given that 45% of the DVDs are about science and 40% are about history, how many of the DVDs are about other subjects?

14. GO DEEPER Mitch planted cabbage, squash, and carrots on his 150-acre farm. He planted half the farm with squash and 22% with carrots. How many acres did he plant with cabbage?

Compare. Write <, >, or =.

15. 45% of 60 ◯ 60% of 45

16. 10% of 90 ◯ 90% of 100

17. 75% of 8 ◯ 8% of 7.5

18. THINK SMARTER Sarah had 12 free throw attempts during a game and made at least 75% of the free throws. What is the greatest number of free throws Sarah could have missed during the game?

19. MATHEMATICAL PRACTICE 3 Chrissie likes to tip a server in a restaurant a minimum of 20%. She and her friend have a lunch bill that is $18.34. Chrissie says the tip will be $3.30. Her friend says that is not a minimum of 20%. Who is correct? Explain.

Unlock the Problem

20. One-third of the juniors in the Linwood High School Marching Band play the trumpet. The band has 50 members and the table shows what percent of the band members are freshmen, sophomores, juniors, and seniors. How many juniors play the trumpet?

Linwood High School Marching Band	
Freshmen	26%
Sophomores	30%
Juniors	24%
Seniors	20%

a. What do you need to find?

____

____

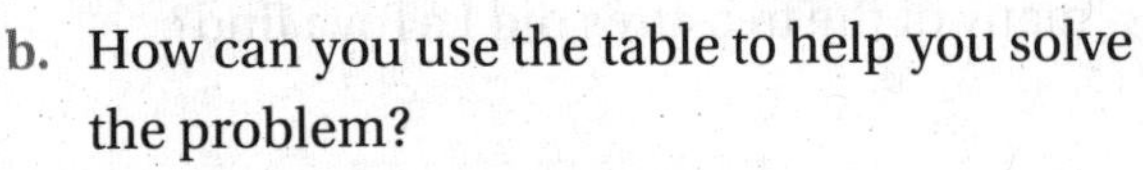

b. How can you use the table to help you solve the problem?

____

____

____

c. What operation can you use to find the number of juniors in the band?

____

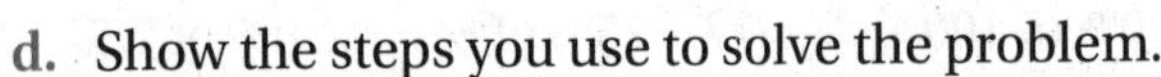

d. Show the steps you use to solve the problem.

e. Complete the sentences.

The band has ______ members. There are ______ juniors in the band. The number of juniors who play the trumpet is ______.

21. THINK SMARTER Compare. Circle $<$, $>$, or $=$.

21a. 25% of 44 [$<$ / $>$ / $=$] 20% of 50

21b. 10% of 30 [$<$ / $>$ / $=$] 30% of 100

21c. 35% of 60 [$<$ / $>$ / $=$] 60% of 35

FOR MORE PRACTICE:
Standards Practice Book

Name ____________________

Problem Solving • Percents

Essential Question How can you use the strategy *use a model* to help you solve a percent problem?

Ratios and Proportional Relationships—6.RP.3c
MATHEMATICAL PRACTICES
MP.1, MP.4, MP.5, MP.6

Unlock the Problem

The recommended daily amount of protein is about 50 grams. One Super Protein Cereal Bar contains 16% of that amount of protein. If Stefon eats one Super Protein Cereal Bar per day, how much protein will he need to get from another source to meet the recommended daily amount?

Use the graphic organizer to help you solve the problem.

Read the Problem

What do I need to find?	What information do I need to use?	How will I use the information?
Write what you need to find. ____________________ ____________________ ____________________ ____________________	Write the important information. ____________________ ____________________ ____________________	What strategy can you use? ____________________ ____________________ ____________________ ____________________

Solve the Problem

Draw a bar model.

100%

Recommended Daily Amount: 50 g

Cereal Bar: ____ 16%

The model shows that 100% = 50 grams,

so 1% of 50 = $\frac{50}{100}$ = ______.

16% of 50 = 16 × ______ = ______

So, the cereal bar contains ____________ of protein.

50 − ______ = ______

So, ____________ of protein should come from another source.

Math Talk — **Mathematical Practices**

How can you use estimation to show that your answer is reasonable?

Try Another Problem

Lee has saved 65% of the money she needs to buy a pair of jeans that cost $24. How much money does Lee have, and how much more money does she need to buy the jeans?

Read the Problem		
What do I need to find?	**What information do I need to use?**	**How will I use the information?**

Solve the Problem

1. Does your answer make sense? Explain how you know.

2. MATHEMATICAL PRACTICE 6 **Explain** how you could solve this problem in a different way.

Mathematical Practices

Compare the model you used to solve this problem with the model on page 213.

Name ________________________________

Share and Show

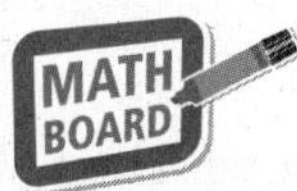

WRITE Math
Show Your Work

1. A geologist visits 40 volcanoes in Alaska and California. 15% of the volcanoes are in California. How many volcanoes does the geologist visit in California and how many in Alaska?

First, draw a bar model.

100%

Total Volcanoes 40

California

15%

Next, find 1%.

$100\% = 40$, so 1% of $40 = \frac{40}{100} =$ ____________

Then, find 15%, the number of volcanoes in California.

15% of $40 = 15 \times$ ____________ $=$ ____________

Finally, subtract to find the number of volcanoes in Alaska.

So, the geologist visited ____________ volcanoes in California and ____________ volcanoes in Alaska.

2. THINK SMARTER **What if** 30% of the volcanoes were in California? How many volcanoes would the geologist have visited in California and how many in Alaska?

____

3. Ricardo has $25 to spend on school supplies. He spends 72% of the money on a backpack and the rest on a large binder. How much does he spend on the backpack? How much does he spend on the binder?

____

4. Kevin is hiking on a trail that is 4.2 miles long. So far, he has hiked 80% of the total distance. How many more miles does Kevin have to hike in order to complete the trail?

____

On Your Own

5. GO DEEPER Jordan takes 50% of the cherries from a bowl. Then Mei takes 50% of the remaining cherries. Finally, Greg takes 50% of the remaining cherries. There are 3 cherries left. How many cherries were in the bowl before Jordan arrived?

______

6. THINK SMARTER Each week, Tasha saves 65% of the money she earns babysitting and spends the rest. This week she earned $40. How much more money did she save than spend this week?

______

7. THINK SMARTER An employee at a state park has 53 photos of animals found at the park. She wants to arrange the photos in rows so that every row except the bottom row has the same number of photos. She also wants there to be at least 5 rows. Describe two different ways she can arrange the photos.

______

______

8. MATHEMATICAL PRACTICE 6 **Explain a Method** Maya wants to mark a length of 7 inches on a sheet of paper, but she does not have a ruler. She has pieces of wood that are 4 inches, 5 inches, and 6 inches long. Explain how she can use these pieces to mark a length of 7 inches.

______

______

______

______

Personal Math Trainer

9. THINK SMARTER + Pierre's family is driving 380 miles from San Francisco to Los Angeles. On the first day, they drive 30% of the distance. On the second day, they drive 50% of the distance. On the third day, they drive the remaining distance and arrive in Los Angeles. How many miles did Pierre's family drive each day? Write the number of miles in the correct box.

76 miles | 190 miles | 114 miles

First Day	Second Day	Third Day

FOR MORE PRACTICE:
Standards Practice Book

Name ______________________________

Find the Whole From a Percent

Essential Question How can you find the whole given a part and the percent?

Ratios and Proportional Relationships—6.RP.3c

MATHEMATICAL PRACTICES
MP.1, MP.4

A percent is equivalent to the ratio of a part to a whole. Suppose there are 20 marbles in a bag and 5 of them are blue. The *whole* is the total number of marbles, 20. The *part* is the number of blue marbles, 5. The ratio of the part to the whole, $\frac{5}{20}$, is equal to the *percent* of marbles that are blue, 25%.

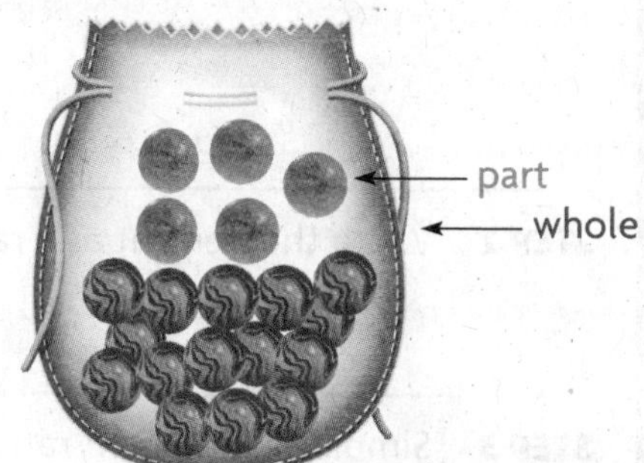

$$\frac{\text{part} \rightarrow 5}{\text{whole} \rightarrow 20} = \frac{5 \times 5}{20 \times 5} = \frac{25}{100} = 25\% \leftarrow \text{percent}$$

You can use the relationship among the part, the whole, and the percent to solve problems.

Unlock the Problem

Emily has sent 28 text messages so far this week. That is 20% of the total number of text messages she is allowed in one week. What is the total number of text messages Emily can send in one week?

One Way Use a double number line.

Think: The *whole* is the total number of messages Emily can send.
The *part* is the number of messages Emily has sent so far.

The double number line shows that 20% represents 28 messages.

Find the number of messages represented by 100%.

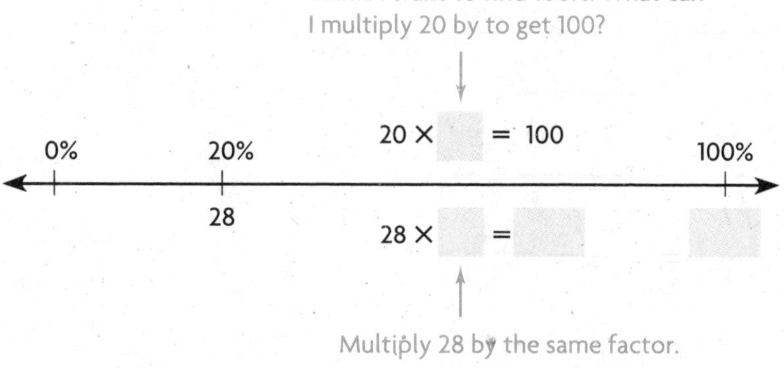

So, 28 is 20% of ____________. Emily can send ____________ messages in one week.

Mathematical Practices

Explain the relationship among the part, the whole, and the percent using the information in this problem.

Another Way Use equivalent ratios.

STEP 1 Write the relationship among the percent, part, and whole.

$$\text{percent} = \frac{\text{part}}{\text{whole}}$$

Think: The percent is ______%. The part is ______ messages. The ______ is unknown.

$$20\% = \frac{\square}{\square}$$

Math Idea

The denominator of the percent ratio will always be 100 because 100% represents the whole.

STEP 2 Write the percent as a ratio.

$$\frac{20}{\square} = \frac{28}{\square}$$

STEP 3 Simplify the known ratio.

$$\frac{20 \div 20}{100 \div \square} = \frac{1}{\square} = \frac{28}{\square}$$

STEP 4 Write an equivalent ratio.

Think: The numerator should be ______.

$$\frac{1 \times 28}{5 \times \square} = \frac{28}{\square}$$

$$\frac{28}{\square} = \frac{28}{\square}$$

So, 28 is 20% of ______. Emily can send ______ messages in one week.

Example 24 is 5% of what number?

STEP 1 Write the relationship among the percent, part, and whole.

$$\text{percent} = \frac{\text{part}}{\text{whole}}$$

Think: The percent is ______%. The part is ______. The ______ is unknown.

$$5\% = \frac{\square}{\square}$$

STEP 2 Write the percent as a ratio.

$$\frac{5}{\square} = \frac{24}{\square}$$

STEP 3 Simplify the known ratio.

$$\frac{5 \div \square}{100 \div \square} = \frac{1}{\square} = \frac{24}{\square}$$

STEP 4 Write an equivalent ratio.

Think: The numerator should be ______.

$$\frac{1 \times \square}{20 \times \square} = \frac{24}{\square}$$

$$\frac{24}{\square} = \frac{24}{\square}$$

So, 24 is 5% of ______.

Math Talk **Mathematical Practices**

Explain how you could check your answer to the Example.

Name ___

Share and Show

Find the unknown value.

1. 9 is 25% of ___

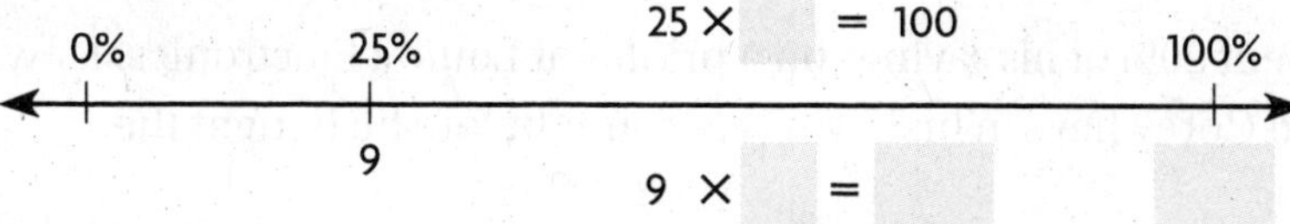

2. 14 is 10% of ___

3. 3 is 5% of ___

4. 12 is 60% of ___

Math Talk — **Mathematical Practices**

Explain how to solve a problem involving a part, a whole, and a percent.

On Your Own

Find the unknown value.

5. 16 is 20% of ___

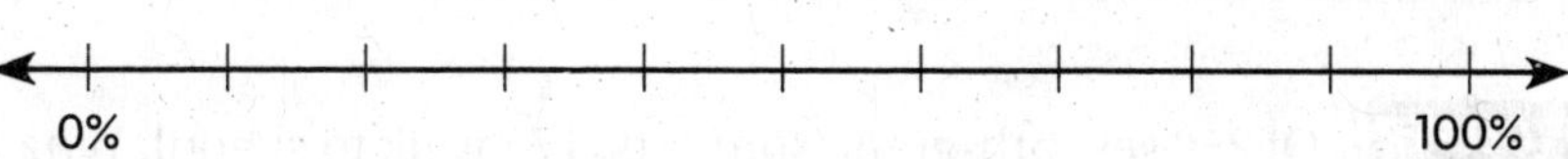

6. 42 is 50% of ___

7. 28 is 40% of ___

8. 60 is 75% of ___

9. 27 is 30% of ___

10. 21 is 60% of ___

11. 12 is 15% of ___

Solve.

12. 40% of the students in the sixth grade at Andrew's school participate in sports. If 52 students participate in sports, how many sixth graders are there at Andrew's school?

___

13. There were 170 people at the concert. If 85% of the seats were filled, how many seats are in the auditorium?

___

MATHEMATICAL PRACTICE 2 Use Reasoning **Algebra** **Find the unknown value.**

14. $40\% = \frac{32}{\square}$ ___

15. $65\% = \frac{91}{\square}$ ___

16. $45\% = \frac{54}{\square}$ ___

Problem Solving • Applications

Use the advertisement for 17 and 18.

17. Corey spent 20% of his savings on a printer at Louie's Electronics. How much did Corey have in his savings account before he bought the printer?

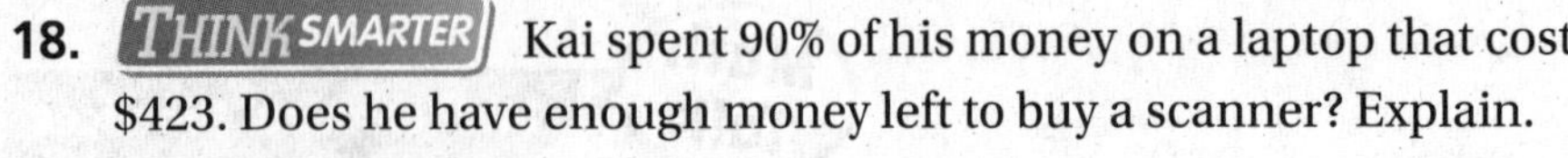

18. THINK SMARTER Kai spent 90% of his money on a laptop that cost $423. Does he have enough money left to buy a scanner? Explain.

Math on the Spot

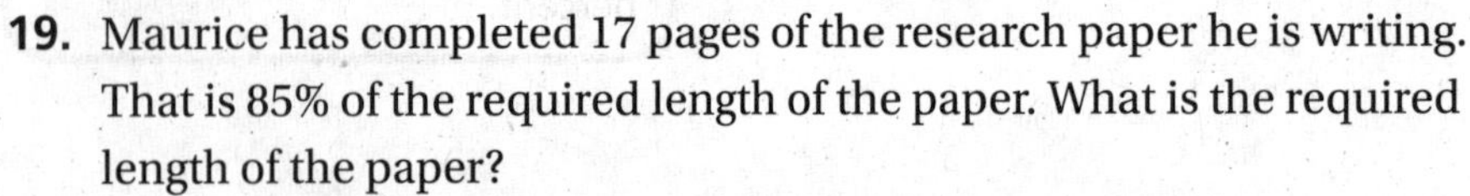

19. Maurice has completed 17 pages of the research paper he is writing. That is 85% of the required length of the paper. What is the required length of the paper?

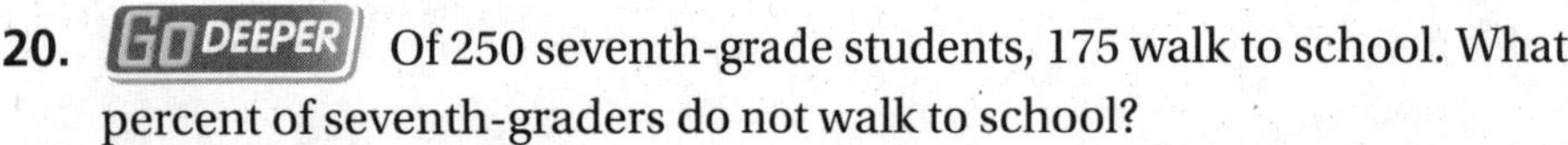

20. GO DEEPER Of 250 seventh-grade students, 175 walk to school. What percent of seventh-graders do not walk to school?

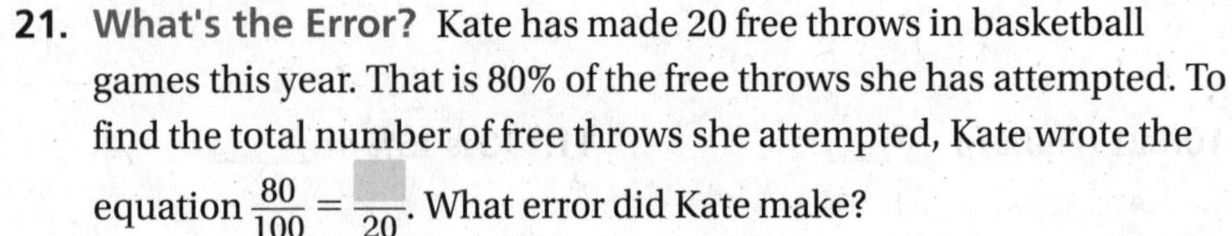

21. **What's the Error?** Kate has made 20 free throws in basketball games this year. That is 80% of the free throws she has attempted. To find the total number of free throws she attempted, Kate wrote the equation $\frac{80}{100} = \frac{\square}{20}$. What error did Kate make?

Personal Math Trainer

22. THINK SMARTER + Maria spent 36% of her savings to buy a smart phone. The phone cost $90. How much money was in Maria's savings account before she purchased the phone? Find the unknown value.

$36\% = \frac{90}{\square}$

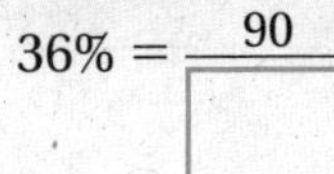

FOR MORE PRACTICE: Standards Practice Book

Name ___________________________________

Chapter 5 Review/Test

1. What percent is represented by the shaded part?

(A) 46%

(B) 60%

(C) 64%

(D) 640%

2. Write a percent to represent the shaded part.

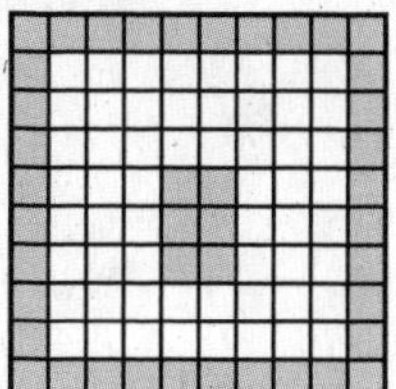

____

3. Rosa made a mosaic wall mural using 42 black tiles, 35 blue tiles and 23 red tiles. Write a percent to represent the number of red tiles in the mural.

____

4. Model 39%.

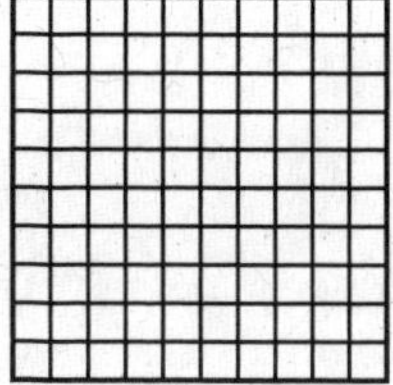

GO DIGITAL Assessment Options Chapter Test

5. For numbers 5a–5d, choose Yes or No to indicate whether the percent and the fraction represent the same amount.

5a. 50% and $\frac{1}{2}$ ○ Yes ○ No

5b. 45% and $\frac{4}{5}$ ○ Yes ○ No

5c. $\frac{3}{8}$ and 37.5% ○ Yes ○ No

5d. $\frac{2}{10}$ and 210% ○ Yes ○ No

6. The school orchestra has 25 woodwinds, 15 percussionists, 31 strings and 30 brass instruments. Select the portion of the instruments that are percussion. Mark all that apply.

○ 15%

○ 1.5

○ $\frac{3}{20}$

○ 0.15

7. For a science project, $\frac{3}{4}$ of the students chose to make a poster and 0.35 of the students wrote a report. Rosa said that more students made a poster than wrote a report. Do you agree with Rosa? Use numbers and words to support your answer.

8. Select other ways to write 0.875. Mark all that apply.

○ 875%

○ 87.5%

○ $\frac{7}{8}$

○ $\frac{875}{100}$

Name ______________________________

9. There are 88 marbles in a bin and 25% of the marbles are red.

There are [22 | 25 | 62 | 66] red marbles in the bin.

10. Harrison has 30 CDs in his music collection. If 40% of the CDs are country music and 30% are pop music, how many CDs are other types of music?

_______ CDs

11. For numbers 11a–11b, choose <, >, or =.

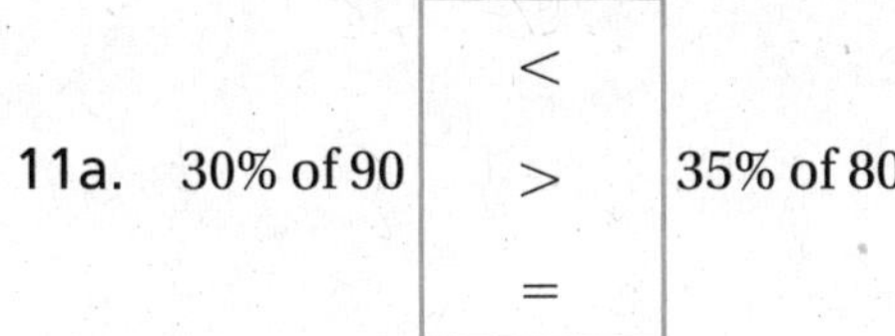

11a. 30% of 90 [< | > | =] 35% of 80

11b. 25% of 16 [< | > | =] 20% of 25

12. There were 200 people who voted at the town council meeting. Of these people, 40% voted for building a new basketball court in the park. How many people voted against building the new basketball court? Use numbers and words to explain your answer.

13. James and Sarah went out to lunch. The price of lunch for both of them was $20. They tipped their server 20% of that amount. How much did each person pay if they shared the price of lunch and the tip equally?

____

14. A sandwich shop has 30 stores and 60% of the stores are in California. The rest of the stores are in Nevada.

Part A

How many stores are in California and how many are in Nevada?

____

Part B

The shop opens 10 new stores. Some are in California, and some are in Nevada. Complete the table.

Locations of Sandwich Shops		
	Percent of Stores	Number of Stores
California		
Nevada	45%	

15. Juanita has saved 35% of the money that she needs to buy a new bicycle. If she has saved $63, how much money does the bicycle cost? Use numbers and words to explain your answer.

Name ______________________________

16. For numbers 16a–16d, choose Yes or No to indicate whether the statement is correct.

16a.	12 is 20% of 60.	○ Yes	○ No
16b.	24 is 50% of 48.	○ Yes	○ No
16c.	14 is 75% of 20.	○ Yes	○ No
16d.	9 is 30% of 30.	○ Yes	○ No

17. Heather and her family are going to the grand opening of a new amusement park. There is a special price on tickets this weekend. Tickets cost $56 each. This is 70% of the cost of a regular price ticket.

Part A

What is the cost of a regular price ticket? Show your work.

Part B

Heather's mom says that they would save more than $100 if they buy tickets for their family on opening weekend. Do you agree or disagree with Heather's mom? Use numbers and words to support your answer. If her statement is incorrect, explain the correct way to solve it.

18. Elise said that 0.2 equals 2%. Use words and numbers to explain her mistake.

19. Write 18% as a fraction.

____

20. Noah wants to put a variety of fish in his new fish tank. His tank is large enough to hold a maximum of 70 fish.

Part A

Complete the table.

Type of Fish	Percent of Maximum Number	Number of Fish in Tank
Rainbow fish	20%	
Swordtail	40%	
Molly	30%	

Part B

Has Noah put the maximum number of fish in his tank? Use number and words to explain how you know. If he has not put the maximum number of fish in the tank, how many more fish could he put in the tank?

Chapter 6

Units of Measure

Show What You Know

Check your understanding of important skills.

Name ____________________

Choose the Appropriate Unit **Circle the more reasonable unit to measure the object.**

1. the length of a car
   inches or feet

2. the length of a soccer field
   meters or kilometers

Multiply and Divide by 10, 100, and 1,000 **Use mental math.**

3. 2.51×10 ________

4. 5.3×100 ________

5. $0.71 \times 1{,}000$ ________

6. $3.25 \div 10$ ________

7. $8.65 \div 100$ ________

8. $56.2 \div 1{,}000$ ________

Convert Units **Complete.**

9. 12 lb = ■ oz
   Think: 1 lb = 16 oz
   ____

10. 8 c = ■ pt
    Think: 2 c = 1 pt
    ____

11. 84 in. = ■ ft
    Think: 12 in. = 1 ft
    ____

A cheetah can run at a rate of 105,600 yards per hour. Be a math detective and find the number of miles the cheetah could run at this rate in 5 minutes.

Personal Math Trainer
Online Assessment and Intervention

Vocabulary Builder

▶ Visualize It

Sort the review words into the Venn diagram. One preview word has been filled in for you.

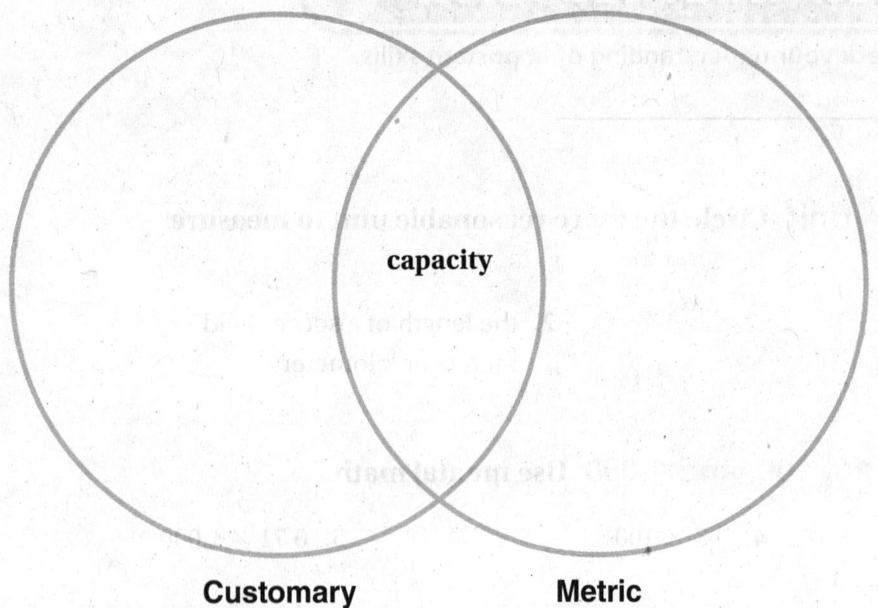

Review Words

✓ gallon
gram
✓ length
liter
✓ mass
meter
ounce
pint
pound
✓ quart
ton
✓ weight

Preview Words

✓ capacity
✓ conversion factor

▶ Understand Vocabulary

Complete the sentences by using the checked words.

1. A rate in which the two quantities are equal but use different units is called a ______________________.

2. ______________________ is the the amount of matter in an object.

3. ______________________ is the amount a container can hold.

4. The ______________________ of an object tells how heavy the object is.

5. Inches, feet, and yards are all customary units used to measure ______________________.

6. A ______________________ is a larger unit of capacity than a quart.

GO DIGITAL
• Interactive Student Edition
• Multimedia eGlossary

Name ____________________

Convert Units of Length

Essential Question How can you use ratio reasoning to convert from one unit of length to another?

Ratios and Proportional Relationships—6.RP.3d

MATHEMATICAL PRACTICES
MP.1, MP.2, MP.6

In the customary measurement system, some of the common units of length are inches, feet, yards, and miles. You can multiply by an appropriate conversion factor to convert between units. A **conversion factor** is a rate in which the two quantities are equal, but use different units.

Customary Units of Length

1 foot (ft) = 12 inches (in.)
1 yard (yd) = 36 inches
1 yard = 3 feet
1 mile (mi) = 5,280 feet
1 mile = 1,760 yards

Unlock the Problem (Real World)

In a soccer game, Kyle scored a goal. Kyle was 33 feet from the goal. How many yards from the goal was he?

Math Idea

When the same unit appears in a numerator and a denominator, you can divide out the common unit before multiplying as you would with a common factor.

Convert 33 feet to yards.

Choose a conversion factor. **Think:** I'm converting *to* yards *from* feet.

1 yard = 3 feet, so use the rate $\frac{1 \text{ yd}}{3 \text{ ft}}$.

Multiply 33 feet by the conversion factor. Units of *feet* appear in a numerator and a denominator, so you can divide out these units before multiplying.

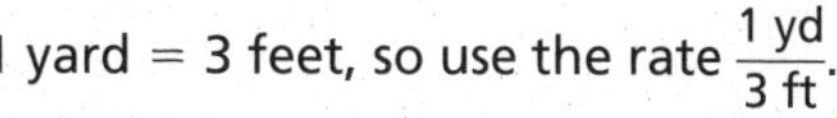

$33 \text{ ft} \times \frac{1 \text{ yd}}{3 \text{ ft}} = \frac{33 \cancel{\text{ft}}}{1} \times \frac{1 \text{ yd}}{3 \cancel{\text{ft}}} =$ ______ yd

So, Kyle was ______ yards from the goal.

How many inches from the goal was Kyle?

Choose a conversion factor. **Think:** I'm converting *to* inches *from* feet.

12 inches = 1 foot, so use the rate $\frac{12 \text{ in.}}{1 \text{ ft}}$.

Multiply 33 ft by the conversion factor.

$33 \text{ ft} \times \frac{12 \text{ in.}}{1 \text{ ft}} = \frac{33 \cancel{\text{ft}}}{1} \times \frac{12 \text{ in.}}{1 \cancel{\text{ft}}} =$ __________ in.

So, Kyle was __________ inches from the goal.

Math Talk — **Mathematical Practices**

Explain how you know which unit to use in the numerator and which unit to use in the denominator of a conversion factor.

Metric Units You can use a similar process to convert metric units. Metric units are used throughout most of the world. One advantage of using the metric system is that the units are related by powers of 10.

Metric Units of Length

1,000 millimeters (mm) = 1 meter (m)
100 centimeters (cm) = 1 meter
10 decimeters (dm) = 1 meter
1 dekameter (dam) = 10 meters
1 hectometer (hm) = 100 meters
1 kilometer (km) = 1,000 meters

Example

A Boeing 777-300 passenger airplane is 73.9 meters long. What is the length of the airplane in centimeters? What is the length in kilometers?

ERROR Alert

Be sure to use the correct conversion factor. The units you are converting from should divide out, leaving only the units you are converting to.

One Way Use a conversion factor.

73.9 meters = ■ centimeters

Choose a conversion factor.

100 cm = 1 m, so use the rate  $\frac{\text{cm}}{\text{m}}$.

Multiply 73.9 meters by the conversion factor. Divide out the common units before multiplying.

$\frac{73.9\ \text{m}}{1} \times \frac{\quad\ \text{cm}}{\text{m}} = \underline{\qquad}\ \text{cm}$

So, 73.9 meters is equal to ________ centimeters.

Another Way Use powers of 10.

Metric units are related to each other by factors of 10.

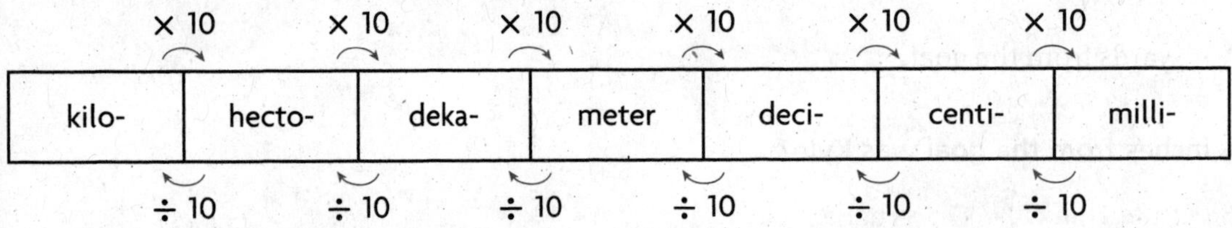

73.9 meters = ■ kilometers

Use the chart.

Kilometers are 3 places to the left of meters in the chart. Move the decimal point 3 places to the left. This is the same as dividing by 1,000.

73.9 0.0739

So, 73.9 meters is equal to ________ kilometer.

Math Talk **Mathematical Practices**

If you convert 285 centimeters to decimeters, will the number of decimeters be greater or less than the number of centimeters? **Explain.**

Name ___

Share and Show

Convert to the given unit.

1. 3 miles = ■ yards

conversion factor: $\frac{\quad}{\quad}\frac{\text{yd}}{\text{mi}}$

3 miles $= \frac{3 \text{ mi}}{1} \times \frac{1{,}760 \text{ yd}}{1 \text{ mi}} =$ ___ yd

2. 43 dm = ___ hm

3. 9 yd = ___ in.

4. 72 ft = ___ yd

5. 7,500 mm = ___ dm

Math Talk **Mathematical Practices**

Explain how to convert from inches to yards and yards to inches.

On Your Own

6. Rohan used 9 yards of ribbon to wrap gifts. How many inches of ribbon did he use?

7. One species of frog can grow to a maximum length of 12.4 millimeters. What is the maximum length of this frog species in centimeters?

8. The height of the Empire State Building measured to the top of the lightning rod is approximately 443.1 meters. What is this height in hectometers?

9. GO DEEPER A snail moves at a speed of 2.5 feet per minute. How many yards will the snail have moved in half of an hour?

Practice: Copy and Solve **Compare. Write <, >, or =.**

10. 32 feet ◯ 11 yards

11. 537 cm ◯ 5.37 m

12. 75 inches ◯ 6 feet

Problem Solving • Applications Real World

What's the Error?

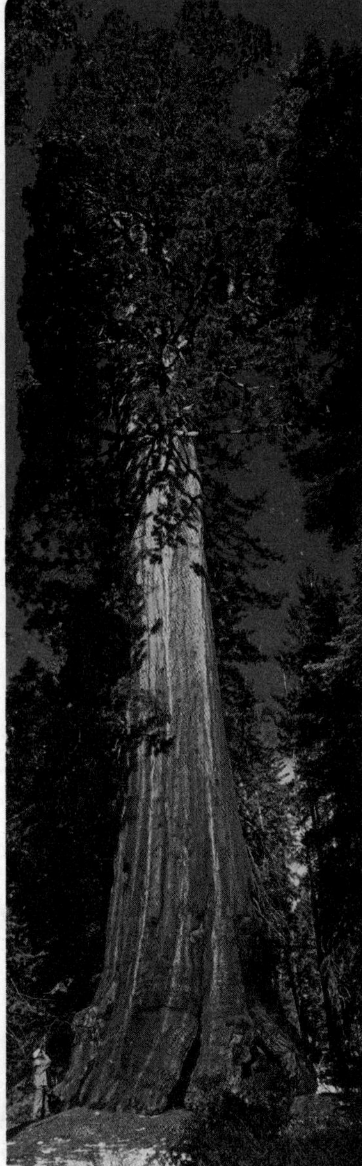

13. THINK SMARTER The Redwood National Park is home to some of the largest trees in the world. Hyperion is the tallest tree in the park, with a height of approximately 379 feet. Tom wants to find the height of the tree in yards.

Tom converted the height this way:

3 feet = 1 yard

conversion factor: $\frac{3 \text{ ft}}{1 \text{ yd}}$

$$\frac{379 \text{ ft}}{1} \times \frac{3 \text{ ft}}{1 \text{ yd}} = 1{,}137 \text{ yd}$$

Find and describe Tom's error. | **Show how to correctly convert from 379 feet to yards.**

So, 379 feet = __________ yards.

-  MATHEMATICAL PRACTICE 6 **Explain** how you knew Tom's answer was incorrect.

____

____

14. THINK SMARTER Choose <, >, or =.

14a. 12 yards 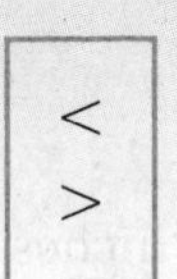 432 inches

14b. 321 cm 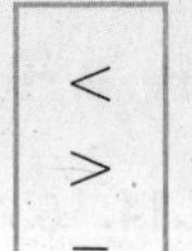 32.1 m

FOR MORE PRACTICE: Standards Practice Book

Name ______________________________

Convert Units of Capacity

Essential Question How can you use ratio reasoning to convert from one unit of capacity to another?

Ratios and Proportional Relationships—6.RP.3d

MATHEMATICAL PRACTICES
MP.2, MP.4, MP.6, MP.8

Capacity measures the amount a container can hold when filled. In the customary measurement system, some common units of capacity are fluid ounces, cups, pints, quarts, and gallons. You can convert between units by multiplying the given units by an appropriate conversion factor.

Customary Units of Capacity

8 fluid ounces (fl oz)	=	1 cup (c)
2 cups	=	1 pint (pt)
2 pints	=	1 quart (qt)
4 cups	=	1 quart
4 quarts	=	1 gallon (gal)

Unlock the Problem

A dairy cow produces about 25 quarts of milk each day. How many gallons of milk does the cow produce each day?

- How are quarts and gallons related?

  ____

- Why can you multiply a quantity by $\frac{1 \text{ gal}}{4 \text{ qt}}$ without changing the value of the quantity?

  ____

  ____

Convert 25 quarts to gallons.

Choose a conversion factor. **Think:** I'm converting *to* gallons *from* quarts.

1 gallon = 4 quarts, so use the rate $\frac{1 \text{ gal}}{4 \text{ qt}}$.

Multiply 25 qt by the conversion factor.

$$25 \text{ qt} \times \frac{1 \text{ gal}}{4 \text{ qt}} = \frac{25 \text{ qt}}{1} \times \frac{1 \text{ gal}}{4 \text{ qt}} = 6\frac{\square}{4} \text{ gal}$$

The fractional part of the answer can be renamed using the smaller unit.

$$6\frac{\square}{4} \text{ gal} \times \_\_\_\_ \text{ gallons, } \_\_\_\_ \text{ quart}$$

So, the cow produces ______ gallons, ______ quart of milk each day.

How many pints of milk does a cow produce each day?

Choose a conversion factor. **Think:** I'm converting *to* pints *from* quarts.

2 pints = 1 quart, so use the rate $\frac{\square \text{ pt}}{\square \text{ qt}}$.

Multiply 25 qt by the conversion factor.

$$25 \text{ qt} \times \frac{\square \text{ pt}}{\square \text{ qt}} = \frac{25 \text{ qt}}{1} \times \frac{\square \text{ pt}}{\square \text{ qt}} = \_\_\_\_ \text{ pt}$$

So, the cow produces ______ pints of milk each day.

Metric Units You can use a similar process to convert metric units of capacity. Just like metric units of length, metric units of capacity are related by powers of 10.

Metric Units of Capacity

1,000 milliliters (mL) = 1 liter (L)
100 centiliters (cL) = 1 liter
10 deciliters (dL) = 1 liter
1 dekaliter (daL) = 10 liters
1 hectoliter (hL) = 100 liters
1 kiloliter (kL) = 1,000 liters

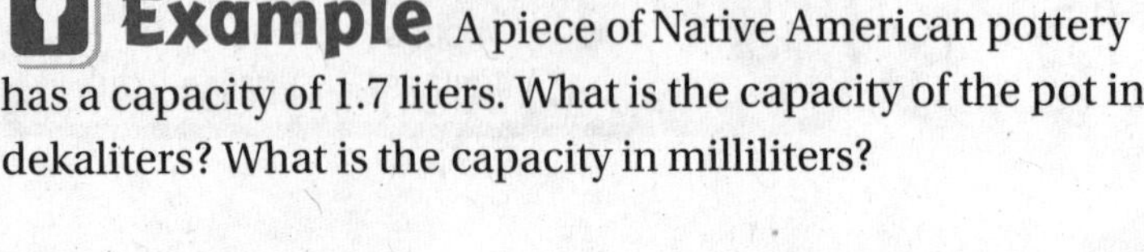

Example

A piece of Native American pottery has a capacity of 1.7 liters. What is the capacity of the pot in dekaliters? What is the capacity in milliliters?

One Way Use a conversion factor.

1.7 liters = ■ dekaliters

Choose a conversion factor. 1 dekaliter = 10 liters, so use the rate

$\frac{\blacksquare \text{ daL}}{\blacksquare \text{ L}}$.

Multiply 1.7 L by the conversion factor. $\frac{1.7 \cancel{L}}{1} \times \frac{\blacksquare \text{ daL}}{\blacksquare \cancel{L}} = \_\_\_\_\_\_ \text{daL}$

So, 1.7 liters is equivalent to ______ dekaliter.

Another Way Use powers of 10.

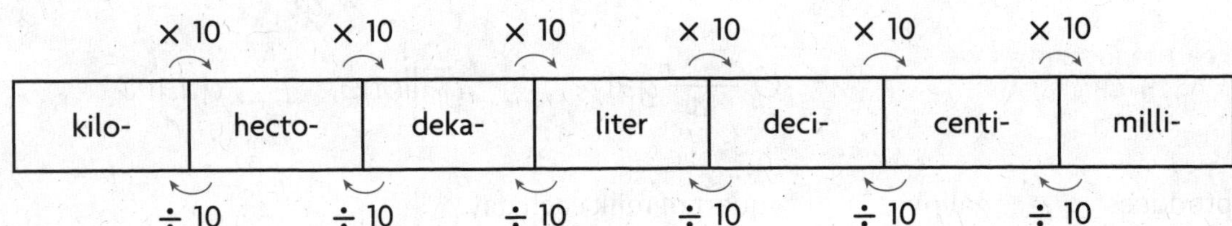

1.7 liters = ■ milliliters

Use the chart.

Milliliters are 3 places to the right of liters. So, move the decimal point 3 places to the right. 1.7 1700.

So, 1.7 liters is equal to ______ milliliters.

Math Talk **Mathematical Practices**

Explain why you cannot convert between units in the customary system by moving the decimal point left or right.

- MATHEMATICAL PRACTICE 6 **Describe a Method** Describe how you would convert kiloliters to milliliters.

Name ______________________

Share and Show

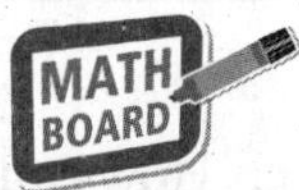

Convert to the given unit.

1. 5 quarts = ▆ cups

conversion factor: $\frac{\square\ c}{qt}$

$5 \text{ quarts} = \frac{5 \text{ qt}}{1} \times \frac{4 \text{ c}}{1 \text{ qt}} = $ ______ c

2. 6.7 liters = ______ hectoliters

✓ 3. 5.3 kL = ______ L

✓ 4. 36 qt = ______ gal

5. 5,000 mL = ______ cL

Math Talk **Mathematical Practices**

Compare the customary and metric systems. In which system is it easier to convert from one unit to another?

On Your Own

6. It takes 41 gallons of water for a washing machine to wash a load of laundry. How many quarts of water does it take to wash one load?

______

7. Sam squeezed 237 milliliters of juice from 4 oranges. How many liters of juice did Sam squeeze?

______

8. MATHEMATICAL PRACTICE 2 **Reason Quantitatively** A bottle contains 3.78 liters of water. Without calculating, determine whether there are more or less than 3.78 deciliters of water in the bottle. Explain your reasoning.

______

______

9. GO DEEPER Tonya has a 1-quart, a 2-quart, and a 3-quart bowl. A recipe asks for 16 ounces of milk. If Tonya is going to triple the recipe, what is the smallest bowl that will hold the milk?

______

Practice: Copy and Solve **Compare. Write <, >, or =.**

10. 700,000 L ◯ 70 kL

11. 6 gal ◯ 30 qt

12. 54 kL ◯ 540,000 dL

13. 10 pt ◯ 5 qt

14. 500 mL ◯ 50 L

15. 14 c ◯ 4 qt

Unlock the Problem

16. THINK SMARTER Jeffrey is loading cases of bottled water onto a freight elevator. There are 24 one-pint bottles in each case. The maximum weight that the elevator can carry is 1,000 pounds. If 1 gallon of water weighs 8.35 pounds, what is the maximum number of full cases Jeffrey can load onto the elevator?

a. What do you need to find?

b. How can you find the weight of 1 case of bottled water? What is the weight?

c. How can you find the number of cases that Jeffrey can load onto the elevator?

d. What is the maximum number of full cases Jeffrey can load onto the elevator?

17. GO DEEPER Monica put 1 liter, 1 deciliter, 1 centiliter, and 1 milliliter of water into a bowl. How many milliliters of water did she put in the bowl?

18. THINK SMARTER Select the conversions that are equivalent to 235 liters. Mark all that apply.

- (A) 235,000 milliliters
- (B) 0.235 milliliters
- (C) 235,000 kiloliters
- (D) 0.235 kiloliters

FOR MORE PRACTICE:
Standards Practice Book

Name ______________________

Convert Units of Weight and Mass

Essential Question How can you use ratio reasoning to convert from one unit of weight or mass to another?

Ratios and Proportional Relationships—6.RP.3d

MATHEMATICAL PRACTICES
MP.1, MP.2, MP.3, MP.4

The weight of an object is a measure of how heavy it is. Units of weight in the customary measurement system include ounces, pounds, and tons.

Customary Units of Weight
1 pound (lb) = 16 ounces (oz)
1 ton (T) = 2,000 pounds

Unlock the Problem

The largest pearl ever found weighed 226 ounces. What was the pearl's weight in pounds?

- How are ounces and pounds related?

____

- Will you expect the number of pounds to be greater than 226 or less than 226? Explain.

____

Convert 226 ounces to pounds.

Choose a conversion factor.
Think: I'm converting *to* pounds *from* ounces.

1 lb = 16 oz, so use the rate $\frac{\square\ \text{lb}}{\square\ \text{oz}}$.

Multiply 226 ounces by the conversion factor.

$$226\ \text{oz} \times \frac{1\ \text{lb}}{16\ \text{oz}} = \frac{226\ \cancel{\text{oz}}}{1} \times \frac{1\ \text{lb}}{16\ \cancel{\text{oz}}} = \square\ \frac{\square}{16}\ \text{lb}$$

Think: The fractional part of the answer can be renamed using the smaller unit.

$$\square\ \frac{\square}{16}\ \text{lb} = \_\_\_\_\ \text{lb},\ \_\_\_\_\ \text{oz}$$

So, the largest pearl weighed ______ pounds, ______ ounces.

The largest emerald ever found weighed 38 pounds. What was its weight in ounces?

Choose a conversion factor.
Think: I'm converting *to* ounces *from* pounds.

16 oz = 1 lb, so use the rate $\frac{\square\ \text{oz}}{\square\ \text{lb}}$.

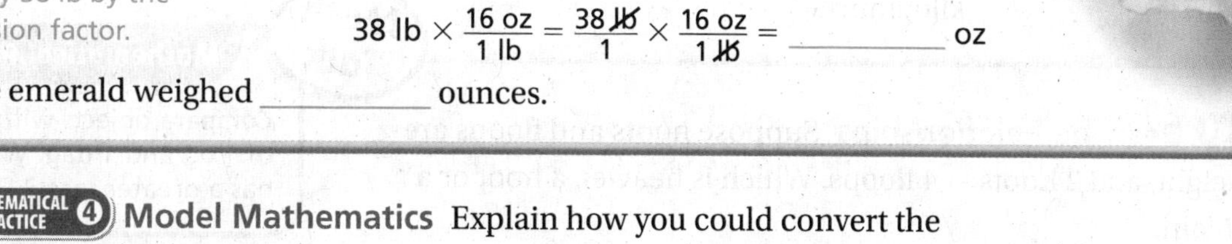

Multiply 38 lb by the conversion factor.

$$38\ \text{lb} \times \frac{16\ \text{oz}}{1\ \text{lb}} = \frac{38\ \cancel{\text{lb}}}{1} \times \frac{16\ \text{oz}}{1\ \cancel{\text{lb}}} = \_\_\_\_\_\_\ \text{oz}$$

So, the emerald weighed ________ ounces.

1. MATHEMATICAL PRACTICE 4 **Model Mathematics** Explain how you could convert the emerald's weight to tons.

____

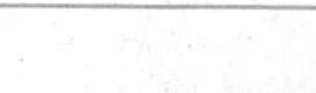

Metric Units The amount of matter in an object is called the mass. Metric units of mass are related by powers of 10.

Metric Units of Mass
1,000 milligrams (mg) = 1 gram (g)
100 centigrams (cg) = 1 gram
10 decigrams (dg) = 1 gram
1 dekagram (dag) = 10 grams
1 hectogram (hg) = 100 grams
1 kilogram (kg) = 1,000 grams

Example

Corinne caught a trout with a mass of 2,570 grams. What was the mass of the trout in centigrams? What was the mass in kilograms?

One Way Use a conversion factor.

2,570 grams to centigrams

Choose a conversion factor. — 100 cg = 1 g, so use the rate $\frac{\underline{\quad} \text{ cg}}{\text{g}}$.

Multiply 2,570 g by the conversion factor. — $\frac{2{,}570 \text{ g}}{1} \times \frac{100 \text{ cg}}{1 \text{ g}} =$ ________ cg.

So, the trout's mass was ________ centigrams.

Another Way Use powers of 10.

Recall that metric units are related to each other by factors of 10.

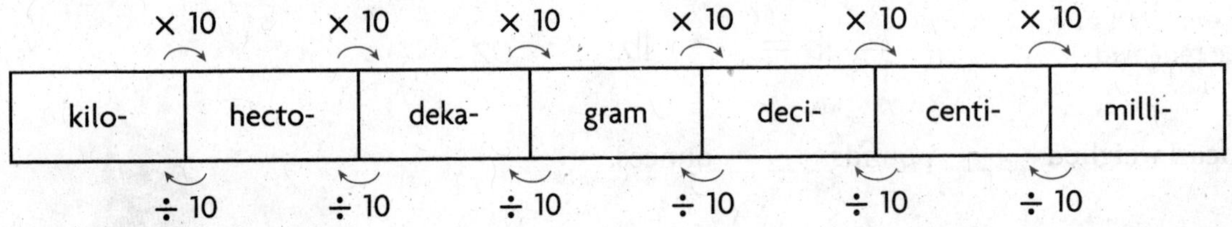

2,570 grams to kilograms

Use the chart.

Kilograms are 3 places to the left of grams. Move the decimal point 3 places to the left. — 2570. 2.570

So, 2,570 grams = ________ kilograms.

Math Talk Mathematical Practices

Compare objects with masses of 1 dg and 1 dag. Which has a greater mass? Explain.

2. MATHEMATICAL PRACTICE 1 **Describe Relationships** Suppose hoots and floops are units of weight, and 2 hoots = 4 floops. Which is heavier, a hoot or a floop? Explain.

Name ______________________________

Share and Show

Convert to the given unit.

1. 9 pounds = ▭ ounces

   conversion factor: $\frac{\square \text{ oz}}{\text{lb}}$

   9 pounds = 9 lb × $\frac{16 \text{ oz}}{1 \text{ lb}}$ = ______ oz

2. 3.77 grams = ______ dekagram

3. Amanda's computer weighs 56 ounces. How many pounds does it weigh?

   ______

4. A honeybee can carry 40 mg of nectar. How many grams of nectar can a honeybee carry?

   ______

Mathematical Practices

Compare metric units of capacity and mass. How are they alike? How are they different?

On Your Own

Convert to the given unit.

5. 4 lb = ______ oz

6. 7.13 g = ______ cg

7. 3 T = ______ lb

8. The African Goliath frog can weigh up to 7 pounds. How many ounces can the Goliath frog weigh?

   ______

9. GO DEEPER The mass of a standard hockey puck must be at least 156 grams. What is the minimum mass of 8 hockey pucks in kilograms?

   ______

Practice: Copy and Solve **Compare. Write <, >, or =.**

10. 250 lb ◯ 0.25 T

11. 65.3 hg ◯ 653 dag

12. 5 T ◯ 5,000 lb

13. THINK SMARTER Masses of precious stones are measured in carats, where 1 carat = 200 milligrams. What is the mass of a 50-dg diamond in carats?

    ______

Problem Solving • Applications

Use the table for 14–17.

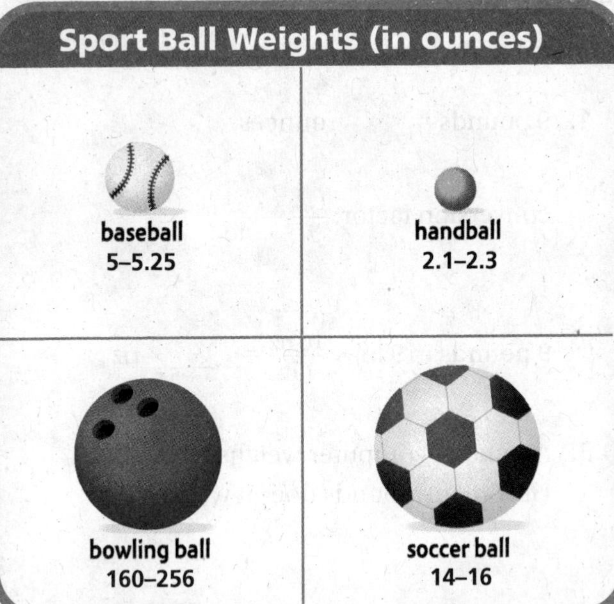

14. Express the weight range for bowling balls in pounds.

15. GO DEEPER How many more pounds does the heaviest soccer ball weigh than the heaviest baseball? Round your answer to the nearest hundredth.

16. THINK SMARTER A manufacturer produces 3 tons of baseballs per day and packs them in cartons of 24 baseballs each. If all of the balls are the minimum allowable weight, how many cartons of balls does the company produce each day?

17. MATHEMATICAL PRACTICE 5 **Communicate** Explain how you could use mental math to estimate the number of soccer balls it would take to produce a total weight of 1 ton.

WRITE ▸ *Math* • **Show Your Work** •

18. THINK SMARTER The Wilson family's newborn baby weighs 84 ounces. Choose the numbers to show the baby's weight in pounds and ounces.

5 6 7	pounds	3 4 5	ounces

FOR MORE PRACTICE:
Standards Practice Book

Name ______________________________

Mid-Chapter Checkpoint

Vocabulary

Vocabulary
capacity
conversion factor
metric system

Choose the best term from the box to complete the sentence.

1. A ____________________ is a rate in which the two quantities are equal, but use different units. (p. 229)

2. ____________________ is the amount a container can hold. (p. 233)

Concepts and Skills

Convert units to solve. (6.RP.3d)

3. A professional football field is 160 feet wide. What is the width of the field in yards?

   ____

4. Julia drinks 8 cups of water per day. How many quarts of water does she drink per day?

   ____

5. The mass of Hinto's math book is 4,458 grams. What is the mass of 4 math books in kilograms?

   ____

6. Turning off the water while brushing your teeth saves 379 centiliters of water. How many liters of water can you save if you turn off the water the next 3 times you brush your teeth?

   ____

Convert to the given unit. (6.RP.3d)

7. 34.2 mm = ______ cm

8. 42 in. = ______ ft

9. 1.4 km = ______ hm

10. 4 gal = ______ qt

11. 53 dL = ______ daL

12. 28 c = ______ pt

13. Trenton's laptop is 32 centimeters wide. What is the width of the laptop in decimeters? (6.RP.3d)

14. A truck is carrying 8 cars weighing an average of 4,500 pounds each. What is the total weight in tons of the cars on the truck? (6.RP.3d)

15. Ben's living room is a rectangle measuring 10 yards by 168 inches. By how many feet does the length of the room exceed the width? (6.RP.3d)

16. Jessie served 13 pints of orange juice at her party. How many quarts of orange juice did she serve? (6.RP.3d)

17. Kaylah's cell phone has a mass of 50,000 centigrams. What is the mass of her phone in grams? (6.RP.3d)

Name ___

Transform Units

Essential Question How can you transform units to solve problems?

Ratios and Proportional Relationships—6.RP.3d

MATHEMATICAL PRACTICES
MP.1, MP.3, MP.5, MP.6

You can sometimes use the units of the quantities in a problem to help you decide how to solve the problem.

Unlock the Problem Real World

A car's gas mileage is the average distance the car can travel on 1 gallon of gas. Maria's car has a gas mileage of 20 miles per gallon. How many miles can Maria travel on 9 gallons of gas?

- Would you expect the answer to be greater or less than 20 miles? Why?

___

___

___

Analyze the units in the problem.

STEP 1 Identify the units.

You know two quantities: the car's gas mileage and the amount of gas.

Gas mileage: 20 miles per gallon = $\frac{20 \quad \_\_\_}{1 \quad \_\_\_}$

Amount of gas: 9 ___

You want to know a third quantity: the distance the car can travel.

Distance: ■ ___

STEP 2 Determine the relationship among the units.

Think: The answer needs to have units of miles. If I multiply $\frac{20 \text{ miles}}{1 \text{ gallon}}$ by 9 gallons, I can divide out units of gallons. The product will have units of

___, which is what I want.

STEP 3 Use the relationship.

$$\frac{20 \text{ mi}}{1 \text{ gal}} \times 9 \text{ gal} = \frac{20 \text{ mi}}{1 \cancel{\text{gal}}} \times \frac{9 \cancel{\text{gal}}}{1} = \_\_\_$$

So, Maria can travel ___ on 9 gallons of gas.

1. Explain why the units of gallons are crossed out in the multiplication step above.

___

___

Sometimes you may need to convert units before solving a problem.

Example

The material for a rectangular awning has an area of 315 square feet. If the width of the material is 5 yards, what is the length of the material in feet? (Recall that the area of a rectangle is equal to its length times its width.)

STEP 1 Identify the units.

You know two quantities: the area of the material and the width of the material.

Area: 315 sq ft = 315 ft × ft

Width: 5 ______

You want to know a third quantity: the length of the material.

Length: ▢ ft

STEP 2 Determine the relationship among the units.

Think: The answer needs to have units of feet. So, I should convert the width from yards to feet.

Width: $\frac{5\text{ yd}}{1} \times \frac{\square\text{ ft}}{1\text{ yd}} = \square$ ft

Think: If I divide the area by the width I can divide out units of feet. The quotient will have units of ______, which is what I want.

STEP 3 Use the relationship.

Divide the area by the width to find the length.

315 sq ft ÷ ______ ft

Write the division using a fraction bar.

$\frac{\square\text{ sq ft}}{15\text{ ft}}$

Write the units of area as a product and divide out the common units.

$\frac{\square\text{ ft} \times \text{ft}}{\square\text{ ft}} = \square$ ft

So, the length of the material is ____________.

Math Idea

You can write units of area as products.

sq ft = ft × ft

Math Talk Mathematical Practices

Discuss how examining the units in a problem can help you solve the problem.

2. MATHEMATICAL PRACTICE 3 **Apply** Explain how knowing how to find the area of a rectangle could help you solve the problem above.

3. MATHEMATICAL PRACTICE 6 **Explain** why the answer is in feet even though units of feet are divided out.

Name ______________________

Share and Show

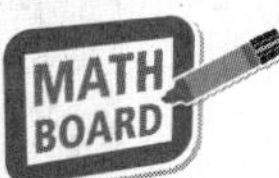

1. A dripping faucet leaks 12 gallons of water per day. How many gallons does the faucet leak in 6 days?

Quantities you know: $\frac{12}{1}$ ______ and ______ days

Quantity you want to know: ______

$\frac{\quad \text{gal}}{1 \text{ day}} \times \quad$ days = ______

So, the faucet leaks ______ in 6 days.

2. Bananas sell for $0.44 per pound. How much will 7 pounds of bananas cost?

3. Grizzly Park is a rectangular park with an area of 24 square miles. The park is 3 miles wide. What is its length in miles?

On Your Own

Multiply or divide the quantities.

4. $\frac{24 \text{ kg}}{1 \text{ min}} \times 15$ min

5. 216 sq cm ÷ 8 cm

6. $\frac{17 \text{ L}}{1 \text{ hr}} \times 9$ hr

7. GO DEEPER The rectangular rug in Marcia's living room measures 12 feet by 108 inches. What is the rug's area in square feet?

8. MATHEMATICAL PRACTICE 1 Make Sense of Problems A box-making machine makes cardboard boxes at a rate of 72 boxes per minute. How many minutes does it take to make 360 boxes?

Personal Math Trainer

9. THINK SMARTER + The area of an Olympic-size swimming pool is 1,250 square meters. The length of the pool is 5,000 centimeters. Select True or False for each statement.

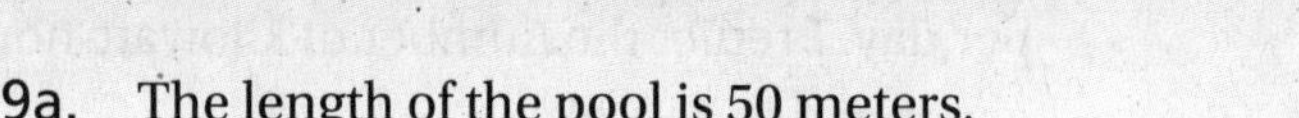

9a. The length of the pool is 50 meters. ○ True ○ False

9b. The width of the pool is 25 meters. ○ True ○ False

9c. The area of the pool is 1.25 square kilometers ○ True ○ False

Connect to Reading

Make Predictions

A *prediction* is a guess about something in the future. A prediction is more likely to be accurate if it is based on facts and logical reasoning.

The Hoover Dam is one of America's largest producers of hydroelectric power. Up to 300,000 gallons of water can move through the dam's generators every second. Predict the amount of water that moves through the generators in half of an hour.

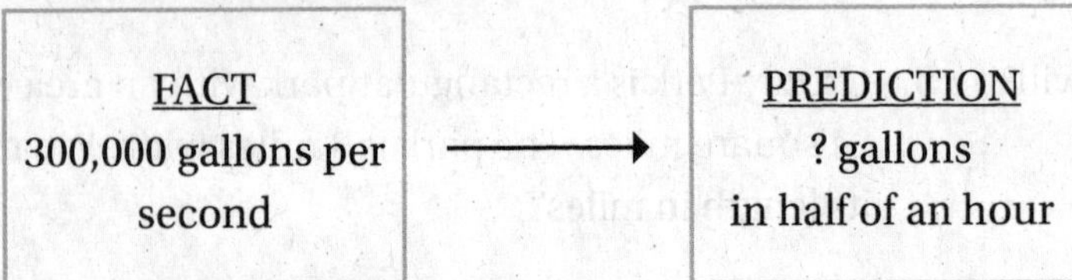

Use what you know about transforming units to make a prediction.

You know the rate of the water through the generators, and you are given an amount of time. — Rate of flow: $\frac{\_\_\_\_ \text{ gal}}{1 \text{ sec}}$; time: $\frac{1}{2}$ ____

You want to find the amount of water. — Amount of water: ■ gallons

Convert the amount of time to seconds to match the units in the rate. — $\frac{1}{2}$ hr = ____ min

$\frac{30 \text{ min}}{1} \times \frac{\_\_\_\_ \text{ sec}}{1 \text{ min}} =$ ________ sec

Multiply the rate by the amount of time to find the amount of water. — $\frac{\_\_\_\_ \text{ gal}}{\text{sec}} \times \frac{\_\_\_\_ \text{ sec}}{1} =$ ________ gal

So, a good prediction of the amount of water that moves through the generators in half of an hour is ____________.

Convert units to solve.

10. An average of 19,230 people tour the Hoover Dam each week. Predict the number of people touring the dam in a year.

____

11. THINK SMARTER The Hoover Dam generates an average of about 11,506,000 kilowatt-hours of electricity per day. Predict the number of kilowatt-hours generated in 7 weeks.

Math on the Spot

____

FOR MORE PRACTICE: Standards Practice Book

Name ____________________

PROBLEM SOLVING
Lesson 6.5

Problem Solving • Distance, Rate, and Time Formulas

Ratios and Proportional Relationships—6.RP.3d

MATHEMATICAL PRACTICES
MP.1, MP.7

Essential Question How can you use the strategy *use a formula* to solve problems involving distance, rate, and time?

You can solve problems involving distance, rate, and time by using the formulas below. In each formula, d represents distance, r represents rate, and t represents time.

Distance, Rate, and Time Formulas		
To find distance, use $d = r \times t$	To find rate, use $r = d \div t$	To find time, use $t = d \div r$

Unlock the Problem

Helena drives 220 miles to visit Niagara Falls. She drives at an average speed of 55 miles per hour. How long does the trip take?

Use the graphic organizer to help you solve the problem.

Read the Problem

What do I need to find?

I need to find the ____________ the trip takes.

What information do I need to use?

I need to use the ____________ Helena travels and the ______ of speed her car is moving.

How will I use the information?

First I will choose the formula ____________ because I need to find time. Next I will substitute for d and r. Then I will ____________ to find the time.

Solve the Problem

- First write the formula for finding time.

$t = d \div r$

- Next substitute the values for d and r.

$t =$ ______ mi $\div \dfrac{\square \text{ mi}}{1 \text{ hr}}$

- Rewrite the division as multiplication by the reciprocal of $\dfrac{55 \text{ mi}}{1 \text{ hr}}$.

$t = \dfrac{\square \text{ mi}}{1} \times \dfrac{1 \text{ hr}}{\square \text{ mi}} =$ ______ hr

Mathematical Practices

Explain how you know which formula to use.

So, the trip takes ______ hours.

Try Another Problem

Santiago's class traveled to the Museum of Natural Science for a field trip. To reach the destination, the bus traveled at a rate of 65 miles per hour for 2 hours. What distance did Santiago's class travel?

Choose a formula.

$d = r \times t$ $\quad r = d \div t$ $\quad t = d \div r$

Use the graphic organizer below to help you solve the problem.

Read the Problem	Solve the Problem
What do I need to find?	
What information do I need to use?	
How will I use the information?	

So, Santiago's class traveled ________ miles.

Math Talk **Mathematical Practices**

Explain how you could check your answer by solving the problem a different way.

1. **What if** the bus traveled at a rate of 55 miles per hour for 2.5 hours? How would the distance be affected?

2. MATHEMATICAL PRACTICE 7 **Identify Relationships** Describe how to find the rate if you are given the distance and time.

Name ______________________________

Share and Show

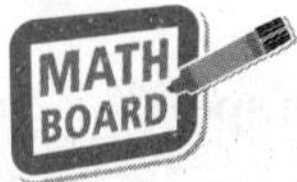

Unlock the Problem

√ Choose the appropriate formula.
√ Include the unit in your answer.

WRITE ▸Math • Show Your Work

1. Mariana runs at a rate of 180 meters per minute. How far does she run in 5 minutes?

   First, choose a formula.

   ____

   Next, substitute the values into the formula and solve.

   ____

   So, Mariana runs ______________ in 5 minutes.

2. THINK SMARTER **What if** Mariana runs for 20 minutes at the same speed? How many kilometers will she run?

   ____

3. A car traveled 130 miles in 2 hours. How fast did the car travel?

   ____

4. A subway car travels at a rate of 32 feet per second. How far does it travel in 16 seconds?

   ____

5. A garden snail travels at a rate of 2.6 feet per minute. At this rate, how long will it take for the snail to travel 65 feet?

   ____

6. GO DEEPER A squirrel can run at a maximum speed of 12 miles per hour. At this rate, how many seconds will it take the squirrel to run 3 miles?

   ____

7. THINK SMARTER A cyclist rides 8 miles in 32 minutes. What is the speed of the cyclist in miles per hour?

   ____

On Your Own

8. A pilot flies 441 kilometers in 31.5 minutes. What is the speed of the airplane?

____

9. GO DEEPER Chris spent half of his money on a pair of headphones. Then he spent half of his remaining money on CDs. Finally, he spent his remaining $12.75 on a book. How much money did Chris have to begin with?

____

WRITE ▸Math
Show Your Work

10. THINK SMARTER André and Yazmeen leave at the same time and travel 75 miles to a fair. André drives 11 miles in 12 minutes. Yazmeen drives 26 miles in 24 minutes. If they continue at the same rates, who will arrive at the fair first? Explain.

____

____

11. MATHEMATICAL PRACTICE 3 **Make Arguments** Bonnie says that if she drives at an average rate of 40 miles per hour, it will take her about 2 hours to drive 20 miles across town. Does Bonnie's statement make sense? Explain.

____

____

Personal Math Trainer

12. THINK SMARTER + Claire says that if she runs at an average rate of 6 miles per hour, it will take her about 2 hours to run 18 miles. Do you agree or disagree with Claire? Use numbers and words to support your answer.

____

____

____

____

FOR MORE PRACTICE:
Standards Practice Book

Name ______________________________

Chapter 6 Review/Test

1. A construction crew needs to remove 2.5 tons of river rock during the construction of new office buildings.

The weight of the rocks is [800 / 2,000 / 5,000] pounds.

2. Select the conversions that are equivalent to 10 yards. Mark all that apply.

(A) 20 feet

(B) 240 inches

(C) 30 feet

(D) 360 inches

3. Meredith runs at a rate of 190 meters per minute. Use the formula $d = r \times t$ to find how far she runs in 6 minutes.

4. The table shows data for 4 cyclists during one day of training. Complete the table by finding the rate of speed for each cyclist. Use the formula $r = d \div t$.

Cyclist	Distance (mi)	Time (hr)	Rate (mi per hr)
Alisha	36	3	
Jose	39	3	
Raul	40	4	
Ruthie	22	2	

GO DIGITAL Assessment Options Chapter Test

5. For numbers 5a–5c, choose <, >, or =.

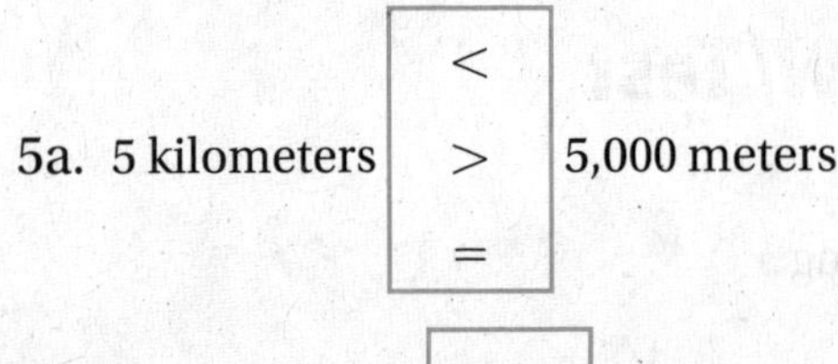

5a. 5 kilometers [< / > / =] 5,000 meters

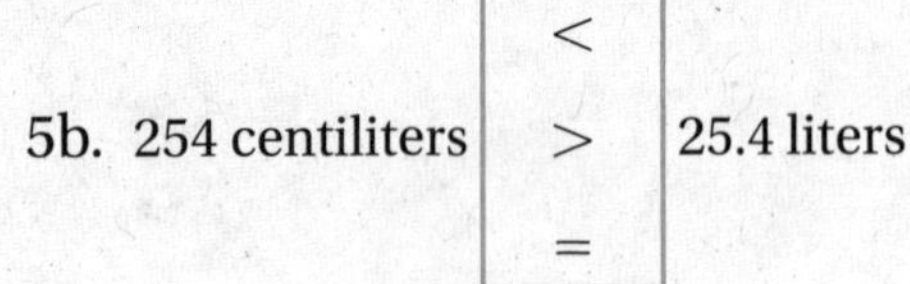

5b. 254 centiliters [< / > / =] 25.4 liters

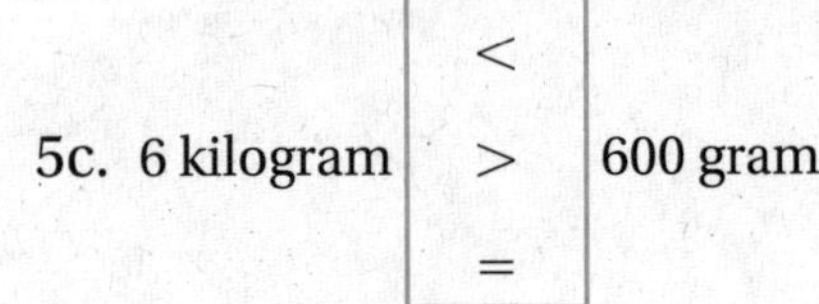

5c. 6 kilogram [< / > / =] 600 gram

6. A recipe calls for 16 fluid ounces of light whipping cream. If Anthony has 1 pint of whipping cream in his refrigerator, does he have enough for the recipe? Explain your answer using numbers and words.

7. For numbers 7a–7d, choose <, >, or =.

7a. 43 feet [< / > / =] 15 yards

7b. 5 tons [< / > / =] 5000 pounds

7c. 10 pints [< / > / =] 5 quarts

7d. 6 miles [< / > / =] 600 yards

8. The distance from Caleb's house to the school is 1.5 miles, and the distance from Ashlee's house to the school is 3,520 feet. Who lives closer to the school, Caleb or Ashlee? Use numbers and words to support your answer.

Name ______________________________

9. Write the mass measurements in order from least to greatest.

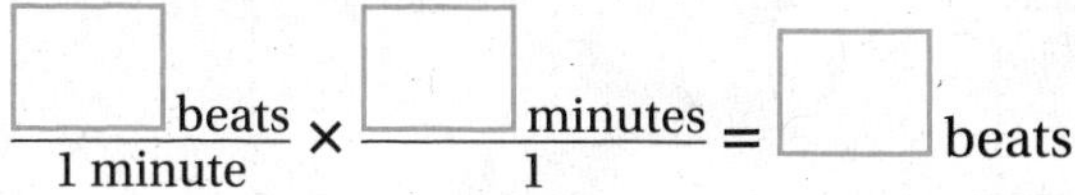

_____________ _____________ _____________

10. An elephant's heart beats 28 times per minute. Complete the product to find how many times its heart beats in 30 minutes.

$\frac{\square \text{ beats}}{1 \text{ minute}} \times \frac{\square \text{ minutes}}{1} = \square$ beats

11. The length of a rectangular football field, including both end zones, is 120 yards. The area of the field is 57,600 square feet. For numbers 11a–11d, select True or False for each statement.

11a. The width of the field is 480 yards. ○ True ○ False

11b. The length of the field is 360 feet. ○ True ○ False

11c. The width of the field is 160 feet. ○ True ○ False

11d. The area of the field is 6,400 square yards. ○ True ○ False

12. Harry received a package for his birthday. The package weighed 357,000 centigrams. Select the conversions that are equivalent to 357,000 centigrams. Mark all that apply.

(A) 3.57 kilograms

(B) 357 dekagrams

(C) 3,570 grams

(D) 3,570,000 decigrams

13. Mr. Martin wrote the following problem on the board.

Juanita's car has a gas mileage of 21 miles per gallon. How many miles can Juanita travel on 7 gallons of gas?

Alex used the expression $\frac{21 \text{ miles}}{1 \text{ gallon}} \times \frac{1}{7 \text{ gallons}}$ to find the answer. Explain Alex's mistake.

14. Mr. Chen filled his son's wading pool with 20 gallons of water.

20 gallons is equivalent to [80 / 60 / 40] quarts.

15. Nadia has a can of vegetables with a mass of 411 grams. Write equivalent conversions in the correct boxes.

4.11 41.1 0.411

kilograms	hectograms	dekagrams

16. Steve is driving 440 miles to visit the Grand Canyon. He drives at an average rate of 55 miles per hour. Explain how you can find the amount of time it will take Steve to get to the Grand Canyon.

Name ____________________

17. Lucy walks one time around the lake. She walks for 1.5 hours at an average rate of 3 miles per hour. What is the distance, in miles, around the lake?

__________ miles

18. The parking lot at a store has a width of 20 yards 2 feet and a length of 30 yards.

20 yards 2 feet

30 yards

Part A

Derrick says that the width could also be written as 22 feet. Explain whether you agree or disagree with Derrick.

Part B

The cost to repave the parking lot is $2 per square foot. Explain how much it would cost to repave the parking lot.

19. Jake is using a horse trailer to take his horses to his new ranch.

Part A

Complete the table by finding the weight, in pounds, of Jake's horse trailer and each horse.

	Weight (T)	Weight (lb)
Horse	0.5	
Trailer	1.25	

Part B

Jake's truck can tow a maximum weight of 5,000 pounds. What is the maximum number of horses he can take in his trailer at one time without going over the maximum weight his truck can tow? Use numbers and words to support your answer.

20. A rectangular room measures 13 feet by 132 inches. Tonya said the area of the room is 1,716 square feet. Explain her mistake, then find the area in square feet.

Critical Area

Expressions and Equations

CRITICAL AREA Writing, interpreting, and using expressions and equations

Great Smoky Mountains National Park is located in the states of North Carolina and Tennessee.

Project

The Great Outdoors

The Moores are planning a family reunion in Great Smoky Mountains National Park. This park includes several campgrounds and over 800 miles of hiking trails. Some trails lead to stunning views of the park's many waterfalls.

Get Started

The Moores want to camp at the park during their reunion. They will have 17 people in their group, and they want to spend no more than $100 on camping fees.

Decide how many and what type of campsites the Moores should reserve, and determine how many nights n the Moores can camp without going over budget. Show your work, and support your answer by writing and evaluating algebraic expressions.

Important Facts

Group Campsite
- Fee of $35 per night
- Holds up to 25 people

Individual Campsite
- Fee of $14 per night
- Holds up to 6 people

Completed by ________________

Chapter

7 Algebra: Expressions

Show What You Know

Check your understanding of important skills.

Name ______________________

▶ Addition Properties **Find the unknown number. Tell whether you used the Identity (or Zero) Property, Commutative Property, or Associative Property of Addition.**

1. $128 + \_\_\_\_ = 128$ ______

2. $(17 + 36) + 14 = 17 + (\_\_\_\_ + 14)$ ______

3. $23 + 15 = \_\_\_\_ + 23$ ______

4. $9 + (11 + 46) = (9 + \_\_\_\_) + 46$ ______

▶ Multiply with Decimals **Find the product.**

5. 1.5×7 ______

6. 5.83×6 ______

7. 3.7×0.8 ______

8. 0.27×0.9 ______

▶ Use Parentheses **Identify which operation to do first. Then find the value of the expression.**

9. $5 \times (3 + 6)$ ______

10. $(24 \div 3) - 2$ ______

11. $40 \div (20 - 16)$ ______

12. $(7 \times 6) + 5$ ______

Greg just moved into an old house and found a mysterious trunk in the attic. The lock on the trunk has a dial numbered 1 to 60. Greg found the note shown at right lying near the trunk. Be a Math Detective and help him figure out the three numbers needed to open the lock.

Lock Combination
Top Secret!

1st number: $3x$

2nd number: $5x - 1$

3rd number: $x^2 + 4$

Hint: $x = 6$

Personal Math Trainer
Online Assessment and Intervention

Vocabulary Builder

▶ Visualize It

Sort the review words into the bubble map.

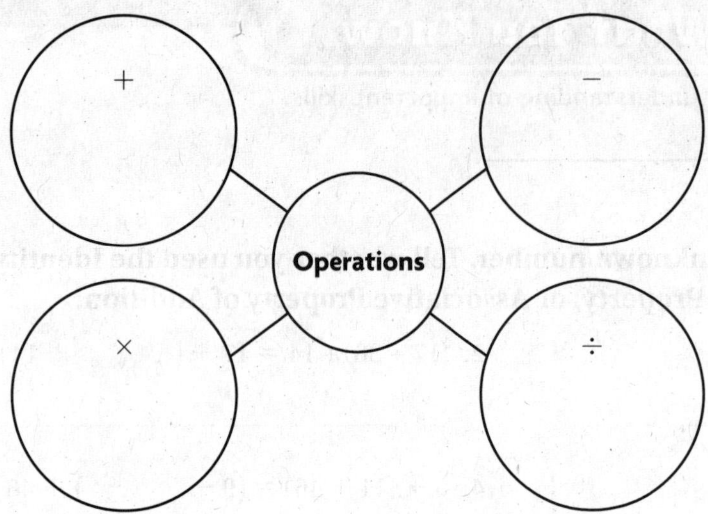

Review Words
addition
difference
division
multiplication
product
quotient
subtraction
sum

Preview Words
algebraic expression
base
coefficient
evaluate
numerical expression
terms
variable

▶ Understand Vocabulary

Complete the sentences using the preview words.

1. An exponent is a number that tells how many times a(n) ____________________ is used as a factor.
2. In the expression 4*a*, the number 4 is a(n) ____________________.
3. To ____________________ an expression, substitute numbers for the variables in the expression.
4. A mathematical phrase that uses only numbers and operation symbols is a(n) ____________________.
5. A letter or symbol that stands for one or more numbers is a(n) ____________________.
6. The parts of an expression that are separated by an addition or subtraction sign are the ____________________ of the expression.

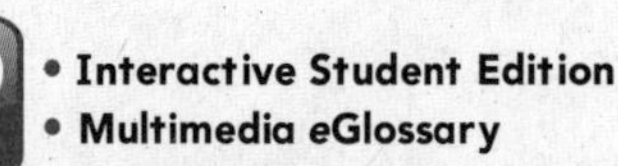

• Interactive Student Edition
• Multimedia eGlossary

Name ____________________

Exponents

Essential Question How do you write and find the value of expressions involving exponents?

Expressions and Equations—6.EE.1

MATHEMATICAL PRACTICES
MP.6, MP.7, MP.8

You can use an exponent and a base to show repeated multiplication of the same factor. An **exponent** is a number that tells how many times a number called the **base** is used as a repeated factor.

$\underbrace{5 \times 5 \times 5}_{\text{3 repeated factors}} = 5^3$ ← exponent, ↖ base

Math Idea

- 5^2 can be read "the 2nd power of 5" or "5 squared."
- 5^3 can be read "the 3rd power of 5" or "5 cubed."

Unlock the Problem — Real World

The table shows the number of bonuses a player can receive in each level of a video game. Use an exponent to write the number of bonuses a player can receive in level D.

Use an exponent to write 3 × 3 × 3 × 3.

The number _______ is used as a repeated factor.

3 is used as a factor _______ times.

Write the base and exponent. _______

So, a player can receive _______ bonuses in level D.

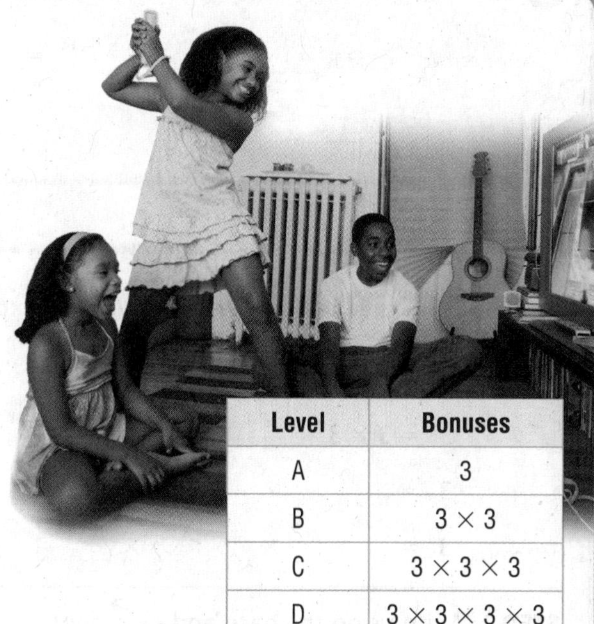

Level	Bonuses
A	3
B	3 × 3
C	3 × 3 × 3
D	3 × 3 × 3 × 3

Math Talk — Mathematical Practices

Explain how you know which number to use as the base and which number to use as the exponent.

Try This! **Use one or more exponents to write the expression.**

A 7 × 7 × 7 × 7 × 7

The number _______ is used as a repeated factor.

7 is used as a factor _______ times.

Write the base and exponent. _______

B 6 × 6 × 8 × 8 × 8

The numbers _______ and _______ are used as repeated factors.

6 is used as a factor _______ times.

8 is used as a factor _______ times.

Write each base with its own exponent. 6 ▢ × 8 ▢

Example 1 Find the value.

A 10^3

STEP 1 Use repeated multiplication to write 10^3.

The repeated factor is ______. 10^3 = ______ × ______ × ______

Write the factor ______ times.

STEP 2 Multiply.

Multiply each pair of factors, working from left to right. $10 \times 10 \times 10 =$ ______ $\times 10$

= ______

B 7^1

The repeated factor is ______. 7^1 = ______

Write the factor ______ time.

Mathematical Practices

In 10^3, what do you notice about the value of the exponent and the product? Is there a similar pattern in other powers of 10? **Explain.**

Example 2 Write 81 with an exponent by using 3 as the base.

STEP 1 Find the correct exponent.

Try 2. $3^2 = 3 \times 3 =$ ______

Try 3. $3^3 =$ ______ × ______ × ______ = ______

Try 4. $3^4 =$ ______ × ______ × ______ × ______ = ______

STEP 2 Write using the base and exponent.

81 = ______

1. Explain how to write repeated multiplication of a factor by using an exponent.

2. THINKSMARTER Is 5^2 equal to 2^5? Explain why or why not.

3. MATHEMATICAL PRACTICE 6 **Describe a Method** Describe how you could have solved the problem in Example 2 by using division.

Name ______________________

Share and Show

1. Write 2^4 by using repeated multiplication. Then find the value of 2^4.

$2^4 = 2 \times 2 \times$ _____ $\times$ _____ $=$ _____

Use one or more exponents to write the expression.

2. $7 \times 7 \times 7 \times 7$ _____

3. $5 \times 5 \times 5 \times 5 \times 5$ _____

4. $3 \times 3 \times 4 \times 4$ _____

Math Talk — Mathematical Practices

In 3^4, does it matter in what order you multiply the factors when finding the value? Explain.

On Your Own

Find the value.

5. 20^2 _____

6. 82^1 _____

7. 3^5 _____

8. Write 32 with an exponent by using 2 as the base.

_____

Complete the statement with the correct exponent.

9. $5^{\square} = 125$

10. $16^{\square} = 16$

11. $30^{\square} = 900$

12. MATHEMATICAL PRACTICE 8 Use Repeated Reasoning Find the values of 4^1, 4^2, 4^3, 4^4, and 4^5. Look for a pattern in your results and use it to predict the ones digit in the value of 4^6.

_____

13. THINKSMARTER Select the expressions that are equivalent to 32. Mark all that apply.

(A) 2^5

(B) 8^4

(C) $2^3 \times 4$

(D) $2 \times 4 \times 4$

Connect to Science

Bacterial Growth

Bacteria are tiny one-celled organisms that live almost everywhere on Earth. Although some bacteria cause disease, other bacteria are helpful to humans, other animals, and plants. For example, bacteria are needed to make yogurt and many types of cheese.

Under ideal conditions, a certain type of bacterium cell grows larger and then splits into 2 "daughter" cells. After 20 minutes, the daughter cells split, resulting in 4 cells. This splitting can happen again and again as long as conditions remain ideal.

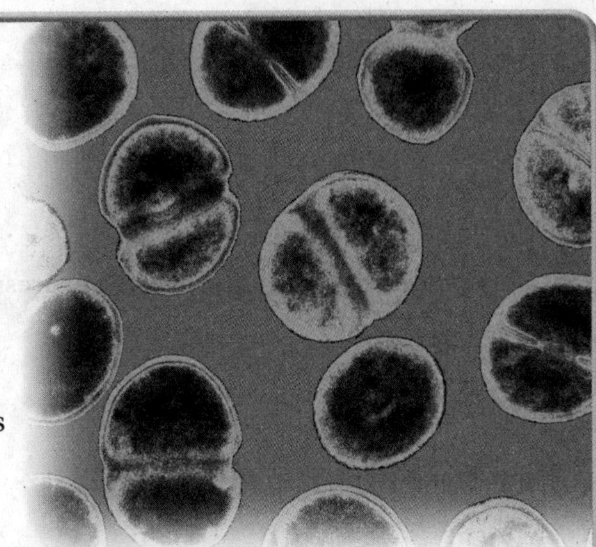

Complete the table.

Bacterial Growth	
Number of Cells	Time (min)
1	0
$2^1 = 2$	20
$2^2 = 2 \times 2 = 4$	40
$2^3 = \_\_\_ \times \_\_\_ \times \_\_\_ = \_\_\_$	60
$2^{\square} = 2 \times 2 \times 2 \times 2 = 16$	80
$2^5 = \_\_\_ \times \_\_\_ \times \_\_\_ \times \_\_\_ \times \_\_\_ = \_\_\_$	100
$2^{\square} = \_\_\_ \times \_\_\_ \times \_\_\_ \times \_\_\_ \times \_\_\_ \times \_\_\_ = \_\_\_$	120
$2^7 = 2 \times 2 \times 2 \times 2 \times 2 \times 2 \times 2 = \_\_\_$	___

Extend the pattern in the table above to answer 14 and 15.

14. GO DEEPER What power of 2 shows the number of cells after 3 hours? How many cells are there after 3 hours?

15. THINK SMARTER How many minutes would it take to have a total of 4,096 cells?

FOR MORE PRACTICE: Standards Practice Book

Name ______________________________

Evaluate Expressions Involving Exponents

Essential Question How do you use the order of operations to evaluate expressions involving exponents?

Expressions and Equations—6.EE.1

MATHEMATICAL PRACTICES
MP.4, MP.6

A **numerical expression** is a mathematical phrase that uses only numbers and operation symbols.

$3 + 16 \times 2^2$ $\qquad$ $4 \times (8 + 5^1)$ $\qquad$ $2^3 + 4$

You **evaluate** a numerical expression when you find its value. To evaluate an expression with more than one operation, you must follow a set of rules called the **order of operations**.

Order of Operations

1. Perform operations in parentheses.
2. Find the values of numbers with exponents.
3. Multiply and divide from left to right.
4. Add and subtract from left to right.

Unlock the Problem

An archer shoots 6 arrows at a target. Two arrows hit the ring worth 8 points, and 4 arrows hit the ring worth 4 points. Evaluate the expression $2 \times 8 + 4^2$ to find the archer's total number of points.

Follow the order of operations.

Write the expression. There are no parentheses.	$2 \times 8 + 4^2$
Find the value of numbers with exponents.	$2 \times 8 +$ ______
______ from left to right.	______ $+ 16$
Then add.	______

So, the archer scores a total of ______ points.

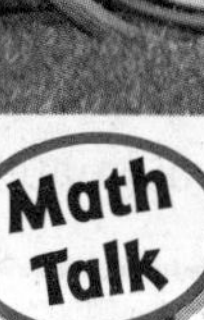

Mathematical Practices

Explain the order you should perform the operations to evaluate the expression $30 - 10 + 5^2$.

Try This! **Evaluate the expression $24 \div 2^3$.**

There are no parentheses.	$24 \div 2^3$
Find the value of numbers with exponents.	$24 \div$ ______
Then divide.	______

Example 1 Evaluate the expression $72 \div (13 - 4) + 5 \times 2^3$.

Write the expression.	$72 \div (13 - 4) + 5 \times 2^3$
Perform operations in ______________.	$72 \div$ ______ $+ 5 \times 2^3$
Find the values of numbers with ______________.	$72 \div 9 + 5 \times$ ______
Multiply and ______________ from left to right.	______ $+ 5 \times 8$
	$8 +$ ______
Then add.	______

Example 2

Last month, an online bookstore had approximately 10^5 visitors to its website. On average, each visitor bought 2 books. Approximately how many books did the bookstore sell last month?

STEP 1 Write an expression.

Think: The number of books sold is equal to the number of visitors times the number of books each visitor bought.

number of visitors | times | number of books bought

↓ ↓ ↓

10^5 $\times$ ______

STEP 2 Evaluate the expression.

Write the expression. There are no parentheses.	$10^5 \times 2$
Find the values of numbers with ______________.	______________ $\times 2$
Multiply.	______________

So, the bookstore sold approximately ______________ books last month.

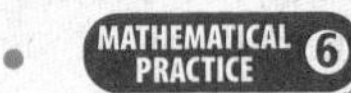

• **Explain** why the order of operations is necessary.

____

____

____

Name ______________________

Share and Show

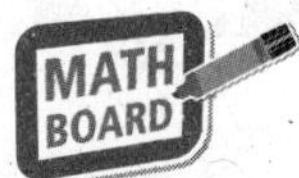

1. Evaluate the expression $9 + (5^2 - 10)$.

$9 + (5^2 - 10)$ Write the expression.

$9 + (\_\_\_\_ - 10)$ Follow the order of operations within the parentheses.

$9 + \_\_\_\_$

$\_\_\_\_$ Add.

Evaluate the expression.

2. $6 + 3^3 \div 9$

3. $(15 - 3)^2 \div 9$

4. $(8 + 9^2) - 4 \times 10$

Math Talk **Mathematical Practices**

Explain how the parentheses make the values of these expressions different: $(2^2 + 8) \div 4$ and $2^2 + (8 \div 4)$.

On Your Own

Evaluate the expression.

5. $10 + 6^2 \times 2 \div 9$

6. $6^2 - (2^3 + 5)$

7. $16 + 18 \div 9 + 3^4$

THINK SMARTER **Place parentheses in the expression so that it equals the given value.**

8. $10^2 - 50 \div 5$
value: 10

9. $20 + 2 \times 5 + 4^1$
value: 38

10. $28 \div 2^2 + 3$
value: 4

Problem Solving • Applications

Use the table for 11–13.

11. MATHEMATICAL PRACTICE 4 **Write an Expression** To find the cost of a window, multiply its area in square feet by the price per square foot. Write and evaluate an expression to find the cost of a knot window.

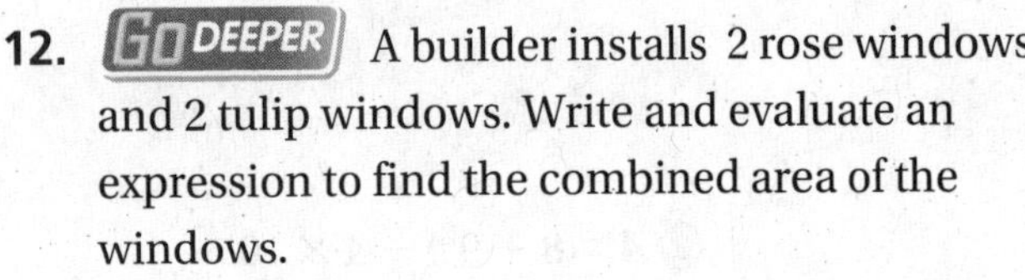

12. GO DEEPER A builder installs 2 rose windows and 2 tulip windows. Write and evaluate an expression to find the combined area of the windows.

Art Glass Windows		
Type	Area (square feet)	Price pe square fo
Knot	2^2	$27
Rose	3^2	$30
Tulip	4^2	$33

13. THINK SMARTER DeShawn bought a tulip window. Emma bought a rose window. Write and evaluate an expression to determine how much more DeShawn paid for his window than Emma paid for hers.

14. **What's the Error?** Darius wrote $17 - 2^2 = 225$. Explain his error.

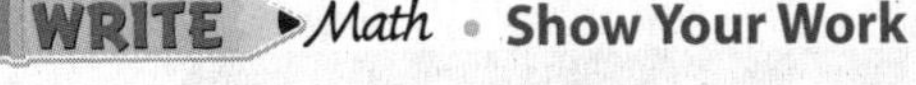

15. THINK SMARTER Ms. Hall wrote the expression $2 \times (3 + 5)^2 \div 4$ on the board. Shyann said the first step is to evaluate 5^2. Explain Shyann's mistake. Then evaluate the expression.

FOR MORE PRACTICE: Standards Practice Book

Name ______________________________

Write Algebraic Expressions

Essential Question How do you write an algebraic expression to represent a situation?

Expressions and Equations—6.EE.2a

MATHEMATICAL PRACTICES
MP.2, MP.4, MP.6

An **algebraic expression** is a mathematical phrase that includes at least one variable. A **variable** is a letter or symbol that stands for one or more numbers.

$x + 10$	$3 \times y$	$3 \times (a + 4)$
↑ variable	↑ variable	↑ variable

Math Idea

There are several ways to show multiplication with a variable. Each expression below represents "3 times y."

$3 \times y$ $3y$ $3(y)$ $3 \cdot y$

Unlock the Problem

An artist charges $5 for each person in a cartoon drawing. Write an algebraic expression for the cost in dollars for a drawing that includes p people.

Write an algebraic expression for the cost.

Think: cost for each person | times | number of ______

↓ ↓ ↓

______ $\times$ p

So, the cost in dollars is ______.

Math Talk | **Mathematical Practices**

Discuss why p is an appropriate variable for this problem. Would it be appropriate to select a different variable? Explain.

Try This! **On Mondays, a bakery adds 2 extra muffins for free with every muffin order. Write an algebraic expression for the number of muffins customers will receive on Mondays when they order m muffins.**

Think: muffins ordered | ______ | extra muffins on Mondays

↓ ↓ ↓

______ + 2

So, customers will receive ____________ muffins on Mondays.

Example 1 **The table at the right shows the number of points that items on a quiz are worth. Write an algebraic expression for the quiz score of a student who gets *m* multiple-choice items and *s* short-answer items correct.**

Quiz Scoring	
Item Type	**Points**
Multiple-choice	2
Short-answer	5

points for multiple-choice items ______ points for short-answer items

↓ ↓ ↓

$(2 \times m)$ + (______)

So, the student's quiz score is ____________ points.

Example 2 **Write an algebraic expression for the word expression.**

A **30 more than the product of 4 and *x***

Think: Start with the product of 4 and *x*. Then find 30 more than the product.

the product of 4 and *x* ______ × ______

30 more than the product ______ $+ 4x$

B **4 times the sum of *x* and 30**

Think: Start with the sum of *x* and 30. Then find 4 times the sum.

the sum of *x* and 30 ______ + ______

4 times the sum ______ $\times (x + 30)$

1. When you write an algebraic expression with two operations, how can you show which operation to do first?

____

2. THINK SMARTER One student wrote $4 + x$ for the word expression "4 more than *x*." Another student wrote $x + 4$ for the same word expression. Are both students correct? Justify your answer.

____

____

____

Name ______________________________

Share and Show

MATH BOARD

1. Write an algebraic expression for the product of 6 and p.

What operation does the word "product" indicate?

____

The expression is ______ $\times$ ______.

Write an algebraic expression for the word expression.

2. 11 more than e

____

3. 9 less than the quotient of n and 5

____

On Your Own

Math Talk — **Mathematical Practices**

Explain why $3x$ is an algebraic expression.

Write an algebraic expression for the word expression.

4. 20 divided by c

____

5. 8 times the product of 5 and t

____

6. There are 12 eggs in a dozen. Write an algebraic expression for the number of eggs in d dozen.

____

7. A state park charges a \$6.00 entry fee plus \$7.50 per night of camping. Write an algebraic expression for the cost in dollars of entering the park and camping for n nights.

____

8. MATHEMATICAL PRACTICE 7 **Look for Structure** At a bookstore, the expression $2c + 8g$ gives the cost in dollars of c comic books and g graphic novels. Next month, the store's owner plans to increase the price of each graphic novel by \$3. Write an expression that will give the cost of c comic books and g graphic novels next month.

____

Unlock the Problem

9. Martina signs up for the cell phone plan described at the right. Write an expression that gives the total cost of the plan in dollars if Martina uses it for m months.

SPECIAL OFFER
CELL PHONE PLAN!
Pay a low monthly fee of $50.
Receive $10 off your first month's fee.

a. What information do you know about the cell phone plan?

____

____

b. Write an expression for the monthly fee in dollars for m months.

____

c. What operation can you use to show the discount of $10 for the first month?

____

d. Write an expression for the total cost of the plan in dollars for m months.

____

10. THINK SMARTER A group of n friends evenly share the cost of dinner. The dinner costs $74. After dinner, each friend pays $11 for a movie. Write an expression to represent what each friend paid for dinner and the movie.

____

11. THINK SMARTER A cell phone company charges $40 per month plus $0.05 for each text message sent. Select the expressions that represent the cost in dollars for one month of cell phone usage and sending m text messages. Mark all that apply.

○ $40m + 0.05$

○ $40 + 0.05m$

○ 40 more than the product of 0.05 and m

○ the product of 40 and m plus 0.05

FOR MORE PRACTICE:
Standards Practice Book

Name ______________________________

Identify Parts of Expressions

Essential Question How can you describe the parts of an expression?

Expressions and Equations—6.EE.2b

MATHEMATICAL PRACTICES
MP.1, MP.2, MP.6

Unlock the Problem

At a gardening store, seed packets cost $2 each. Martin bought 6 packets of lettuce seeds and 7 packets of pea seeds. The expression $2 \times (6 + 7)$ represents the cost in dollars of Martin's seeds. Identify the parts of the expression. Then write a word expression for $2 \times (6 + 7)$.

- Explain how you could find the cost of each type of seed.

____

____

Describe the parts of the expression $2 \times (6 + 7)$.

Identify the operations in the expression.

multiplication and __________

Describe the part of the expression in parentheses, and tell what it represents.

- The part in parentheses shows the ______ of 6 and ______.
- The sum represents the number of packets of __________ seeds plus the number of packets of __________ seeds.

Describe the multiplication, and tell what it represents.

- One of the factors is ______. The other factor is the ______ of 6 and 7.
- The product represents the ______ per packet times the number of __________ Martin bought.

So, a word expression for $2 \times (6 + 7)$ is "the __________ of 2 and the ______ of ______ and 7."

- **MATHEMATICAL PRACTICE 6** **Attend to Precision** Explain how the expression $2 \times (6 + 7)$ differs from $2 \times 6 + 7$. Then write a word expression for $2 \times 6 + 7$.

____

____

____

The **terms** of an expression are the parts of the expression that are separated by an addition or subtraction sign. A **coefficient** is a number that is multiplied by a variable.

$4k + 5$ — The expression has two terms, $4k$ and 5. The coefficient of the term $4k$ is 4.

Example

Identify the parts of the expression. Then write a word expression for the algebraic expression.

A $2x + 8$

Identify the terms in the expression. — The expression is the sum of ______ terms.

The terms are ______ and 8.

Describe the first term. — The first term is the product of the coefficient ______ and the variable ______.

Describe the second term. — The second term is the number ______.

A word expression for $2x + 8$ is "8 more than the ____________ of ______ and *x*."

Math Talk — **Mathematical Practices**

Explain why the terms of the expression are $2x$ and 8, not x and 8.

B $3a - 4b$

Identify the terms in the expression. — The expression is the ____________ of 2 terms. The terms are ______ and ______.

Describe the first term. — The first term is the product of the ____________ 3 and the variable ______.

Describe the second term. — The second term is the product of the coefficient ______ and the variable ______.

A word expression for the algebraic expression is "the difference of ______ times ______ and 4 ____________ *b*.

Math Talk — **Mathematical Practices**

Identify the coefficient of y in the expression $12 + y$. Explain your reasoning.

Name ____________________

Share and Show

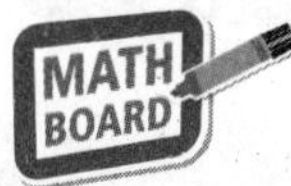

Identify the parts of the expression. Then write a word expression for the numerical or algebraic expression.

1. $7 \times (9 - 4)$

   The part in parentheses shows the __________ of ______ and ______.

   One factor of the multiplication is ______, and the other factor is $9 - 4$.

   Word expression: ____________________

2. $5m + 2n$

   ____

   ____

   ____

Mathematical Practices

Describe the expression $9 \times (a + b)$ as a product of two factors.

On Your Own

Practice: Copy and Solve **Identify the parts of the expression. Then write a word expression for the numerical or algebraic expression.**

3. $8 + (10 - 7)$
4. $1.5 \times 6 + 8.3$
5. $b + 12x$
6. $4a \div 6$

Identify the terms of the expression. Then give the coefficient of each term.

7. $k - 3d$

   ____

   ____

8. $0.5x + 2.5y$

   ____

   ____

9. MATHEMATICAL PRACTICE 2 **Connect Symbols and Words** Ava said she wrote an expression with three terms. She said the first term has the coefficient 7, the second term has the coefficient 1, and the third term has the coefficient 0.1. Each term involves a different variable. Write an expression that could be the expression Ava wrote.

   ____

Problem Solving • Applications

Use the table for 10–12.

10. GO DEEPER A football team scored 2 touchdowns and 2 extra points. Their opponent scored 1 touchdown and 2 field goals. Write a numerical expression for the points scored in the game.

____

11. Write an algebraic expression for the number of points scored by a football team that makes t touchdowns, f field goals, and e extra points.

____

12. Identify the parts of the expression you wrote in Exercise 11.

____

____

____

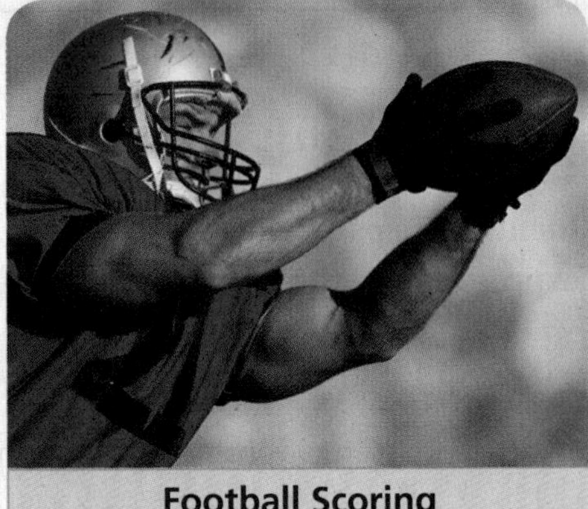

Football Scoring	
Type	**Points**
Touchdown	6
Field Goal	3
Extra Point	1

WRITE Math
Show Your Work

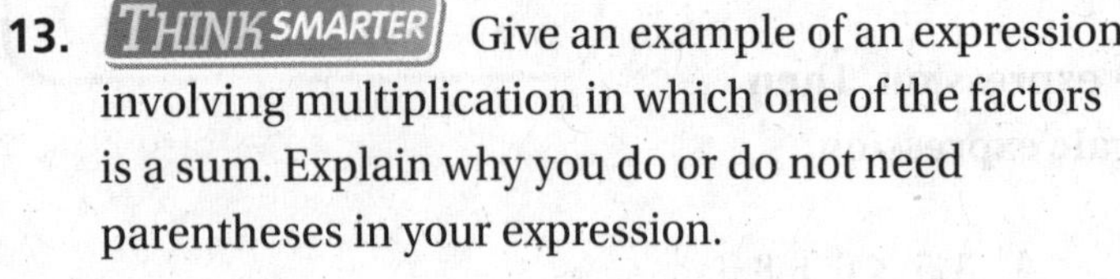

13. THINK SMARTER Give an example of an expression involving multiplication in which one of the factors is a sum. Explain why you do or do not need parentheses in your expression.

____

____

____

____

14. THINK SMARTER Kennedy bought a pounds of almonds at \$5 per pound and p pounds of peanuts at \$2 per pound. Write an algebraic expression for the cost of Kennedy's purchase.

____

FOR MORE PRACTICE:
Standards Practice Book

Name ______________________

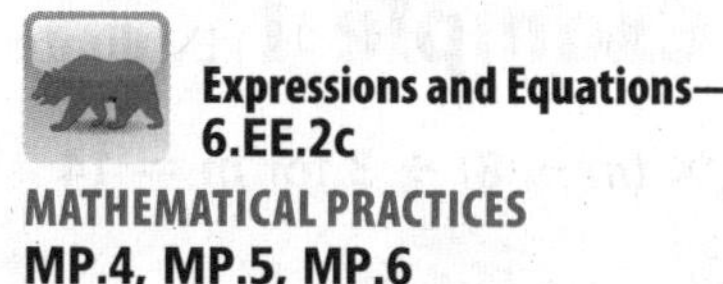

Evaluate Algebraic Expressions and Formulas

Essential Question How do you evaluate an algebraic expression or a formula?

Expressions and Equations—6.EE.2c

MATHEMATICAL PRACTICES
MP.4, MP.5, MP.6

To evaluate an algebraic expression, substitute numbers for the variables and then follow the order of operations.

Unlock the Problem (Real World)

Amir is saving money to buy an MP3 player that costs \$120. He starts with \$25, and each week he saves \$9. The expression $25 + 9w$ gives the amount in dollars that Amir will have saved after w weeks.

- Which operations does the expression $25 + 9w$ include?

  ____

- In what order should you perform the operations?

  ____

A **How much will Amir have saved after 8 weeks?**

Evaluate the expression for $w = 8$.

Write the expression. $25 + 9w$

Substitute 8 for w. $25 + 9 =$ ____

Multiply. $25 +$ ____

Add. ____

So, Amir will have saved \$ ____ after 8 weeks.

B **After how many weeks will Amir have saved enough money to buy the MP3 player?**

Make a table to find the week when the amount saved is at least \$120.

Week	Value of $25 + 9w$	Amount Saved
9	$25 + 9 \times 9 = 25 +$ ____ $= 106$	
10	$25 + 9 \times 10 = 25 +$ ____ $=$ ____	
11	$25 + 9 \times 11 = 25 +$ ____ $=$ ____	

So, Amir will have saved enough money for the MP3 player after ____ weeks.

Math Talk **Mathematical Practices**

Explain what it means to substitute a value for a variable.

Example 1 Evaluate the expression for the given value of the variable.

A $4 \times (m - 8) \div 3$ for $m = 14$

Write the expression.	$4 \times (m - 8) \div 3$
Substitute 14 for m.	$4 \times (\_\_\_\_ - 8) \div 3$
Perform operations in parentheses.	$4 \times \_\_\_\_ \div 3$
Multiply and divide from left to right.	$\_\_\_\_ \div 3$
	$\_\_\_\_$

B $3 \times (y^2 + 2)$ for $y = 4$

Write the expression.	$3 \times (y^2 + 2)$
Substitute 4 for y.	$3 \times (\_\_\_\_^2 + 2)$
Follow the order of operations within the parentheses.	$3 \times (\_\_\_\_ + 2)$
	$3 \times \_\_\_\_$
Multiply.	$\_\_\_\_$

ERROR Alert

When squaring a number, be sure to multiply the number by itself.

$4^2 = 4 \times 4$

Recall that a *formula* is a set of symbols that expresses a mathematical rule.

Example 2

The formula $P = 2\ell \times 2w$ gives the perimeter P of a rectangle with length ℓ and width w. What is the perimeter of a rectangular garden with a length of 2.4 meters and a width of 1.2 meters?

Write the expression for the perimeter of a rectangle.	$2\ell + 2w$
Substitute 2.4 for ℓ and ____ for w.	$2 \times \_\_\_\_ + 2 \times \_\_\_\_$
Multiply from left to right.	$\_\_\_\_ + 2 \times 1.2$
	$4.8 + \_\_\_\_$
Add.	$\_\_\_\_$

So, the perimeter of the garden is ____ meters.

Math Talk **Mathematical Practices**

Describe how evaluating an algebraic expression is different from evaluating a numerical expression.

Name ___________________________

Share and Show

1. Evaluate $5k + 6$ for $k = 4$.

Write the expression. ________

Substitute 4 for *k*. $5 \times$ ______ $+ 6$

Multiply. ______ $+ 6$

Add. ______

Evaluate the expression for the given value of the variable.

2. $m - 9$ for $m = 13$

3. $16 - 3b$ for $b = 4$

4. $p^2 + 4$ for $p = 6$

5. The formula $A = \ell w$ gives the area A of a rectangle with length ℓ and width w. What is the area in square feet of a United States flag with a length of 12 feet and a width of 8 feet?

Mathematical Practices

Tell what information you need to evaluate an algebraic expression.

On Your Own

Practice: Copy and Solve **Evaluate the expression for the given value of the variable.**

6. $7s + 5$ for $s = 3$

7. $21 - 4d$ for $d = 5$

8. $(t - 6)^2$ for $t = 11$

9. $6 \times (2v - 3)$ for $v = 5$

10. $2 \times (k^2 - 2)$ for $k = 6$

11. $5 \times (f - 32) \div 9$ for $f = 95$

12. GO DEEPER The formula $P = 4s$ gives the perimeter P of a square with side length s. How much greater is the perimeter of a square with a side length of $5\frac{1}{2}$ inches than a square with a side length of 5 inches?

Problem Solving • Applications Real World

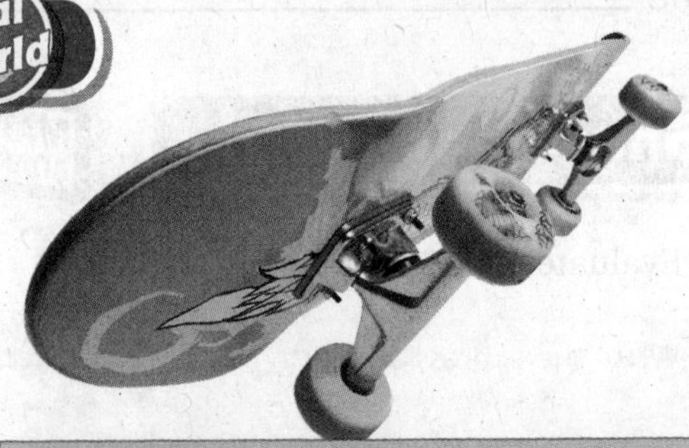

The table shows how much a company charges for skateboard wheels. Each pack of 8 wheels costs \$50. Shipping costs \$7 for any order. Use the table for 13–15.

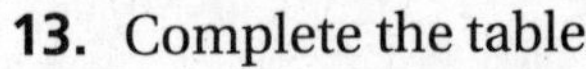

13. Complete the table.

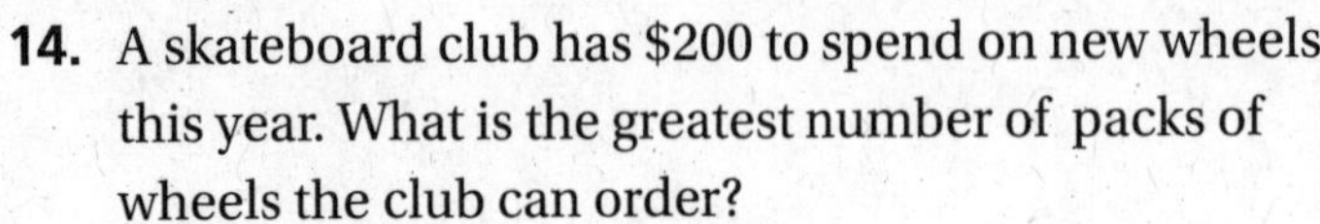

14. A skateboard club has \$200 to spend on new wheels this year. What is the greatest number of packs of wheels the club can order?

____

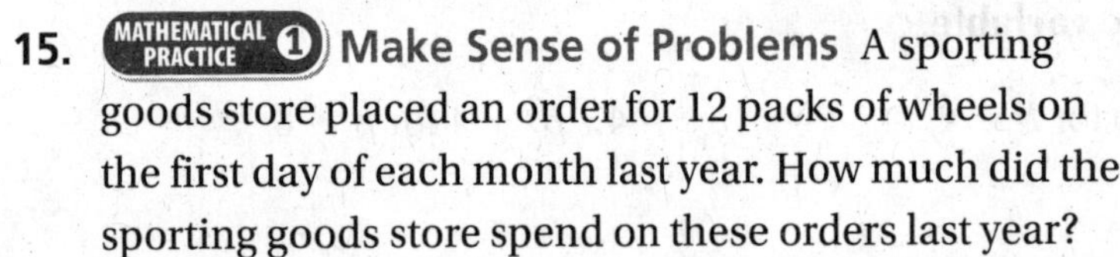

15. MATHEMATICAL PRACTICE 1 **Make Sense of Problems** A sporting goods store placed an order for 12 packs of wheels on the first day of each month last year. How much did the sporting goods store spend on these orders last year?

____

Costs for Skateboard Wheels

Packs	$50 \times n + 7$	Cost
1	$50 \times 1 + 7$	\$57
2		
3		
4		
5		

WRITE Math • Show Your Work •

16. THINK SMARTER **What's the Error?** Bob used these steps to evaluate $3m - 3 \div 3$ for $m = 8$. Explain his error.

$3 \times 8 - 3 \div 3 = 24 - 3 \div 3$

$= 21 \div 3$

$= 7$

____

____

____

____

17. THINK SMARTER The surface area of a cube can be found by using the formula $6s^2$, where s represents the length of the side of the cube.

The surface area of a cube that has a side length of 3 meters is [54 / 108 / 2,916] meters squared.

FOR MORE PRACTICE: Standards Practice Book

Name ________________________

Vocabulary

Vocabulary
coefficient
exponent
numerical expression

Choose the best term from the box to complete the sentence.

1. A(n) ________________ tells how many times a base is used as a factor. (p. 261)

2. The mathematical phrase $5 + 2 \times 18$ is an example of a(n) ________________. (p. 265)

Concepts and Skills

Find the value. (6.EE.1)

3. 5^4

4. 21^2

5. 8^3

Evaluate the expression. (6.EE.1)

6. $9^2 \times 2 - 4^2$

7. $2 \times (10 - 2) \div 2^2$

8. $30 - (3^3 - 8)$

Write an algebraic expression for the word expression. (6.EE.2a)

9. the quotient of c and 8

10. 16 more than the product of 5 and p

11. 9 less than the sum of x and 5

Evaluate the expression for the given value of the variable. (6.EE.2c)

12. $5 \times (h + 3)$ for $h = 7$

13. $2 \times (c^2 - 5)$ for $c = 4$

14. $7a - 4a$ for $a = 8$

15. The greatest value of any U.S. paper money ever printed is 10^5 dollars. What is this amount written in standard form? (6.EE.1)

16. A clothing store is raising the price of all its sweaters by \$3.00. Write an expression that could be used to find the new price of a sweater that originally cost d dollars. (6.EE.2a)

17. Kendra bought a magazine for \$3 and 4 paperback books for \$5 each. The expression $3 + 4 \times 5$ represents the total cost in dollars of her purchases. What are the terms in this expression? (6.EE.2b)

18. The expression $5c + 7m$ gives the number of people who can ride in c cars and m minivans. What are the coefficients in this expression? (6.EE.2b)

19. The formula $P = a + b + c$ gives the perimeter P of a triangle with side lengths a, b, and c. A triangular field has sides that measure 33 yards, 56 yards, and 65 yards. What is the perimeter of the field? (6.EE.2c)

Name ______________________________

Use Algebraic Expressions

Essential Question How can you use variables and algebraic expressions to solve problems?

Expressions and Equations—6.EE.6

MATHEMATICAL PRACTICES
MP.1, MP.2, MP.4

Sometimes you are missing a number that you need to solve a problem. You can represent a problem like this by writing an algebraic expression in which a variable represents the unknown number.

Unlock the Problem (Real World)

Rafe's flight from Los Angeles to New York took 5 hours. He wants to know the average speed of the plane in miles per hour.

A **Write an expression to represent the average speed of the plane.**

Use a variable to represent the unknown quantity.

Think: The plane's average speed is equal to the distance traveled divided by the time traveled.

Use a variable to represent the unknown quantity. — Let d represent the __________ traveled in units of __________.

Write an algebraic expression for the average speed. — $\frac{d \text{ mi}}{\square \text{ hr}}$

B **Rafe looks up the distance between Los Angeles and New York on the Internet and finds that the distance is 2,460 miles. Use this distance to find the average speed of Rafe's plane.**

Evaluate the expression for d = 2,460.

Write the expression. — $\frac{d \text{ mi}}{5 \text{ hr}}$

Substitute 2,460 for d. — $\frac{\square \text{ mi}}{5 \text{ hr}}$

Divide to find the unit rate. — $\frac{2{,}460 \text{ mi} \div \square}{5 \text{ hr} \div 5} = \frac{\square \text{ mi}}{1 \text{ hr}}$

So, the plane's average speed was __________ miles per hour.

Math Talk — **Mathematical Practices**

Explain how you could check whether you found the plane's average speed correctly.

In the problem on the previous page, the variable represented a single value—the distance in miles between Los Angeles and New York. In other situations, a variable may represent any number in a particular set of numbers, such as the set of positive numbers.

Example

Joanna makes and sells candles online. She charges \$7 per candle, and shipping is \$5 per order.

A Write an expression that Joanna can use to find the total cost for any candle order.

Think: The number of candles a customer buys will vary from order to order.

Let n represent the number of ________ a customer buys, where n is a whole number greater than 0.

The cost per order equals	the charge per candle	times	the number of candles	plus	the shipping charge.
	↓	↓	↓	↓	↓
	______	×	______	+	______

So, an expression for the total cost of a candle order is ________.

B In March, one of Joanna's customers placed an order for 4 candles. In May, the same customer placed an order for 6 candles. What was the total charge for both orders?

STEP 1 Find the charge in dollars for each order.

	March	**May**
Write the expression.	$7n + 5$	$7n + 5$
Substitute the number of candles ordered for n.	$7 \times$ ______ $+ 5$	$7 \times$ ______ $+ 5$
Follow the order of operations.	______ $+ 5$	______ $+ 5$
	______	______

STEP 2 Find the charge in dollars for both orders.

Add the charge in dollars for March to the charge in dollars for May.

______ + ______ = ______

So, the total charge for both orders was ______.

Math Talk **Mathematical Practices**

Explain why the value of the variable n in the Example is restricted to the set of whole numbers greater than 0.

Name ______________________________

Share and Show

MATH BOARD

Louisa read that the highest elevation of Mount Everest is 8,848 meters. She wants to know how much higher Mount Everest is than Mount Rainier. Use this information for 1–2.

1. Write an expression to represent the difference in heights of the two mountains. Tell what the variable in your expression represents.

2. Louisa researches the highest elevation of Mount Rainier and finds that it is 4,392 meters. Use your expression to find the difference in the mountains' heights.

Math Talk — **Mathematical Practices**

Explain whether the variable in Exercise 1 represents a single unknown number or any number in a particular set.

On Your Own

A muffin recipe calls for 3 times as much flour as sugar. Use this information for 3–5.

3. Write an expression that can be used to find the amount of flour needed for a given amount of sugar. Tell what the variable in your expression represents.

4. Use your expression to find the amount of flour needed when $\frac{3}{4}$ cup of sugar is used.

5. MATHEMATICAL PRACTICE 2 **Reason Quantitatively** Is the value of the variable in your expression restricted to a particular set of numbers? Explain.

Practice: Copy and Solve **Write an algebraic expression for each word expression. Then evaluate the expression for these values of the variable: $\frac{1}{2}$, 4, and 6.5.**

6. the quotient of p and 4

7. 4 less than the sum of x and 5

Problem Solving • Applications

Use the graph for 8–10.

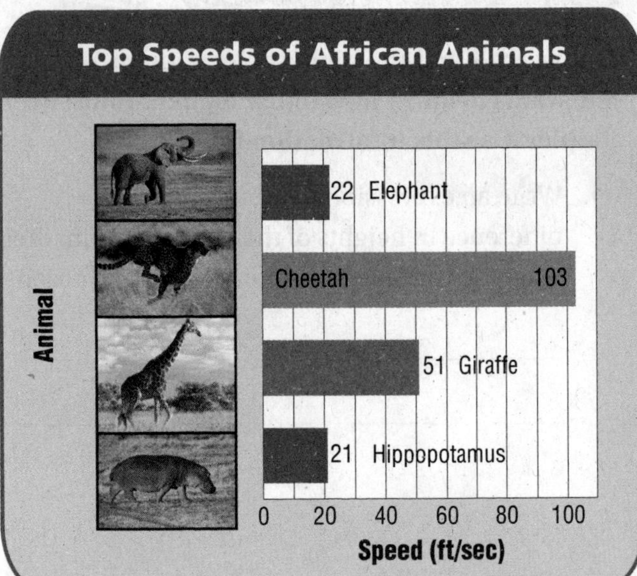

8. Write expressions for the distance in feet that each animal could run at top speed in a given amount of time. Tell what the variable in your expressions represents.

____

____

____

____

9. GO DEEPER How much farther could a cheetah run in 20 seconds at top speed than a hippopotamus could?

____

10. THINK SMARTER A giraffe runs at top speed toward a tree that is 400 feet away. Write an expression that represents the giraffe's distance in feet from the tree after s seconds.

____

Personal Math Trainer

11. THINK SMARTER + A carnival charges \$7 for admission and \$2 for each ride. An expression for the total cost of going to the carnival and riding n rides is $7 + 2n$.

Complete the table by finding the total cost of going to the carnival and riding n rides.

Number of rides, n	$7 + 2n$	Total Cost
1		
2		
3		
4		

WRITE Math • Show Your Work

FOR MORE PRACTICE: Standards Practice Book

Name ________________

Problem Solving • Combine Like Terms

Essential Question How can you use the strategy *use a model* to combine like terms?

Expressions and Equations—6.EE.3
MATHEMATICAL PRACTICES
MP.1, MP.4, MP.5

Like terms are terms that have the same variables with the same exponents. Numerical terms are also like terms.

Algebraic Expression	Terms	Like Terms
$5x + 3y - 2x$	$5x$, $3y$, and $2x$	$5x$ and $2x$
$8z^2 + 4z + 12z^2$	$8z^2$, $4z$, and $12z^2$	$8z^2$ and $12z^2$
$15 - 3x + 5$	15, $3x$, and 5	15 and 5

Unlock the Problem

Baseball caps cost \$9, and patches cost \$4. Shipping is \$8 per order. The expression $9n + 4n + 8$ gives the cost in dollars of buying caps with patches for n players. Simplify the expression $9n + 4n + 8$ by combining like terms.

Use the graphic organizer to help you solve the problem.

Read the Problem

What do I need to find?	What information do I need to use?	How will I use the information?
I need to simplify the expression ________.	I need to use the like terms $9n$ and ______.	I can use a bar model to find the sum of the ______ terms.

Solve the Problem

Draw a bar model to add ______ and ______. Each square represents n, or $1n$.

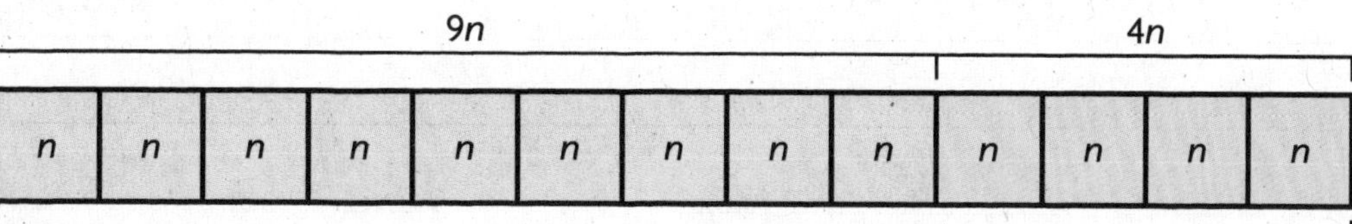

______n

The model shows that $9n + 4n =$ ______.

$9n + 4n + 8 =$ ______ $+ 8$

So, a simplified expression for the cost in dollars is ____________.

Mathematical Practices

Explain how the bar model shows that your answer is correct.

Try Another Problem

Paintbrushes normally cost \$5 each, but they are on sale for \$1 off. A paintbrush case costs \$12. The expression $5p - p + 12$ can be used to find the cost in dollars of buying p paintbrushes on sale plus a case for them. Simplify the expression $5p - p + 12$ by combining like terms.

Use the graphic organizer to help you solve the problem.

Read the Problem

What do I need to find?	What information do I need to use?	How will I use the information?

Solve the Problem

So, a simplified expression for the cost in dollars is ______.

1. **MATHEMATICAL PRACTICE 4** **Use Models** Explain how the bar model shows that your answer is correct.

2. Explain how you could combine like terms without using a model.

Name ________________________

Share and Show

MATH BOARD

1. Museum admission costs \$7, and tickets to the mammoth exhibit cost \$5. The expression $7p + 5p$ represents the cost in dollars for p people to visit the museum and attend the exhibit. Simplify the expression by combining like terms.

First, draw a bar model to combine the like terms.

Next, use the bar model to simplify the expression.

____

So, a simplified expression for the cost in dollars is ______.

2. THINK SMARTER **What if** the cost of tickets to the exhibit were reduced to \$3? Write an expression for the new cost in dollars for p people to visit the museum and attend the exhibit. Then simplify the expression by combining like terms.

____

3. A store receives tomatoes in boxes of 40 tomatoes each. About 4 tomatoes per box cannot be sold due to damage. The expression $40b - 4b$ gives the number of tomatoes that the store can sell from a shipment of b boxes. Simplify the expression by combining like terms.

____

4. Each cheerleading uniform includes a shirt and a skirt. Shirts cost \$12 each, and skirts cost \$18 each. The expression $12u + 18u$ represents the cost in dollars of buying u uniforms. Simplify the expression by combining like terms.

____

5. A shop sells vases holding 9 red roses and 6 white roses. The expression $9v + 6v$ represents the total number of roses needed for v vases. Simplify the expression by combining like terms.

____

Unlock the Problem

- Read the entire problem carefully before you begin to solve it.
- Check your answer by using a different method.

WRITE Math
Show Your Work

On Your Own

6. GO DEEPER Marco received a gift card. He used it to buy 2 bike lights for $10.50 each. Then he bought a handlebar bag for $18.25. After these purchases, he had $0.75 left on the card. How much money was on the gift card when Marco received it?

____

Sea snail shells

Scallop shell

7. Lydia collects shells. She has 24 sea snail shells, 16 conch shells, and 32 scallop shells. She wants to display the shells in equal rows, with only one type of shell in each row. What is the greatest number of shells Lydia can put in each row?

____

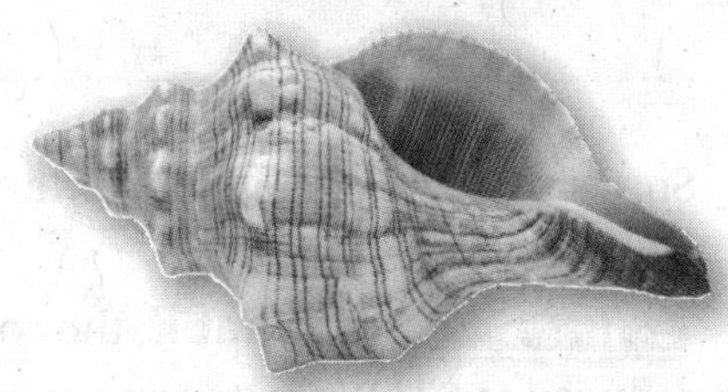

Conch shell

8. THINK SMARTER The three sides of a triangle measure $3x + 6$ inches, $5x$ inches, and $6x$ inches. Write an expression for the perimeter of the triangle in inches. Then simplify the expression by combining like terms.

____

9. MATHEMATICAL PRACTICE 3 **Verify the Reasoning of Others** Karina states that you can simplify the expression $20x + 4$ by combining like terms to get $24x$. Does Karina's statement make sense? Explain.

____

____

____

Personal Math Trainer

10. THINK SMARTER + Vincent is ordering accessories for his surfboard. A set of fins costs $24 each and a leash costs $15. The shipping cost is $4 per order. The expression $24b + 15b + 4$ can be used to find the cost in dollars of buying b fins and b leashes plus the cost of shipping.

For numbers 10a–10c, select True or False for each statement.

10a. The terms are $24b$, $15b$ and 4. ○ True ○ False

10b. The like terms are $24b$ and $15b$. ○ True ○ False

10c. The simplified expression is $43b$. ○ True ○ False

FOR MORE PRACTICE:
Standards Practice Book

Name ______________________________

Generate Equivalent Expressions

Essential Question How can you use properties of operations to write equivalent algebraic expressions?

Expressions and Equations—6.EE.3

MATHEMATICAL PRACTICES
MP.2, MP.3, MP.8

Equivalent expressions are equal to each other for any values of their variables. For example, $x + 3$ and $3 + x$ are equivalent. You can use properties of operations to write equivalent expressions.

$x + 3$	$3 + x$
$4 + 3$	$3 + 4$
7	7

Properties of Addition

Commutative Property of Addition If the order of terms changes, the sum stays the same.	$12 + a = a + 12$
Associative Property of Addition When the grouping of terms changes, the sum stays the same.	$5 + (8 + b) = (5 + 8) + b$
Identity Property of Addition The sum of 0 and any number is that number.	$0 + c = c$

Properties of Multiplication

Commutative Property of Multiplication If the order of factors changes, the product stays the same.	$d \times 9 = 9 \times d$
Associative Property of Multiplication When the grouping of factors changes, the product stays the same.	$11 \times (3 \times e) = (11 \times 3) \times e$
Identity Property of Multiplication The product of 1 and any number is that number.	$1 \times f = f$

Unlock the Problem

Nelson ran 2 miles, 3 laps, and 5 miles. The expression $2 + 3\ell + 5$ represents the total distance in miles Nelson ran, where ℓ is the length in miles of one lap. Write an equivalent expression with only two terms.

Rewrite the expression $2 + 3\ell + 5$ with only two terms.

The like terms are 2 and _______. Use the _______________ Property to reorder the terms. $2 + 3\ell + 5 = 3\ell +$ _______ $+ 5$

Use the _______________ Property to regroup the terms. $= 3\ell + ($_______ $+$ _______$)$

Add within the parentheses. $= 3\ell +$ _______

So, an equivalent expression for the total distance in miles is _______________.

Distributive Property

Multiplying a sum by a number is the same as multiplying each term by the number and then adding the products.

$5 \times (g + 9) = (5 \times g) + (5 \times 9)$

The Distributive Property can also be used with multiplication and subtraction. For example, $2 \times (10 - h) = (2 \times 10) - (2 \times h)$.

Example 1 Use properties of operations to write an expression equivalent to $5a + 8a - 16$ by combining like terms.

Use the Commutative Property of Multiplication to rewrite the like terms $5a$ and $8a$. $5a + 8a - 16 = a \times$ _____ $+ a \times$ _____ $- 16$

Use the Distributive Property to rewrite $a \times 5 + a \times 8$. $=$ _____ $\times (5 + 8) - 16$

Add within the parentheses. $= a \times$ _____ $- 16$

Use the Commutative Property of Multiplication to rewrite $a \times 13$. $=$ _____ $- 16$

So, the expression ________ is equivalent to $5a + 8a - 16$.

Example 2 Use the Distributive Property to write an equivalent expression.

A $6(y + 7)$

Use the Distributive Property. $6(y + 7) = (6 \times$ _____$) + (6 \times$ _____$)$

Multiply within the parentheses. $= 6y +$ _____

So, the expression ________ is equivalent to $6(y + 7)$.

Math Idea

When one factor in a product is in parentheses, you can leave out the multiplication sign. So, $6 \times (y + 7)$ can be written as $6(y + 7)$.

B $12a + 8b$

Find the greatest common factor (GCF) of the coefficients of the terms. The GCF of 12 and 8 is _____.

Write the first term, $12a$, as the product of the GCF and another factor. $12a + 8b = 4 \times 3a + 8b$

Write the second term, $8b$, as the product of the GCF and another factor. $= 4 \times 3a + 4 \times$ _____

Use the Distributive Property. $= 4 \times ($_____ $+ 2b)$

So, the expression ________ is equivalent to $12a + 8b$.

Math Talk **Mathematical Practices**

Give a different expression that is equivalent to $12a + 8b$. **Explain** what property you used.

Name ________________

Share and Show

Use properties of operations to write an equivalent expression by combining like terms.

1. $3.7r - 1.5r$ ______

2. $20a + 18 + 16a$ ______

3. $7s + 8t + 10s + 12t$ ______

Use the Distributive Property to write an equivalent expression.

4. $8(h + 1.5)$ ______

5. $4m + 4p$ ______

6. $3a + 9b$ ______

Math Talk **Mathematical Practices**

List three expressions with two terms that are equivalent to $5x$. Compare and discuss your list with a partner's.

On Your Own

Practice: Copy and Solve **Use the Distributive Property to write an equivalent expression.**

7. $3.5(w + 7)$

8. $\frac{1}{2}(f + 10)$

9. $4(3z + 2)$

10. $20b + 16c$

11. $30d + 18$

12. $24g - 8h$

13. MATHEMATICAL PRACTICE 4 **Write an Expression** The lengths of the sides of a triangle are $3t$, $2t + 1$, and $t + 4$. Write an expression for the perimeter (sum of the lengths). Then write an equivalent expression with 2 terms.

______

14. GO DEEPER Use properties of operations to write an expression equivalent to the sum of the expressions $3(g + 5)$ and $2(3g - 6)$.

______

Problem Solving • Applications (Real World)

15. THINK SMARTER **Sense or Nonsense** Peter and Jade are using what they know about properties to write an expression equivalent to $2 \times (n + 6) + 3$. Whose answer makes sense? Whose answer is nonsense? **Explain** your reasoning.

Peter's Work

Expression:	$2 \times (n + 6) + 3$
Associative Property of Addition:	$2 \times n + (6 + 3)$
Add within parentheses:	$2 \times n + 9$
Multiply:	$2n + 9$

Jade's Work

Expression:	$2 \times (n + 6) + 3$
Distributive Property:	$(2 \times n) + (2 \times 6) + 3$
Multiply within parentheses:	$2n + 12 + 3$
Associative Property of Addition:	$2n + (12 + 3)$
Add within parentheses:	$2n + 15$

For the answer that is nonsense, correct the statement.

16. THINK SMARTER Write the algebraic expression in the box that shows an equivalent expression.

$6(z + 5)$ $6z + 5z$ $2 + 6z + 3$

$6z + 5$	$11z$	$6z + 30$

FOR MORE PRACTICE: Standards Practice Book

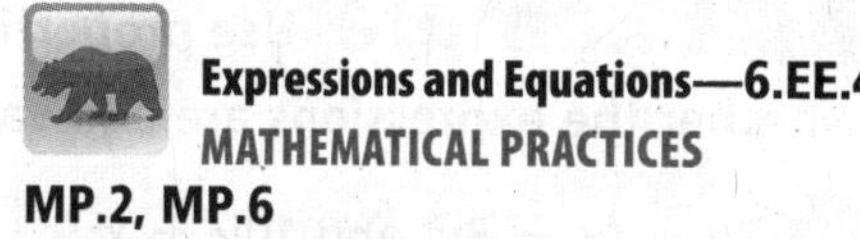

Name ______________________________

Identify Equivalent Expressions

Essential Question How can you identify equivalent algebraic expressions?

Expressions and Equations—6.EE.4
MATHEMATICAL PRACTICES
MP.2, MP.6

Unlock the Problem Real World

Each train on a roller coaster has 10 cars, and each car can hold 4 riders. The expression $10t \times 4$ can be used to find the greatest number of riders when there are t trains on the track. Is this expression equivalent to $14t$? Use properties of operations to support your answer.

- What is one property of operations that you could use to write an expression equivalent to $10t \times 4$?

____

____

Determine whether $10t \times 4$ is equivalent to $14t$.

The expression $14t$ is the product of a number and a variable, so rewrite $10t \times 4$ as a product of a number and a variable.

Use the Commutative Property of Multiplication. $10t \times 4 = 4 \times$ ______

Use the ______________ Property of Multiplication. $= (4 \times$ ______$) \times t$

Multiply within the parentheses. $=$ ______

Compare the expressions $40t$ and $14t$.

Think: 40 times a number is not equal to 14 times the number, except when the number is 0.

Check by choosing a value for t and evaluating $40t$ and $14t$.

Write the expressions.	$40t$	$14t$
Use 2 as a value for t.	$40 \times$ ______	$14 \times$ ______
Multiply. The expressions have different values.	______	______

So, the expressions $10t \times 4$ and $14t$ are ______________.

Math Talk **Mathematical Practices**

Explain why the expressions $7a$ and $9a$ are not equivalent, even though they have the same value when $a = 0$.

Example Use properties of operations to determine whether the expressions are equivalent.

A $7y + (x + 3y)$ **and** $10y + x$

The expression $10y + x$ is a sum of two terms, so rewrite $7y + (x + 3y)$ as a sum of two terms.

Use the Commutative Property of Addition to rewrite $x + 3y$. $7y + (x + 3y) = 7y + (\_\_\_\_ + \_\_\_\_)$

Use the ________ Property of Addition to group like terms. $= (\_\_\_\_ + 3y) + x$

Combine like terms. $= \_\_\_\_ + x$

Compare the expressions $10y + x$ and $10y + x$: They are the same.

So, the expressions $7y + (x + 3y)$ and $10y + x$ are ________.

Math Talk **Mathematical Practices**

Explain how you can decide whether two algebraic expressions are equivalent.

B $10(m + n)$ **and** $10m + n$

The expression $10m + n$ is a sum of two terms, so rewrite $10(m + n)$ as a sum of two terms.

Use the Distributive Property. $10(m + n) = (10 \times \_\_\_\_) + (10 \times \_\_\_\_)$

Multiply within the parentheses. $= 10m + \_\_\_\_$

Compare the expressions $10m + 10n$ and $10m + n$.

Think: The first terms of both expressions are ________, but the second terms are different.

Check by choosing values for m and n and evaluating $10m + 10n$ and $10m + n$.

	$10m + 10n$	$10m + n$
Write the expressions.	$10m + 10n$	$10m + n$
Use 2 as a value for m and 4 as a value for n.	$10 \times \_\_\_\_ + 10 \times \_\_\_\_$	$10 \times \_\_\_\_ + \_\_\_\_$
Multiply.	$\_\_\_\_ + \_\_\_\_$	$\_\_\_\_ + \_\_\_\_$
Add. The expressions have different values.	____	____

So, the expressions $10(m + n)$ and $10m + n$ are ________.

Math Talk **Mathematical Practices**

Explain how you know that the terms $10n$ and n from Part B are not equivalent.

Name ____________________

Share and Show

Use properties of operations to determine whether the expressions are equivalent.

1. $7k + 4 + 2k$ and $4 + 9k$

Rewrite $7k + 4 + 2k$. Use the Commutative Property of Addition. $7k + 4 + 2k = 4 +$ ______ $+ 2k$

Use the Associative Property of Addition. $= 4 + ($______ $+$ ______$)$

Add like terms. $= 4 +$ ______

The expressions $7k + 4 + 2k$ and $4 + 9k$ are ______.

2. $9a \times 3$ and $12a$

______

3. $8p + 0$ and $8p \times 0$

______

4. $5(a + b)$ and $(5a + 2b) + 3b$

______

Math Talk — **Mathematical Practices**

Explain how you can use logical reasoning to show that $x + 5$ is not equivalent to $x + 8$.

On Your Own

Use properties of operations to determine whether the expressions are equivalent.

5. $3(v + 2) + 7v$ and $16v$

______

6. $14h + (17 + 11h)$ and $25h + 17$

______

7. $4b \times 7$ and $28b$

______

8. GO DEEPER Each case of dog food contains c cans. Each case of cat food contains 12 cans. Four students wrote the expressions below for the number of cans in 6 cases of dog food and 1 case of cat food. Which of the expressions are correct?

$6c + 12$ $6c \times 12$ $6(c + 2)$ $(2c + 4) \times 3$

______

Problem Solving • Applications (Real World)

Use the table for 9–11.

Collectible Cards	
Type	**Number per Packet**
Baseball	b
Cartoon	c
Movie	m
Animal	a

9. Marcus bought 4 packets of baseball cards and 4 packets of animal cards. Write an algebraic expression for the total number of cards Marcus bought.

____

10. MATHEMATICAL PRACTICE 3 **Make Arguments** Is the expression for the number of cards Marcus bought equivalent to $4(a + b)$? Justify your answer.

____

____

____

____

WRITE ▶Math • Show Your Work •

11. THINK SMARTER Angelica buys 3 packets of movie cards and 6 packets of cartoon cards and adds these to the 3 packets of movie cards she already has. Write three equivalent algebraic expressions for the number of cards Angelica has now.

____

____

12. THINK SMARTER Select the expressions that are equivalent to $3(x + 2)$. Mark all that apply.

Ⓐ $3x + 6$

Ⓑ $3x + 2$

Ⓒ $5x$

Ⓓ $x + 5$

 FOR MORE PRACTICE: Standards Practice Book

Name ____________________

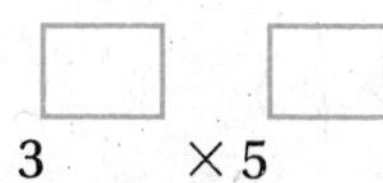

Chapter 7 Review/Test

1. Use exponents to write the expression.

$3 \times 3 \times 3 \times 3 \times 5 \times 5$

$3^{\square} \times 5^{\square}$

2. A plumber charges $10 for transportation and $55 per hour for repairs. Write an expression that can be used to find the cost in dollars for a repair that takes h hours.

____

3. Ellen is 2 years older than her brother Luke. Let k represent Luke's age. Identify the expression that can be used to find Ellen's age.

Ⓐ $k - 2$

Ⓑ $k + 2$

Ⓒ $2k$

Ⓓ $\frac{k}{2}$

4. Write 4^3 using repeated multiplication. Then find the value of 4^3.

____

5. Jasmine is buying beans. She bought r pounds of red beans that cost $3 per pound and b pounds of black beans that cost $2 per pound. The total amount of her purchase is given by the expression $3r + 2b$. Select the terms of the expression. Mark all that apply.

Ⓐ 2

Ⓑ $2b$

Ⓒ 3

Ⓓ $3r$

GO DIGITAL Assessment Options Chapter Test

6. Choose the number that makes the sentence true.
The formula $V = s^3$ gives the volume V of a cube with side length s.
The volume of a cube that has a side length of 8 inches

is [24 / 64 / 512] inches cubed.

7. Liang is ordering new chairs and cushions for his dining room table. A new chair costs \$88 and a new cushion costs \$12. Shipping costs \$34. The expression $88c + 12c + 34$ gives the total cost for buying c sets of chairs and cushions. Simplify the expression by combining like terms.

____

8. Mr. Ruiz writes the expression $5 \times (2 + 1)^2 \div 3$ on the board. Chelsea says the first step is to evaluate 1^2. Explain Chelsea's mistake. Then evaluate the expression.

9. Jake writes this word expression.

the product of 7 and m

Write an algebraic expression for the word expression. Then, evaluate the expression for $m = 4$. Show your work.

Name ____________________

10. Sora has some bags that each contain 12 potatoes. She takes 3 potatoes from each bag. The expression $12p - 3p$ represents the number of potatoes p left in the bags. Simplify the expression by combining like terms. Draw a line to match the expression with the simplified expression.

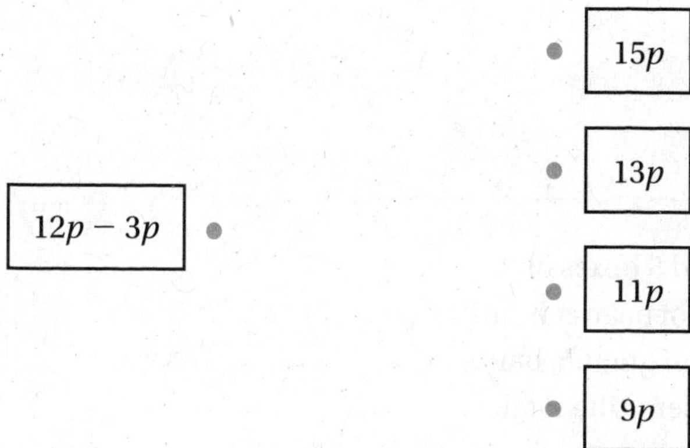

11. Logan works at a florist. He earns $600 per week plus $5 for each floral arrangement he delivers. The expression $600 + 5f$ gives the amount in dollars that Logan earns for delivering f floral arrangements. How much will Logan earn if he delivers 45 floral arrangements in one week? Show your work.

12. Choose the word that makes the sentence true.
Dara wrote the expression $7 \times (d + 4)$ in her notebook. She used the

Associative Commutative Distributive	Property to write the equivalent expression $7d + 28$.

13. Use properties of operations to determine whether $5(n + 1) + 2n$ and $7n + 1$ are equivalent expressions.

14. Alisha buys 5 boxes of peanut butter granola bars and 5 boxes of cinnamon granola bars. Let p represent the number of peanut butter granola bars and c represent the number of cinnamon granola bars. Jaira and Emma each write an expression that represents the total number of granola bars Alisha bought. Are the expressions equivalent? Justify your answer.

Jaira	Emma
$5p + 5c$	$5(p + c)$

15. Abe is 3 inches taller than Chen. Select the expressions that represent Abe's height if Chen's height is h inches. Mark all that apply.

- ○ $h - 3$
- ○ $h + 3$
- ○ the sum of h and 3
- ○ the difference between h and 3

16. Write the algebraic expression in the box that shows an equivalent expression.

$3(k + 2)$ $3k + 2k$ $2 + 6k + 3$

$6k + 5$	$5k$	$3k + 6$

Name ___________________________________

17. Draw a line to match the property with the statement that shows the same property.

Associative Property of Addition •	• $0 + 14 = 14$
Commutative Property of Addition •	• $14 + b = b + 14$
Identity Property of Addition •	• $6 + (8 + b) = (6 + 8) + b$

18. A bike rental company charges $10 to rent a bike plus $2 for each hour the bike is rented. An expression for the total cost of renting a bike for h hours is $10 + 2h$. Complete the table to find the total cost of renting a bike for h hours.

Number of Hours, h	$10 + 2h$	Total Cost
1	$10 + 2 \times 1$	
2		
3		
4		

19. An online sporting goods store charges $12 for a pair of athletic socks. Shipping is $2 per order.

Part A

Write an expression that Hana can use to find the total cost in dollars for ordering n pairs of socks.

____

Part B

Hana orders 3 pairs of athletic socks and her friend, Charlie, orders 2 pairs of athletic socks. What is the total cost, including shipping, for both orders? Show your work.

20. Fernando evaluates the expression $(6 + 2)^2 - 4 \times 3$.

Part A

Fernando shows his work on the board. Use numbers and words to explain his mistake.

$(6 + 2)^2 - 4 \times 3$

$(6 + 4) - 4 \times 3$

$10 - 4 \times 3$

6×3

18

Part B

Evaluate the expression $(6 + 2)^2 - 4 \times 3$ using the order of operations.

Chapter 8

Algebra: Equations and Inequalities

Show What You Know

Check your understanding of important skills.

Name ______________________________

Multiplication Properties **Find the unknown number. Write which multiplication property you used.**

1. $42 \times$ _____ $= 42$

____

2. $9 \times 6 =$ _____ $\times 9$

____

Evaluate Algebraic Expressions **Evaluate the expression.**

3. $4a - 2b$ for $a = 5$ and $b = 3$

____

4. $7x + 9y$ for $x = 7$ and $y = 1$

____

5. $8c \times d - 6$ for $c = 10$ and $d = 2$

____

6. $4s \div t + 10$ for $s = 9$ and $t = 3$

____

Add Fractions and Decimals **Find the sum. Write the sum in simplest form.**

7. $35.68 + 17.84 =$ _____

8. $24.38 + 25.3 =$ _____

9. $\frac{3}{4} + \frac{1}{8} =$ _____

10. $\frac{2}{5} + \frac{1}{4} =$ _____

The equation $m = 19.32v$ can be used to find the mass m in grams of a pure gold coin with volume v in cubic centimeters. Carl has a coin with a mass of 37.8 grams. The coin's volume is 2.1 cubic centimeters. Be a Math Detective and decide if the coin could be pure gold. Explain your reasoning.

Personal Math Trainer
Online Assessment and Intervention

Vocabulary Builder

Visualize It

Use the review words to complete the tree diagram. You may use some words more than once.

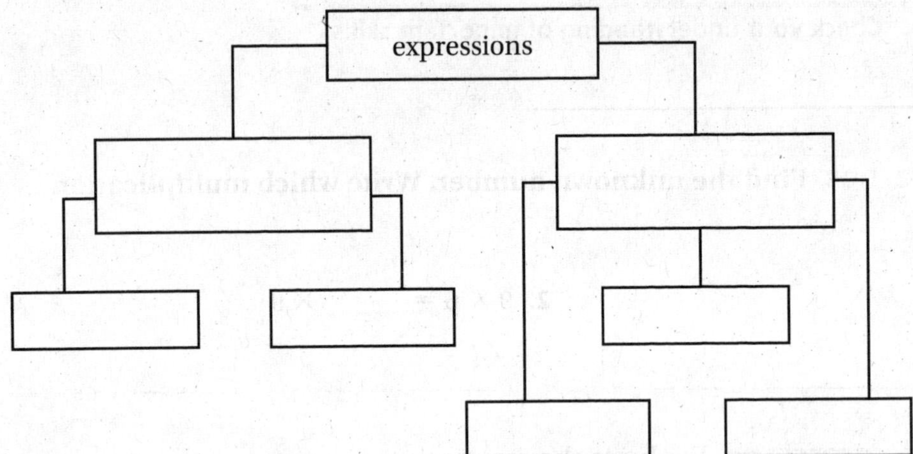

Review Words
algebraic expressions
numbers
numerical expressions
operations
variables

Preview Words
Addition Property of Equality
equation
inequality
inverse operations
solution of an equation
Subtraction Property of Equality

Understand Vocabulary

Draw a line to match the preview word with its definition.

Preview Words	Definitions
1. Addition Property of Equality	operations that undo each other
2. inequality	a value of a variable that makes an equation true
3. inverse operations	property that states that if you add the same number to both sides of an equation, the two sides will remain equal
4. equation	a mathematical statement that compares two expressions by using the symbol <, >, ≤, ≥, or ≠
5. solution of an equation	property that states that if you subtract the same number from both sides of an equation, the two sides will remain equal
6. Subtraction Property of Equality	a statement that two mathematical expressions are equal

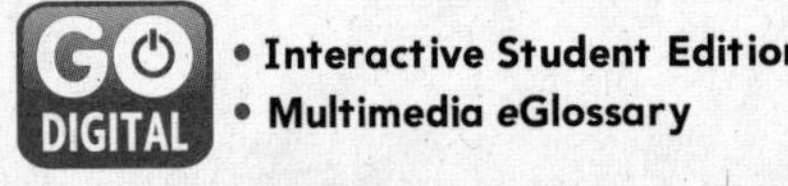

- Interactive Student Edition
- Multimedia eGlossary

Name ________________________________

Solutions of Equations

Essential Question How do you determine whether a number is a solution of an equation?

Expressions and Equations—6.EE.5

MATHEMATICAL PRACTICES
MP.2, MP.4, MP.6

An **equation** is a statement that two mathematical expressions are equal. These are examples of equations:

$8 + 12 = 20$ $\quad$ $14 = a - 3$ $\quad$ $2d = 14$

A **solution of an equation** is a value of a variable that makes an equation true.

$x + 3 = 5$ $\quad$ $x = 2$ is the solution of the equation because $2 + 3 = 5$.

Unlock the Problem — Real World

In the 2009–2010 season, the women's basketball team of Duke University lost 5 of their 29 games. The equation $w + 5 = 29$ can be used to find the team's number of wins w. Determine whether $w = 14$ or $w = 24$ is a solution of the equation, and tell what the solution means.

Use substitution to determine the solution.

STEP 1 Check whether $w = 14$ is a solution.

Write the equation. $\quad w + 5 = 29$

Substitute 14 for w. $\quad$ ______ $+ 5 \stackrel{?}{=} 29$

Add. $\quad$ ______ $\neq 29$

The equation is not true when $w = 14$, so $w = 14$ is not a solution.

Math Idea

The symbol $\neq$ means "is not equal to."

STEP 2 Check whether $w = 24$ is a solution.

Write the equation. $\quad w + 5 = 29$

Substitute 24 for w. $\quad$ ______ $+ 5 \stackrel{?}{=} 29$

Add. $\quad$ ______ $= 29$

The equation is true when $w = 24$, so $w = 24$ is a solution.

So, the solution of the equation $w + 5 = 29$ is $w =$ ______,

which means that the team won ______ games.

Math Talk — **Mathematical Practices**

Describe how an algebraic equation, such as $x + 1 = 4$, is different from a numerical equation, such as $3 + 1 = 4$.

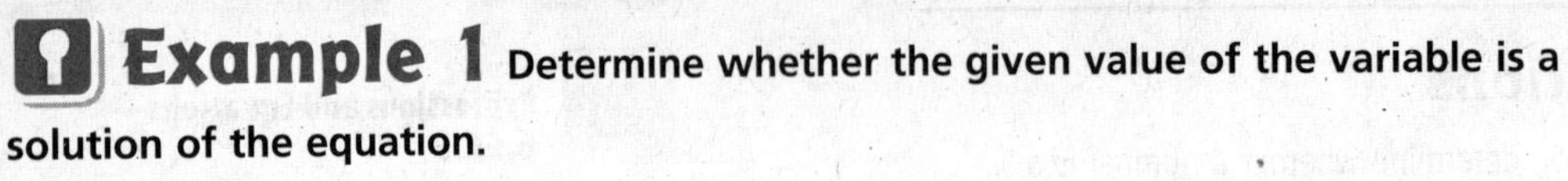

Example 1 **Determine whether the given value of the variable is a solution of the equation.**

A $x - 0.7 = 4.3$; $x = 3.6$

Write the equation. $x - 0.7 = 4.3$

Substitute the given value for the variable. $\_\_\_\_\_ - 0.7 \stackrel{?}{=} 4.3$

Subtract. Write = or ≠. $\_\_\_\_\_ \bigcirc 4.3$

The equation ________ true when $x = 3.6$, so $x = 3.6$

________ a solution.

B $\frac{1}{3}a = \frac{1}{4}$; $a = \frac{3}{4}$

Write the equation. $\frac{1}{3}a = \frac{1}{4}$

Substitute the given value for the variable. $\frac{1}{3} \times \_\_\_\_\_ \stackrel{?}{=} \frac{1}{4}$

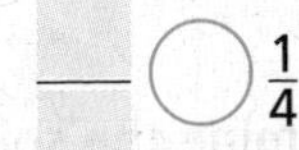

Simplify factors and multiply. Write = or ≠. $\_\_\_\_\_ \bigcirc \frac{1}{4}$

The equation _____ true when $a = \frac{3}{4}$, so $a = \frac{3}{4}$

_____ a solution.

Example 2 **The sixth-grade class president serves a term of 8 months. Janice has already served 5 months of her term as class president. The equation $m + 5 = 8$ can be used to determine the number of months m Janice has left. Use mental math to find the solution of the equation.**

Think: What number plus 5 is equal to 8? _____ plus 5 is equal to 8.

Use substitution to check whether $m = 3$ is a solution.

Write the equation. $m + 5 = 8$

Substitute 3 for m. $\_\_\_\_\_ + 5 \stackrel{?}{=} 8$

Add. Write = or ≠. $\_\_\_\_\_ \bigcirc 8$

So, $m =$ _____ is the solution of the equation, and

_____ months of Janice's term remain.

Mathematical Practices

Give an example of an equation whose solution is $y = 7$. **Explain** how you know that the equation has this solution.

Name ________________

Share and Show

Determine whether the given value of the variable is a solution of the equation.

1. $x + 12 = 29; x = 7$

   ______ $+ 12 \stackrel{?}{=} 29$

   ______ $\neq 29$

   ______

2. $n - 13 = 2; n = 15$

   ______

3. $\frac{1}{2}c = 14; c = 28$

   ______

4. $m + 2.5 = 4.6; m = 2.9$

   ______

5. $d - 8.7 = 6; d = 14.7$

   ______

6. $k - \frac{3}{5} = \frac{1}{10}; k = \frac{7}{10}$

   ______

Mathematical Practices

Explain why $2x - 6$ is not an equation.

On Your Own

Determine whether the given value of the variable is a solution of the equation.

7. $17.9 + v = 35.8; v = 17.9$

   ______

8. $c + 35 = 57; c = 32$

   ______

9. $18 = \frac{2}{3}h; h = 12$

   ______

Practice: Copy and Solve **Use mental math to find the solution of the equation. Use substitution to check your answer.**

10. $x + 5 = 12$

11. $t - 3 = 6$

12. $8z = 40$

13. Antonia pays for a cat toy with a $10 bill and receives $4.35 in change. The equation $10 - c = 4.35$ gives the cost in dollars of the cat toy. Determine whether $c = 5.35$, $c = 5.65$, or $c = 6.35$ is a solution of the equation, and tell what the solution means.

______

Problem Solving • Applications

Use the table for 14–16.

Length of Day

Planet	Length of Day (hours)
Earth	24.0
Mars	24.7
Jupiter	9.9

14. MATHEMATICAL PRACTICE 2 **Connect Symbols and Words** The length of a day on Saturn is 14 hours less than a day on Mars. The equation $24.7 - s = 14$ gives the length s in hours of a day on Saturn. Determine whether $s = 9.3$ or $s = 10.7$ is a solution of the equation, and tell what the solution means.

____

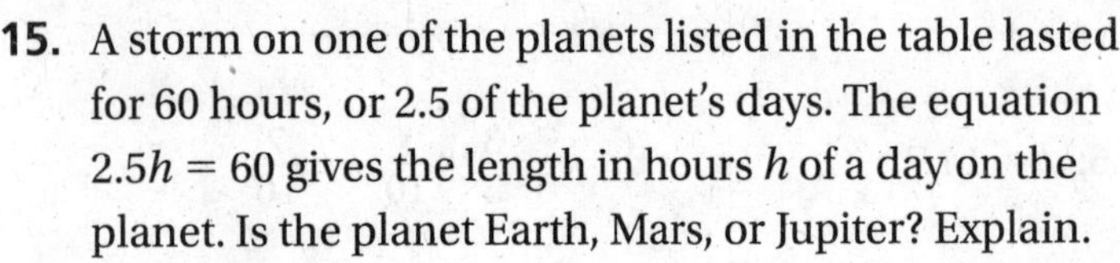

15. A storm on one of the planets listed in the table lasted for 60 hours, or 2.5 of the planet's days. The equation $2.5h = 60$ gives the length in hours h of a day on the planet. Is the planet Earth, Mars, or Jupiter? Explain.

____

____

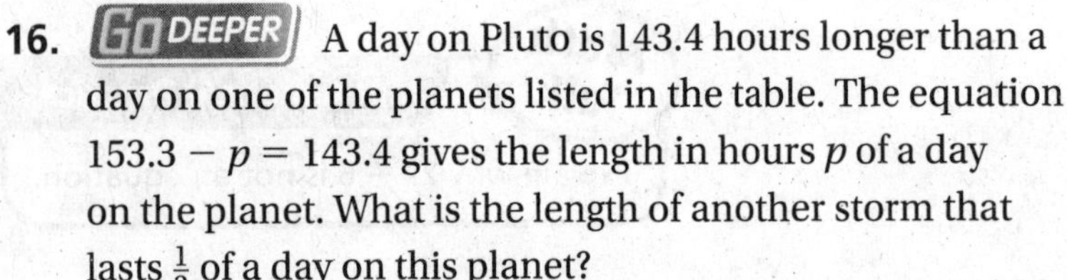

16. GO DEEPER A day on Pluto is 143.4 hours longer than a day on one of the planets listed in the table. The equation $153.3 - p = 143.4$ gives the length in hours p of a day on the planet. What is the length of another storm that lasts $\frac{1}{3}$ of a day on this planet?

____

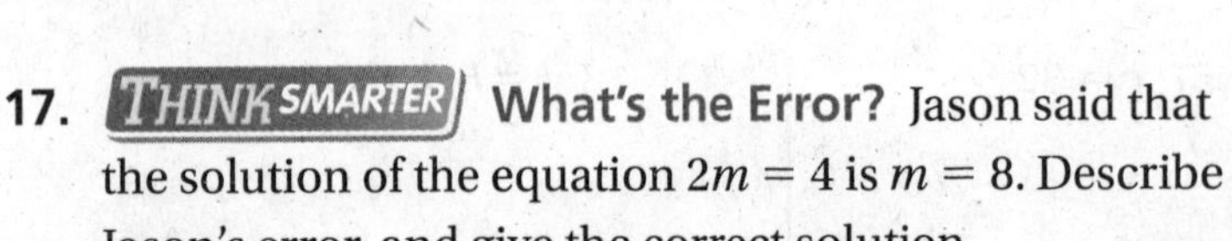

17. THINK SMARTER **What's the Error?** Jason said that the solution of the equation $2m = 4$ is $m = 8$. Describe Jason's error, and give the correct solution.

____

____

____

18. THINK SMARTER The marking period is 45 school days long. Today is the twenty-first day of the marking period. The equation $x + 21 = 45$ can be used to find the number of days left in the marking period. Using substitution, Rachel determines

there are [20 / 24 / 26] days left in the marking period.

FOR MORE PRACTICE:
Standards Practice Book

Name ______________________________

Write Equations

Essential Question How do you write an equation to represent a situation?

Expressions and Equations—6.EE.7

MATHEMATICAL PRACTICES
MP.2, MP.3, MP.4, MP.6

CONNECT You can use what you know about writing algebraic expressions to help you write algebraic equations.

Unlock the Problem

A circus recently spent \$1,650 on new trapezes. The trapezes cost \$275 each. Write an equation that could be used to find the number of trapezes t that the circus bought.

- Circle the information that you need to write the equation.
- What expression could you use to represent the cost of t trapezes?

____

Write an equation for the situation.

Think:

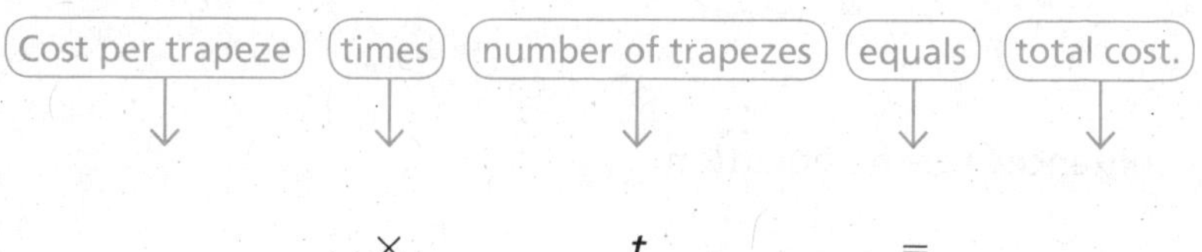

______ $\times$ t $=$ ______

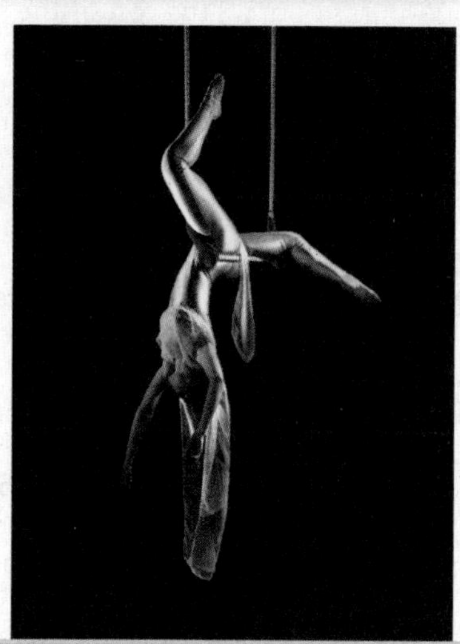

So, an equation that could be used to find the number of trapezes t is ____________________.

Try This! **Ben is making a recipe for salsa that calls for $3\frac{1}{2}$ cups of tomatoes. He chops 4 tomatoes, which fill $2\frac{1}{4}$ cups. Write an equation that could be used to find how many more cups c that Ben needs.**

Think: Cups filled → plus → cups needed → equals → total cups for recipe.

______ $+$ ______ $=$ ______

So, an equation that could be used to find the number of additional cups c is ____________________.

Math Talk **Mathematical Practices**

Describe another equation you could use to model the problem.

Example 1 Write an equation for the word sentence.

A Six fewer than a number is 46.33.

Think: Let *n* represent the unknown number. The phrase "fewer than" indicates

_____.

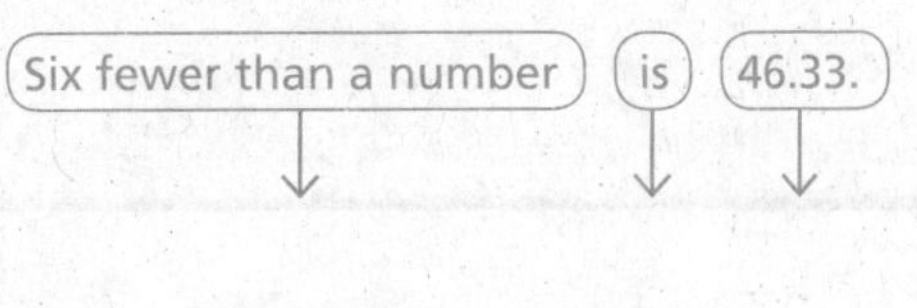

_____ − _____ = _____

ERROR Alert

The expression $n - 6$ means "6 fewer than *n*." The expression $6 - n$ means "*n* fewer than 6."

B Two-thirds of the cost of the sweater is $18.

Think: Let *c* represent the _____ of the sweater in dollars. The word "of"

indicates _____.

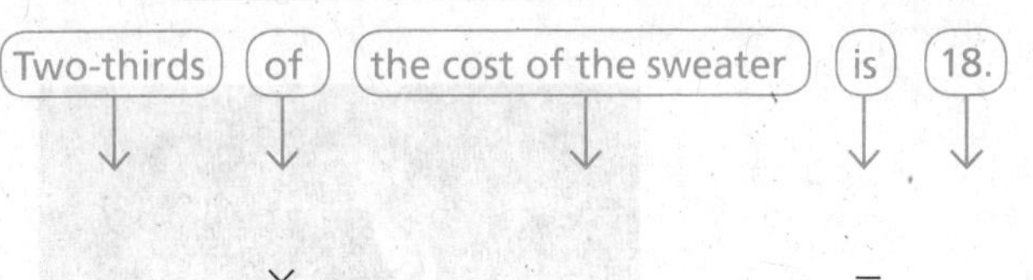

_____ × _____ = _____

Example 2 Write two word sentences for the equation.

A $a + 15 = 24$

- The _____ of *a* and 15 _____ 24.
- 15 _____ than *a* _____ 24.

B $r \div 0.2 = 40$

- The _____ of *r* and 0.2 _____ 40.
- *r* _____ by 0.2 _____ 40.

1. Explain how you can rewrite the equation $n + 8 = 24$ so that it involves subtraction rather than addition.

_____

_____

2. MATHEMATICAL PRACTICE 3 **Compare Representations** One student wrote $18 \times d = 54$ for the sentence "The product of 18 and *d* equals 54." Another student wrote $d \times 18 = 54$ for the same sentence. Are both students correct? Justify your answer.

_____

_____

Name ______________________

Share and Show

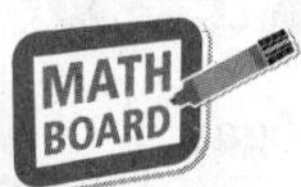

1. Write an equation for the word sentence "25 is 13 more than a number."

   What operation does the phrase "more than" indicate? ______________

   The equation is ____________ = ____________ + ____________.

Write an equation for the word sentence.

2. The difference of a number and 2 is $3\frac{1}{3}$.

3. Ten times the number of balloons is 120.

Write a word sentence for the equation.

4. $x - 0.3 = 1.7$

5. $25 = \frac{1}{4}n$

Math Talk — **Mathematical Practices**

Describe how an equation differs from an expression.

On Your Own

Write an equation for the word sentence.

6. The quotient of a number and 20.7 is 9.

7. 24 less than the number of snakes is 35.

8. 75 is $18\frac{1}{2}$ more than a number.

9. d degrees warmer than 50 degrees is 78 degrees.

Write a word sentence for the equation.

10. $15g = 135$

11. $w \div 3.3 = 0.6$

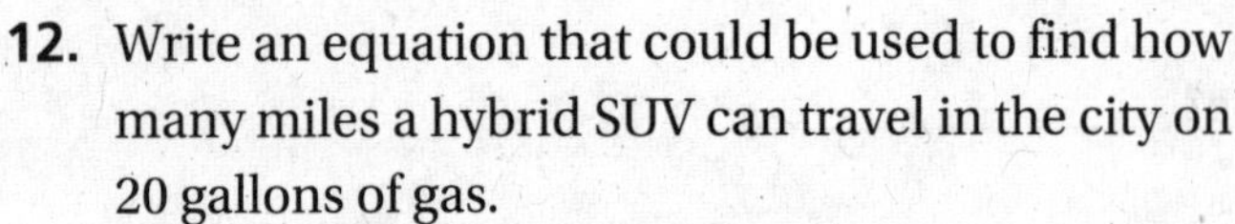

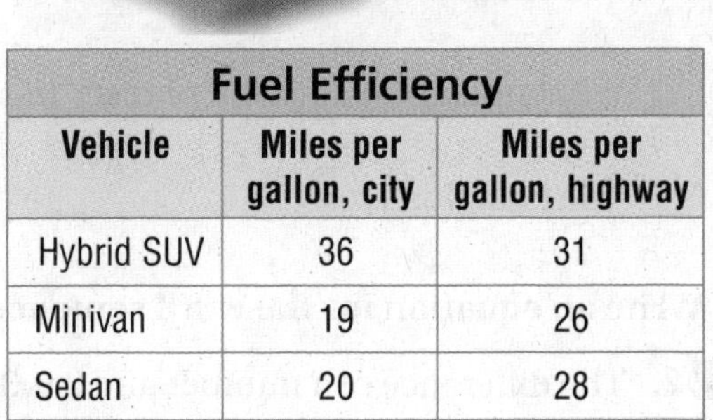

To find out how far a car can travel on a certain amount of gas, multiply the car's fuel efficiency in miles per gallon by the gas used in gallons. Use this information and the table for 12–13.

Fuel Efficiency		
Vehicle	Miles per gallon, city	Miles per gallon, highway
Hybrid SUV	36	31
Minivan	19	26
Sedan	20	28
SUV	22	26

12. Write an equation that could be used to find how many miles a hybrid SUV can travel in the city on 20 gallons of gas.

13. A sedan traveled 504 miles on the highway on a full tank of gas. Write an equation that could be used to find the number of gallons the tank holds.

WRITE Math
Show Your Work

14. MATHEMATICAL PRACTICE 2 **Connect Symbols to Words** Sonya was born in 1998. Carmen was born 11 years after Sonya. If you wrote an equation to find the year in which Carmen was born, what operation would you use in your equation?

15. GO DEEPER A magazine has 110 pages. There are 23 full-page ads and 14 half-page ads. The rest of the magazine consists of articles. Write an equation that can be used to find the number of pages of articles in the magazine.

16. THINK SMARTER **What's the Error?** Tony is traveling 560 miles to visit his cousins. He travels 313 miles the first day. He says that he can use the equation $m - 313 = 560$ to find the number of miles he has left on his trip. Describe Tony's error.

17. THINK SMARTER Jamie is making cookies for a bake sale. She triples the recipe in order to have enough cookies to sell. Jamie uses 12 cups of flour to make the triple batch. Write an equation that can be used to find out how much flour f is needed for one batch of cookies.

 FOR MORE PRACTICE: Standards Practice Book

Name ______________________________

Model and Solve Addition Equations

Essential Question How can you use models to solve addition equations?

Expressions and Equations—6.EE.7

MATHEMATICAL PRACTICES
MP.3, MP.4, MP. 5

You can use algebra tiles to help you find solutions of equations.

Algebra Tiles

x tile   1 tile

Investigate

Hands On

Materials ■ MathBoard, algebra tiles

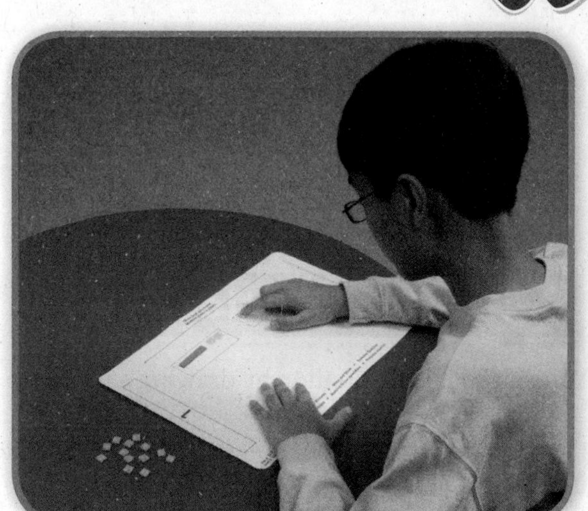

Thomas has \$2. He wants to buy a poster that costs \$7. Model and solve the equation $x + 2 = 7$ to find the amount x in dollars that Thomas needs to save in order to buy the poster.

A. Draw 2 rectangles on your MathBoard to represent the two sides of the equation.

B. Use algebra tiles to model the equation. Model $x + 2$ in the left rectangle, and model 7 in the right rectangle.

- What type of tiles and number of tiles did you use to model $x + 2$?

  ____

C. To solve the equation, get the x tile by itself on one side. If you remove a tile from one side, you can keep the two sides equal by removing the same type of tile from the other side.

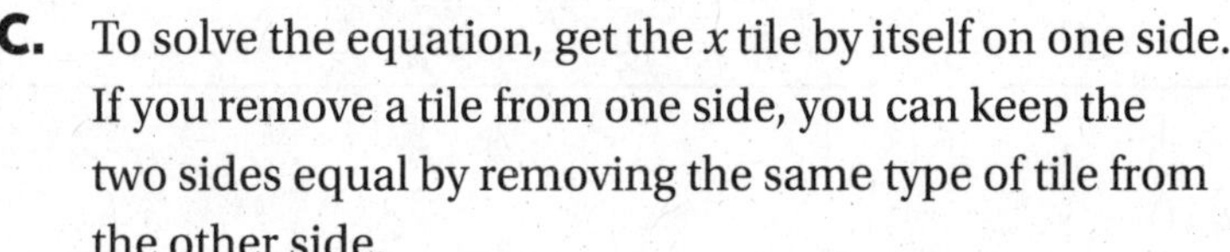

- How many 1 tiles do need to remove from each side to get the x tile by itself on the left side? ______
- When the x tile is by itself on the left side, how many 1 tiles are on the right side? ______

D. Write the solution of the equation: $x =$ ______.

So, Thomas needs to save \$ ______ in order to buy the poster.

Math Talk **Mathematical Practices**

Tell what operation you modeled when you removed tiles.

Draw Conclusions

1. MATHEMATICAL PRACTICE 5 **Use Appropriate Tools** Describe how you could use your model to check your solution.

____

____

____

2. Tell how you could use algebra tiles to model the equation $x + 4 = 8$.

____

____

3. THINKSMARTER What would you do to solve the equation $x + 9 = 12$ without using a model?

____

Make Connections

You can solve an equation by drawing a model to represent algebra tiles.

Let a rectangle represent the variable. Let a small square represent 1.

Solve the equation $x + 3 = 7$.

STEP 1

Draw a model of the equation.

STEP 2

Get the variable by itself on one side of the model by doing the same thing to both sides.

Cross out ______ squares on the left side and ______ squares on the right side.

STEP 3

Draw a model of the solution.

There is 1 rectangle on the left side. There are ______ squares on the right side.

So, the solution of the equation $x + 3 = 7$ is $x =$ ______.

Name ______________________

Share and Show

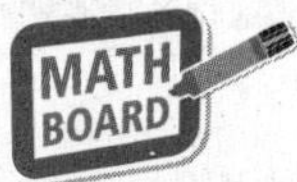

Model and solve the equation by using algebra tiles.

1. $x + 5 = 7$ ________

✓2. $8 = x + 1$ ________

3. $x + 2 = 5$ ________

4. $x + 6 = 8$ ________

5. $5 + x = 9$ ________

6. $5 = 4 + x$ ________

Solve the equation by drawing a model.

7. $x + 1 = 5$ ________

✓8. $3 + x = 4$ ________

9. $6 = x + 4$ ________

10. $8 = 2 + x$ ________

11. MATHEMATICAL PRACTICE 6 **Describe a Method** Describe how you would draw a model to solve the equation $x + 5 = 10$.

____

____

____

____

Problem Solving • Applications

12. MATHEMATICAL PRACTICE 4 **Interpret a Result** The table shows how long several animals have lived at a zoo. The giraffe has lived at the zoo 4 years longer than the mountain lion. The equation $5 = 4 + y$ can be used to find the number of years y the mountain lion has lived at the zoo. Solve the equation. Then tell what the solution means.

Zoo Animals

Animal	Time at zoo (years)
Giraffe	5
Hippopotamus	6
Kangaroo	2
Zebra	9

13. GO DEEPER Carlos walked 2 miles on Monday and 5 miles on Saturday. The number of miles he walked on those two days is 3 miles more than the number of miles he walked on Friday. Write and solve an addition equation to find the number of miles Carlos walked on Friday.

14. THINK SMARTER **Sense or Nonsense?** Gabriela is solving the equation $x + 1 = 6$. She says that the solution must be less than 6. Is Gabriela's statement sense or nonsense? Explain.

Personal Math Trainer

15. THINK SMARTER + The Hawks beat the Tigers by 5 points in a football game. The Hawks scored a total of 12 points.

Use numbers and words to explain how this model can be used to solve the equation $x + 5 = 12$.

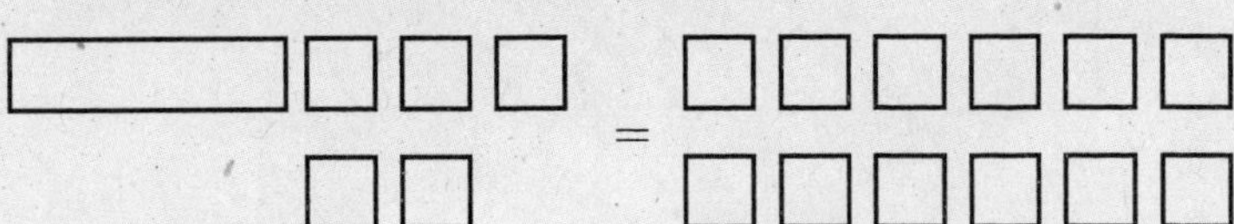

Name ______________________________

Solve Addition and Subtraction Equations

Essential Question How do you solve addition and subtraction equations?

Expressions and Equations—6.EE.7

MATHEMATICAL PRACTICES MP.2, MP.8

CONNECT To solve an equation, you must get the variable on one side of the equal sign by itself. You have solved equations by using models. You can also solve equations by using Properties of Equality.

Subtraction Property of Equality

If you subtract the same number from both sides of an equation, the two sides will remain equal.

$3 + 4 = 7$

$3 + 4 - 4 = 7 - 4$

$3 + 0 = 3$

$3 = 3$

Unlock the Problem

Real World

The longest distance jumped on a pogo stick is 23 miles. Emilio has jumped 5 miles on a pogo stick. The equation $d + 5 = 23$ can be used to find the remaining distance d in miles he must jump to match the record. Solve the equation, and explain what the solution means.

Solve the addition equation.

To get d by itself, you must undo the addition by 5. Operations that undo each other are called **inverse operations**. Subtracting 5 is the inverse operation of adding 5.

Write the equation. $d + 5 = 23$

Use the Subtraction Property of Equality. $d + 5 - 5 = 23 -$ ____

Subtract. $d + 0 =$ ____

Use the Identity Property of Addition. ____ $= 18$

Check the solution.

Write the equation. $d + 5 = 23$

Substitute ____ for d. ____ $+ 5 = 23$

The solution checks. ____ $= 23$

So, the solution means that Emilio must jump ____ more miles.

Math Talk — **Mathematical Practices**

Explain how you know what number to subtract from both sides of the equation.

When you solve an equation that involves subtraction, you can use addition to get the variable by itself on one side of the equal sign.

Addition Property of Equality	
If you add the same number to both sides of an equation, the two sides will remain equal.	$7 - 4 = 3$ $7 - 4 + 4 = 3 + 4$ $7 + 0 = 7$ $7 = 7$

Example

While cooking dinner, Carla pours $\frac{5}{8}$ cup of milk from a carton. This leaves $\frac{7}{8}$ cup of milk in the carton. Write and solve an equation to find how much milk was in the carton when Carla started cooking.

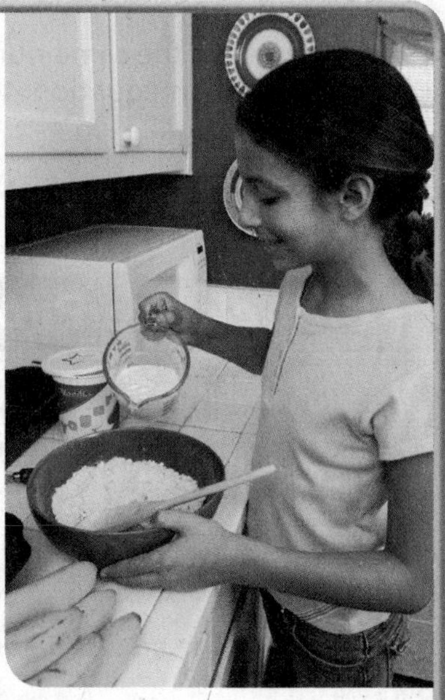

STEP 1 Write an equation.

Let *a* represent the amount of milk in cups in the carton when Carla started cooking.

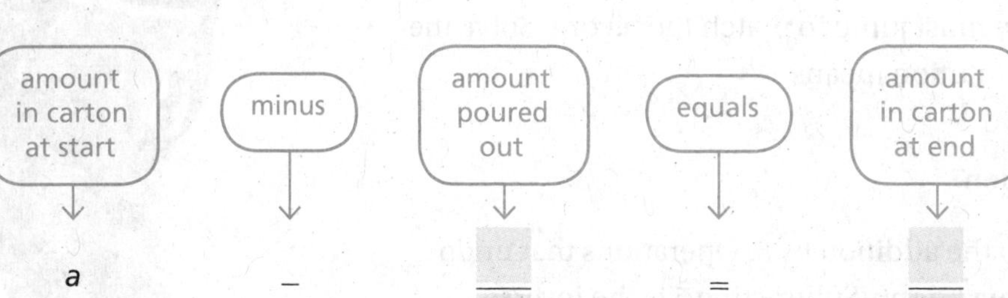

$a - \frac{\square}{\square} = \frac{\square}{\square}$

STEP 2 Solve the equation.

Think: $\frac{5}{8}$ is subtracted from *a*, so add $\frac{5}{8}$ to both sides to undo the subtraction.

Write the equation. $a - \frac{5}{8} = \frac{7}{8}$

Use the Addition Property of Equality. $a - \frac{5}{8} + \frac{\square}{\square} = \frac{7}{8} + \frac{\square}{\square}$

Add. $a = \frac{\square}{\square}$

Write the fraction greater than 1 as a mixed number, and simplify. $a =$ ______

So, there were ______ cups of milk in the carton when Carla started cooking.

Math Talk **Mathematical Practices**

Explain how you can check the solution of the equation.

Name ___

Share and Show

1. Solve the equation $n + 35 = 80$.

$n + 35 = 80$

$n + 35 - 35 = 80 -$ ___ Use the ___ Property of Equality.

$n =$ ___ Subtract.

Solve the equation, and check the solution.

2. $16 + x = 42$

3. $y + 6.2 = 9.1$

4. $m + \frac{3}{10} = \frac{7}{10}$

5. $z - \frac{1}{3} = 1\frac{2}{3}$

6. $12 = x - 24$

7. $25.3 = w - 14.9$

Math Talk — **Mathematical Practices**

Explain how to get the variable by itself on one side of a subtraction equation.

On Your Own

Practice: Copy and Solve **Solve the equation, and check the solution.**

8. $y - \frac{3}{4} = \frac{1}{2}$

9. $75 = n + 12$

10. $m + 16.8 = 40$

11. $w - 36 = 56$

12. $8\frac{2}{5} = d + 2\frac{2}{5}$

13. $8.7 = r - 1.4$

14. The temperature dropped 8 degrees between 6:00 P.M. and midnight. The temperature at midnight was 26°F. Write and solve an equation to find the temperature at 6:00 P.M.

___

15. MATHEMATICAL PRACTICE ② **Reason Abstractly** Write an addition equation that has the solution $x = 9$.

___

Unlock the Problem

16. GO DEEPER In July, Kimberly made two deposits into her bank account. She made no withdrawals. At the end of July, her account balance was \$120.62. Write and solve an equation to find Kimberly's balance at the beginning of July.

Bank Statement: Kimberly Gilson

Deposits	
July 12	\$45.50
July 25	\$43.24
Withdrawals	
None	

a. What do you need to find?

b. What information do you need from the bank statement?

c. Write an equation you can use to solve the problem. Explain what the variable represents.

d. Solve the equation. Show your work and describe each step.

e. Write Kimberly's balance at the beginning of July.

17. THINK SMARTER If $x + 6 = 35$, what is the value of $x + 4$? Explain how to find the value without solving the equation.

18. THINK SMARTER Select the equations that have the solution $n = 23$. Mark all that apply.

Ⓐ $16 + n = 39$

Ⓑ $n - 4 = 19$

Ⓒ $25 = n - 2$

Ⓓ $12 = n - 11$

FOR MORE PRACTICE: Standards Practice Book

Name ______________________________

Model and Solve Multiplication Equations

Essential Question How can you use models to solve multiplication equations?

Expressions and Equations—6.EE.7
MATHEMATICAL PRACTICES
MP.1, MP.4, MP.5, MP.6

You can use algebra tiles to model and solve equations that involve multiplication.

Algebra Tiles

To model an expression involving multiplication of a variable, you can use more than one x tile. For example, to model the expression $4x$, you can use four x tiles.

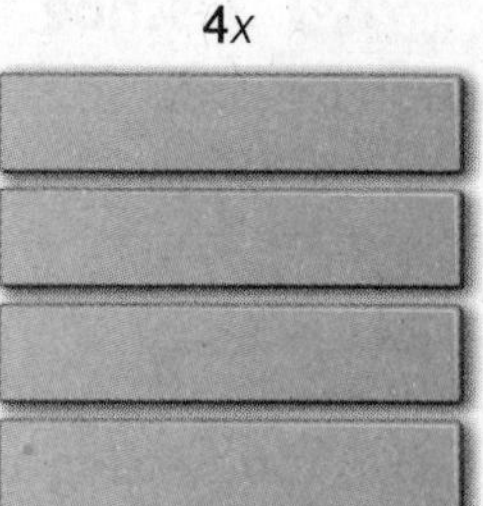

Investigate

Hands On

Materials ■ MathBoard, algebra tiles

Tennis balls are sold in cans of 3 tennis balls each. Daniel needs 15 tennis balls for a tournament. Model and solve the equation $3x = 15$ to find the number of cans x that Daniel should buy.

A. Draw 2 rectangles on your MathBoard to represent the two sides of the equation.

B. Use algebra tiles to model the equation. Model $3x$ in the left rectangle, and model 15 in the right rectangle.

C. There are three x tiles on the left side of your model. To solve the equation by using the model, you need to find the value of one x tile. To do this, divide each side of your model into 3 equal groups.

- When the tiles on each side have been divided into 3 equal groups, how many 1 tiles are in each group on the right side? ______

D. Write the solution of the equation: $x =$ ______.

So, Daniel should buy ______ cans of tennis balls.

Math Talk **Mathematical Practices**

Tell what operation you modeled in Step C.

Draw Conclusions

1. Explain how you could use your model to check your solution.

2. MATHEMATICAL PRACTICE 6 **Describe** how you could use algebra tiles to model the equation $6x = 12$.

3. THINK SMARTER What would you do to solve the equation $5x = 35$ without using a model?

Make Connections

You can also solve multiplication equations by drawing a model to represent algebra tiles. Let a rectangle represent x. Let a square represent 1. Solve the equation $2x = 6$.

STEP 1 Draw a model of the equation.

STEP 2 Find the value of one rectangle.

Divide each side of the model into _______ equal groups.

STEP 3 Draw a model of the solution.

There is 1 rectangle on the left side. There are _______ squares on the right side.

So, the solution of the equation $2x = 6$ is $x =$ _______.

Name ______________________________

Share and Show

Model and solve the equation by using algebra tiles.

1. $4x = 16$ ______

2. $3x = 12$ ______

3. $4 = 4x$ ______

4. $3x = 9$ ______

5. $2x = 10$ ______

6. $15 = 5x$ ______

Solve the equation by drawing a model.

7. $4x = 8$ ______

8. $3x = 18$ ______

Problem Solving • Applications

9. MATHEMATICAL PRACTICE 5 **Communicate** Explain the steps you use to solve a multiplication equation with algebra tiles.

The bar graph shows the number of countries that competed in the first four modern Olympic Games. Use the bar graph for 10–11.

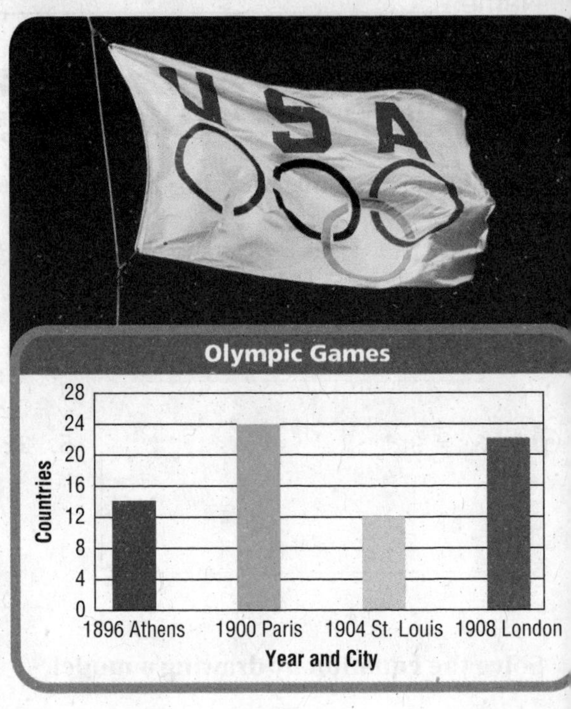

10. GO DEEPER Naomi is doing a report about the 1900 and 1904 Olympic Games. Each page will contain information about 4 of the countries that competed each year. Write and solve an equation to find the number of pages Naomi will need.

____

11. THINK SMARTER **Pose a Problem** Use the information in the bar graph to write and solve a problem involving a multiplication equation.

____

____

____

____

____

12. The equation $7s = 21$ can be used to find the number of snakes s in each cage at a zoo. Solve the equation. Then tell what the solution means.

____

13. THINK SMARTER A choir is made up of 6 vocal groups. Each group has an equal number of singers. There are 18 singers in the choir. Solve the equation $6p = 18$ to find the number of singers in each group. Use a model.

FOR MORE PRACTICE:
Standards Practice Book

Name ______________________________

Solve Multiplication and Division Equations

Essential Question How do you solve multiplication and division equations?

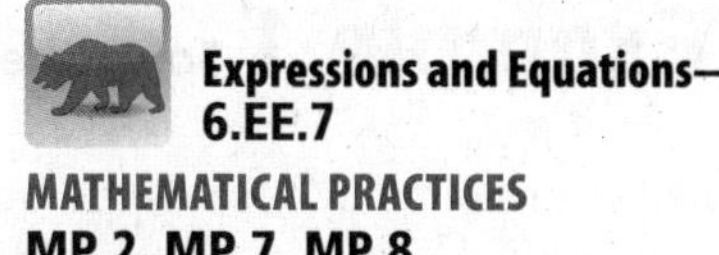

MATHEMATICAL PRACTICES
MP.2, MP.7, MP.8

CONNECT You can use Properties of Equality and inverse operations to solve multiplication and division equations.

Division Property of Equality

If you divide both sides of an equation by the same nonzero number, the two sides will remain equal.

$$2 \times 6 = 12$$
$$\frac{2 \times 6}{2} = \frac{12}{2}$$
$$1 \times 6 = 6$$
$$6 = 6$$

Unlock the Problem

Mei ran 14 laps around a track for a total of 4,200 meters. The equation $14d = 4{,}200$ can be used to find the distance d in meters she ran in each lap. Solve the equation, and explain what the solution means.

- What operation is indicated by $14d$? ______________

Solve a multiplication equation.

To get d by itself, you must undo the multiplication by 14. Dividing by 14 is the inverse operation of multiplying by 14.

Write the equation. $14d = 4{,}200$

Use the Division Property of Equality. $\frac{14d}{\square} = \frac{4{,}200}{\square}$

Divide. $1 \times d =$ ______

Use the Identity Property of Multiplication. ______ $= 300$

Check the solution.

Write the equation. $14d = 4{,}200$

Substitute ______ for d. $14 \times$ ______ $= 4{,}200$

The solution checks. ______ $= 4{,}200$

So, the solution means that Mei ran ______ meters in each lap.

Math Talk **Mathematical Practices**

Explain how you know what number to divide both sides of the equation by.

Example 1 Solve the equation $\frac{2}{3}n = \frac{1}{4}$.

Think: n is multiplied by $\frac{2}{3}$, so divide both sides by $\frac{2}{3}$ to undo the division.

Write the equation. $\frac{2}{3}n = \frac{1}{4}$

Use the ______________ Property of Equality. $\frac{2}{3}n \div \frac{2}{3} = \frac{1}{4} \div \frac{\square}{\square}$

To divide by $\frac{2}{3}$, multiply by its reciprocal. $\frac{2}{3}n \times \frac{3}{2} = \frac{1}{4} \times \frac{\square}{\square}$

Multiply. $n = \frac{\square}{\square}$

Multiplication Property of Equality

If you multiply both sides of an equation by the same number, the two sides will remain equal.

$\frac{12}{4} = 3$

$4 \times \frac{12}{4} = 4 \times 3$

$1 \times 12 = 12$

$12 = 12$

Example 2

A biologist divides a water sample equally among 8 test tubes. Each test tube contains 24.5 milliliters of water. Write and solve an equation to find the volume of the water sample.

STEP 1 Write an equation. Let v represent the volume in milliliters.

Think: The volume divided by 8 equals the volume in each test tube. $\frac{v}{\square} =$ ______

STEP 2 Solve the equation. v is divided by 8, so multiply both sides by 8 to undo the division.

Write the equation. $\frac{v}{8} = 24.5$

Use the ______________ Property of Equality. ______ $\times \frac{v}{8} =$ ______ $\times 24.5$

Multiply. $v =$ ______

So, the volume of the water sample is ______ milliliters.

Math Talk **Mathematical Practices**

Explain how you can use the Multiplication Property of Equality to solve Example 1.

Name ______________________

Share and Show

1. Solve the equation $2.5m = 10$.

$2.5m = 10$

$\frac{2.5m}{2.5} = \frac{10}{}$ Use the ____________ Property of Equality.

$m =$ ____ Divide.

Solve the equation, and check the solution.

2. $3x = 210$

3. $2.8 = 4t$

4. $\frac{1}{3}n = 15$

5. $\frac{1}{2}y = \frac{1}{10}$

6. $25 = \frac{a}{5}$

7. $1.3 = \frac{c}{4}$

Math Talk — **Mathematical Practices**

Explain how to get the variable by itself on one side of a division equation.

On Your Own

Practice: Copy and Solve **Solve the equation, and check the solution.**

8. $150 = 6m$

9. $14.7 = \frac{b}{7}$

10. $\frac{1}{4} = \frac{3}{5}s$

11. GO DEEPER There are 100 calories in 8 fluid ounces of orange juice and 140 calories in 8 fluid ounces of pineapple juice. Tia mixed 4 fluid ounces of each juice. Write and solve an equation to find the number of calories in each fluid ounce of Tia's juice mixture.

____

12. THINK SMARTER Write a division equation that has the solution $x = 16$.

____

Problem Solving • Applications

What's the Error?

13. THINK SMARTER Melinda has a block of clay that weighs 14.4 ounces. She divides the clay into 6 equal pieces. To find the weight w in ounces of each piece, Melinda solved the equation $6w = 14.4$.

Look at how Melinda solved the equation. Find her error.

This is how Melinda solved the equation:

$$6w = 14.4$$

$$\frac{6w}{6} = 6 \times 14.4$$

$$w = 86.4$$

Melinda concludes that each piece of clay weighs 86.4 ounces.

Correct the error. Solve the equation, and explain your steps.

So, $w =$ ______.

This means each piece of clay weighs ____________.

- MATHEMATICAL PRACTICE 1 **Describe** the error that Melinda made.

____

____

14. THINK SMARTER For numbers 14a–14d, choose Yes or No to indicate whether the equation has the solution $x = 15$.

14a. $15x = 30$ ○ Yes ○ No

14b. $4x = 60$ ○ Yes ○ No

14c. $\frac{x}{5} = 3$ ○ Yes ○ No

14d. $\frac{x}{3} = 5$ ○ Yes ○ No

FOR MORE PRACTICE:
Standards Practice Book

Name ______________________________

Problem Solving • Equations with Fractions

Essential Question How can you use the strategy *solve a simpler problem* to solve equations involving fractions?

Expressions and Equations—6.EE.7

MATHEMATICAL PRACTICES
MP.2, MP.6, MP.7, MP.8

You can change an equation involving a fraction to an equation involving only whole numbers. To do so, multiply both sides of the equation by the denominator of the fraction.

Unlock the Problem

On canoe trips, people sometimes carry their canoes between bodies of water. Maps for canoeing use a unit of length called a *rod* to show distances. Victoria and Mick carry their canoe 40 rods. The equation $40 = \frac{2}{11}d$ gives the distance d in yards that they carried the canoe. How many yards did they carry the canoe?

Use the graphic organizer to help you solve the problem.

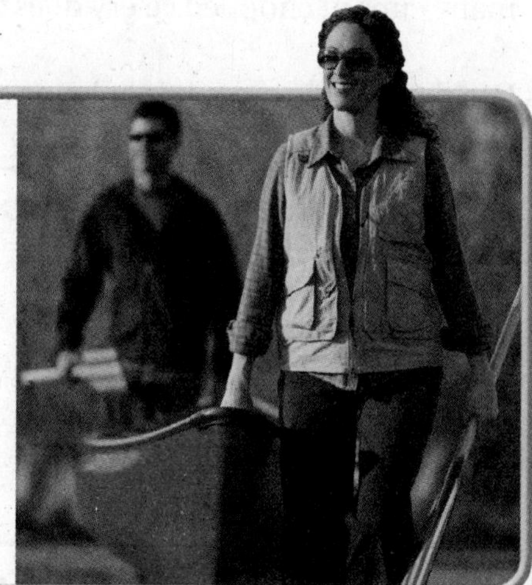

Read the Problem	Solve the Problem
What do I need to find? I need to find ______________________ ______________________.	• Write a simpler equation. Write the equation. $40 = \frac{2}{11}d$ Multiply both sides by the denominator. $11 \times 40 = \_\_\_\_ \times \frac{2}{11}d$ Multiply. $\_\_\_\_ = 2d$
What information do I need to use? I need to use ______________________.	• Solve the simpler equation. Write the equation. $440 = 2d$
How will I use the information? I can solve a simpler problem by changing the equation to an equation involving only whole numbers. Then I can solve the simpler equation.	Use the Division Property of Equality. $\frac{440}{\_\_\_\_} = \frac{2d}{\_\_\_\_}$ Divide. $\_\_\_\_ = d$

So, Victoria and Mick carried their canoe ______ yards.

Math Talk **Mathematical Practices**

Explain how you can check that your answer to the problem is correct.

If an equation contains more than one fraction, you can change it to an equation involving only whole numbers by multiplying both sides of the equation by the product of the denominators of the fractions.

Try Another Problem

Trevor is making $\frac{2}{3}$ of a recipe for chicken noodle soup. He adds $\frac{1}{2}$ cup of chopped celery. The equation $\frac{2}{3}c = \frac{1}{2}$ can be used to find the number of cups c of chopped celery in the original recipe. How many cups of chopped celery does the original recipe call for?

Use the graphic organizer to help you solve the problem.

Read the Problem	Solve the Problem
What do I need to find?	
What information do I need to use?	
How will I use the information?	

So, the original recipe calls for ______ cup of chopped celery.

- MATHEMATICAL PRACTICE 6 **Describe a Method** Describe another method that you could use to solve the problem.

____

____

Math Talk **Mathematical Practices**

Explain how you know that your answer is reasonable.

Name ______________________________

Share and Show

1. Connor ran 3 kilometers in a relay race. His distance represents $\frac{3}{10}$ of the total distance of the race. The equation $\frac{3}{10}d = 3$ can be used to find the total distance d of the race in kilometers. What was the total distance of the race?

First, write a simpler equation by multiplying both sides by the denominator of the fraction.

____

Next, solve th e simpler equation.

____

So, the race is ____________ long.

2. THINK SMARTER What if Connor's distance of 3 kilometers represented only $\frac{2}{10}$ of the total distance of the race. What would the total distance of the race have been?

____

3. The lightest puppy in a litter weighs 9 ounces, which is $\frac{3}{4}$ of the weight of the heaviest puppy. The equation $\frac{3}{4}w = 9$ can be used to find the weight w in ounces of the heaviest puppy. How much does the heaviest puppy weigh?

____

4. Sophia took home $\frac{2}{5}$ of the pizza that was left over from a party. The amount she took represents $\frac{1}{2}$ of a whole pizza. The equation $\frac{2}{5}p = \frac{1}{2}$ can be used to find the number of pizzas p left over from the party. How many pizzas were left over?

____

5. A city received $\frac{3}{4}$ inch of rain on July 31. This represents $\frac{3}{10}$ of the total amount of rain the city received in July. The equation $\frac{3}{10}r = \frac{3}{4}$ can be used to find the amount of rain r in inches the city received in July. How much rain did the city receive in July?

____

Unlock the Problem

- ✓ Circle the important information.
- ✓ Use the Properties of Equality when you solve equations.
- ✓ Check your solution by substituting it into the original equation.

WRITE ▸*Math* • **Show Your Work**

On Your Own

6. GO DEEPER Carole ordered 4 dresses for \$80 each, a \$25 sweater, and a coat. The cost of the items without sales tax was \$430. What was the cost of the coat?

7. THINK SMARTER A dog sled race is 25 miles long. The equation $\frac{5}{8}k = 25$ can be used to estimate the race's length k in kilometers. Approximately how many hours will it take a dog sled team to finish the race if it travels at an average speed of 30 kilometers per hour?

8. MATHEMATICAL PRACTICE 6 **Explain a Method** Explain how you could use the strategy *solve a simpler problem* to solve the equation $\frac{3}{4}x = \frac{3}{10}$.

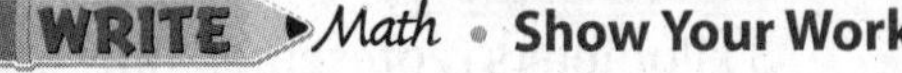

9. THINK SMARTER In a basket of fruit, $\frac{5}{6}$ of the pieces of fruit are apples. There are 20 apples in the display. The equation $\frac{5}{6}f = 20$ can be used to find how many pieces of fruit f are in the basket. Use words and numbers to explain how to solve the equation to find how many pieces of fruit are in the basket.

FOR MORE PRACTICE: Standards Practice Book

Name ________________________________

Mid-Chapter Checkpoint

Vocabulary

Vocabulary
equation
inverse operations
solution of an equation

Choose the best term from the box to complete the sentence.

1. A(n) ____________________ is a statement that two mathematical expressions are equal. (p. 307)

2. Adding 5 and subtracting 5 are ____________________. (p. 319)

Concepts and Skills

Write an equation for the word sentence. (6.EE.7)

3. The sum of a number and 4.5 is 8.2.

4. Three times the cost is $24.

Determine whether the given value of the variable is a solution of the equation. (6.EE.5)

5. $x - 24 = 58; x = 82$

6. $\frac{1}{3}c = \frac{3}{8}; c = \frac{3}{4}$

Solve the equation, and check the solution. (6.EE.7)

7. $a + 2.4 = 7.8$

8. $b - \frac{1}{4} = 3\frac{1}{2}$

9. $3x = 27$

10. $\frac{1}{3}s = \frac{1}{5}$

11. $\frac{t}{4} = 16$

12. $\frac{w}{7} = 0.3$

13. A stadium has a total of 18,000 seats. Of these, 7,500 are field seats, and the rest are grandstand seats. Write an equation that could be used to find the number of grandstand seats s. (6.EE.7)

____

14. Aaron wants to buy a bicycle that costs \$128. So far, he has saved \$56. The equation $a + 56 = 128$ can be used to find the amount a in dollars that Aaron still needs to save. What is the solution of the equation? (6.EE.7)

____

15. Ms. McNeil buys 2.4 gallons of gasoline. The total cost is \$7.56. The equation $2.4p = 7.56$ can be used to find the price p in dollars of one gallon of gasoline. What is the price of one gallon of gasoline? (6.EE.7)

____

16. Crystal is picking blueberries. So far, she has filled $\frac{2}{3}$ of her basket, and the blueberries weigh $\frac{3}{4}$ pound. The equation $\frac{2}{3}w = \frac{3}{4}$ can be used to estimate the weight w in pounds of the blueberries when the basket is full. About how much will the blueberries in Crystal's basket weigh when it is full? (6.EE.7)

____

Name ___________________

Solutions of Inequalities

Essential Question How do you determine whether a number is a solution of an inequality?

Expressions and Equations—6.EE.5

MATHEMATICAL PRACTICES
MP.2, MP.3, MP.6

An **inequality** is a mathematical sentence that compares two expressions using the symbol $<$, $>$, $\leq$, $\geq$, or $\neq$. These are examples of inequalities:

$8 < 11$ $9 > {}^{-}4$ $a \leq 50$ $x \geq 3.2$

Math Idea

- The symbol $\leq$ means "is less than or equal to."
- The symbol $\geq$ means "is greater than or equal to."

A **solution of an inequality** is a value of a variable that makes the inequality true. Inequalities can have more than one solution.

Unlock the Problem (Real World)

A library has books from the Middle Ages. The books are more than 650 years old. The inequality $a > 650$ represents the possible ages a in years of the books. Determine whether $a = 678$ or $a = 634$ is a solution of the inequality, and tell what the solution means.

 **Use substitution to determine the solution.**

STEP 1 Check whether $a = 678$ is a solution.

Write the inequality. $a > 650$

Substitute 678 for a. ________ $\stackrel{?}{>}$ 650

Compare the values. 678 is ________ than 650.

The inequality is true when $a = 678$, so $a = 678$ is a solution.

STEP 2 Check whether $a = 634$ is a solution.

Write the inequality. $a > 650$

Substitute 634 for a. ________ $\stackrel{?}{>}$ 650

Compare the values. 634 ________ greater than 650.

The inequality ________ true when $a = 634$, so $a = 634$ ________ a solution.

The solution $a = 678$ means that a book in the library from the Middle Ages could be ________ years old.

Mathematical Practices

Give another solution of the inequality $a > 650$. **Explain** how you determined the solution.

Example 1 Determine whether the given value of the variable is a solution of the inequality.

A $b < 0.3$; $b = {}^{-}0.2$

Write the inequality. $b < 0.3$

Substitute the given value for the variable. ______ $\overset{?}{<} 0.3$

Compare the values. $^{-}0.2$ is ______ than 0.3.

The inequality ______ true when $b = {}^{-}0.2$, so $b = {}^{-}0.2$ ______ a solution.

B $m \geq \frac{2}{3}$; $m = \frac{3}{5}$

Write the inequality. $m \geq \frac{2}{3}$

Substitute the given value for the variable. ______ $\overset{?}{\geq} \frac{2}{3}$

Rewrite the fractions with a common denominator. $\frac{\quad}{15} \overset{?}{\geq} \frac{\quad}{15}$

Compare the values. $\frac{9}{15}$ ______ greater than or equal to $\frac{10}{15}$.

The inequality ______ true when $m = \frac{3}{5}$, so $m = \frac{3}{5}$ ______ a solution.

Example 2

An airplane can hold no more than 416 passengers. The inequality $p \leq 416$ represents the possible number of passengers p on the airplane, where p is a whole number. Give two solutions of the inequality, and tell what the solutions mean.

Think: The solutions of the inequality are whole numbers ______ than or ______ to 416.

- $p = 200$ is a solution because 200 is ______ than ______.
- $p =$ ______ is a solution because ______ is ______ than 416.

These solutions mean that the number of passengers on the plane could be ______ or ______.

Math Talk **Mathematical Practices**

Give an example of a value of p that is not a solution of the inequality. **Explain** why it is not a solution.

Name ____________________

Share and Show

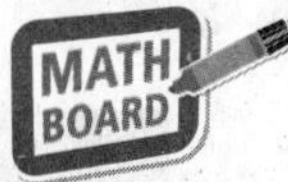

Determine whether the given value of the variable is a solution of the inequality.

1. $a \geq {}^{-}6$; $a = {}^{-}3$

   ______ $\overset{?}{\geq} {}^{-}6$

   ______

2. $y < 7.8$; $y = 8$

   ______

3. $c > \frac{1}{4}$; $c = \frac{1}{5}$

   ______

4. $x \leq 3$; $x = 3$

   ______

5. $d < {}^{-}0.52$; $d = {}^{-}0.51$

   ______

6. $t \geq \frac{2}{3}$; $t = \frac{3}{4}$

   ______

Math Talk **Mathematical Practices**

Explain how you could use a number line to check your answer to Exercise 5.

On Your Own

Practice: Copy and Solve **Determine whether the given value of the variable is a solution of the inequality.**

7. $s > {}^{-}1$; $s = 0$

8. $v \leq 1\frac{5}{6}$; $v = 1\frac{3}{4}$

9. $x < 0.43$; $x = 0.48$

Give two solutions of the inequality.

10. $e < 3$

    ______

11. $p > {}^{-}12$

    ______

12. $y \geq 5.8$

    ______

13. MATHEMATICAL PRACTICE ② **Connect Symbols and Words** A person must be at least 18 years old to vote. The inequality $a \geq 18$ represents the possible ages a in years at which a person can vote. Determine whether $a = 18$, $a = 17\frac{1}{2}$, and $a = 91.5$ are solutions of the inequality, and tell what the solutions mean.

______

______

Problem Solving • Applications

The table shows ticket and popcorn prices at five movie theater chains. Use the table for 14–15.

14. GO DEEPER The inequality $p < 4.75$ represents the prices p in dollars that Paige is willing to pay for popcorn. The inequality $p < 8.00$ represents the prices p in dollars that Paige is willing to pay for a movie ticket. At how many theaters would Paige be willing to buy a ticket and popcorn?

____

Movie Theater Prices

Ticket Price ($)	Popcorn Price ($)
8.00	4.25
8.50	5.00
9.00	4.00
7.50	4.75
7.25	4.50

15. THINK SMARTER **Sense or Nonsense?** Edward says that the inequality $d \geq 4.00$ represents the popcorn prices in the table, where d is the price of popcorn in dollars. Is Edward's statement sense or nonsense? Explain.

____

____

____

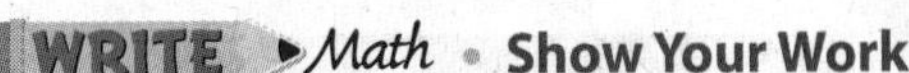

16. MATHEMATICAL PRACTICE 6 **Use Math Vocabulary** Explain why the statement $t > 13$ is an inequality.

____

____

Personal Math Trainer

17. THINK SMARTER + The minimum wind speed for a storm to be considered a hurricane is 74 miles per hour. The inequality $w \geq 74$ represents the possible wind speeds of a hurricane.

Two possible solutions for the inequality $w \geq 74$ are [71 / 73 / 75] and [80. / 60. / 40.]

FOR MORE PRACTICE: Standards Practice Book

Name ______________________________

Write Inequalities

Essential Question How do you write an inequality to represent a situation?

Expressions and Equations—6.EE.8

MATHEMATICAL PRACTICES
MP.2, MP.4

CONNECT You can use what you know about writing equations to help you write inequalities.

Unlock the Problem

The highest temperature ever recorded at the South Pole was 8°F. Write an inequality to show that the temperature t in degrees Fahrenheit at the South Pole is less than or equal to 8°F.

- Underline the words that tell you which inequality symbol to use.
- Will you use an equal sign in your inequality? Explain.

____

____

 **Write an inequality for the situation.**

Think:

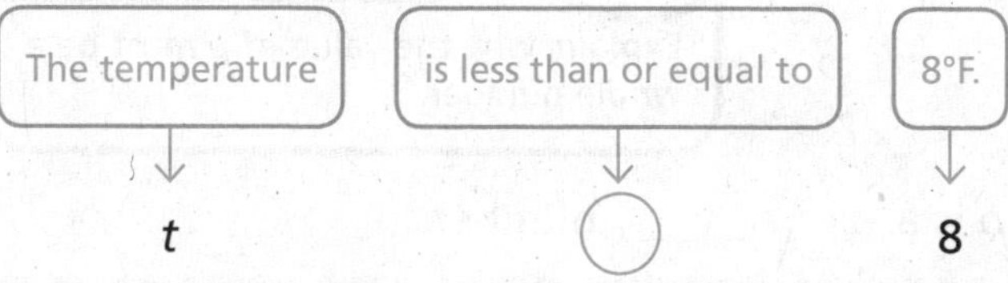

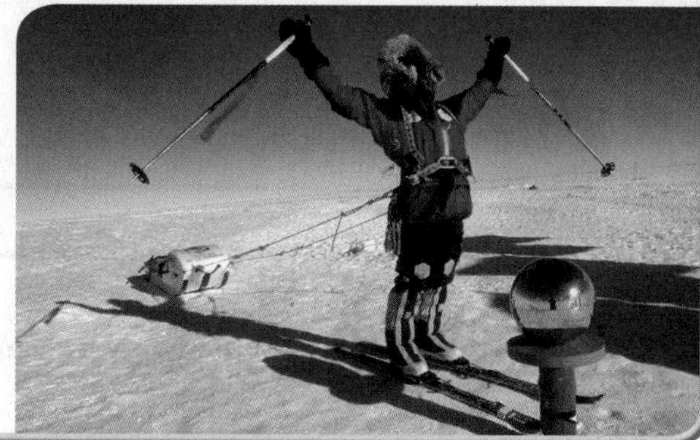

So, an inequality that describes the temperature t in degrees Fahrenheit at the South Pole is __________.

Try This! **The directors of an animal shelter need to raise more than $50,000 during a fundraiser. Write an inequality that represents the amount of money *m* in dollars that the directors need to raise.**

Think:

The amount of money	is more than	$50,000.
↓	↓	↓
m	◯	__________

So, an inequality that describes the amount of money m in dollars is __________.

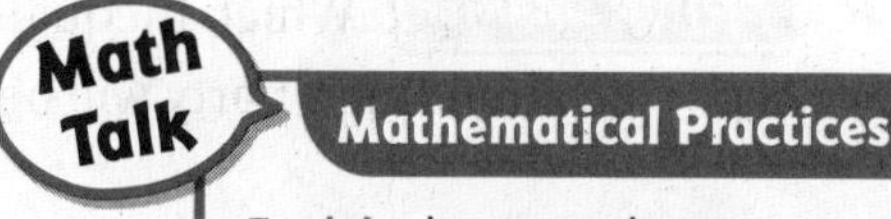

Explain how you knew which inequality symbol to use in the Try This! problem.

Example 1 Write an inequality for the word sentence. Tell what type of numbers the variable in the inequality can represent.

A The weight is less than $3\frac{1}{2}$ pounds.

Think: Let *w* represent the unknown weight in pounds.

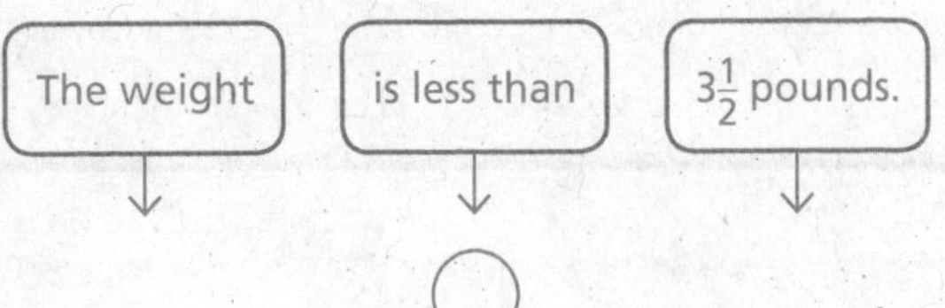

______ ◯ ______, where *w* is a positive number

B There must be at least 65 police officers on duty.

Think: Let *p* represent the number of police officers. The phrase "at least" is equivalent to "is ____________ than or equal to."

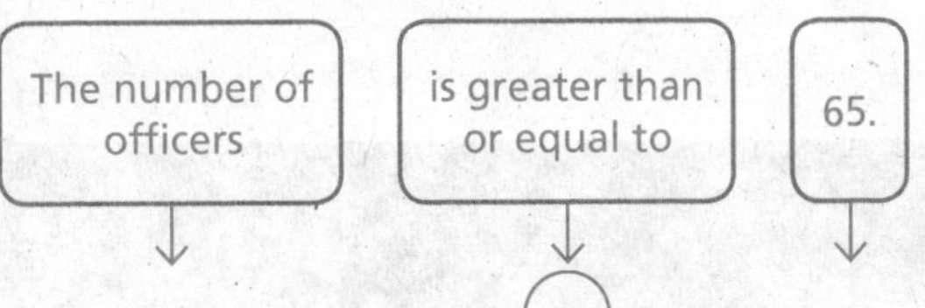

______ ◯ ______, where *p* is a ____________ number

Mathematical Practices

Explain why the value of *p* must be a whole number.

Example 2 Write two word sentences for the inequality.

A $n \leq 0.3$

- *n* is ____________ than or ____________ to 0.3.
- *n* is no ____________ than 0.3.

B $a > {}^{-}4$

- *a* is ____________ than ${}^{-}4$.
- *a* is ____________ than ${}^{-}4$.

- **THINK SMARTER** Which inequality symbol would you use to show that the number of people attending a party will be at most 14? Explain.

____

____

Name ______________________________

Share and Show

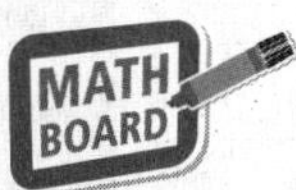

Write an inequality for the word sentence. Tell what type of numbers the variable in the inequality can represent.

1. The elevation e is greater than or equal to 15 meters.

2. A passenger's age a must be more than 4 years.

Write a word sentence for the inequality.

3. $b < \frac{1}{2}$

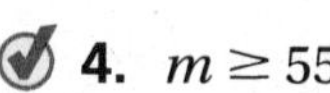

4. $m \geq 55$

On Your Own

5. MATHEMATICAL PRACTICE 6 **Compare** Explain the difference between $t \leq 4$ and $t < 4$.

6. GO DEEPER A children's roller coaster is limited to riders whose height is at least 30 inches and at most 48 inches. Write two inequalities that represent the height h of riders for the roller coaster.

7. THINK SMARTER Match the inequality with the word sentence it represents.

- $r > 10$
- $s \leq 10$
- $t \geq 10$
- $w < 10$

- Walter sold more than 10 tickets.
- Fewer than 10 children are at the party.
- No more than 10 people can be seated at a table.
- At least 10 people need to sign up for the class.

Connect to Reading

Make Generalizations

The reading skill *make generalizations* can help you write inequalities to represent situations. A generalization is a statement that is true about a group of facts.

Sea otters spend almost their entire lives in the ocean. Their thick fur helps them to stay warm in cold water. Sea otters often float together in groups called *rafts*. A team of biologists weighed the female sea otters in one raft off the coast of Alaska. The chart shows their results.

Weights of Female Sea Otters	
Otter Number	Weight (pounds)
1	50
2	61
3	62
4	69
5	71
6	54
7	68
8	62
9	58
10	51
11	61
12	66

Write two inequalities that represent generalizations about the sea otter weights.

First, list the weights in pounds in order from least to greatest.

50, 51, 54, _____, _____, _____, _____, _____,

_____, _____, _____, _____

Next, write an inequality to describe the weights by using the least weight in the list. Let w represent the weights of the otters in pounds.

Think: The least weight is _____ pounds, so all of the weights are greater than or equal to 50 pounds.

$w \bigcirc 50$

Now, write an inequality to describe the weights by using the greatest weight in the list.

Think: The greatest weight is _____ pounds, so all of the weights are _____ than or equal to _____ pounds.

$w \bigcirc 71$

So, the inequalities ________ and ________ represent generalizations about the weights w in pounds of the otters.

10. THINK SMARTER Use the chart at the right to write two inequalities that represent generalizations about the number of sea otter pups per raft.

____

____

Sea Otter Pups per Raft	
Raft Number	Number of Pups
1	7
2	10
3	15
4	23
5	6
6	16
7	20
8	6

FOR MORE PRACTICE: Standards Practice Book

Name ________________________________

Graph Inequalities

Essential Question How do you represent the solutions of an inequality on a number line?

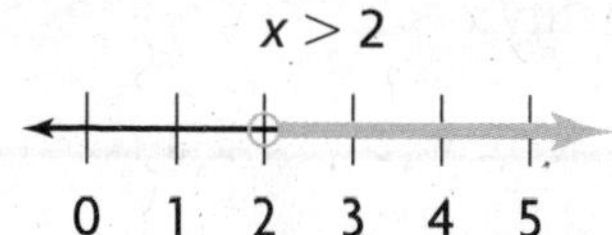

MATHEMATICAL PRACTICES
MP.4, MP.5, MP.6

Inequalities can have an infinite number of solutions. The solutions of the inequality $x > 2$, for example, include all numbers greater than 2. You can use a number line to represent all of the solutions of an inequality.

The number line at right shows the solutions of the inequality $x > 2$.

$x > 2$

The empty circle at 2 shows that 2 is not a solution. The shading to the right of 2 shows that values greater than 2 are solutions.

Unlock the Problem Real World

Forest fires are most likely to occur when the air temperature is greater than 60°F. The inequality $t > 60$ represents the temperatures t in degrees Fahrenheit for which forest fires are most likely. Graph the solutions of the inequality on a number line.

Show the solutions of $t > 60$ on a number line.

Think: I need to show all solutions that are greater than 60.

Draw an empty circle at _______ to show that 60 is not a solution.

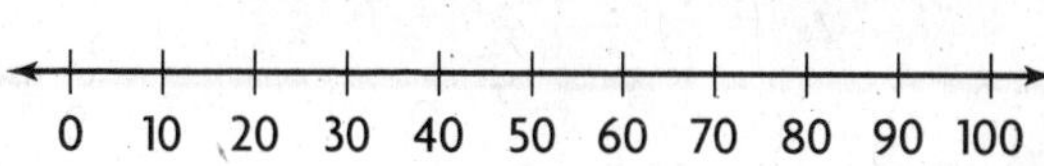

Shade to the _______________ of _______ to show that values greater than 60 are solutions.

Try This! **Graph the solutions of the inequality $y < 5$.**

Draw an empty circle at _______ to show that 5 is not a solution.

Shade to the _______________ of _______ to show that values less than 5 are solutions.

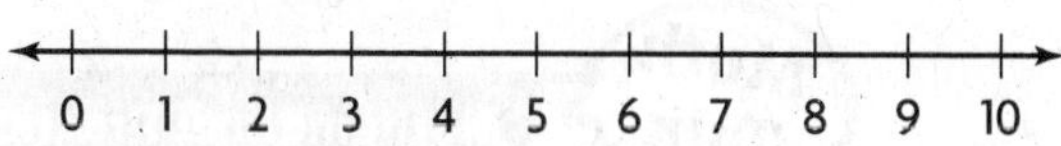

- MATHEMATICAL PRACTICE 6 **Make Connections** Explain why $y = 5$ is not a solution of the inequality $y < 5$.

____

You can also use a number line to show the solutions of an inequality that includes the symbol ≤ or ≥.

The number line at right shows the solutions of the inequality $x \geq 2$.

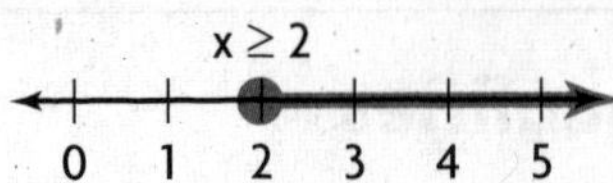

The filled-in circle at 2 shows that 2 is a solution. The shading to the right of 2 shows that values greater than 2 are also solutions.

Example 1 Graph the solutions of the inequality on a number line.

A $w \leq 0.8$

Draw a filled-in circle at ______ to show that 0.8 is a solution.

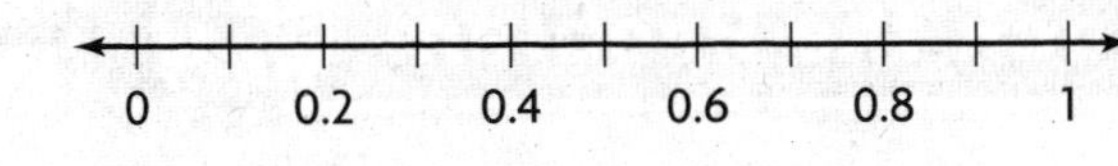

Shade to the ____________ of ______ to show that values less than 0.8 are also solutions.

B $n \geq {}^{-}3$

Draw a filled-in circle at ______ to show that ⁻3 is a solution.

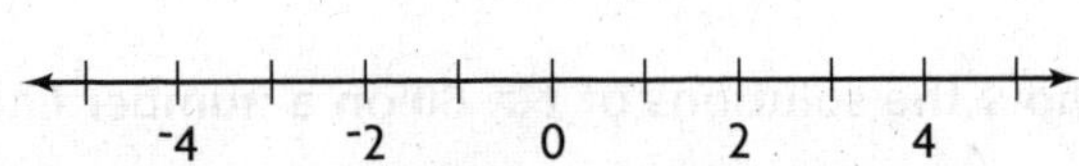

Shade to the ____________ of ______ to show that values greater than ⁻3 are also solutions.

Example 2 Write the inequality represented by the graph.

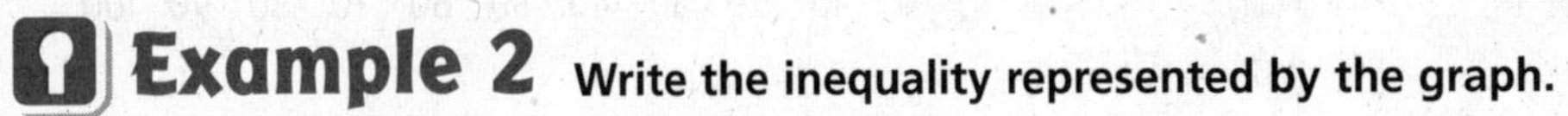

Use x (or another letter) for the variable in the inequality.

The ____________ circle at ______ shows that ⁻2

____________ a solution.

The shading to the ____________ of ______ shows that values

____________ than ⁻2 are solutions.

So, the inequality represented by the graph is ____________.

Math Talk **Mathematical Practices**

Explain how you know whether to shade to the right or to the left when graphing an inequality.

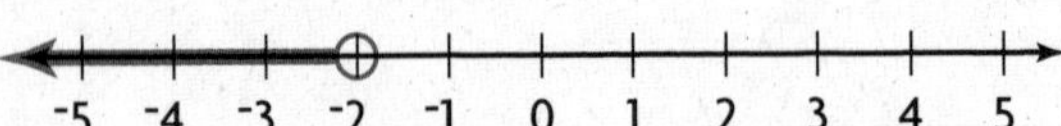

Name ______________________________

Share and Show

Graph the inequality.

1. $m < 15$

Draw an empty circle at ______ to show that 15 is not a solution. Shade to the ____________ of ______ to show that values less than 15 are solutions.

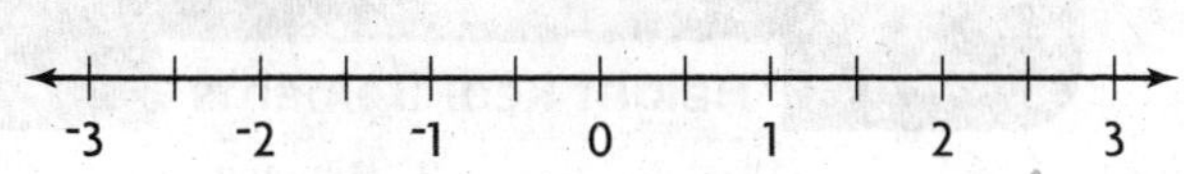

2. $c \geq {}^{-}1.5$

3. $b \leq \frac{5}{8}$

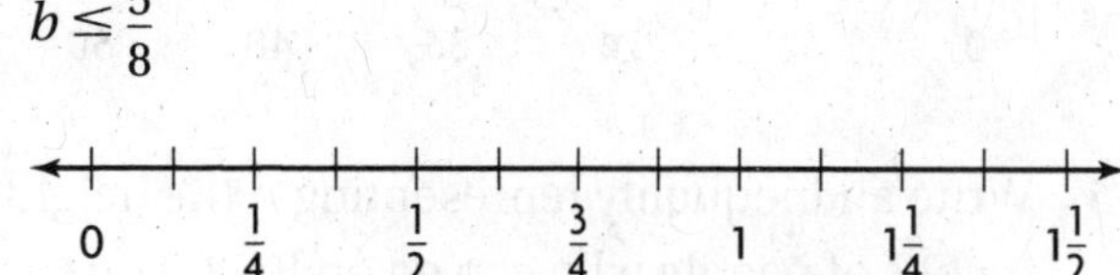

Math Talk — **Mathematical Practices**

Explain why it is easier to graph the solutions of an inequality than it is to list them.

On Your Own

Practice: Copy and Solve Graph the inequality.

4. $a < \frac{2}{3}$

5. $x > {}^{-}4$

6. $k \geq 0.3$

7. $t \leq 6$

Write the inequality represented by the graph.

8.

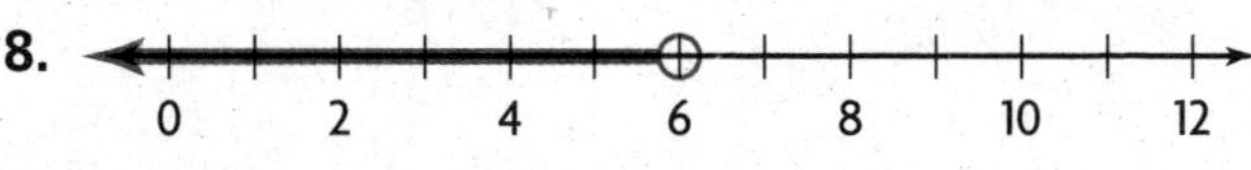

9.

-10 -8 -6 -4 -2 0 2

____

____

10. MATHEMATICAL PRACTICE 4 **Model Mathematics** The inequality $w \geq 60$ represents the wind speed w in miles per hour of a tornado. Graph the solutions of the inequality on the number line.

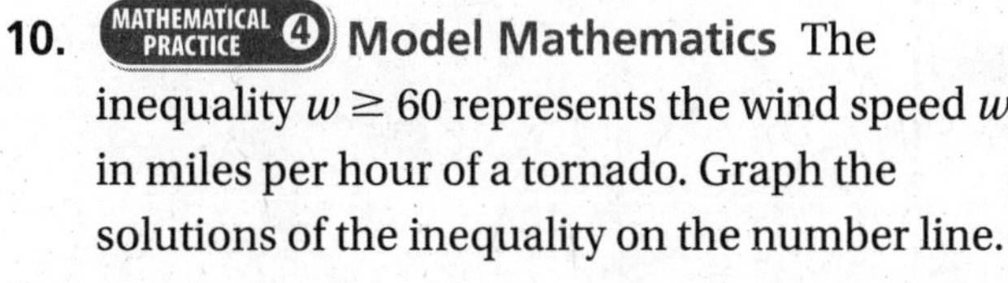

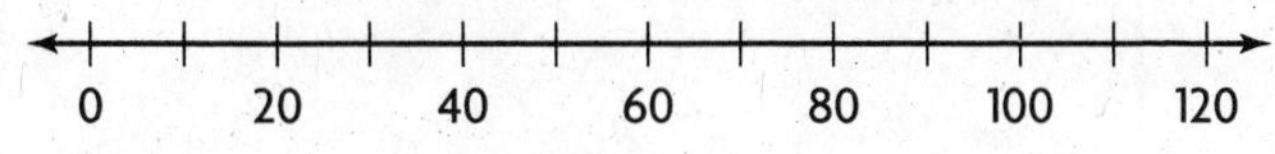

11. GO DEEPER Graph the solutions of the inequality $c < 12 \div 3$ on the number line.

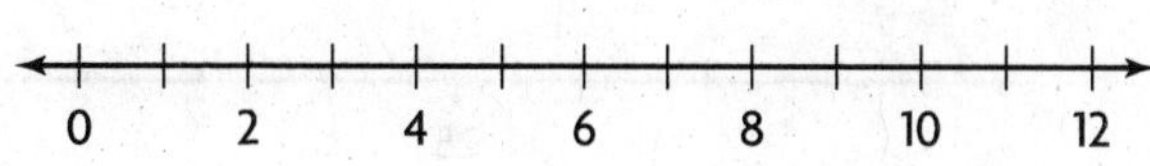

Problem Solving • Applications Real World

The table shows the height requirements for rides at an amusement park. Use the table for 12–16.

Height Requirements

Ride	Minimum height (in.)
Mighty Mountain	44
Race Track	42
River Rapids	38
Twirl & Whirl	48

12. Write an inequality representing t, the heights in inches of people who can go on Twirl & Whirl.

13. Graph your inequality from Exercise 12.

0 12 24 36 48 60 72

14. Write an inequality representing r, the heights in inches of people who can go on Race Track.

15. Graph your inequality from Exercise 14.

0 12 24 36 48 60 72

16. THINK SMARTER Write an inequality representing b, the heights in inches of people who can go on *both* River Rapids and Mighty Mountain. Explain how you determined your answer.

WRITE Math • Show Your Work

17. THINK SMARTER Alena graphed the inequality $c \leq 25$.

Darius said that 25 is not part of the solution of the inequality. Do you agree or disagree with Darius? Use numbers and words to support your answer.

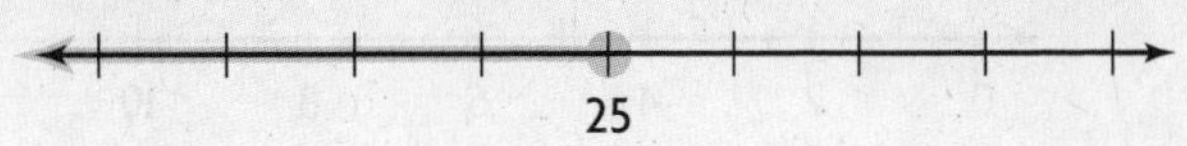

FOR MORE PRACTICE: Standards Practice Book

Name ___________________________

Chapter 8 Review/Test

1. For numbers 1a–1c, choose Yes or No to indicate whether the given value of the variable is a solution of the equation.

1a. $\frac{2}{5}v = 10$; $v = 25$ ○ Yes ○ No

1b. $n + 5 = 15$; $n = 5$ ○ Yes ○ No

1c. $5z = 25$; $z = 5$ ○ Yes ○ No

2. The distance from third base to home plate is 88.9 feet. Romeo was 22.1 feet away from third base when he was tagged out. The equation $88.9 - t = 22.1$ can be used to determine how far he needed to run to get to home plate. Using substitution, the coach determines that Romeo needed

to run [66 / 66.8 / 111] feet to get to home plate.

3. There are 84 grapes in a bag. Four friends are sharing the grapes. Write an equation that can be used to find out how many grapes *g* each friend will get if each each friend gets the same number of grapes.

____

4. Match each scenario with the equation that can be used to solve it.

Scenario	Equation
Jane's dog eats 3 pounds of food a week. How many days long will a 24-pound bag last?	• $3x = 39$
There are 39 students in the gym, and there are an equal number of students in each class. If three classes are in the gym, how many students are in each class?	• $4x = 24$
There are 4 games at the carnival. Kevin played all the games in 24 minutes. How many minutes did he spend at each game if he spent an equal amount of time at each?	• $3x = 24$

GO DIGITAL Assessment Options Chapter Test

5. Frank's hockey team attempted 15 more goals than Spencer's team. Frank's team attempted 23 goals. Write and solve an equation that can be used to find how many goals Spencer's team attempted.

____

6. Ryan solved the equation $10 + y = 17$ by drawing a model. Use numbers and words to explain how Ryan's model can be used to find the solution.

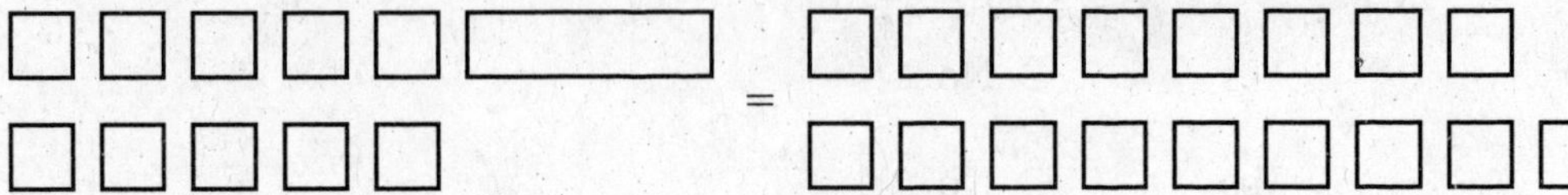

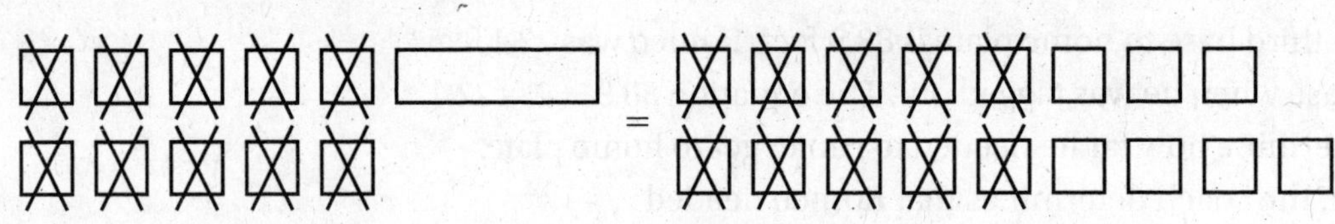

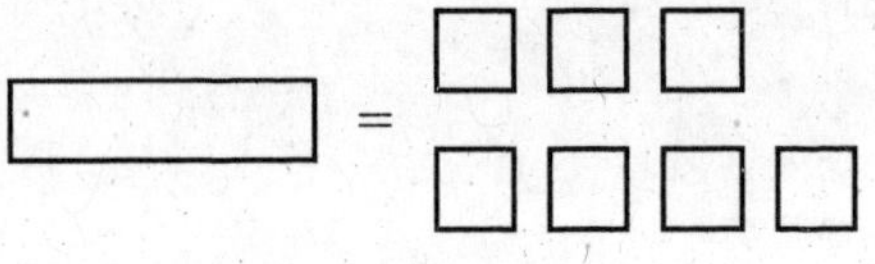

7. Gabriella and Max worked on their math project for a total of 6 hours. Max worked on the project for 2 hours by himself. Solve the equation $x + 2 = 6$ to find out how many hours Gabriella worked on the project.

____

8. Select the equations that have the solution $m = 17$. Mark all that apply.

Ⓐ $3 + m = 21$

Ⓑ $m - 2 = 15$

Ⓒ $14 = m - 3$

Ⓓ $2 = m - 15$

Name ________________________________

9. Describe how you could use algebra tiles to model the equation $4x = 20$.

10. For numbers 10a–10d, choose Yes or No to indicate whether the equation has the solution $x = 12$.

10a. $\frac{3}{4}x = 9$ ○ Yes ○ No

10b. $3x = 36$ ○ Yes ○ No

10c. $5x = 70$ ○ Yes ○ No

10d. $\frac{x}{3} = 4$ ○ Yes ○ No

11. Bryan rides the bus to and from work on the days he works at the library. In one month, he rode the bus 24 times. Solve the equation $2x = 24$ to find the number of days Bryan worked at the library. Use a model.

12. Betty needs $\frac{3}{4}$ of a yard of fabric to make a skirt. She bought 9 yards of fabric.

Part A

Write and solve an equation to find how many skirts x she can make from 9 yards of fabric.

Part B

Explain how you determined which operation was needed to write the equation.

13. Karen is working on her math homework. She solves the equation $\frac{b}{8} = 56$ and says that the solution is $b = 7$. Do you agree or disagree with Karen? Use words and numbers to support your answer. If her answer is incorrect, find the correct answer.

Name ______________________________

14. There are 70 historical fiction books in the school library. Historical fiction books make up $\frac{1}{10}$ of the library's collection. The equation $\frac{1}{10}b = 70$ can be used to find out how many books the library has. Solve the equation to find the total number of books in the library's collection. Use numbers and words to explain how to solve $\frac{1}{10}b = 70$.

15. Andy drove 33 miles on Monday morning. This was $\frac{3}{7}$ of the total number of miles he drove on Monday. Solve the equation $\frac{3}{7}m = 33$ to find the total number of miles Andy drove on Monday.

16. The maximum number of players allowed on a lacrosse team is 23. The inequality $t \leq 23$ represents the total number of players t allowed on the team.

Two possible solutions for the inequality are [23 / 25 / 27] and [26. / 24. / 22.]

17. Mr. Charles needs to have at least 10 students sign up for homework help in order to use the computer lab. The inequality $h \geq 10$ represents the number of students h who must sign up. Select possible solutions of the inequality. Mark all that apply.

- (A) 7
- (B) 8
- (C) 9
- (D) 10
- (E) 11
- (F) 12

18. The maximum capacity of the school auditorium is 420 people. Write an inequality for the situation. Tell what type of numbers the variable in the inequality can represent.

____

19. Match the inequality to the word sentence it represents.

$w < 70$ •	• The temperature did not drop below 70 degrees.
$x \leq 70$ •	• Dane saved more than $70.
$y > 70$ •	• Fewer than 70 people attended the game.
$z \geq 70$ •	• No more than 70 people can participate.

20. Cydney graphed the inequality $d \leq 14$.

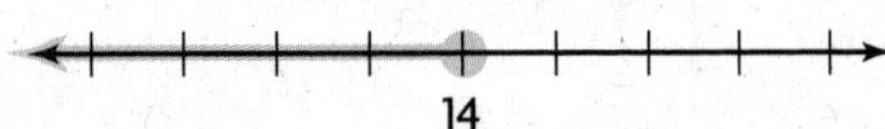

Part A

Dylan said that 14 is not part of the solution of the inequality. Do you agree or disagree with Dylan? Use numbers and words to support your answer.

Part B

Suppose Cydney's graph had an empty circle at 14. Write the inequality represented by this graph.

____

Chapter 9

Algebra: Relationships Between Variables

Show What You Know

Check your understanding of important skills.

Name ____________________

▶ **Number Patterns** **Write a rule to explain the pattern. Use the rule to find the missing numbers.**

1. 127, 123, 119, ■, 111, ■

____

2. 5,832, ■, 648, 216, 72, ■, 8

____

▶ **Identify Points on a Coordinate Grid** **Use the ordered pair to name the point on the grid.**

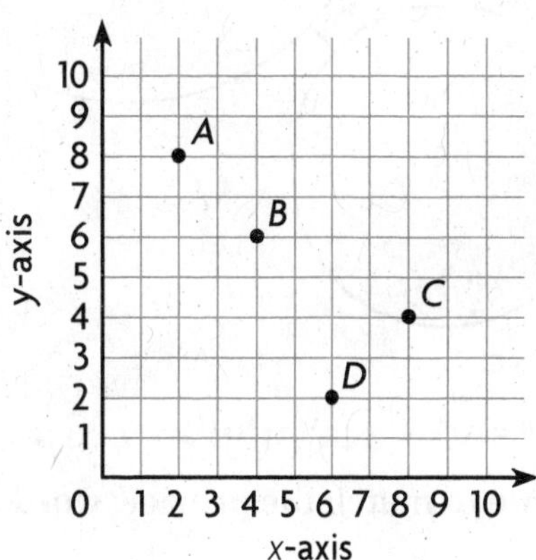

3. (4, 6) ____________

4. (8, 4) ____________

5. (2, 8) ____________

▶ **Evaluate Expressions** **Evaluate the expression.**

6. $18 + 4 - 7$ ____________

7. $59 - 20 + 5$ ____________

8. $(40 - 15) + 30$ ____________

9. $77 - (59 - 18)$ ____________

Terrell plotted points on the coordinate plane as shown. He noticed that the points lie on a straight line. Be a Math Detective and help him write an equation that shows the relationship between the *x*- and *y*-coordinate of each point he plotted. Then use the equation to find the *y*-coordinate of a point on the line with an *x*-coordinate of 20.

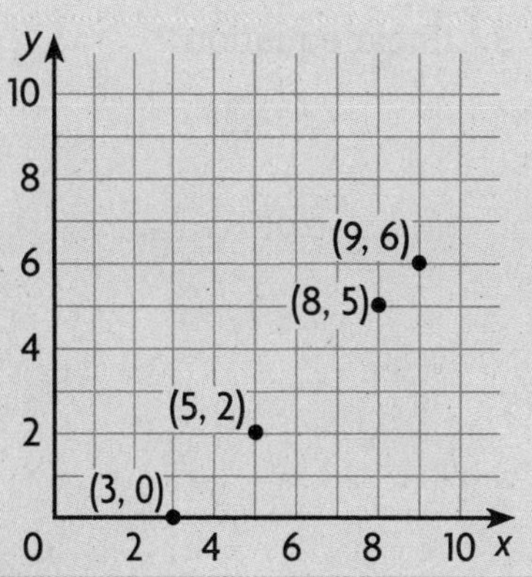

Personal Math Trainer
Online Assessment and Intervention

Vocabulary Builder

▶ Visualize It

Use the review words to complete the bubble map.

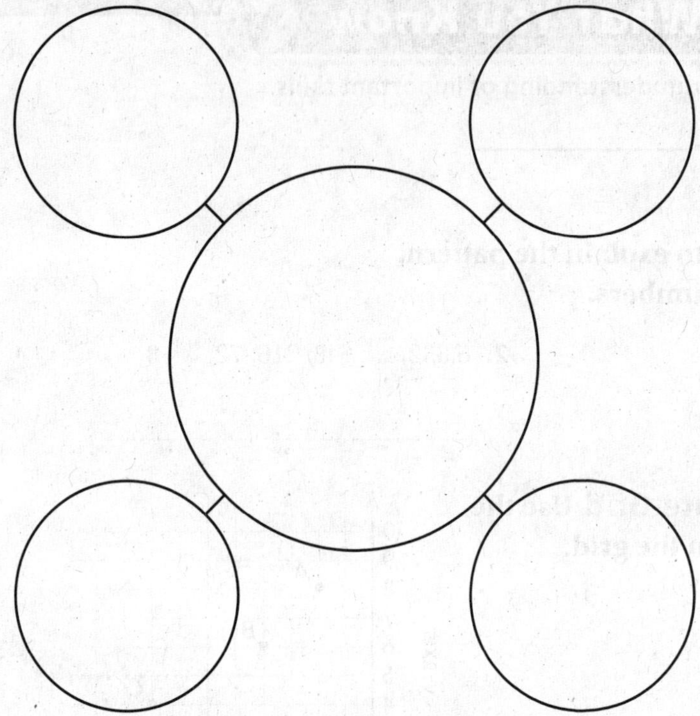

Review Words

coordinate plane
ordered pair
quadrants
x-coordinate
y-coordinate

Preview Words

dependent variable
independent variable
linear equation

▶ Understand Vocabulary

Draw a line to match the preview word with its definition.

Preview Words	Definitions
1. dependent variable •	• has a value that determines the value of another quantity
2. independent variable •	• names the point where the axes in the coordinate plane intersect
3. linear equation •	• has a value that depends on the value of another quantity
	• forms a straight line when graphed

GO DIGITAL
• Interactive Student Edition
• Multimedia eGlossary

Name ________________________________

Independent and Dependent Variables

Essential Question How can you write an equation to represent the relationship between an independent variable and a dependent variable?

Expressions and Equations—6.EE.9
MATHEMATICAL PRACTICES
MP.1, MP.4, MP.6, MP.7

You can use an equation with two variables to represent a relationship between two quantities. One variable is called the *independent variable*, and the other is called the *dependent variable*. The value of the **independent variable** determines the value of the **dependent variable**.

Unlock the Problem (Real World)

Jeri burns 5.8 calories for every minute she jogs. Identify the independent and dependent variables in this situation. Then write an equation to represent the relationship between the number of minutes Jeri jogs and the total number of calories she burns.

- Why do you need to use a variable?

____

- How many variables are needed to write the equation for this problem?

____

Identify the independent and dependent variables. Then use the variables to write an equation.

Let c represent the total number of ____________ Jeri burns.

Let m represent the number of ____________ Jeri jogs.

Think: The total number of calories Jeri burns **depends** on the number of minutes she jogs.

______ is the dependent variable.

______ is the independent variable.

Write an equation to represent the situation.

Think: The total calories burned | is equal to | 5.8 | times | the number of minutes jogged.

______ = 5.8 × ______

So, the equation ____________ represents the number of calories c Jeri burns if she jogs m minutes, where ______ is the dependent variable and ______ is the independent variable.

Math Talk — **Mathematical Practices**

Explain how you know that the value of c is dependent on the value of m.

Example

Lorelei is spending the afternoon bowling with her friends. Each game she plays costs \$3.25, and there is a one-time shoe-rental fee of \$2.50.

A Identify the independent and dependent variables in this situation. Then write an equation to represent the relationship between the number of games and the total cost.

Think: The total cost in dollars c depends on the number of games g Lorelei plays.

_____ is the dependent variable.

_____ is the independent variable.

ERROR Alert

Note that the fee for the shoes, \$2.50, is a one-time fee, and therefore is not multiplied by the number of games.

Think:

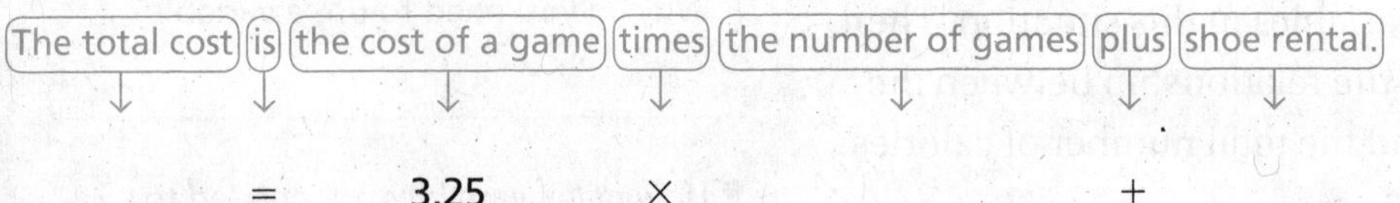

_____ = 3.25 × _____ + _____

So, the equation _______________ represents the total cost in dollars c that Lorelei spends if she bowls g games, where _____ is the dependent variable and _____ is the independent variable.

B Use your equation to find the total cost for Lorelei to play 3 games.

Think: Find the value of c when $g = 3$.

Write the equation.	$c = 3.25g + 2.50$
Substitute 3 for g.	$c = 3.25($_____$) + 2.50$
Follow the order of operations to solve for c.	$b =$ _____ $+ 2.50 =$ _____

So, it will cost Lorelei __________ to play 3 games.

1. THINK SMARTER **What if** there were no fee for shoe rentals? How would the equation be different?

2. MATHEMATICAL PRACTICE 1 **Evaluate Reasonableness** How can you use estimation to check that your answer is reasonable?

Name ______________________________

Share and Show

Identify the independent and dependent variables. Then write an equation to represent the relationship between them.

1. An online store lets customers have their name printed on any item they buy. The total cost c in dollars is the price of the item p in dollars plus $3.99 for the name.

   The __________ depends on the ______________.

   dependent variable: _____

   independent variable: _____

   equation: _____ = _____

✓ 2. A raft travels downriver at a rate of 6 miles per hour. The total distance d in miles that the raft travels is equal to the rate times the number of hours h.

   dependent variable: _____

   independent variable: _____

   equation: __________

✓ 3. Apples are on sale for $1.99 a pound. Sheila buys p pounds of apples for a total cost of c dollars.

   dependent variable: _____

   independent variable: _____

   equation: __________

Math Talk — **Mathematical Practices**

Explain how you know which variable in a relationship is dependent and which is independent.

On Your Own

Identify the independent and dependent variables. Then write an equation to represent the relationship between them.

4. Sean can make 8 paper birds in an hour. The total number of birds b is equal to the number of birds he makes per hour times the number of hours h.

   dependent variable: _____

   independent variable: _____

   equation: __________

5. Billy has $25. His father is going to give him more money. The total amount t Billy will have is equal to the amount m his father gives him plus the $25 Billy already has.

   dependent variable: _____

   independent variable: _____

   equation: __________

6. MATHEMATICAL PRACTICE 2 **Connect Symbols and Words** Describe a situation that can be represented by the equation $c = 12b$.

   ____

   ____

   ____

7. GO DEEPER Belinda pays $4.25 for each glass she buys. The total cost c is equal to the price per glass times the number of glasses n plus $9.95 for shipping and handling. Write an equation and use it to find how much it will cost Belinda to buy 12 glasses.

   ____

Unlock the Problem

8. Benji decides to save \$15 per week to buy a computer program. Write an equation that models the total amount t in dollars Benji will have saved in w weeks.

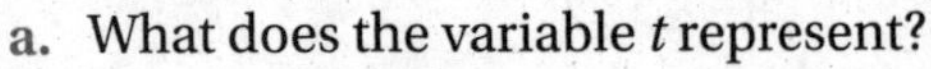

a. What does the variable t represent?

____

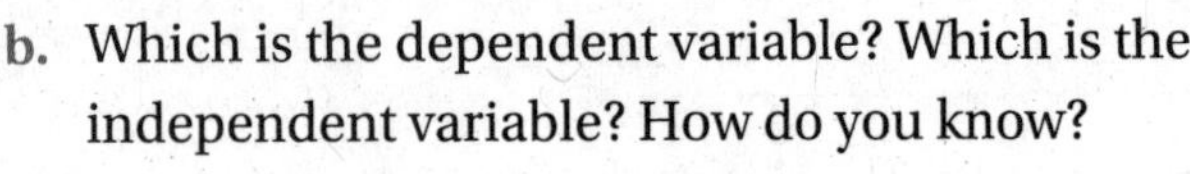

b. Which is the dependent variable? Which is the independent variable? How do you know?

____

____

____

____

____

____

c. How can you find the total amount saved in w weeks?

____

____

d. Write an equation for the total amount that Benji will have saved.

____

9. GO DEEPER Coach Diaz is buying hats for the baseball team. The total cost c is equal to the number of hats n that he buys times the sum of the price per hat h and a \$2 charge per hat to the have the team name printed on it. Write an equation that can be used to find the cost of the hats.

____

10. THINK SMARTER A steel cable that is $\frac{1}{2}$ inch in diameter weighs 0.42 pound per foot. The total weight in pounds w is equal to 0.42 times of the number of feet f of steel cable. Choose the letter or equation that makes each sentence true.

The independent variable is [f. / w.] The dependent variable is [f. / w.]

The equation that represents the relationship between the variables is [$w = 0.42f$. / $f = 0.42w$.]

FOR MORE PRACTICE:
Standards Practice Book

Name ________________________________

Equations and Tables

Essential Question How can you translate between equations and tables?

Expressions and Equations— 6.EE.9

MATHEMATICAL PRACTICES
MP.2, MP.3, MP.4, MP.7

When an equation describes the relationship between two quantities, the variable x often represents the independent variable, and y often represents the dependent variable.

A value of the independent variable is called the *input* value, and a value of the dependent variable is called the *output* value.

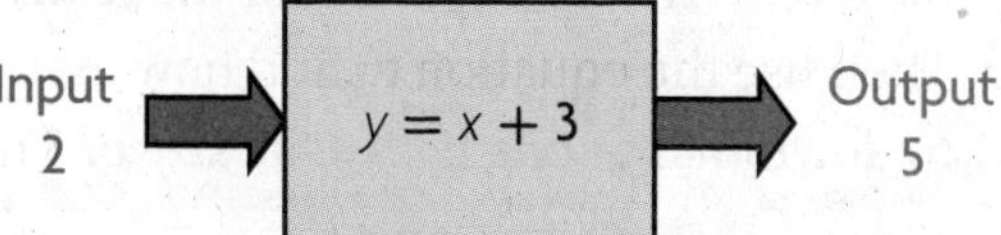

Input 4 → $y = x + 3$ → Output 7

Unlock the Problem (Real World)

A skating rink charges $3.00 for each hour of skating, plus $1.75 to rent skates. Write an equation for the relationship that gives the total cost y in dollars for skating x hours. Then make a table that shows the cost of skating for 1, 2, 3, and 4 hours.

Write an equation for the relationship, and use the equation to make a table.

- What is the independent variable? What is the dependent variable?

____

____

STEP 1 Write an equation.

Think:

The total cost	is	________	for each	hour	plus	________.
↓	↓	↓	↓	↓	↓	↓
______	=	3	·	______	+	1.75

So, the equation for the relationship is ________________.

STEP 2 Make a table.

Input	Rule	Output
Time (hr), x	$3x + 1.75$	Cost ($), y
1	$3 \cdot 1 + 1.75$	4.75
2		
3		
4		

Replace x with each input value, and then evaluate the rule to find each output value.

Mathematical Practices

Explain how you could use the equation to find the total cost of skating for 6 hours.

Example

Jamal downloads songs on his MP3 player. The table shows how the time it takes him to download a song depends on the song's file size. Write an equation for the relationship shown in the table. Then use the equation to find how many seconds it takes Jamal to download a song with a file size of 7 megabytes (MB).

Download Times	
File Size (MB), x	Time (s), y
4	48
5	60
6	72
7	?
8	96

STEP 1 Write an equation.

Look for a pattern between the file sizes and the download times.

File Size (MB), x	4	5	6	8
Time (s), y	48	60	72	96
	$12 \cdot 4$	$12 \cdot 5$	$12 \cdot$ ______	$12 \cdot$ ______

Think: You can find each download time by multiplying the file size by ______.

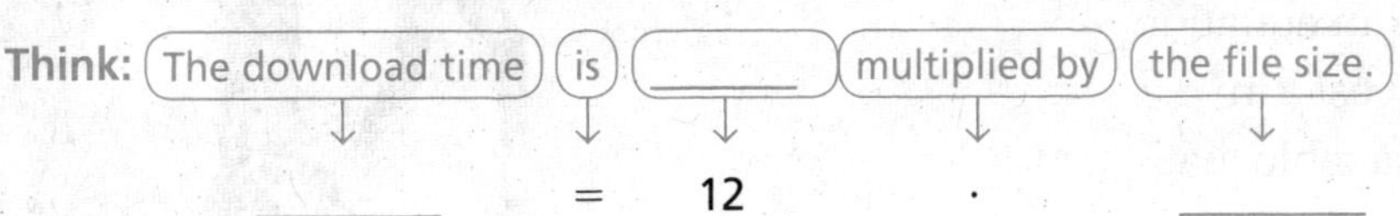

So, the equation for the relationship is ____________.

STEP 2 Use the equation to find the download time for a file size of 7 megabytes.

Write the equation. $y = 12x$

Replace x with 7. $y = 12 \cdot$ ______

Solve for y. $y =$ ______

So, it takes Jamal ______ seconds to download a 7-megabyte song.

1. Explain how you can check that your equation for the relationship is correct.

____

____

2. MATHEMATICAL PRACTICE 3 **Compare Representations** Describe a situation in which it would be more useful to represent a relationship between two quantities with an equation than with a table of values.

____

____

Name ________________________________

Share and Show

Use the equation to complete the table.

1. $y = x + 3$

Input	Rule	Output
x	$x + 3$	y
6	6 + 3	
8	8 + 3	
10		

2. $y = 2x + 1$

Input	Output
x	y
4	
7	
10	

On Your Own

Write an equation for the relationship shown in the table. Then find the unknown value in the table.

3.

x	8	9	10	11
y	16	18	?	22

____

4.

x	10	20	30	40
y	5	10	15	?

____

5. GO DEEPER The table shows the current cost of buying apps for a cell phone. Next month, the price of each app will double. Write an equation you can use to find the total cost y of buying x apps next month.

____

Cell Phone Apps	
Number of apps, x	Total cost ($), y
3	9
4	12
5	15

6. THINK SMARTER A beach resort charges $1.50 per hour plus $4.50 to rent a bicycle. The equation $c = 1.50x + 4.50$ gives the total cost c of renting a bicycle for x hours. Use numbers and words to explain how to find the cost c of renting a bicycle for 6 hours.

____

____

____

Input	Output
Time (hr), x	Cost ($), c
1	6.00
2	7.50
3	9.00
4	10.50

Connect to Reading

Cause and Effect

The reading skill *cause and effect* can help you understand how a change in one variable may cause a change in another variable.

In karate, a person's skill level is often shown by the color of his or her belt. At Sara's karate school, students must pass a test to move from one belt level to the next. Each test costs \$23. Sara hopes to move up 3 belt levels this year. How will this affect her karate expenses?

Cause: Sara moves to higher belt levels.	→	Effect: Sara's karate expenses go up.

Write an equation to show the relationship between cause and effect. Then use the equation to solve the problem.

Let x represent the number of belt levels Sara moves up, and let y represent the increase in dollars in her karate expenses.

Write the equation. $y =$ ______ $\cdot x$

Sara plans to move up 3 levels, so replace x with ______. $y = 23 \cdot$ ______

Solve for y. $y =$ ______

So, if Sara moves up 3 belt levels this year, her karate expenses will increase by \$______.

Write an equation to show the relationship between cause and effect. Then use the equation to solve the problem.

7. THINK SMARTER Classes at Tony's karate school cost \$29.50 per month. This year he plans to take 2 more months of classes than he did last year. How will this affect Tony's karate expenses?

8. MATHEMATICAL PRACTICE 4 **Write an Equation** A sporting goods store regularly sells karate uniforms for \$35.90 each. The store is putting karate uniforms on sale for 10% off. How will this affect the price of a karate uniform?

FOR MORE PRACTICE: Standards Practice Book

Name ______________________________

Problem Solving • Analyze Relationships

Essential Question How can you use the strategy *find a pattern* to solve problems involving relationships between quantities?

Expressions and Equations—6.EE.9

MATHEMATICAL PRACTICES
MP.1, MP.4, MP.8

Unlock the Problem

The table shows the amount of water pumped through a fire hose over time. If the pattern in the table continues, how long will it take a firefighter to spray 3,000 gallons of water on a fire using this hose?

Fire Hose Flow Rate

Time (min)	1	2	3	4
Amount of water (gal)	150	300	450	600

Use the graphic organizer to help you solve the problem.

Read the Problem

What do I need to find?

I need to find ______________________________

______________________________.

What information do I need to use?

I need to use the relationship between ______________

and ______________________.

How will I use the information?

I will find a ______________ in the table and write an

______________________.

Solve the Problem

Use the table above to find the relationship between the time and the amount of water.

Think: Let t represent the time in minutes, and w represent the amount of water in gallons. The amount of water in gallons is ______ multiplied by the time in minutes.

______ = 150 · ______

Use the equation to find how long it will take to spray 3,000 gallons.

Write the equation. $w = 150t$

Substitute 3,000 for w. $3{,}000 = 150t$

Solve for t. Divide both sides by 150. $\frac{3{,}000}{} = \frac{150t}{}$

______ $= t$

So, it will take ______ minutes to spray 3,000 gallons of water.

Math Talk Mathematical Practices

Explain how you can check that your answer is correct.

Try Another Problem

Dairy cows provide 90% of the world's milk supply. The table shows the amount of milk produced by a cow over time. If the pattern in the table continues, how much milk can a farmer get from a cow in 1 year (365 days)?

Cow Milk Production				
Time (days), x	2	7	10	30
Amount of milk (L), y	50	175	250	750

Read the Problem

What do I need to find?	What information do I need to use?	How will I use the information?

Solve the Problem

Math Talk **Mathematical Practices**

Explain how you wrote an equation to represent the pattern in the table.

So, in 365 days, the farmer can get __________ liters of milk from the cow.

- Explain how you could find the number of days it would take the cow to produce 500 liters of milk.

____

____

____

Name ______________________

Share and Show

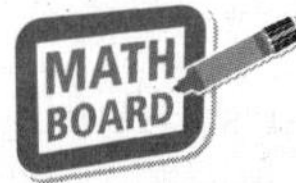

1. A soccer coach is ordering shirts for the players. The table shows the total cost based on the number of shirts ordered. How much will it cost the coach to order 18 shirts?

First, find a pattern and write an equation.

The cost is ______ multiplied by ______________.

______ = ______ · ______

Next, use the equation to find the cost of 18 shirts.

So, the cost of 18 shirts is ______.

2. THINKSMARTER What if the coach spent $375 to purchase a number of shirts? Could you use the same equation to find how many shirts the coach bought? Explain.

____

____

3. GO DEEPER The table shows the number of miles the Carter family drove over time. If the pattern continues, will the Carter family have driven more than 400 miles in 8 hours? Explain.

____

____

____

4. MATHEMATICAL PRACTICE 7 **Look for a Pattern** The Carter family drove a total of 564 miles. Describe how to use the pattern in the table to find the number of hours they spent driving.

____

____

____

Unlock the Problem

- √ Find a pattern in the table.
- √ Write an equation to represent the pattern.
- √ Check your answer.

Soccer Shirts

Number of Shirts, n	2	3	5	6
Cost ($), c	30	45	75	90

Carter Family Trip

Time (hr), x	Distance (mi), y
1	47
3	141
5	235
6	282

On Your Own

5. A group of dancers practiced for 4 hours in March, 8 hours in April, 12 hours in May, and 16 hours in June. If the pattern continues, how many hours will they practice in November?

6. GO DEEPER The table shows the number of hours Jacob worked and the amount he earned each day.

Jacob's Earnings					
Time (hr), h	5	7	6	8	4
Amount earned ($), d	60	84	72	96	48

At the end of the week, he used his earnings to buy a new pair of skis. He had $218 left over. How much did the skis cost?

7. THINK SMARTER **Pose a Problem** Look back at Problem 6. Use the data in the table to write a new problem in which you could use the strategy *find a pattern*. Then solve the problem.

8. MATHEMATICAL PRACTICE 8 **Draw Conclusions** Marlon rode his bicycle 9 miles the first week, 18 miles the second week, and 27 miles the third week. If the pattern continues, will Marlon ride exactly 100 miles in a week at some point? Explain how you determined your answer.

Personal Math Trainer

9. THINK SMARTER + A diving instructor ordered snorkels. The table shows the cost based on the number of snorkels ordered.

Number of Snorkels, s	1	2	3	4
Cost ($), c	32	64	96	128

If the diving instructor spent $1,024, how many snorkels did he order? Use numbers and words to explain your answer.

FOR MORE PRACTICE: Standards Practice Book

Name ______________________________

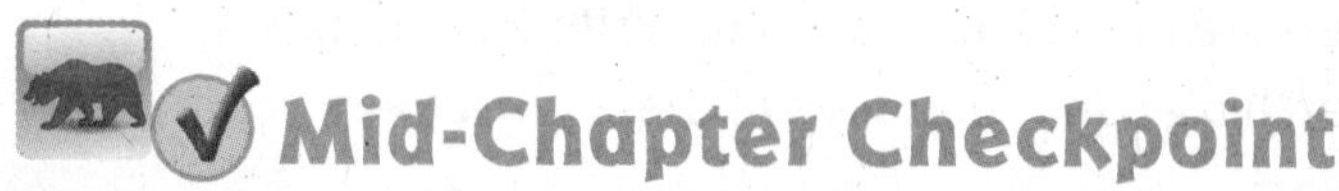

Mid-Chapter Checkpoint

Vocabulary

Vocabulary
dependent variable
equation
independent variable

Choose the best term from the box to complete the sentence.

1. A(n) ____________ has a value that determines the value of another quantity. (p. 357)

2. A variable whose value is determined by the value of another quantity is called a(n) ____________. (p. 357)

Concepts and Skills

Identify the independent and dependent variables. (6.EE.9)

3. Marco spends a total of *d* dollars on postage to mail party invitations to each of *g* guests.

   dependent variable: ______

   independent variable: ______

4. Sophie has a doll collection with 36 dolls. She decides to sell *s* dolls to a museum and has *r* dolls remaining.

   dependent variable: ______

   independent variable: ______

Write an equation for the relationship shown in the table. Then find the unknown value in the table. (6.EE.9)

5.

x	6	7	8	9
y	42	?	56	63

____

6.

x	20	40	60	80
y	4	8	?	16

____

Write an equation that describes the pattern shown in the table. (6.EE.9)

7. The table shows how the number of pepperoni slices used depends on the number of pizzas made.

Pepperonis Used				
Pizzas, *x*	2	3	5	9
Pepperoni slices, *y*	34	51	85	153

____

8. Brayden is training for a marathon. The table shows how the number of miles he runs depends on which week of training he is in.

Miles Run During Training				
Week, *w*	3	5	8	12
Miles, *m*	8	10	13	17

____

9. The band has a total of 152 members. Some of the members are in the marching band, and the rest are in the concert band. Write an equation that models how many marching band members m there are if there are c concert band members. (6.EE.9)

10. A coach is ordering baseball jerseys from a website. The jerseys cost \$15 each, and shipping is \$8 per order. Write an equation that can be used to determine the total cost y, in dollars, for x jerseys. (6.EE.9)

11. Amy volunteers at an animal shelter. She worked 10 hours in March, 12 hours in April, 14 hours in May, and 16 hours in June. If the pattern continues, how many hours will she work in December? (6.EE.9)

12. Aaron wants to buy a new snowboard. The table shows the amount that he has saved. If the pattern in the table continues, how much will he have saved after 1 year? (6.EE.9)

Aaron's Savings

Time (months)	Money saved (\$)
3	135
4	180
6	270
7	315

Name ______________________________

Graph Relationships

Essential Question How can you graph the relationship between two quantities?

Expressions and Equations—6.EE.9

MATHEMATICAL PRACTICES
MP.4, MP.6, MP.7

CONNECT You have learned that tables and equations are two ways to represent the relationship between two quantities. You can also represent a relationship between two quantities by using a graph.

Unlock the Problem

A cafeteria has a pancake-making machine. The table shows the relationship between the time in hours and the number of pancakes the machine can make. Graph the relationship represented by the table.

Pancake Production	
Time (hours)	Pancakes Made
1	200
2	400
3	600
4	800
5	1,000

Use the table values to graph the relationship.

STEP 1 Write ordered pairs.

Let x represent the time in hours and y represent the number of pancakes made. Use each row of the table to write an ordered pair.

(1, 200) (2, ________) (3, ________) (____, ________) (____, ________)

STEP 2 Choose an appropriate scale for each axis of the graph. Label the axes and give the graph a title.

____

STEP 3 Graph a point for each ordered pair.

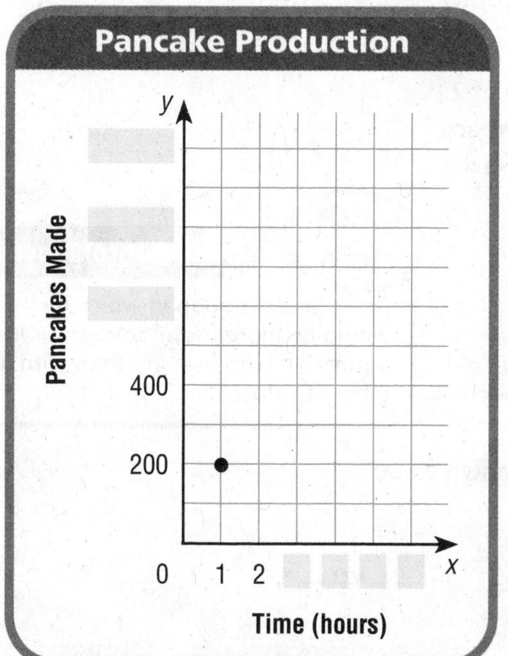

Math Talk **Mathematical Practices**

Describe any patterns you notice in the set of points you graphed.

Example

The table shows the relationship between the number of bicycles y Shawn has left to assemble and the number of hours x he has worked. Graph the relationship represented by the table to find the unknown value of y.

Time (hours), *x*	Bicycles Left to Assemble, *y*
0	10
1	8
2	?
3	4
4	2

STEP 1 Write ordered pairs.

Use each row of the table to write an ordered pair. Skip the row with the unknown *y*-value.

(0, 10) (1, ______) (3, ______) (______, ______)

STEP 2 Graph a point for each ordered pair on a coordinate plane.

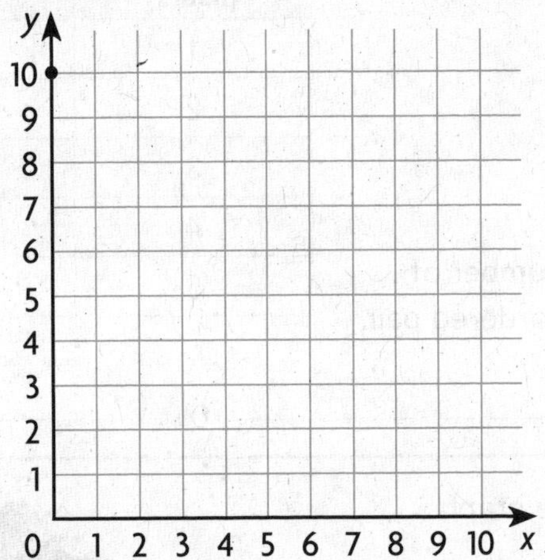

Remember

The first value in an ordered pair represents the independent variable *x*. The second value represents the dependent variable *y*.

STEP 3 Find the unknown *y*-value.

The points on the graph appear to lie on a line. Use a ruler to draw a dashed line through the points.

Use the line to find the *y*-value that corresponds to an *x*-value of 2. Start at the origin, and move 2 units right. Move up until you reach the line you drew. Then move left to find the *y*-value on the *y*-axis.

When *x* has a value of 2, *y* has a value of ______.

So, after 2 hours, Shawn has ______ bicycles left to assemble.

Math Talk **Mathematical Practices**

Describe a situation in which it would be more useful to represent a function with a graph than with a table of values.

- MATHEMATICAL PRACTICE 6 **Describe** another way you could find the unknown value of *y* in the table.

Name ________________________________

Share and Show

Graph the relationship represented by the table.

1.

x	1	2	3	4
y	50	100	150	200

Write ordered pairs. Then graph.

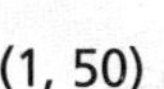

(1, 50)

(2, ________)

(3, ________)

(________, ________)

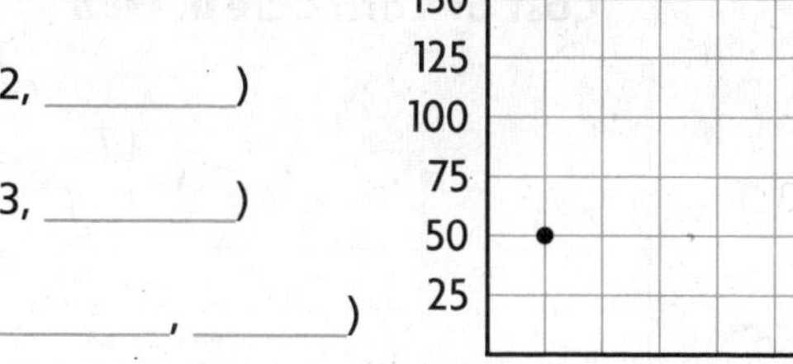

2.

x	20	40	60	80
y	100	200	300	400

Graph the relationship represented by the table to find the unknown value of y.

3.

x	4	5	6	7	8
y	9	7	5		1

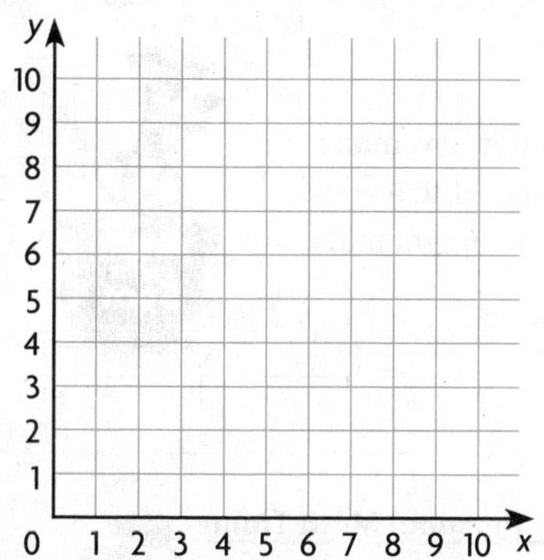

4.

x	1	3	5	7	9
y	3	4	5		7

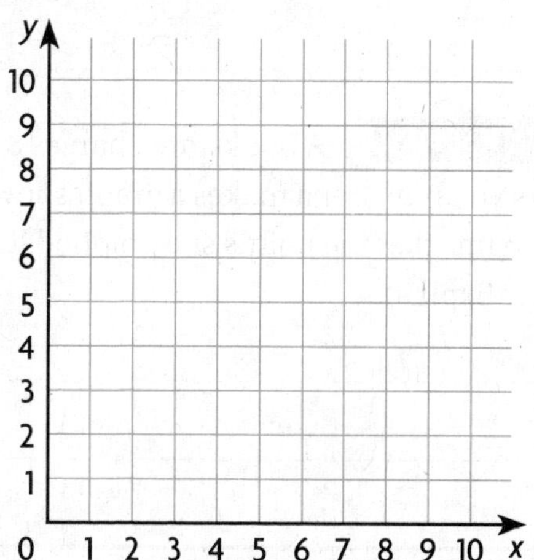

Math Talk — **Mathematical Practices**

Explain how to use a graph to find an unknown y-value in a table.

On Your Own

Practice: Copy and Solve **Graph the relationship represented by the table to find the unknown value of y.**

5.

x	1	3	5	7	9
y	7	6		4	3

6.

x	1	2	4	6	7
y	2	3	5		8

Problem Solving • Applications

The table at the right shows the typical price of a popular brand of corn cereal over time. Use the table for 7–8.

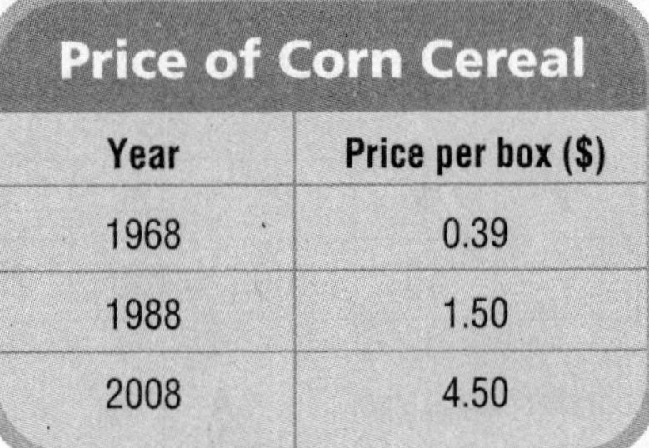

Price of Corn Cereal

Year	Price per box ($)
1968	0.39
1988	1.50
2008	4.50

7. MATHEMATICAL PRACTICE 4 **Use Graphs** Complete the table below to show the cost of buying 1 to 5 boxes of corn cereal in 1988. Then graph the relationship on the coordinate plane at right.

Boxes	1	2	3	4	5
Cost in 1988 ($)	1.50				

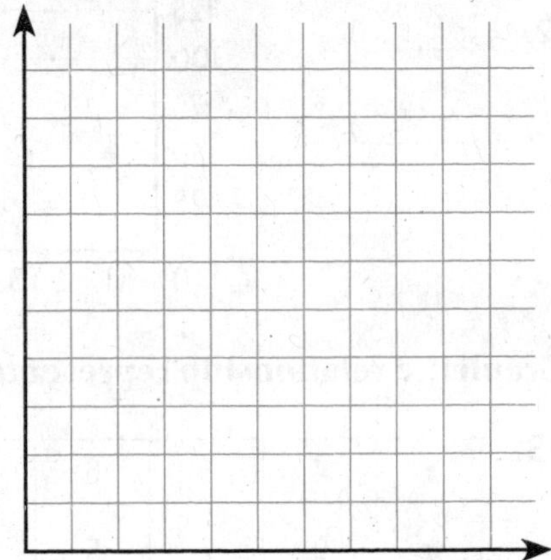

8. GO DEEPER Suppose you graphed the cost of buying 1 to 5 boxes of corn cereal using the 1968 price and the 2008 price. Explain how those graphs would compare to the graph you made using the 1988 price.

____

____

____

____

____

9. THINK SMARTER A bookstore charges $4 for shipping, no matter how many books you buy. Irena makes a graph showing the shipping cost for 1 to 5 books. She claims that the points she graphed lie on a line. Does her statement make sense? Explain.

____

____

Personal Math Trainer

10. THINK SMARTER + Graph the relationship represented by the table to find the unknown value of y.

x	1	2	3	4
y	2	2.5		3.5

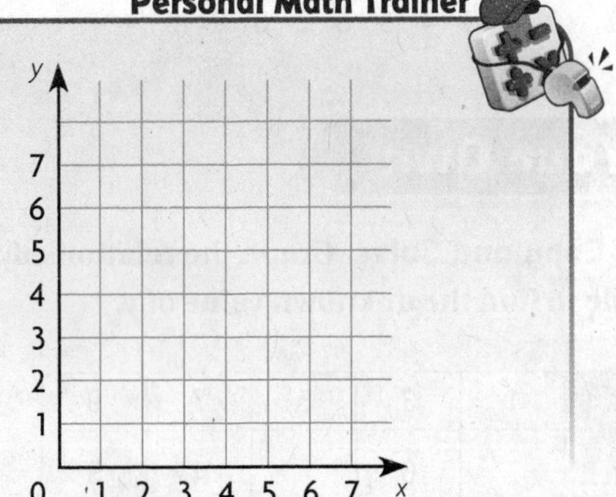

FOR MORE PRACTICE: Standards Practice Book

Name ______________________________

Equations and Graphs

Essential Question How can you translate between equations and graphs?

Expressions and Equations—6.EE.9

MATHEMATICAL PRACTICES
MP.3, MP.4, MP.5

The solution of an equation in two variables is an ordered pair that makes the equation true. For example, (2, 5) is a solution of the equation $y = x + 3$ because $5 = 2 + 3$.

A **linear equation** is an equation whose solutions form a straight line on the coordinate plane. Any point on the line is a solution of the equation.

Unlock the Problem

A blue whale is swimming at an average rate of 3 miles per hour. Write a linear equation that gives the distance y in miles that the whale swims in x hours. Then graph the relationship.

- What formula can you use to help you write the equation?

____

Write and graph a linear equation.

STEP 1 Write an equation for the relationship.

Think: Distance → equals → rate → multiplied by → time.

_______ = _______ · _______

STEP 2 Find ordered pairs that are solutions of the equation.

Choose several values of x and find the corresponding values of y.

x	$3x$	y	Ordered Pair
1	$3 \cdot 1$	3	(1, 3)
2	$3 \cdot$		(2,)
3	$3 \cdot$		(,)
4	$3 \cdot$		(,)

STEP 3 Graph the relationship.

Graph the ordered pairs. Draw a line through the points to show all the solutions of the linear equation.

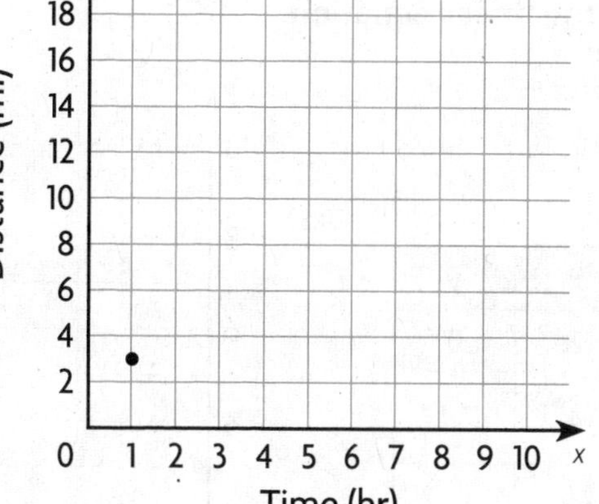

Math Talk **Mathematical Practices**

Explain why the graph does not show negative values of x or y.

Example The graph shows the number of beaded necklaces *y* that Ginger can make in *x* hours. Write the linear equation for the relationship shown by the graph.

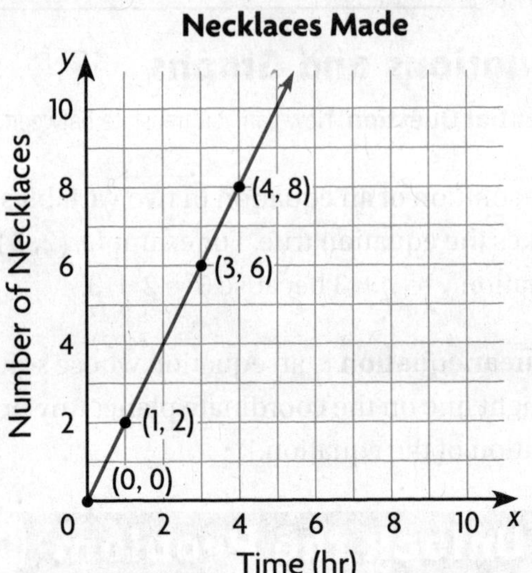

STEP 1 Use ordered pairs from the graph to complete the table of values below.

STEP 2 Look for a pattern in the table.

Compare each *y*-value with the corresponding *x*-value.

x	0	1	3	4
y	0			

$2 \cdot 0$ $2 \cdot 1$ $2 \cdot$ _____ $2 \cdot$ _____

Think: Each *y*-value is ______ times the corresponding *x*-value.

So, the linear equation for the relationship is $y =$ ______.

1. Explain how to graph a linear equation. __________

____

____

2. MATHEMATICAL PRACTICE 3 **Compare Representations** Describe a situation in which it would be more useful to represent a relationship with an equation than with a graph.

____

____

Share and Show

Graph the linear equation.

1. $y = x - 2$

Make a table of values. Then graph.

x	*y*
2	0
4	
6	
8	

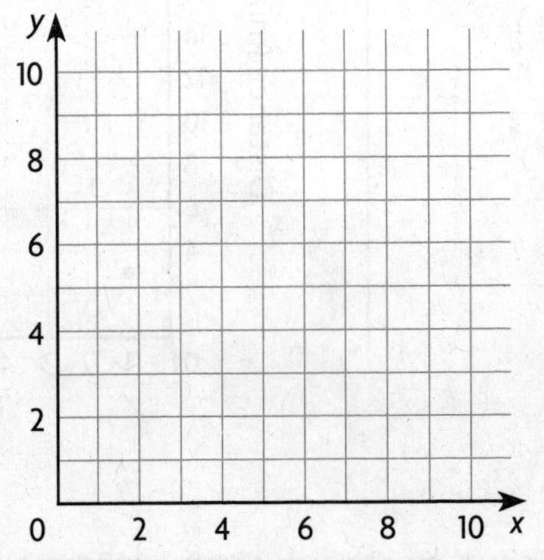

2. $y = 3x$

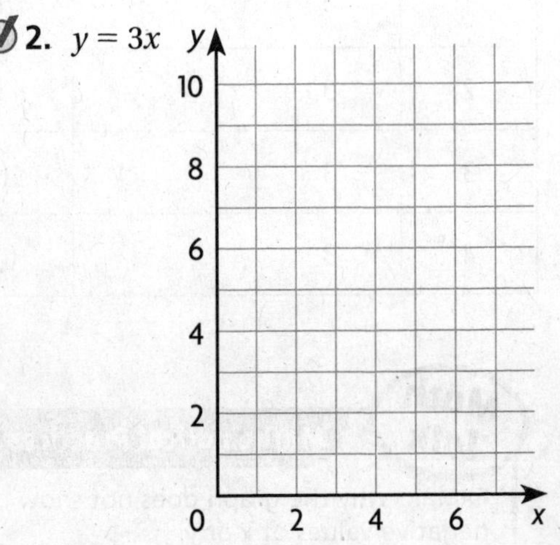

Name ____________________

Write the linear equation for the relationship shown by the graph.

3.

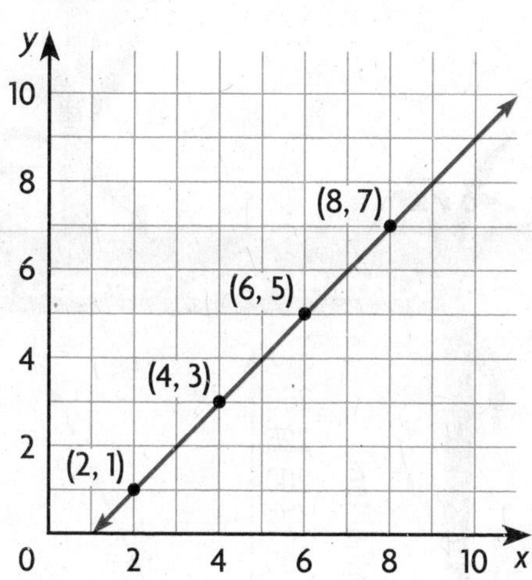

4.

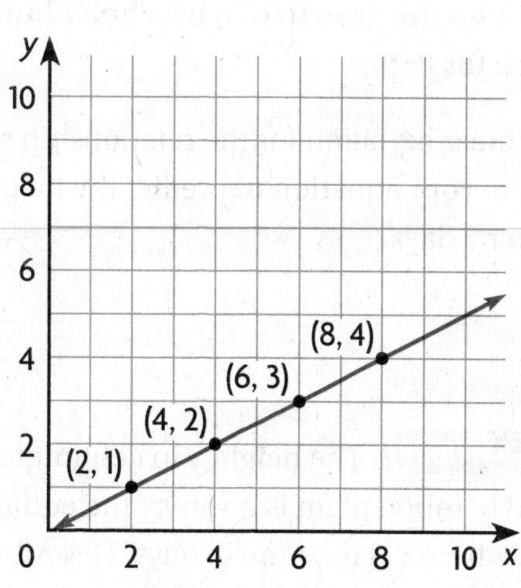

Math Talk **Mathematical Practices**

Explain how you can tell whether you have graphed a linear equation correctly.

On Your Own

Graph the linear equation.

5. $y = x + 1$

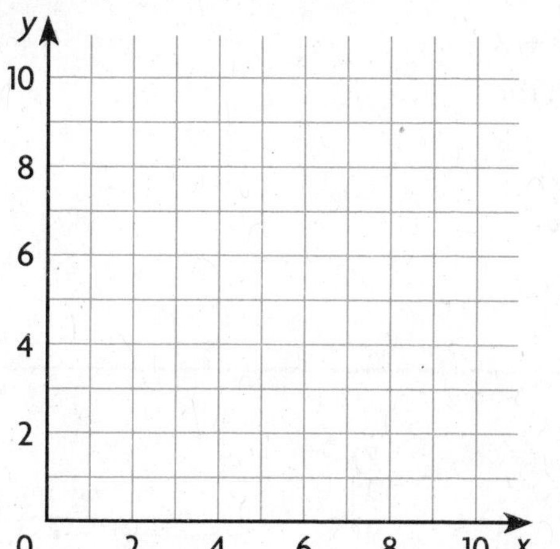

6. $y = 2x - 1$

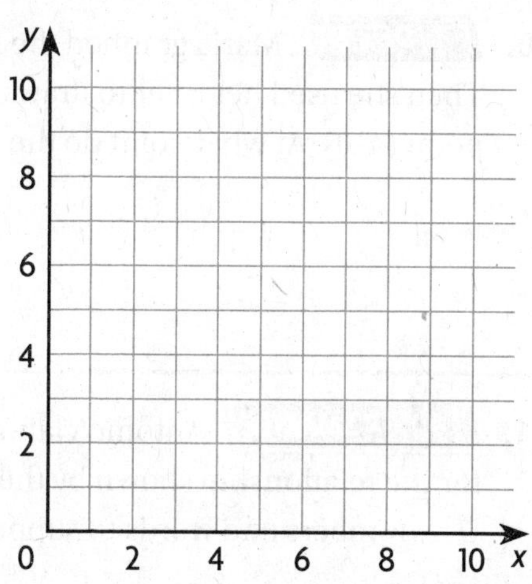

7. MATHEMATICAL PRACTICE 7 **Identify Relationships** The graph shows the number of loaves of bread y that Kareem bakes in x hours. Write the linear equation for the relationship shown by the graph.

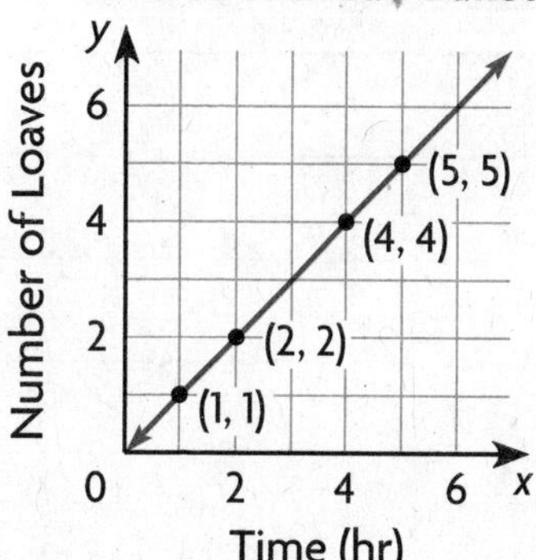

Problem Solving • Applications

The graph shows the growth of a bamboo plant. Use the graph for 8–9.

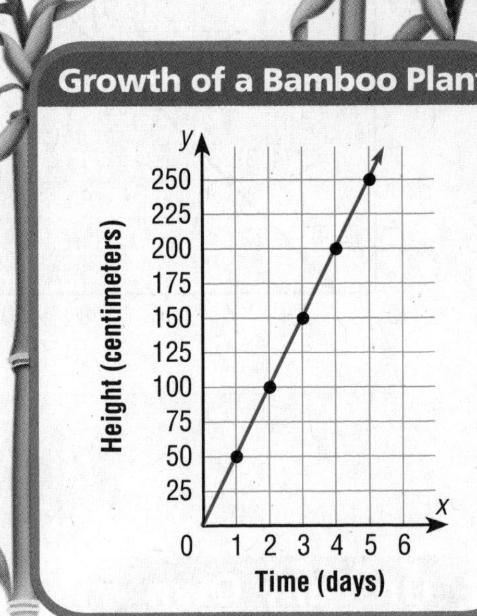

8. Write a linear equation for the relationship shown by the graph. Use your equation to predict the height of the bamboo plant after 7 days.

____

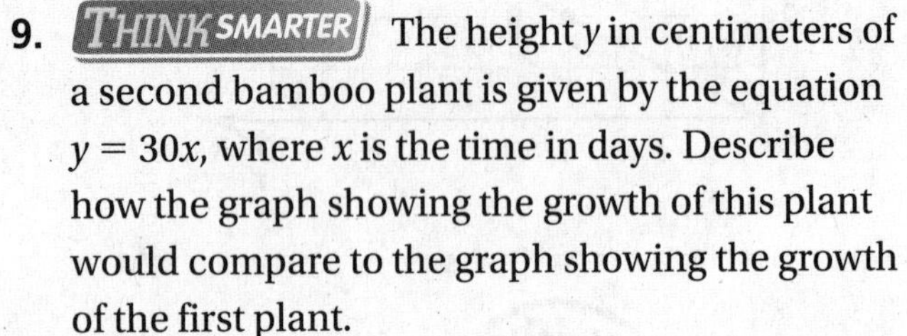

9. THINK SMARTER The height y in centimeters of a second bamboo plant is given by the equation $y = 30x$, where x is the time in days. Describe how the graph showing the growth of this plant would compare to the graph showing the growth of the first plant.

____

____

____

10. GO DEEPER Maria graphed the linear equation $y = x + 3$. Then she used her ruler to draw a vertical line through the point (4, 0). At what point do the two lines intersect?

____

11. THINK SMARTER Antonio claims the linear equation for the relationship shown by the graph is $y = \frac{1}{2}x + 2$. Use numbers and words to support Antonio's claim.

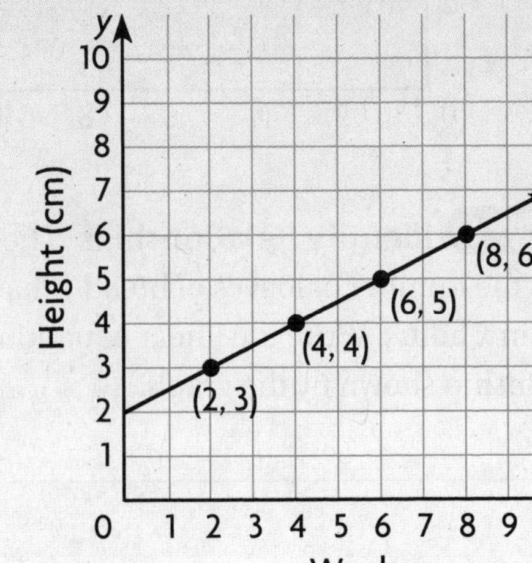

____

____

____

____

____

FOR MORE PRACTICE: Standards Practice Book

Name ______________________

Chapter 9 Review/Test

1. A box of peanut butter crackers contains 12 individual snacks. The total number of individual snacks *s* is equal to 12 times the number of boxes of crackers *b*.

The independent variable is [*b*. / *s*.]   The dependent variable is [*b*. / *s*.]

The equation that represents the relationship between the variables is [$b = 12s$. / $s = 12b$.]

2. A stationery store charges \$8 to print logos on paper purchases. The total cost *c* is the price of the paper *p* plus \$8 for printing the logo.

For numbers 2a–2d, select True or False for each statement.

2a. The total cost *c* depends on the price of the paper. ○ True ○ False

2b. *c* is the dependent variable. ○ True ○ False

2c. *p* is the independent variable. ○ True ○ False

2d. The equation that represents the relationship between the variables is $c = 8p$. ○ True ○ False

3. An electrician charges \$75 an hour for labor and an initial fee of \$65. The total cost *c* equals 75 times the number of hours *x* plus 65. Write an equation for the relationship and use the equation to complete the table.

Time (hr), *x*	Cost (\$), *c*
1	
2	
3	
4	

equation ______________

GO DIGITAL Assessment Options Chapter Test

4. The community center offers classes in arts and crafts. There is a registration fee of $125 and each class costs $79. The total cost *c* equals 79 times the number of classes *n* plus 125.

Input	Output
Number of Classes, *n*	Cost ($), *c*
1	204
2	283
3	362
4	441

For numbers 4a–4d, select True or False for each statement.

4a. The registration fee is $120. ○ True ○ False

4b. *n* is the independent variable. ○ True ○ False

4c. *c* is the dependent variable. ○ True ○ False

4d. The cost for 7 classes is $678. ○ True ○ False

5. Ms. Walsh is buying calculators for her class. The table shows the total cost based on the number of calculators purchased.

Number of Calculators, *n*	1	2	3	4
Cost ($), *c*	15	30	45	60

If Ms. Walsh spent a total of $525, how many calculators did she buy? Use numbers and words to explain your answer.

Name ______________________________

6. The table shows the number of cups of lemonade that can be made from cups of lemon juice.

Lemon Juice (cups), j	2	4	5	7
Lemonade (cups), l	14	28	35	49

Mary Beth says the number of cups of lemon juice j depends on the number of cups of lemonade l. She says the equation $j = 7l$ represents the relationship between the cups of lemon juice j and the cups of lemonade l. Is Mary Beth correct? Use words and numbers to explain why or why not.

7. For numbers 7a–7d, choose Yes or No to indicate whether the points on a graph of the ordered pairs would lie on a line.

7a. (1, 6), (2, 4), (3, 2), (4, 0) ○ Yes ○ No

7b. (1, 1), (2, 4), (3, 9), (4, 16) ○ Yes ○ No

7c. (1, 3), (2, 5), (3, 7), (4, 9) ○ Yes ○ No

7d. (1, 8), (2, 10), (3, 12), (4, 14) ○ Yes ○ No

8. Graph the relationship represented by the table to find the unknown value.

Time (seconds), x	40	50	60	70
Water in Tub (gal), y	13	11.5		8.5

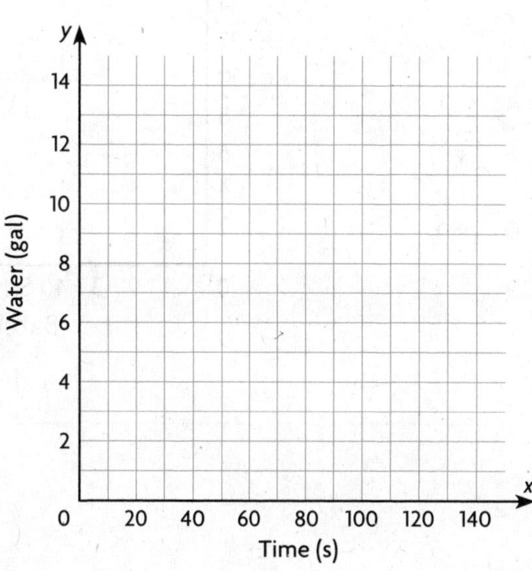

9. Graph the relationship represented by the table.

Time (hr), x	3	4	5	6
Distance (mi), y	240	320	400	480

y
560
480
400
320
240
160
80
Distance (mi)
0 1 2 3 4 5 6 7 8 9 10
x
Time (hr)

10. Miranda's wages are $15 per hour. Write a linear equation that gives the wages w in dollars that Miranda earns in h hours.

____

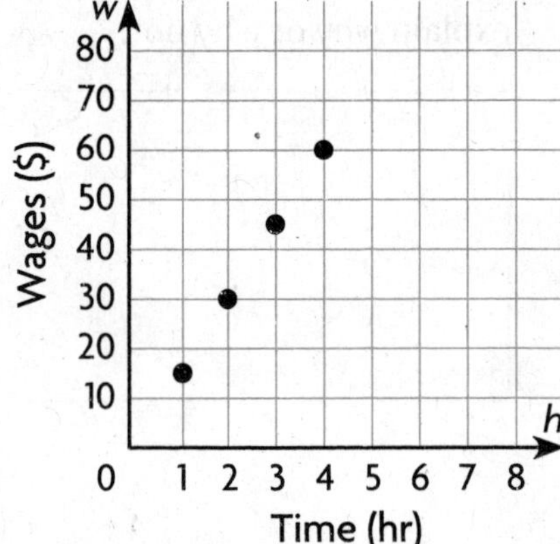

11. The table shows the number of apples a that Lucinda uses in b batches of applesauce.

Batches, b	1	2	3	4
Apples, a	4	8	12	16

Graph the relationship between batches b and apples a. Then write the equation that shows the relationship.

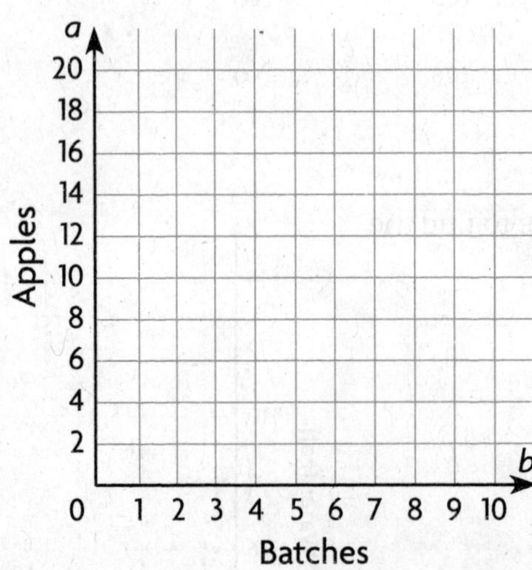

____

Name ______________________________

12. Delonna walks 4 miles per day for exercise. The total number of miles *m* she walks equals 4 times the number of days *d* she walks.

What is the dependent variable? ____________

What is the independent variable? ____________

Write the equation that represents the relationship between the *m* and *d*.

____

13. Lacy is staying at a hotel that costs $85 per night. The total cost of Lacy's stay is 85 times the number of nights *n* she stays.

For numbers 13a–13d, select True or False for each statement.

13a. The number of nights *n* is dependent on the cost *c*. ○ True ○ False

13b. *n* is the independent variable. ○ True ○ False

13c. *c* is the dependent variable. ○ True ○ False

13d. The equation that represents the total cost is $c = 85n$. ○ True ○ False

14. A taxi cab company charges an initial fee of $5 and then $4 per mile for a ride. Use the equation $c = 4x + 5$ to complete the table.

Input	Output
Miles (mi), *x*	Cost ($), *c*
2	
4	
6	
8	

15. A grocery display of cans is arranged in the form of a pyramid with 1 can in the top row, 3 in the second row from the top, 5 in the third row, and 7 in the fourth row. The total number of cans c in each row equals 2 times the row r minus 1. Use the equation $c = 2r - 1$ to complete the table.

Row, r	Cans, c
5	
6	
7	
8	

16. The graph shows the number of words Mason read in a given amount of minutes. If Mason continues to read at the same rate, how many words will he have read in 5 minutes?

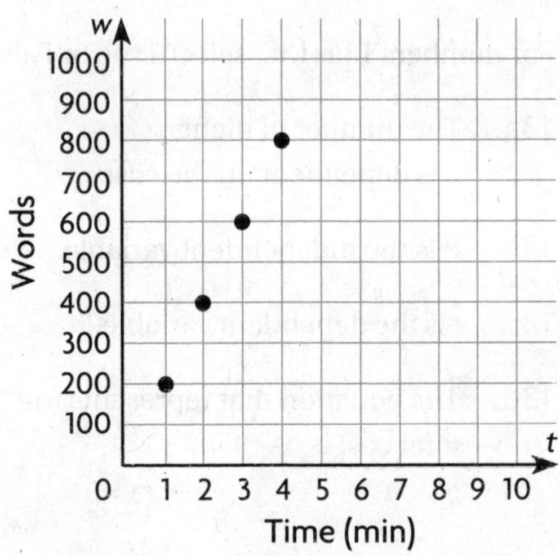

____

17. Casey claims the linear equation for the relationship shown by the graph is $c = 25j$. Use numbers and words to support Casey's claim.

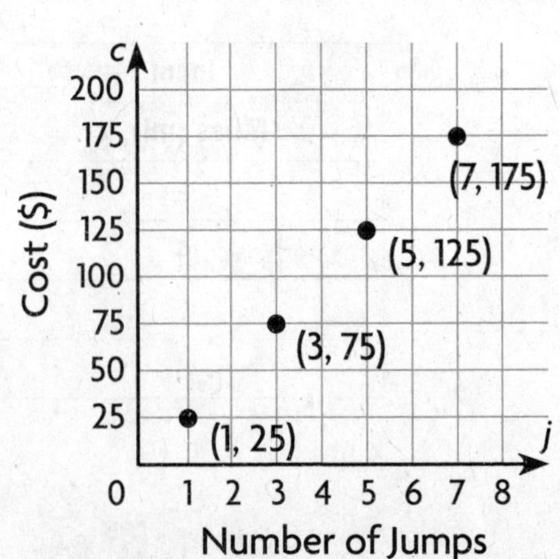

____

____

____

____

Critical Area

Geometry and Statistics

CRITICAL AREA

Solve real-world and mathematical problems involving area, surface area, and volume.

Developing understanding of statistical thinking

The San Francisco zoo in San Francisco, California, is home to hundreds of different animals, including this Bengal tiger.

Project

This Place is a Zoo!

Planning a zoo is a difficult task. Each animal requires a special environment with different amounts of space and different features.

Get Started

You are helping to design a new section of a zoo. The table lists some of the new attractions planned for the zoo. Each attraction includes notes about the type and the amount of space needed. The zoo owns a rectangle of land that is 100 feet long and 60 feet wide. Find the dimensions of each of the attractions and draw a sketch of the plan for the zoo.

Important Facts

Attraction	Minimum Floor Space (sq ft)	Notes
American Alligators	400	rectangular pen with one side at least 24 feet long
Amur Tigers	750	trapezoid-shaped area with one side at least 40 feet long
Howler Monkeys	450	parallelogram-shaped cage with one side at least 30 feet long
Meerkat Village	250	square pen with glass sides
Red Foxes	350	rectangular pen with length twice as long as width
Tropical Aquarium	200	triangular bottom with base at least 20 feet long

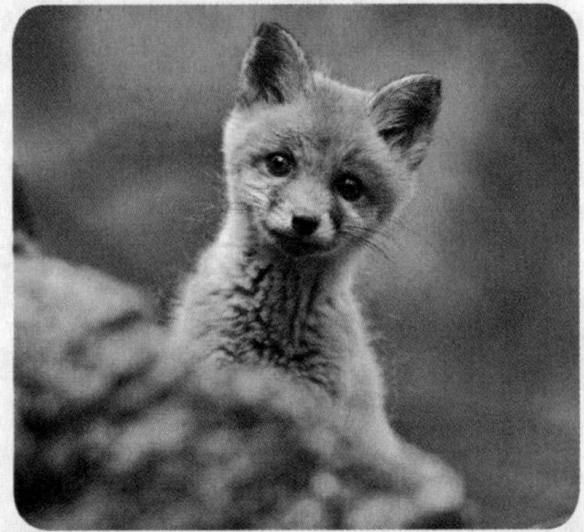

Completed by ______________________________

Chapter

10 Area

Show What You Know

Check your understanding of important skills.

Name ______________________

▶ Perimeter Find the perimeter.

1. 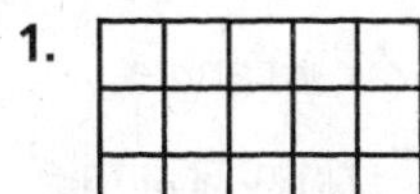 $P =$ ______ units

2. 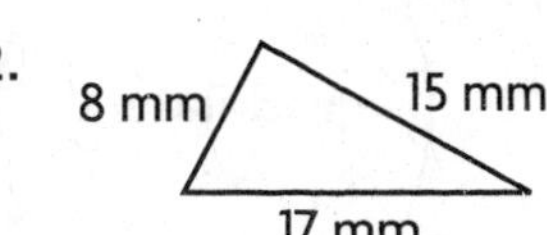

$P =$ ______ mm

▶ Identify Polygons Name each polygon based on the number of sides.

3. 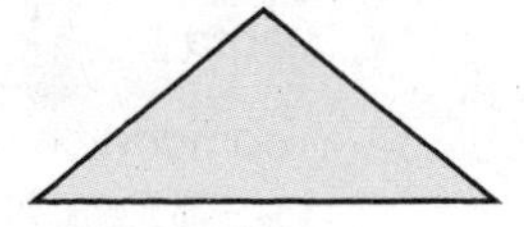
______

4. 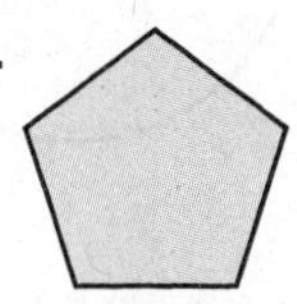
______

5. ______

▶ Evaluate Algebraic Expressions Evaluate the expression.

6. $5x + 2y$ for $x = 7$ and $y = 9$
______

7. $6a \times 3b + 4$ for $a = 2$ and $b = 8$
______

8. $s^2 + t^2 - 2^3$ for $s = 4$ and $t = 6$
______

Ross needs to paint the white boundary lines of one end zone on a football field. The area of the end zone is 4,800 square feet, and one side of the end zone measures 30 feet. One can of paint is enough to paint 300 feet of line. Be a Math Detective and find out if one can is enough to line the perimeter of the end zone.

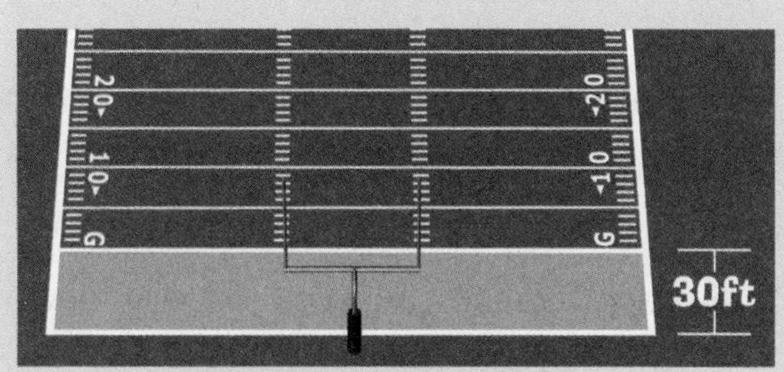

Personal Math Trainer
Online Assessment and Intervention

Vocabulary Builder

▶ Visualize It

Complete the bubble map by using the checked words that are types of quadrilaterals.

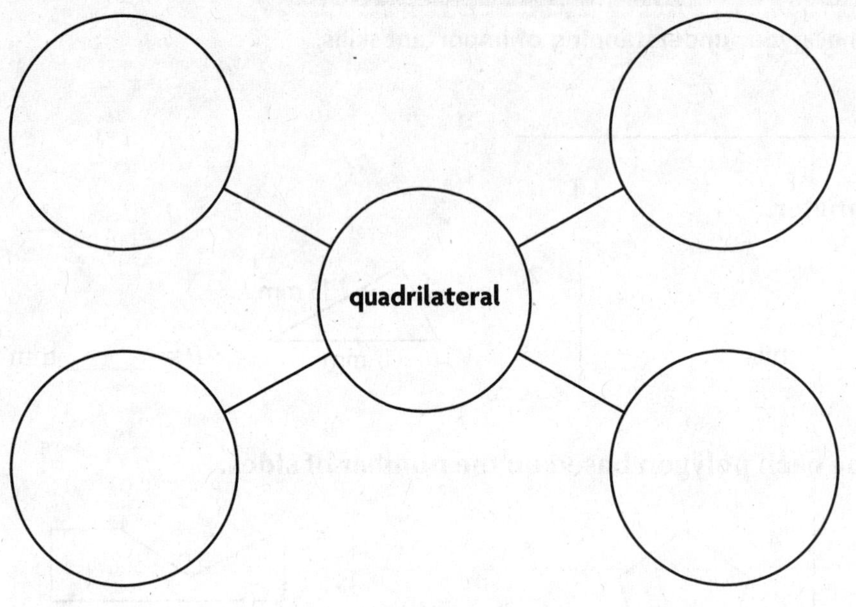

Review Words

acute triangle
base
height
obtuse triangle
✓ polygon
quadrilateral
✓ rectangle
right triangle
✓ square

Preview Words

area
composite figure
congruent
✓ parallelogram
regular polygon
✓ trapezoid

▶ Understand Vocabulary

Complete the sentences using the preview words.

1. The ____________________ of a figure is the number of square units needed to cover it without any gaps or overlaps.

2. A polygon in which all sides are the same length and all angles have the same measure is called a(n) ____________________.

3. A(n) ____________________ is a quadrilateral with exactly one pair of parallel sides.

4. ____________________ figures have the same size and shape.

5. A quadrilateral with two pairs of parallel sides is called a ____________________.

6. A(n) ____________________ is made up of more than one shape.

GO DIGITAL • Interactive Student Edition • Multimedia eGlossary

Name ____________________________________

ALGEBRA Lesson 10.1

Area of Parallelograms

Essential Question How can you find the area of parallelograms?

Geometry—6.G.1 *Also 6.EE.2c, 6.EE.7*

MATHEMATICAL PRACTICES
MP.4, MP.5, MP.6, MP.8

CONNECT The **area** of a figure is the number of square units needed to cover it without any gaps or overlaps. The area of a rectangle is the product of the length and the width. The rectangle shown has an area of 12 square units. For a rectangle with length l and width w, $A = l \times w$, or $A = lw$.

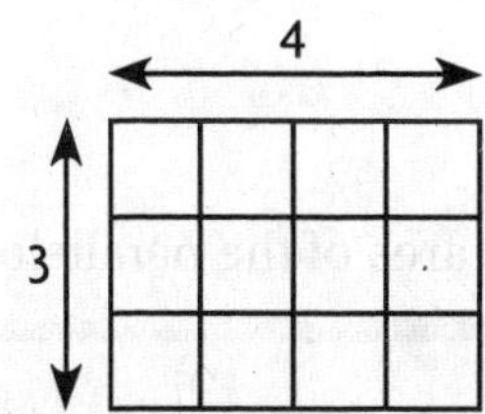

Recall that a rectangle is a special type of parallelogram. A parallelogram is a quadrilateral with two pairs of parallel sides.

Unlock the Problem

Victoria is making a quilt. She is using material in the shape of parallelograms to form the pattern. The base of each parallelogram measures 9 cm and the height measures 4 cm. What is the area of each parallelogram?

Activity Use the area of a rectangle to find the area of the parallelogram.

Materials ■ grid paper ■ scissors

- Draw the parallelogram on grid paper and cut it out.
- Cut along the dashed line to remove a triangle.
- Move the triangle to the right side of the figure to form a rectangle.

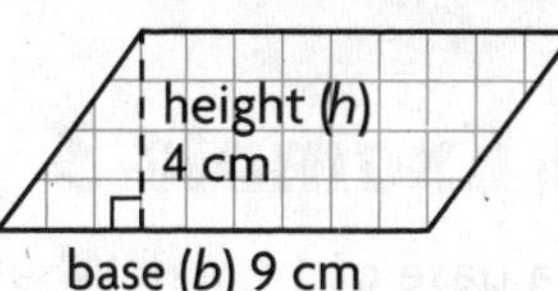

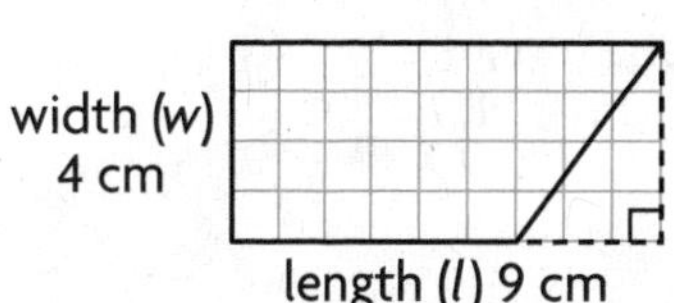

- What is the area of the rectangle? ______________
- What is the area of the parallelogram? ______________
- base of parallelogram = ____________ of rectangle

  height of parallelogram = ____________ of rectangle

  area of parallelogram = ____________ of rectangle
- For a parallelogram with base b and height h, $A =$ ____________

Area of parallelogram $= b \times h = 9 \text{ cm} \times 4 \text{ cm} =$ ______ sq cm

So, the area of each parallelogram in the quilt is ______ sq cm.

Math Idea

The height of a parallelogram forms a 90° angle with the base.

Math Talk Mathematical Practices

Explain how you know that the area of the parallelogram is the same as the area of the rectangle.

Example 1 Use the formula $A = bh$ to find the area of the parallelogram.

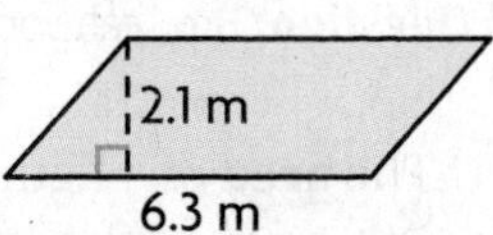

Write the formula. $A = bh$

Replace b and h with their values. $A = 6.3 \times$ ______

Multiply. $A =$ ______

So, the area of the parallelogram is ______ square meters.

A square is a special rectangle in which the length and width are equal. For a square with side length s, $A = l \times w = s \times s = s^2$, or $A = s^2$.

Example 2 Find the area of a square with sides measuring 9.5 cm.

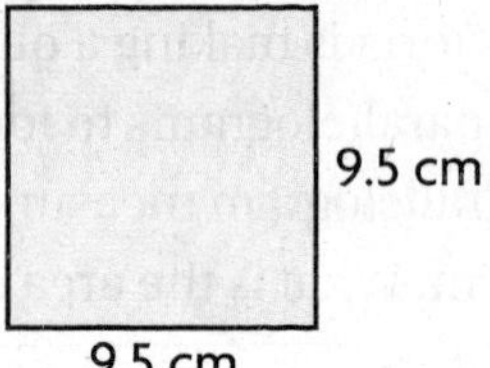

Write the formula. $A = s^2$

Substitute 9.5 for s. Simplify. $A = ($ ______ $)^2 =$ ______

So, the area of the square is ______ cm^2.

Example 3 A parallelogram has an area of 98 square feet and a base of 14 feet. What is the height of the parallelogram?

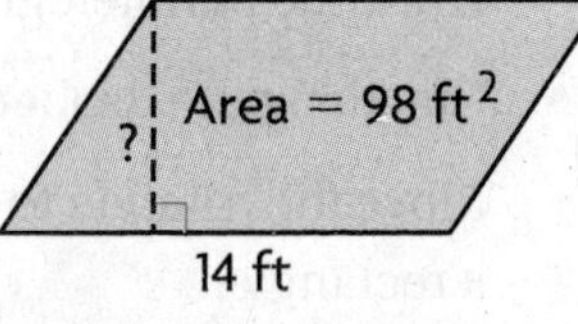

Write the formula. $A = bh$

Replace A and b with their values. ______ = ______ $\times h$

Use the Division Property of Equality. $\frac{98}{\square} = \frac{14h}{\square}$

Solve for h. ______ $= h$

So, the height of the parallelogram is ______ feet.

- MATHEMATICAL PRACTICE 6 **Compare** Explain the difference between the height of a rectangle and the height of a parallelogram.

______

______

______

Name ______________________

Share and Show

Find the area of the figure.

1. $A = bh$

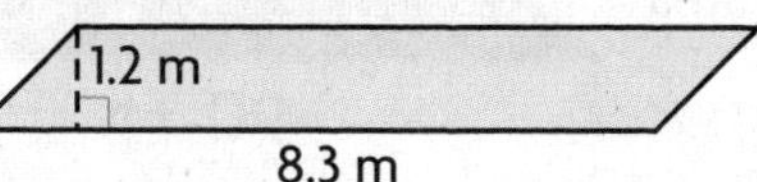

$A = 8.3 \times 1.2$

$A =$ ________ m^2

2.

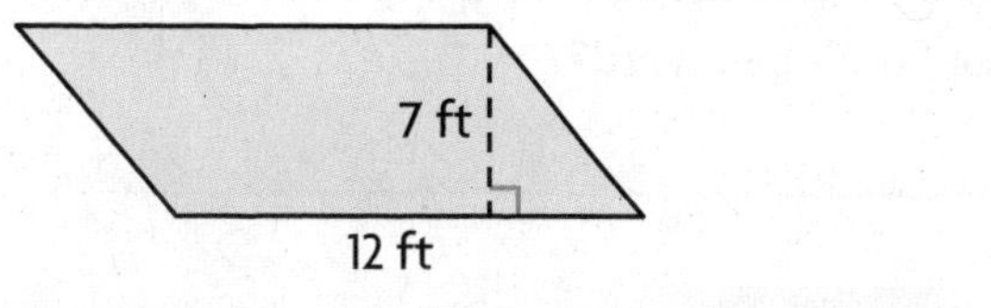

________ ft^2

3.

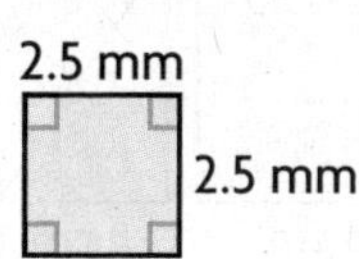

________ mm^2

4.

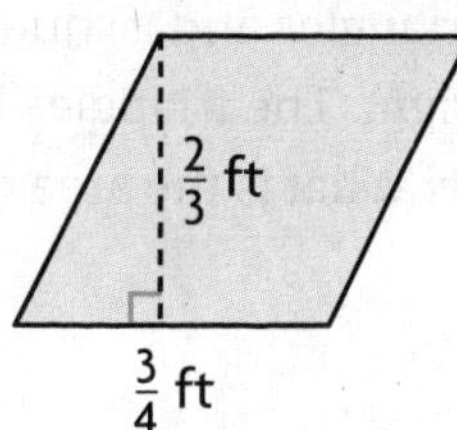

________ ft^2

Find the unknown measurement for the figure.

5. Area = 11 yd^2

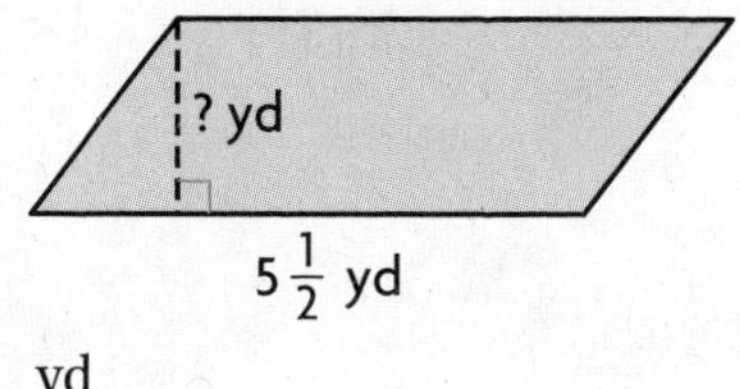

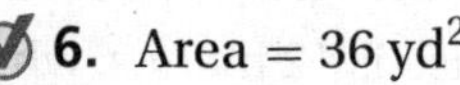

________ yd

6. Area = 36 yd^2

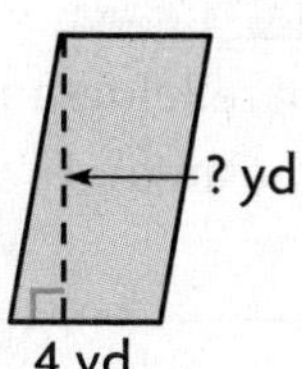

________ yd

Math Talk — **Mathematical Practices**

Explain how the areas of some parallelograms and rectangles are related.

On Your Own

Find the area of the figure.

7.

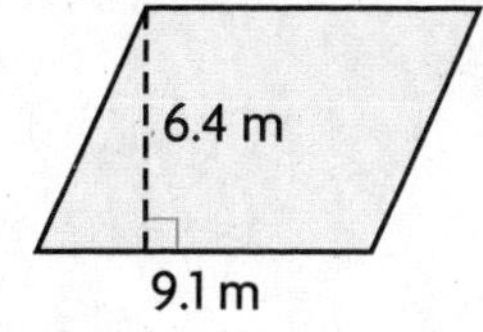

________ m^2

8. 8 ft; 21 ft

________ ft^2

Find the unknown measurement for the figure.

9. square

$A =$ ________

$s = 15$ ft

10. parallelogram

$A = 32\ m^2$

$b =$ ________

$h = 8$ m

11. parallelogram

$A = 51\frac{1}{4}\ in.^2$

$b = 8\frac{1}{5}$ in.

$h =$ ________

12. parallelogram

$A = 121\ mm^2$

$b = 11$ mm

$h =$ ________

13. THINK SMARTER The height of a parallelogram is four times the base. The base measures $3\frac{1}{2}$ ft. Find the area of the parallelogram.

____

Problem Solving • Applications

14. Jane's backyard is shaped like a parallelogram. The base of the parallelogram is 90 feet, and the height, measured from the back of the yard to the front, is 25 feet. What is the area of Jane's backyard?

____

15. THINK SMARTER Jack made a parallelogram by putting together two congruent triangles and a square, like the figures shown at the right. The triangles have the same height as the square. What is the area of Jack's parallelogram?

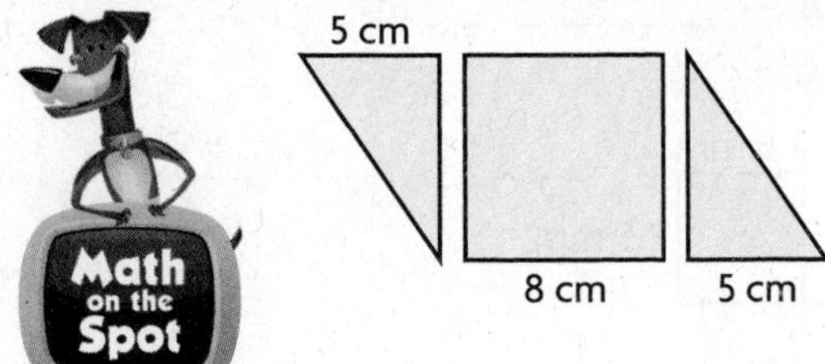

____

16. GO DEEPER The base of a parallelogram is 2 times the parallelogram's height. If the base is 12 inches, what is the area?

____

17. MATHEMATICAL PRACTICE 3 **Verify the Reasoning of Others** Li Ping says that a square with 3-inch sides has a greater area than a parallelogram that is not a square but has sides that have the same length. Does Li Ping's statement make sense? Explain.

____

____

____

____

____

18. THINK SMARTER Find the area of the parallelogram.

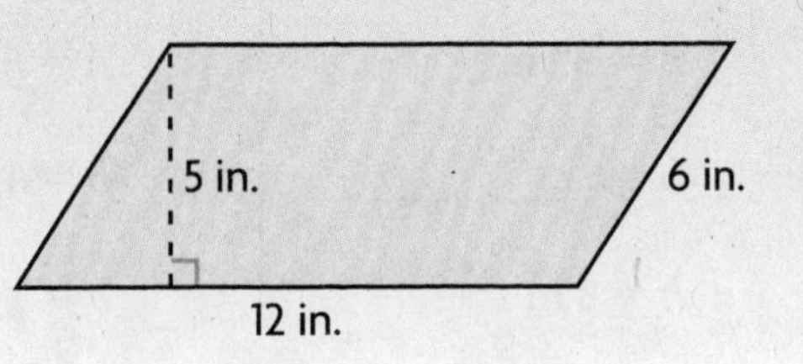

The area is _______ in^2.

FOR MORE PRACTICE: Standards Practice Book

Name ______________________________

Explore Area of Triangles

Essential Question What is the relationship among the areas of triangles, rectangles, and parallelograms?

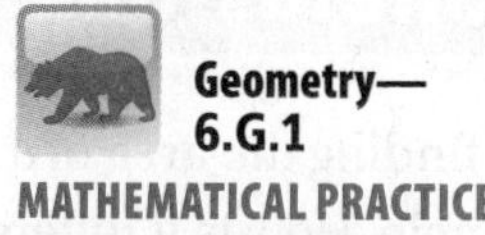

Geometry—6.G.1

MATHEMATICAL PRACTICES
MP.1, MP7, MP.8

Investigate

Materials ■ tracing paper ■ ruler ■ scissors

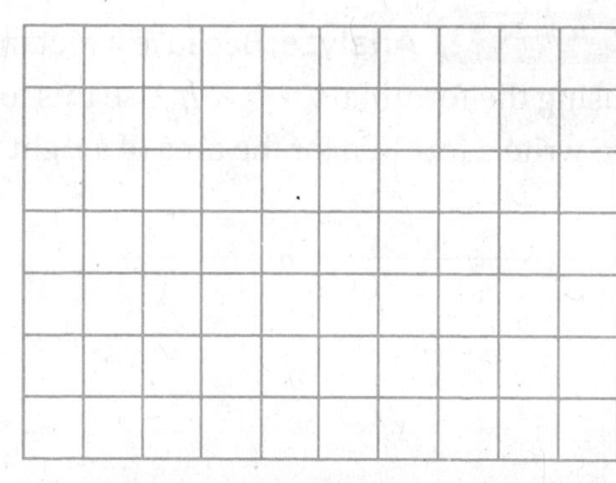

A. On the grid, draw a rectangle with a base of 6 units and a height of 5 units.

- What is the area of the rectangle?

____

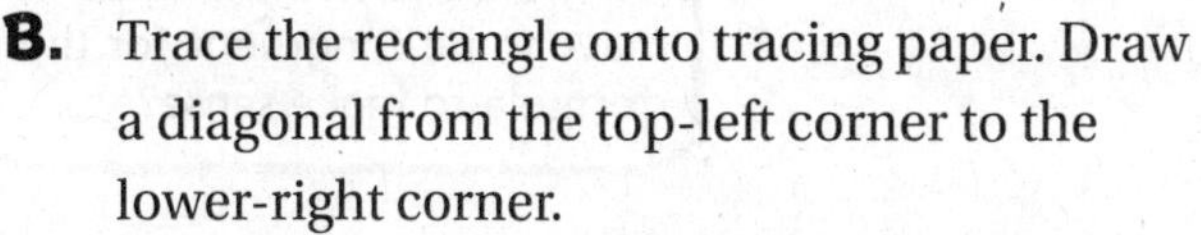

B. Trace the rectangle onto tracing paper. Draw a diagonal from the top-left corner to the lower-right corner.

- A diagonal is a line segment that connects two nonadjacent vertices of a polygon.

C. Cut out the rectangle. Then cut along the diagonal to divide the rectangle into two right triangles. Compare the two triangles.

- **Congruent** figures are the same shape and size. Are the two right triangles congruent?

____

____

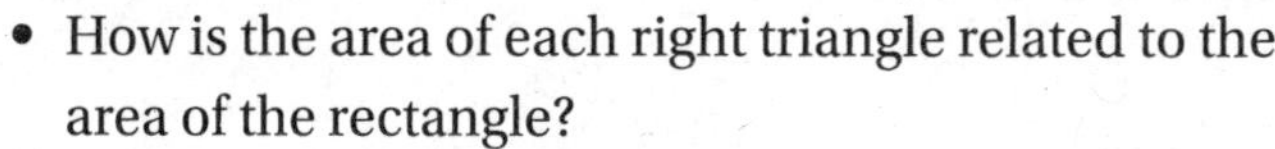

- How is the area of each right triangle related to the area of the rectangle?

____

____

- What is the area of each right triangle?

____

Draw Conclusions

1. Explain how finding the area of a rectangle is like finding the area of a right triangle. How is it different?

____

____

2. MATHEMATICAL PRACTICE 1 **Analyze** Because a rectangle is a parallelogram, its area can be found using the formula $A = b \times h$. Use this formula and your results from the Investigate to write a formula for the area of a right triangle with base b and height h.

____

Math Talk — **Mathematical Practices**

Why did the two triangles have to be congruent for the formula to make sense?

Make Connections

The area of any parallelogram, including a rectangle, can be found using the formula $A = b \times h$. You can use a parallelogram to look at more triangles.

A. Trace and cut out two copies of the acute triangle.

B. Arrange the two triangles to make a parallelogram.

- Are the triangles congruent? ______
- If the area of the parallelogram is 10 square centimeters, what is the area of each triangle? Explain how you know.

____

____

____

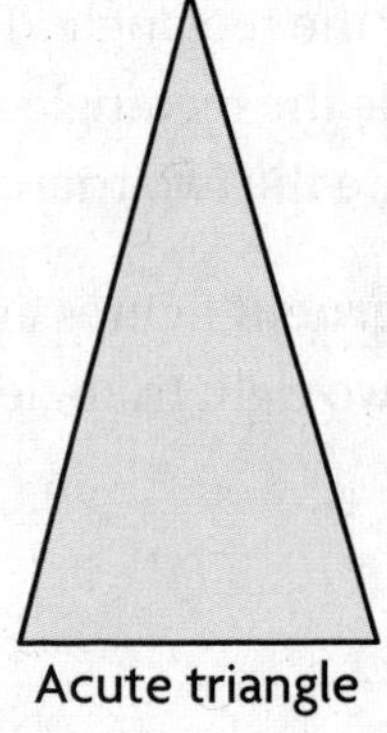

Acute triangle

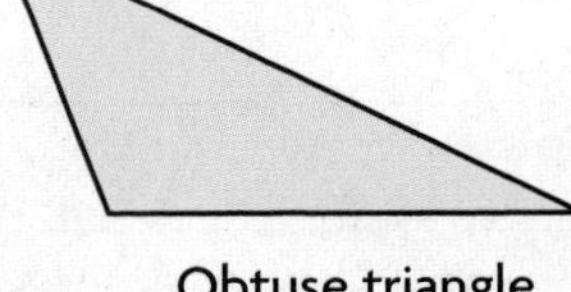

Obtuse triangle

C. Repeat Steps A and B with the obtuse triangle.

3. MATHEMATICAL PRACTICE 8 **Generalize** Can you use the formula $A = \frac{1}{2} \times b \times h$ to find the area of any triangle? Explain.

____

____

Name ______________________

Share and Show

1. Trace the parallelogram, and cut it into two congruent triangles. Find the areas of the parallelogram and one triangle, using square units.

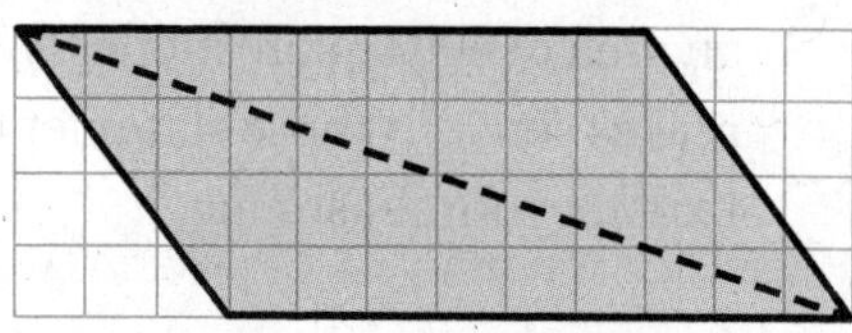

____

Find the area of each triangle.

2. 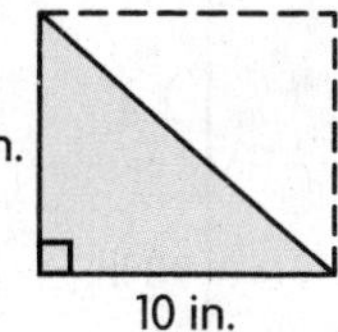

______ in.^{2}

3. 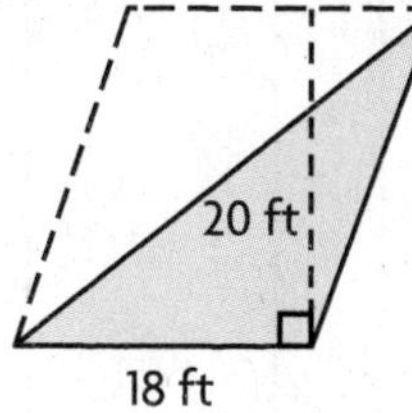

______ ft^2

4. 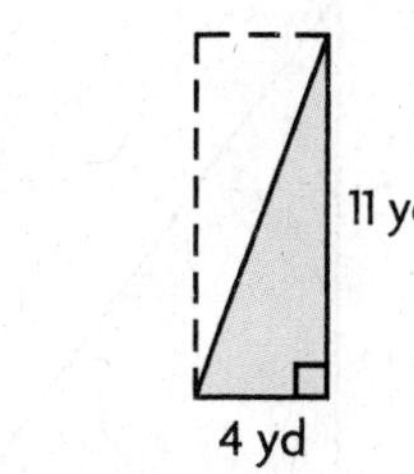

______ yd^2

5. 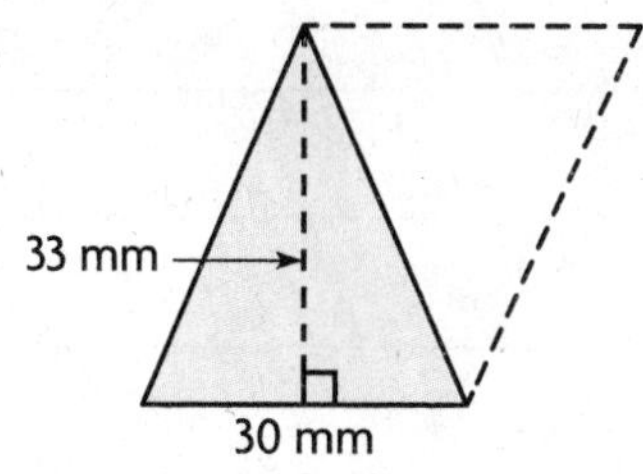

______ mm^2

6. 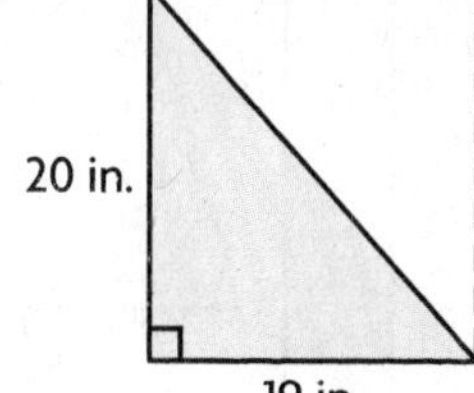

______ in.^{2}

7. 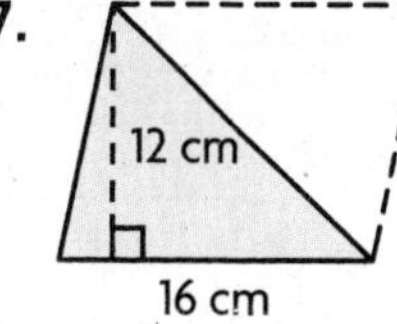

______ cm^2

Problem Solving • Applications

8. MATHEMATICAL PRACTICE 5 **Communicate** Describe how you can use two triangles of the same shape and size to form a parallelogram.

____

____

____

9. GO DEEPER A school flag is in the shape of a right triangle. The height of the flag is 36 inches and the base is $\frac{3}{4}$ of the height. What is the area of the flag?

____

THINK SMARTER Sense or Nonsense?

10. Cyndi and Tyson drew the models below. Each said his or her drawing represents a triangle with an area of 600 square inches. Whose statement makes sense? Whose statement is nonsense? Explain your reasoning.

Tyson's Model

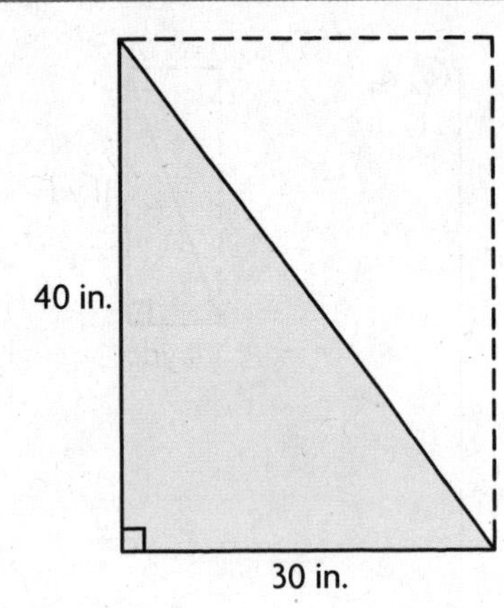

Cyndi's Model

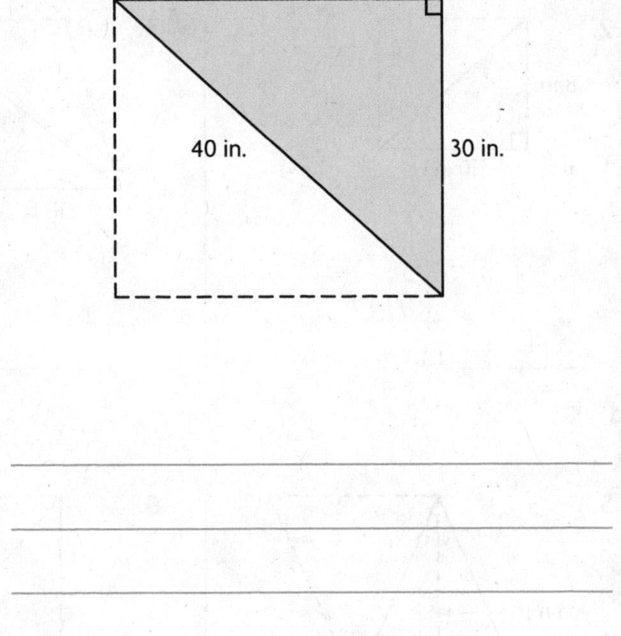

11. THINK SMARTER A flag is separated into two different colors. Find the area of the white region. Show your work.

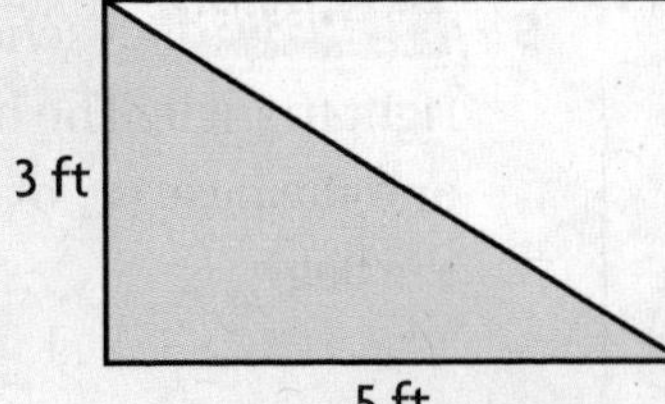

FOR MORE PRACTICE: Standards Practice Book

Name ______________________________

Geometry—6.G.1 *Also 6.EE.1*
MATHEMATICAL PRACTICES
MP.1, MP.5, MP.8

Area of Triangles

Essential Question How can you find the area of triangles?

Any parallelogram can be divided into two congruent triangles. The area of each triangle is half the area of the parallelogram, so the area of a triangle is half the product of its base and its height.

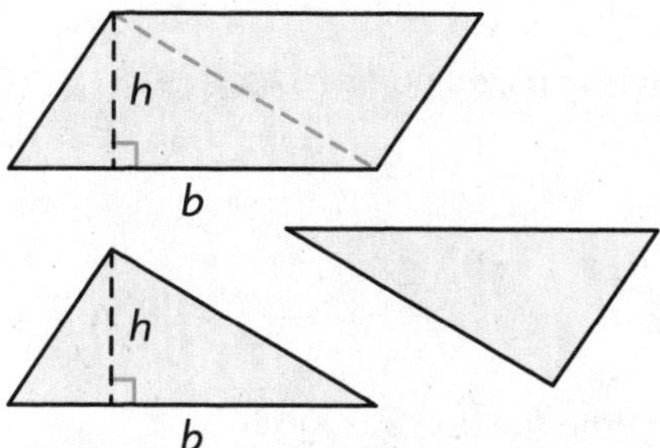

Area of a Triangle

$$A = \frac{1}{2}bh$$

where b is the base and h is the height

Unlock the Problem

The Flatiron Building in New York is well known for its unusual shape. The building was designed to fit the triangular plot of land formed by 22nd Street, Broadway, and Fifth Avenue. The diagram shows the dimensions of the triangular foundation of the building. What is the area of the triangle?

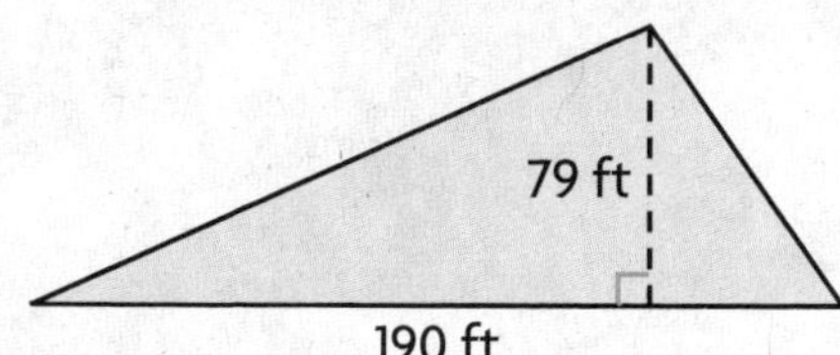

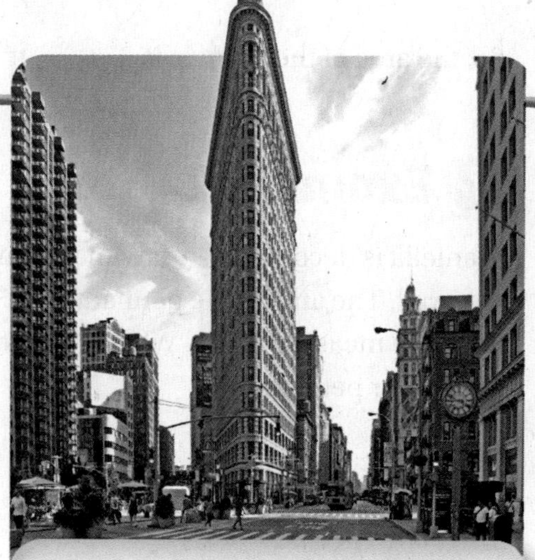

- How can you identify the base and the height of the triangle?

____

____

____

____

Find the area of the triangle.

Write the formula.	$A = \frac{1}{2}bh$
Substitute 190 for b and 79 for h.	$A = \frac{1}{2} \times$ ______ $\times$ ______
Multiply the base and height.	$A = \frac{1}{2} \times$ ______
Multiply by $\frac{1}{2}$.	$A =$ ______

So, the area of the triangle is ______ ft^2.

Math Talk Mathematical Practices

Explain how the area of a triangle relates to the area of a rectangle with the same base and height.

Example 1 Find the area of the triangle.

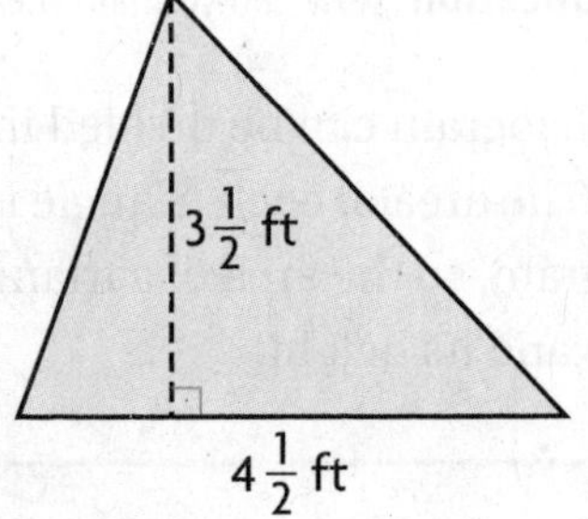

Write the formula. $A = \frac{1}{2}bh$

Substitute $4\frac{1}{2}$ for b and $3\frac{1}{2}$ for h. $A = \frac{1}{2} \times$ ______ $\times$ ______

Rewrite the mixed numbers as fractions. $A = \frac{1}{2} \times \frac{\square}{2} \times \frac{\square}{2}$

Multiply. $A = \frac{\square}{8}$

Rewrite the fraction as a mixed number. $A =$ ______

So, the area of the triangle is ______ ft^2.

Example 2

Daniella is decorating a triangular pennant for her wall. The area of the pennant is 225 $in.^2$ and the base measures 30 in. What is the height of the triangular pennant?

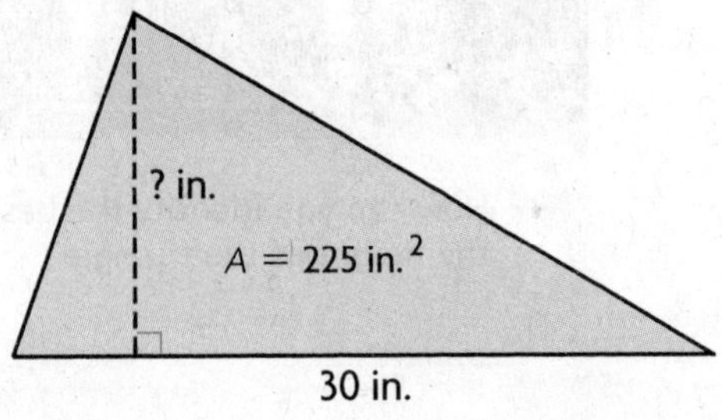

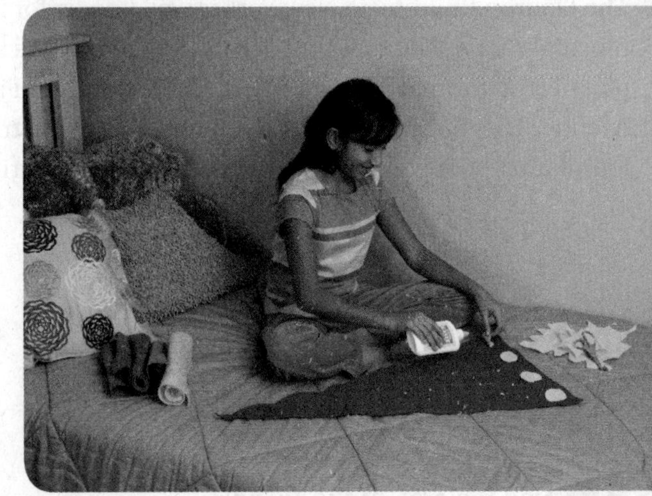

Write the formula. $A = \frac{1}{2}bh$

Substitute 225 for A and 30 for b. ______ $= \frac{1}{2} \times$ ______ $\times h$

Multiply $\frac{1}{2}$ and 30. $225 =$ ______ $\times h$

Use the Division Property of Equality. $\frac{225}{\square} = \frac{\square \times h}{\square}$

Simplify. ______ $= h$

So, the height of the triangular pennant is ______ in.

Name ____________________

Share and Show

1. Find the area of the triangle.

$A = \frac{1}{2}bh$

$A = \frac{1}{2} \times 14 \times$ ______

$A =$ ______ cm^2

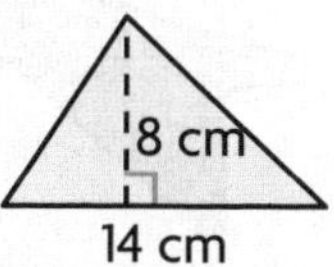

2. The area of the triangle is 132 in.^2 Find the height of the triangle.

$h =$ ______

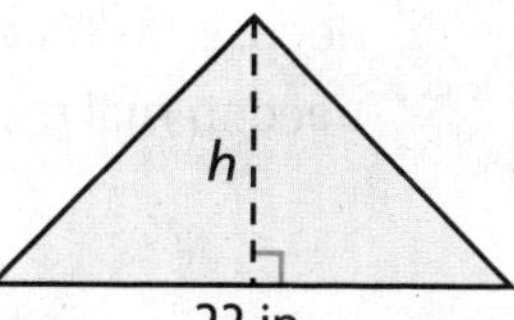

Find the area of the triangle.

3.

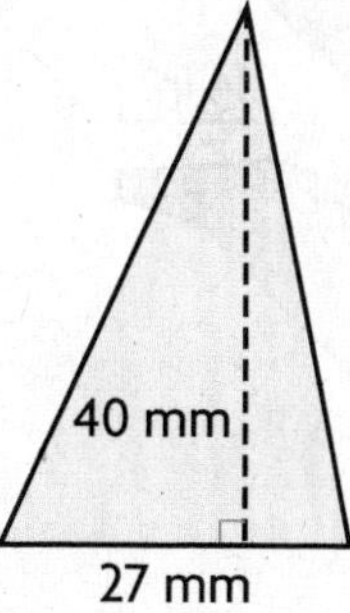

$A =$ ______

4.

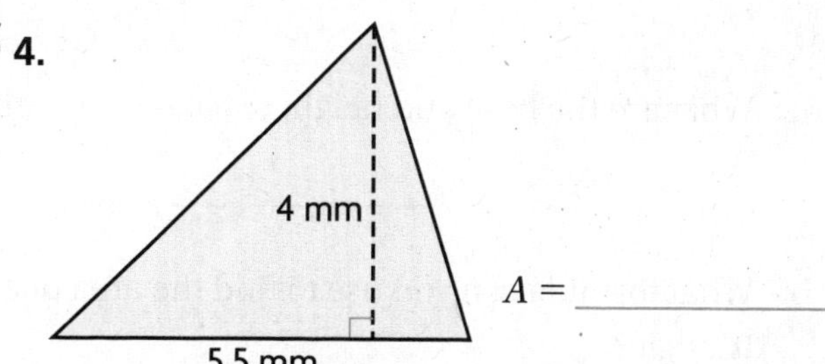

$A =$ ______

Math Talk — **Mathematical Practices**

Explain how you can identify the height of a triangle.

On Your Own

THINK SMARTER **Find the unknown measurement for the figure.**

5.

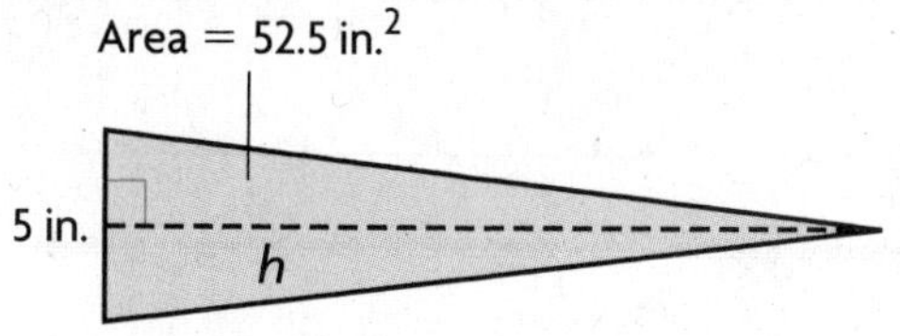

$h =$ ______

6.

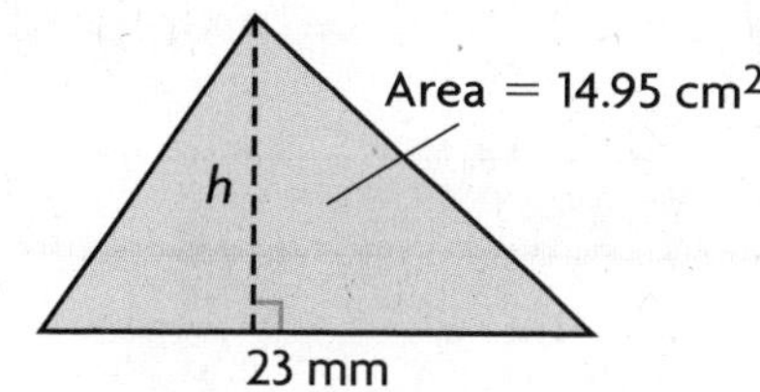

$h =$ ______

7. MATHEMATICAL PRACTICE 3 **Verify the Reasoning of Others** The height of a triangle is twice the base. The area of the triangle is 625 in.^2 Carson says the base of the triangle is at least 50 in. Is Carson's estimate reasonable? Explain.

____

____

____

Unlock the Problem 

8. GO DEEPER Alani is building a set of 4 shelves. Each shelf will have 2 supports in the shape of right isosceles triangles. Each shelf is 14 inches deep. How many square inches of wood will she need to make all of the supports?

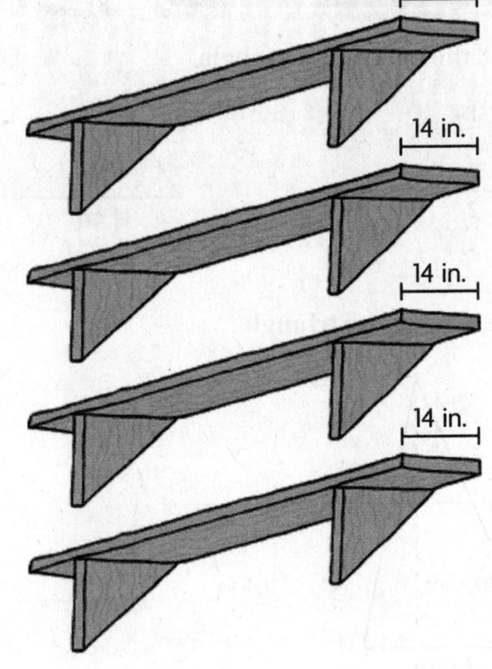

a. What are the base and height of each triangle?

b. What formula can you use to find the area of a triangle?

c. Explain how you can find the area of one triangular support.

d. How many triangular supports are needed to build 4 shelves?

e. How many square inches of wood will Alani need to make all the supports?

9. THINK SMARTER The area of a triangle is 97.5 cm^2. The height of the triangle is 13 cm. Find the base of the triangle. Explain your work.

10. THINK SMARTER The area of a triangle is 30 ft^2. For numbers 10a–10d, select Yes or No to tell if the dimensions given could be the height and base of the triangle.

10a. $h = 3, b = 10$ ○ Yes ○ No

10b. $h = 3, b = 20$ ○ Yes ○ No

10c. $h = 5, b = 12$ ○ Yes ○ No

10d. $h = 5, b = 24$ ○ Yes ○ No

FOR MORE PRACTICE: Standards Practice Book

Name ______________________________

Explore Area of Trapezoids

Essential Question What is the relationship between the areas of trapezoids and parallelograms?

Geometry—6.G.1

MATHEMATICAL PRACTICES MP.4, MP.7, MP.8

CONNECT A **trapezoid** is a quadrilateral with exactly one pair of parallel sides. The parallel sides are the *bases* of the trapezoid. A line segment drawn at a 90° angle to the two bases is the *height* of the trapezoid. You can use what you know about the area of a parallelogram to find the area of a trapezoid.

base 2

height

base 1

Investigate

Hands On

Materials ■ grid paper ■ ruler ■ scissors

3 units

4 units

6 units

A. Draw two copies of the trapezoid on grid paper.

B. Cut out the trapezoids.

C. Arrange the trapezoids to form a parallelogram, as shown. Examine the parallelogram.

- How can you find the length of the base of the parallelogram?

____

____

- The base of the parallelogram is ______ + ______ = ______ units.
- The height of the parallelogram is ______ units.
- The area of the parallelogram is ______ × ______ = ______ square units.

D. Examine the trapezoids.

- How does the area of one trapezoid relate to the area of the parallelogram?

____

____

- Find the area of one trapezoid. Explain how you found the area.

____

____

Draw Conclusions

1. MATHEMATICAL PRACTICE 7 **Identify Relationships** Explain how knowing how to find the area of a parallelogram helped you find the area of the trapezoid.

____

2. Use your results from the Investigate to describe how you can find the area of any trapezoid.

____

____

____

3. MATHEMATICAL PRACTICE 8 **Generalize** Can you use the method you described above to find the area of a trapezoid if two copies of the trapezoid can be arranged to form a rectangle? Explain.

____

____

Make Connections

You can use the formula for the area of a rectangle to find the area of some types of trapezoids.

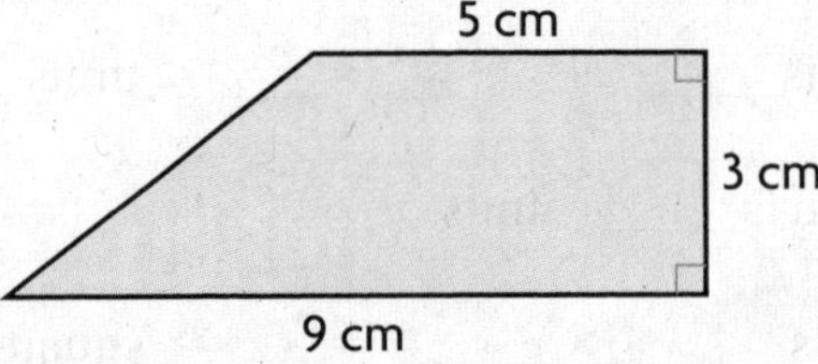

A. Trace and cut out two copies of the trapezoid.

B. Arrange the two trapezoids to form a rectangle. Examine the rectangle.

- The length of the rectangle is ______ + ______ = ______ cm.
- The width of the rectangle is ______ cm.
- The area of the rectangle is ______ × ______ = ______ cm^2.

C. Examine the trapezoids.

- How does the area of each trapezoid relate to the area of the rectangle?

  ____

- The area of the given trapezoid is $\frac{1}{2}$ × ______ = ______ cm^2.

Name ______________________

Share and Show

1. Trace and cut out two copies of the trapezoid. Arrange the trapezoids to form a parallelogram. Find the areas of the parallelogram and one trapezoid using square units.

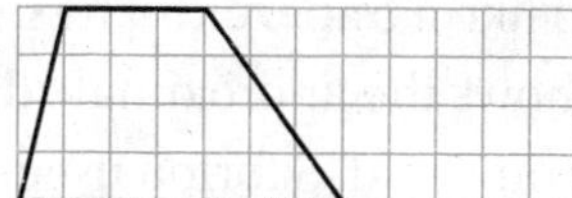

____

Find the area of the trapezoid.

2.

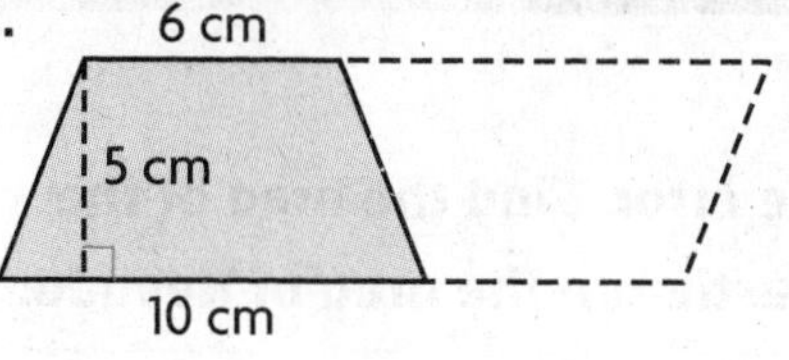

______ cm^2

3.

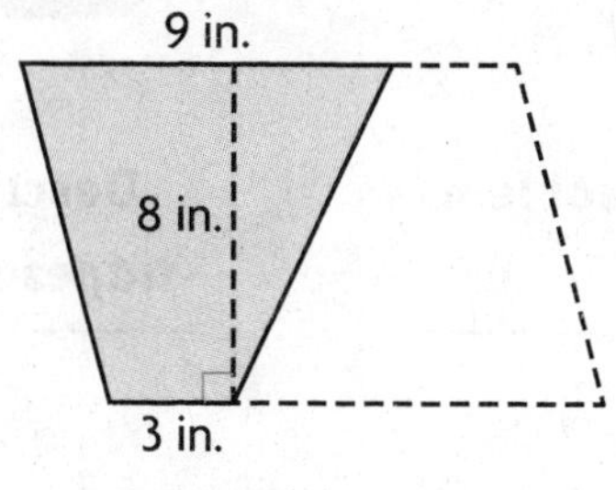

______ $in.^2$

4.

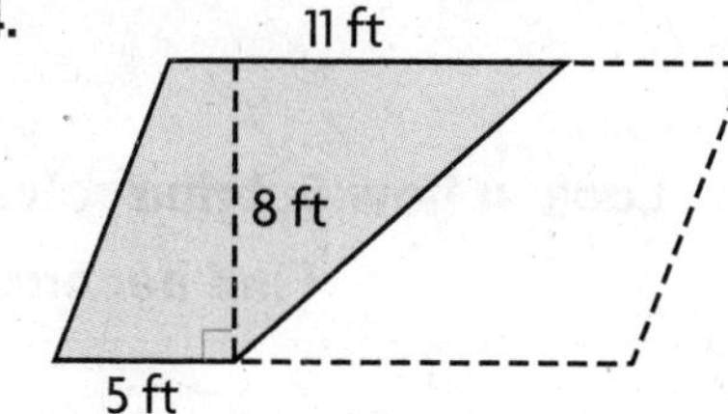

______ ft^2

5.

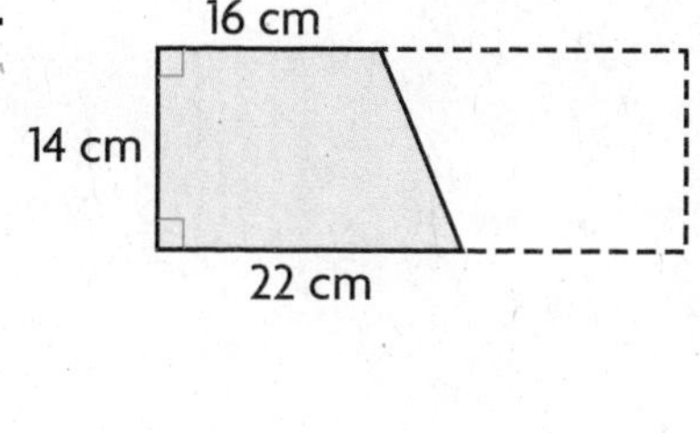

______ cm^2

6.

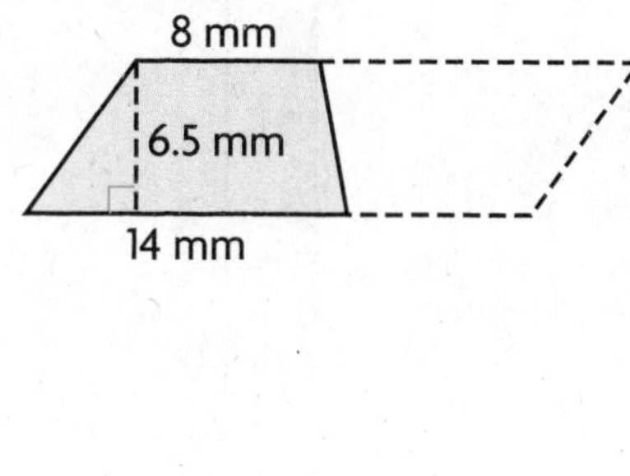

______ mm^2

7.

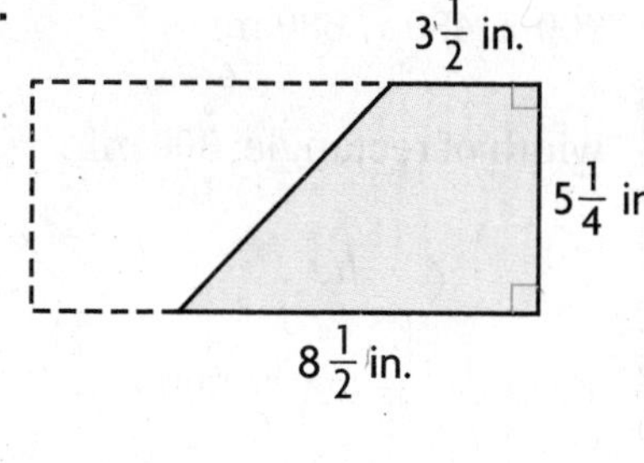

______ $in.^2$

Problem Solving • Applications

8. MATHEMATICAL PRACTICE 4 **Describe a Method** Explain one way to find the height of a trapezoid if you know the area of the trapezoid and the length of both bases.

____

____

____

9. GO DEEPER A patio is in the shape of a trapezoid. The length of the longer base is 18 feet. The length of the shorter base is two feet less than half the longer base. The height is 8 feet. What is the area of the patio?

____

THINK SMARTER What's the Error?

10. Except for a small region near its southeast corner, the state of Nevada is shaped like a trapezoid. The map at the right shows the approximate dimensions of the trapezoid. Sabrina used the map to estimate the area of Nevada.

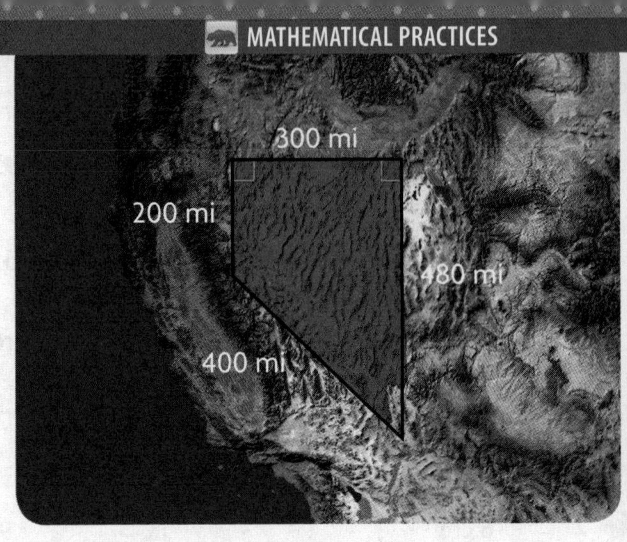

Look at how Sabrina solved the problem. Find her error.

Two copies of the trapezoid can be put together to form a rectangle.

length of rectangle:

$200 + 480 = 680$ mi

width of rectangle: 300 mi

$A = lw$

$= 680 \times 300$

$= 204{,}000$

The area of Nevada is about 204,000 square miles.

Describe the error. Find the area of the trapezoid to estimate the area of Nevada.

11. THINK SMARTER A photo was cut in half at an angle. What is the area of one of the cut pieces?

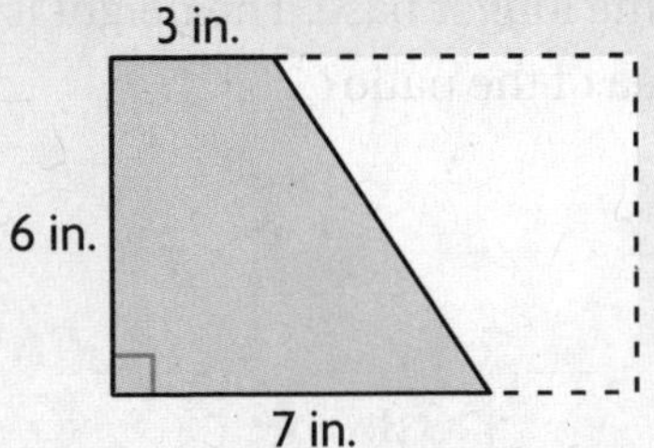

The area is _______ ft^2.

FOR MORE PRACTICE: Standards Practice Book

Name ______________________________

Area of Trapezoids

Essential Question How can you find the area of trapezoids?

Geometry—6.G.1
Also 6.EE.2C

MATHEMATICAL PRACTICES
MP.1, MP.3, MP.7

Any parallelogram can be divided into two trapezoids with the same shape and size. The bases of the trapezoids, b_1 and b_2, form the base of the parallelogram. The area of each trapezoid is half the area of the parallelogram. So, the area of a trapezoid is half the product of its height and the sum of its bases.

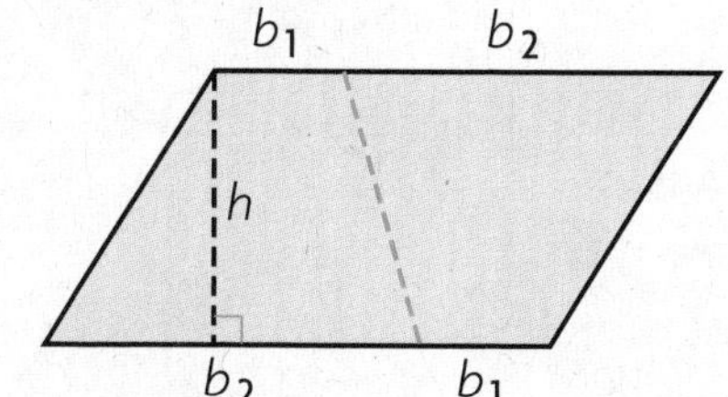

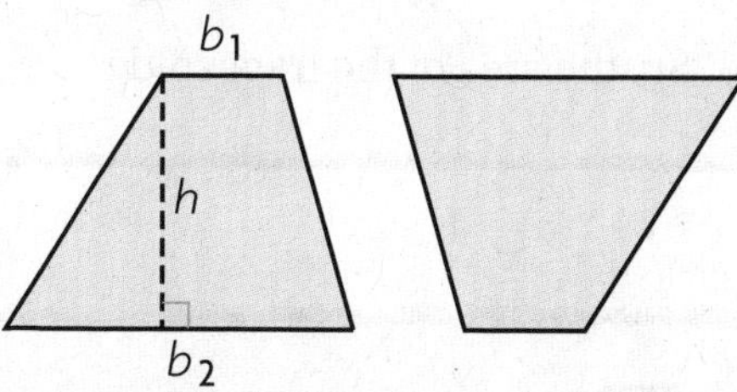

Area of a Trapezoid

$$A = \frac{1}{2}(b_1 + b_2)h$$

where b_1 and b_2 are the two bases and h is the height

Unlock the Problem

Mr. Desmond has tables in his office with tops shaped like trapezoids. The diagram shows the dimensions of each tabletop. What is the area of each tabletop?

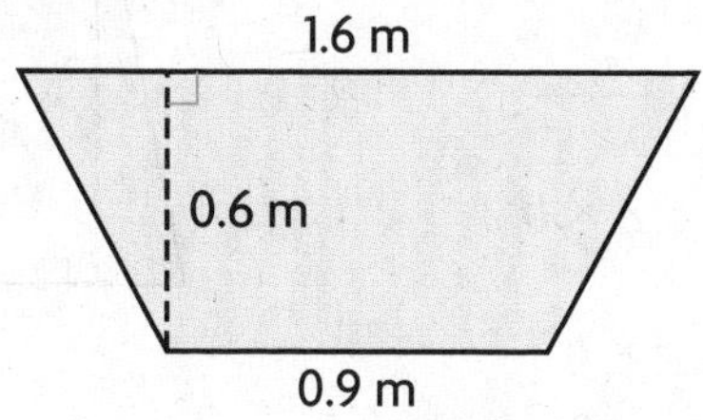

- How can you identify the bases?

____

____

- How can you identify the height?

____

____

Find the area of the trapezoid.

Write the formula. $A = \frac{1}{2}(b_1 + b_2)h$

Substitute 1.6 for b_1, 0.9 for b_2, and 0.6 for h. $A = \frac{1}{2} \times (\_\_\_\_ + \_\_\_\_) \times \_\_\_\_$

Add within the parentheses. $A = \frac{1}{2} \times \_\_\_\_ \times 0.6$

Multiply. $A = \frac{1}{2} \times \_\_\_\_ = \_\_\_\_$

So, the area of each tabletop is ______ m^2.

Mathematical Practices

Describe the relationship between the area of a trapezoid and the area of a parallelogram with the same height and a base equal to the sum of the trapezoid's bases.

Example 1 Find the area of the trapezoid.

4.6 cm

4.5 cm

9.4 cm

Write the formula. $A = \frac{1}{2}(b_1 + b_2)h$

Substitute 4.6 for b_1, 9.4 for b_2, and 4.5 for h. $A = \frac{1}{2} \times (\_\_\_\_ + \_\_\_\_) \times 4.5$

Add. $A = \frac{1}{2} \times \_\_\_\_ \times 4.5$

Multiply. $A = \_\_\_\_ \times 4.5 = \_\_\_\_$

So, the area of the trapezoid is ____________ cm^2.

Example 2 The area of the trapezoid is 702 in.^{2} Find the height of the trapezoid.

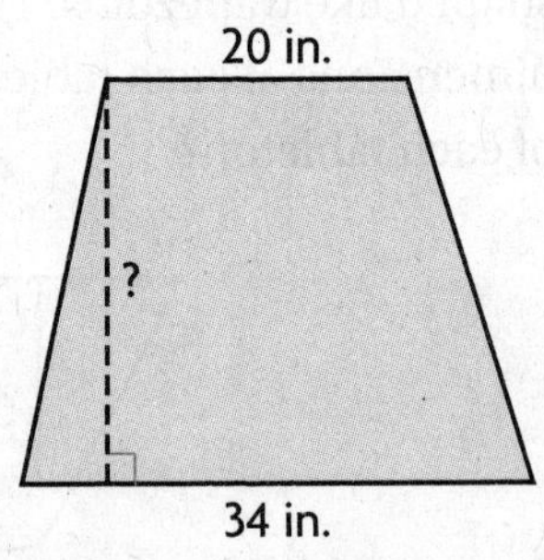

Write the formula. $A = \frac{1}{2}(b_1 + b_2)h$

Substitute 702 for A, 20 for b_1, and 34 for b_2. $702 = \frac{1}{2} \times (20 + \_\_\_\_) \times h$

Add within the parentheses. $702 = \frac{1}{2} \times \_\_\_\_ \times h$

Multiply $\frac{1}{2}$ and 54. $702 = \_\_\_\_ \times h$

Use the Division Property of Equality. $\frac{702}{\_\_\_\_} = \frac{\_\_\_\_ \times h}{\_\_\_\_}$

Simplify. $\_\_\_\_ = h$

So, the height of the trapezoid is ______ in.

Math Talk **Mathematical Practices**

Explain how to find the height of a trapezoid if you know the area and the lengths of both bases.

- MATHEMATICAL PRACTICE 1 **Analyze Relationships** Explain why the formula for the area of a trapezoid contains the expression $b_1 + b_2$.

____

____

____

____

Name ______________________________

Share and Show

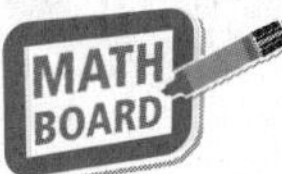

1. Find the area of the trapezoid.

$A = \frac{1}{2}(b_1 + b_2)h$

$A = \frac{1}{2} \times (\_\_\_\_\_ + \_\_\_\_\_) \times 4$

$A = \frac{1}{2} \times \_\_\_\_\_ \times 4$

$A = \_\_\_\_\_$ cm^2

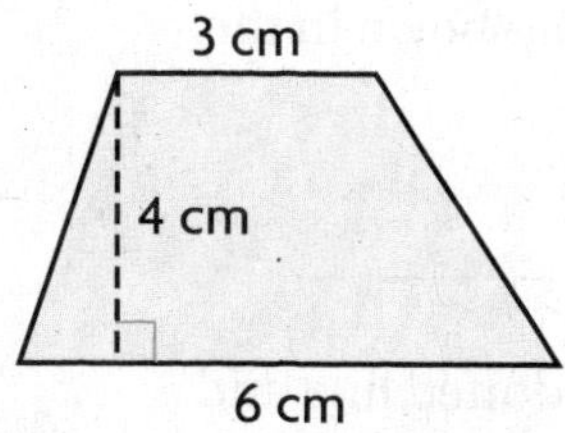

2. The area of the trapezoid is 45 ft^2. Find the height of the trapezoid.

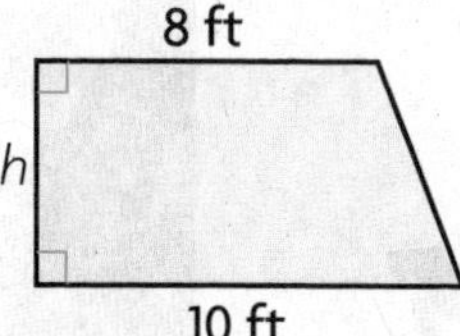

$h =$ ____________

3. Find the area of the trapezoid.

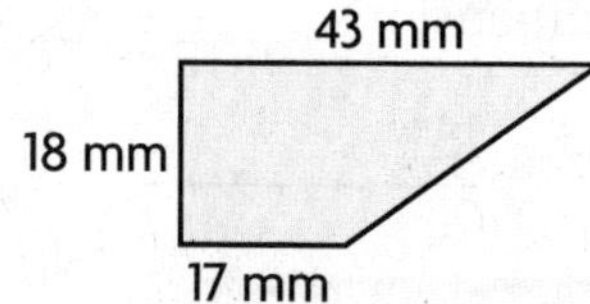

$A =$ ____________

Mathematical Practices

Two trapezoids have the same bases and the same height. Are the areas equal? Must the trapezoids have the same shape? **Explain.**

On Your Own

Find the area of the trapezoid.

4.

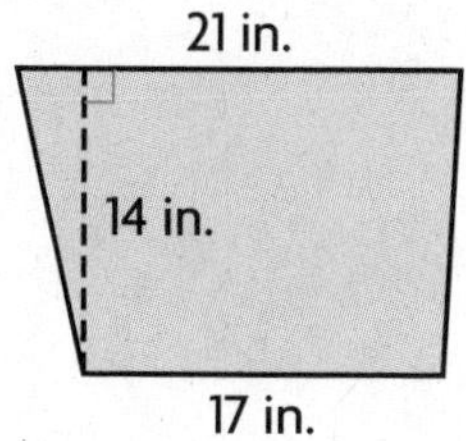

$A =$ ____________

5.

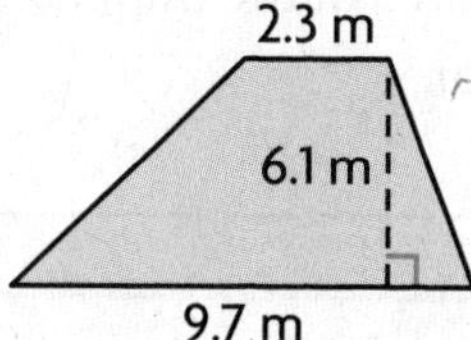

$A =$ ____________

Find the height of the trapezoid.

6.

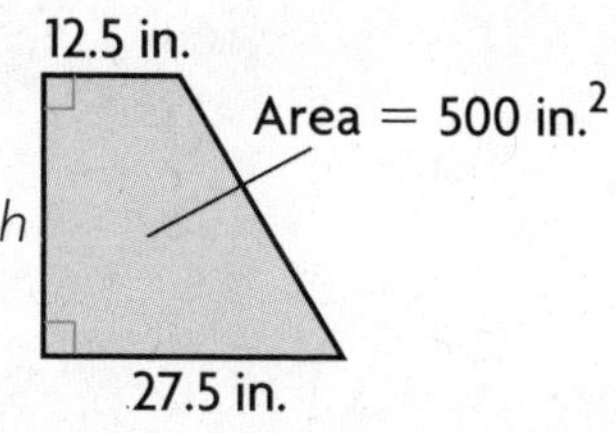

$h =$ ____________

7.

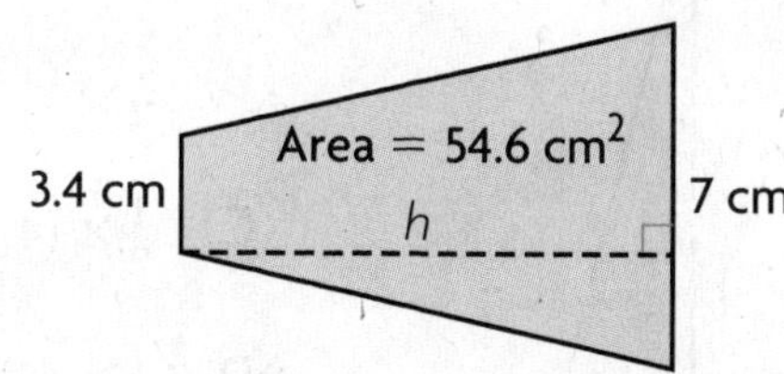

$h =$ ____________

Problem Solving • Applications

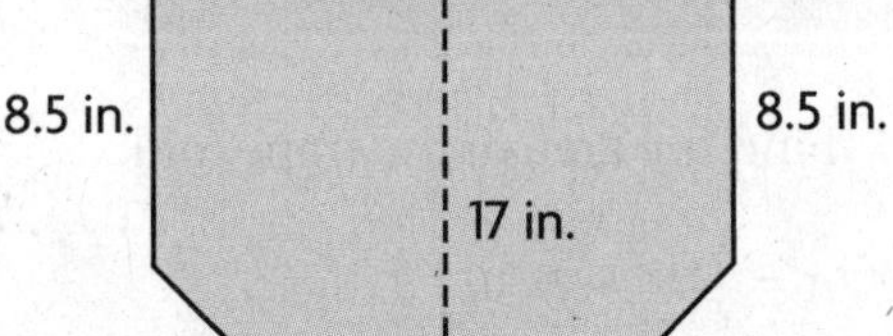

Use the diagram for 8–9.

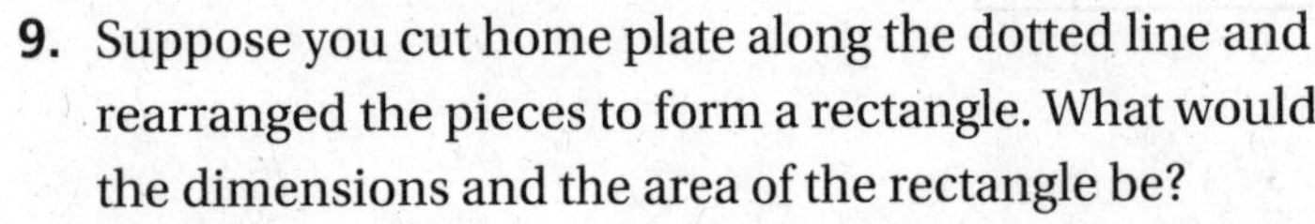

8. GO DEEPER A baseball home plate can be divided into two trapezoids with the dimensions shown in the drawing. Find area of home plate.

____

9. Suppose you cut home plate along the dotted line and rearranged the pieces to form a rectangle. What would the dimensions and the area of the rectangle be?

dimensions: _______________

area: _______________

10. THINK SMARTER A pattern used for tile floors is shown. A side of the inner square measures 10 cm, and a side of the outer square measures 30 cm. What is the area of one of the yellow trapezoid tiles?

____

WRITE ▸ Math • Show Your

11. MATHEMATICAL PRACTICE 3 **Verify the Reasoning of Others** A trapezoid has a height of 12 cm and bases with lengths of 14 cm and 10 cm. Tina says the area of the trapezoid is 288 cm^2. Find her error, and correct the error.

____

12. THINK SMARTER Which expression can be used to find the area of the trapezoid? Mark all that apply.

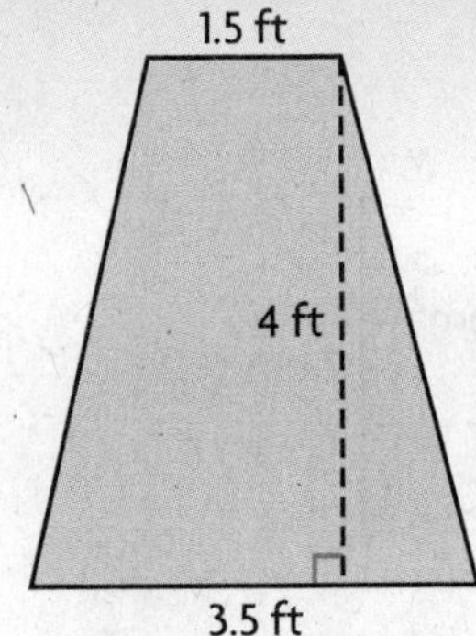

Ⓐ $\frac{1}{2} \times (4 + 1.5) \times 3.5$

Ⓑ $\frac{1}{2} \times (1.5 + 3.5) \times 4$

Ⓒ $\frac{1}{2} \times (4 + 3.5) \times 1.5$

Ⓓ $\frac{1}{2} \times (5) \times 4$

FOR MORE PRACTICE:
Standards Practice Book

Name ______________________________

Mid-Chapter Checkpoint

Vocabulary

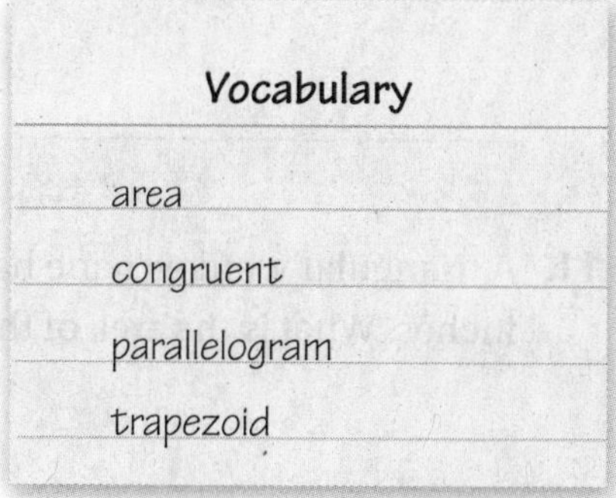

Vocabulary
area
congruent
parallelogram
trapezoid

Choose the best term from the box to complete the sentence.

1. A ________________ is a quadrilateral with two pairs of parallel sides. (p. 387)

2. The number of square units needed to cover a surface without any gaps or overlaps is called the ________________. (p. 387)

3. Figures with the same size and shape are ________________. (p. 393)

Concepts and Skills

Find the area. (6.G.1, 6.EE.2c)

4.

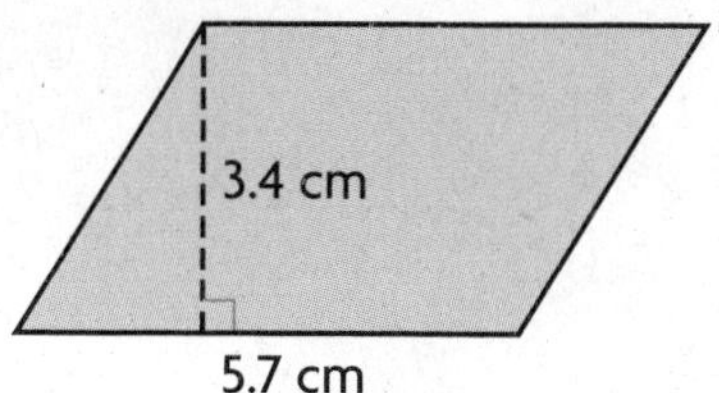

5.

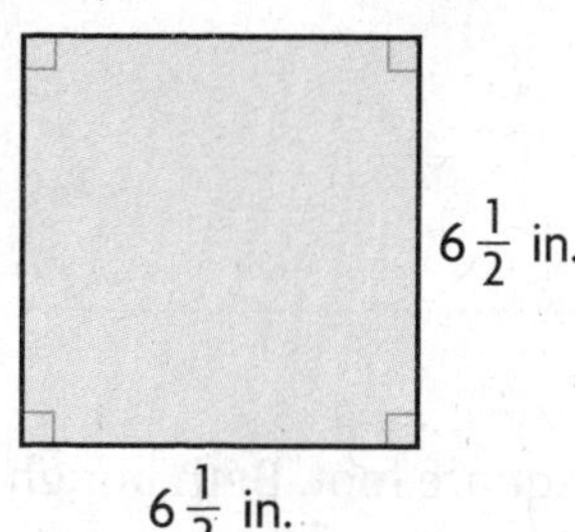

6.

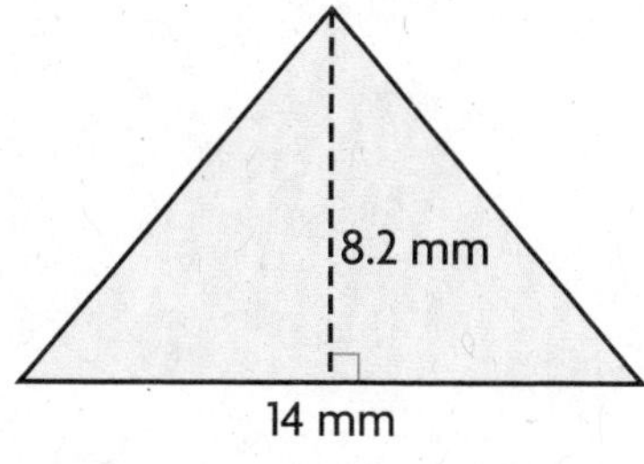

7.

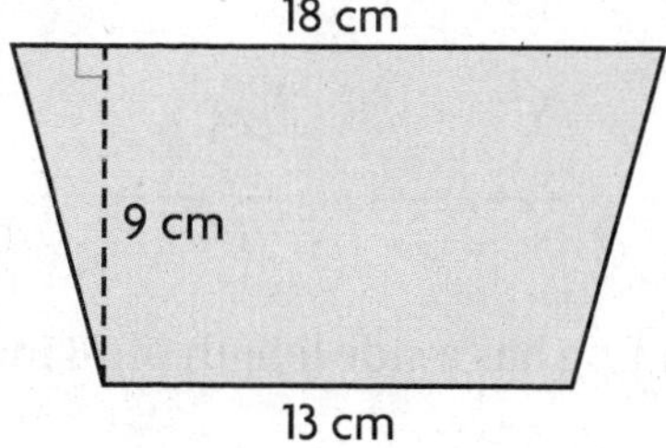

8. A parallelogram has an area of 276 square meters and a base measuring 12 meters. What is the height of the parallelogram?

9. The base of a triangle measures 8 inches and the area is 136 square inches. What is the height of the triangle?

10. The height of a parallelogram is 3 times the base. The base measures 4.5 cm. What is the area of the parallelogram? (6.G.1)

11. A triangular window pane has a base of 30 inches and a height of 24 inches. What is the area of the window pane? (6.G.1)

12. The courtyard behind Jennie's house is shaped like a trapezoid. The bases measure 8 meters and 11 meters. The height of the trapezoid is 12 meters. What is the area of the courtyard? (6.G.1)

13. Rugs sell for $8 per square foot. Beth bought a 9-foot-long rectangular rug for $432. How wide was the rug? (6.G.1, 6.EE.2c)

14. A square painting has a side length of 18 inches. What is the area of the painting? (6.G.1, 6.EE.2c)

Name ______________________________

Area of Regular Polygons

Essential Question How can you find the area of regular polygons?

Geometry—6.G.1
Also 6.EE.2c

MATHEMATICAL PRACTICES
MP.7, MP.8

Unlock the Problem

Emory is making a patch for his soccer ball. The patch he is using is a regular polygon. A **regular polygon** is a polygon in which all sides have the same length and all angles have the same measure. Emory needs to find the area of a piece of material shaped like a regular pentagon.

Activity

You can find the area of a regular polygon by dividing the polygon into congruent triangles.

- Draw line segments from each vertex to the center of the pentagon to divide it into five congruent triangles.
- You can find the area of one of the triangles if you know the side length of the polygon and the height of the triangle.

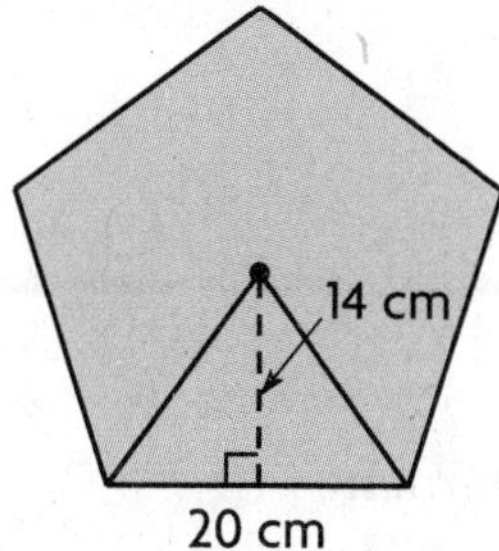

Math Talk — **Mathematical Practices**

Explain how to determine the number of congruent triangles a regular polygon should be divided into in order to find the area.

- Find the area of one triangle.

Write the formula. $A = \frac{1}{2}bh$

Substitute 20 for *b* and 14 for *h*. $A = \frac{1}{2} \times$ ______ $\times$ ______

Simplify. $A =$ ______ cm^2

- Find the area of the regular polygon by multiplying the number of triangles by the area of one triangle.

$A =$ ______ $\times$ ______ $=$ ______ cm^2

So, the area of the pentagon-shaped piece is ____________.

Example Find the area of the regular polygon.

STEP 1 Draw line segments from each vertex to the center of the hexagon.

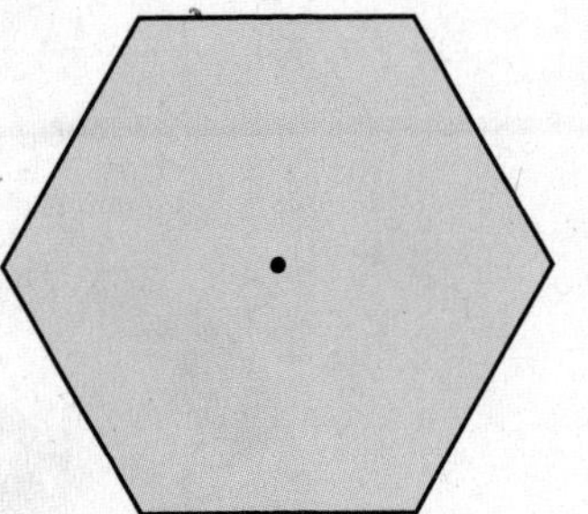

Into how many congruent triangles did you divide the figure? ______

STEP 2 Find the area of one triangle.

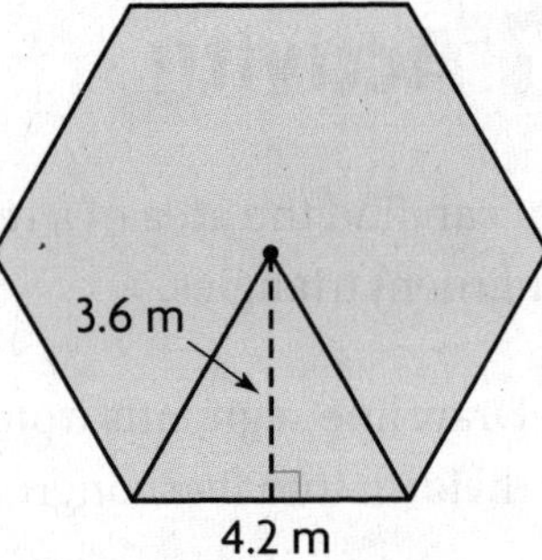

Write the formula. $A = \frac{1}{2}bh$

Substitute 4.2 for b and 3.6 for h. $A = \frac{1}{2} \times$ ______ $\times$ ______

Simplify. $A =$ ______ m^2

STEP 3 Find the area of the hexagon.

$A =$ ______ $\times$ ______ $=$ ______ m^2

So, the area of the hexagon is ______ m^2

1. MATHEMATICAL PRACTICE 8 **Use Repeated Reasoning** Into how many congruent triangles can you divide a regular decagon by drawing line segments from each vertex to the center of the decagon? Explain.

2. THINK SMARTER In an *irregular polygon,* the sides do not all have the same length and the angles do not all have the same measure. Could you find the area of an irregular polygon using the method you used in this lesson? Explain your reasoning.

Name ______________________________

Share and Show

Find the area of the regular polygon.

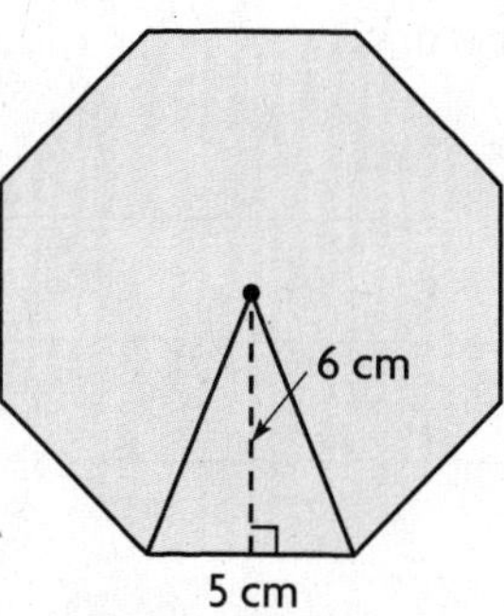

1. number of congruent triangles inside the figure: ______

   area of each triangle: $\frac{1}{2}$ × ______ × ______ = ______ cm^2

   area of octagon: ______ × ______ = ______ cm^2

2.

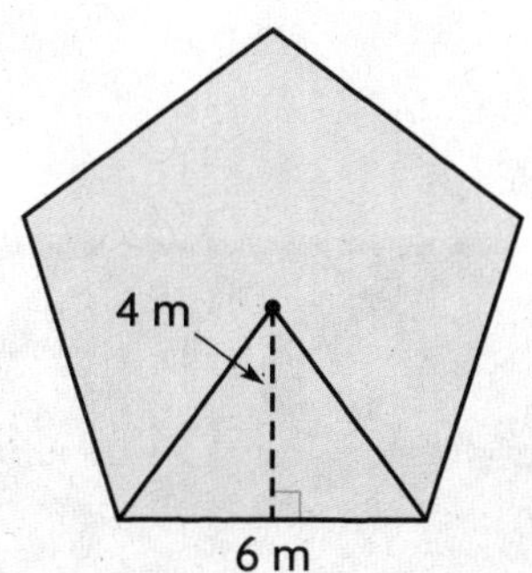

3.

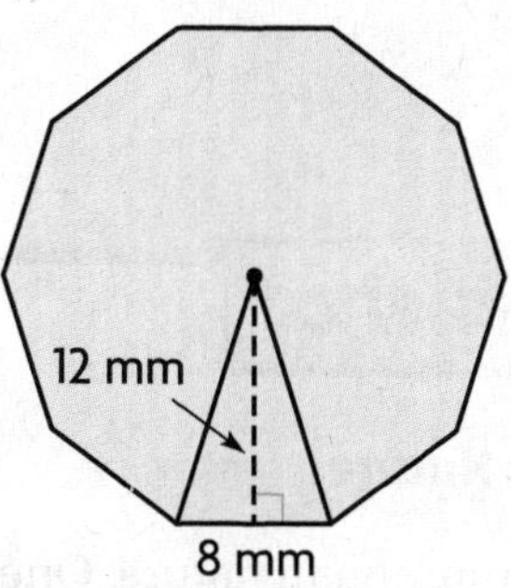

Math Talk — **Mathematical Practices**

Describe the information you must have about a regular polygon in order to find its area.

On Your Own

Find the area of the regular polygon.

4.

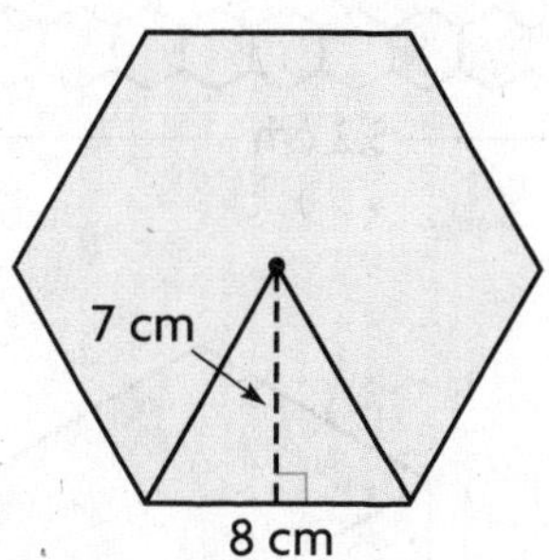

5.

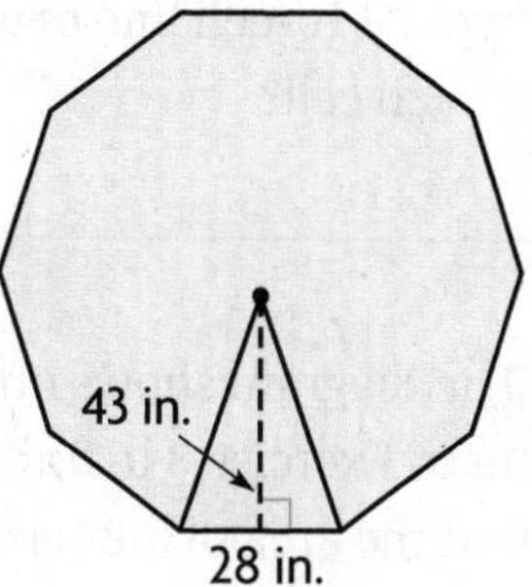

6. MATHEMATICAL PRACTICE 6 **Explain** A regular pentagon is divided into congruent triangles by drawing a line segment from each vertex to the center. Each triangle has an area of 24 cm^2. Explain how to find the area of the pentagon.

7. THINK SMARTER Name the polygon and find its area. Show your work.

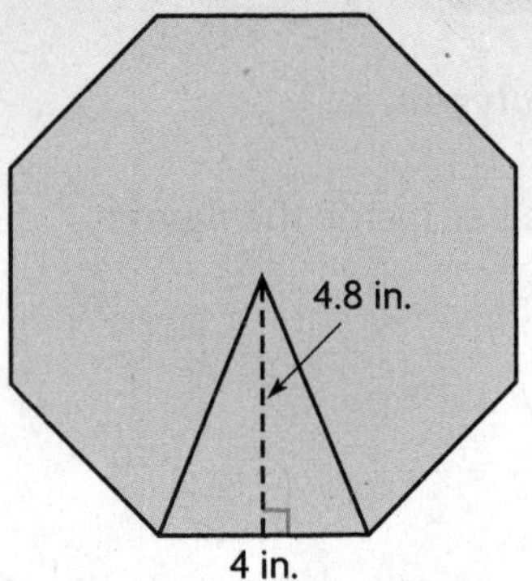

Connect to Science

Regular Polygons in Nature

Regular polygons are common in nature. One of the best-known examples of regular polygons in nature is the small hexagonal cells in honeycombs constructed by honeybees. The cells are where bee larvae grow. Honeybees store honey and pollen in the hexagonal cells. Scientists can measure the health of a bee population by the size of the cells.

8. Cells in a honeycomb vary in width. To find the average width of a cell, scientists measure the combined width of 10 cells, and then divide by 10.

The figure shows a typical 10-cell line of worker bee cells. What is the width of each cell?

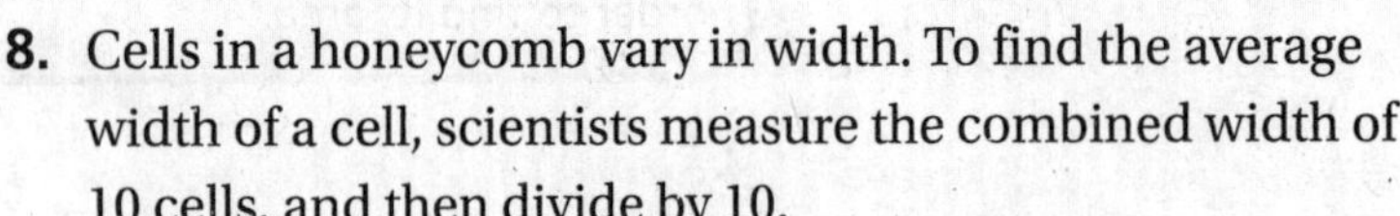

9. THINK SMARTER The diagram shows one honeycomb cell. Use your answer to Exercise 8 to find h, the height of the triangle. Then find the area of the hexagonal cell.

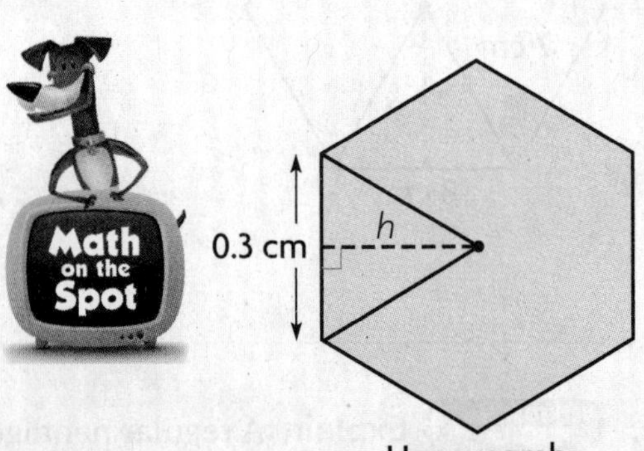

10. GO DEEPER A rectangular honeycomb measures 35.1 cm by 32.4 cm. Approximately how many cells does it contain?

FOR MORE PRACTICE: Standards Practice Book

Name ______________________________

Composite Figures

Essential Question How can you find the area of composite figures?

Geometry—6.G.1
Also 6.EE.2c

MATHEMATICAL PRACTICES
MP.1, MP.2, MP.5

A **composite figure** is made up of two or more simpler figures, such as triangles and quadrilaterals.

Unlock the Problem

The new entryway to the fun house at Happy World Amusement Park is made from the shapes shown in the diagram. It will be painted bright green. Juanita needs to know the area of the entryway to determine how much paint to buy. What is the area of the entryway?

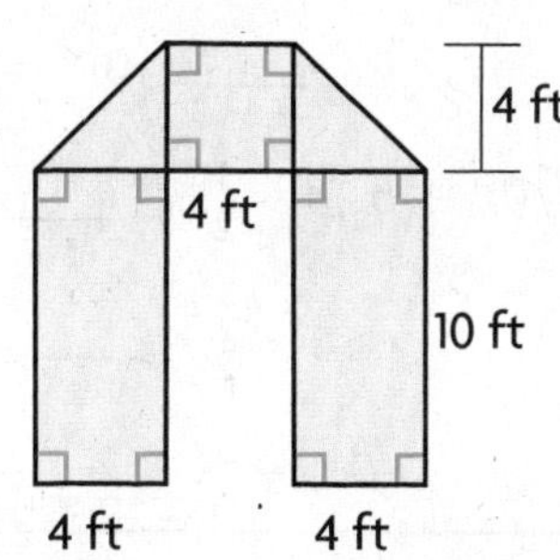

Find the area of the entryway.

STEP 1 Find the area of the rectangles.

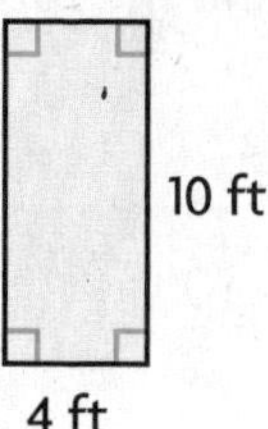

Write the formula. $A = lw$

Substitute the values for *l* and *w* and evaluate. $A = 10 \times$ ______ = ______

Find the total area of two rectangles. $2 \times$ ______ = ______ ft^2

STEP 2 Find the area of the triangles.

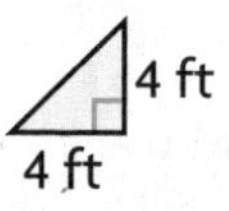

Write the formula. $A = \frac{1}{2}bh$

Substitute the values for *b* and *h* and evaluate. $A = \frac{1}{2} \times 4 \times$ ______ = ______

Find the total area of two triangles. $2 \times$ ______ = ______ ft^2

STEP 3 Find the area of the square.

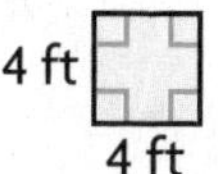

Write the formula. $A = s^2$

Substitute the value for *s*. $A = ($______$)^2$ = ______ ft^2

STEP 4 Find the total area of the composite figure.

Add the areas. $A = 80\ ft^2 +$ ______ $ft^2 +$ ______ $ft^2 =$ ______ ft^2

So, Juanita needs to buy enough paint to cover ______ ft^2.

Math Talk **Mathematical Practices**

Discuss other ways you could divide up the composite figure.

Example 1 Find the area of the composite figure shown.

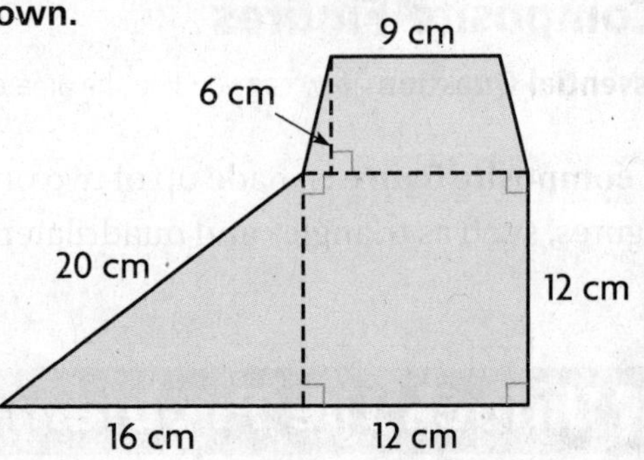

STEP 1 Find the area of the triangle, the square, and the trapezoid.

area of triangle $A = \frac{1}{2}bh = \frac{1}{2} \times 16 \times$ ______

$=$ ______ cm^2

area of square $A = s^2 = ($______$)^2$

$=$ ______ cm^2

area of trapezoid $A = \frac{1}{2}(b_1 + b_2)h = \frac{1}{2} \times ($______ $+$ ______$) \times$ ______

$= \frac{1}{2} \times$ ______ $\times 6$

$=$ ______ cm^2

STEP 2 Find the total area of the figure.

total area $A =$ ______ $\text{cm}^2 +$ ______ $\text{cm}^2 +$ ______ cm^2

$=$ ______ cm^2

So, the area of the figure is ______ cm^2.

Example 2 Find the area of the shaded region.

3 in.
3 in.
6 in.
1 ft

STEP 1 Find the area of the rectangle and the square.

area of rectangle (1 ft = 12 in.) $A = lw =$ ______ $\times$ ______

$A =$ ______ in.^2

area of square $A = s^2 = ($______$)^2$

$A =$ ______ in.^2

STEP 2 Subtract the area of the square from the area of the rectangle.

area of shaded region $A =$ ______ $\text{in.}^2 -$ ______ in.^2

$A =$ ______ in.^2

So, the area of the shaded region is ______ in.^2

Name ______________________________

Share and Show

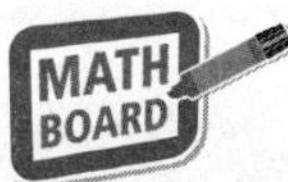

1. Find the area of the figure.

8 ft
3 ft
10 ft
5 ft
5 ft

area of one rectangle $A = lw$

$A =$ ______ $\times$ ______ $=$ ______ ft^2

area of two rectangles $A = 2 \times$ ______ $=$ ______ ft^2

length of base of triangle $b =$ ______ ft + ______ ft + ______ ft

$=$ ______ ft

area of triangle $A = \frac{1}{2}bh$

$A = \frac{1}{2} \times$ ______ $\times$ ______ $=$ ______ ft^2

area of composite figure $A =$ ______ $\text{ft}^2 +$ ______ $\text{ft}^2 =$ ______ ft^2

Find the area of the figure.

2.

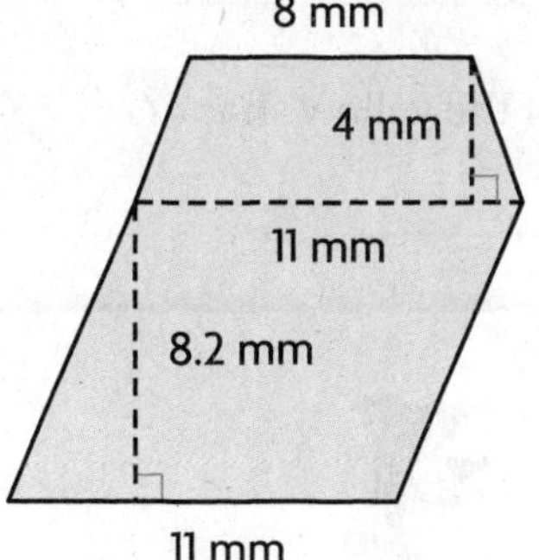

3.

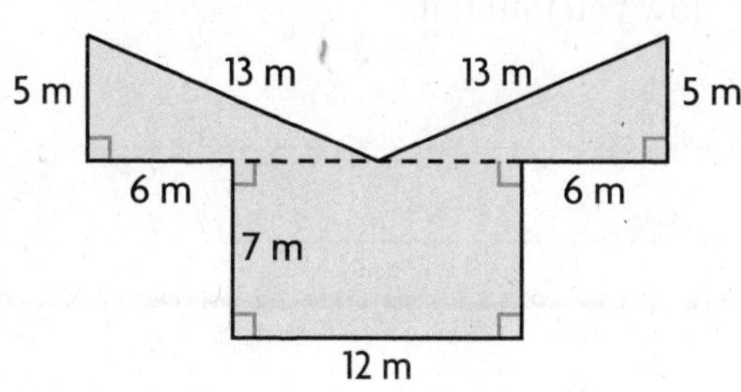

Math Talk — **Mathematical Practices**

Explain how to find the area of a composite figure.

On Your Own

4. Find the area of the figure.

8 in.
10 in.
6 in.
8 in.
16 in.

5. MATHEMATICAL PRACTICE 6 **Attend to Precision** Find the area of the shaded region.

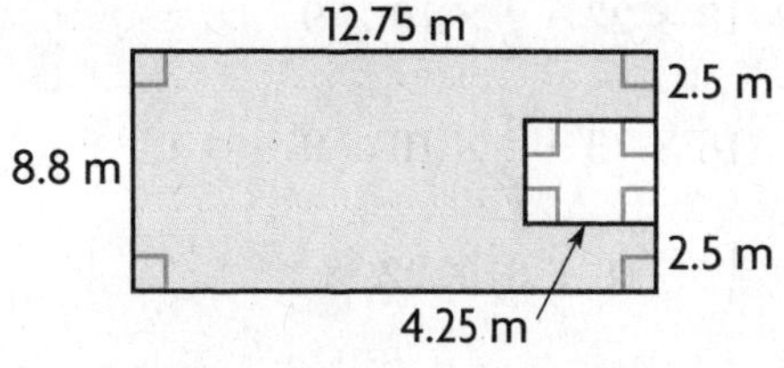

Unlock the Problem

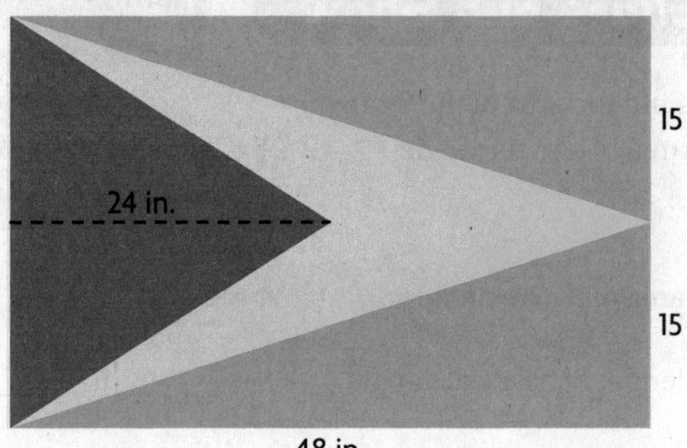

6. GO DEEPER Marco made the banner shown at the right. What is the area of the yellow shape?

a. Explain how you could find the area of the yellow shape if you knew the areas of the green and red shapes and the area of the entire banner .

b. What is the area of the entire banner? Explain how you found it.

c. What is the area of the red shape? What is the area of each green shape?

d. What equation can you write to find A, the area of the yellow shape?

e. What is the area of the yellow shape?

7. There are 6 rectangular flower gardens each measuring 18 feet by 15 feet in a rectangular city park measuring 80 feet by 150 feet. How many square feet of the park are not used for flower gardens?

Personal Math Trainer

8. THINK SMARTER + Sabrina wants to replace the carpet in a few rooms of her house. Select the expression she can use to find the total area of the floor that will be covered. Mark all that apply.

Ⓐ $8 \times 22 + 130 + \frac{1}{2} \times 10 \times 9$

Ⓑ $18 \times 22 - \frac{1}{2} \times 10 \times 9$

Ⓒ $18 \times 13 + \frac{1}{2} \times 10 \times 9$

Ⓓ $\frac{1}{2} \times (18 + 8) \times 22$

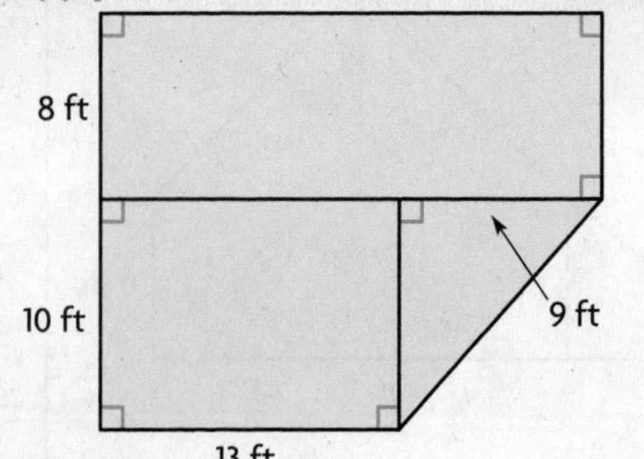

FOR MORE PRACTICE:
Standards Practice Book

Name ________________________________

Problem Solving • Changing Dimensions

Essential Question How can you use the strategy *find a pattern* to show how changing dimensions affects area?

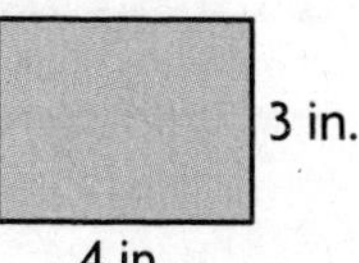

Geometry—
6.G.1

MATHEMATICAL PRACTICES
MP.1, MP.3, MP.8

Unlock the Problem 

Jason has created a 3-in. by 4-in. rectangular design to be made into mouse pads. To manufacture the pads, the dimensions will be multiplied by 2 or 3. How will the area of the design be affected?

3 in.

4 in.

Use the graphic organizer to help you solve the problem.

Read the Problem

What do I need to find?	What information do I need to use?	How will I use the information?
I need to find how ____________ will be affected by changing the ____________.	I need to use ____________ of the original design and ____________ ____________ ____________.	I can draw a sketch of each rectangle and calculate ____________ of each. Then I can look for ____________ in my results.

Solve the Problem

Sketch	Dimensions	Multiplier	Area
	3 in. by 4 in.	none	$A = 3 \times 4 = 12$ in.^{2}
6 in.; 8 in.	6 in. by 8 in.	2	$A =$ ______ $\times$ ______ $=$ ______ in.^{2}
9 in.; 12 in.			

So, when the dimensions are multiplied by 2, the area is multiplied by ______. When the dimensions are multiplied by 3, the area is multiplied by ______.

Mathematical Practices

Predict what would happen to the area of a rectangle if the dimensions were multiplied by 4.

Try Another Problem

A stained-glass designer is reducing the dimensions of an earlier design. The dimensions of the triangle shown will be multiplied by $\frac{1}{2}$ or $\frac{1}{4}$. How will the area of the design be affected? Use the graphic organizer to help you solve the problem.

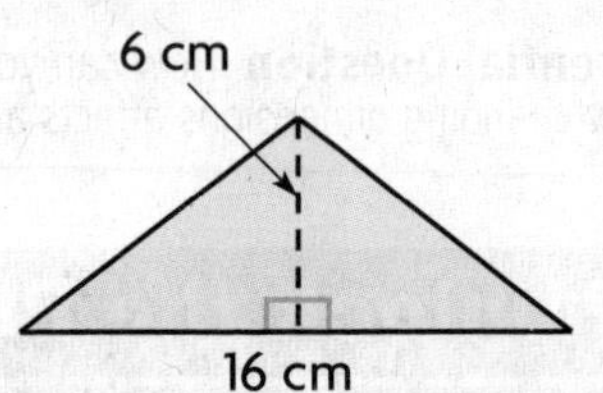

Read the Problem

What do I need to find?	What information do I need to use?	How will I use the information?

Solve the Problem

Sketch	Multiplier	Area
	none	$A = \frac{1}{2} \times 16 \times$ ______ $=$ ______ cm^2
3 cm 8 cm	$\frac{1}{2}$	

So, when the dimensions are multiplied by $\frac{1}{2}$, the area is multiplied by ______. When the dimensions are multiplied by ______, the area is multiplied by ______.

Mathematical Practices

Explain what happens to the area of a triangle when the dimensions are multiplied by a number *n*.

Name ________________________________

Share and Show

1. The dimensions of a 2-cm by 6-cm rectangle are multiplied by 5. How is the area of the rectangle affected?

   First, find the original area:

   ____

   Next, find the new area:

   ____

   So, the area is multiplied by ______.

2. THINKSMARTER What if the dimensions of the original rectangle in Exercise 1 had been multiplied by $\frac{1}{2}$? How would the area have been affected?

   ____

   ____

   ____

   ____

3. Evan bought two square rugs. The larger one measured 12 ft square. The smaller one had an area equal to $\frac{1}{4}$ the area of the larger one. What fraction of the side lengths of the larger rug were the side lengths of the smaller one?

   ____

4. GO DEEPER On Silver Island, a palm tree, a giant rock, and a buried treasure form a triangle with a base of 100 yd and a height of 50 yd. On a map of the island, the three landmarks form a triangle with a base of 2 ft and a height of 1 ft. How many times the area of the triangle on the map is the area of the actual triangle?

   ____

Unlock the Problem

- √ Plan your solution by deciding on the steps you will use.
- √ Find the original area and the new area, and then compare the two.
- √ Look for patterns in your results.

WRITE Math • Show Your Work

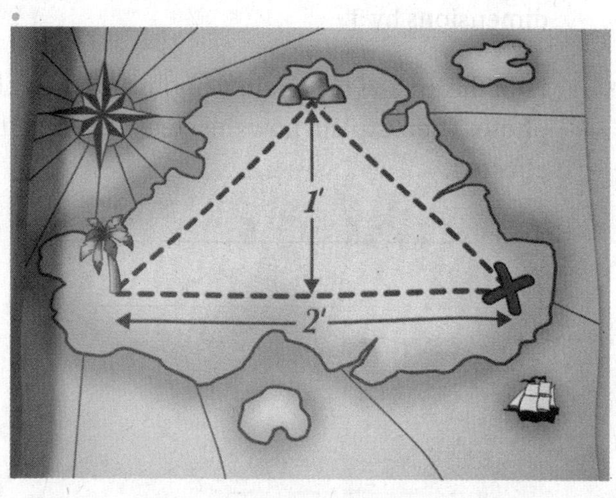

On Your Own

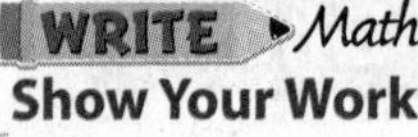

Show Your Work

5. A square game board is divided into smaller squares, each with sides one-ninth the length of the sides of the board. Into how many squares is the game board divided?

____

6. THINK SMARTER Flynn County is a rectangle measuring 9 mi by 12 mi. Gibson County is a rectangle with an area 6 times the area of Flynn County and a width of 16 mi. What is the length of Gibson County?

____

7. MATHEMATICAL PRACTICE 4 **Use Diagrams** Carmen left her house and drove 10 mi north, 15 mi east, 13 mi south, 11 mi west, and 3 mi north. How far was she from home?

____

8. GO DEEPER Bernie drove from his house to his cousin's house in 6 hours at an average rate of 52 mi per hr. He drove home at an average rate of 60 mi per hr. How long did it take him to drive home?

____

Personal Math Trainer

9. THINK SMARTER + Sophia wants to enlarge a 5-inch by 7-inch rectangular photo by multiplying the dimensions by 3.

Find the area of the original photo and the enlarged photo. Then explain how the area of the original photo is affected.

____

____

____

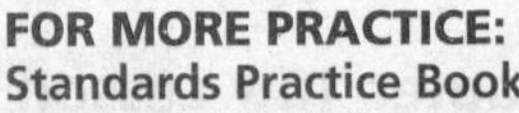
FOR MORE PRACTICE: Standards Practice Book

Name ______________________

Figures on the Coordinate Plane

Essential Question How can you plot polygons on a coordinate plane and find their side lengths?

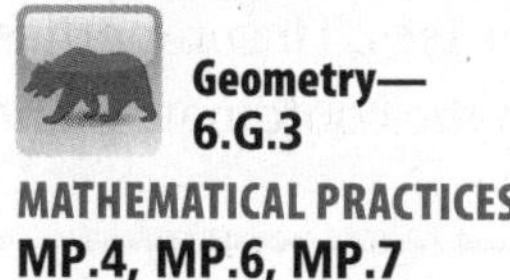

Geometry—6.G.3

MATHEMATICAL PRACTICES
MP.4, MP.6, MP.7

Unlock the Problem

The world's largest book is a collection of photographs from the Asian nation of Bhutan. A book collector models the rectangular shape of the open book on a coordinate plane. Each unit of the coordinate plane represents one foot. The book collector plots the vertices of the rectangle at $A(9, 3)$, $B(2, 3)$, $C(2, 8)$, and $D(9, 8)$. What are the dimensions of the open book?

- What two dimensions do you need to find?

____

____

Plot the vertices and find the dimensions of the rectangle.

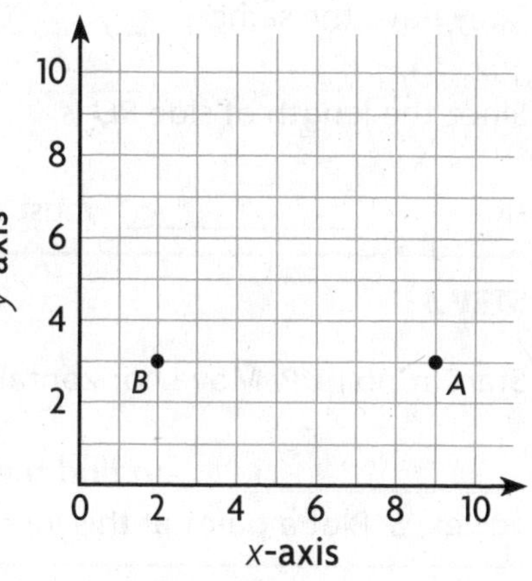

STEP 1 Complete the rectangle on the coordinate plane.

Plot points $C(2, 8)$ and $D(9, 8)$.
Connect the points to form a rectangle.

STEP 2 Find the length of the rectangle.

Find the distance between points $A(9, 3)$ and $B(2, 3)$.

The y-coordinates are the same, so the points lie on a ______ line.

Think of the horizontal line passing through A and B as a number line.

Horizontal distance of A from 0: $|9|$ = ______ ft

Horizontal distance of B from 0: $|2|$ = ______ ft

Subtract to find the distance from A to B: ______ − ______ = ______ ft.

STEP 3 Find the width of the rectangle.

Find the distance between points C (2, 8) and $B(2, 3)$.

The x-coordinates are the same, so the points lie on a ______ line.

Think of the vertical line passing through C and B as a number line.

Vertical distance of C from 0: $|8|$ = ______ ft

Vertical distance of B from 0: $|3|$ = ______ ft

Subtract to find the distance from C to B: ______ − ______ = ______ ft.

So, the dimensions of the open book are ______ ft by ______ ft.

Math Talk — **Mathematical Practices**

Explain how you know whether to add or subtract the absolute values to find the distance between the vertices of the rectangle.

CONNECT You can use properties of quadrilaterals to help you find unknown vertices. The properties can also help you graph quadrilaterals on the coordinate plane.

Example Find the unknown vertex, and then graph.

Three vertices of parallelogram *PQRS* are *P*(4, 2), *Q*(3, $^-3$), and *R*($^-3$, $^-3$). Give the coordinates of vertex *S* and graph the parallelogram.

Math Idea

The name of a polygon, such as parallelogram *PQRS*, gives the vertices in order as you move around the polygon.

STEP 1

Plot the given points on the coordinate plane.

STEP 2

The opposite sides of a parallelogram are ________.

They have the same ____________.

Since the length of side $\overline{RQ}$ is _____ units, the length of

side ____________ must also be _____ units.

STEP 3

Start at point *P*. Move horizontally _____ units to the

__________ to find the location of the remaining vertex, *S*. Plot a point at this location.

STEP 4

Draw the parallelogram. Check that opposite sides are parallel and congruent.

So, the coordinates of the vertex *S* are ________.

1. **MATHEMATICAL PRACTICE 6 Attend to Precision** Explain why vertex *S* must be to the left of vertex *P* rather than to the right of vertex *P*.

2. Describe how you could find the area of parallelogram *PQRS* in square units.

Name ______________________________

Share and Show

MATH BOARD

1. The vertices of triangle ABC are $A(^{-}1, 3)$, $B(^{-}4, ^{-}2)$, and $C(2, ^{-}2)$. Graph the triangle and find the length of side $\overline{BC}$.

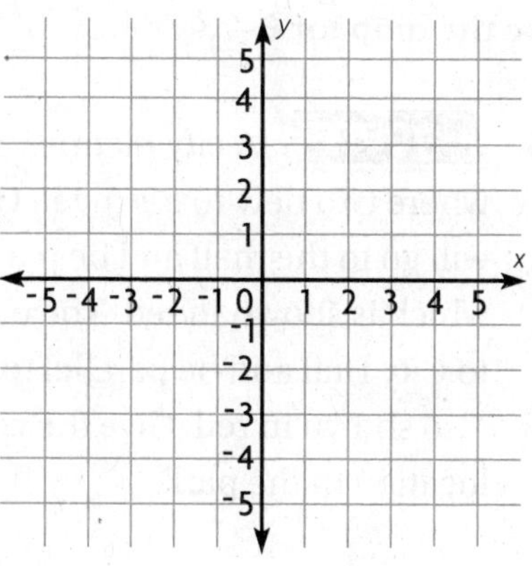

Horizontal distance of B from 0: $|^{-}4|$ = ______ units

Horizontal distance of C from 0: $|2|$ = ______ units

The points are in different quadrants, so add to find the distance from B to C: ______ + ______ = ______ units.

Give the coordinates of the unknown vertex of rectangle *JKLM*, and graph.

2.

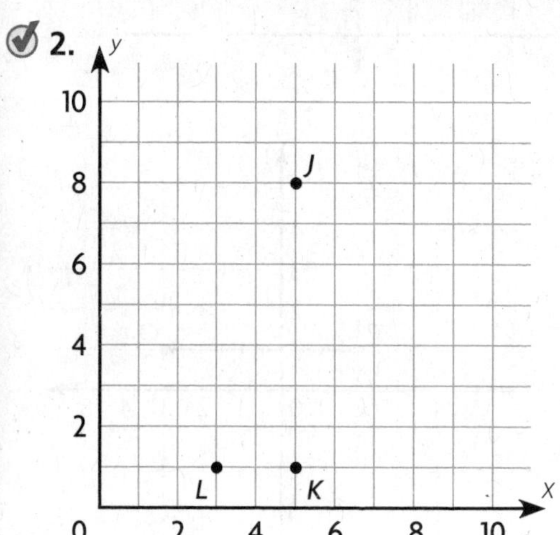

____

3.

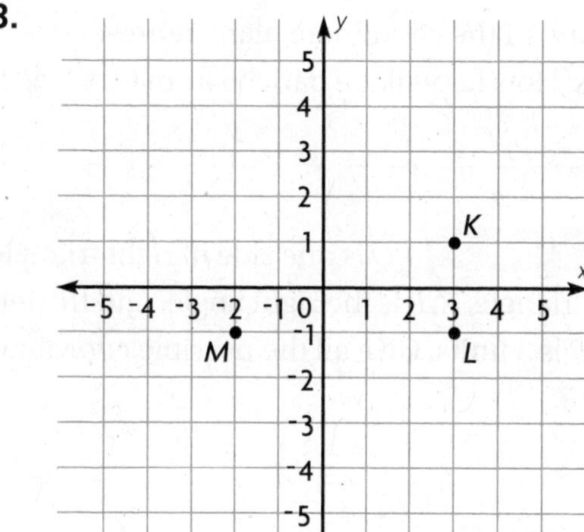

____

On Your Own

4. Give the coordinates of the unknown vertex of rectangle $PQRS$, and graph.

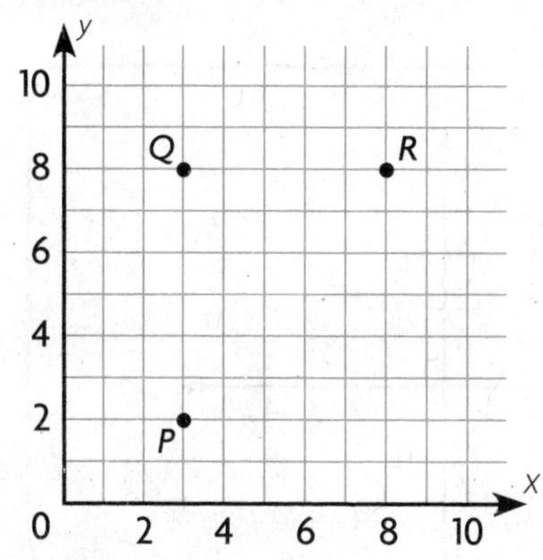

____

5. The vertices of pentagon $PQRST$ are $P(9, 7)$, $Q(9, 3)$, $R(3, 3)$, $S(3, 7)$, and $T(6, 9)$. Graph the pentagon and find the length of side $\overline{PQ}$.

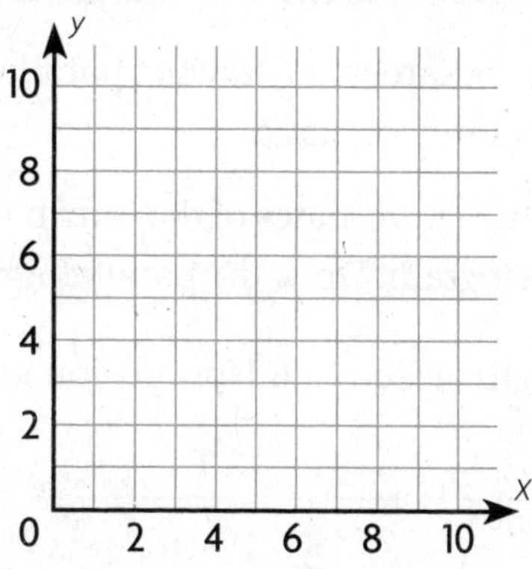

____

Problem Solving • Applications

The map shows the location of some city landmarks. Use the map for 6–7.

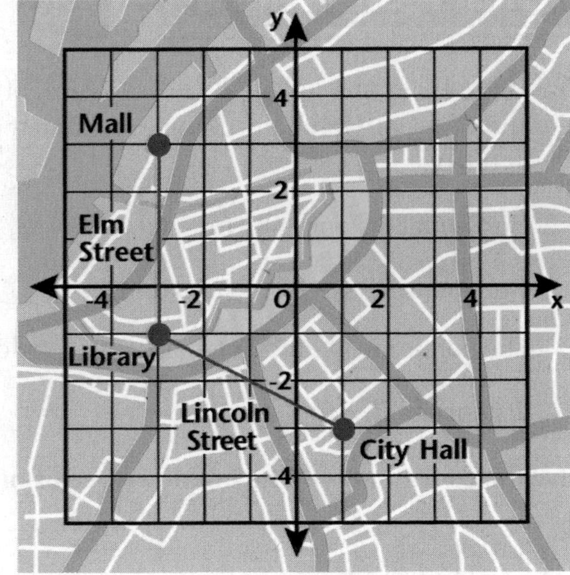

6. GO DEEPER A city planner wants to locate a park where two new roads meet. One of the new roads will go to the mall and be parallel to Lincoln Street which is shown in red. The other new road will go to City Hall and be parallel to Elm Street which is also shown in red. Give the coordinates for the location of the park.

7. Each unit of the coordinate plane represents 2 miles. How far will the park be from City Hall?

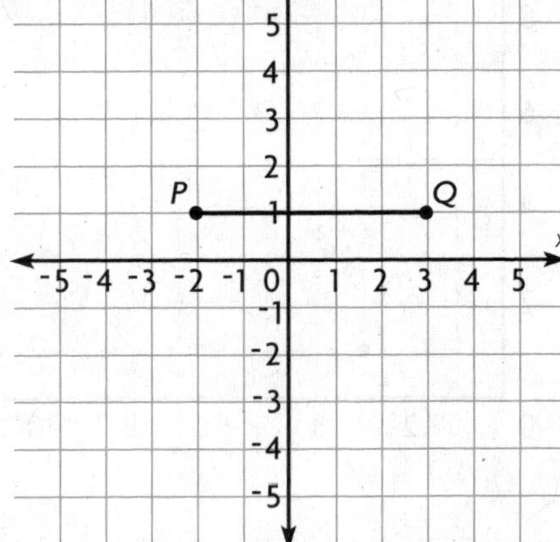

8. THINK SMARTER $\overline{PQ}$ is one side of right triangle PQR. In the triangle, $\angle P$ is the right angle, and the length of side $\overline{PR}$ is 3 units. Give all the possible coordinates for vertex R.

9. MATHEMATICAL PRACTICE 6 **Use Math Vocabulary** Quadrilateral $WXYZ$ has vertices with coordinates $W(^-4, 0)$, $X(^-2, 3)$, $Y(2, 3)$, and $Z(2, 0)$. Classify the quadrilateral using the most exact name possible and explain your answer.

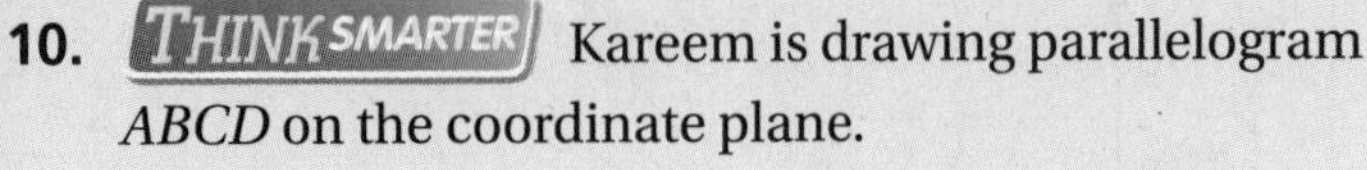

10. THINK SMARTER Kareem is drawing parallelogram $ABCD$ on the coordinate plane.

Find and label the coordinates of the fourth vertex, D, of the parallelogram. Draw the parallelogram.

What is the length of side CD? How do you know?

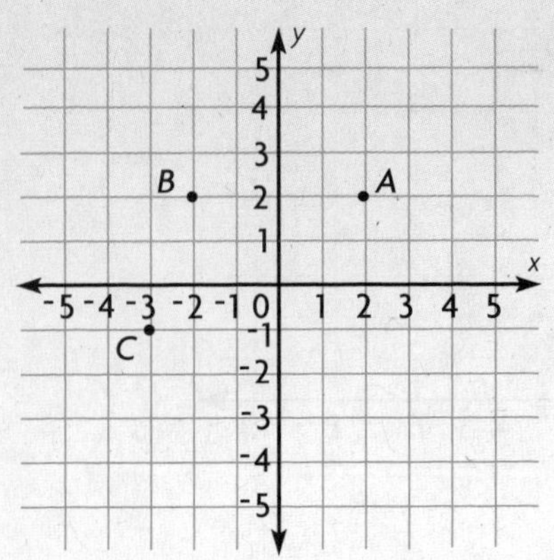

FOR MORE PRACTICE:
Standards Practice Book

Name ________________________________

Chapter 10 Review/Test

1. Find the area of the parallelogram.

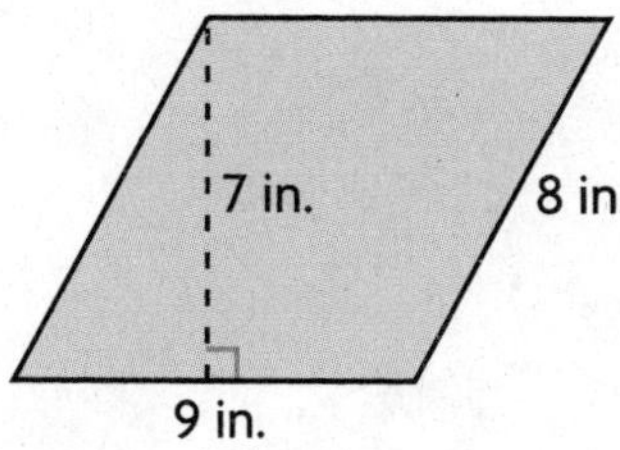

The area is ______ in^2.

2. A wall tile is two different colors. What is the area of the white part of the tile? Explain how you found your answer.

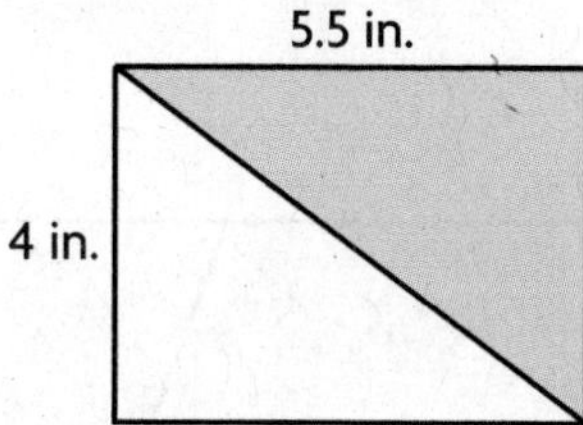

3. The area of a triangle is 36 ft^2. For numbers 3a–3d, select Yes or No to tell if the dimensions could be the height and base of the triangle.

3a. $h = 3, b = 12$ ○ Yes ○ No

3b. $h = 3, b = 24$ ○ Yes ○ No

3c. $h = 4, b = 18$ ○ Yes ○ No

3d. $h = 4, b = 9$ ○ Yes ○ No

4. Mario traced this trapezoid. Then he cut it out and arranged the trapezoids to form a rectangle. What is the area of the rectangle?

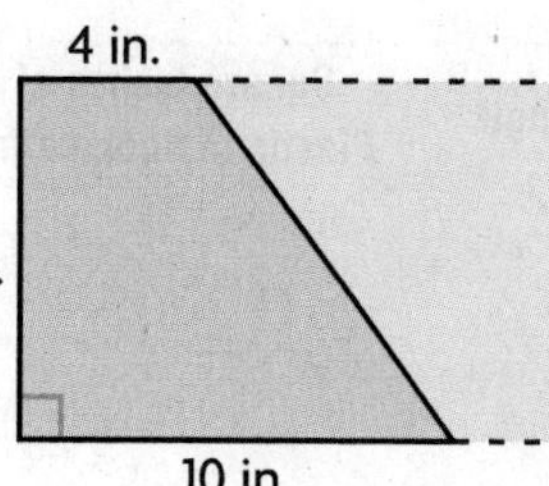

______ in^2.

GO DIGITAL Assessment Options Chapter Test

5. The area of the triangle is 24 ft^2. Use the numbers to label the height and base of the triangle.

2 4 6 8 10 20

☐ ft

☐ ft

6. A rectangle has an area of 50 cm^2. The dimensions of the rectangle are multiplied to form a new rectangle with an area of 200 cm^2. By what number were the dimensions multiplied?

____

7. Sami put two trapezoids with the same dimensions together to make a parallelogram.

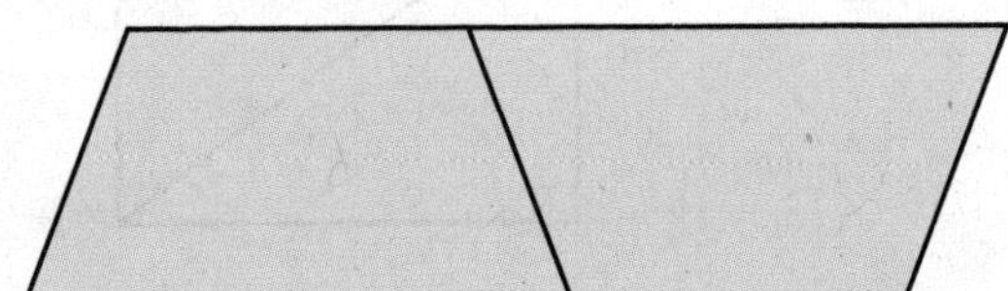

The formula for the area of a trapezoid is $A = \frac{1}{2}(b_1 + b_2)h$. Explain why the bases of a trapezoid need to be added in the formula.

8. A rectangular plastic bookmark has a triangle cut out of it. Use the diagram of the bookmark to complete the table.

Area of Rectangle	Area of Triangle	Square Inches of Plastic in Bookmark

5 in.

2 in.

1 in.

1 in.

Name ______________________________

9. A trapezoid has an area of 32 in^2. If the lengths of the bases are 6 in. and 6.8 in., what is the height?

__________ in.

10. A pillow is in the shape of a regular pentagon. It is made from 5 pieces of fabric that are congruent triangles. Each triangle has an area of 22 in^2. What is the area of the pillow?

__________ $in.^2$

11. Which expressions can be used to find the area of the trapezoid? Mark all that apply.

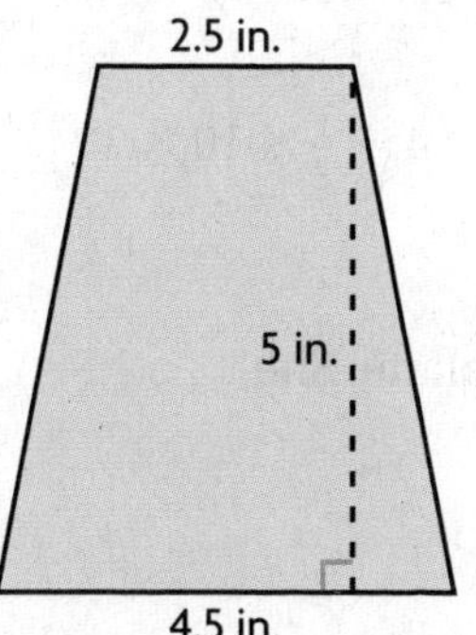

Ⓐ $\frac{1}{2} \times (5 + 2.5) \times 4.5$

Ⓑ $\frac{1}{2} \times (2.5 + 4.5) \times 5$

Ⓒ $\frac{1}{2} \times (5 + 4.5) \times 2.5$

Ⓓ $\frac{1}{2} \times (7) \times 5$

12. Name the polygon and find its area. Show your work.

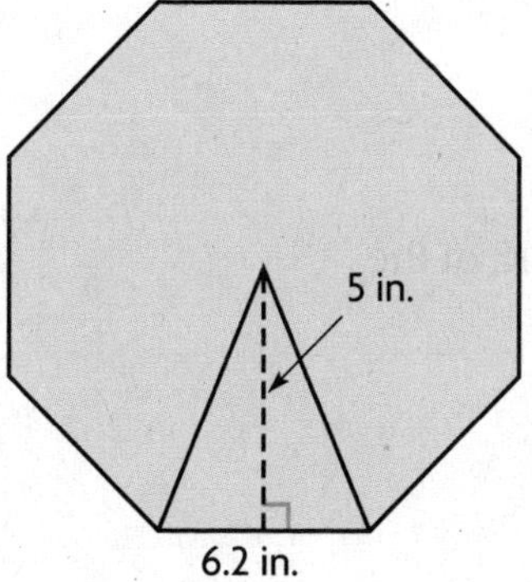

polygon: __________ area: __________

13. A carpenter needs to replace some flooring in a house.

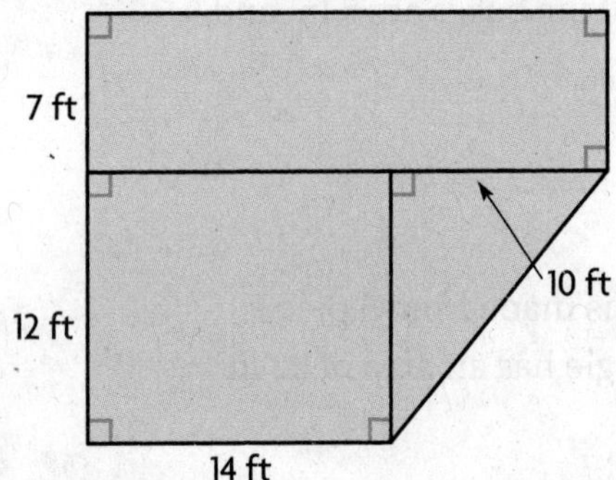

Select the expression that can be used to find the total area of the flooring to be replaced. Mark all that apply.

Ⓐ 19×14

Ⓑ $168 + 12 \times 14 + 60$

Ⓒ $19 \times 24 - \frac{1}{2} \times 10 \times 12$

Ⓓ $7 \times 24 + 12 \times 14 + \frac{1}{2} \times 10 \times 12$

14. Ava wants to draw a parallelogram on the coordinate plane. She plots these 3 points.

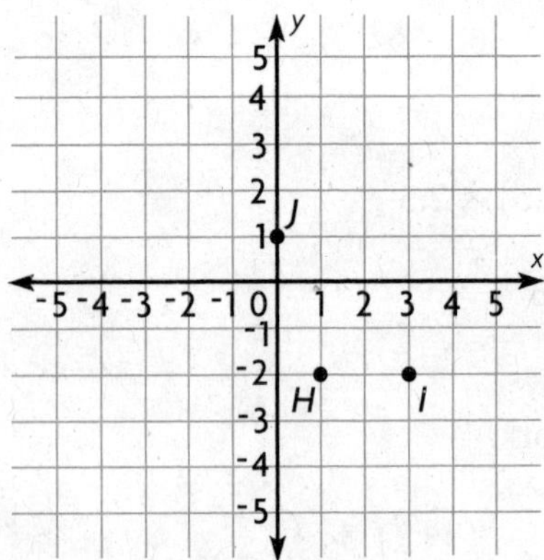

Part A

Find and label the coordinates of the fourth vertex, *K*, of the parallelogram. Draw the parallelogram.

Part B

What is the length of side *JK*? How do you know?

Name ___

15. Joan wants to reduce the area of her posters by one-third. Draw lines to match the original dimensions in the left column with the correct new area in the right column. Not all dimensions will have a match.

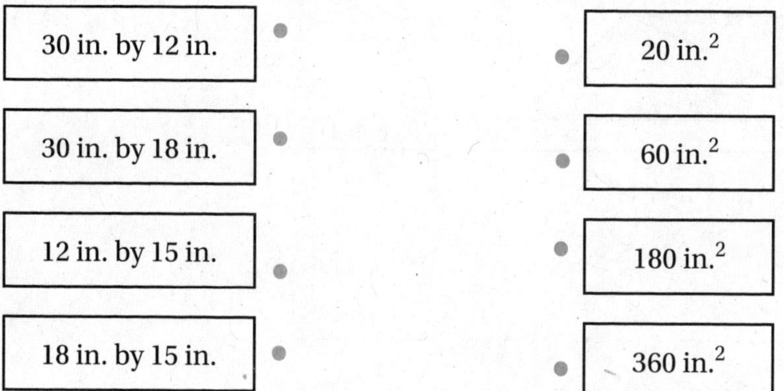

16. Alex wants to enlarge a 4-ft by 6-ft vegetable garden by multiplying the dimensions of the garden by 2.

Part A

Find each area.

Area of original garden: ___

Area of enlarged garden: ___

Part B

Explain how the area of the original garden will be affected.

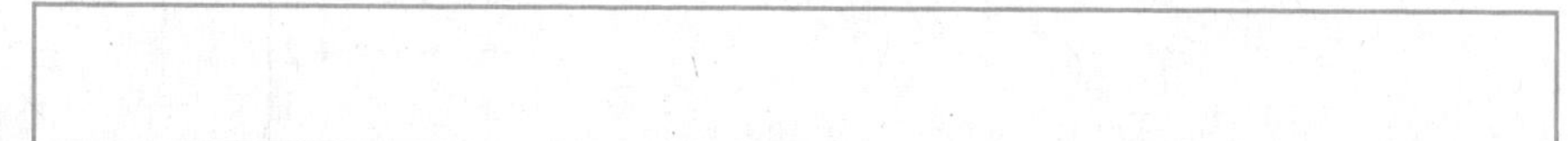

17. Suppose the point (3, 2) is changed to (3, 1) on this rectangle. What other point must change so the figure remains a rectangle? What is the area of the new rectangle?

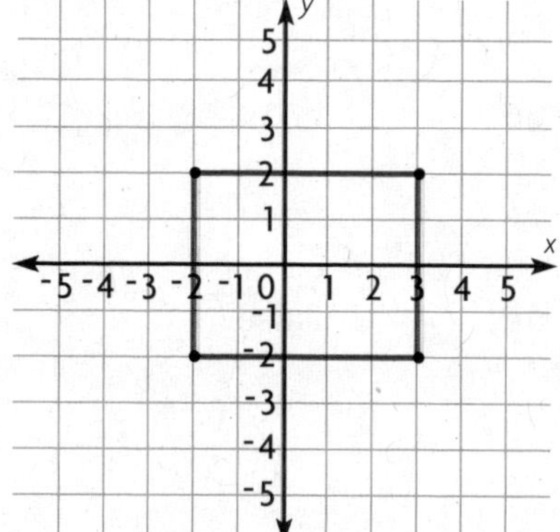

Point: ___ would change to ___.

The area of the new rectangle is ___ square units.

18. Look at the figure below. The area of the parallelogram and the areas of the two congruent triangles formed by a diagonal are related. If you know the area of the parallelogram, how can you find the area of one of the triangles?

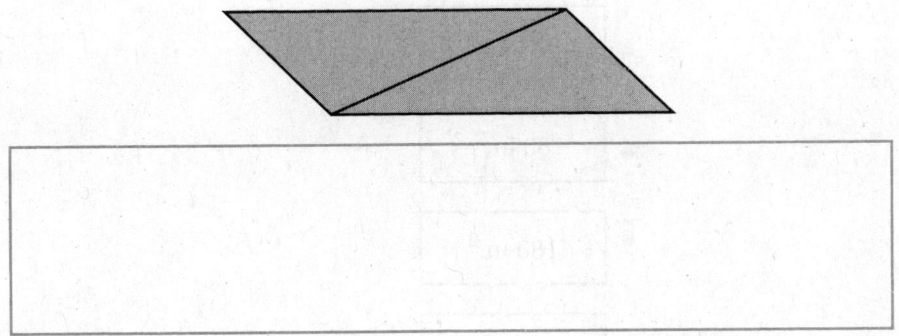

19. The roof of Kamden's house is shaped like a parallelogram. The base of the roof is 13 m and the area is 110.5 m^2. Choose a number and unit to make a true statement.

The height of the roof is [123.5 / 97.5 / 17 / 8.5] [m. / m^2. / m^3.]

20. Eliana is drawing a figure on the coordinate grid. For numbers 20a–20d, select True or False for each statement.

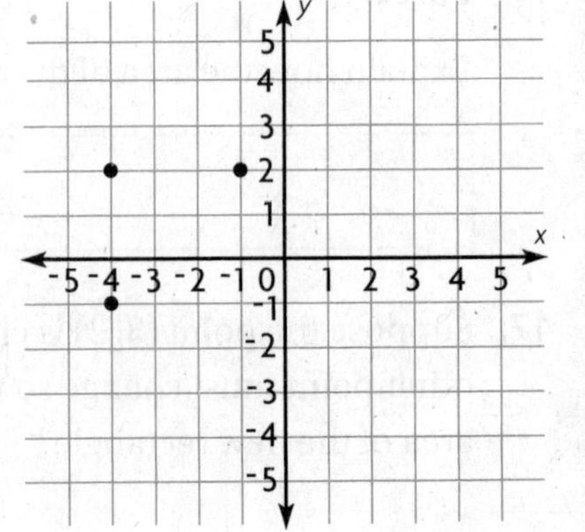

20a. The point ($^-1$, 1) would be the fourth vertex of a square. ○ True ○ False

20b. The point (1, 1) would be the fourth vertex of a trapezoid. ○ True ○ False

20c. The point (2, $^-1$) would be the fourth vertex of a trapezoid. ○ True ○ False

20d. The point ($^-1$, $^-1$) would be the fourth vertex of a square. ○ True ○ False

Chapter 11

Surface Area and Volume

Show What You Know

Check your understanding of important skills.

Name ____________________

Estimate and Find Area **Multiply to find the area.**

1. 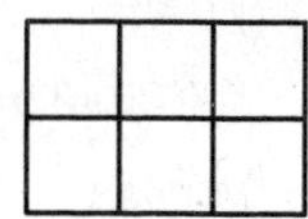

____

2. _______________

Area of Squares, Rectangles, and Triangles **Find the area.**

3. 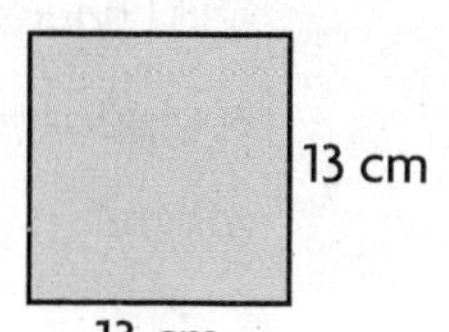

$A = s^2$

Area = _______________

4. 

$A = lw$

Area = _______________

5. 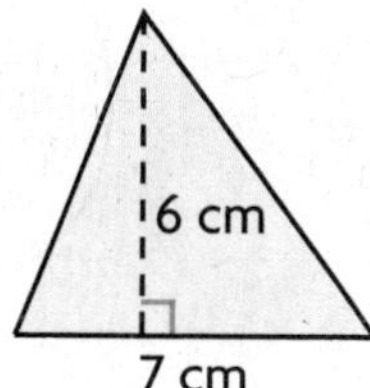

$A = \frac{1}{2}(b \times h)$

Area = _______________

Evaluate Expressions **Evaluate the expression.**

6. $3 \times (2 + 4)$ _______

7. $6 + 6 \div 3$ _______

8. $4^2 + 4 \times 5 - 2$ _______

Jerry is building an indoor beach volleyball court. He has ordered 14,000 cubic feet of sand. The dimensions of the court will be 30 feet by 60 feet. Jerry needs to have a 10-foot boundary around the court for safety. Be a math detective and determine how deep the sand will be if Jerry uses all the sand.

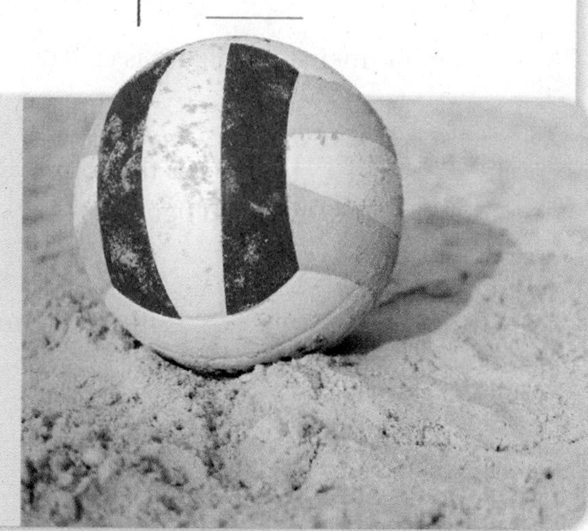

Personal Math Trainer
Online Assessment and Intervention

Vocabulary Builder

▶ Visualize It

Complete the bubble map. Use the review terms that name solid figures.

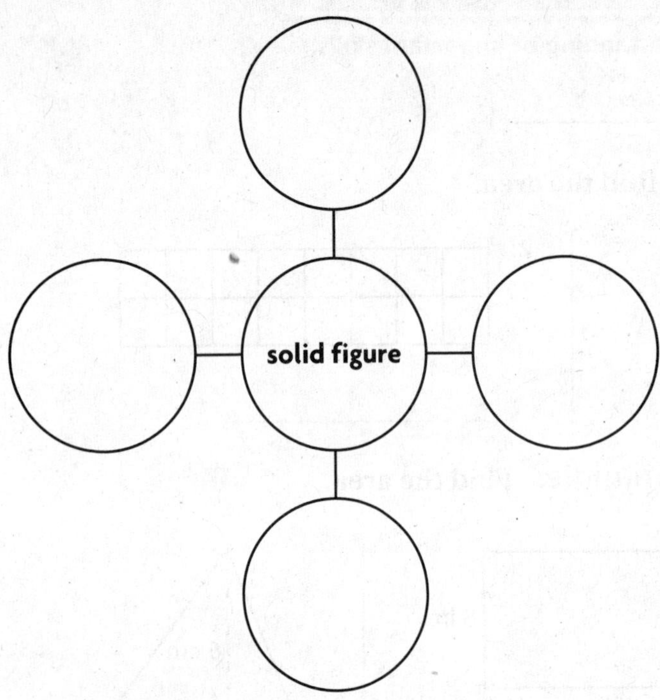

Review Words
base
cube
lateral face
polygon
polyhedron
prism
pyramid
vertex

Preview Words
net
solid figure
surface area
volume

▶ Understand Vocabulary

Complete the sentences using the preview words.

1. A three-dimensional figure having length, width, and height is called a(n) ________________.

2. A two-dimensional pattern that can be folded into a three-dimensional figure is called a(n) ________________.

3. ________________ is the sum of the areas of all the faces, or surfaces, of a solid figure.

4. ________________ is the measure of space a solid figure occupies.

GO DIGITAL
- Interactive Student Edition
- Multimedia eGlossary

Name ____________________

Three-Dimensional Figures and Nets

Essential Question How do you use nets to represent three-dimensional figures?

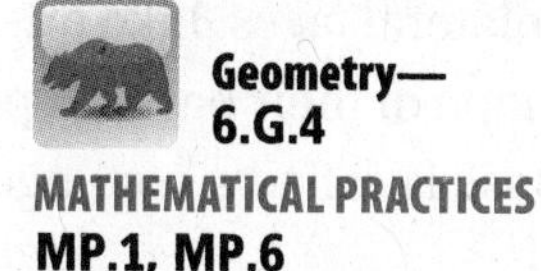

MATHEMATICAL PRACTICES
MP.1, MP.6

A **solid figure** is a three-dimensional figure because it has three dimensions—length, width, and height. Solid figures can be identified by the shapes of their bases, the number of bases, and the shapes of their lateral faces.

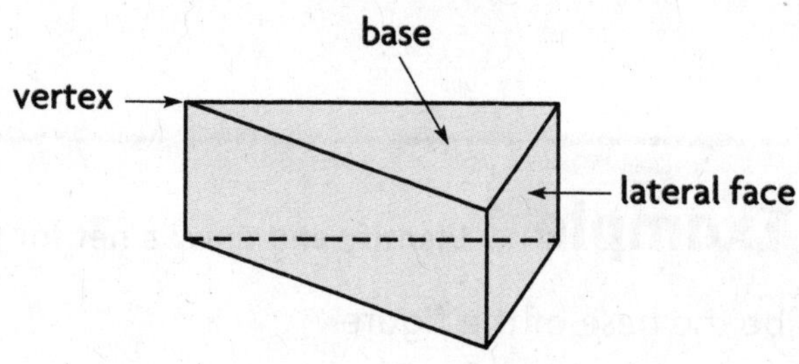

Triangular Prism

Unlock the Problem Real World

A designer is working on the layout for the cereal box shown. Identify the solid figure and draw a net that the designer can use to show the placement of information and artwork on the box.

- How many bases are there? ____________
- Are the bases congruent? ____________
- What shape are the bases? ____________

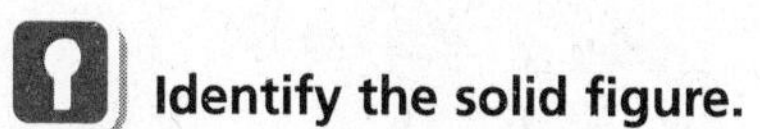
Identify the solid figure.

Recall that a prism is a solid figure with two congruent, parallel bases. Its lateral faces are rectangles. It is named for the shape of its bases.

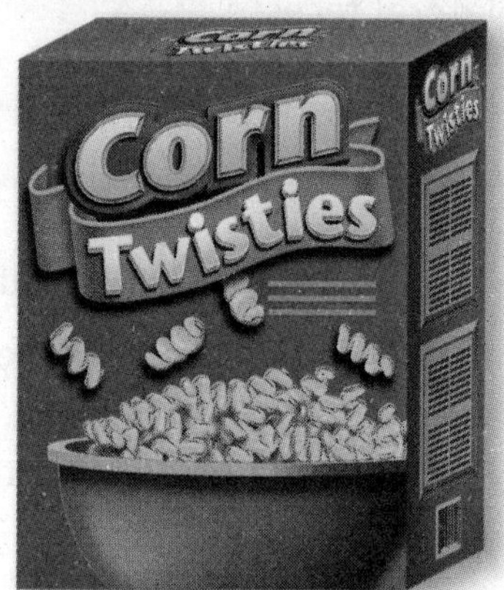

Is the cereal box a prism? ____________

What shape are the bases? ____________

So, the box is a ____________________.

Draw a net for the figure.

A **net** is a two-dimensional figure that can be folded into a solid figure.

STEP 1

Make a list of the shapes you will use.

top and bottom bases: ____________

left and right faces: ____________

front and back faces: ____________

STEP 2

Draw the net using the shapes you listed in Step 1. One possible net is shown.

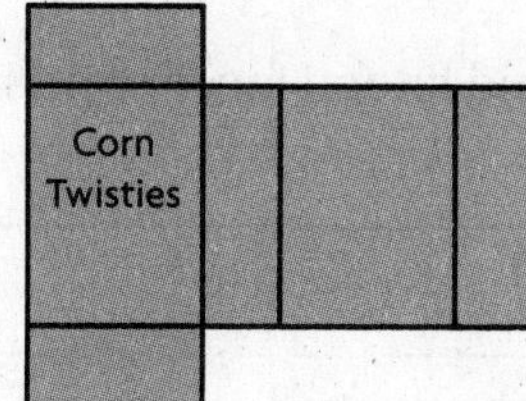

A *pyramid* is a solid figure with a polygon-shaped base and triangles for lateral faces. Like prisms, pyramids are named by the shape of their bases. A pyramid with a rectangle for a base is called a rectangular pyramid.

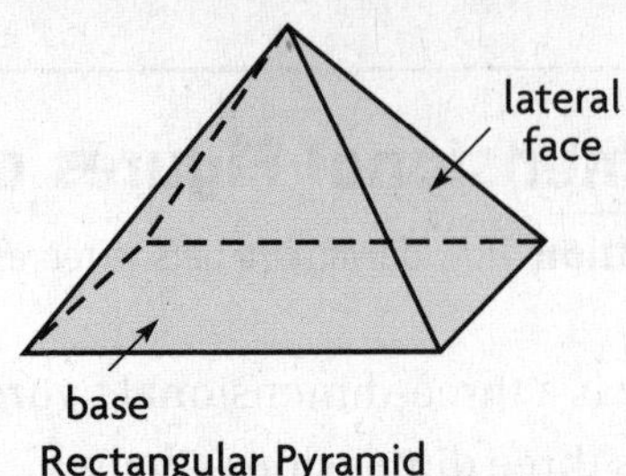

Rectangular Pyramid

Example 1 Identify and draw a net for the solid figure.

Describe the base of the figure.

____

Describe the lateral faces.

____

The figure is a ______________.

Shapes to use in the net:

base: __________

lateral faces: __________

Net:

Example 2 Identify and sketch the solid figure that could be formed by the net.

The net has only ______ triangles, so it cannot be a

______________.

The triangles must be the ______________ for a

______________.

- MATHEMATICAL PRACTICE 6 **Compare** the bases and lateral faces of prisms and pyramids.

____

____

____

Name ______________________________

Share and Show

Identify and draw a net for the solid figure.

1. 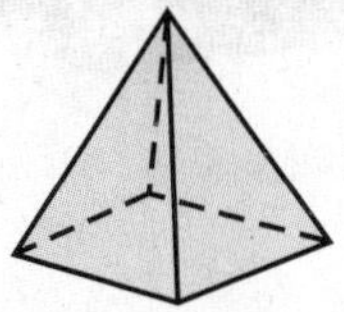

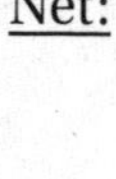

Net:

base: ______________

lateral faces: ______________

figure: ______________

 2. 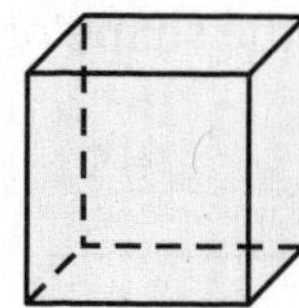

____

Identify and sketch the solid figure that could be formed by the net.

3. 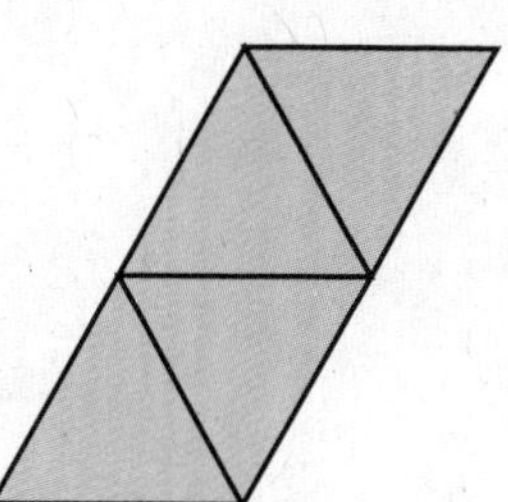

____

4. 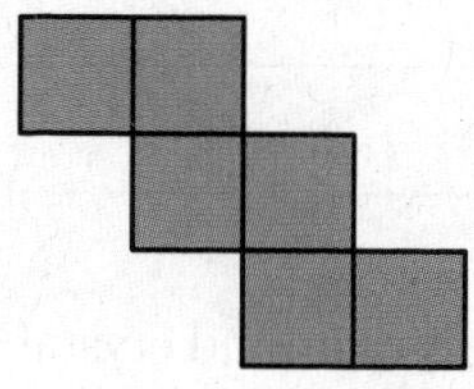

____

Math Talk — **Mathematical Practices**

Describe the characteristics of a solid figure that you need to consider when making its net.

On Your Own

Identify and draw a net for the solid figure.

5. 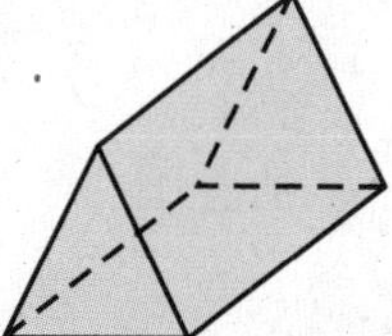

____

6. 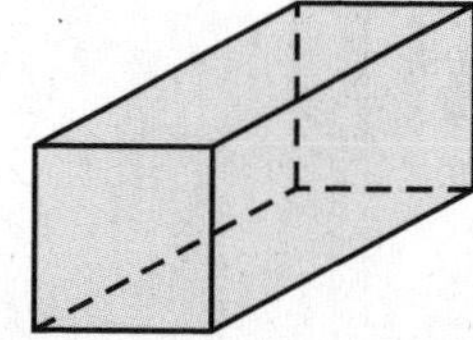

____

Problem Solving • Applications Real World

Solve.

7. The lateral faces and bases of crystals of the mineral galena are congruent squares. Identify the shape of a galena crystal.

____

8. THINK SMARTER Rhianon draws the net below and labels each square. Can Rhianon fold her net into a cube that has letters A through G on its faces? Explain.

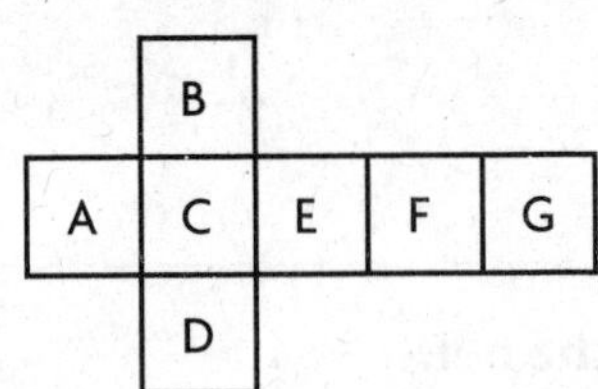

Math on the Spot

____

____

WRITE Math • Show Your Work

9. MATHEMATICAL PRACTICE 1 **Describe** A diamond crystal is shown. Describe the figure in terms of the solid figures you have seen in this lesson.

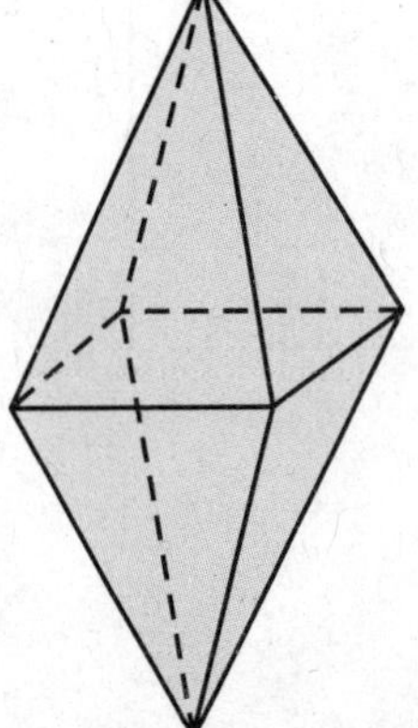

____

____

____

____

10. THINK SMARTER Sasha makes a triangular prism from paper.

The bases are [rectangles. / squares. / triangles.]

The lateral faces are [rectangles. / squares. / triangles.]

FOR MORE PRACTICE:
Standards Practice Book

Lesson 11.2

Name ______________________________

Explore Surface Area Using Nets

Essential Question What is the relationship between a net and the surface area of a prism?

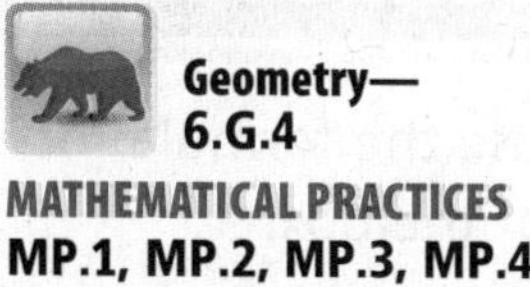

Geometry—
6.G.4

MATHEMATICAL PRACTICES
MP.1, MP.2, MP.3, MP.4

CONNECT The **surface area** of a solid figure is the sum of the areas of all the faces or surfaces of the figure. Surface area is measured in square units. You can use a net to help you find the surface area of a solid figure.

Investigate

Hands On

Materials ■ centimeter grid paper, ruler, scissors

A box is shaped like a rectangular prism. The box is 8 cm long, 6 cm wide, and 4 cm high. What is the surface area of the box?

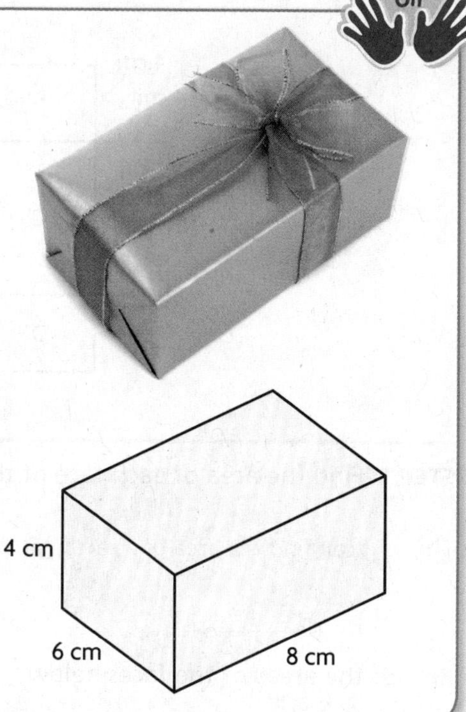

Find the surface area of the rectangular prism.

A. Draw a net of the prism on centimeter grid paper.

B. Cut out the net.

C. Fold the net to confirm that it represents a rectangular prism measuring 8 cm by 6 cm by 4 cm.

D. Count the grid squares on each face of the net.

So, the surface area of the box is __________ cm^2.

ERROR Alert

Make sure you include all surfaces in the net of a three-dimensional figure, not just the surfaces you can see in the diagram of the figure.

Draw Conclusions

1. Explain how you used the net to find the surface area of the box.

____

____

2. THINK SMARTER Describe how you could find the area of each face of the prism without counting grid squares on the net.

____

____

Make Connections

You can also use the formula for the area of a rectangle to find the surface area of the box.

Find the surface area of the box in the Investigate, which measures 8 cm by 6 cm by 4 cm.

STEP 1 Label the rectangles in the net A through F. Then label the dimensions.

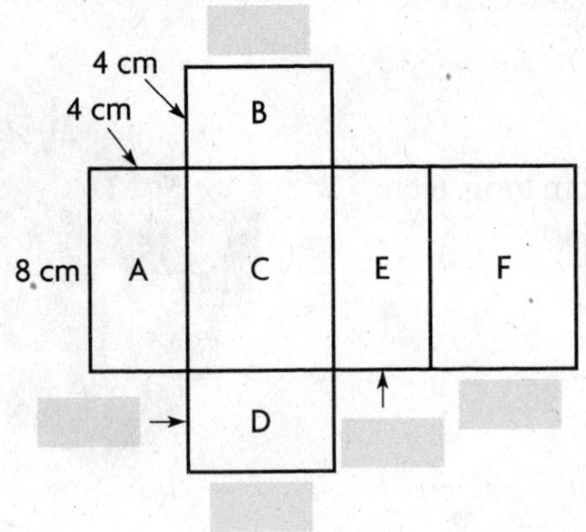

STEP 2 Find the area of each face of the prism.

Think: I can find the area of a rectangle by multiplying the rectangle's ________

times its ________.

Record the areas of the faces below.

Face A: $4 \times 8 = 32$ cm^2 Face B: ______ cm^2 Face C: ______ cm^2

Face D: ______ cm^2 Face E: ______ cm^2 Face F: ______ cm^2

STEP 3 Add the areas to find the surface area of the prism.

The surface area of the prism is ______ cm^2.

Math Talk **Mathematical Practices**

Compare the surface area you found by adding the areas of the faces to the surface area you found by counting grid squares. Explain your results.

3. MATHEMATICAL PRACTICE 2 **Use Reasoning** Identify any prism faces that have equal areas. How could you use that fact to simplify the process of finding the surface area of the prism?

______

______

______

4. Describe how you could find the surface area of a cube.

______

Name ______________________

Share and Show

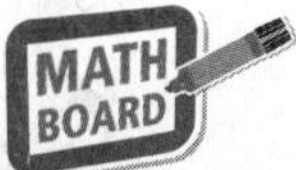

Use the net to find the surface area of the prism.

1.

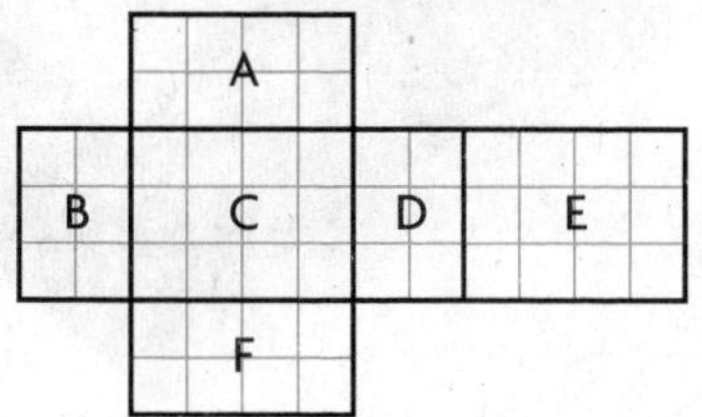

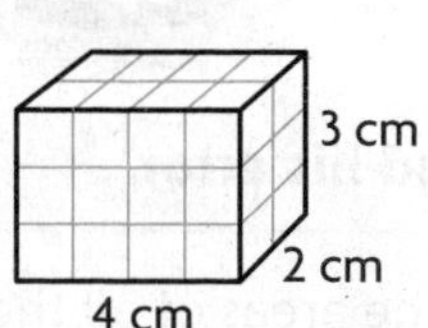

Face A: ______ cm^2 Face D: ______ cm^2

Face B: ______ cm^2 Face E: ______ cm^2

Face C: ______ cm^2 Face F: ______ cm^2

Surface area: ______ cm^2

Find the surface area of the rectangular prism.

2.

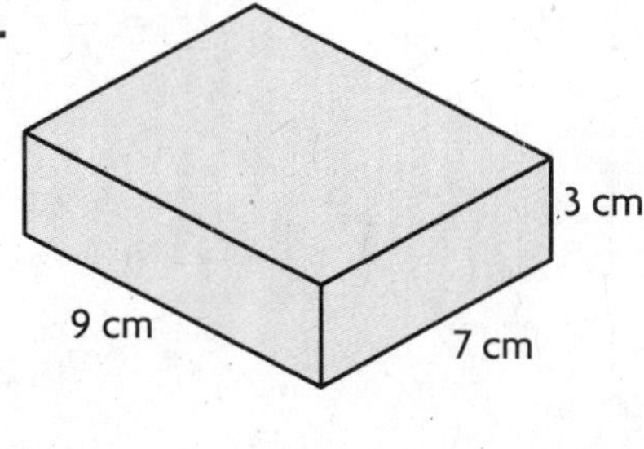

____

3.

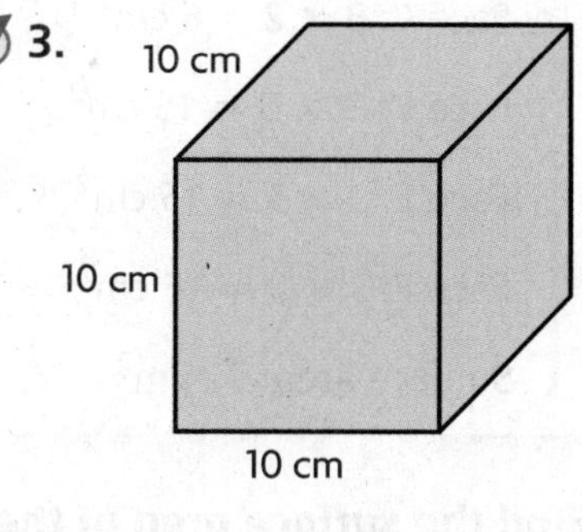

____

4.

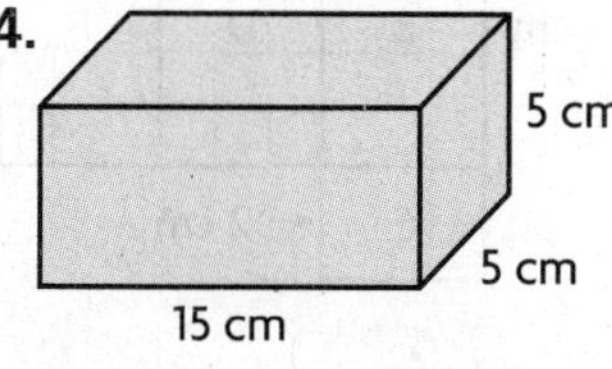

____

Problem Solving • Applications

5. A cereal box is shaped like a rectangular prism. The box is 20 cm long, by 5 cm wide by 30 cm high. What is the surface area of the cereal box?

____

6. GO DEEPER Darren is painting a wooden block as part of his art project. The block is a rectangular prism that is 12 cm long by 9 cm wide by 5 cm high. What is the surface area, in square meters, that Darren has to paint?

____

7. MATHEMATICAL PRACTICE 1 **Describe** the rectangles that make up the net for the prism in Exercise 6.

____

____

What's the Error?

8. THINK SMARTER Emilio is designing the packaging for a new mp3 player. The box for the mp3 player is 5 cm by 3 cm by 2 cm. Emilio needs to find the surface area of the box.

Look at how Emilio solved the problem. Find his error.

STEP 1 Draw a net.

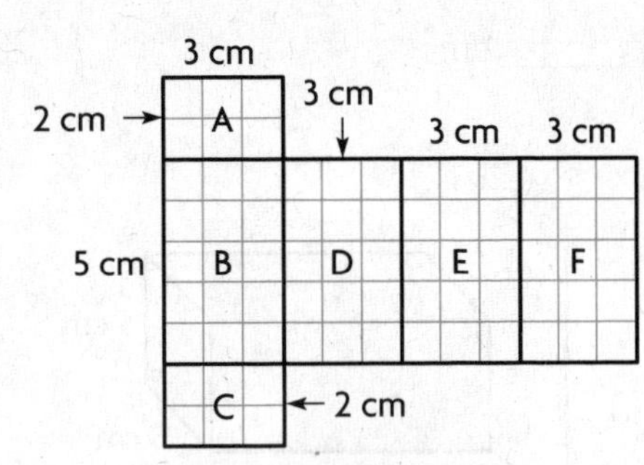

STEP 2 Find the areas of all the faces and add them.

Face A: $3 \times 2 = 6 \text{ cm}^2$

Face B: $3 \times 5 = 15 \text{ cm}^2$

Face C: $3 \times 2 = 6 \text{ cm}^2$

Face D: $3 \times 5 = 15 \text{ cm}^2$

Face E: $3 \times 5 = 15 \text{ cm}^2$

Face F: $3 \times 5 = 15 \text{ cm}^2$

Surface area: 72 cm^2

Correct the error. Find the surface area of the prism.

So, the surface area of the prism is ____________.

9. THINK SMARTER For numbers 9a–9d, select True or False for each statement.

9a. The area of face A is 10 cm^2. ○ True ○ False

9b. The area of face B is 10 cm^2. ○ True ○ False

9c. The area of face C is 40 cm^2. ○ True ○ False

9d. The surface area of the prism is 66 cm^2. ○ True ○ False

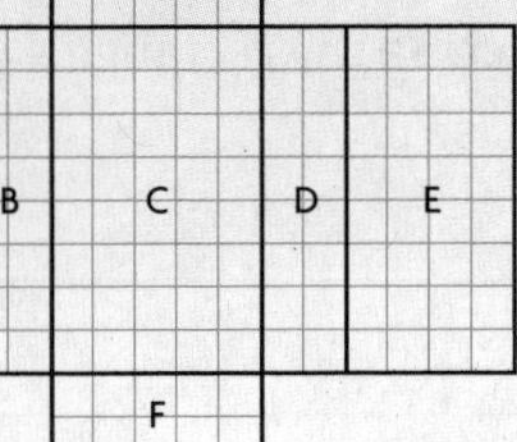

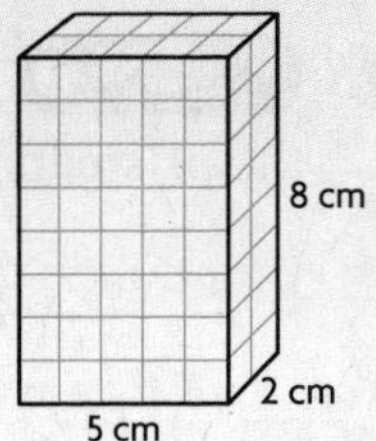

FOR MORE PRACTICE: Standards Practice Book

Name ___________________________

ALGEBRA
Lesson 11.3

Surface Area of Prisms

Essential Question How can you find the surface area of a prism?

You can use a net to find the surface area of a solid figure, such as a prism.

Geometry—6.G.4
Also 6.EE.2c

MATHEMATICAL PRACTICES
MP.2, MP.4, MP.8

Unlock the Problem Real World

Alex is designing wooden boxes for his books. Each box measures 15 in. by 12 in. by 10 in. Before he buys wood, he needs to find the surface area of each box. What is the surface area of each box?

- What is the shape of each face?

____

- What are the dimensions of each face?

____

____

Use a net to find the surface area.

12 in.

10 in. A

10 in. 10 in. 12 in.

B C D E 15 in.

10 in. F

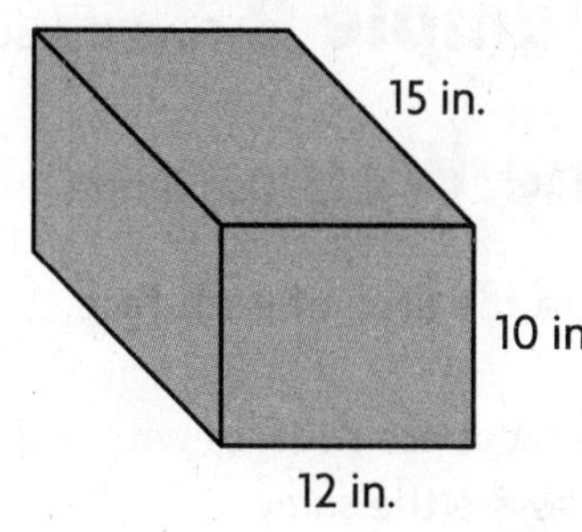

STEP 1 Find the area of each lettered face.

Face A: $12 \times 10 = 120$ in.^{2} Face B: $15 \times 10 =$ ______ in.^{2}

Face C: ______ $\times$ ______ $=$ ______ in.^{2} Face D: ______ $\times$ ______ $=$ ______ in.^{2}

Face E: ______ $\times$ ______ $=$ ______ in.^{2} Face F: ______ $\times$ ______ $=$ ______ in.^{2}

STEP 2 Find the sum of the areas of the faces. ____________

So, the surface area of each box is ____________.

Math Talk **Mathematical Practices**

Describe What do you notice about the opposite faces of the box that could help you find its surface area?

Example 1 Use a net to find the surface area of the triangular prism.

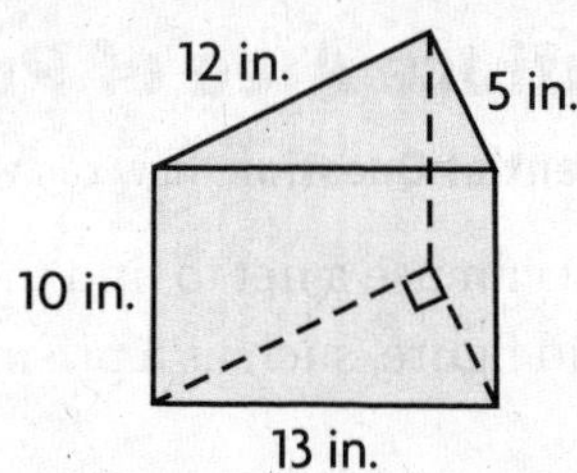

The surface area equals the sum of the areas of the three rectangular faces and two triangular bases. Note that the bases have the same area.

A
5 in.
13 in.
12 in.
5 in.
10 in.
D
C
B
10 in.
E
5 in.

area of bases A and E: $A = \frac{1}{2}bh = \frac{1}{2} \times 12 \times$ ______ = ______

area of face B: $A = lw = 5 \times 10 =$ ______

area of face C: $A = lw =$ ______ $\times$ ______ = ______

area of face D: $A = lw =$ ______ $\times$ ______ = ______

Surface area: $2 \times$ ______ + ______ + ______ + ______ = ______

So, the surface area of the triangular prism is ______________.

Math Talk **Mathematical Practices**

Explain why the area of one triangular base was multiplied by 2.

Example 2 Find the surface area of the cube.

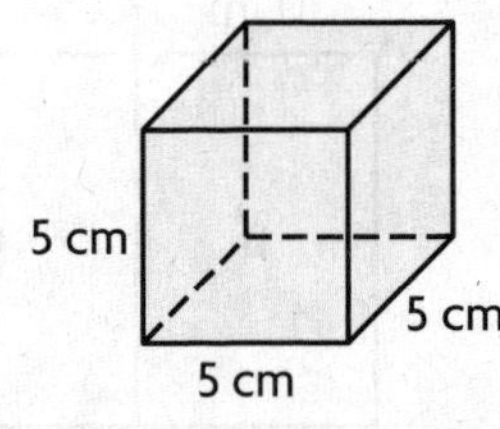

One Way Use a net.

STEP 1 Find the area of each face.

All of the faces are squares with a side length of __________, so the areas of all the squares are the same.

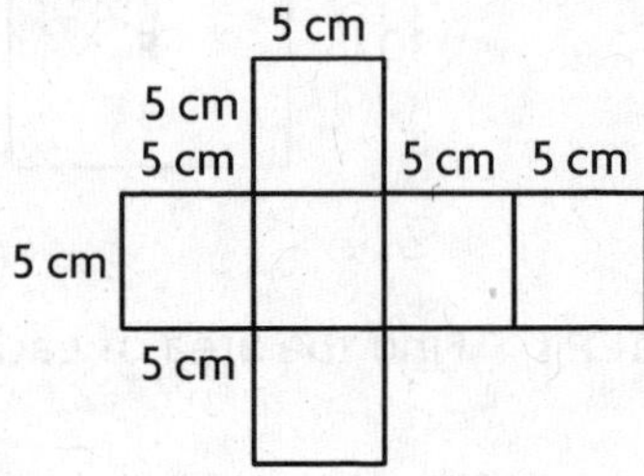

Area of one face: $A =$ ______ $\times$ ______ = __________

STEP 2 Find the sum of the areas of all ______ faces.

______ + ______ + ______ + ______ + ______ + ______ = __________

Another Way Use a formula.

You can also find the surface area of a cube using the formula $S = 6s^2$, where S is the surface area and s is the side length of the cube.

Write the formula. $S = 6s^2$

Replace s with 5. $S = 6($ ______ $)^2$

Simplify. $S = 6($ ______ $) =$ ______

The surface area of the cube is __________.

Name ____

Share and Show

Use a net to find the surface area.

1.

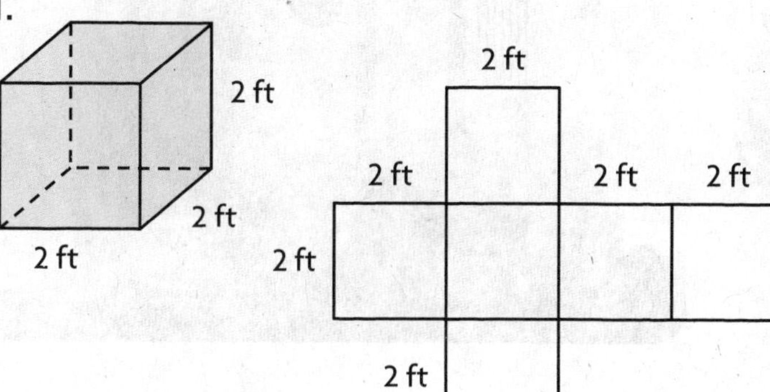

area of each face: ______ × ______ = ______

number of faces: ______

surface area = ______ × ______ = ______ ft^2

2.

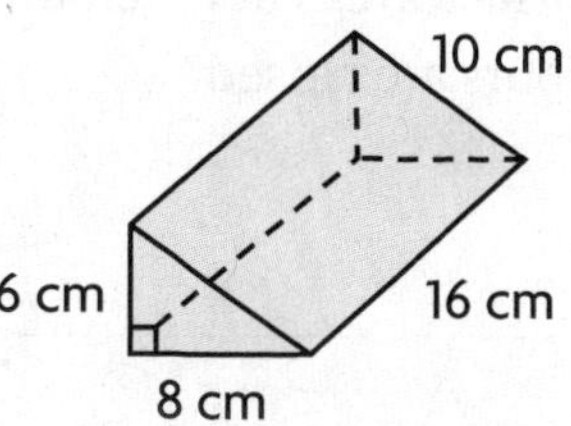

____

3.

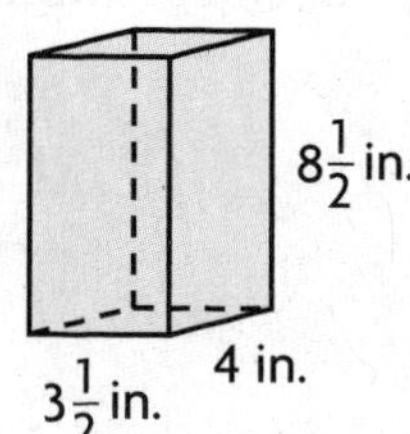

____

Math Talk **Mathematical Practices**

Explain how to find the surface area of a rectangular prism with a length of 8 ft, a width of 2 ft, and a height of 3 ft. Then find the surface area.

On Your Own

Use a net to find the surface area.

4.

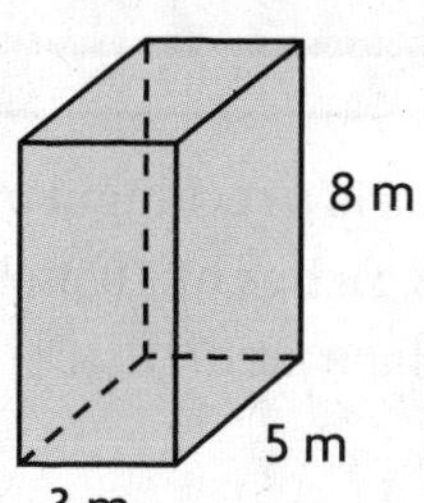

____

5.

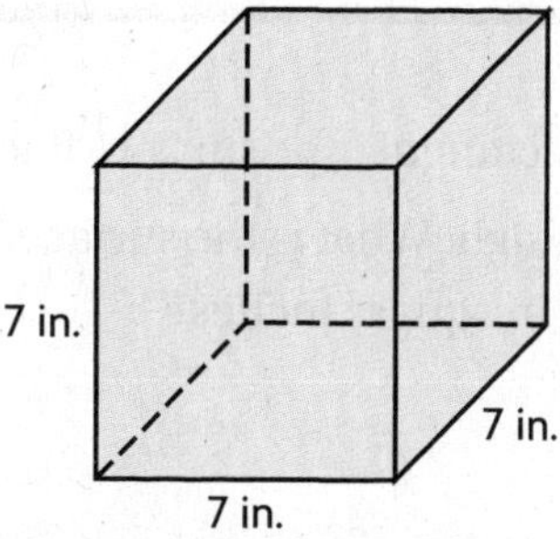

____

6. MATHEMATICAL PRACTICE 6 **Attend to Precision** Calculate the surface area of the cube in Exercise 5 using the formula $S = 6s^2$. Show your work.

____

Unlock the Problem

7. THINK SMARTER The Vehicle Assembly Building at Kennedy Space Center is a rectangular prism. It is 218 m long, 158 m wide, and 160 m tall. There are four 139 m tall doors in the building, averaging 29 in width. What is the building's outside surface area when the doors are open?

Math on the Spot

a. Draw each face of the building, not including the floor.

b. What are the dimensions of the 4 walls?

______

______

c. What are the dimensions of the roof?

______

d. Find the building's surface area (not including the floor) when the doors are closed.

______

e. Find the area of the four doors.

______

f. Find the building's surface area (not including the floor) when the doors are open.

______

8. GO DEEPER A rectangular prism is $1\frac{1}{2}$ ft long, $\frac{2}{3}$ ft wide, and $\frac{5}{6}$ ft high. What is the surface area of the prism in square inches?

______

9. THINK SMARTER A gift box is a rectangular prism. The box measures 8 inches by 10 inches by 3 inches. What is its surface area?

______

FOR MORE PRACTICE:
Standards Practice Book

Name ______________________________

Surface Area of Pyramids

ALGEBRA
Lesson 11.4

Essential Question How can you find the surface area of a pyramid?

Geometry—6.G.4
Also 6.EE.2c

MATHEMATICAL PRACTICES
MP.4, MP.5, MP.6

Most people think of Egypt when they think of pyramids, but there are ancient pyramids throughout the world. The Pyramid of the Sun in Mexico was built around 100 C.E. and is one of the largest pyramids in the world.

Unlock the Problem

Cara is making a model of the Pyramid of the Sun for a history project. The base is a square with a side length of 12 in. Each triangular face has a height of 7 in. What is the surface area of Cara's model?

Find the surface area of the square pyramid.

STEP 1

Label the dimensions on the net of the pyramid.

STEP 2

Find the area of the base and each triangular face.

Base:

Write the formula for the area of a square. $A = s^2$

Substitute ______ for s and simplify. $A =$ ______ $=$ ______ in.^{2}

Face:

Write the formula for the area of a triangle. $A = \frac{1}{2}bh$

Substitute ______ for b and ______ for h and simplify. $A = \frac{1}{2}$(______)(______)

$=$ ______ in.^{2}

STEP 3

Add the areas to find the surface area of the pyramid.

$S =$ ______ $+ 4 \times$ ______ $=$ ______ $+$ ______ $=$ ______ in.^{2}

So, the surface area of Cara's model is __________.

Mathematical Practices

Explain why you multiplied the area of the triangular face by 4 when finding the surface area.

Sometimes you need to find the total area of the lateral faces of a solid figure, but you don't need to include the area of the base. The **lateral area** L of a solid figure is the sum of the areas of the lateral faces.

Example

Kwan is making a tent in the shape of a triangular pyramid. The three sides of the tent are made of fabric, and the bottom will be left open. The faces have a height of 10 ft and a base of 6 ft. What is the area of the fabric Kwan needs to make the tent?

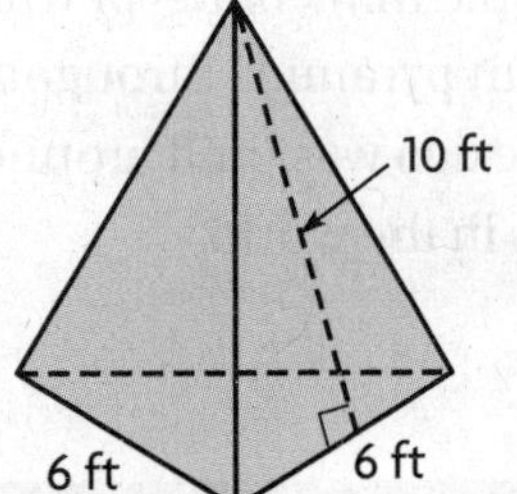

Find the lateral area of the triangular pyramid.

STEP 1

Draw and label a net for the pyramid.

STEP 2

Shade the lateral area of the net.

STEP 3

Find the area of one of the lateral faces of the pyramid.

Write the formula for the area of a triangle $A = \frac{1}{2}bh$

Substitute ______ for b and ______ for h. $A = \frac{1}{2}(\_\_\_\_\_)(\_\_\_\_\_)$

Simplify $A =$ ______ ft^2

STEP 4

To find the lateral area, find the area of all three lateral faces of the pyramid.

$L = 3 \times$ ______ $=$ ______ ft^2

So, the area of fabric Kwan needs is ____________.

1. MATHEMATICAL PRACTICE 6 **Compare** Explain the difference between finding the surface area and the lateral area of a three-dimensional figure.

2. Explain how you could find the amount of fabric needed if Kwan decided to make a fabric base for the tent. The height of the triangular base is about 5 ft.

Name ______________________________

Share and Show

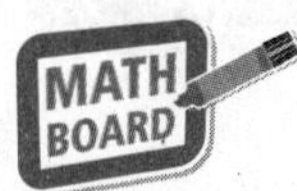

1. Use a net to find the surface area of the square pyramid.

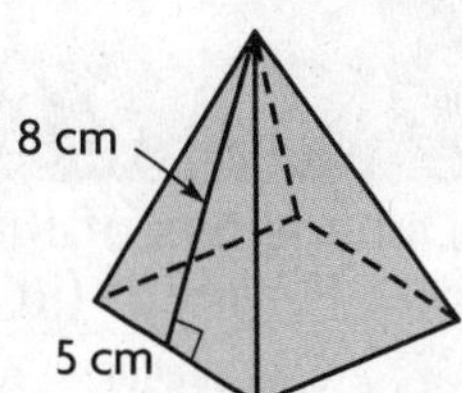

Base: $A =$ ______ $=$ ______ cm^2

Face: $A = \frac{1}{2}$(______)(______) $=$ ______ cm^2

Surface area of pyramid: $S =$ ______ $+ 4 \times$ ______

$=$ ______ $+$ ______ $=$ ______ cm^2

2. A triangular pyramid has a base with an area of 43 cm^2 and lateral faces with bases of 10 cm and heights of 8.6 cm. What is the surface area of the pyramid?

____

3. A square pyramid has a base with a side length of 3 ft and lateral faces with heights of 2 ft. What is the lateral area of the pyramid?

____

Math Talk — **Mathematical Practices**

Explain how to find the surface area of a square pyramid if you know the height of each face and the perimeter of the base.

On Your Own

Use a net to find the surface area of the square pyramid.

4.

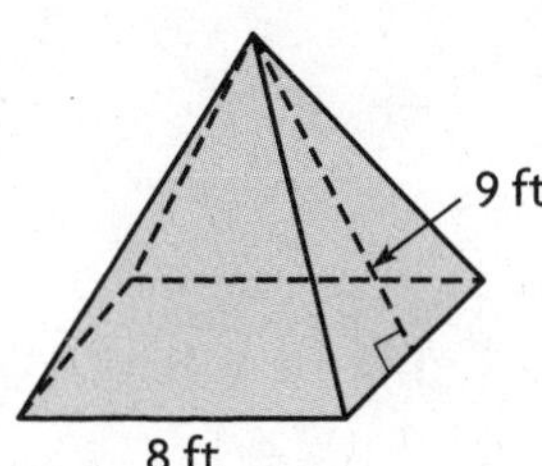

____

5.

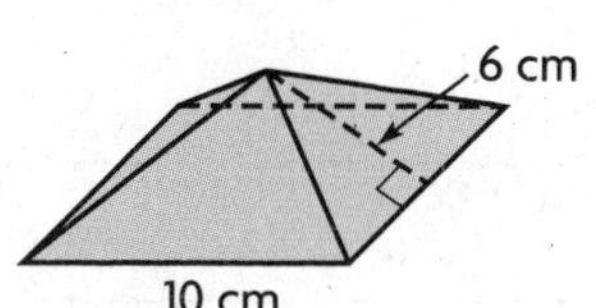

____

6.

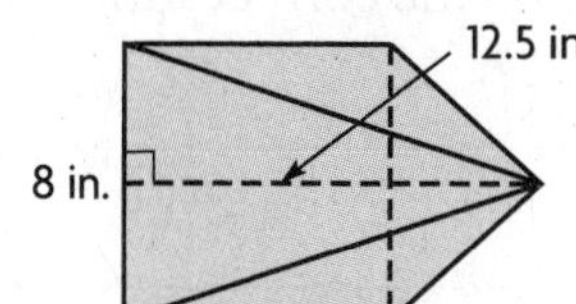

____

7. The Pyramid Arena is located in Memphis, Tennessee. It is in the shape of a square pyramid, and the lateral faces are made almost completely of glass. The base has a side length of about 600 ft and the lateral faces have a height of about 440 ft. What is the total area of the glass in the Pyramid Arena?

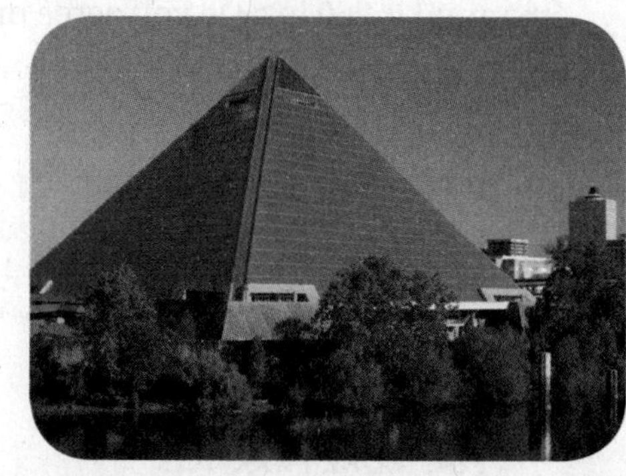

____

Problem Solving • Applications

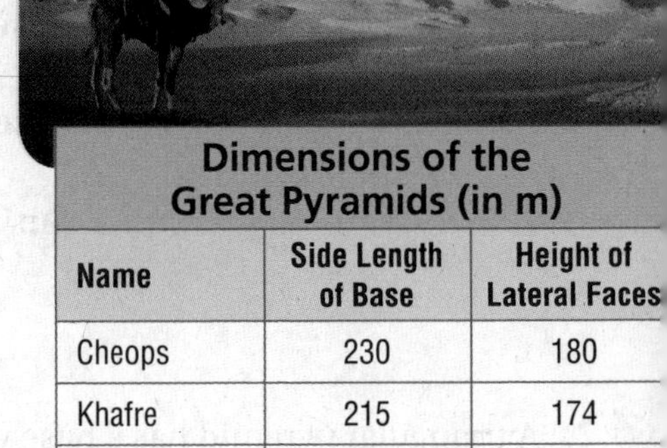

Use the table for 8–9.

Dimensions of the Great Pyramids (in m)		
Name	**Side Length of Base**	**Height of Lateral Faces**
Cheops	230	180
Khafre	215	174
Menkaure	103	83

8. The Great Pyramids are located near Cairo, Egypt. They are all square pyramids, and their dimensions are shown in the table. What is the lateral area of the Pyramid of Cheops?

______

9. GO DEEPER What is the difference between the surface areas of the Pyramid of Khafre and the Pyramid of Menkaure?

______

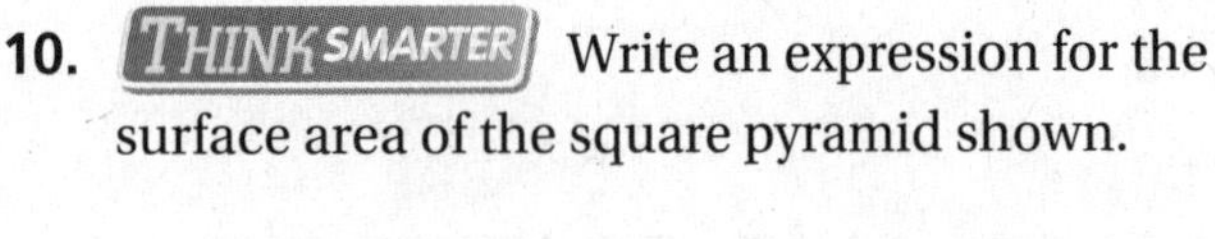

10. THINK SMARTER Write an expression for the surface area of the square pyramid shown.

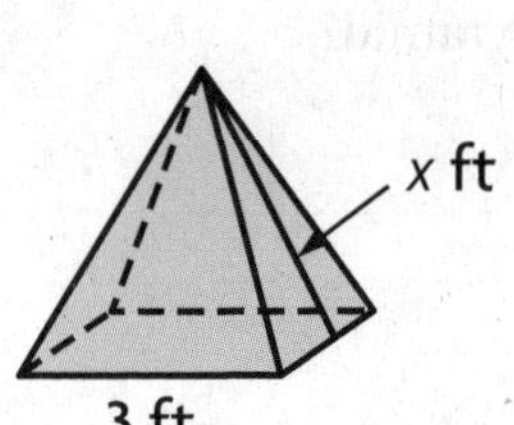

______

11. MATHEMATICAL PRACTICE 3 **Make Arguments** A square pyramid has a base with a side length of 4 cm and triangular faces with a height of 7 cm. Esther calculated the surface area as $(4 \times 4) + 4(4 \times 7) = 128 \text{ cm}^2$. Explain Esther's error and find the correct surface area.

______

______

______

Personal Math Trainer

12. THINK SMARTER + Jose says the lateral area of the square pyramid is 260 in.^{2} Do you agree or disagree with Jose? Use numbers and words to support your answer.

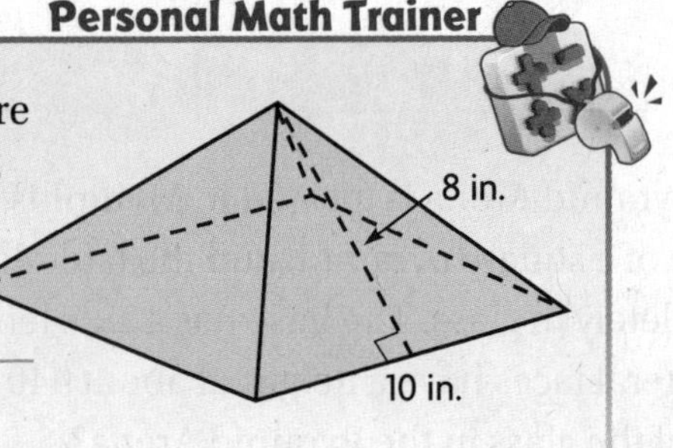

______

______

______

 FOR MORE PRACTICE: Standards Practice Book

Name ________________________________

Mid-Chapter Checkpoint

Vocabulary

Choose the best term from the box to completes the sentence.

Vocabulary
lateral area
net
solid figure
surface area

1. ______________ is the sum of the areas of all the faces, or surfaces, of a solid figure. (p. 435)

2. A three-dimensional figure having length, width, and height is called a(n) ______________. (p. 439)

3. The ______________ of a solid figure is the sum of the areas of its lateral faces. (p. 448)

Concepts and Skills

4. Identify and draw a net for the solid figure. (6.G.4)

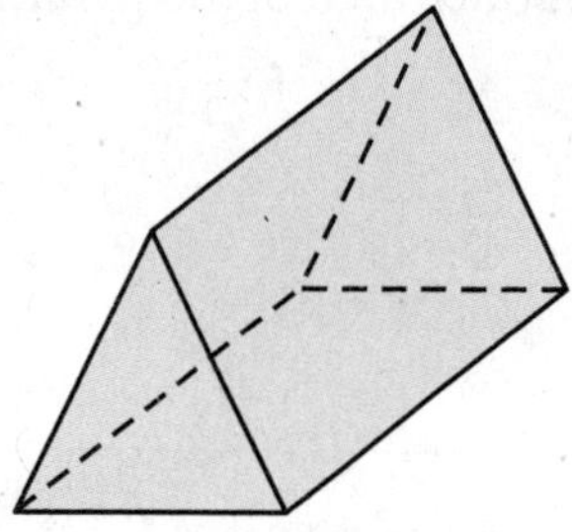

____

5. Use a net to find the lateral area of the square pyramid. (6.G.4)

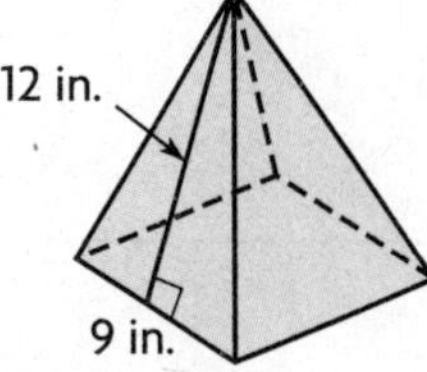

____

6. Use a net to find the surface area of the prism. (6.G.4)

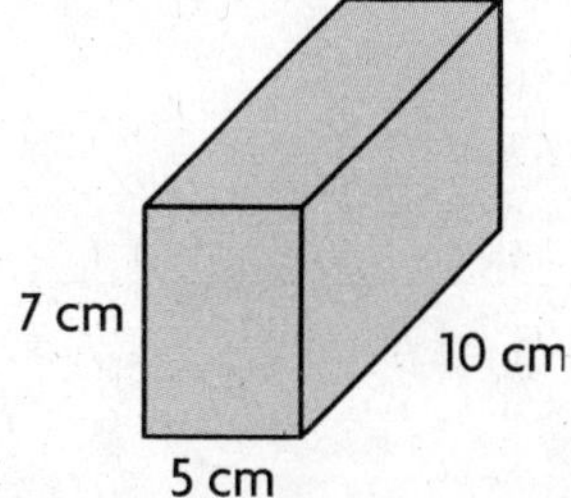

____

7. A machine cuts nets from flat pieces of cardboard. The nets can be folded into triangular pyramids used as pieces in a board game. What shapes appear in the net? How many of each shape are there? (6.G.4)

8. Fran's filing cabinet is 6 feet tall, $1\frac{1}{3}$ feet wide, and 3 feet deep. She plans to paint all sides except the bottom of the cabinet. Find the area of the sides she intends to paint. (6.G.4)

9. A triangular pyramid has lateral faces with bases of 6 meters and heights of 9 meters. The area of the base of the pyramid is 15.6 square meters. What is the surface area of the pyramid? (6.G.4)

10. What is the surface area of a storage box that measures 15 centimeters by 12 centimeters by 10 centimeters? (6.G.4)

11. A small refrigerator is a cube with a side length of 16 inches. Use the formula $S = 6s^2$ to find the surface area of the cube. (6.EE.2c)

Name ______________________________

Fractions and Volume

Essential Question What is the relationship between the volume and the edge lengths of a prism with fractional edge lengths?

Geometry—6.G.2

MATHEMATICAL PRACTICES MP.5, MP.6, MP.7, MP.8

CONNECT **Volume** is the number of cubic units needed to occupy a given space without gaps or overlaps. You can find the volume of a rectangular prism by seeing how many unit cubes it takes to fill the prism. Recall that a unit cube is a cube with a side length of 1.

Investigate

Hands On

Materials net of a rectangular prism, cubes, scissors, tape

A jewelry box has a length of $3\frac{1}{2}$ units, a width of $1\frac{1}{2}$ units, and a height of 2 units. What is the volume of the box in cubic units?

A. Each of the cubes in this activity has a side length of $\frac{1}{2}$ unit.

How many cubes with side length $\frac{1}{2}$ does it take to form a unit cube? ______

So, each smaller cube represents ______ of a unit cube.

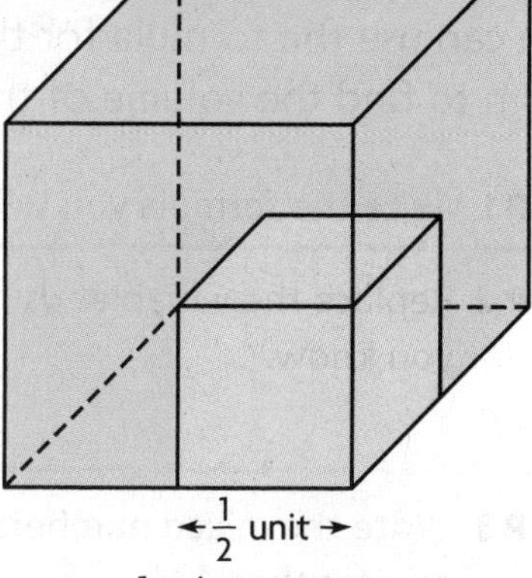

B. Cut out the net. Then fold and tape the net into a rectangular prism. Leave one face open so you can pack the prism with cubes.

C. Pack the prism with cubes.

How many cubes with side length $\frac{1}{2}$ does it take to fill the prism?

______

D. To find the volume of the jewelry box in cubic units, determine how many unit cubes you could make from the smaller cubes you used to pack the prism.

Think: It takes 8 smaller cubes to make 1 unit cube.

Divide the total number of smaller cubes by 8. Write the remainder as a fraction.

______ ÷ 8 = ______ = ______

So, the volume of the jewelry box is ______ cubic units.

Math Talk — **Mathematical Practices**

Explain how you determined how many cubes with side length $\frac{1}{2}$ it takes to form a unit cube.

Draw Conclusions

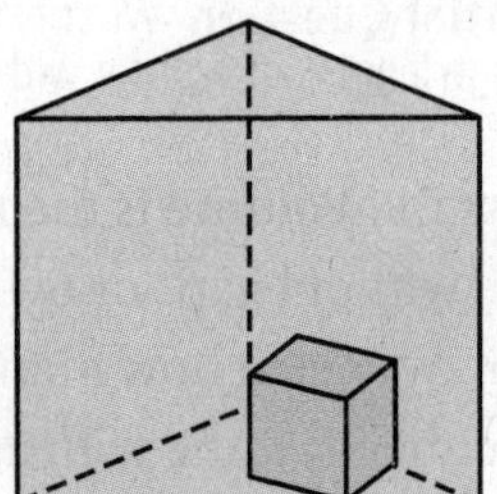

1. MATHEMATICAL PRACTICE 8 **Draw Conclusions** Could you use the method of packing cubes to find the volume of a triangular prism? Explain.

____

____

____

____

2. THINK SMARTER How many cubes with a side length of $\frac{1}{2}$ unit do you need to form 3 unit cubes? Explain how you know.

____

____

____

Make Connections

You can use the formula for the volume of a rectangular prism to find the volume of the jewelry box.

Remember

The volume of a rectangular prism is the product of the length, the width, and the height: $V = l \times w \times h$.

STEP 1 Write the formula you will use. $V = l \times w \times h$

STEP 2 Replace the variables using the values you know. $V = 3\frac{1}{2} \times \square \times \square$

STEP 3 Write the mixed numbers as fractions greater than 1. $V = \frac{\square}{\square} \times \frac{3}{2} \times 2$

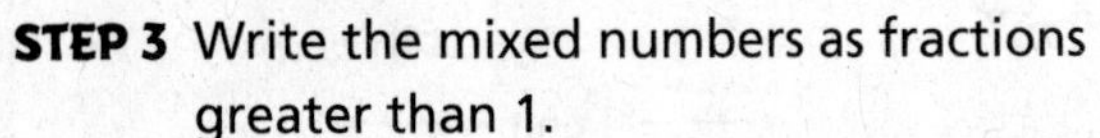

STEP 4 Multiply. $V = \frac{\square}{\square}$

STEP 5 Write the fraction as a mixed number. $V = \square\frac{2}{4} = \square$

So, the volume of the jewelry box is _______ cubic units.

Math Talk **Mathematical Practices**

Tell how the volume you found by using the formula compares to the volume you found by packing the prism with cubes.

Name ______________________

Share and Show

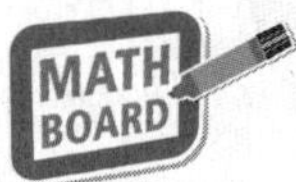

1. A prisim is filled with 38 cubes with a side length of $\frac{1}{2}$ unit. What is the volume of the prism in cubic units?

   $38 \div 8 =$ ______ $=$ ______

   volume = ______ cubic units

2. A prism is filled with 58 cubes with a side length of $\frac{1}{2}$ unit. What is the volume of the prism in cubic units?

   ____

Find the volume of the rectangular prism.

3. 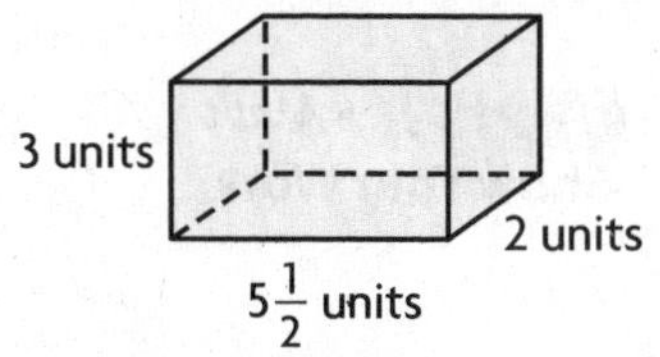

   ____

4. 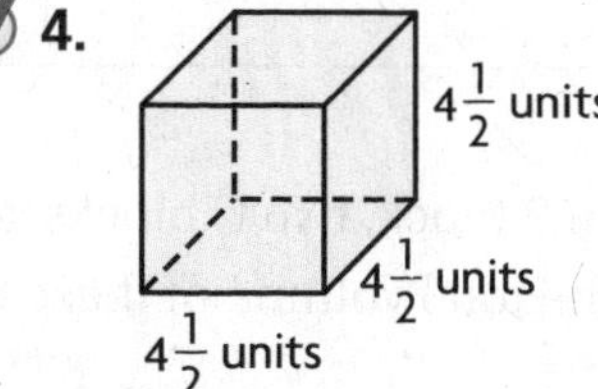

   ____

5. GO DEEPER Theodore wants to put three flowering plants in his window box. The window box is shaped like a rectangular prism that is 30.5 in. long, 6 in. wide, and 6 in. deep. The three plants need a total of 1,200 in.^{3} of potting soil to grow well. Is the box large enough? Explain.

   ____

   ____

   ____

6. WRITE ▸Math Explain how use the formula $V = l \times w \times h$ to verify that a cube with a side length of $\frac{1}{2}$ unit has a volume of $\frac{1}{8}$ of a cubic unit.

   ____

   ____

   ____

Problem Solving • Applications

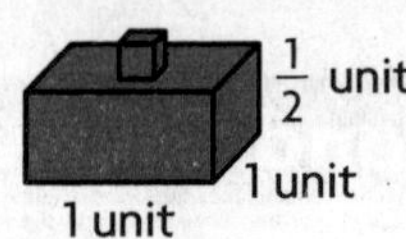

B
1 unit
1 unit
1 unit

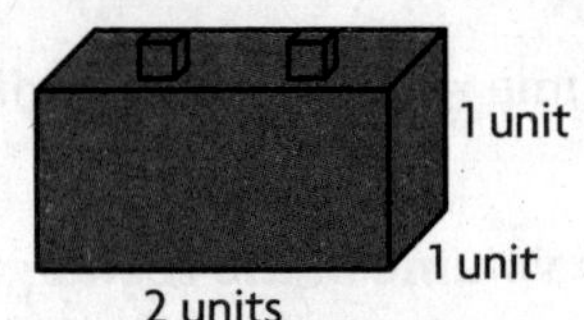

Use the diagram for 7–10.

7. Karyn is using a set of building blocks shaped like rectangular prisms to make a model. The three types of blocks she has are shown at right. What is the volume of an A block? (Do not include the pegs on top.)

____

8. How many A blocks would you need to take up the same amount of space as a C block?

____

WRITE ▸ *Math*
Show Your Work

9. GO DEEPER Karyn puts a B block, two C blocks, and three A blocks together. What is the total volume of these blocks?

____

10. THINK SMARTER Karyn uses the blocks to make a prism that is 2 units long, 3 units wide, and $1\frac{1}{2}$ units high. The prism is made of two C blocks, two B blocks, and some A blocks. What is the total volume of A blocks used?

____

11. MATHEMATICAL PRACTICE 3 **Verify the Reasoning of Others** Jo says that you can use $V = l \times w \times h$ or $V = h \times w \times l$ to find the volume of a rectangular prism. Does Jo's statement make sense? Explain.

____

____

____

12. THINK SMARTER A box measures 5 units by 3 units by $2\frac{1}{2}$ units. For numbers 12a–12b, select True or False for the statement.

12a. The greatest number of cubes with a side length of $\frac{1}{2}$ unit that can be packed inside the box is 300. ○ True ○ False

12b. The volume of the box is $37\frac{1}{2}$ cubic units. ○ True ○ False

FOR MORE PRACTICE: Standards Practice Book

Name ______________________________

Volume of Rectangular Prisms

Essential Question How can you find the volume of rectangular prisms with fractional edge lengths?

Geometry— 6.G.2
Also 6.EE.2C

MATHEMATICAL PRACTICES
MP.2, MP.5, MP.6

You can use the formula $V = l \times w \times h$ to find the volume of a rectangular prism when you know the length, width, and height of the prism.

Unlock the Problem

A bento is a single-portion meal that is common in Japan. The meal is usually served in a box. A small bento box is a rectangular prism that is 5 inches long, 4 inches wide, and $2\frac{1}{2}$ inches high. How much food fits in the box?

- Underline the sentence that tells you what you are trying to find.
- Circle the numbers you need to use.

Find the volume of a rectangular prism

You can use the formula $V = l \times w \times h$ to find the volume of a rectangular prism when you know the length, width, and height of the prism.

STEP 1

Sketch the rectangular prism.

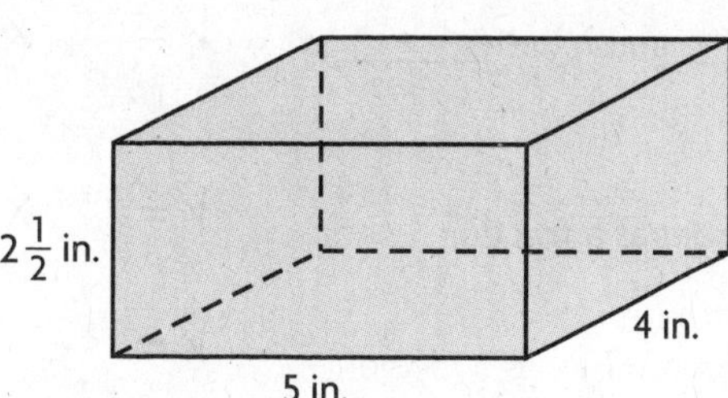

STEP 2 Identify the value for each variable.

The length l is 5 in.

The width w is ________ in.

The height h is ________ in.

STEP 3 Evaluate the formula.

Write the formula. $V = l \times w \times h$

Replace l with 5, w with ________, and h with ________. $V =$ ______ $\times$ ______ $\times$ ______

Multiply. $V =$ ______ in.^{3}

So, ________ in.^{3} of food fits in the box.

Math Talk **Mathematical Practices**

Explain how you know what units to use for the volume of the box.

CONNECT You know that the volume of a rectangular prism is the product of its length, width, and height. Since the product of the length and width is the area of one base, the volume is also the product of the area of one base and the height.

> **Volume of a Prism**
>
> Volume = area of one base × height | $V = Bh$

Example 1 Find the volume of the prism.

STEP 1 Identify the value for each variable.

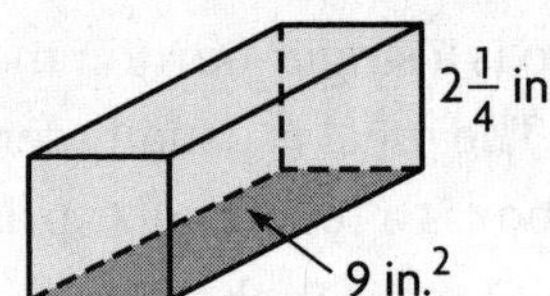

The height h is ________ in.

The area of the base B is ________ in.^{2}

STEP 2 Evaluate the formula.

Write the formula. $V = Bh$

Replace B with ________ and h with ________. $V = \square \times \square$

Write the mixed number as a fraction greater than 1. $V = \square \times \frac{\square}{4}$

Multiply and write the product as a mixed number. $V = \square = \square\frac{1}{4}$ in.^{3}

So, the volume of the prism is ____________.

Example 2 Find the volume of the cube.

$3\frac{1}{2}$ ft

$3\frac{1}{2}$ ft

$3\frac{1}{2}$ ft

Write the formula. The area of the square base is s^2. The height of a cube is also s, so $V = Bh = s^3$. $V = s^3$

Substitute ________ for s. $V = (\square)^3$

Write the mixed number as a fraction greater than 1. Then use repeated multiplication.

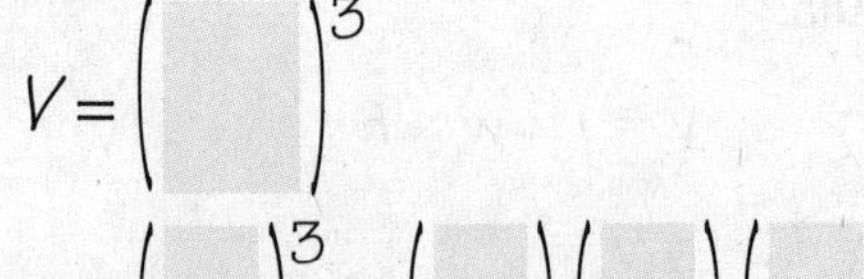

$V = (\square)^3 = (\square)(\square)(\square)$

Simplify. $V = \frac{\square}{8} = 42\frac{\square}{8}$ ft^3

So, the volume of the cube is ____________.

Name ____________________

Share and Show

Find the volume.

1. 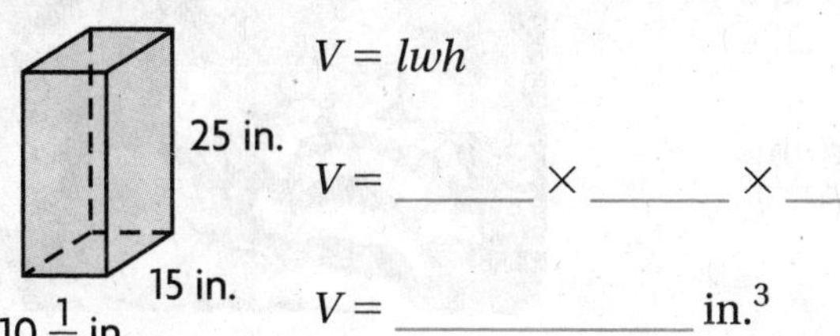

$V = lwh$

$V =$ ______ $\times$ ______ $\times$ ______

$V =$ ______ $in.^3$

2. 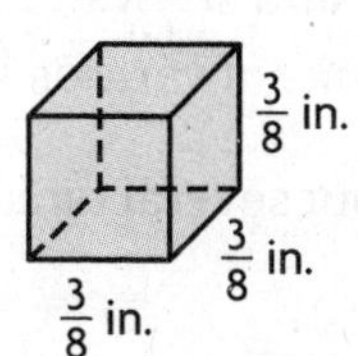

Math Talk **Mathematical Practices**

Describe the steps for finding the volume of a cube.

On Your Own

Find the volume of the prism.

3. 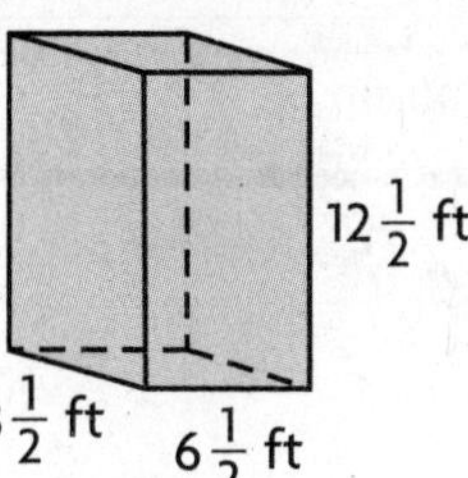

______

4. 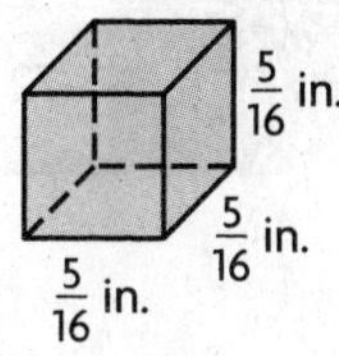

______

5. 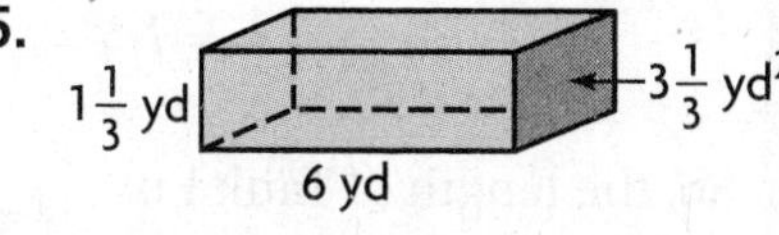

______

6. **GO DEEPER** Wayne's gym locker is a rectangular prism with a width and height of $14\frac{1}{2}$ inches. The length is 8 inches greater than the width. What is the volume of the locker?

______

7. **THINK SMARTER** Abraham has a toy box that is in the shape of a rectangular prism.

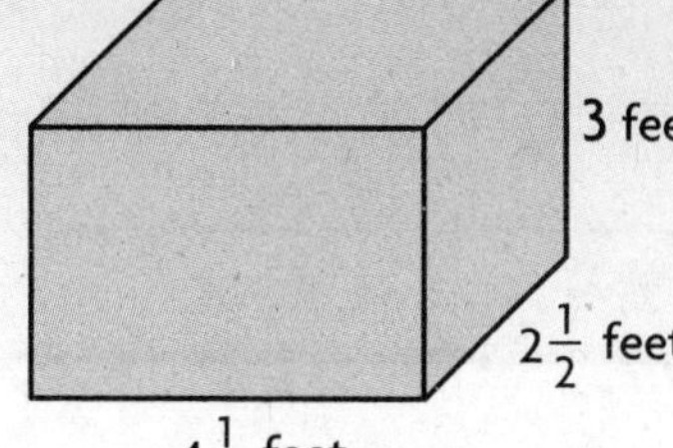

The volume is
- $33\frac{3}{4}$ ft^3.
- $35\frac{1}{2}$ ft^3.
- $64\frac{1}{2}$ ft^3.

Connect to Science

Aquariums

Large public aquariums like the Tennessee Aquarium in Chattanooga have a wide variety of freshwater and saltwater fish species from around the world. The fish are kept in tanks of various sizes.

The table shows information about several tanks in the aquarium. Each tank is a rectangular prism.

Find the length of Tank 1.

$V = lwh$

$52{,}500 = l \times$ ______ $\times$ ______

$52{,}500 = l \times$ ______

$\frac{52{,}500}{\quad} = l$

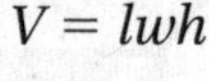

______ $= l$

So, the length of Tank 1 is ________.

Aquarium Tanks

	Length	Width	Height	Volume
Tank 1		30 cm	35 cm	52,500 cm^3
Tank 2	12 m		4 m	384 m^3
Tank 3	18 m	12 m		2,160 m^3
Tank 4	72 cm	55 cm	40 cm	

Solve.

8. Find the width of Tank 2 and the height of Tank 3.

9. THINK SMARTER To keep the fish healthy, there should be the correct ratio of water to fish in the tank. One recommended ratio is 9 L of water for every 2 fish. Find the volume of Tank 4. Then use the equivalencies $1\ cm^3 = 1$ mL and 1,000 mL $= 1$ L to find how many fish can be safely kept in Tank 4.

10. MATHEMATICAL PRACTICE 2 **Use Reasoning** Give another set of dimensions for a tank that would have the same volume as Tank 2. Explain how you found your answer.

Name ________________________

Problem Solving • Geometric Measurements

Essential Question How can you use the strategy *use a formula* to solve problems involving area, surface area, and volume?

Geometry—6.G.4 *Also 6.G.1, 6.G.2*
MATHEMATICAL PRACTICES
MP.1, MP.2

Unlock the Problem

Shedd Aquarium in Chicago has one of the country's few full-scale animal hospitals linked to an aquarium. One tank for sick fish is a rectangular prism measuring 75 cm long, 60.cm wide, and 36 cm high along the outside. The glass on the tank is 2 cm thick. How much water can the tank hold? How much water is needed to fill the tank?

Use the graphic organizer to help you solve the problem.

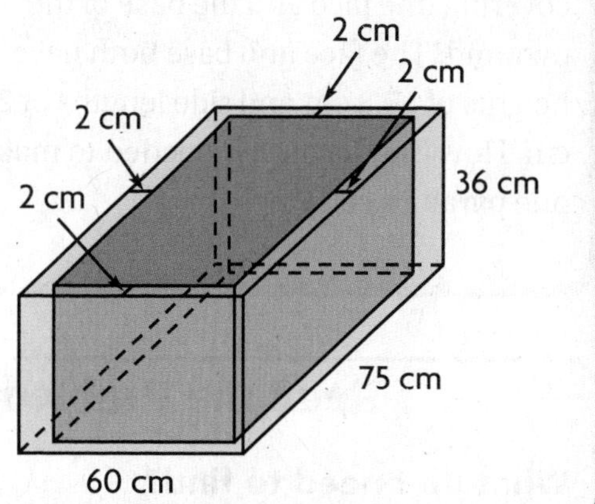

Read the Problem

What do I need to find?

I need to find ________________ and ________________.

What information do I need to use?

I need to use ________________ and ________________.

How will I use the information?

First I will decide ________________.

Then I will choose a ________________ I can use to calculate the measure. Finally, I will substitute the values for the ________________, and I will ________________ the formula.

Solve the Problem

- Choose the measure that specifies the amount of water that will fill a tank.

____

- Choose an appropriate formula.

____

- Subtract the width of the glass twice from the length and width and once from the height to find the inner dimensions.

Find the length. 75 cm − 4 cm = ______ cm

Find the width. 60 cm − 4 cm = ______ cm

Find the height. 36 cm − 2 cm = ______ cm

- Substitute and evaluate.

$V = 71 \times$ ______ = ______ = ______ cm^3

Math Talk **Mathematical Practices**

Explain why volume is the correct measure to use to solve the problem.

So, the volume of the tank is ________________.

Try Another Problem

Alexander Graham Bell, the inventor of the telephone, also invented a kite made out of "cells" shaped like triangular pyramids.

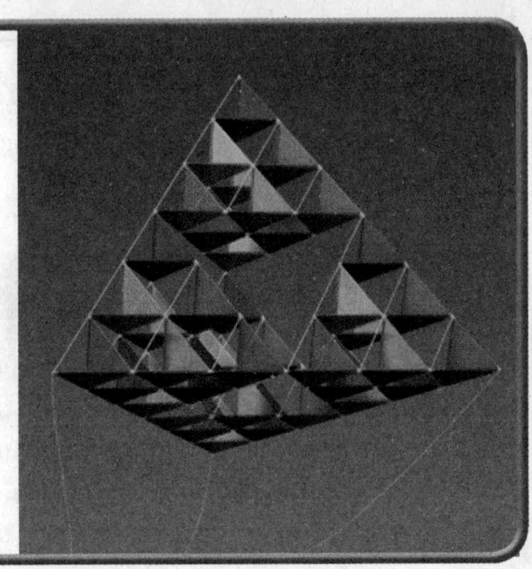

A kite is made of triangular pyramid-shaped cells with fabric covering one face and the base of the pyramid. The face and base both have heights of 17.3 cm and side lengths of 20 cm. How much fabric is needed to make one pyramid cell?

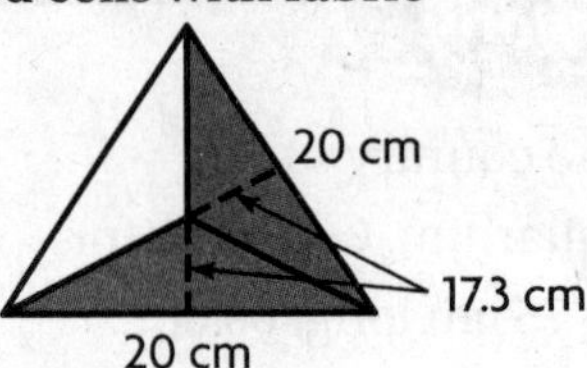

Read the Problem	Solve the Problem
What do I need to find?	
What information do I need to use?	
How will I use the information?	

So, ______ cm^2 of fabric is needed.

- Explain how you knew which units to use for your answer.

______

Math Talk — **Mathematical Practices**

Explain how the strategy of using a formula helped you solve the problem.

Name ______________________

Share and Show

1. An aquarium tank in the shape of a rectangular prism is 60 cm long, 30 cm wide, and 24 cm high. The top of the tank is open, and the glass used to make the tank is 1 cm thick. How much water can the tank hold?

   First identify the measure and choose an appropriate formula.

   ____

   Next find the inner dimensions and replace the variables with the correct values.

   ____

   Finally, evaluate the formula.

   ____

   So, the tank can hold ____________ of water.

2. THINK SMARTER **What if,** to provide greater strength, the glass bottom were increased to a thickness of 4 cm? How much less water would the tank hold?

   ____

3. An aquarium tank in the shape of a rectangular prism is 40 cm long, 26 cm wide, and 24 cm high. If the top of the tank is open, how much tinting is needed to cover the glass on the tank? Identify the measure you used to solve the problem.

   ____

4. The Louvre Museum in Paris, France, has a square pyramid made of glass in its central courtyard. The four triangular faces of the pyramid have bases of 35 meters and heights of 27.8 meters. What is the area of glass used for the four triangular faces of the pyramid?

   ____

Unlock the Problem

- √ Draw a diagram.
- √ Identify the measure needed.
- √ Choose an appropriate formula.

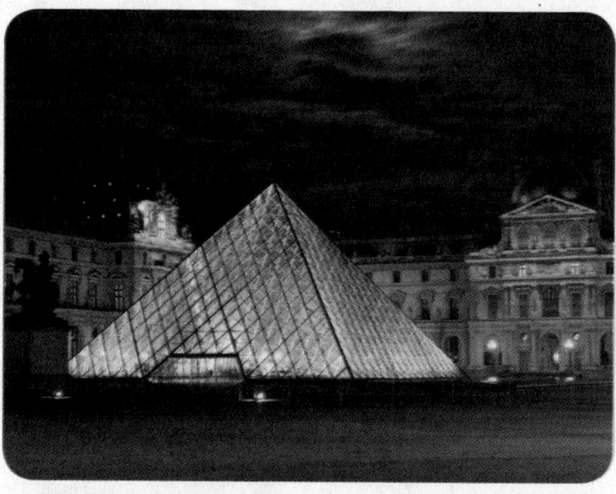

The Louvre Museum in Paris, France

WRITE Math • Show Your Work

On Your Own

5. THINK SMARTER A rectangular-prism-shaped block of wood measures 3 m by $1\frac{1}{2}$ m by $1\frac{1}{2}$ m. How much of the block must a carpenter carve away to obtain a prism that measures 2 m by $\frac{1}{2}$ m by $\frac{1}{2}$ m?

____

6. GO DEEPER The carpenter (Problem 5) varnished the outside of the smaller piece of wood, all except for the bottom, which measures $\frac{1}{2}$ m by $\frac{1}{2}$ m. Varnish costs $2.00 per square meter. What was the cost of varnishing the wood?

____

7. A wax candle is in the shape of a cube with a side length of $2\frac{1}{2}$ in. What volume of wax is needed to make the candle?

____

8. MATHEMATICAL PRACTICE 1 **Describe** A rectangular prism-shaped box measures 6 cm by 5 cm by 4 cm. A cube-shaped box has a side length of 2 cm. How many of the cube-shaped boxes will fit into the rectangular prism-shaped box? Describe how you found your answer.

____

____

____

____

____

Personal Math Trainer

9. THINK SMARTER + Justin is covering the outside of an open shoe box with colorful paper for a class project. The shoe box is 30 cm long, 20 cm wide, and 13 cm high. How many square centimeters of paper are needed to cover the outside of the open shoe box? Explain your strategy.

____

____

____

____

____

FOR MORE PRACTICE:
Standards Practice Book

Name ______________________________

Chapter 11 Review/Test

1. Elaine makes a rectangular pyramid from paper.

The base is a [rectangle. / square. / triangle.] The lateral faces are [rectangles. / squares. / triangles.]

2. Darrell paints all sides except the bottom of the box shown below.

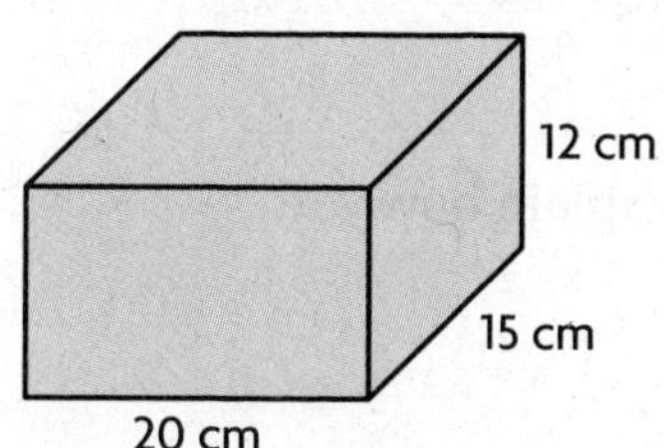

Select the expressions that show how to find the surface area that Darrell painted. Mark all that apply.

Ⓐ 240 + 240 + 180 + 180 + 300 + 300

Ⓑ 2(20 × 12) + 2(15 × 12) + (20 × 15)

Ⓒ (20 × 12) + (20 × 12) + (15 × 12)+ (15 × 12)+ (20 × 15)

Ⓓ 20 × 15 × 12

3. A prism is filled with 44 cubes with $\frac{1}{2}$-unit side lengths. What is the volume of the prism in cubic units?

______ cubic units

4. A triangular pyramid has a base with an area of 11.3 square meters, and lateral faces with bases of 5.1 meters and heights of 9 meters.

Write an expression that can be used to find the surface area of the triangular pyramid.

____

GO DIGITAL Assessment Options Chapter Test

5. Jeremy makes a paperweight for his mother in the shape of a square pyramid. The base of the pyramid has a side length of 4 centimeters, and the lateral faces have heights of 5 centimeters. After he finishes, he realizes that the paperweight is too small and decides to make another one. To make the second pyramid, he doubles the length of the base in the first pyramid.

For numbers 5a–5c, choose Yes or No to indicate whether the statement is correct.

5a. The surface area of the second pyramid is 144 cm^2. ○ Yes ○ No

5b. The surface area doubled from the first pyramid to the second pyramid. ○ Yes ○ No

5c. The lateral area doubled from the first pyramid to the second pyramid. ○ Yes ○ No

6. Identify the figure shown and find its surface area. Explain how you found your answer.

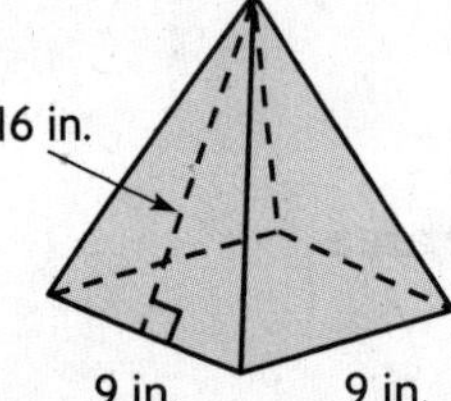

7. Dominique has a box of sewing buttons that is in the shape of a rectangular prism.

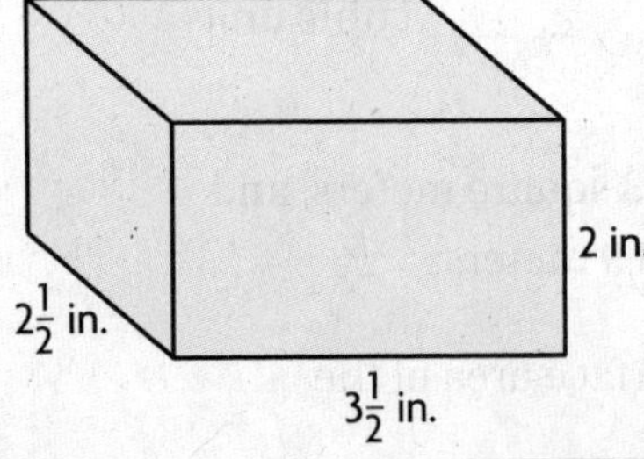

The volume of the box is $2\frac{1}{2}$ in. × $3\frac{1}{2}$ in. × [2 in. / $2\frac{1}{2}$ in. / $3\frac{1}{2}$ in.] = [8 in.^{3} / $17\frac{1}{2}$ in.^{3} / 35 in.^{3}]

Name ______________________________

8. Emily has a decorative box that is shaped like a cube with a height of 5 inches. What is the surface area of the box?

______ in.^{2}

9. Albert recently purchased a fish tank for his home. Match each question with the geometric measure that would be most appropriate for each scenario.

Question		Measure
How much water can the fish tank hold? •		• The area of the base of the fish tank
How much material would it take to cover the entire fish tank? •		• The surface area of the fish tank
How much space would the fish tank occupy on the table? •		• The volume of the fish tank

10. Select the expressions that show the volume of the rectangular prism. Mark all that apply.

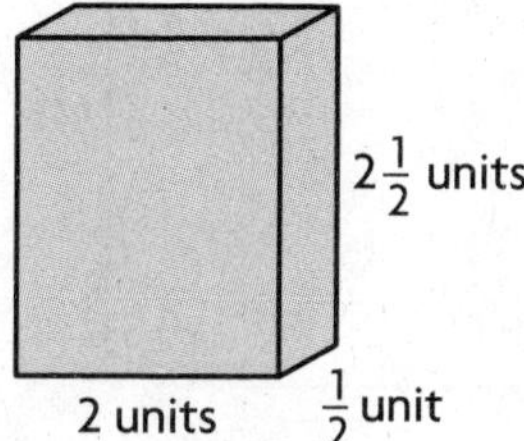

(A) $2(2 \text{ units} \times 2\frac{1}{2} \text{ units}) + 2(2 \text{ units} \times \frac{1}{2} \text{ unit}) + 2(\frac{1}{2} \text{ unit} \times 2\frac{1}{2} \text{ units})$

(B) $2(2 \text{ units} \times \frac{1}{2} \text{ unit}) + 4(2 \text{ units} \times 2\frac{1}{2} \text{ units})$

(C) $2 \text{ units} \times \frac{1}{2} \text{ unit} \times 2\frac{1}{2} \text{ units}$

(D) 2.5 cubic units

11. For numbers 11a–11d, select True or False for the statement.

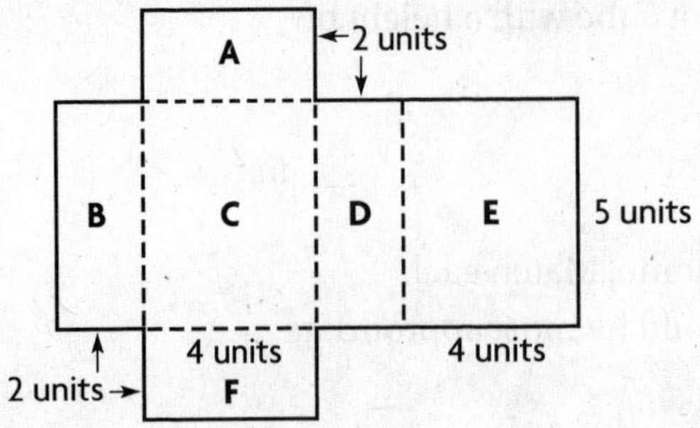

11a. The area of face A is 8 square units.	○ True	○ False
11b. The area of face B is 10 square units.	○ True	○ False
11c. The area of face C is 8 square units.	○ True	○ False
11d. The surface area of the prism is 56 square units.	○ True	○ False

12. Stella received a package in the shape of a rectangular prism. The box has a length of $2\frac{1}{2}$ feet, a width of $1\frac{1}{2}$ feet, and a height of 4 feet.

Part A

Stella wants to cover the box with wrapping paper. How much paper will she need? Explain how you found your answer.

Part B

Can the box hold 16 cubic feet of packing peanuts? Explain how you know.

Name ___

13. A box measures 6 units by $\frac{1}{2}$ unit by $2\frac{1}{2}$ units.

For numbers 13a–13b, select True or False for the statement.

13a. The greatest number of cubes with a side length of $\frac{1}{2}$ unit that can be packed inside the box is 60. ○ True ○ False

13b. The volume of the box is $7\frac{1}{2}$ cubic units. ○ True ○ False

14. Bella says the lateral area of the square pyramid is 1,224 in.^{2} Do you agree or disagree with Bella? Use numbers and words to support your answer. If you disagree with Bella, find the correct answer.

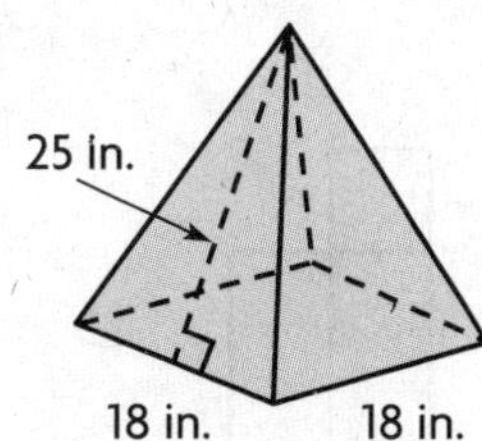

15. Lourdes is decorating a toy box for her sister. She will use self-adhesive paper to cover all of the exterior sides except for the bottom of the box. The toy box is 4 feet long, 3 feet wide, and 2 feet high. How many square feet of adhesive paper will Lourdes use to cover the box?

___

16. Gary wants to build a shed shaped like a rectangular prism in his backyard. He goes to the store and looks at several different options. The table shows the dimensions and volumes of four different sheds.

Use the formula $V = l \times w \times h$ to complete the table.

	Length (ft)	Width (ft)	Height (ft)	Volume (ft^3)
Shed 1		10	8	960
Shed 2	18		10	2,160
Shed 3	12	4		288
Shed 4	10	12	10	

17. Tina cut open a cube-shaped microwave box to see the net. How many square faces does this box have?

_______ square faces

18. Charles is painting a treasure box in the shape of a rectangular prism.

Which nets can be used to represent Charles' treasure box?
Mark all that apply.

Ⓐ

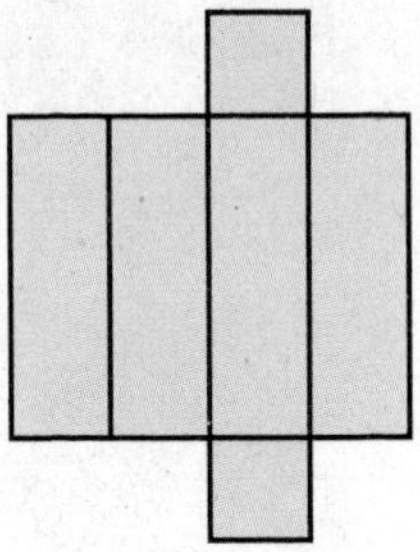

Ⓒ

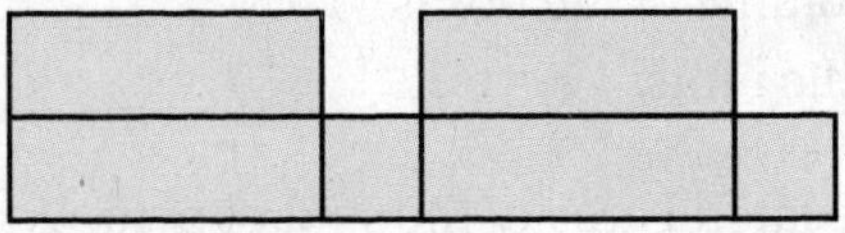

Ⓑ

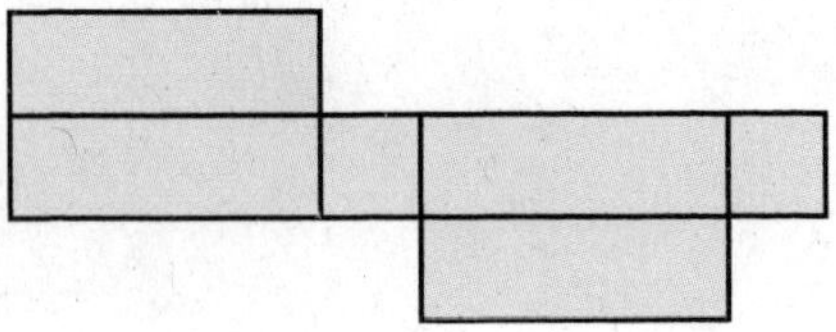

Ⓓ

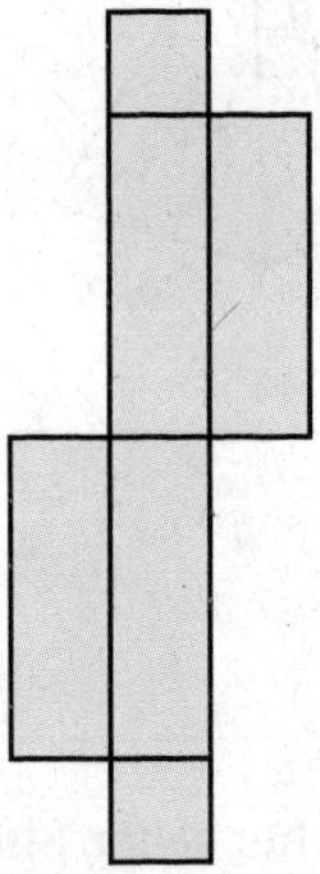

19. Julianna is lining the inside of a basket with fabric. The basket is in the shape of a rectangular prism that is 29 cm long, 19 cm wide, and 10 cm high. How much fabric is needed to line the inside of the basket if the basket does not have a top? Explain your strategy.

Chapter 12

Data Displays and Measures of Center

Show What You Know

Check your understanding of important skills

Name ______________________

▶ **Read a Bar Graph** **Use the bar graph to answer the questions.**

1. Who has the highest test score?

____

2. Who has a score between 70 and 80?

____

3. What is the difference between the highest and lowest scores?

____

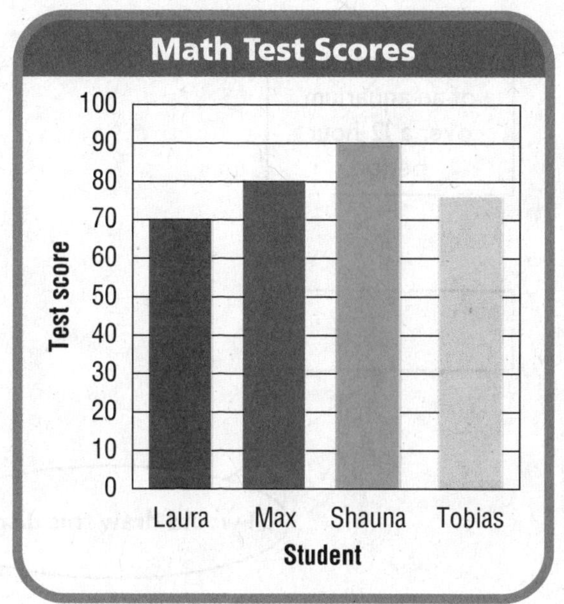

▶ **Division** **Find the quotient.**

4. $35\overline{)980}$ | 5. $16\overline{)352}$ | 6. $24\overline{)3,456}$ | 7. $42\overline{)3,276}$

▶ **Compare Decimals** **Compare. Write <, >, or =.**

8. 2.48 ◯ 2.53 | 9. 0.3 ◯ 0.04 | 10. 4.63 ◯ 4.3 | 11. 1.7 ◯ 1.70

Kayla scored 110 in the first game she bowled, but she can't remember her score from the second game. The average of the two scores is 116. Be a Math Detective and help her figure out what her second score was.

____

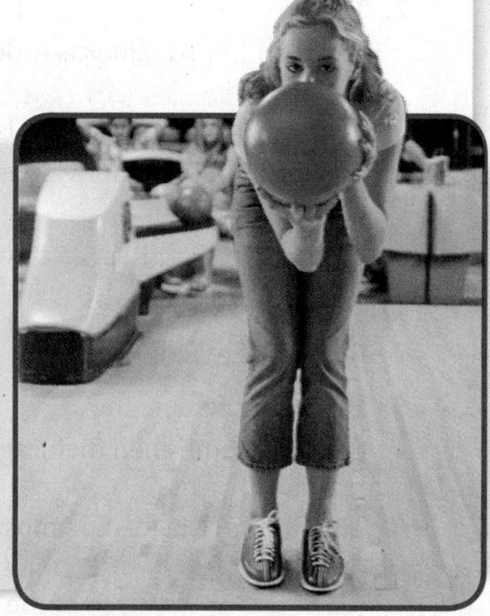

Personal Math Trainer
Online Assessment and Intervention

Vocabulary Builder

▶ Visualize It

Sort the review words into the chart.

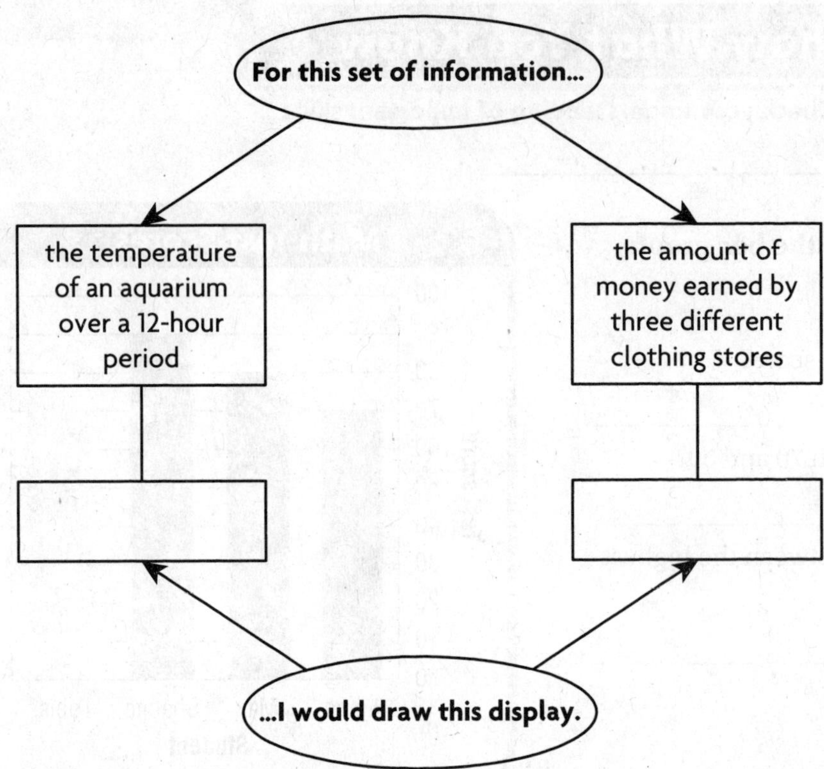

Review Words
bar graph
line graph

Preview Words
dot plot
frequency
histogram
mean
median
mode
outlier
statistical question

▶ Understand Vocabulary

Complete the sentences using the preview words.

1. A(n) ____________ is a bar graph that shows the frequency of data in specific intervals.

2. The ____________ is the middle value when a data set with an odd number of values is ordered from least to greatest.

3. A(n) ____________ is a value that is much less or much greater than the other values in a data set.

4. A(n) ____________ is a number line with dots that show the ____________ of the values in a data set.

5. You can calculate the ____________ of a data set by adding the values and then dividing the sum by the number of values.

6. The item(s) that occurs most often in a data set is called the ____________ of the data.

- Interactive Student Edition
- Multimedia eGlossary

Name ______________________________

Recognize Statistical Questions

Essential Question How do you identify a statistical question?

Statistics and Probability—6.SP.1

MATHEMATICAL PRACTICES
MP.1

If you measure the heights of your classmates, you are collecting data. A set of **data** is a set of information collected about people or things. A question that asks about a set of data that can vary is called a **statistical question**.

"What are the heights of my classmates on July 1?" is a statistical question because height usually varies in a group of people. "What is Sasha's height on July 1?" is not a statistical question because it asks for only one piece of information at one time.

Unlock the Problem — Real World

The New England Aquarium in Boston is home to over 80 penguins. Which of the following is a statistical question a biologist could ask about the penguins? Explain your reasoning.

A **How much does the penguin named Pip weigh this morning?**

B **How much does the penguin named Pip weigh each morning on 30 different days?**

Identify the statistical question.

Question A asks for Pip's weight at ____________ time(s),

so it ____________ ask about a set of data that varies.

Question A ____________ a statistical question.

Question B asks for Pip's weight at ____________ time(s), and it is

likely that Pip's weight ____________ vary during this period.

Question B asks about a set of data that can vary, so it ____________ a statistical question.

- Another biologist asks how old the penguin named Royal Pudding is. Is this a statistical question? Explain your reasoning.

____

____

A statistical question can ask about an entire set of data that can vary or a value that describes that set of data. For example, "What is the height of the tallest person in my class?" is a statistical question because it will tell you the greatest value in a set of data that can vary. You will learn other ways to describe a set of data later in this chapter.

Example

Bongos are a kind of antelope that live in central Africa. Bongos are unusual because both males and females have horns. Write two statistical questions a biologist could ask about a group of bongos.

1. What is the ____________ in inches of the horns on the bongo that has the ____________ horns in the group?

   Different bongos will have different horn lengths. This question asks about a value in a set of data that ______ vary, so it ______ a statistical question.

2. What is the weight of the ____________ bongo in the group?

   Different bongos will have different weights. This question asks about a value in a set of data that ______ vary, so it ______ a statistical question.

Math Talk **Mathematical Practices**

Give a different statistical question you could ask about the heights of students in your class.

Try This! **Write a statistical question you could ask in the situations described below.**

A **A researcher knows the amount of electricity used in 20 different homes on a Monday.**

____

____

____

____

____

B **A museum director records the number of students in each tour group that visits the museum during one week.**

____

____

____

____

____

Name ___________________________

Share and Show

MATH BOARD

Identify the statistical question. Explain your reasoning.

1. **A.** What was the low temperature in Chicago each day in March?

   B. What was the low temperature in Chicago on March 7?

   Question A asks for the low temperature at ______ time(s),

   and it is likely the temperature ____________.

   Question B asks for the low temperature at ______ time(s).

   Question ______ is a statistical question.

2. **A.** How long did it take you to get to school this morning?

   B. How long did it take you to get to school each morning this week?

   ____

   ____

Write a statistical question you could ask in the situation.

3. A student recorded the number of pets in the households of 50 sixth-graders.

   ____

Math Talk — **Mathematical Practices**

Explain how to determine whether a question is a statistical question.

On Your Own

Identify the statistical question. Explain your reasoning.

4. **A.** How many gold medals has Finland won at each of the last 10 Winter Olympics?

   B. How many gold medals did Finland win at the 2008 Winter Olympics?

   ____

   ____

Write a statistical question you could ask in the situation.

5. A wildlife biologist measured the length of time that 17 grizzly bears hibernated.

   ____

6. A doctor recorded the birth weights of 48 babies.

   ____

Problem Solving • Applications Real World

Use the table for 7 and 8.

7. Give a statistical question that you could ask about the data recorded in the table.

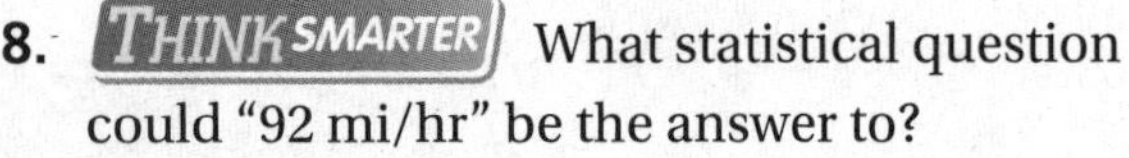

8. THINK SMARTER What statistical question could "92 mi/hr" be the answer to?

Name	Height (ft)	Maximum Speed (mi/hr)
Rocket	256	83
Thunder Dolphin	281	87
Varmint	240	81
Screamer	302	92

Roller Coaster Data

9. MATHEMATICAL PRACTICE 6 **Explain** A video game company will make a new game. The manager must choose between a role-playing game and an action game. He asks his sales staff which of the last 10 released games sold the most copies. Explain why this is a statistical question.

10. GO DEEPER Think of a topic. Record a set of data for the topic. Write a statistical question that you could ask about your data.

11. THINK SMARTER For numbers 11a–11d, choose Yes or No to indicate whether the question is a statistical question.

11a. How many minutes did it take Ethan to complete his homework last night? ○ Yes ○ No

11b. How many minutes did it take Madison to complete her homework each night this week? ○ Yes ○ No

11c. How many more minutes did Andrew spend on homework on Tuesday than on Thursday? ○ Yes ○ No

11d. What was the longest amount of time Abigail spent on homework this week? ○ Yes ○ No

FOR MORE PRACTICE:
Standards Practice Book

Name ____________________________

Describe Data Collection

Essential Question How can you describe how a data set was collected?

Statistics and Probability—6.SP.5a, 6.SP.5b

MATHEMATICAL PRACTICES
MP.3, MP.5, MP.6

Unlock the Problem

One way to describe a set of data is by stating the number of *observations*, or measurements, that were made. Another way is by listing the attributes that were measured. An *attribute* is a property or characteristic of the item being measured, such as its color or length.

Jeffrey's hobby is collecting rocks and minerals. The chart gives data on garnets he found during a recent mineral-hunting trip. Identify:

- The attribute being measured
- The unit of measure
- The likely means by which measurements were made
- The number of observations

Garnet Data			
Garnet	Mass (g)	Garnet	Mass (g)
1	7.2	7	4.6
2	3.5	8	5.6
3	4.0	9	9.0
4	3.9	10	3.6
5	5.2	11	3.8
6	5.8	12	4.3

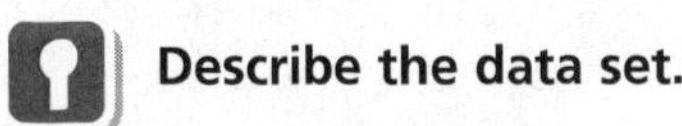

Describe the data set.

Think: What property or characteristic of the garnets did Jeffrey measure?

- The attribute Jeffrey measured was the ____________ of the garnets.
- The unit used to measure the mass of the garnets was ____________.
- To measure mass in grams, Jeffrey probably used a ____________.
- The number of observations Jeffrey made was ____________.

1. Would Jeffrey likely have gotten the same data set if he had measured a different group of garnets? Explain.

____

____

2. What other attributes of the garnets could Jeffrey have measured?

____

____

Activity Collect a data set.

Hands On

Materials ■ ruler

In this activity, you will work with other students to collect data on the length of the students' index fingers in your group. You will present the data in a chart.

- Describe the attribute you will measure. What unit will you use?
- Describe how you will make your measurements.
- Describe the data you will record in your chart.
- In the space at the right, make a chart of your data.
- How many observations did you make?

Math Talk **Mathematical Practices**

Explain what statistical question your data set in the Activity answers.

3. MATHEMATICAL PRACTICE 3 **Make Arguments** One of your classmates made 3 observations and another made 10 observations to answer a statistical question. Who do you think arrived at a better answer to the statistical question? Explain.

Name ________________________

Share and Show

Describe the data set by listing the attribute measured, the unit of measure, the likely means of measurement, and the number of observations.

100-Meter Run Data			
Race	Time (sec)	Race	Time (sec)
1	12.8	5	13.5
2	12.5	6	13.7
3	12.9	7	12.6
4	13.4		

1. Greg's 100-meter race results

   attribute: ____________

   unit of measure: ____________

   likely means by which measurements were taken: ____________

   number of observations: ______

Daily Water Use (gal)				
153.7	161.8	151.5	153.7	160.1
161.9	155.5	152.3	166.7	158.3
155.8	167.5	150.8	154.6	

2. The Andrews family's water use

   ____

   ____

   ____

Math Talk **Mathematical Practices**

Explain why it is important to make more than one observation when attempting to answer a statistical question.

On Your Own

3. **Practice: Copy and Solve** Collect data on one of the topics listed below. You may wish to work with other students. Make a chart of your results. Then describe the data set.

   - Weights of cereal boxes, soup cans, or other items
   - Numbers of family members
   - Lengths of time to multiply two two-digit numbers
   - Numbers of pets in families
   - Lengths of forearm (elbow to fingertip)
   - Numbers of pages in books

4. THINK SMARTER Describe the data set by writing the attribute measured, the unit of measure, the likely means of measurement, and the number of observations in the correct location on the chart.

Heights of 6th Graders (in.)						
50	58	56	60	58	52	50
53	54	61	48	59	48	59
55	59	62	49	57	56	61

21

yardstick

inches

heights of 6th graders

Attribute	Unit of Measure	Likely Means of Measurement	Number of Observations

Connect to Reading

Summarize

When you *summarize* a reading passage, you restate the most important information in a shortened form. This allows you to understand more easily what you have read. Read the followng passage:

A biologist is studying green anacondas. The green anaconda is the largest snake in the world. Finding the length of any snake is difficult because the snake can curl up or stretch out while being measured. Finding the length of a green anaconda is doubly difficult because of the animal's great size and strength. The standard method for measuring a green anaconda is to calm the snake, lay a piece of string along its entire length, and then measure the length of the string. The table at the right gives data collected by the biologist using the string method.

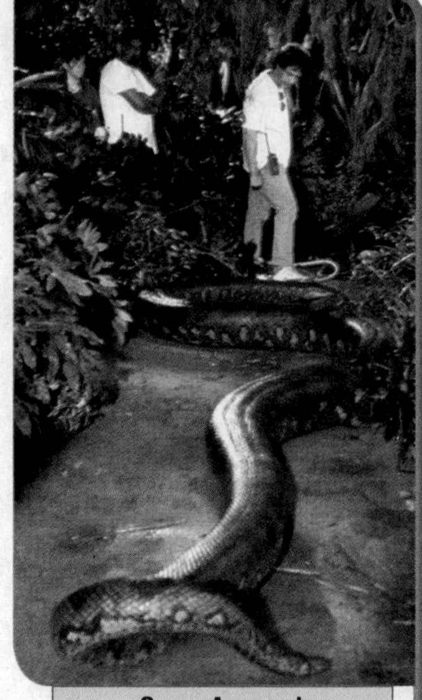

Green Anaconda Lengths (cm)			
357.2	407.6	494.5	387.0
417.6	305.3	189.4	267.7
441.3	507.5	413.2	469.8
168.9	234.0	366.2	499.1
370.0	488.8	219.2	

5. MATHEMATICAL PRACTICE 1 **Analyze** Summarize the passage in your own words.

6. THINK SMARTER Use your summary to name the attribute the biologist was measuring. Describe how the biologist measured this attribute.

7. Give any other information that is important for describing the data set.

8. GO DEEPER Write the greatest green anaconda length that the biologist measured in feet. Round your answer to the nearest foot. (Hint: 1 foot is equal to about 30 centimeters.)

FOR MORE PRACTICE:
Standards Practice Book

Name ______________________________

Dot Plots and Frequency Tables

Essential Question How can you use dot plots and frequency tables to display data?

Statistics and Probability—6.SP.4

MATHEMATICAL PRACTICES
MP.4, MP.5, MP.6

A **dot plot** is a number line with marks that show the frequency of data. **Frequency** is the number of times a data value occurs.

Unlock the Problem

Hannah is training for a walkathon. The table shows the number of miles she walks each day. She has one day left in her training. How many miles is she most likely to walk on the last day?

- What do you need to find?

____

Make a dot plot.

Distance Hannah Walked (mi)				
4	2	9	3	3
5	5	1	6	2
5	2	5	4	5
4	9	3	2	4

STEP 1

Draw a number line with an appropriate scale.

Numbers vary from ______ to ______, so use a scale from 0 to 10.

STEP 2

For each piece of data, plot a dot above the number that corresponds to the number of miles Hannah walked.

Complete the dot plot by making the correct number of dots above the numbers 5 through 10.

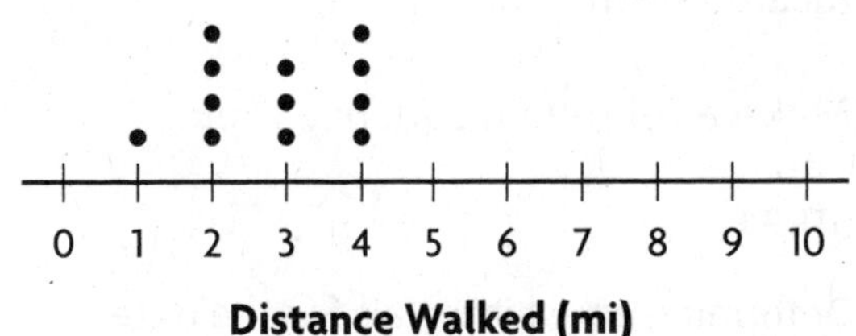

The number of miles Hannah walked most often is the value with the tallest stack of dots. The tallest stack in this dot plot is for

______________________________.

So, the number of miles Hannah is most likely to walk on the last day of her training is

______________.

Math Idea
A dot plot is sometimes called a line plot.

- MATHEMATICAL PRACTICE 5 **Communicate** Explain why a dot plot is useful for solving this problem.

____

____

A **frequency table** shows the number of times each data value or range of values occurs. A **relative frequency table** shows the percent of time each piece of data or group of data occurs.

Example 1

Jill kept a record of her workout times. How many of Jill's workouts lasted exactly 90 minutes?

Jill's Workout Times (minutes)						
30	60	30	90	60	30	60
90	60	120	30	60	90	90
60	120	60	60	60	30	30
120	30	120	60	120	60	120

Make a frequency table.

STEP 1

List the workout times in the first column.

STEP 2

Record the frequency of each time in the Frequency column.

Jill's Workout Times

Minutes	Frequency
30	7
60	
90	
120	

Complete the frequency table.

So, ______ of Jill's workouts lasted exactly 90 minutes.

Example 2

The table shows the number of laps Ricardo swam each day. What percent of the days did Ricardo swim 18 or more laps?

Ricardo's Lap Swimming				
10	10	15	5	12
12	5	19	3	19
16	14	17	18	13
6	17	16	11	8

Make a relative frequency table.

STEP 1

Determine equal intervals for the data. List the intervals in the first column.

STEP 2

Count the number of data values in each interval. Record this in the Frequency column.

STEP 3

Divide each frequency by the total number of data values. Write the result as a percent in the Relative Frequency column.

Ricardo's Lap Swimming

Number of Laps	Frequency	Relative Frequency
3–7	4	20%
8–12	6	30%
13–17	7	
18–22	3	

There are 20 data values.

$\frac{4}{20} = 0.2 = 20\%$

$\frac{6}{20} = 0.3 = 30\%$

Complete the relative frequency table.

So, Ricardo swam 18 or more laps on ______ of the days.

Math Talk — Mathematical Practices

Explain how you could find the percent of days on which Ricardo swam 13 or more laps.

Name ______________________

Share and Show

For 1–4, use the data at right.

1. Complete the dot plot.

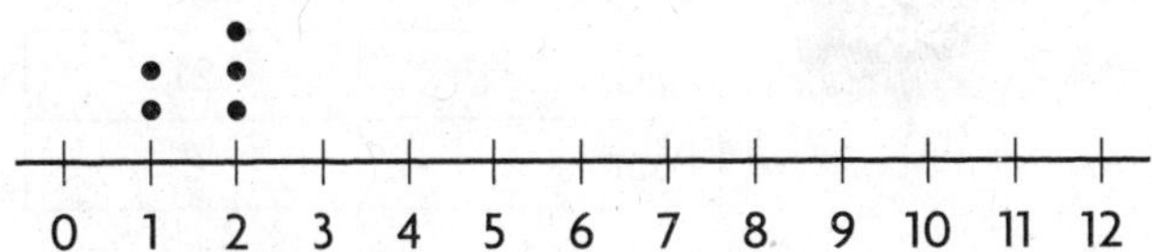

Daily Distance Lionel Biked (km)				
3	5	12	2	1
8	5	8	6	3
11	8	6	4	10
10	9	6	6	6
5	2	1	2	3

2. What was the most common distance Lionel biked? How do you know?

3. Make a frequency table. Use the intervals 1–3 km, 4–6 km, 7–9 km, and 10–12 km.

4. Make a relative frequency table. Use the same intervals as in Exercise 3.

On Your Own

Practice: Copy and Solve **For 5–9, use the table.**

5. Make a dot plot of the data.

6. Make a frequency table of the data with three intervals.

7. Make a relative frequency table of the data with three intervals.

8. MATHEMATICAL PRACTICE 1 **Describe** how you decided on the intervals for the frequency table.

Gloria's Daily Sit-Ups				
13	3	14	13	12
12	13	4	15	12
15	13	14	3	11
13	13	12	14	15
11	14	13	15	11

9. THINK SMARTER Could someone use the information in the frequency table to make a dot plot? Explain.

Unlock the Problem

10. THINK SMARTER The manager of a fitness center asked members to rate the fitness center. The results of the survey are shown in the frequency table. What percent of members in the survey rated the center as excellent or good?

Fitness Center Survey	
Response	**Frequency**
Excellent	18
Good	15
Fair	21
Poor	6

a. What do you need to find?

____

b. How can you use relative frequency to help you solve the problem?

____

____

c. Show the steps you use to solve the problem.

d. Complete the sentences.

The percent of members who rated the center as excellent is ______.

The percent of members who rated the center as good is ______.

The percent of members who rated the center as excellent or good is ______.

11. GO DEEPER Use the table above. What is the difference in percent of the members in the survey that rated the fitness center as poor versus excellent?

____

Personal Math Trainer

12. THINK SMARTER + Julie kept a record of the number of minutes she spent reading for 20 days. Complete the frequency table by finding the frequency and the relative frequency (%).

Julie's Reading Times (min)				
15	30	15	30	30
30	60	15	60	45
15	45	30	45	15
60	45	30	30	30

Julie's Reading Times		
Minutes	**Frequency**	**Relative Frequency (%)**
15	5	25
30		
45		
60		

FOR MORE PRACTICE:
Standards Practice Book

Name ______________________________

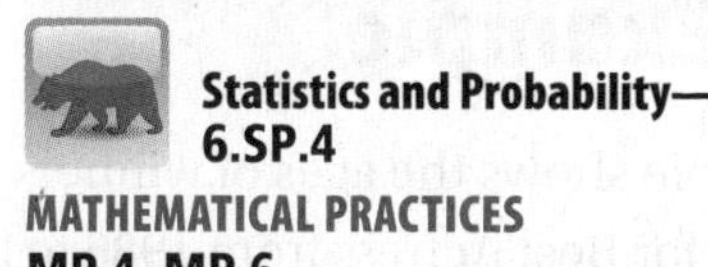

Statistics and Probability—6.SP.4

MATHEMATICAL PRACTICES MP.4, MP.6

Histograms

Essential Question How can you use histograms to display data?

When there is a large number of data values, it is helpful to group the data into intervals. A **histogram** is a bar graph that shows the frequency of data in intervals. Unlike a bar graph, there are no gaps between the bars in a histogram.

Unlock the Problem

The histogram shows the ages of winners of the Academy Award for Best Actor from 1990 to 2009. How many winners were under 40 years old?

Ages of Best Actor Winners, 1990–2009

Frequency: 0 1 2 3 4 5 6 7 8 9

Age: 20–29, 30–39, 40–49, 50–59, 60–69

Interpret the histogram.

The height of each bar shows how many data values are in the interval the bar represents.

How many winners were 20–29 years old?

____

Which other bar represents people under 40?

____

How many winners were 30–39 years old? __________

To find the total number of winners who were under 40 years old, add the frequencies for the intervals 20–29 and 30–39.

______ + ______ = ______

So, ______ of the winners were under 40 years old.

1. MATHEMATICAL PRACTICE 4 **Use Graphs** Explain whether it is possible to know from the histogram if any winner was 37 years old.

____

Example

The table shows the ages of winners of the Academy Award for Best Actress from 1986 to 2009. How many of the winners were under 40 years old?

Ages of Best Actress Winners					
45	21	41	26	80	42
29	33	36	45	49	39
34	26	25	33	35	35
28	30	29	61	32	33

Make a histogram.

STEP 1

Make a frequency table using intervals of 10.

Interval	20–29	30–39	40–49	50–59	60–69	70–79	80–89
Frequency	7			0			1

STEP 2

Set up the intervals along the ________ axis of the graph. The intervals must be all the same size. In this case, every interval includes 10 years.

Write a scale for the frequencies on the ________ axis.

STEP 3

Graph the number of winners in each interval.

STEP 4

Give the graph a title and label the axes.

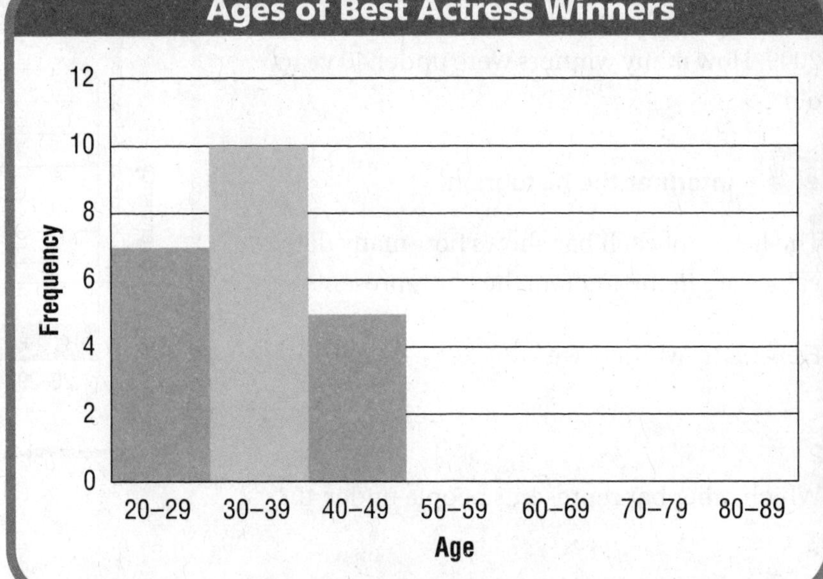

Complete the histogram by drawing the bars for the intervals 60–69, 70–79, and 80–89.

To find the number of winners who were under 40 years old, add the frequencies for the intervals 20–29 and 30–39.

______ + ______ = ______

So, ______ of the winners were under 40 years old.

2. MATHEMATICAL PRACTICE 6 **Explain** how you can tell from the histogram which age group has the most winners.

______

______

Name ______________________

Share and Show

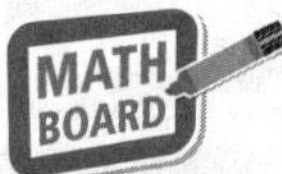

For 1–3, use the data at right.

Ages of People at a Health Club (yr)				
21	25	46	19	33
38	18	22	30	29
26	34	48	22	31

1. Complete the frequency table for the age data in the table at right.

Interval	10–19	20–29	30–39	40–49
Frequency	2			

2. Complete the histogram for the data.

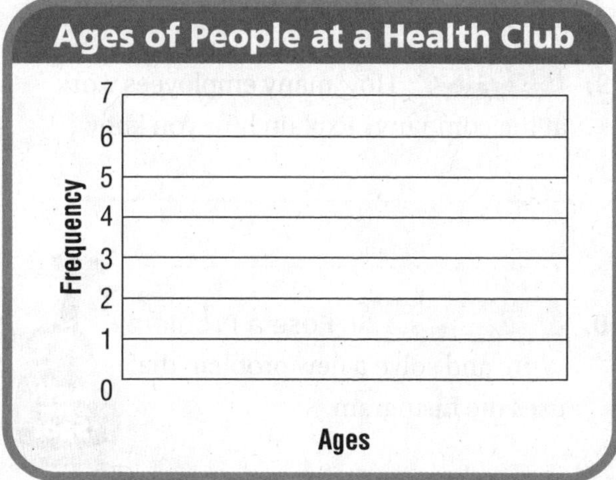

3. Use your histogram to find the number of people at the health club who are 30 or older.

____

4. GO DEEPER Use your histogram to determine the percent of the people at the health club who are 20–29 years old.

____

Math Talk — Mathematical Practices

Explain whether you could use the histogram to find the number of people who are 25 or older.

On Your Own

Practice: Copy and Solve For 5–7, use the table.

Weights of Dogs (lb)				
16	20	15	24	32
33	26	30	15	21
21	12	19	21	37
10	39	21	17	35

5. Make a histogram of the data using the intervals 10–19, 20–29, and 30–39.

6. Make a histogram of the data using the intervals 10–14, 15–19, 20–24, 25–29, 30–34, and 35–39.

7. MATHEMATICAL PRACTICE 6 **Compare** Explain how using different intervals changed the appearance of your histogram.

____

____

____

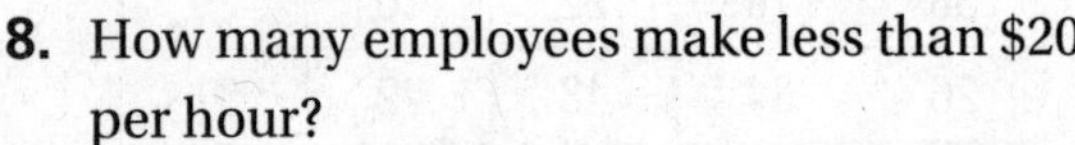

The histogram shows the hourly salaries, to the nearest dollar, of the employees at a small company. Use the histogram to solve 8–11.

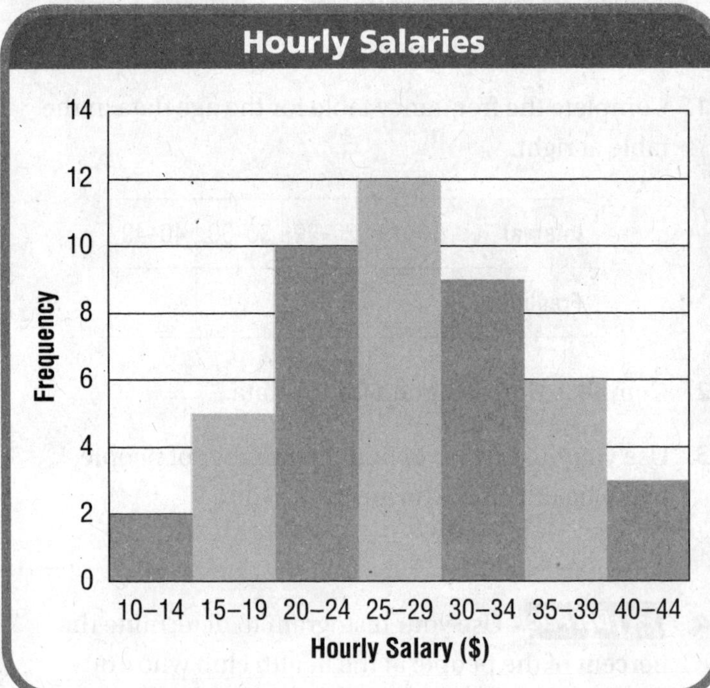

8. How many employees make less than $20 per hour?

9. GO DEEPER How many employees work at the company? Explain how you know.

10. THINK SMARTER **Pose a Problem** Write and solve a new problem that uses the histogram.

11. MATHEMATICAL PRACTICE 6 **Analyze** Describe the overall shape of the histogram. What does this tell you about the salaries at the company?

Personal Math Trainer

12. THINK SMARTER + The frequency table shows the TV ratings for the show American Singer. Complete the histogram for the data.

TV ratings	
Rating	**Frequency**
14.1-14.5	2
14.6-15.0	6
15.1-15.5	6
15.6-16.0	5
16.1-16.5	1

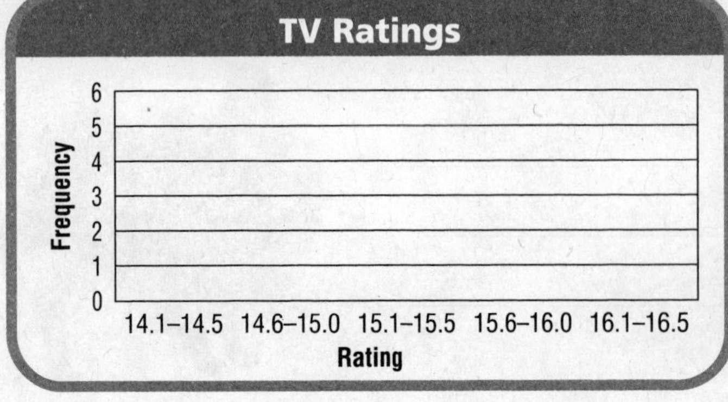

FOR MORE PRACTICE:
Standards Practice Book

Name ___________________________

Mid-Chapter Checkpoint

Vocabulary

Vocabulary
dot plot
histogram
statistical question

Choose the best term from the box to complete the sentence.

1. A _________________ is a kind of bar graph that shows the frequency of data grouped into intervals. (p. 485)

2. A question that asks about a set of data that varies is called a

_________________. (p. 473)

Concepts and Skills

3. A sports reporter records the number of touchdowns scored each week during the football season. What statistical question could the reporter ask about the data? (6.SP.1)

____

____

4. Flora records her pet hamster's weight once every week for one year. How many observations does she make? (6.SP.5a)

____

5. The number of runs scored by a baseball team in 20 games is given below. Draw a dot plot of the data and use it to find the most common number of runs scored in a game. (6.SP.4)

Runs Scored									
3	1	4	3	4	2	1	7	2	3
5	3	2	9	4	3	2	1	1	4

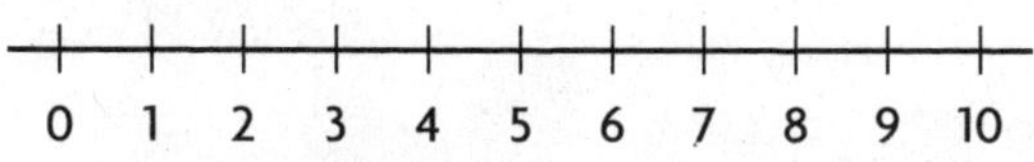

Number of Runs Scored

____

6. Write a statistical question you could ask about a set of data that shows the times visitors arrived at an amusement park. (6.SP.1)

7. A school principal is trying to decide how long the breaks should be between periods. He plans to time how long it takes several students to get from one classroom to another. Name a tool he could use to collect the data. (6.SP.5b)

8. The U.S. Mint uses very strict standards when making coins. On a tour of the mint, Casey asks, "How much copper is in each penny?" Lenny asks, "What is the value of a nickel?" Who asked a statistical question? (6.SP.1)

9. Chen checks the temperature at dawn and at dusk every day for a week for a science project. How many observations does he make? (6.SP.5a)

10. The table shows the lengths of the songs played by a radio station during a 90-minute period. Alicia is making a histogram of the data. What frequency should she show for the interval 160–169 seconds? (6.SP.4)

Song Lengths (sec)				
166	157	153	194	207
150	175	168	209	206
151	201	187	162	152
209	194	168	165	156

Name ______________________________

Mean as Fair Share and Balance Point

Essential Question How does the mean represent a fair share and balance point?

Statistics and Probability—6.SP.5c

MATHEMATICAL PRACTICES
MP.1, MP.2, MP.8

Hands On

Materials ■ counters

On an archaeological dig, five students found 1, 5, 7, 3, and 4 arrowheads. The students agreed to divide the arrowheads evenly. How many arrowheads should each student get?

A. Use counters to show how many arrowheads each of the five students found. Use one stack of counters for each student.

B. Remove a counter from the tallest stack and move it to the shortest. Keep moving counters from taller stacks to shorter stacks until each stack has the same height.

C. Count the number of counters in each stack.

The number of counters in each stack is the *mean*, or average, of the data. The mean represents the number of arrowheads each student should get if the arrowheads are shared equally.

There are 5 stacks of ______ counters.

So, each student should get ______ arrowheads.

Mathematical Practices

What is the mean ofthe data set 3, 3, 3, 3, 3? **Explain** how you know.

Draw Conclusions

1. Explain what is "fair" about a fair share of a group of items.

____

____

____

2. THINK SMARTER How could you find the fair share of arrowheads using the total number of arrowheads and division?

____

____

Make Connections

The mean can also be seen as a kind of balance point.

Ms. Burnham's class holds a walk-a-thon to help raise money to update the computer lab. Five of the students walked 1, 1, 2, 4, and 7 miles. The mean distance walked is 3 miles.

Complete the dot plot of the data set.

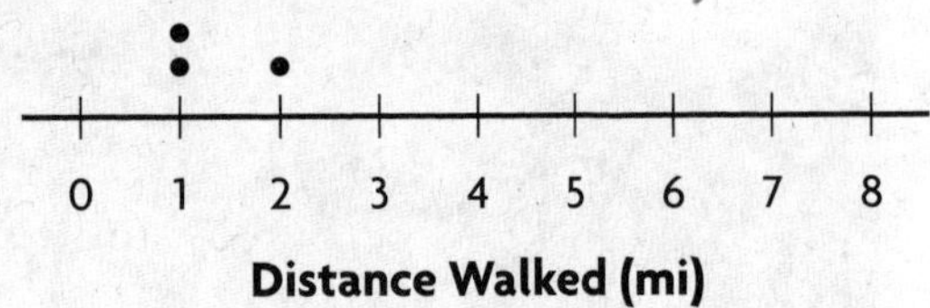

Circle the number that represents the mean.

Complete the table to find the distances of the data points from the mean.

	Values Less than the Mean			Values Greater than the Mean	
Data point	1 mi	1 mi	mi	4 mi	mi
Distance from the mean	2 mi	mi	mi	mi	mi

The total distance from the mean for values less than the mean is:

2 miles + 2 miles + 1 mile = ______ miles

The total distance from the mean for values greater than the mean is:

______ mile + ______ miles = ______ miles

The total distance of the data values less than the mean is ____________ the total distance of the data values greater than the mean. The mean represents a balance point for data values less than the mean and greater than the mean.

3. Explain how you found the distance of each data value from the mean.

____

____

4. MATHEMATICAL PRACTICE 8 **Generalize** Can all of the values in a data set be greater than the mean? Explain why or why not.

____

____

Name ______________________________

Share and Show

MATH BOARD

Use counters to find the mean of the data set.

1. On the first day of a school fundraiser, five students sell 1, 1, 2, 2, and 4 gift boxes of candy.

   Make ______ stacks of counters with heights 1, 1, 2, 2, and 4.

   Rearrange the counters so that all ______ stacks have the same height.

   After rearranging, every stack has ______ counters.

   So, the mean of the data set is ______.

Make a dot plot for the data set and use it to check whether the given value is a balance point for the data set.

2. Rosanna's friends have 0, 1, 1, 2, 2, and 12 pets at home. Rosanna says the mean of the data is 3. Is Rosanna correct?

   0 1 2 3 4 5 6 7 8 9 10 11 12

   Number of Pets

   The total distance from 3 for data values less than 3 is ______.

   The total distance from 3 for data values greater than 3 is ______.

   The mean of 3 __________ a balance point.

   So, Rosanna __________ correct.

Problem Solving • Applications

Real World

3. GO DEEPER Four people go to lunch, and the costs of their orders are \$6, \$9, \$10, and \$11. They want to split the bill evenly. Find each person's fair share. Explain your work.

   ____

   ____

   ____

Use the table for 4–6.

Fruit Baskets			
Basket	Apples	Oranges	Pears
A	4	2	2
B	1	2	1
C	4	2	5

4. A grocer is preparing fruit baskets to sell as holiday presents. If the grocer rearranges the apples in baskets A, B, and C so that each has the same number, how many apples will be in each basket? Use counters to find the fair share.

5. MATHEMATICAL PRACTICE 3 **Make Arguments** Can the pears be rearranged so that there is an equal whole number of pears in each basket? Explain why or why not.

6. THINK SMARTER Use counters to find the mean of the number of pears originally in baskets B and C. Draw a dot plot of the data set. Use your plot to explain why the mean you found is a balance point.

7. THINK SMARTER Four friends go to breakfast and the costs of their breakfasts are \$5, \$8, \$9, and \$10. Select True or False for each statement.

7a. The mean of the cost of the breakfasts can be found by adding each of the costs and dividing that total by 4. ○ True ○ False

7b. The mean cost of the four breakfasts is \$10. ○ True ○ False

7c. The difference between the greatest cost and the mean is \$2. ○ True ○ False

7d. The difference between the least cost and the mean is \$2. ○ True ○ False

FOR MORE PRACTICE:
Standards Practice Book

Name ______________________________

Measures of Center

Essential Question How can you describe a set of data using mean, median, and mode?

Statistics and Probability—6.SP.5c
Also 6.SP.2, 6.SP.3

MATHEMATICAL PRACTICES
MP.3, MP.6, MP.7

A **measure of center** is a single value used to describe the middle of a data set. A measure of center can be a useful way to summarize a data set, especially when the data set is large.

Unlock the Problem

Kara made a paper airplane. She flew her airplane 6 times and recorded how long it stayed in the air during each flight. The times in seconds for the flights are 5.8, 2.9, 6.7, 1.6, 2.9, and 4.7. What are the mean, median, and mode of the data?

What unit of time is used in the problem?

____

How many flight times are given?

____

Find the mean, median, and mode.

The **mean** is the sum of the data items divided by the number of data items.

$$\text{Mean} = \frac{5.8 + 2.9 + 6.7 + 1.6 + 2.9 + 4.7}{} = \frac{}{} = $$

The **median** is the middle value when the data are written in order. If the number of data items is even, the median is the mean of the two middle values.

Order the values from least to greatest.

1.6, 2.9, 2.9, 4.7, 5.8, 6.7

The data set has an __________ number of values, so the median is the mean of the two middle values. Circle the two middle values of the data set.

Now find the mean of the two middle values.

$$\frac{ + }{} = \frac{}{} = $$

The **mode** is the data value or values that occur most often.

______ occurs twice, and all the other values occur once.

__________ is the mode.

Math Talk **Mathematical Practices**

Explain how you could use a dot plot and the idea of a balance point to check your answer for the mean.

Try This! In 2009, an engineer named Takuo Toda set a world record for flight time for a paper airplane. His plane flew for 27.9 sec. If Toda's time was included in Kara's set of times, what would the median be?

____

Example 1

Mrs. O'Donnell's class has a fundraiser for a field trip to a wildlife preservation. Five of the donations are $15, $25, $30, $28, and $27. Find the mean, median, and mode of the donations.

Mean = $\frac{\square + \square + \square + \square + \square}{\square}$

= $\frac{\square}{\square}$ = $\square$

Order the data from least to greatest to find the median.

______, ______, ______, ______, ______

Median = ______

If all of the values in a data set occur with equal frequency, then the data set has no mode.

The data set has no repeated values, so there is no __________.

Example 2

Keith surveys his classmates about how many brothers and sisters they have. Six of the responses were 1, 3, 1, 2, 2, and 0. Find the mean, median, and mode of the data.

Mean = $\frac{\square + \square + \square + \square + \square + \square}{\square}$ = $\frac{\square}{\square}$ = $\square$

Order the data from least to greatest to find the median.

______, ______, ______, ______, ______, ______

The number of data values is even, so find the mean of the two middle values.

Median = $\frac{\square + \square}{\square}$ = $\frac{\square}{\square}$ = $\square$

The data values ______ and ______ appear twice in the set. If two or more values appear in the data set the most number of times, then the data set has two or more modes.

Modes = ______ and ______

Name ___________________________

Share and Show

1. Terrence records the number of e-mails he receives per day. During one week, he receives 7, 3, 10, 5, 5, 6, and 6 e-mails. What are the mean, median, and mode of the data?

Mean = ________ Median = ________ Mode(s) = ________

2. Julie goes to several grocery stores and researches the price of a 12 oz bottle of juice. Find the mean, median, and mode of the prices shown.

Juice Prices		
$0.95	$1.09	$0.99
$1.25	$0.99	$1.99

Mean = ________ Median = ________ Mode(s) = ________

Mathematical Practices

Explain how to find the median of a set of data with an even number of values.

On Your Own

3. T.J. is training for the 200-meter dash event for his school's track team. Find the mean, median, and mode of the times shown in the table.

T.J.'s Times (sec)		
22.3	22.4	23.3
24.5	22.5	

Mean = ________ Median = ________ Mode(s) = ________

4. MATHEMATICAL PRACTICE 6 **Make Connections Algebra** The values of a data set can be represented by the expressions x, $2x$, $4x$, and $5x$. Write the data set for $x = 3$ and find the mean.

____

5. GO DEEPER In the last six months, Sonia's family used 456, 398, 655, 508, 1,186, and 625 minutes on their cell phone plan. To save money, Sonia's family wants to keep their mean cell phone usage below 600 minutes per month. By how many minutes did they go over their goal in the last six months?

____

Problem Solving • Applications

Sense or Nonsense?

6. Jeremy scored 85, 90, 72, 88, and 92 on five math tests, for a mean of 85.4. On the sixth test he scored a 95. He calculates his mean score for all 6 tests as shown below, but Deronda says he is incorrect. Whose answer makes sense? Whose answer is nonsense? Explain your reasoning.

Jeremy's Work

The mean of my first 5 test scores was 85.4, so to find the mean of all 6 test scores, I just need to find the mean of 85.4 and 95.

$$\text{Mean} = \frac{85.4 + 95}{2} = \frac{180.4}{2} = 90.2$$

So, my mean score for all 6 tests is 90.2.

Deronda's Work

To find the mean of all 6 test scores, you need to add up all 6 scores and divide by 6.

$$\text{Mean} = \frac{85 + 90 + 72 + 88 + 92 + 95}{6}$$

$$= \frac{522}{6} = 87$$

So, Jeremy's mean score for all 6 tests is 87.

7. THINK SMARTER Alex took a standardized test 4 times. His test scores were 16, 28, 24, and 32.

The mean of the test scores is [24. / 25. / 26.]

The median of the test scores is [24. / 26. / 28.]

The mode of the test scores is [16. / 32. / no mode.]

FOR MORE PRACTICE:
Standards Practice Book

Name ______________________________

Effects of Outliers

Essential Question How does an outlier affect measures of center?

Statistics and Probability—6.SP.5d

MATHEMATICAL PRACTICES
MP.2, MP.3, MP.4, MP.6

An **outlier** is a value that is much less or much greater than the other values in a data set. An outlier may greatly affect the mean of a data set. This may give a misleading impression of the data.

Unlock the Problem (Real World)

The table gives the number of days that the 24 members of the Garfield Middle School volleyball team were absent from school last year.

Volleyball Team Absences (days)							
4	6	7	4	5	5	3	6
6	7	3	5	8	16	5	4
5	6	5	7	6	4	5	4

Does the data set contain any outliers?

- Why might a dot plot be helpful in determining if there is an outlier?

____

____

____

____

____

____

Use a dot plot to find the outlier(s).

STEP 1 Plot the data on the number line.

0 1 2 3 4 5 6 7 8 9 10 11 12 13 14 15 16 17 18

Team Absences (days)

STEP 2 Find any values that are much greater or much less than the other values.

Most of the data values are between ______ and ______.

The value ______ is much greater than the rest, so ______ is an outlier.

1. MATHEMATICAL PRACTICE 6 **Generalize** What effect do you think an outlier greater than the other data would have on the mean of the data set? Justify your answer.

____

____

____

Example

The high temperatures for the week in Foxdale, in degrees Fahrenheit, were 43, 43, 45, 42, 26, 43, and 45. The mean of the data is 41°F, and the median is 43°F. Identify the outlier and describe how the mean and median are affected by it.

STEP 1 Draw a dot plot of the data and identify the outlier.

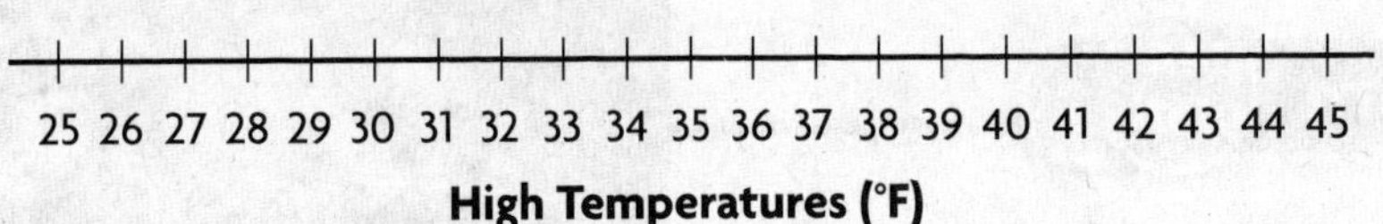

The outlier is ______ °F.

STEP 2 Find the mean and median of the temperatures *without* the outlier.

$$\text{Mean} = \frac{43 + \square + \square + \square + \square + \square}{\square}$$

$$= \frac{\square}{6} = \square \text{ °F}$$

Values ordered least to greatest: 42, ______, ______, ______, ______, ______

$$\text{Median} = \frac{43 + \square}{2} = \square \text{ °F}$$

The mean with the outlier is ______ °F, and the mean without the outlier is ______ °F.

The outlier made the mean ____________.

The median with the outlier is ______ °F, and the median without the outlier is ______ °F.

The outlier ____________ affect the median.

2. MATHEMATICAL PRACTICE ② **Use Reasoning** Explain why the mean without the outlier could be a better description of the data set than the mean with the outlier.

____

____

____

3. If the outlier had been 59°F rather than 26°F, how would the mean have been affected by the outlier? Explain your reasoning.

____

____

Name ___________________________

Share and Show

1. Find the outlier by drawing a dot plot of the data.

Foul Shots Made						
2	3	1	3	2	2	1
15	2	1	3	1	3	

0 1 2 3 4 5 6 7 8 9 10 11 12 13 14 15 16 17 18

Foul Shots Made

The outlier is ______.

2. The prices of the X-40 Laser Printer at five different stores are \$99, \$68, \$98, \$105, and \$90. The mean price is \$92, and the median price is \$98. Identify the outlier and describe how the mean and median are affected by it.

The outlier is ______.

without the outlier: Mean = \$______

Median = \$______

____

Math Talk **Mathematical Practices**

The mean of a certain data set is much greater than the median. **Explain** how this can happen.

On Your Own

3. Identify the outlier in the data set of melon weights. Then describe the effect the outlier has on the mean and median.

Melon Weights (oz)					
47	45	48	45	49	47
14	45	51	46	47	

The outlier is ______ oz.

____

____

4. MATHEMATICAL PRACTICE 2 **Use Reasoning** In a set of Joanne's test scores, there is an outlier. On the day of one of those tests, Joanne had the flu. Do you think the outlier is greater or less than the rest of her scores? Explain.

____

____

Problem Solving • Applications Real World

Use the table for 5–7.

Baseball All-Time Stolen Base Leaders	
Player	**Stolen Bases**
Rickey Henderson	1,406
Lou Brock	938
Billy Hamilton	914
Ty Cobb	897
Tim Raines	808

▲ Ty Cobb steals a base.

5. Which player's number of stolen bases is an outlier?

6. GO DEEPER What effect does the outlier have on the median of the data set?

7. THINK SMARTER Miguel wrote that the mean of the data set is 992.6. Is this the mean with or without the outlier? Explain how you can tell without doing a calculation.

8. THINK SMARTER Does an outlier have any effect on the mode of a data set? Explain.

9. THINK SMARTER The prices of mesh athletic shorts at five different stores are \$9, \$16, \$18, \$20, and \$22. The mean price is \$17 and the median price is \$18. Identify the outlier and describe how the mean and median are affected by it.

WRITE ▸Math • Show Your Work

FOR MORE PRACTICE:
Standards Practice Book

Name ______________________________

Lesson 12.8

Problem Solving • Data Displays

Essential Question How can you use the strategy *draw a diagram* to solve problems involving data?

Statistics and Probability—6.SP.4
MATHEMATICAL PRACTICES
MP.1, MP.4, MP.5

Unlock the Problem (Real World)

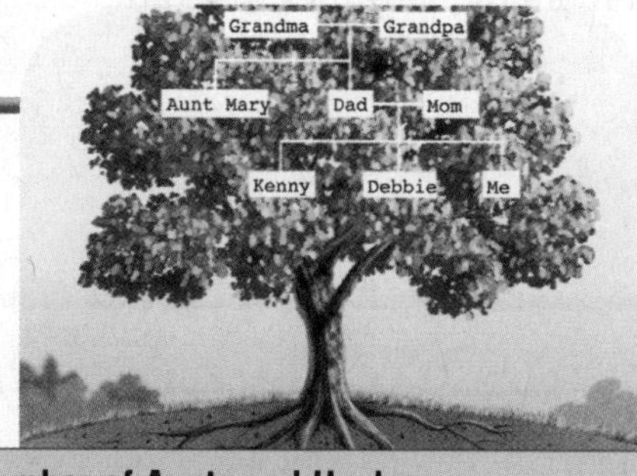

The 32 students in the History Club are researching their family histories so they can draw family trees. The data set at the right shows the numbers of aunts and uncles the students have. What is the most common number of aunts and uncles among the students in the club?

Use the graphic organizer to help you solve the problem.

Number of Aunts and Uncles							
4	3	2	4	5	7	0	3
1	4	2	4	6	3	5	1
2	5	0	6	3	2	4	5
4	1	3	0	4	2	8	3

Read the Problem

What do I need to find?

I need to find the ______________ number of aunts and uncles among students in the club.

The most common number in the data is the __________.

What information do I need to use?

I need to use the number of ______________ each student has from the table.

How will I use the information?

I can draw a diagram that shows the __________ of each value in the data set. A good way to show the frequency of each value in a data set is a __________.

Solve the Problem

- Make a dot plot of the data.

  Check: Are there the same number of dots on the plot as there are data values?

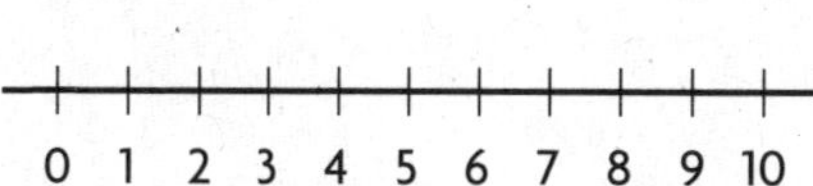

Number of Aunts and Uncles

- Use the plot to determine the mode. The mode is the data value with the ________ dots. The data value with the most dots is _____.

So, the most common number of aunts and uncles is _____.

Math Talk Mathematical Practices

Explain why displaying the data in a dot plot is a better choice for solving this problem than displaying the data in a histogram.

Try Another Problem

The table shows the attendance for the Pittsburgh Pirates' last 25 home games of the 2009 baseball season. What percent of the games were attended by at least 25,000 people?

Attendance at 25 Pittsburgh Pirates Games (in thousands)				
12	13	23	33	21
17	17	24	15	27
19	15	18	11	26
20	24	13	16	16
16	19	36	27	17

Read the Problem

What do I need to find?	What information do I need to use?	How will I use the information?

Solve the Problem

So, ______ of the last 25 home games were attended by at least 25,000 people.

Math Talk — **Mathematical Practices**

What other type of display might you have used to solve this problem? **Explain** how you could have used the display.

Name ______________________________

Share and Show

1. The table shows the number of goals scored by the Florida Panthers National Hockey League team in the last 20 games of the 2009 season. What was the most common number of goals the team scored?

Goals Scored									
1	3	3	2	1	1	2	2	2	1
4	5	1	3	3	3	0	2	4	2

First, draw a dot plot of the data.

Next, use the plot to find the mode of the data: The value ______ appears ______ times.

So, the most common number of goals the Panthers scored was ______.

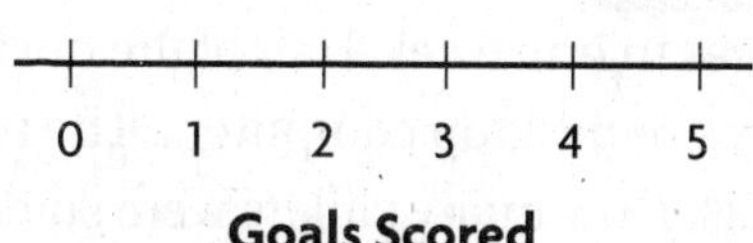

Goals Scored

2. Draw a histogram of the hockey data. Use it to find the percent of the games in which the Panthers scored more than 3 goals.

____

3. MATHEMATICAL PRACTICE 5 **Use Appropriate Tools** If you needed to find the mean of a data set, which data display—dot plot or histogram—would you choose? Explain your reasoning.

____

____

____

Unlock the Problem

- ✓ Read the question carefully to be sure you understand what you need to find.
- ✓ Check that you plot every data value exactly once.
- ✓ Check that you answered the question.

WRITE ▸ Math • Show Your Work

On Your Own

4. THINK SMARTER Corey collected data on the ages of the parents of his classmates. Make a data display and use it to find the percent of parents at least 30 years old but under 50 years old.

42, 36, 35, 49, 52, 43, 41, 32, 45, 39, 50, 38, 27, 29, 37, 39

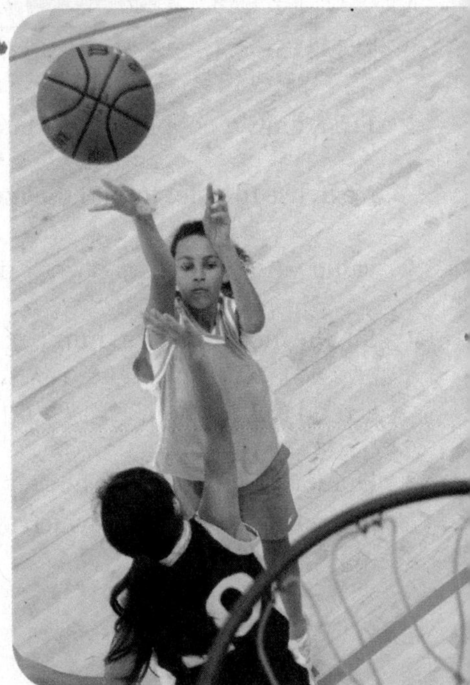

5. What is the mode of the data in Exercise 4?

6. MATHEMATICAL PRACTICE 6 **Explain** An online retail store sold 500 electronic devices in one week. Half of the devices were laptop computers and 20% were desktop computers. The remaining devices sold were tablets. How many tablets were sold? Explain how you found your answer.

7. GO DEEPER A recipe for punch calls for apple juice and cranberry juice. The ratio of apple juice to cranberry juice is 3:2. Tyrone wants to make at least 20 cups of punch, but no more than 30 cups of punch. Describe two different ways he can use apple juice and cranberry juice to make the punch.

8. THINK SMARTER The data set shows the total points scored by the middle school basketball team in the last 14 games. What is the most common number of points scored in a game? Explain how to find the answer using a dot plot.

Total Points Scored						
42	36	35	49	52	43	41
32	45	39	50	38	37	39

Name ___

Chapter 12 Review/Test

1. The data set shows the total number of sandwiches sold each day for 28 days. What is the most common number of sandwiches sold in a day?

Number of sandwiches sold each day						
10	14	11	12	19	13	24
12	12	18	9	17	15	20
20	21	10	13	13	16	19
21	22	18	13	15	14	10

___

2. Michael's teacher asks, "How many items were sold on the first day of the fund raiser?" Explain why this is not a statistical question.

3. Describe the data set by writing the attribute measured, the unit of measure, the likely means of measurement, and the number of observations in the correct location on the chart.

Daily Temperature (°F)						
64	53	61	39	36	43	48

7 | thermometer | degrees Fahrenheit | daily temperature

Attribute	Unit of Measure	Likely Means of Measurement	Number of Observations

GO DIGITAL Assessment Options Chapter Test

4. The numbers of points scored by a football team in 7 different games are 26, 38, 33, 20, 27, 3, and 28. For numbers 4a–4d, select True or False to indicate whether the statement is correct.

4a. The outlier in the data set is 3. ○ True ○ False

4b. The difference between the outlier and the lowest number of points scored is 17. ○ True ○ False

4c. The outlier in this set of data affects the mean by increasing it. ○ True ○ False

5. Mr. Jones gave a quiz to his math class. The students' scores are listed in the table. Make a dot plot of the data.

Math Test Scores				
100	90	40	70	70
90	80	50	70	60
90	70	60	80	100
70	50	80	90	90
80	70	80	90	70

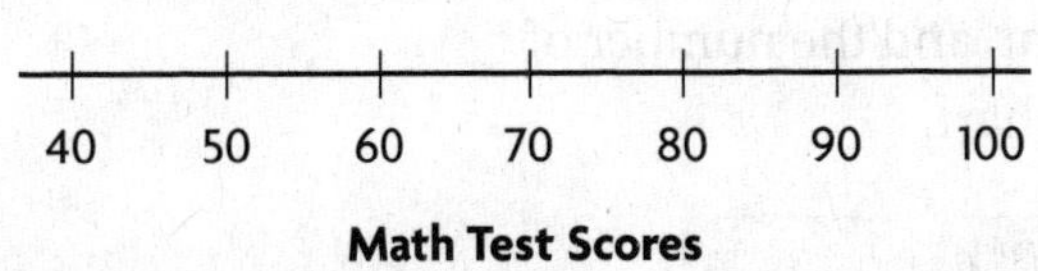

6. Melanie scored 10, 10, 11, and 13 points in her last 4 basketball games.

The mean of the test scores is [10. / 11. / 13.]

The median of the test scores is [10. / 10.5. / 11.]

The mode of the test scores is [10. / 11. / no mode.]

Name ___________________________

7. The Martin family goes out for frozen yogurt to celebrate the last day of school. The costs of their frozen yogurts are $1, $1, $2, and $4. Select True or False for each statement.

7a. The mean cost for the frozen yogurts can be found by adding each cost and dividing that total by 4. ○ True ○ False

7b. The mean cost of the four frozen yogurts is $2. ○ True ○ False

7c. The difference between the greatest cost and the mean is $1. ○ True ○ False

7d. The difference between the least cost and the mean is $1. ○ True ○ False

8. The histogram shows the amount of time students spent on homework for the week. For numbers 8a–8d, choose True or False to indicate whether the statement is correct.

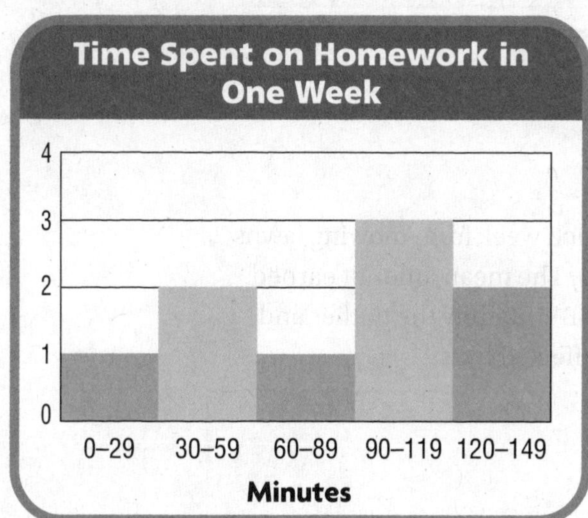

8a. The number of students that spent between 30 minutes and 59 minutes on homework is 2. ○ True ○ False

8b. The greatest number of students spent between 90 minutes and 119 minutes on homework. ○ True ○ False

8c. Five of the students spent less than 60 minutes on homework for the week. ○ True ○ False

8d. Six of the students spent 60 minutes or more on homework for the week. ○ True ○ False

9. The dot plot shows how many games of chess 8 different members of the chess club played in one month. If Jackson is a new member of the chess club, how many games of chess is he likely to play in one month? Explain how the dot plot helped you find the answer.

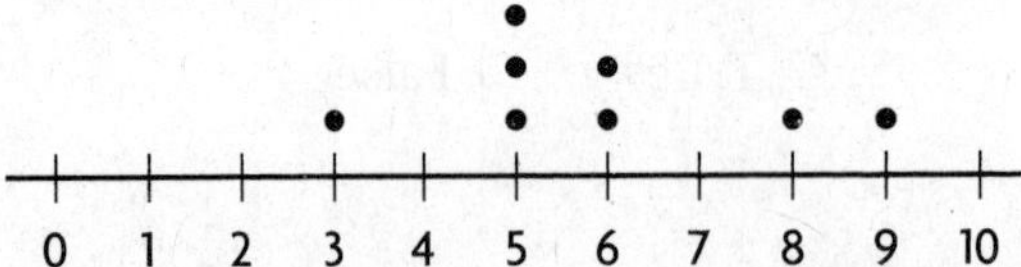

Number of Games Played in One Month

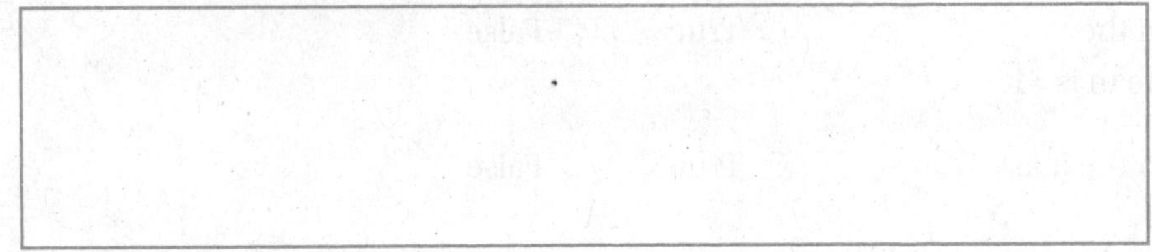

10. Larry is training for a bicycle race. He records how far he rides each day in a table. Find the mode of the data.

Miles Larry Rides each Day					
Monday	Tuesday	Wednesday	Thursday	Friday	Saturday
15	14	12	16	15	15

____

11. The amounts of money Connor earned each week from mowing lawns for 5 weeks are \$12, \$61, \$71, \$52, and \$64. The mean amount earned is \$52 and the median amount earned is \$61. Identify the outlier and describe how the mean and median are affected by it.

12. The frequency table shows the height, in inches, of 12 basketball players. What fraction of the players are 70 inches or taller?

Heights of Basketball Players	
Inches	Frequency
60-69	3
70-79	6
80-89	3

____

Name ____

13. A teacher surveys her students to find out how much time the students spent eating lunch on Monday.

She uses [hours / minutes / seconds] as the unit of measure.

Monday Lunch Time (min)			
15	18	18	14
15	20	16	15
15	19	15	19

14. For numbers 14a–14d, choose Yes or No to indicate whether the question is a statistical question.

14a. What is the height of the tallest tree in the park? ○ Yes ○ No

14b. What is the difference in height between the tallest tree and the shortest tree? ○ Yes ○ No

14c. How tall is the cypress tree on the north side of the lake this morning? ○ Yes ○ No

14d. How many trees are taller than 30 feet? ○ Yes ○ No

15. Five friends have 8, 6, 5, 2, and 4 baseball cards to divide equally among themselves.

The fair share of cards for each friend is [4 / 5 / 6] cards.

16. The data set shows the ages of the members of the cheerleading squad. What is the most common age of the members of the squad? Explain how to find the answer using a dot plot.

Ages of Cheerleaders (years)				
8	11	13	12	14
12	10	11	9	11

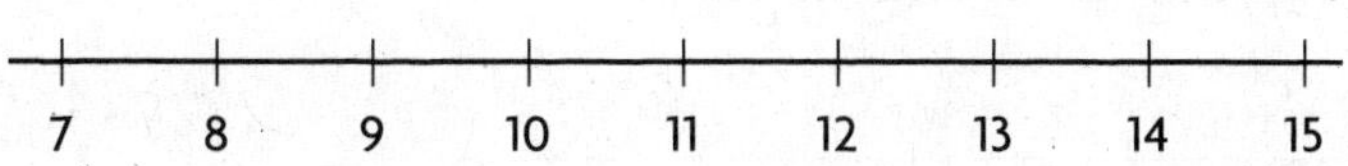

17. The band director kept a record of the number of concert tickets sold by 20 band members. Complete the frequency table by finding the frequency and the relative frequency.

Number of Concert Tickets Sold				
4	6	6	7	7
8	8	9	9	9
8	11	12	11	13
15	14	18	20	19

Number of Concert Tickets Sold		
Number of Tickets Sold	Frequency	Relative Frequency (%)
1-5	1	5
6-10		
11-15		
16-20		

18. Gilbert is training for a marathon by running each week. The table shows the distances, in miles, that he ran each week during the first 7 weeks.

Week	1	2	3	4	5	6	7
Distance (miles)	8	10	9	10	15	18	21

Part A

Gilbert set a goal that the mean number of miles he runs in 7 weeks is at least 14 miles. Did Gilbert reach his goal? Use words and numbers to support your answer.

Part B

Suppose Gilbert had run 18 miles during week 5 and 22 miles during week 6. Would he have reached his goal? Use words and numbers to support your answer.

Chapter

13 Variability and Data Distributions

Show What You Know

Check your understanding of important skills.

Name ______________________

Place the First Digit Tell where to place the first digit. Then divide.

1. $4\overline{)872}$ __________ place

2. $8\overline{)256}$ __________ place

Order of Operations Evaluate the expression.

3. $9 + 4 \times 8$ __________

4. $2 \times 7 + 5$ __________

5. $6 \div (3 - 2)$ __________

6. $(12 - 3^2) \times 5$ __________

7. $2^3 \times (22 \div 2)$ __________

8. $(8 - 2)^2 - 9$ __________

9. $(9 - 2^3) + 8$ __________

10. $(27 + 9) \div 3$ __________

Mean Find the mean for the set of data.

11. 285, 420, 345, 390 __________

12. 0.2, 0.23, 0.16, 0.21, 0.2 __________

13. \$33, \$48, \$55, \$52 __________

14. 8.1, 7.2, 8.4 __________

Raina watched two of her friends play a game of darts. She has to pick one of them to be her partner in a tournament. Be a Math Detective and help her figure out which of her friends is a more consistent dart player.

____

____

Dart Scores						
Hector	15	5	7	19	3	19
Marin	12	10	11	11	10	14

Vocabulary Builder

▶ Visualize It

Sort the review words into the chart.

Review Words
histogram
mean
median
mode

Preview Words
box plot
lower quartile
interquartile range
measure of variability
range
upper quartile

Measures of Center

How Do I Find It?

Find the sum of all the data values and divide the sum by the number of data values.	Order the data and find the middle value or the mean of the two middle values if the number of values is even.	Find the data value(s) that occurs most often.

▶ Understand Vocabulary

Complete the sentences using the preview words.

1. The median of the upper half of a data set is the ________________.

2. The ________________ is the difference between the greatest value and the least value in a data set.

3. A(n) ________________ is a graph that shows the median, quartiles, least value, and greatest value of a data set.

4. A data set's ________________ is the difference between its upper and lower quartiles.

5. You can describe how spread out a set of data is using a(n) ________________.

GO DIGITAL
• Interactive Student Edition
• Multimedia eGlossary

Name ______________________________

Patterns in Data

Essential Question How can you describe overall patterns in a data set?

Statistics and Probability—6.SP.5c
Also 6.SP.2

MATHEMATICAL PRACTICES
MP.5, MP.7, MP.8

CONNECT Seeing data sets in graphs, such as dot plots and histograms, can help you find and understand patterns in the data.

Unlock the Problem (Real World)

Many lakes and ponds contain freshwater fish species such as bass, pike, bluegills, and trout. Jacob and his friends went fishing at a nearby lake. The dot plot shows the sizes of the fish that the friends caught. What patterns do you see in the data?

Fish Caught

Length (inches)	5	6	7	8	9	10	11	12	13	14
Dots	1	3	2	0	0	0	2	3	1	1

- Circle any spaces with no data.
- Place a box around any groups of data.

Analyze the dot plot.

A *gap* is an interval that contains no data.

Does the dot plot contain any gaps?

If so, where? ______________

A *cluster* is a group of data points that lie within a small interval.

There is a cluster from ______ to ______ and another cluster from ______ to ______.

So, there were no fish from ______ to ______ inches long,

and there were two clusters of fish measuring from ______ to ______ inches long and from ______ to ______ inches long.

Math Talk Mathematical Practices

What is the mode(s) of the data? **Explain** how you know.

1. Summarize the information shown in the dot plot.

____

____

2. MATHEMATICAL PRACTICE 8 **Draw Conclusions** What conclusion can you draw about why the data might have this pattern?

____

____

You can also analyze patterns in data that are displayed in histograms. Some data sets have symmetry about a peak, while others do not.

Example Analyze a histogram.

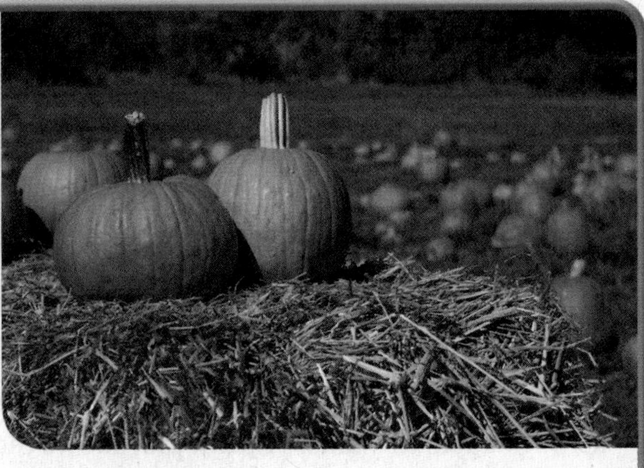

Erica made this histogram to show the weights of the pumpkins grown at her father's farm in October. What patterns do you see in the data?

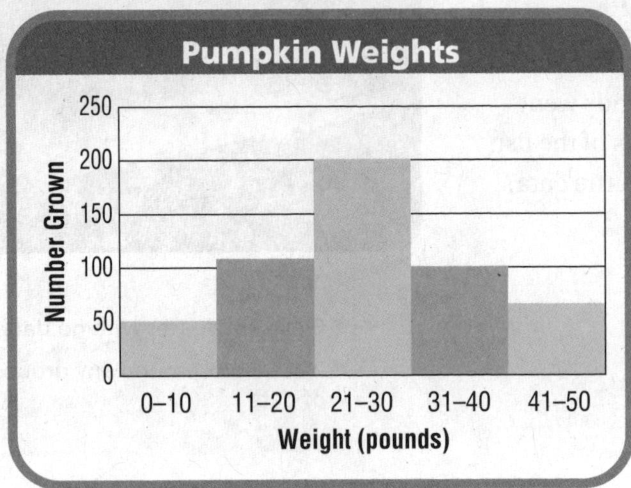

STEP 1 Identify any peaks in the data.

The histogram has ______ peak(s).

The interval representing the greatest number of pumpkins is for weights between ______ and ______ pounds.

STEP 2 Describe how the data changes across the intervals.

The number of pumpkins increases from 0 to ______ pounds and ____________ from 30 to 50 pounds.

STEP 3 Describe any symmetry the graph has.

If I draw a vertical line through the interval for ______ to ______ pounds, the left and right parts of the histogram are very close to being mirror images. The histogram ____________ line symmetry.

Remember

A geometric figure has line symmetry if you can draw a line through it so that the two parts are mirror images of each other.

So, the data values increase to one peak in the interval for ______ to ______ pounds and then decrease. The data set ____________ line symmetry about the peak.

Name ______________________

Share and Show

For 1–3, use the dot plot.

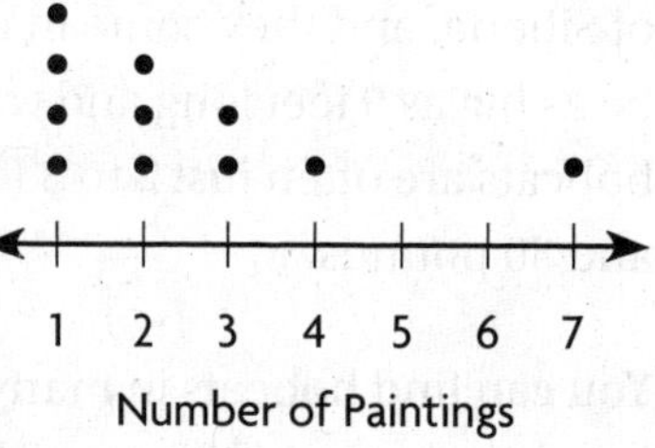

1. The dot plot shows the number of paintings students in the art club displayed at the art show. Does the dot plot contain any gaps?

If so, where? ______________________

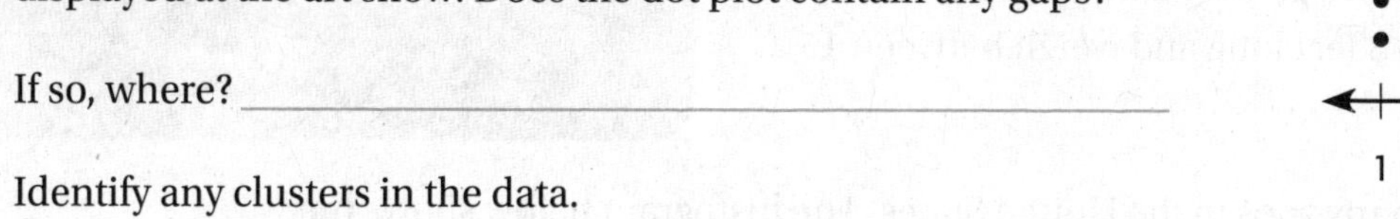

2. Identify any clusters in the data.

____

3. Summarize the information in the dot plot.

____

____

On Your Own

4. GO DEEPER What patterns do you see in the histogram data?

____

____

____

____

____

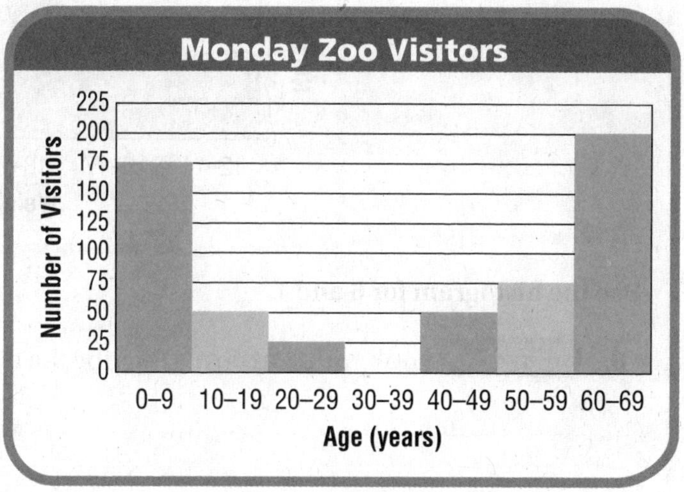

Monday Zoo Visitors

Number of Visitors: 0, 25, 50, 75, 100, 125, 150, 175, 200, 225

Age (years): 0–9, 10–19, 20–29, 30–39, 40–49, 50–59, 60–69

5. THINK SMARTER The dot plot shows the number of errors made by a baseball team in the first 16 games of the season. For numbers 7a-7e, choose Yes or No to indicate whether the statement is correct.

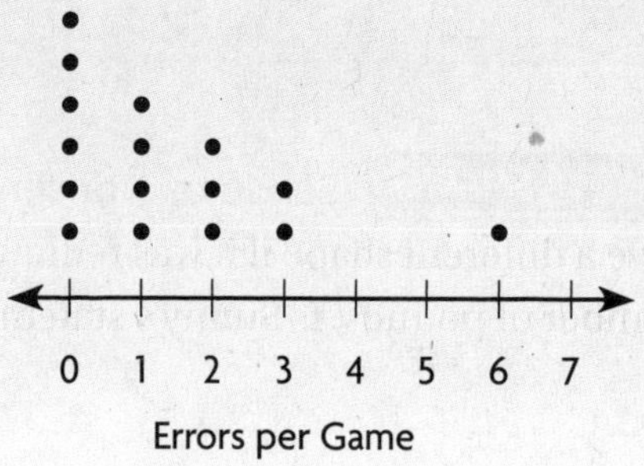

0 1 2 3 4 5 6 7

Errors per Game

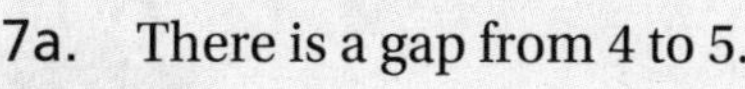 

7a. There is a gap from 4 to 5. ○ Yes ○ No

7b. There is a peak at 0. ○ Yes ○ No

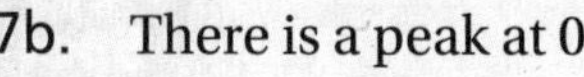 

7c. The dot plot has line symmetry. ○ Yes ○ No

7d. There are two modes. ○ Yes ○ No

7e. There is one cluster. ○ Yes ○ No

Connect to Science

Big Cats

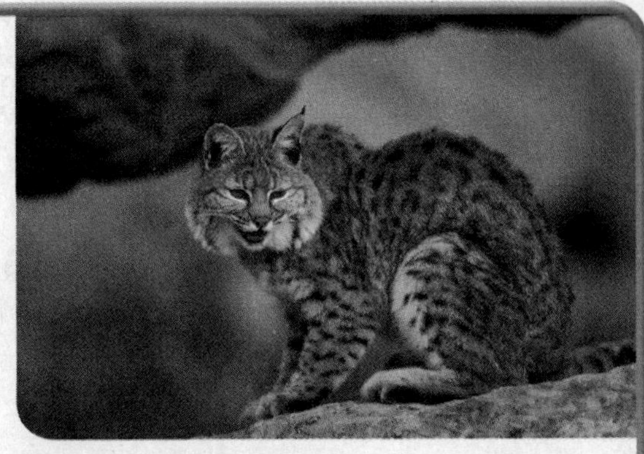

There are 41 species of cats living in the world today. Wild cats live in places as different as deserts and the cold forests of Siberia, and they come in many sizes. Siberian tigers may be as big as 9 feet long and weigh over 2,000 pounds, while bobcats are often just 2 to 3 feet long and weigh between 15 and 30 pounds.

You can find bobcats in many zoos in the United States. The histogram below shows the weights of several bobcats. The weights are rounded to the nearest pound.

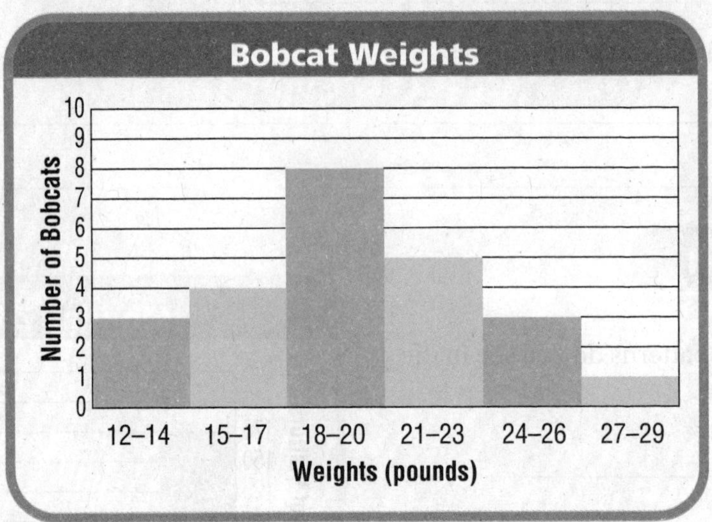

Use the histogram for 6 and 7.

6. MATHEMATICAL PRACTICE 7 **Look for a Pattern** Describe the overall shape of the histogram.

____

____

____

____

7. THINK SMARTER **Sense or Nonsense?** Sunny says that the graph might have a different shape if it was redrawn as a bar graph with one bar for each number of pounds. Is Sunny's statement sense or nonsense? Explain.

____

____

____

FOR MORE PRACTICE: Standards Practice Book

Name ______________________________

Box Plots

Essential Question How can you use box plots to display data?

Statistics and Probability—6.SP.4

MATHEMATICAL PRACTICES
MP.3, MP.4, MP.6

The median is the middle value, or the mean of the two middle values, when data is written in order. The **lower quartile** is the median of the lower half of a data set, and the **upper quartile** is the median of the upper half of a data set.

Unlock the Problem

In 1885, a pair of jeans cost $1.50. Today, the cost of jeans varies greatly. The chart lists the prices of jeans at several different stores. What are the median, lower quartile, and upper quartile of the data?

Prices of Jeans								
$35	$28	$42	$50	$24	$75	$47	$32	$60

Find the median, lower quartile, and upper quartile.

STEP 1 Order the numbers from least to greatest.

$24 $28 $32 $35 $42 $47 $50 $60 $75

STEP 2 Circle the middle number, the median.

The median is $______.

STEP 3 Calculate the upper and lower quartiles.

Find the median of each half of the data set.

Think: If a data set has an even number of values, the median is the mean of the two middle values.

ERROR Alert

When a data set has an odd number of values, do not include the median when finding the lower and upper quartiles.

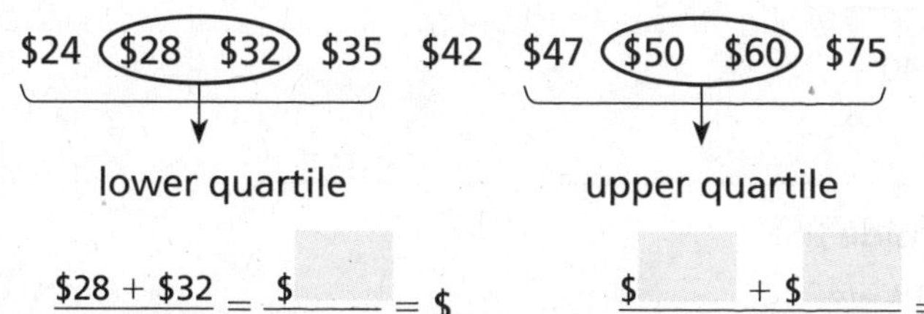

$\frac{\$28 + \$32}{2} = \frac{\$\_\_\_}{2} = \$\_\_\_\_\_$ $\frac{\$\_\_\_ + \$\_\_\_}{2} = \frac{\$\_\_\_}{2} = \$\_\_\_\_\_$

So, the median is $______, the lower quartile is $______, and the upper quartile is $______.

A **box plot** is a type of graph that shows how data are distributed by using the least value, the lower quartile, the median, the upper quartile, and the greatest value. Below is a box plot showing the data for jean prices from the previous page.

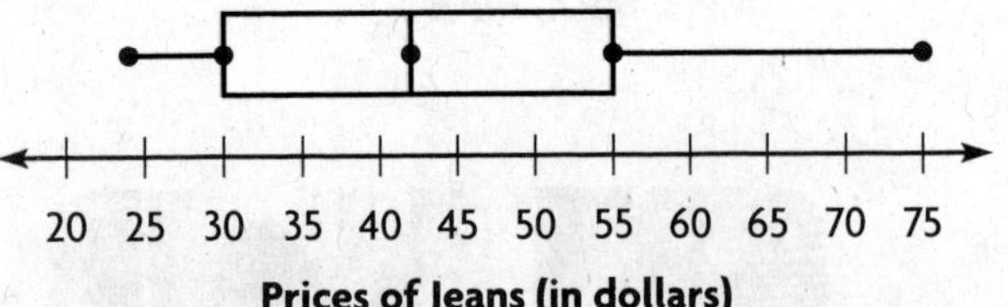

Example Make a box plot.

The data set below represents the ages of the top ten finishers in a 5K race. Use the data to make a box plot.

Ages of Top 10 Runners (in years)									
33	18	21	23	35	19	38	30	23	25

STEP 1 Order the data from least to greatest. Then find the median and the lower and upper quartiles.

18, ______, ______, ______, ______, ______, ______, ______, ______, ______

Median = $\frac{\square + \square}{2}$ = ______ years

Lower quartile = ______ years — The lower quartile is the median of the lower half of the data set, which goes from 18 to 23.

Upper quartile = ______ years — The upper quartile is the median of the upper half of the data set, which goes from 25 to 38.

STEP 2 Draw a number line. Above the number line, plot a point for the least value, the lower quartile, the median, the upper quartile, and the greatest value.

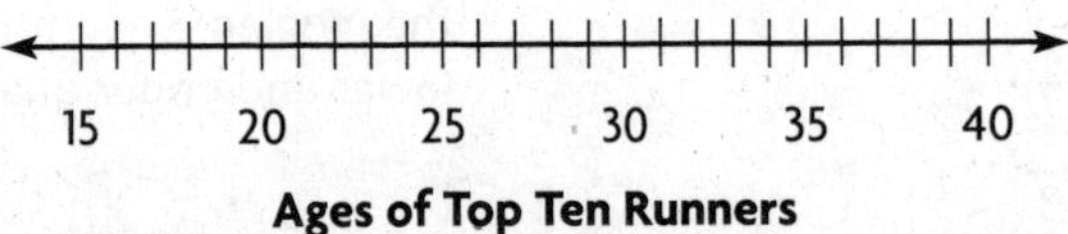

Ages of Top Ten Runners

STEP 3 Draw a box from the lower to upper quartile. Inside the box, draw a vertical line segment through the median. Then draw line segments from the box to the least and greatest values.

Mathematical Practices

Describe the steps for making a box plot.

- MATHEMATICAL PRACTICE 6 **Explain** Would the box plot change if the data point for 38 years were replaced with 40 years? Explain.

____

Name ______________________________

Share and Show

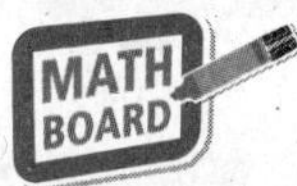

Find the median, lower quartile, and upper quartile of the data.

1. the scores of 11 students on a geography quiz:
87, 72, 80, 95, 86, 80, 78, 92, 88, 76, 90

Order the data from least to greatest. 72, 76, 78, 80, 80, 86, 87, 88, 90, 92, 95

median: ______ lower quartile: ______ upper quartile: ______

2. the lengths, in seconds, of 9 videos posted online:
50, 46, 51, 60, 62, 50, 65, 48, 53

median: ______ lower quartile: ______ upper quartile: ______

3. Make a box plot to display the data set in Exercise 2.

Mathematical Practices

How are box plots and dot plots similar? How are they different?

On Your Own

Find the median, lower quartile, and upper quartile of the data.

4. 13, 24, 37, 25, 56, 49, 43, 20, 24

median: ______

lower quartile: ______

upper quartile: ______

5. 61, 23, 49, 60, 83, 56, 51, 64, 84, 27

median: ______

lower quartile: ______

upper quartile: ______

6. The chart shows the height of trees in a park. Display the data in a box plot.

Tree Heights (feet)											
8	12	20	30	25	18	18	8	10	28	26	29

5 10 15 20 25 30 35

Tree Heights (feet)

7. MATHEMATICAL PRACTICE 1 **Analyze** Eric made this box plot for the data set below. Explain his error.

Number of Books Read								
5	13	22	8	31	37	25	24	10

Problem Solving • Applications

THINK SMARTER Pose a Problem

8. The box plots show the number of flights delayed per day for two different airlines. Which data set is more spread out?

Find the distance between the least and greatest values for each data set.

Airline A: greatest value − least value =

______ − ______ = ______

Airline B: greatest value − least value =

______ − ______ = ______

So, the data for __________ is more spread out.

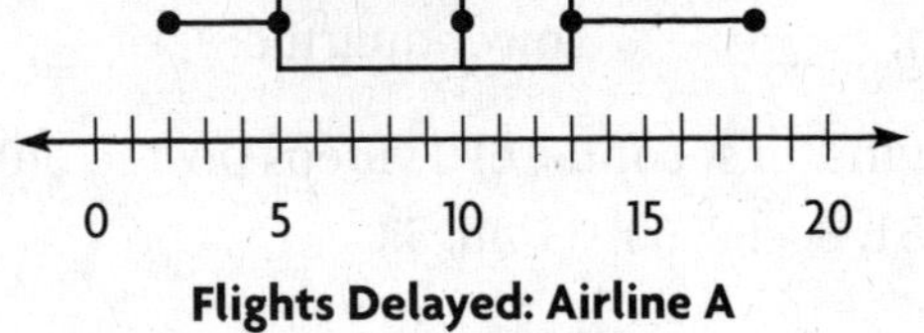

Flights Delayed: Airline A

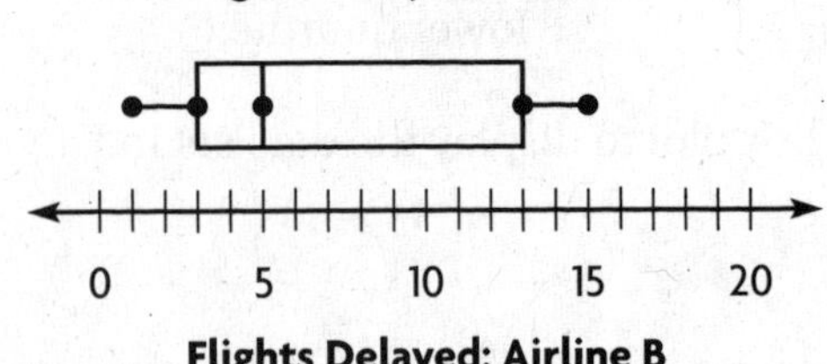

Flights Delayed: Airline B

Write a new problem that can be solved using the data in the box plots.

Pose a Problem

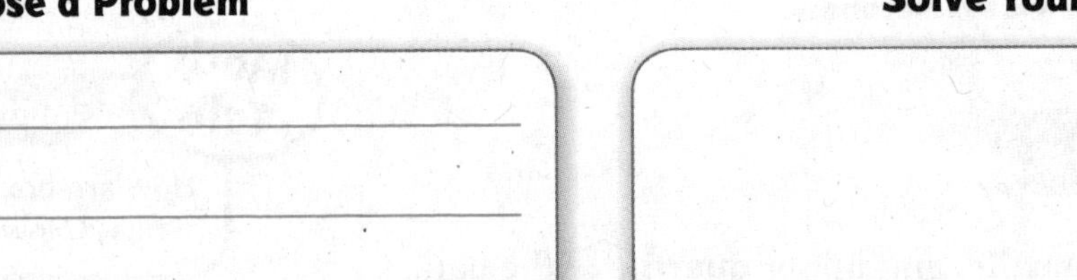

Solve Your Problem

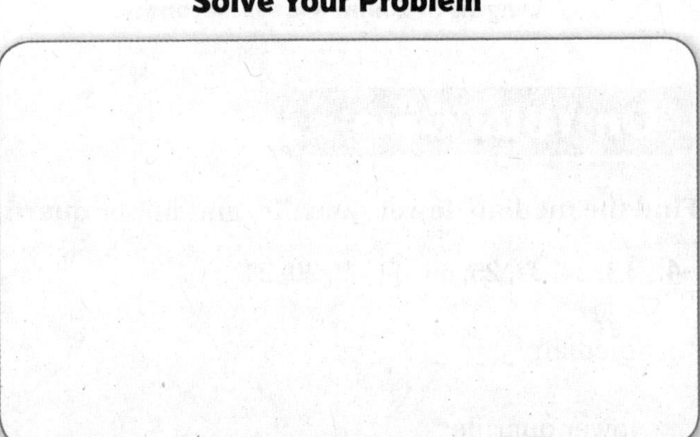

9. THINK SMARTER The data set shows the cost of the dinner specials at a restaurant on Friday night.

Cost of Dinner Specials ($)										
30	24	24	16	24	25	19	28	18	19	26

The median is [19. / 24. / 25.] The lower quartile is [16. / 18. / 19.] The upper quartile is [26. / 28. / 30.]

FOR MORE PRACTICE:
Standards Practice Book

Name ______________________________

Mean Absolute Deviation

Essential Question How do you calculate the mean absolute deviation of a data set?

Statistics and Probability—6.SP.5c

MATHEMATICAL PRACTICES
MP.4, MP.6, MP.8

One way to describe a set of data is with the mean. However, two data sets may have the same mean but look very different when graphed. When interpreting data sets, it is important to consider how far away the data values are from the mean.

Investigate

Hands On

Materials ■ counters, large number line from 0–10

The number of magazine subscriptions sold by two teams of students for a drama club fundraiser is shown below. The mean number of subscriptions for each team is 4.

Team A				
3	3	4	5	5

Team B				
0	1	4	7	8

A. Make a dot plot of each data set using counters for the dots. Draw a vertical line through the mean.

B. Count to find the distance between each counter and the mean. Write the distance underneath each counter.

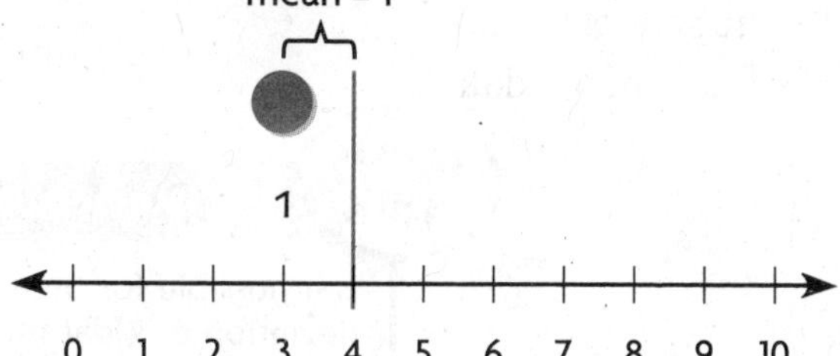

C. Find the mean of the distances for each data set.

Team A

$\frac{1 + \square + \square + \square + \square}{5} = \frac{\square}{5} = \square$

Team B

$\frac{\square + \square + \square + \square + \square}{\square} = \frac{\square}{\square} = \square$

Draw Conclusions

1. THINK SMARTER Which data set, Team A or B, looks more spread out in your dot plots? Which data set had a greater average distance from the mean? Explain how these two facts are connected.

2. MATHEMATICAL PRACTICE 2 **Reason Quantitatively** The table shows the average distance from the mean for the heights of players on two basketball teams. Tell which set of heights is more spread out. Explain how you know.

Heights of Players

Team	Average Distance from Mean (in.)
Chargers	2.8
Wolverines	1.5

Make Connections

The mean of the distances of data values from the mean of the data set is called the **mean absolute deviation**. As you learned in the Investigation, mean absolute deviation is a way of describing how spread out a data set is.

The dot plot shows the ages of gymnasts registered for the school team. The mean of the ages is 10. Find the mean absolute deviation of the data.

STEP 1 Label each dot with its distance from the mean.

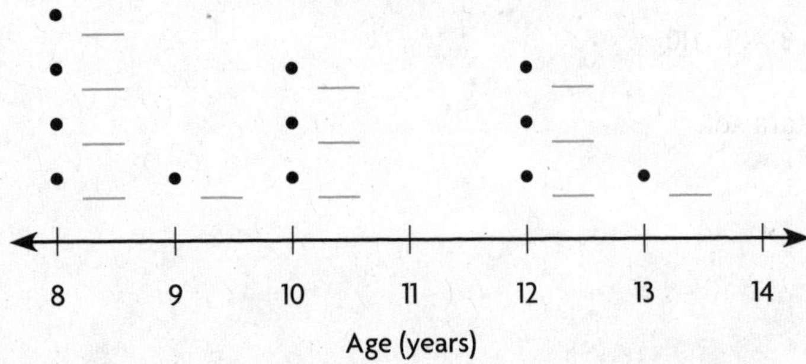

Math Talk **Mathematical Practices**

Is it possible for the mean absolute deviation of a data set to be zero? Explain.

STEP 2 Find the mean of the distances.

$\frac{\_ + \_ + \_ + \_ + \_ + \_ + \_ + \_ + \_ + \_ + \_ + \_}{\_} = \frac{\_}{\_} = \_$

So, the mean absolute deviation of the data is ______ years.

Name ______________________________

Share and Show

Use counters or a dot plot to find the mean absolute deviation of the data.

1. Find the mean absolute deviation for both data sets. Explain which data set is more spread out.

the number of laps Shawna swam on 5 different days:

5, 6, 6, 8, 10

mean = 7

$\frac{2 + \square + \square + \square + \square}{\square} = \frac{\square}{\square} = \square$

mean absolute deviation = ______ laps

the number of laps Lara swam on 5 different days:

1, 3, 7, 11, 13

mean = 7

mean absolute deviation = ______ laps

The data set of ____________ laps is more spread out because the mean absolute deviation of her data is ____________.

Use the dot plot to find the mean absolute deviation of the data.

2. mean = 7 books

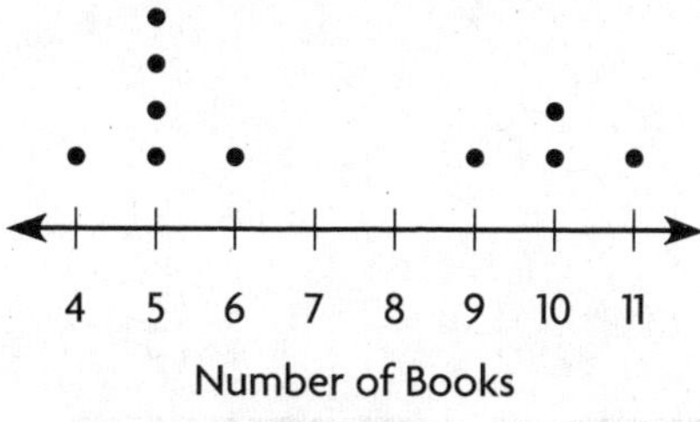

mean absolute deviation = ____________

3. mean = 29 pounds

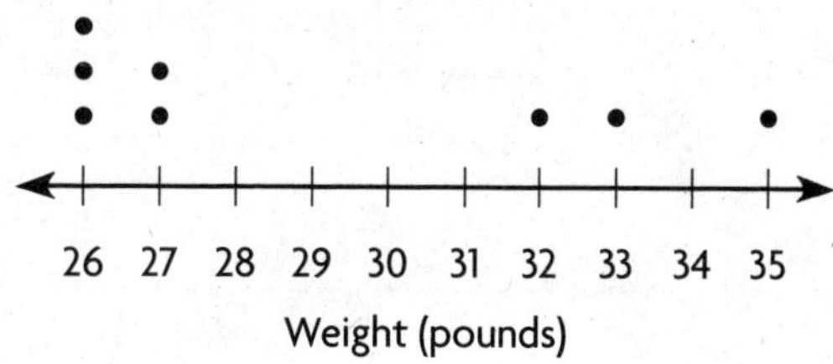

mean absolute deviation = ____________

4. **WRITE** ▸*Math* The mean absolute deviation of the number of daily visits to Scott's website for February is 167.7. In March, the absolute mean deviation is 235.9. In which month did the number of visits to Scott's website vary more? Explain how you know.

____

5. **MATHEMATICAL PRACTICE 4** **Write an Inequality** **Algebra** In April, the data for Scott's website visits are less spread out than they were in February. Use a to represent the mean absolute deviation for April. Write an inequality to describe the possible values of a.

____

Problem Solving • Applications

9. GO DEEPER Use the dot plot.

Days of Precipitation											
Jan	Feb	Mar	Apr	May	Jun	Jul	Aug	Sep	Oct	Nov	Dev
10	12	13	18	10	8	7	6	16	14	8	10

The mean of the data is 11. What is the mean absolute deviation of the data?

____

7. THINK SMARTER Suppose all of the players on a basketball team had the same height. Explain how you could use reasoning to find the mean absolute deviation of the players' heights.

____

____

____

8. MATHEMATICAL PRACTICE 6 Explain Tell how an outlier that is much greater than the mean would affect the mean absolute deviation of the data set. Explain your reasoning.

____

____

____

9. THINK SMARTER The data set shows the number of soccer goals scored by players in 3 games.

Number of Goals Scored			
Player A	1	2	1
Player B	2	2	2
Player C	3	2	1

For numbers 9a–9c, choose Yes or No to indicate whether the statement is correct.

9a. The mean absolute deviation of Player A is 1. ○ Yes ○ No

9b. The mean absolute deviation of Player B is 0. ○ Yes ○ No

9c. The mean absolute deviation of Player C is greater than the mean absolute deviation of Player A. ○ Yes ○ No

FOR MORE PRACTICE:
Standards Practice Book

Name ______________________________

Measures of Variability

Essential Question How can you summarize a data set by using range, interquartile range, and mean absolute deviation?

Statistics and Probability— 6.SP.5c
Also 6.SP.2, 6.SP.3

MATHEMATICAL PRACTICES
MP.1, MP.7, MP.8

CONNECT A **measure of variability** is a single value used to describe how spread out a set of data values are. The mean absolute deviation is a measure of variability.

Unlock the Problem

In gym class, the students recorded how far they could jump. The data set below gives the distances in inches that Manuel jumped. What is the mean absolute deviation of the data set?

Manuel's Jumps (in inches)					
54	58	56	59	60	55

Find the mean absolute deviation.

STEP 1 Find the mean of the data set.

Add the data values and divide the sum by the number of data values.

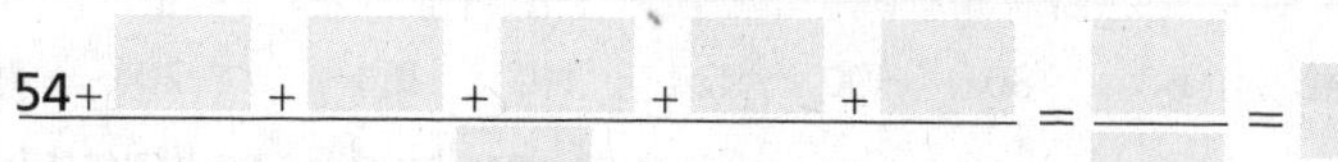

$\frac{54 + \square + \square + \square + \square + \square}{\square} = \frac{\square}{\square} = \square$

The mean of the data set is ______ inches.

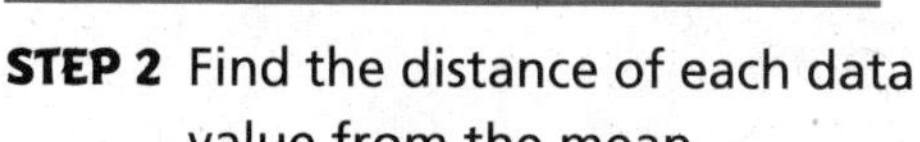

STEP 2 Find the distance of each data value from the mean.

Subtract the lesser value from the greater value.

Data Value	Subtract (Mean = 57)	Distance between data value and the mean
54	57 − 54 =	3
58	58 − 57 =	
56	57 − 56 =	
59	59 − 57 =	
60	60 − 57 =	
55	57 − 55 =	
Total of distances from the mean:		

STEP 3 Add the distances.

STEP 4 Find the mean of the distances.

Divide the sum of the distances by the number of data values.

______ ÷ 6 = ______

So, the mean absolute deviation of the data is ______ inches.

Math Talk — **Mathematical Practices**

Give an example of a data set that has a small mean absolute deviation. **Explain** how you know that the mean absolute deviation is small without doing any calculations.

Range is the difference between the greatest value and the least value in a data set. **Interquartile range** is the difference between the upper quartile and the lower quartile of a data set. Range and interquartile range are also measures of variability.

Example Use the range and interquartile range to compare the data sets.

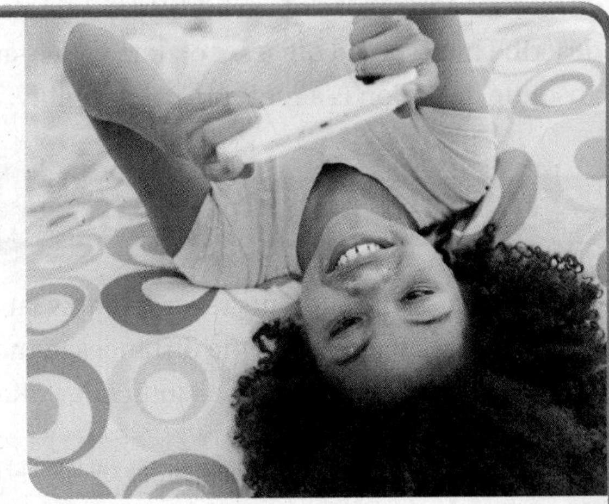

The box plots show the price in dollars of the handheld game players at two different electronic stores. Find the range and interquartile range for each data set. Then compare the variability of the prices of the handheld game players at the two stores.

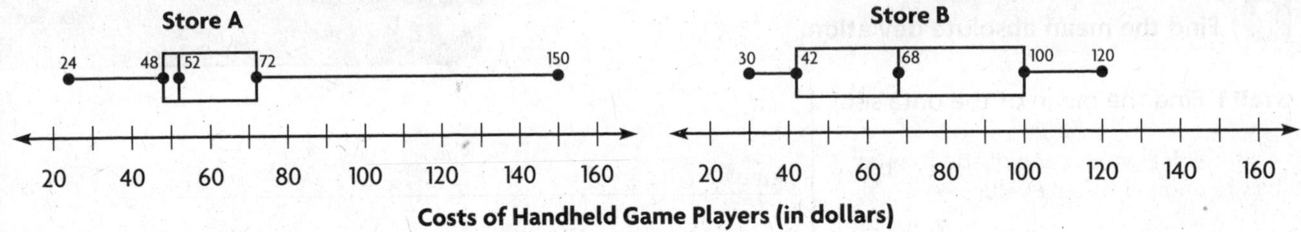

	STORE A	STORE B
Calculate the range. Find the difference between the greatest and least values.	150 − 24 = ______ The range for Store A is ______.	120 − ______ = ______ The range for Store B is ______.
Calculate the interquartile range. Find the difference between the upper quartile and lower quartile.	72 − 48 = ______ The interquartile range for Store A is ______.	100 − ______ = ______ The interquartile range for Store B is ______.

So, Store A has a greater ______________, but Store B has a greater ______________.

Math Talk **Mathematical Practices**

Explain how range and interquartile range are alike and how they are different.

Name ______________________

Share and Show

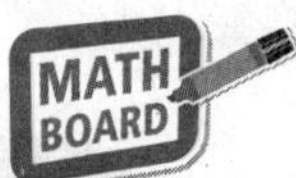

1. Find the range and interquartile range of the data in the box plot.

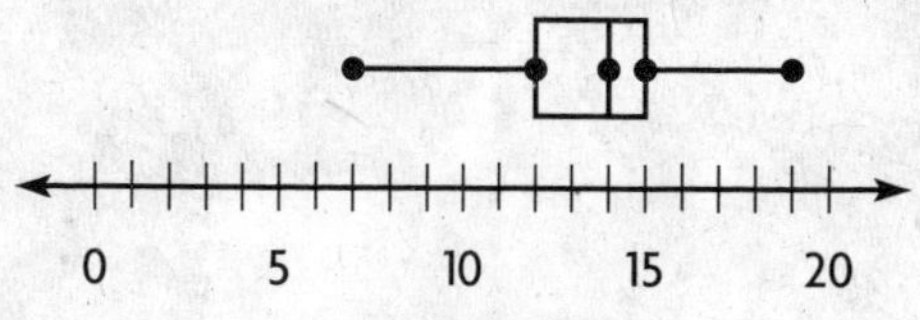

For the range, find the difference between the greatest and least values.

_____ − _____ = _____

range: $ _____

For the interquartile range, find the difference between the upper and lower quartiles.

_____ − _____ = _____

interquartile range: $ _____

Practice: Copy and Solve Find the mean absolute deviation for the data set.

2. heights in inches of several tomato plants:

16, 18, 18, 20, 17, 20, 18, 17

mean absolute deviation: __________

3. times in seconds for students to run one lap:

68, 60, 52, 40, 64, 40

mean absolute deviation: __________

Mathematical Practices

Explain how to find mean absolute deviation of a data set.

On Your Own

Use the box plot for 4 and 5.

4. What is the range of the data? _____

5. What is the interquartile range of the data?

____

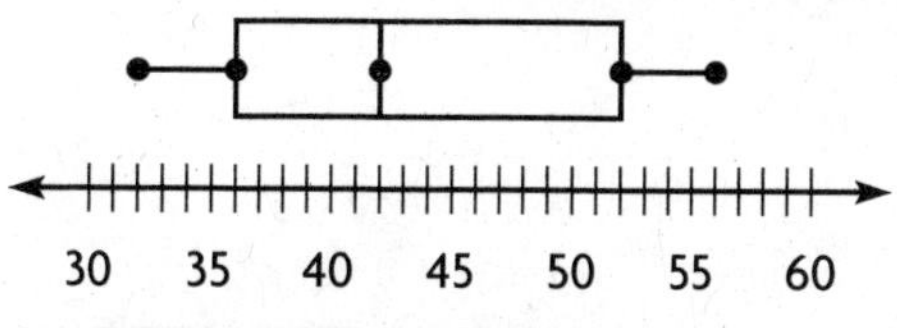

Practice: Copy and Solve Find the mean absolute deviation for the data set.

6. times in minutes spent on a history quiz

35, 35, 32, 34, 34, 32, 34, 36

mean absolute deviation: __________

7. number of excused absences for one semester:

1, 2, 1, 10, 9, 9, 10, 6, 1, 1

mean absolute deviation: __________

8. The chart shows the price of different varieties of dog food at a pet store. Find the range, interquartile range, and the mean absolute deviation of the data set.

Cost of Bag of Dog Food ($)									
18	24	20	26	24	20	32	20	16	20

____

____

Problem Solving • Applications

9. GO DEEPER Hyato's family began a walking program. They walked 30, 45, 25, 35, 40, 30, and 40 minutes each day during one week. At the right, make a box plot of the data. Then find the interquartile range.

____

10. MATHEMATICAL PRACTICE 6 **Compare** Jack recorded the number of minutes his family walked each day for a month. The range of the data is 15. How does this compare to the data for Hyato's family?

____

____

____

20 25 30 35 40 45 50 55 60

Time Spent Walking (in minutes)

11. THINK SMARTER **Sense or Nonsense?** Nathan claims that the interquartile range of a data set can never be greater than its range. Is Nathan's claim sense or nonsense? Explain.

____

____

____

12. THINK SMARTER The box plot shows the heights of corn stalks from two different farms.

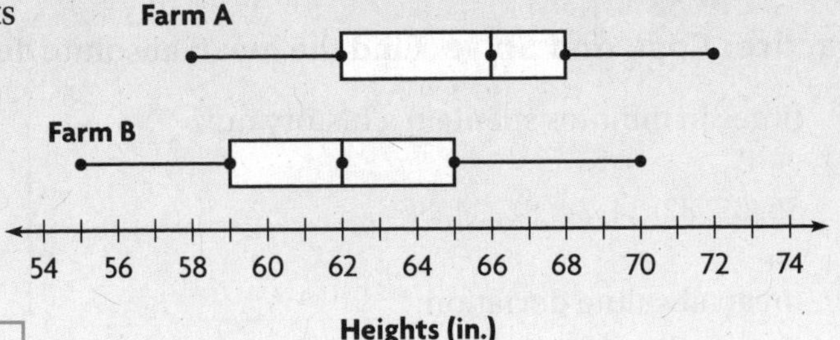

The range of Farm A's heights is [the same as / less than / greater than] the range of Farm B's heights.

FOR MORE PRACTICE:
Standards Practice Book

Name ______________________________

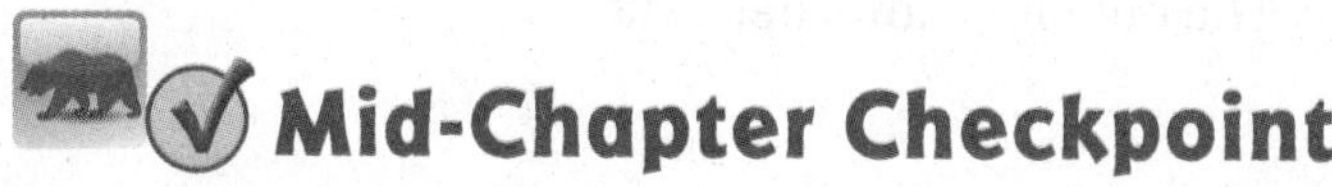

Mid-Chapter Checkpoint

Vocabulary

Vocabulary
box plot
interquartile range
mean absolute deviation
measure of variability
range

Choose the best term from the box to complete the sentence.

1. The ______________ is the difference between the median of the upper half and the median of the lower half of a data set. (p. 527)

2. A graph that shows the median, quartiles, and least and greatest values of a data set is called a(n) ______________. (p. 520)

3. The difference between the greatest value and the least value in a data set is the ______________. (p. 528)

4. The ______________ is the mean of the distances between the values of a data set and the mean of the data set. (p. 524)

Concepts and Skills

5. Make a box plot for this data set: 73, 65, 68, 72, 70, 74. (6.SP.4)

Find the mean absolute deviation of the data. (6.SP.5c)

6. 43, 46, 48, 40, 38

7. 26, 20, 25, 21, 24, 27, 26, 23

8. 99, 70, 78, 85, 76, 81

Find the range and interquartile range of the data. (6.SP.5c)

9. 2, 4, 8, 3, 2

10. 84, 82, 86, 87, 88, 83, 84

11. 39, 22, 33, 45, 42, 40, 28

12. Yasmine keeps track of the number of hockey goals scored by her school's team at each game. The dot plot shows her data.

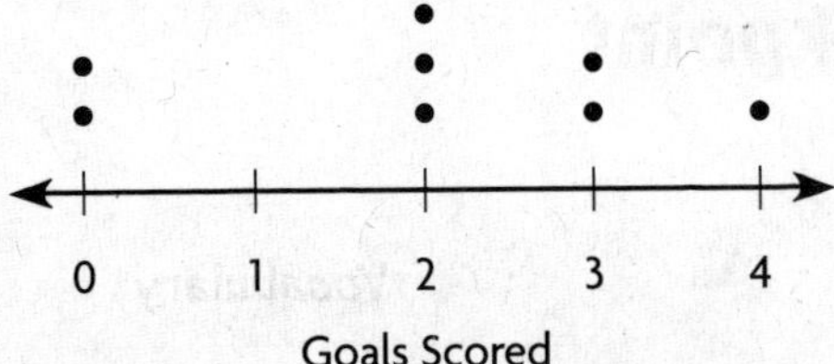

Where is there a gap in the data? (6.SP.5c)

____

13. What is the interquartile range of the data shown in the dot plot with Question 12? (6.SP.5c)

____

14. Randall's teacher added up the class scores for the quarter and used a histogram to display the data. How many peaks does the histogram have? (6.SP.5c)

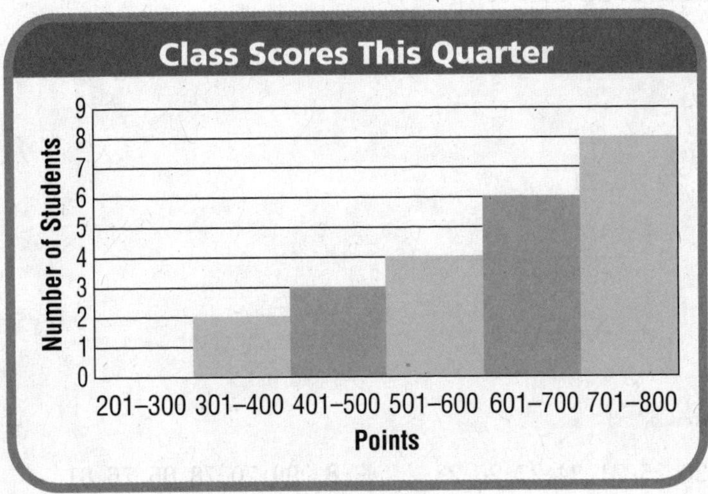

____

15. In a box plot of the data below, where would the box be drawn? (6.SP.4)

55, 37, 41, 62, 50, 49, 64

____

Name ____________________

Choose Appropriate Measures of Center and Variability

Statistics and Probabiltiy—6.SP.5d

MATHEMATICAL PRACTICES
MP.1, MP.2, MP.3

Essential Question How can you choose appropriate measures of center and variability to describe a data set?

Outliers, gaps, and clusters in a set of data can affect both the measures of center and variability. Some measures of center and variability may describe a particular set of data better than others.

Unlock the Problem (Real World)

Thomas is writing an article for the school newsletter about a paper airplane competition. In the distance category, Kara's airplanes flew 17 ft, 16 ft, 18 ft, 15 ft, and 2 ft. Should Thomas use the mean, median, or mode to best describe Kara's results? Explain your reasoning.

- Do you need to order the numbers?

____

____

____

____

Find the mean, median, and mode and compare them.

Mean = $\frac{\square + \square + \square + \square + \square}{\square}$

$= \frac{\square}{\square} = \square$

Order the data from least to greatest to find the median.

______, ______, ______, ______, ______

Median = ______

The data set has no repeated values so there is no __________.

The mean is __________ than 4 of the 5 values, so it is not a good description of the center of the data. The __________ is closer to most of the values, so it is the best way to describe Kara's results.

So, Thomas should use the __________ to describe Kara's results.

Math Idea

The measures of center for some data sets may be very close together. If that is the case, you can list more than one measure as the best way to describe the data.

1. Explain why the two modes may be a better description than the mean or median of the data set 2, 2, 2, 2, 7, 7, 7, 7.

____

____

Example **Mr. Tobin is buying a book online. He compares prices of the book at several different sites. The table shows his results. Make a box plot of the data. Then use the plot to find the range and interquartile range. Which measure better describes the data? Explain your reasoning.**

Prices of Book	
Site	**Price ($)**
1	15
2	35
3	17
4	18
5	5
6	16
7	17

STEP 1 Make a box plot.

Write the data in order from least to greatest. _____, _____, _____, _____, _____, _____, _____

Find the median of the data. median = _____

Find the lower quartile—the median of the lower half of the data. lower quartile = _____

Find the upper quartile—the median of the upper half of the data. upper quartile = _____

Make the plot.

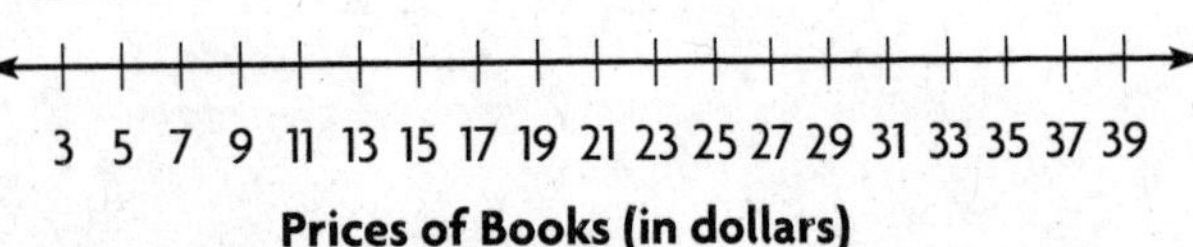

Math Talk **Mathematical Practices**

Describe a data set for which the range is a better description than the interquartile range.

STEP 2 Use the box plot to find the range and the interquartile range.

range = _____ − _____ = _____

interquartile range = _____ − _____ = _____

________ of the seven prices are within the __________.
The other two prices are much higher or lower.

So, the __________ better describes the data because the __________ makes it appear that the data values vary more than they actually do.

2. **THINK SMARTER** How can you tell from the box plot how varied the data are? Explain.

Name ____________________

Share and Show

1. The distances in miles students travel to get to school are 7, 1, 6, 8, 9, and 8. Decide which measure(s) of center best describes the data set. Explain your reasoning.

mean = ____________

median = ____________

mode = ____________

The ____________ is less than 4 of the 6 data points, and the ____________ describes only 2 of the data points. So, the ____________ best describes the data.

2. MATHEMATICAL PRACTICE 4 **Use Graphs** The numbers of different brands of orange juice carried in several stores are 2, 1, 3, 1, 12, 1, 2, 2, and 5. Make a box plot of the data and find the range and interquartile range. Decide which measure better describes the data set and explain your reasoning.

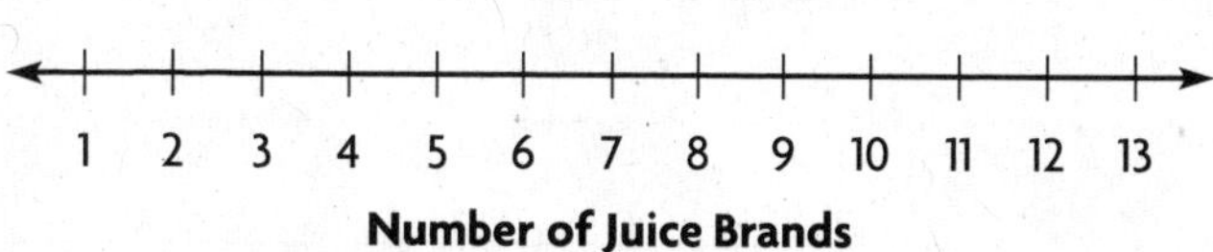

range = ______

interquartile range = ______

____

____

Mathematical Practices

Explain how an outlier affects the range of a data set.

On Your Own

3. MATHEMATICAL PRACTICE 3 **Use Reasoning** The ages of students in a computer class are 14, 13, 14, 15, 14, 35, 14. Decide which measure of center(s) best describes the data set. Explain your reasoning.

mean = ____________

median = ____________

mode = ____________

____

____

4. GO DEEPER Mateo scored 98, 85, 84, 80, 81, and 82 on six math tests. When a seventh math test score is added, the measure of center that best describes his scores is the median. What could the seventh test score be? Explain your reasoning.

____

____

Unlock the Problem 

5. THINK SMARTER Jaime is on the community swim team. The table shows the team's results in the last 8 swim meets. Jaime believes they can place in the top 3 at the next swim meet. Which measure of center should Jaime use to persuade her team that she is correct? Explain.

Swim Team Results	
Meet	**Place**
Meet 1	1
Meet 2	2
Meet 3	3
Meet 4	18
Meet 5	1
Meet 6	2
Meet 7	3
Meet 8	2

a. What do you need to find?

b. What information do you need to solve the problem?

c. What are the measures of center?

d. Which measure of center should Jaime use? Explain.

Personal Math Trainer

8. THINK SMARTER + The numbers of sit-ups students completed in one minute are 10, 42, 46, 50, 43, and 49. The mean of the data values is 40 and the median is 44.5. Which measure of center better describes the data, the mean or median? Use words and numbers to support your answer.

FOR MORE PRACTICE:
Standards Practice Book

Name ______________________________

Apply Measures of Center and Variability

Statistics and Probability—6.SP.3
Also 6.SP.2

MATHEMATICAL PRACTICES
MP.4, MP.6, MP.7

Essential Question What do measures of center and variability indicate about a data set?

Unlock the Problem

Julia is collecting data on her favorite sports teams for a report. The table shows the median and interquartile range of the heights of the players on her favorite baseball and basketball teams. How do the heights of the two teams compare?

Sports Team Data

	Median	Interquartile Range
Baseball Team Heights	70 in.	6 in.
Basketball Team Heights	78 in.	4 in.

Compare the medians and interquartile ranges of the two teams.

Median

The median of the __________ players' heights is ______ inches greater than the median of the __________ players' heights.

Interquartile Range

The interquartile range of the baseball team is __________ the interquartile range of the basketball team, so the heights of the baseball players vary __________ the heights of the basketball team.

So, the players on the __________ team are typically taller than the players on the __________ team, and the heights of the __________ team vary more than the those of the __________ team.

Math Talk — **Mathematical Practices**

What if the mean of the heights of players on the baseball team is 75 in.? **Explain** what this could tell you about the data.

1. Julia randomly picks one player from the basketball team and one player from the baseball team. Given data in the table, can you say that the basketball player will definitely be taller than the baseball player? Explain your reasoning.

____

____

____

Example

Kamira and Joey sold T-shirts during lunch to raise money for a charity. The table shows the number of T-shirts each student sold each day for two weeks. Find the mean and range of each data set, and use these measures to compare the data.

T-Shirts Sold	
Kamira	5, 1, 2, 1, 3, 3, 1, 4, 5, 5
Joey	0, 1, 2, 13, 2, 1, 3, 4, 4, 0

STEP 1 Find the mean of each data set.

Kamira:

Mean = $\frac{\square + \square + \square + \square + \square + \square + \square + \square + \square + \square}{\square}$

$= \frac{\square}{\square} = \square$

Joey:

Mean = $\frac{\square + \square + \square + \square + \square + \square + \square + \square + \square + \square}{\square}$

$= \frac{\square}{\square} = \square$

ERROR Alert

Make sure you include zeroes when you count the total number of data values.

STEP 2 Find the range of each data set.

Kamira:

Range = $\square - \square = \square$

Joey:

Range = $\square - \square = \square$

STEP 3 Compare the mean and range.

The mean of Joey's sales is ______________ the mean of Kamira's sales

The range of Joey's sales is ______________ the range of Kamira's sales.

So, the typical number of shirts Joey sold each day was ______________ the typical number of shirts Kamira sold. However, since the range of Joey's data was ____________ than Kamira's, the number of shirts Joey sold varied ____________ from day to day than the number of shirts Kamira sold.

2. MATHEMATICAL PRACTICE 6 **Explain** Which measure of center would better describe Joey's data set? Explain.

____

____

Name ______________________________

Share and Show

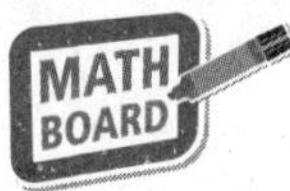

1. Zoe collected data on the number of points her favorite basketball players scored in several games. Use the information in the table to compare the data.

Points Scored		
	Mean	Interquartile Range
Player 1	24	8
Player 2	33	16

The mean of Player 1's points is ____________ the mean of Player 2's points.

The interquartile range of Player 1's points is ____________ the interquartile range of Player 2's points.

So, Player 2 typically scores ____________ points than Player 1, but

Player 2's scores typically vary ____________ Player 1's scores.

2. Mark collected data on the weights of puppies at two animal shelters. Find the median and range of each data set, and use these measures to compare the data.

Puppy Weight, in pounds
Shelter A: 7, 10, 5, 12, 15, 7, 7
Shelter B: 4, 11, 5, 11, 15, 5, 13

____

____

____

____

On Your Own

Kwan analyzed data about the number of hours musicians in her band practice each week. The table shows her results. Use the table for Exercises 3–5.

3. Which two students typically practiced the same amount each week, with about the same variation in practice times?

____

4. Which two students typically practiced the same number of hours, but had very different variations in their practice times?

____

5. Which two students had the same variation in practice times, but typically practiced a different number of hours per week?

____

Hours of Practice per Week		
	Mean	Range
Sally	5	2
Matthew	9	12
Tim	5	12
Jennifer	5	3

Problem Solving • Applications

6. MATHEMATICAL PRACTICE 6 **Compare** The table shows the number of miles Johnny ran each day for two weeks. Find the median and the interquartile range of each data set, and use these measures to compare the data sets.

Miles Run
Week 1 2, 1, 5, 2, 3, 3, 4
Week 2 3, 8, 1, 8, 1, 3, 1

7. THINK SMARTER **Sense or Nonsense?** Yashi made the box plots at right to show the data he collected on plant growth. He thinks that the variation in bean plant growth was about the same as the variation in tomato plant growth. Does Yashi's conclusion make sense? Why or why not?

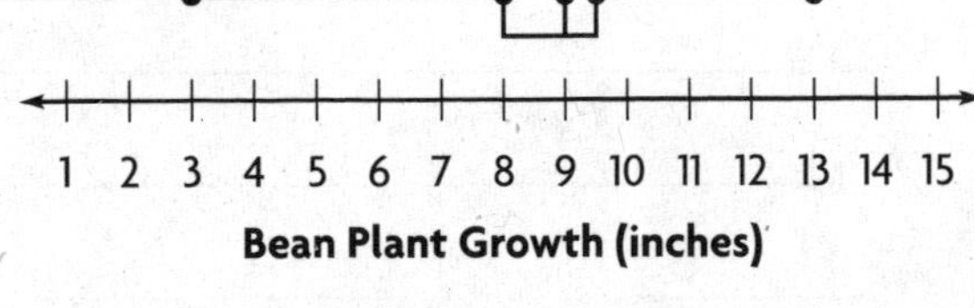

Bean Plant Growth (inches)

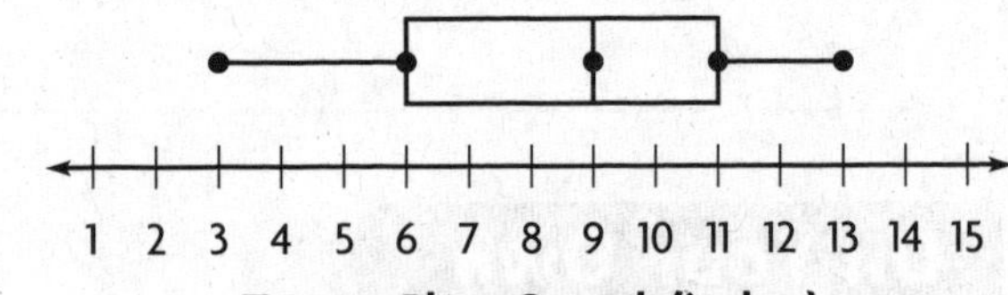

Tomato Plant Growth (inches)

Personal Math Trainer

8. THINK SMARTER + Kylie's teacher collected data on the heights of boys and girls in a sixth grade class. Use the information in the table to compare the data.

Heights (in.)							
Girls	55	60	56	51	60	63	65
Boys	72	68	70	56	58	62	64

The mean of the boys' heights is [the same as / less than / greater than] the mean of the girls' heights.

The range of the boys' heights is [the same as / less than / greater than] the range of the girls' heights.

FOR MORE PRACTICE:
Standards Practice Book

Name ______________________________

Describe Distributions

Essential Question How can you describe the distribution of a data set collected to answer a statistical question?

Statistics and Probability—6.SP.2

MATHEMATICAL PRACTICES
MP.1, MP.3, MP.6

Activity

Ask at least 20 students in your school how many pets they have. Record your results in a frequency table like the one shown.

Pet Survey	
Number of Pets	Frequency
0	
1	
2	
3	
4	

- What statistical question could you use your data to answer?

____

____

Unlock the Problem (Real World)

You can graph your data set to see the center, spread, and overall shape of the data.

Make a dot plot or a histogram of your data.

- What type of graph will you use?

____

- How will you label your graph?

____

____

Math Talk — Mathematical Practices

Explain why you chose the display you used.

Think about the overall distribution of your data.

- Are there any clusters?
- Are there peaks in the data?
- Are there gaps in the data?
- Does the graph have symmetry?

1. MATHEMATICAL PRACTICE 1 **Use Math Vocabulary** Describe the overall distribution of the data. Include information about clusters, gaps, peaks, and symmetry.

____

____

Example **Find the mean, median, mode, interquartile range, and range of the data you collected.**

STEP 1 Find the mean, median, and mode.

Mean: ____________ Median: ____________

Model: ____________

STEP 2 Draw a box plot of your data and use it to find the interquartile range and range.

Interquartile range: ____________ Range: ____________

2. Which measure of center do you think best describes your data? Why?

____

____

3. Does the interquartile range or range best describe your data? Why?

____

____

4. What is the answer to the statistical question you wrote on the previous page?

____

____

Math Talk **Mathematical Practices**

Compare your data set to the data set of one of your classmates. **Describe** how the data sets are similar and how they are different.

Name ______________________

Share and Show

MATH BOARD

Connie asked people their ages as they entered the food court at the mall. Use the histogram of the data she collected for 1–5.

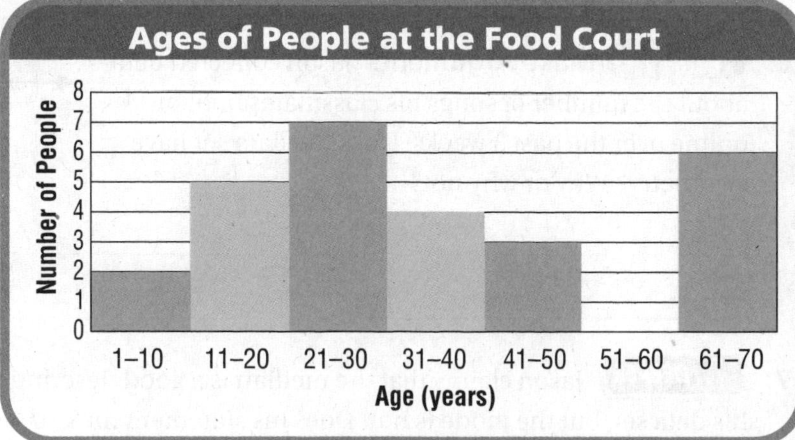

1. What statistical question could Connie ask about her data?

____

____

____

2. Describe any peak or gap in the data.

____

____

3. Does the graph have symmetry? Explain your reasoning.

____

____

On Your Own

4. The lower quartile of the data set is 16.5 years, and the upper quartile is 51.5 years. Find the interquartile range. Is it a better description of the data than the range? Explain your reasoning.

____

____

____

Math Talk — **Mathematical Practices**

Explain what, if any, information you would need to answer the statistical question you wrote in Exercise 1 and what calculations you would need to do.

5. MATHEMATICAL PRACTICE 3 **Make Arguments** The mode of the data is 16 years old. Is the mode a good description of the center of the data? Explain.

____

____

Problem Solving • Applications

Use the dot plot for 6–8.

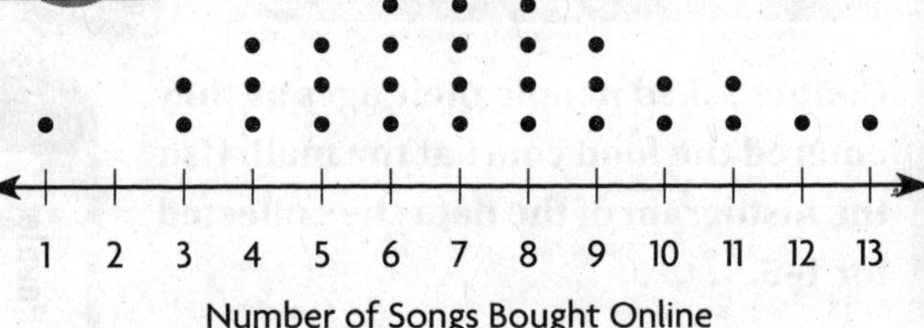

6. MATHEMATICAL PRACTICE 1 **Make Arguments** Jason collected data about the number of songs his classmates bought online over the past 3 weeks. Does the data set have symmetry? Why or why not?

7. GO DEEPER Jason claims that the median is a good description of his data set, but the mode is not. Does his statement make sense? Explain.

8. THINK SMARTER Trinni surveyed her classmates about how many siblings they have. A dot plot of her data increases from 0 siblings to a peak at 1 sibling, and then decreases steadily as the graph goes to 6 siblings. How is Trinnis dot plot similar to Jason's? How is it different?

9. THINK SMARTER Diego collected data on the number of movies seen last month by a random group of students.

Number of Movies Seen Last Month												
0	1	3	2	1	0	5	12	2	3	2	2	3

Draw a box plot of the data and use it to find the interquartile range and range.

Interquartile range ______

Range ______

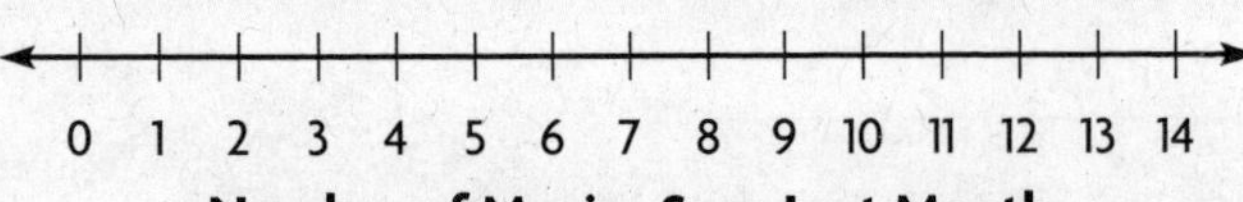

FOR MORE PRACTICE: Standards Practice Book

Name ___________________________

Problem Solving • Misleading Statistics

Essential Question How can you use the strategy *work backward* to draw conclusions about a data set?

Statistics and Probability—6.SP.2
MATHEMATICAL PRACTICES
MP.1, MP.3, MP.6

Unlock the Problem

Mr. Owen wants to move to a town where the daily high temperature is in the 70s most days. A real estate agent tells him that the mean daily high temperature in a certain town is 72°. Other statistics about the town are given in the table. Does this location match what Mr. Owen wants? Why or why not?

Town Statistics for the Past Year (Daily High Temperature)	
Minimum	62°
Maximum	95°
Median	69°
Mean	72°

Use the graphic organizer to help you solve the problem.

Read the Problem

What do I need to find?

I need to decide if the daily high temperature in the town

___________________.

What information do I need?

I need the ___________ in the table.

How will I use the information?

I will work backward from the statistics to draw conclusions

about the ___________ of data.

Solve the Problem

The minimum high temperature is _____.

Think: The high temperature is sometimes ___________ than 70°.

The maximum high temperature is _____.

Think: The high temperature is sometimes ___________ than 80°.

The median of the data set is _____.

Think: The median is the middle value in the data set.

Because the median is 69°, at least half of the days must have high temperatures less than or equal to 69°.

So, the location does not match what Mr. Owen wants. The median

indicates that most days ___________ have a high temperature in the 70s.

Math Talk **Mathematical Practices**

Explain why the mean temperature is misleading in this example.

Try Another Problem

Ms. Gracia is buying a new car. She would like to visit a dealership that has a wide variety of cars for sale at many different price ranges. The table gives statistics about one dealership in her town. Does the dealership match Ms. Gracia's requirements? Explain your reasoning.

Statistics for New Car Prices	
Lowest Price	$12,000
Highest Price	$65,000
Lower Quartile Price	$50,000
Median Price	$55,000
Upper Quartile Price	$60,000

Read the Problem

What do I need to find?	What information do I need?	How will I use the information?

Solve the Problem

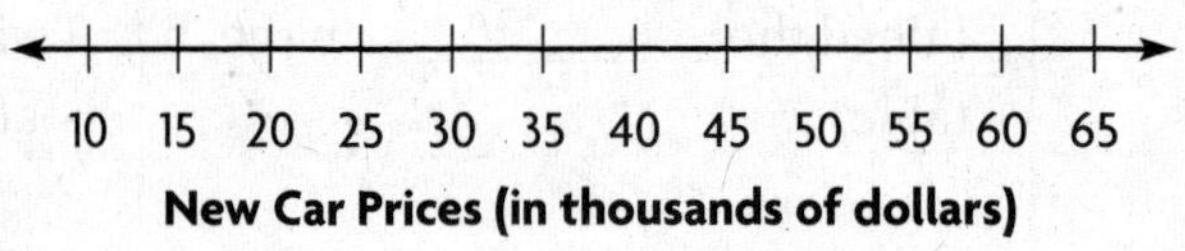

- What would the box plot look like for a dealership that does meet Ms. Gracia's requirements?

Name ___________________________________

Share and Show

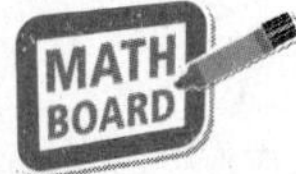

1. Josh is playing a game at the carnival. If his arrow lands on a section marked 25 or higher, he gets a prize. Josh will only play if most of the players win a prize. The carnival worker says that the average (mean) score is 28. The box plot shows other statistics about the game. Should Josh play the game? Explain your reasoning.

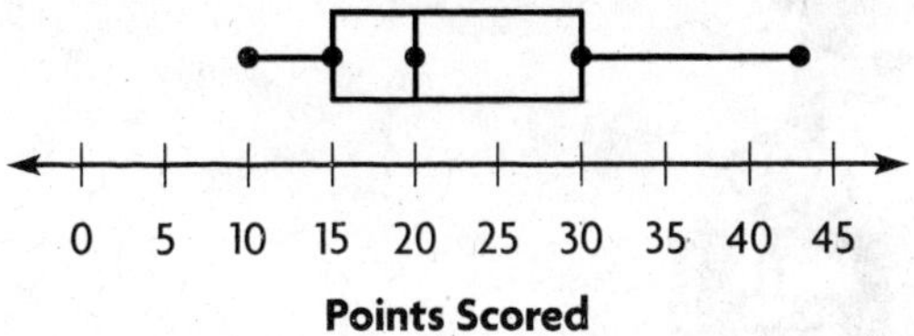

First, look at the median. The median is ______ points.

Next, work backward from the statistics.

The median is the ____________ value of the data.

So, at least ____________ of the values are scores less than or equal to ______.

Finally, use the statistics to draw a conclusion.

____

____

Unlock the Problem

- ✓ Circle important facts.
- ✓ Organize the information.
- ✓ Choose a strategy.
- ✓ Check to make sure you answered the question.

2. THINKSMARTER **What if** a score of 15 or greater resulted in a prize? How would that affect Josh's decision? Explain.

____

____

3. GO DEEPER A store collects data on the sales of DVD players each week for 3 months. The manager determines that the data has a range of 62 players and decides that the weekly sales were very inconsistent. Use the statistics in the table to decide if the manager is correct. Explain your answer.

Weekly DVD Player Sales	
Minimum	16
Maximum	78
Lower quartile	58
Upper quartile	72

____

____

____

On Your Own

4. GO DEEPER Gerard is fencing in a yard that is 21 feet by 18 feet. How many yards of fencing material does Gerrard need? Explain how you found your answer.

5. THINK SMARTER Susanna wants to buy a fish that grows to be about 4 in. long. Mark suggests she buys the same type of fish he has. He has five of these fish with lengths of 1 in., 1 in., 6 in., 6 in., and 6 in., with a mean length of 4 in. Should Susanna buy the type of fish that Mark suggests? Explain.

6. MATHEMATICAL PRACTICE 7 **Look for a Pattern** The graph shows the number of stamps that Luciano collected over several weeks. If the pattern continues, how many stamps will Luciano collect in Week 8? Explain.

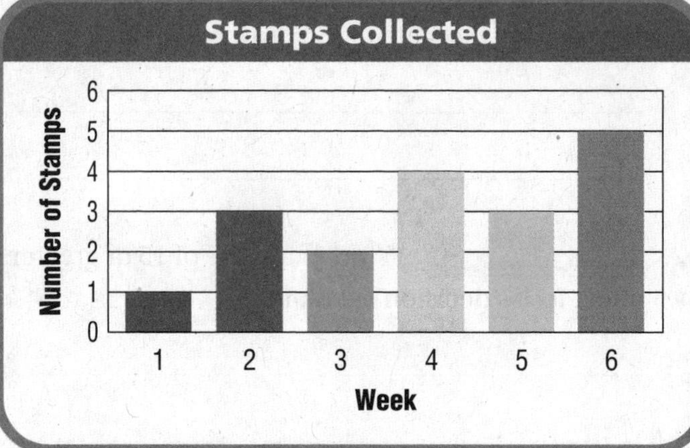

7. THINK SMARTER The data set shows the number of hours Luke plays the piano each week. Luke says he usually plays the piano 3 hours per week. Why is Luke's statement misleading?

Hours Playing the Piano						
1	2	1	3	2	10	2

FOR MORE PRACTICE:
Standards Practice Book

Name ____________________

Chapter 13 Review/Test

1. The dot plot shows the number of chin-ups done by a gym class.

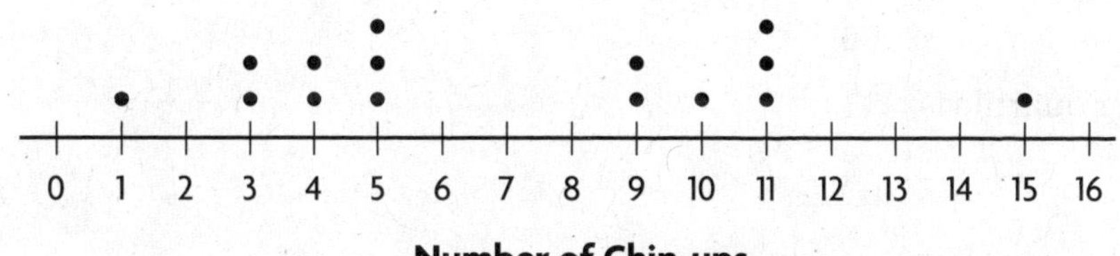

For numbers 1a–1e, choose Yes or No to indicate whether the statement is correct.

1a.	There are two peaks.	○ Yes	○ No
1b.	There are no clusters.	○ Yes	○ No
1c.	There is a gap between 6 and 8.	○ Yes	○ No
1d.	The most chin-ups anyone did was 15.	○ Yes	○ No
1e.	The modes are 3, 4, and 9.	○ Yes	○ No

2. The histogram shows the high temperatures in degrees Fahrenheit of various cities for one day in March.

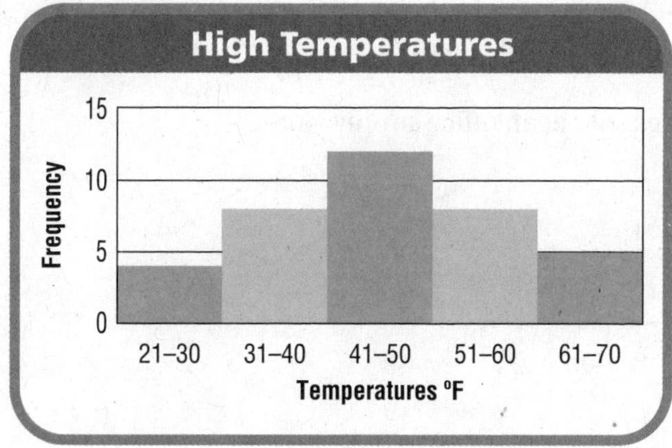

Select the best word to complete each sentence.

The histogram has [zero / one / two] peak(s). The histogram [has / does not have] line symmetry.

3. The data set shows the scores of the players on the winning team of a basketball game.

Scores of Players on Winning Team												
0	17	47	13	4	1	22	0	5	6	9	1	30

The median is [6. / 9. / 13.]

The lower quartile is

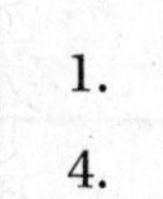

The upper quartile is [26. / 30. / 51.]

4. The data set shows the number of desks in 12 different classrooms.

Classroom Desks											
24	21	18	17	21	19	17	20	21	22	20	16

Find the values of the points on the box plot.

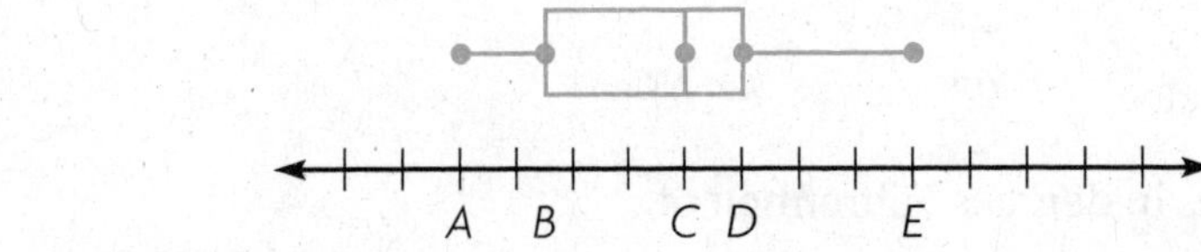

$A =$ ☐ $B =$ ☐ $C =$ ☐ $D =$ ☐ $E =$ ☐

5. The box plot shows the number of boxes sold at an office supply store each day for a week.

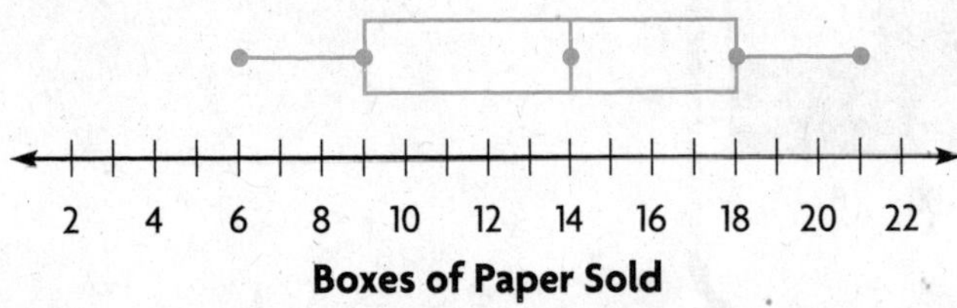

For numbers 5a–5d, select True or False for each statement.

5a. The median is 18. ○ True ○ False

5b. The range is 15. ○ True ○ False

5c. The interquartile range is 9. ○ True ○ False

5d. The upper quartile is 18. ○ True ○ False

Name ______________________________

6. The data set shows the number of glasses of water Dalia drinks each day for a week.

Glasses of Water						
6	7	9	9	8	7	10

Part A

What is the mean number of glasses of water Dalia drinks each day?

____

Part B

What is the mean absolute deviation of the number of glasses of water Dalia drinks each day? Round your answer to the nearest tenth. Use words and number to support your answer.

7. The numbers of emails Megan received each hour are 9, 10, 9, 8, 7, and 2. The mean of the data values is 7.5 and the median is 8.5. Which measure of center better describes the data, the mean or median? Use words and numbers to support your answer.

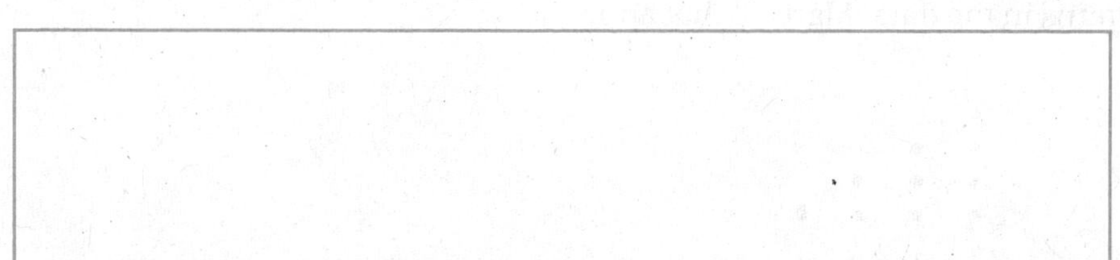

8. The number of miles Madelyn drove between stops was 182, 180, 181, 184, 198, and 185. Which measure of center best describes the data?

Ⓐ mean

Ⓑ median

Ⓒ mode

9. The histogram shows the weekly earnings of part-time workers. What are the most common weekly earnings?

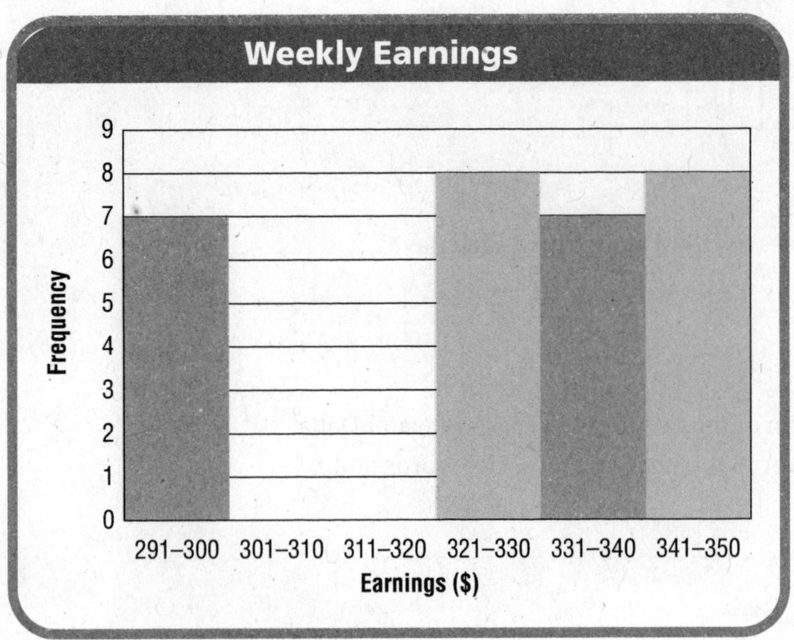

____

10. Jordan surveyed a group of randomly selected smartphone users and asked them how many applications they have downloaded onto their phones. The dot plot shows the results of Jordan's survey. Select the statements that describe patterns in the data. Mark all that apply.

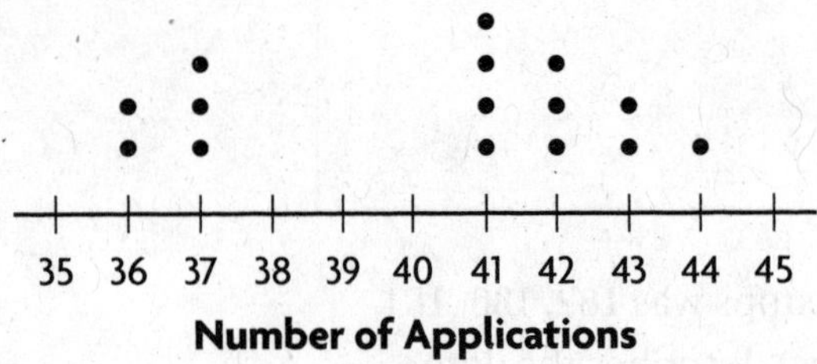

Ⓐ The modes are 37 and 42.

Ⓑ There is a gap from 38 to 40.

Ⓒ There is a cluster from 41 to 44.

Ⓓ There is a cluster from 35 to 36.

Name ______________________________

11. Mrs. Gutierrez made a histogram of the birth month of the students in her class. Describe the patterns in the histogram by completing the chart.

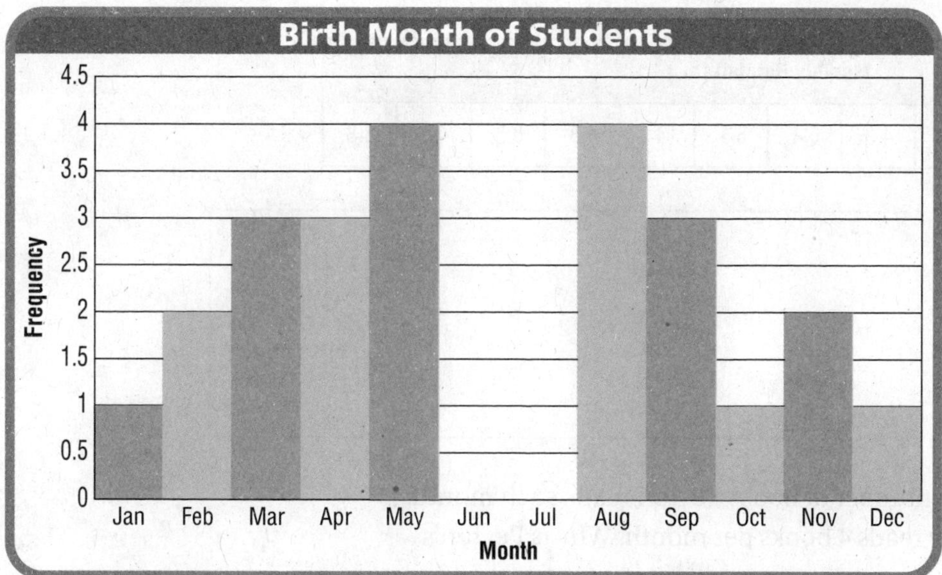

Identify any peaks.	Indentify any increases across the intervals.	Indentify any decreases across the intervals.

12. Ian collected data on the number of children in 13 different families.

Number of Children												
1	2	4	3	2	1	0	8	1	1	0	2	3

Draw a box plot of the data and use it to find the interquartile range and range.

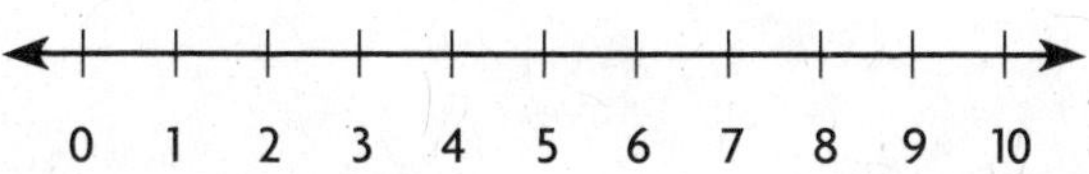

Interquartile range: ______ Range: ______

13. Gavin wants to move to a county where it rains about 5 inches every month. The data set shows the monthly rainfall in inches for a county. The mean of the data is 5 and the median is 4.35. After analyzing the data, Gavin says that this county would not be a good place to move. Do you agree or disagree with Gavin? Use words and numbers to support your answer.

Monthly Rainfall (in.)											
4.4	3.7	6	2.9	4.3	5.4	6.1	14.1	4.3	0.5	4.5	3.8

14. The data set shows the number of books Peyton reads each month. Peyton says she usually reads 4 books per month. Why is Peyton's statement misleading?

Books Read						
2	3	2	4	3	11	3

15. The data set shows the scores of three players for a board game.

Board Game Scores			
Player A	90	90	90
Player B	110	100	90
Player C	95	100	95

For numbers 15a–15d, choose Yes or No to indicate whether the statement is correct.

15a. The mean absolute deviation of Player B is 0. ○ Yes ○ No

15b. The mean absolute deviation of Player A is 0. ○ Yes ○ No

15c. The mean absolute deviation of Player B is greater than the mean absolute deviation of Player C. ○ Yes ○ No

Glossary

Pronunciation Key

a	add, map	f	fit, half	n	nice, tin	p	pit, stop	û(r)	burn, term
ā	ace, rate	g	go, log	ng	ring, song	r	run, poor	yo͞o	fuse, few
â(r)	care, air	h	hope, hate	o	odd, hot	s	see, pass	v	vain, eve
ä	palm, father	i	it, give	ō	open, so	sh	sure, rush	w	win, away
b	bat, rub	ī	ice, write	ô	order, jaw	t	talk, sit	y	yet, yearn
ch	check, catch	j	joy, ledge	oi	oil, boy	th	thin, both	z	zest, muse
d	dog, rod	k	cool, take	ou	pout, now	t͟h	this, bathe	zh	vision, pleasure
e	end, pet	l	look, rule	o͝o	took, full	u	up, done		
ē	equal, tree	m	move, seem	o͞o	pool, food	ù	pull book		

ə the schwa, an unstressed vowel representing the sound spelled *a* in above, *e* in sicken, *i* in possible, *o* in melon, *u* in circus

Other symbols:
- • separates words into syllables
- ʼ indicates stress on a syllable

absolute value [ab′sə•lo͞ot val′yo͞o] **valor absoluto** The distance of an integer from zero on a number line (p. 119)

acute angle [ə•kyo͞ot′ ang′gəl] **ángulo agudo** An angle that has a measure less than a right angle (less than 90° and greater than 0°)
Example:

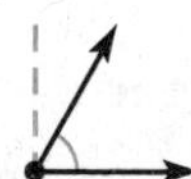

acute triangle [ə•kyo͞ot′ trī′ang•gəl] **triángulo acutángulo** A triangle that has three acute angles

addend [ad′end] **sumando** A number that is added to another in an addition problem

addition [ə•dish′ən] **suma** The process of finding the total number of items when two or more groups of items are joined; the inverse operation of subtraction

Addition Property of Equality [ə•dish′ən präp′ər•tē əv ē•kwôl′ə•tē] **propiedad de suma de la igualdad** The property that states that if you add the same number to both sides of an equation, the sides remain equal

additive inverse [ad′ə•tiv in′v ûrs] **inverso aditivo** The number which, when added to the given number, equals zero

algebraic expression [al•jə•brā′ik ek•spresh′ən] **expresión algebraica** An expression that includes at least one variable (p. 269)
Examples: $x + 5$, $3a - 4$

angle [ang′gəl] **ángulo** A shape formed by two rays that share the same endpoint
Example:

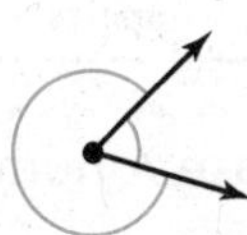

area [âr′ē•ə] **área** The number of square units needed to cover a surface without any gaps or overlaps (p. 389)

array [ə•rā′] **matriz** An arrangement of objects in rows and columns
Example:

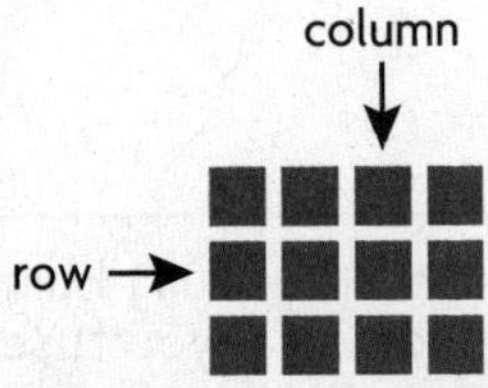

Associative Property of Addition [ə•sō′shē•ə•āt•iv präp′ər•tē əv ə•dish′ən] **propiedad asociativa de la suma** The property that states that when the grouping of addends is changed, the sum is the same
Example: (5 + 8) + 4 = 5 + (8 + 4)

Associative Property of Multiplication [ə•sō′shē•ə•tiv präp′ər•tē əv mul•tə•pli•kā′shən] **propiedad asociativa de la multiplicación** The property that states that when the grouping of factors is changed, the product is the same
Example: (2 × 3) × 4 = 2 × (3 × 4)

bar graph [bär graf] **gráfica de barras** A graph that uses horizontal or vertical bars to display countable data
Example:

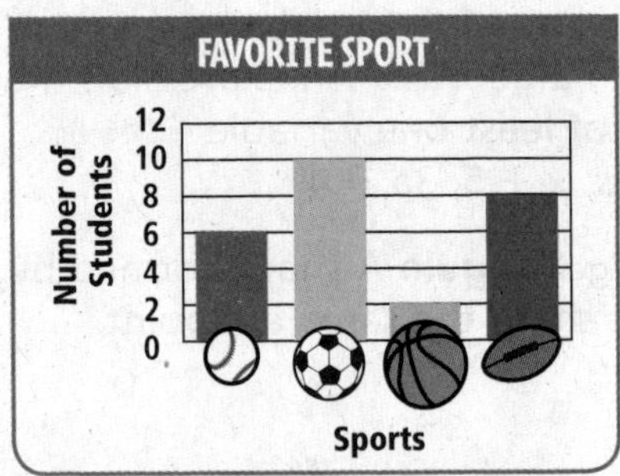

base [bās] (arithmetic) **base** A number used as a repeated factor (p. 261)
Example: $8^3 = 8 \times 8 \times 8$. The base is 8.

base [bās] (geometry) **base** In two dimensions, one side of a triangle or parallelogram which is used to help find the area. In three dimensions, a plane figure, usually a polygon or circle, which is used to partially describe a solid figure and to help find the volume of some solid figures. See also *height*
Examples:

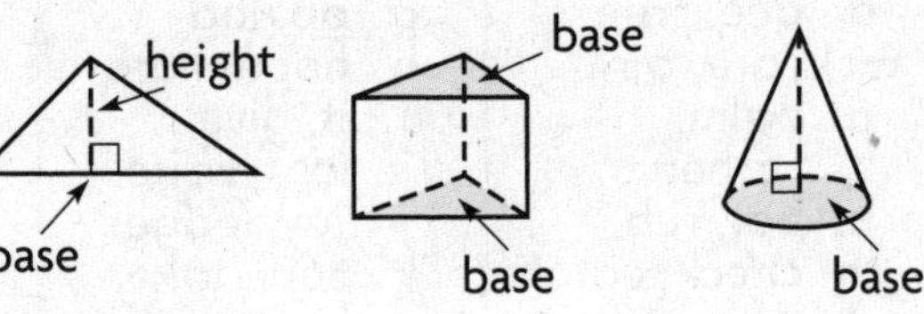

benchmark [bench′märk] **punto de referencia** A familiar number used as a point of reference

billion [bil′yən] **millardo** 1,000 millions; written as 1,000,000,000

box plot [bäks plät] **diagrama de caja** A graph that shows how data are distributed using the median, quartiles, least value, and greatest value (p. 520)
Example:

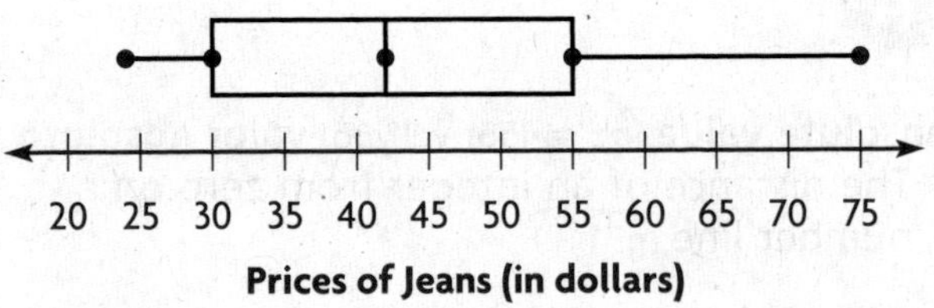

capacity [kə•pas′i•tē] **capacidad** The amount a container can hold (p. 233)
Examples: $\frac{1}{2}$ gallon, 2 quarts

Celsius (°C) [sel′sē•əs] **Celsius (°C)** A metric scale for measuring temperature

closed figure [klōzd fig′yər] **figura cerrada** A figure that begins and ends at the same point

coefficient [kō•ə•fish′ənt] **coeficiente** A number that is multiplied by a variable (p. 274)
Example: 6 is the coefficient of x in $6x$

common denominator [käm′ən dē•näm′ə•nāt•ər] **denominador común** A common multiple of two or more denominators
Example: Some common denominators for $\frac{1}{4}$ and $\frac{5}{6}$ are 12, 24, and 36.

common factor [käm′ən fak′tər] **factor común** A number that is a factor of two or more numbers (p. 17)

common multiple [käm′ən mul′tə•pəl] **múltiplo común** A number that is a multiple of two or more numbers

Commutative Property of Addition [kə•myo͞ot′ ə•tiv präp′ər•tē əv ə•dish′ən] **propiedad conmutativa de la suma** The property that states that when the order of two addends is changed, the sum is the same
Example: $4 + 5 = 5 + 4$

Commutative Property of Multiplication [kə•myo͞ot′ə•tiv präp′ər•tē əv mul•tə•pli•kāsh′ən] **propiedad conmutativa de la multiplicación** The property that states that when the order of two factors is changed, the product is the same
Example: $4 \times 5 = 5 \times 4$

compatible numbers [kəm•pat′ə•bəl num′bərz] **números compatibles** Numbers that are easy to compute with mentally

composite figure [kəm•päz′it fig′yər] **figura compuesta** A figure that is made up of two or more simpler figures, such as triangles and quadrilaterals (p. 415)
Example:

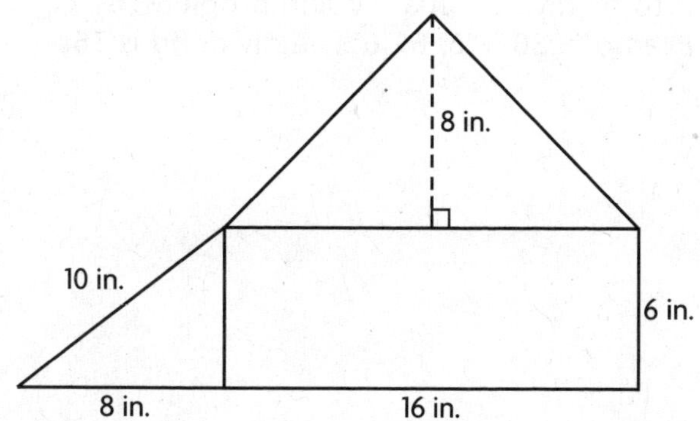

composite number [kəm•päz′it num′bər] **número compuesto** A number having more than two factors
Example: 6 is a composite number, since its factors are 1, 2, 3, and 6.

cone [kōn] **cono** A solid figure that has a flat, circular base and one vertex
Example:

congruent [kən•gro͞o′ənt] **congruente** Having the same size and shape (p. 393)
Example:

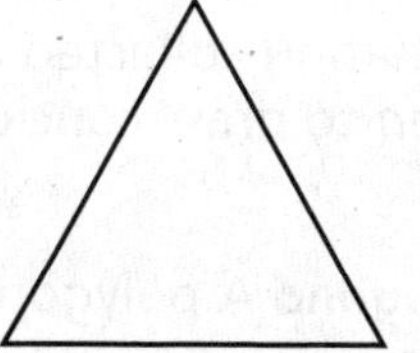
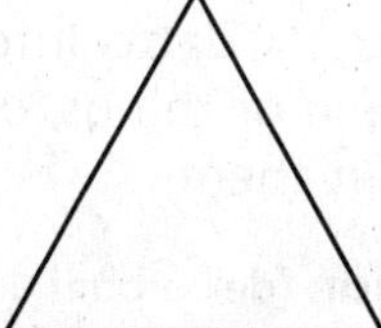

conversion factor [kən•vûr′zhən fak′tər] **factor de conversión** A rate in which two quantities are equal, but use different units (p. 229)

coordinate plane [kō•ôrd′n•it plān] **plano cartesiano** A plane formed by a horizontal line called the x-axis and a vertical line called the y-axis (p. 127)
Example:

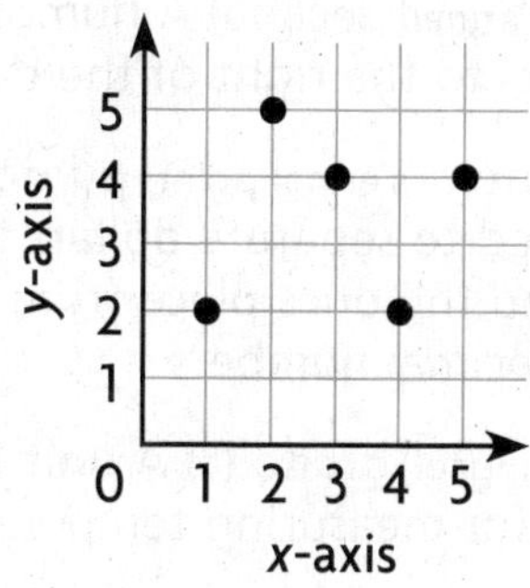

cube [kyo͞ob] **cubo** A solid figure with six congruent square faces
Example:

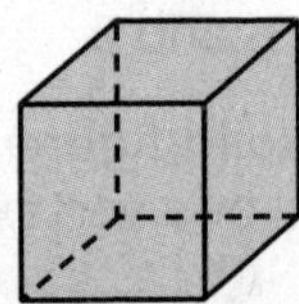

cubic unit [kyo͞o′bik yo͞o′nit] **unidad cúbica** A unit used to measure volume such as cubic foot (ft^3), cubic meter (m^3), and so on

D

data [dāt′ə] **datos** Information collected about people or things, often to draw conclusions about them (p. 473)

decagon [dek′ə•gän] **decágono** A polygon with 10 sides and 10 angles
Examples:

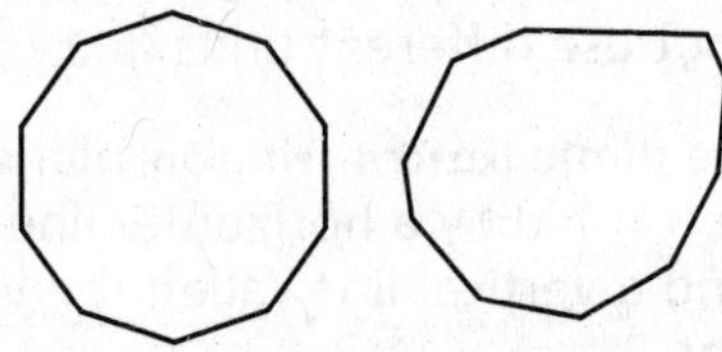

decimal [des′ə•məl] **decimal** A number with one or more digits to the right of the decimal point

decimal point [des′ə•məl point] **punto decimal** A symbol used to separate dollars from cents in money, and the ones place from the tenths place in decimal numbers

degree (°) [di•grē′] **grado (°)** A unit for measuring angles or for measuring temperature

degree Celsius (°C) [di•grē′ sel′sē•əs] **grado Celcius** A metric unit for measuring temperature

degree Fahrenheit (°F) [di•grē′ fâr′ən•hīt] **grado Fahrenheit** A customary unit for measuring temperature

denominator [dē•näm′ə•nāt•ər] **denominador** The number below the bar in a fraction that tells how many equal parts are in the whole or in the group

Example: $\frac{3}{4}$ ← denominator

dependent variable [dē•pen′dənt vâr′ē•ə•bəl] **variable dependiente** A variable whose value depends on the value of another quantity (p. 357)

difference [dif′ər•əns] **diferencia** The answer to a subtraction problem

digit [dij′it] **dígito** Any one of the ten symbols 0, 1, 2, 3, 4, 5, 6, 7, 8, 9 used to write numbers

dimension [də•men′shən] **dimensión** A measure in one direction

distribution [dis•tri•byo͞o′shən] **distribución** The overall shape of a data set

Distributive Property [di•strib′yo͞o•tiv präp′ər•tē] **propiedad distributiva** The property that states that multiplying a sum by a number is the same as multiplying each addend in the sum by the number and then adding the products (p. 18)
Example: $3 \times (4 + 2) = (3 \times 4) + (3 \times 2)$
$3 \times 6 = 12 + 6$
$18 = 18$

divide [də•vīd′] **dividir** To separate into equal groups; the inverse operation of multiplication

dividend [div′ə•dend] **dividendo** The number that is to be divided in a division problem
Example: $36 \div 6$; $6\overline{)36}$ The dividend is 36.

divisible [də•viz′ə•bəl] **divisible** A number is divisible by another number if the quotient is a counting number and the remainder is zero
Example: 18 is divisible by 3.

division [də•vizh′ən] **división** The process of sharing a number of items to find how many groups can be made or how many items will be in a group; the operation that is the inverse of multiplication

Division Property of Equality [də•vizh′ən präp′ər•tē əv ē•kwôl′ə•tē] **propiedad de división de la igualdad** The property that states that if you divide both sides of an equation by the same nonzero number, the sides remain equal

divisor [də•vī′zər] **divisor** The number that divides the dividend
Example: $15 \div 3$; $3\overline{)15}$ The divisor is 3.

dot plot [dot plät] **diagrama de puntos** A graph that shows frequency of data along a number line (p. 481)
Example:

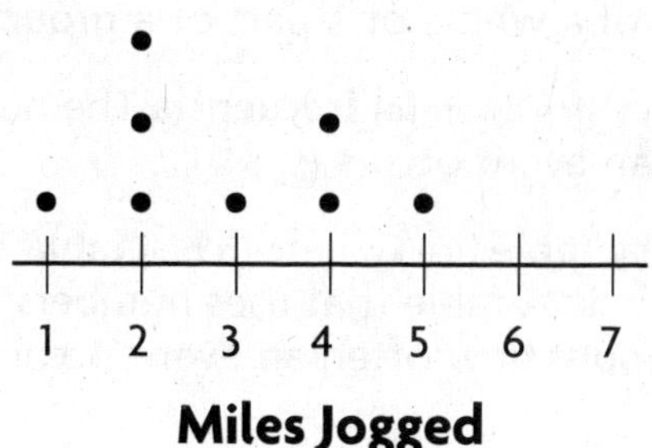

edge [ej] **arista** The line where two faces of a solid figure meet
Example:

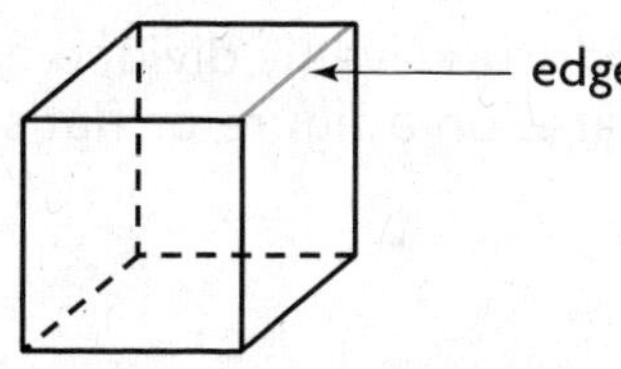

equation [i•kwā′zhən] **ecuación** An algebraic or numerical sentence that shows that two quantities are equal (p. 307)

equilateral triangle [ē•kwi•lat′ər•əl trī′ang•gəl] **triángulo equilátero** A triangle with three congruent sides
Example:

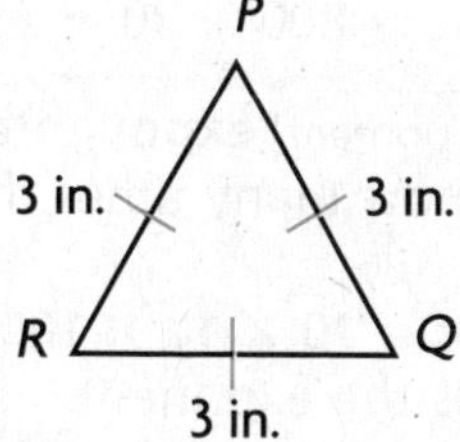

equivalent [ē•kwiv′ə•lənt] **equivalente** Having the same value

equivalent decimals [ē•kwiv′ə•lənt des′ə•məlz] **decimales equivalentes** Decimals that name the same number or amount
Example: $0.4 = 0.40 = 0.400$

equivalent expressions [ē•kwiv′ə•lənt ek•spresh′ənz] **expresiones equivalentes** Expressions that are equal to each other for any values of their variables (p. 291)
Example: $2x + 4x = 6x$

equivalent fractions [ē•kwiv′ə•lənt frak′shənz] **fracciones equivalentes** Fractions that name the same amount or part
Example: $\frac{3}{4} = \frac{6}{8}$

equivalent ratios [ē•kwiv′ə•lənt rā′shē•ōz] **razones equivalents** Ratios that name the same comparison (p. 161)

estimate [es′tə•mit] *noun* **estimación (s)** A number close to an exact amount

estimate [es′tə•māt] *verb* **estimar (v)** To find a number that is close to an exact amount

evaluate [ē•val'yo͞o•āt] **evaluar** To find the value of a numerical or algebraic expression (p. 265)

even [ē'vən] **par** A whole number that has a 0, 2, 4, 6, or 8 in the ones place

expanded form [ek•span'did fôrm] **forma desarrollada** A way to write numbers by showing the value of each digit
Example: 832 = 800 + 30 + 2

exponent [eks'pōn•ənt] **exponente** A number that shows how many times the base is used as a factor (p. 261)
Example: $10^3 = 10 \times 10 \times 10$; 3 is the exponent.

Word History

Exponent comes from the combination of the Latin roots *ex* ("out of") + *ponere* ("to place"). In the 17th century, mathematicians began to use complicated quantities. The idea of positioning a number by raising it "out of place" is traced to René Descartes.

expression [ek•spresh'ən] **expresión** A mathematical phrase or the part of a number sentence that combines numbers, operation signs, and sometimes variables, but does not have an equal or inequality sign

face [fās] **cara** A polygon that is a flat surface of a solid figure
Example:

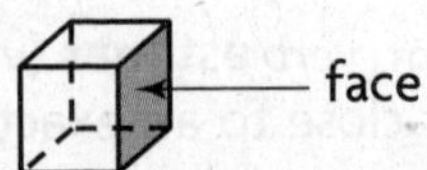

fact family [fakt fam'ə•lē] **familia de operaciones** A set of related multiplication and division, or addition and subtraction, equations
Example: $7 \times 8 = 56$; $8 \times 7 = 56$; $56 \div 7 = 8$; $56 \div 8 = 7$

factor [fak'tər] **factor** A number multiplied by another number to find a product

factor tree [fak'tər trē] **árbol de factores** A diagram that shows the prime factors of a number
Example:

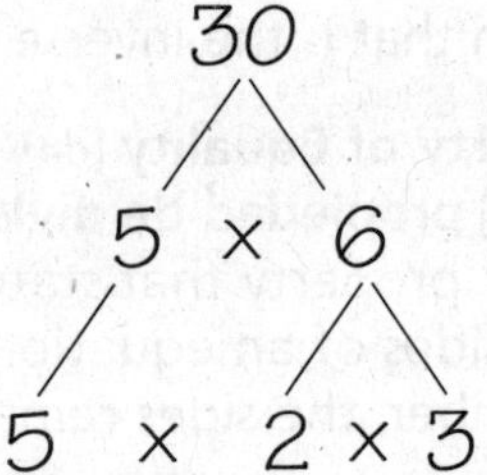

Fahrenheit (°F) [fâr'ən•hīt] **Fahrenheit (°F)** A customary scale for measuring temperature

formula [fôr'myo͞o•lə] **fórmula** A set of symbols that expresses a mathematical rule
Example: $A = b \times h$

fraction [frak'shən] **fracción** A number that names a part of a whole or a part of a group

frequency [frē'kwən•sē] **frecuencia** The number of times an event occurs (p. 481)

frequency table [frē'kwən•sē tā'bəl] **tabla de frecuencia** A table that uses numbers to record data about how often an event occurs (p. 482)

greatest common factor (GCF) [grāt'est käm'ən fak'tər] **máximo común divisor (MCD)** The greatest factor that two or more numbers have in common (p. 17)
Example: 6 is the GCF of 18 and 30.

grid [grid] **cuadrícula** Evenly divided and equally spaced squares on a figure or flat surface

height [hīt] **altura** The length of a perpendicular from the base to the top of a plane figure or solid figure
Example:

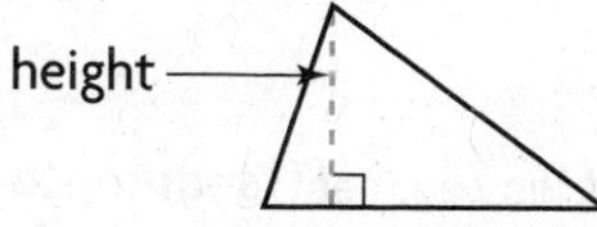

hexagon [hek′sə•gän] **hexágono** A polygon with six sides and six angles
Examples:

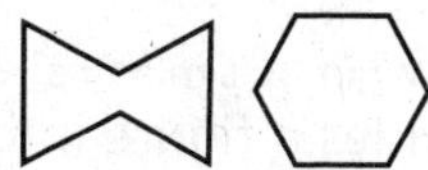

histogram [his′tə•gram] **histograma** A type of bar graph that shows the frequencies of data in intervals. (p. 485)
Example:

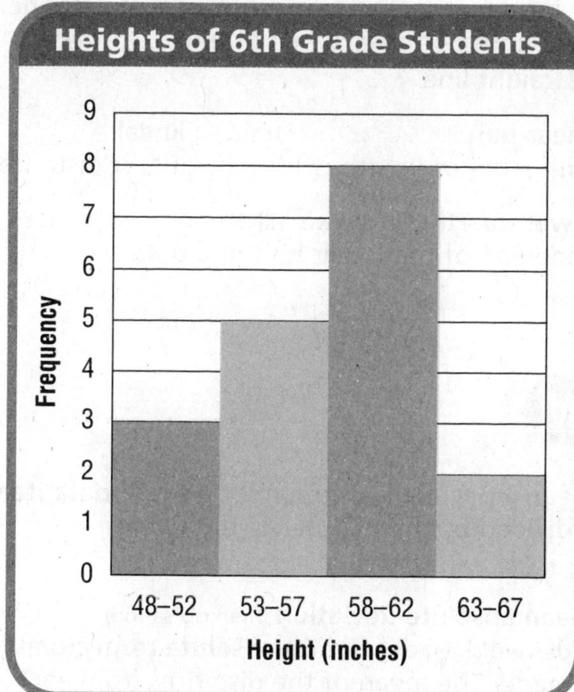

horizontal [hôr•i•zänt′əl] **horizontal** Extending left and right

hundredth [hun′drədth] **centésimo** One of one hundred equal parts
Examples: 0.56, $\frac{56}{100}$, fifty-six hundredths

independent variable [in•dē•pen′dənt′ vâr′ē•ə•bəl] **variable independiente** A variable whose value determines the value of another quantity (p. 357)

Identity Property of Addition [ī•den′tə•tē präp′ər•tē əv ə•dish′ən] **propiedad de identidad de la suma** The property that states that when you add zero to a number, the result is that number

Identity Property of Multiplication [ī•den′tə•tē präp′ər•tē əv mul•tə•pli•kā′shən] **propiedad de identidad de la multiplicación** The property that states that the product of any number and 1 is that number

inequality [in•ē•kwôl′ə•tē] **desigualdad** A mathematical sentence that contains the symbol $<$, $>$, $\leq$, $\geq$, or $\neq$ (p. 357)

integers [in′tə•jərz] **enteros** The set of whole numbers and their opposites (p. 101)

interquartile range [in′tûr•kwôr′tīl rānj] **rango intercuartil** The difference between the upper and lower quartiles of a data set (p. 528)

intersecting lines [in•tər•sekt′ing līnz] **líneas secantes** Lines that cross each other at exactly one point
Example:

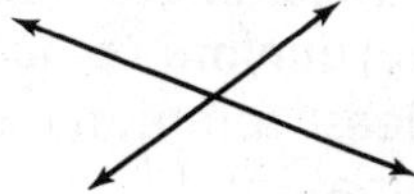

inverse operations [in′vûrs äp•pə•rā′shənz] **operaciones inversas** Opposite operations, or operations that undo each other, such as addition and subtraction or multiplication and division (p. 319)

key [kē] **clave** The part of a map or graph that explains the symbols

kite [kīt] **cometa** A quadrilateral with exactly two pairs of congruent sides that are next to each other; no two sides are parallel
Example:

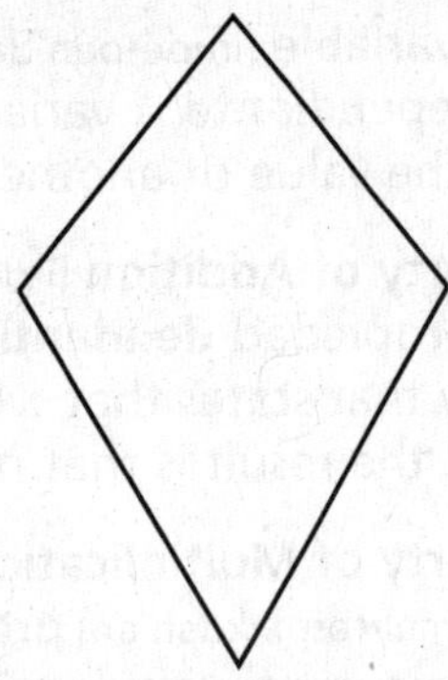

ladder diagram [lad′ər dī′ə•gram] **diagrama de escalera** A diagram that shows the steps of repeatedly dividing by a prime number until the quotient is 1 (p. 10)

lateral area [lat′ər•əl âr′ē•ə] **cara área** The sum of the areas of the lateral faces of a solid

lateral face [lat′ər•əl fās] **cara lateral** Any surface of a polyhedron other than a base

least common denominator (LCD) [lēst käm′ən dē•näm′ə•nāt•ər] **mínimo común denominador (m.c.d.)** The least common multiple of two or more denominators

Example: The LCD for $\frac{1}{4}$ and $\frac{5}{6}$ is 12.

least common multiple (LCM) [lēst käm′ən mul′tə•pəl] **mínimo común múltiplo (m.c.m.)** The least number that is a common multiple of two or more numbers (p. 13)

like terms [līk tûrmz] **términos semejantes** Expressions that have the same variable with the same exponent (p. 287)

line [līn] **línea** A straight path in a plane, extending in both directions with no endpoints
Example:

line graph [līn graf] **gráfica lineal** A graph that uses line segments to show how data change over time

line segment [līn seg′mənt] **segmento** A part of a line that includes two points called endpoints and all the points between them
Example:

line of symmetry [līn əv sim′ə•trē] **eje de simetría** A line that divides a figure into two halves that are reflections of each other (p. 132)

line symmetry [līn sim′ə•trē] **simetría axial** A figure has line symmetry if it can be folded about a line so that its two parts match exactly. (p. 132)

linear equation [lin′ē•ər ē•kwā′zhən] **ecuación lineal** An equation that, when graphed, forms a straight line (p. 375)

linear unit [lin′ē•ər yōō′nit] **unidad lineal** A measure of length, width, height, or distance

lower quartile [lō′ər kwôr′tīl] **primer cuartil** The median of the lower half of a data set (p. 519)

mean [mēn] **media** The sum of a set of data items divided by the number of data items (p. 495)

mean absolute deviation [mēn ab′sə•lōōt dē•vē•ā′shən] **desviación absoluta respecto ala media** The mean of the distances from each data value in a set to the mean of the set (p. 524)

measure of center [mezh′ər əv sent′ər] **medida de tendencia central** A single value used to describe the middle of a data set (p. 495)
Examples: mean, median, mode

measure of variability [mezh′ər əv vâr′ē•ə•bil′ə•tē] **medida de dispersión** A single value used to describe how the values in a data set are spread out (p. 527)
Examples: range, interquartile range, mean absolute deviation

median [mē′dēən] **mediana** The middle value when a data set is written in order from least to greatest, or the mean of the two middle values when there is an even number of items (p. 495)

midpoint [mid′point] **punto medio** A point on a line segment that is equally distant from either endpoint

million [mil′yən] **millón** 1,000 thousands; written as 1,000,000

mixed number [mikst num′bər] **número mixto** A number that is made up of a whole number and a fraction
Example: $1\frac{5}{8}$

mode [mōd] **moda** The value(s) in a data set that occurs the most often (p. 495)

multiple [mul′tə•pəl] **múltiplo** The product of two counting numbers is a multiple of each of those numbers

multiplication [mul•tə•pli•kā′shən] **multiplicación** A process to find the total number of items made up of equal-sized groups, or to find the total number of items in a given number of groups; It is the inverse operation of division.

Multiplication Property of Equality [mul•tə•pli•kā′shən präp′ər•tē əv ē•kwôl′ə•tē] **propiedad de multiplicación de la igualdad** The property that states that if you multiply both sides of an equation by the same number, the sides remain equal

multiplicative inverse [mul′tə•pli•kāt•iv in′vûrs] **Inverso multiplicativo** A reciprocal of a number that is multiplied by that number resulting in a product of 1 (p. 78)

multiply [mul′tə•plī] **multiplicar** When you combine equal groups, you can multiply to find how many in all; the inverse operation of division

negative integer [neg′ə•tiv in′tə•jər] **entero negativo** Any integer less than zero
Examples: $^{-}4$, $^{-}5$, and $^{-}6$ are negative integers.

net [net] **plantilla** A two-dimensional pattern that can be folded into a three-dimensional polyhedron (p. 435)
Example:

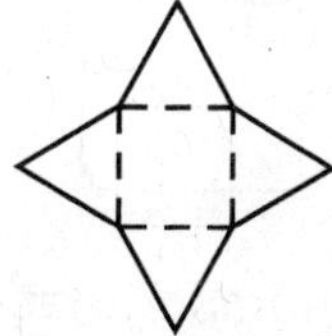
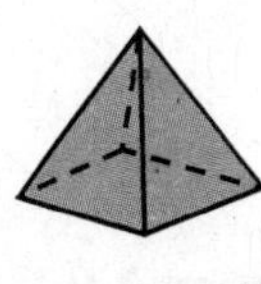

not equal to (≠) [not ē′kwəl to͞o] **no igual a** A symbol that indicates one quantity is not equal to another

number line [num′bər līn] **recta numérica** A line on which numbers can be located
Example:

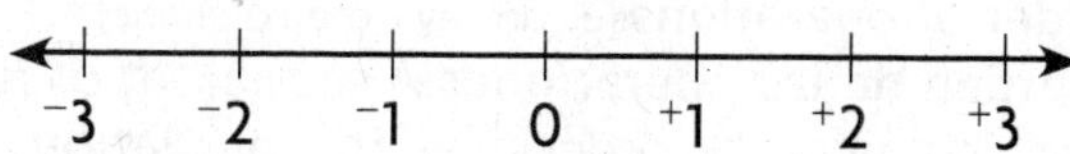

numerator [no͞o′mər•āt•ər] **numerador** The number above the bar in a fraction that tells how many equal parts of the whole are being considered
Example: $\frac{3}{4}$ ← numerator

numerical expression [no͞o•mer′i•kəl ek•spresh′ən] **expresión numérica** A mathematical phrase that uses only numbers and operation signs (p. 265)

obtuse angle [äb•to͞os′ ang′gəl] **ángulo obtuso** An angle whose measure is greater than 90° and less than 180°
Example:

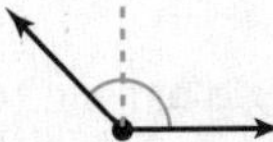

obtuse triangle [äb•to͞os′ trī′ang•gəl] **triángulo obtusángulo** A triangle that has one obtuse angle

octagon [äk′tə•gän] **octágono** A polygon with eight sides and eight angles
Examples:

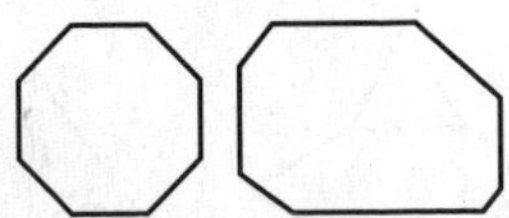

odd [od] **impar** A whole number that has a 1, 3, 5, 7, or 9 in the ones place

open figure [ō′pən fig′yər] **figura abierta** A figure that does not begin and end at the same point

opposites [äp′ə•zits] **opuestos** Two numbers that are the same distance, but in opposite directions, from zero on a number line (p. 101)

order of operations [ôr′dər əv äp•ə•rā′shənz] **orden de las operaciones** A special set of rules which gives the order in which calculations are done in an expression (p. 265)

ordered pair [ôr′dərd pâr] **par ordenado** A pair of numbers used to locate a point on a grid. The first number tells the left-right position and the second number tells the up-down position. (p. 127)

origin [ôr′ə•jin] **origen** The point where the two axes of a coordinate plane intersect; (0,0) (p. 127)

outlier [out′lī•ər] **valor atípico** A value much higher or much lower than the other values in a data set (p. 499)

overestimate [ō′vər•es•tə•mit] **sobrestimar** An estimate that is greater than the exact answer

parallel lines [pâr′ə•lel līnz] **líneas paralelas** Lines in the same plane that never intersect and are always the same distance apart
Example:

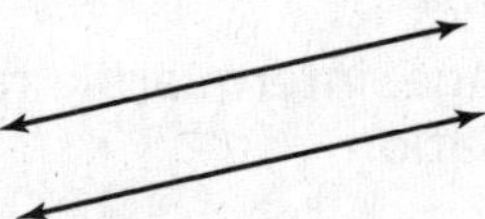

parallelogram [pâr•ə•lel′ə•gram] **paralelogramo** A quadrilateral whose opposite sides are parallel and congruent (p. 389)
Example:

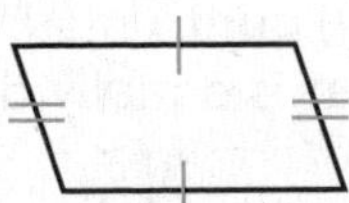

parentheses [pə•ren′thə•sēz] **paréntesis** The symbols used to show which operation or operations in an expression should be done first

partial product [pär′shəl präd′əkt] **producto parcial** A method of multiplying in which the ones, tens, hundreds, and so on are multiplied separately and then the products are added together

pattern [pat′ərn] **patrón** An ordered set of numbers or objects; the order helps you predict what will come next
Examples: 2, 4, 6, 8, 10

pentagon [pen′tə•gän] **pentágono** A polygon with five sides and five angles
Examples:

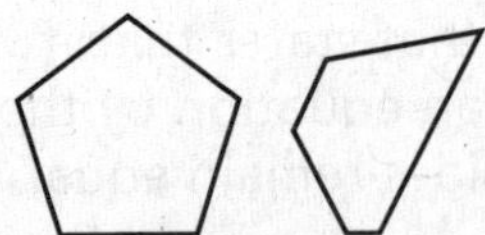

percent [pər•sent′] **porcentaje** The comparison of a number to 100; percent means "per hundred" (p. 195)

perimeter [pə•rim′ə•tər] **perímetro** The distance around a closed plane figure

period [pir′ē•əd] **período** Each group of three digits separated by commas in a multidigit number
Example: 85,643,900 has three periods.

perpendicular lines [pər•pən•dik′yo͞o•lər līnz] **líneas perpendiculares** Two lines that intersect to form four right angles
Example:

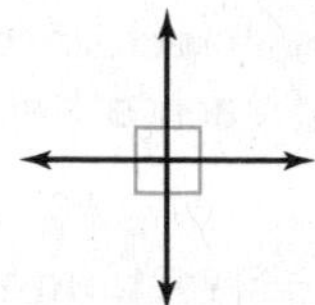

pictograph [pik′tə•graf] **pictografía** A graph that displays countable data with symbols or pictures
Example:

HOW WE GET TO SCHOOL	
Walk	⊛ ⊛ ⊛
Ride a Bike	⊛ ⊛ ⊛ ⊛
Ride a Bus	⊛ ⊛ ⊛ ⊛ ⊛ ◖
Ride in a Car	⊛ ⊛

Key: Each ⊛ = 10 students

place value [plās val′yo͞o] **valor posicional** The value of each digit in a number based on the location of the digit

plane [plān] **plano** A flat surface that extends without end in all directions
Example:

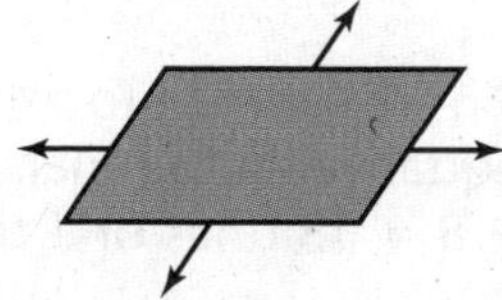

plane figure [plān fig′yər] **figura plana** A figure that lies in a plane; a figure having length and width

point [point] **punto** An exact location in space

polygon [päl′i•gän] **polígono** A closed plane figure formed by three or more line segments
Examples:

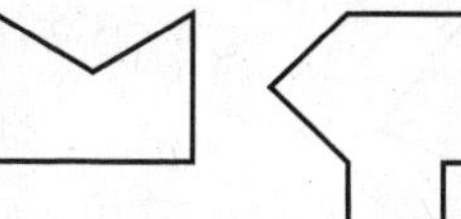

Polygons

Not Polygons

polyhedron [päl•i•hē′drən] **poliedro** A solid figure with faces that are polygons (p. 434)
Examples:

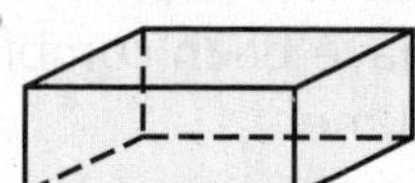

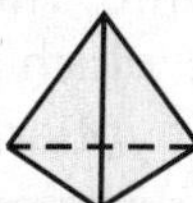

positive integer [päz′ə•tiv in′tə•jər] **entero positivo** Any integer greater than zero

prime factor [prīm fak′tər] **factor primo** A factor that is a prime number

prime factorization [prīm fak•tə•rə•zā′shən] **descomposición en factores primos** A number written as the product of all its prime factors (p. 9)

prime number [prīm num′bər] **número primo** A number that has exactly two factors: 1 and itself
Examples: 2, 3, 5, 7, 11, 13, 17, and 19 are prime numbers. 1 is not a prime number.

prism [priz′əm] **prisma** A solid figure that has two congruent, polygon-shaped bases, and other faces that are all parallelograms
Examples:

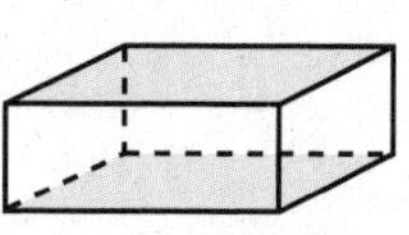

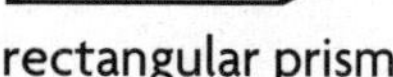

rectangular prism

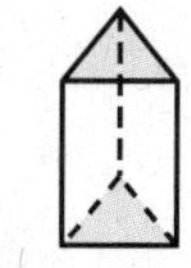

triangular prism

product [präd′əkt] **producto** The answer to a multiplication problem

pyramid [pir′ə•mid] **pirámide** A solid figure with a polygon base and all other faces as triangles that meet at a common vertex
Example:

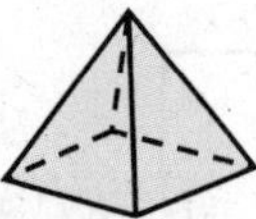

Word History

A fire is sometimes in the shape of a pyramid, with a point at the top and a wider base. This may be how *pyramid* got its name. The Greek word for fire was *pura*, which may have been combined with the Egyptian word *mer*.

Q

quadrants [kwä′drənts] **cuadranes** The four regions of the coordinate plane separated by the *x*- and *y*-axes (p. 131)

quadrilateral [kwä•dri•lat′ər•əl] **cuadrilátero** A polygon with four sides and four angles
Example:

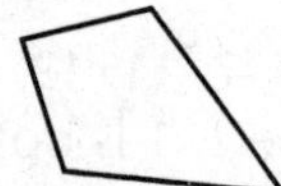

quotient [kwō′shənt] **cociente** The number that results from dividing
Example: 8 ÷ 4 = 2. The quotient is 2.

R

range [rānj] **rango** The difference between the greatest and least numbers in a data set (p. 528)

rate [rāt] **tasa** A ratio that compares two quantities having different units of measure (p. 158)

ratio [rā′shē•ō] **razón** A comparison of two numbers, *a* and *b*, that can be written as a fraction $\frac{a}{b}$ (p. 153)

rational number [rash′•ən•əl num′bər] **número racional** Any number that can be written as a ratio $\frac{a}{b}$ where *a* and *b* are integers and $b \neq 0$. (p. 109)

ray [rā] **semirrecta** A part of a line; it has one endpoint and continues without end in one direction
Example:

reciprocal [ri•sip′rə•kəl] **reciproco** Two numbers are reciprocals of each other if their product equals 1. (p. 78)

rectangle [rek′tang•gəl] **rectángulo** A parallelogram with four right angles
Example:

rectangular prism [rek•tang′gyə•lər priz′əm] **prisma rectangular** A solid figure in which all six faces are rectangles
Example:

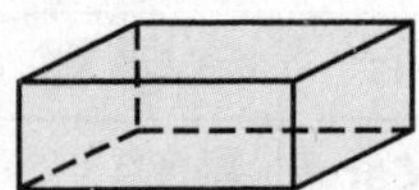

reflection [ri•flek′shən] **reflexión** A movement of a figure to a new position by flipping it over a line; a flip
Example:

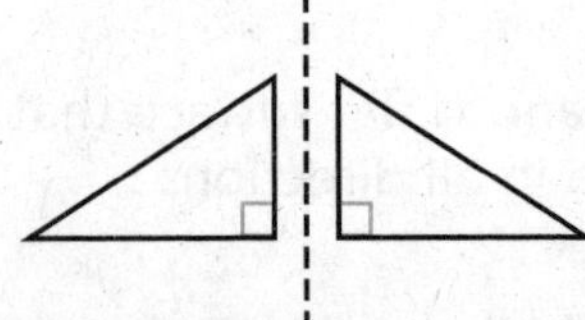

regroup [rē•grōōp′] **reagrupar** To exchange amounts of equal value to rename a number
Example: 5 + 8 = 13 ones or 1 ten 3 ones

regular polygon [reg′yə•lər päl′i•gän] **polígono regular** A polygon in which all sides are congruent and all angles are congruent (p. 411)

relative frequency table [rel′ə•tiv frē′kwən•sē tā′bəl] **tabla de frecuencia relativa** A table that shows the percent of time each piece of data occurs (p. 482)

remainder [ri•mān′dər] **residuo** The amount left over when a number cannot be divided equally

rhombus [räm′bəs] **rombo** A parallelogram with four congruent sides
Example:

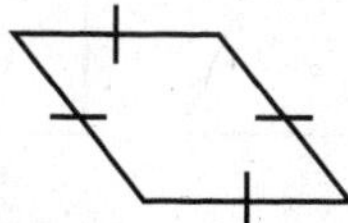

Word History

Rhombus is almost identical to its Greek origin, *rhombos.* The original meaning was "spinning top" or "magic wheel," which is easy to imagine when you look at a rhombus, an equilateral parallelogram.

right triangle [rīt trī′ang•gəl] **triángulo rectángulo** A triangle that has a right angle
Example:

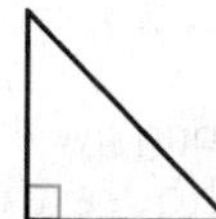

round [round] **redondear** To replace a number with one that is simpler and is approximately the same size as the original number
Example: 114.6 rounded to the nearest ten is 110 and to the nearest unit is 115.

sequence [sē′kwəns] **secuencia** An ordered set of numbers

simplest form [sim′pləst fôrm] **mínima expresión** A fraction is in simplest form when the numerator and denominator have only 1 as a common factor

simplify [sim′plə•fī] **simplificar** The process of dividing the numerator and denominator of a fraction or ratio by a common factor

solid figure [sä′lid fig′yər] **cuerpo geométrico** A three-dimensional figure having length, width, and height (p. 435)

solution of an equation [sə•lo͞o′shən əv an ē•kwā′zhən] **solución de una ecuación** A value that, when substituted for the variable, makes an equation true (p. 307)

solution of an inequality [sə•lo͞o′shən əv an in•ē•kwôl′ə•tē] **solución de una desigualdad** A value that, when substituted for the variable, makes an inequality true (p. 337)

square [skwâr] **cuadrado** A polygon with four equal, or congruent, sides and four right angles

square pyramid [skwâr pir′ə•mid] **pirámide cuadrada** A solid figure with a square base and with four triangular faces that have a common vertex
Example:

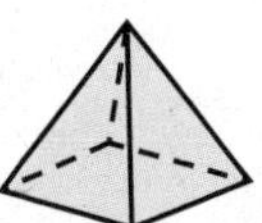

square unit [skwâr yo͞o′nit] **unidad cuadrada** A unit used to measure area such as square foot (ft^2), square meter (m^2), and so on

standard form [stan′dərd fôrm] **forma normal** A way to write numbers by using the digits 0–9, with each digit having a place value
Example: 456 ← standard form

statistical question [stə•tis′ti•kəl kwes′chən] **pregunta estadística** A question that asks about a set of data that can vary (p. 473)
Example: How many desks are in each classroom in my school?

Substitution Property of Equality [sub•stə•too′shən präp′ər•tē əv ē•kwôl′ə•tē] **propiedad de sustitución de la iqualdad** The property that states that if you have one quantity equal to another, you can substitute that quantity for the other in an equation

subtraction [səb•trak′shən] **resta** The process of finding how many are left when a number of items are taken away from a group of items; the process of finding the difference when two groups are compared; the inverse operation of addition

Subtraction Property of Equality [səb•trak′shən präp′ər•tē əv ē•kwôl′ə•tē] **propiedad de resta de la igualdad** The property that states that if you subtract the same number from both sides of an equation, the sides remain equal

sum [sum] **suma o total** The answer to an addition problem

surface area [sûr′fis âr′ē•ə] **área total** The sum of the areas of all the faces, or surfaces, of a solid figure (p. 439)

tally table [tal′ē tā′bəl] **tabla de conteo** A table that uses tally marks to record data

terms [tûrmz] **términos** The parts of an expression that are separated by an addition or subtraction sign (p. 274)

tenth [tenth] **décimo** One of ten equal parts
Example: 0.7 = seven tenths

thousandth [thou′zəndth] **milésimo** One of one thousand equal parts
Example: 0.006 = six thousandths

three-dimensional [thrē də•men′shə•nəl] **tridimensional** Measured in three directions, such as length, width, and height

three-dimensional solid [thrē də•men′shə•nəl säl′id] **figura tridimensional** See *solid figure*

trapezoid [trap′i•zoid] **trapecio** A quadrilateral with exactly one pair of parallel sides (p. 401)
Examples:

tree diagram [trē dī′ə•gram] **diagrama de árbol** A branching diagram that shows all possible outcomes of an event (p. 9)

trend [trend] **tendencia** A pattern over time, in all or part of a graph, where the data increase, decrease, or stay the same

triangle [trī′ang•gəl] **triángulo** A polygon with three sides and three angles
Examples:

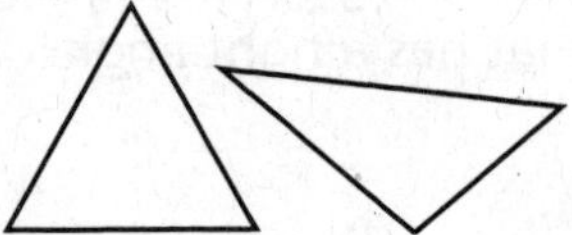

triangular prism [trī•ang′gyə•lər priz′əm] **prisma triangular** A solid figure that has two triangular bases and three rectangular faces

two-dimensional [too də•men′shə•nəl] **bidimensional** Measured in two directions, such as length and width

two-dimensional figure [too də•men′shə•nəl fig′yər] **figura bidimensional** See *plane figure*

underestimate [un•dər•es′tə•mit] **subestimar** An estimate that is less than the exact answer

unlike fractions [un′līk frak′shənz] **fracciónes no semejantes** Fractions with different denominators

unit fraction [yōō′nit frak′shən] **fracción unitaria** A fraction that has 1 as a numerator

unit rate [yōō′nit rāt] **tasa por unidad** A rate expressed so that the second term in the ratio is one unit (p. 158)
Example: 55 ml per hr

upper quartile [up′ər kwôr′tīl] **tercer cuartil** The median of the upper half of a data set (p. 519)

variable [vâr′ē•ə•bəl] **variable** A letter or symbol that stands for an unknown number or numbers (p. 269)

Venn diagram [ven dī′ə•gram] **diagrama de Venn** A diagram that shows relationships among sets of things
Example:

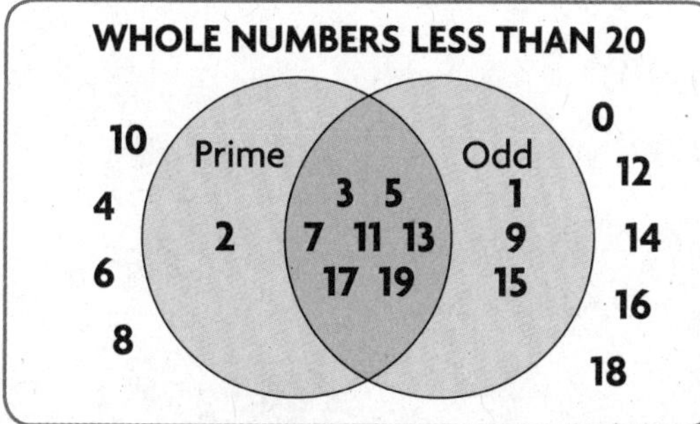

vertical [vûr′ti•kəl] **vertical** Extending up and down

vertex [vûr′teks] **vértice** The point where two or more rays meet; the point of intersection of two sides of a polygon; the point of intersection of three (or more) edges of a solid figure; the top point of a cone; the plural of *vertex* is *vertices*
Examples:

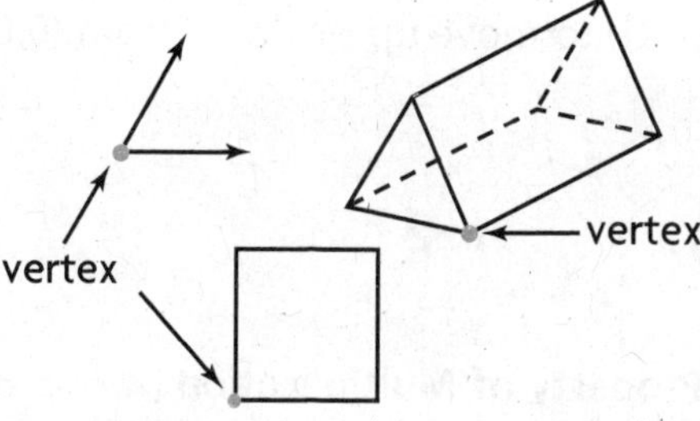

volume [väl′yōōm] **volumen** The measure of the space a solid figure occupies (p. 453)

weight [wāt] **peso** How heavy an object is

whole number [hōl num′bər] **número entero** One of the numbers 0, 1, 2, 3, 4, . . . ; the set of whole numbers goes on without end

x*-axis** [eks ak′sis] **eje de la *x The horizontal number line on a coordinate plane (p. 127)

x*-coordinate** [eks kō•ôrd′n•it] **coordenada *x The first number in an ordered pair; tells the distance to move right or left from (0,0) (p. 127)

y*-axis** [wī ak′sis] **eje de la *y The vertical number line on a coordinate plane (p. 127)

y*-coordinate** [wī kō•ôrd′•n•it] **coordenada *y The second number in an ordered pair; tells the distance to move up or down from (0,0) (p. 127)

Zero Property of Multiplication [zē′rō präp′ər•tē əv mul•tə•pli•kā′shən] **propiedad del cero de la multiplicación** The property that states that when you multiply by zero, the product is zero

CALIFORNIA COMMON CORE STATE STANDARDS

Standards You Will Learn

Standards You Will Learn		Student Edition Lessons
Mathematical Practices		
MP.1	Make sense of problems and persevere in solving them.	Lessons 1.1, 2.6, 2.9, 6.1, 6.3, 6.5, 12.8, 13.4, 13.7
MP.2	Reason abstractly and quantitatively.	Lessons 1.2, 1.8, 1.9, 7.3, 7.4, 7.6, 12.5, 12.7, 13.5
MP.3	Construct viable arguments and critique the reasoning of others.	Lessonss 1.7, 2.4, 3.5, 6.4, 7.8, 8.3, 13.5, 13.7, 13.8
MP.4	Model with mathematics.	Lessons 1.4, 2.5, 2.8, 5.6, 6.2, 7.6, 12.8, 13.2, 13.3
MP.5	Use appropriate tools strategically.	Lessons 2.8, 3.1, 3.2, 6.4, 7.5, 7.7, 12.3, 12.8, 13.1
MP.6	Attend to precision.	Lessons 1.6, 2.9, 3.7, 7.4, 7.9, 8.1, 13.6, 13.7, 13.8
MP.7	Look for and make use of structure.	Lessons 1.2, 2.7, 3.1, 5.2, 6.5, 8.7, 13.1, 13.4, 13.6
MP.8	Look for and express regularity in repeated reasoning.	Lessons 1.9, 2.7, 3.2, 4.5, 5.2, 6.2, 12.5, 13.1, 13.3
Domain: Ratios and Proportional Relationships		
Understand ratio concepts and use ratio reasoning to solve problems.		
6.RP.1	Understand the concept of a ratio and use ratio language to describe a ratio relationship between two quantities. For example, "The ratio of wings to beaks in the bird house at the zoo was 2:1, because for every 2 wings there was 1 beak." *"For every vote candidate A received, candidate C received nearly three votes."*	Lessons 4.1, 4.2
6.RP.2	Understand the concept of a unit rate *a*/*b* associated with a ratio *a*:*b* with $b \neq 0$, and use rate language in the context of a ratio relationship. For example, *"This recipe has a ratio of 3 cups of flour to 4 cups of sugar, so there is 3/4 cup of flour for each cup of sugar." "We paid $75 for 15 hamburgers, which is a rate of $5 per hamburger."*	Lessons 4.2, 4.6

Standards You Will Learn		Student Edition Lessons
Ratios and Proportional Relationships *(Continued)*		
6.RP.3	Use ratio and rate reasoning to solve real-world and mathematical problems, e.g., by reasoning about tables of equivalent ratios, tape diagrams, double number line diagrams, or equations.	
	a. Make tables of equivalent ratios relating quantities with whole-number measurements, find missing values in the tables, and plot the pairs of values on the coordinate plane. Use tables to compare ratios.	Lessons 4.3, 4.4, 4.5, 4.8
	b. Solve unit rate problems including those involving unit pricing and constant speed. *For example, if it took 7 hours to mow 4 lawns, then at that rate, how many lawns could be mowed in 35 hours? At what rate were lawns being mowed?*	Lessons 4.6, 4.7
	c. Find a percent of a quantity as a rate per 100 (e.g., 30% of a quantity means 30/100 times the quantity); solve problems involving finding the whole, given a part and the percent.	Lessons 5.1, 5.2, 5.3, 5.4, 5.5, 5.6
	d. Use ratio reasoning to convert measurement units; manipulate and transform units appropriately when multiplying or dividing quantities.	Lessons 6.1, 6.2, 6.3, 6.4, 6.5

Standards You Will Learn		Student Edition Lessons
Domain: The Number System		
Apply and extend previous understandings of multiplications and division to divide fractions by fractions.		
6.NS.1	Interpret and compute quotients of fractions, and solve word problems involving division of fractions by fractions, e.g., by using visual fraction models and equations to represent the problem. *For example, create a story context for (2/3) ÷ (3/4) and use a visual fraction model to show the quotient; use the relationship between multiplication and division to explain that (2/3) ÷ (3/4) – 8/9 because 3/4 of 8/9 is 2/3. (In general, (a/b) ÷ (c/d) = ad/bc.) How much chocolate will each person get if 3 people share 1/2 lb of chocolate equally? How many 3/4-cup servings are in 2/3 of a cup of yogurt? How wide is a rectangular strip of land with length 3/4 mi and area 1/2 square mi?*	Lessons 2.5, 2.6, 2.7, 2.8, 2.9, 2.10
Compute fluently with multi-digit numbers and find common factors and multiples.		
6.NS.2	Fluently divide multi-digit numbers using the standard algorithm.	Lesson 1.1
6.NS.3	Fluently add, subtract, multiply, and divide multi-digit decimals using the standard algorithm for each operation.	Lessons 1.6, 1.7, 1.8, 1.9
6.NS.4	Find the greatest common factor of two whole numbers less than or equal to 100 and the least common multiple of two whole numbers less than or equal to 12. Use the distributive property to express a sum of two whole numbers 1–100 with a common factor as a multiple of a sum of two whole numbers with no common factor. *For example, express 36 + 8 as 4 (9 + 2).*	Lessons 1.2, 1.3, 1.4, 1.5, 2.3, 2.4

Standards You Will Learn

	Apply and extend previous understandings of numbers to the system of rational numbers.	Student Edition Lessons
6.NS.5	Understand that positive and negative numbers are used together to describe quantities having opposite directions or values (e.g., temperature above/below zero, elevation above/below sea level, credits/ debits, positive/negative electric charge); use positive and negative numbers to represent quantities in real-world contexts, explaining the meaning of 0 in each situation.	Lesson 3.1
6.NS.6	Understand a rational number as a point on the number line. Extend number line diagrams and coordinate axes familiar from previous grades to represent points on the line and in the plane with negative number coordinates.	
	a. Recognize opposite signs of numbers as indicating locations on opposite sides of 0 on the number line; recognize that the opposite of the opposite of a number is the number itself, e.g., $-(-3) = 3$, and that 0 is its own opposite.	Lessons 3.1, 3.3
	b. Understand signs of numbers in ordered pairs as indicating locations in quadrants of the coordinate plane; recognize that when two ordered pairs differ only by signs, the locations of the points are related by reflections across one or both axes.	Lesson 3.8
	c. Find and position integers and other rational numbers on a horizontal or vertical number line diagram; find and position pairs of integers and other rational numbers on a coordinate plane.	Lessons 2.1, 2.2, 3.3, 3.7

Standards You Will Learn

	Standards You Will Learn	Student Edition Lessons
Apply and extend previous understandings of numbers to the system of rational numbers. *(Continued)*		
6.NS.7	Understand ordering and absolute value of rational numbers.	
	a. Interpret statements of inequality as statements about the relative position of two numbers on a number line diagram. *For example, interpret* $-3 > -7$ *as a statement that* -3 *is located to the right of* -7 *on a number line oriented from left to right.*	Lessons 3.2, 3.4
	b. Write, interpret, and explain statements of order for rational numbers in real-world contexts. *For example, write* $-3°C > -7°C$ *to express the fact that* $-3°C$ *is warmer than* $-7°C$.	Lessons 3.2, 3.4
	c. Understand the absolute value of a rational number as its distance from 0 on the number line; interpret absolute value as magnitude for a positive or negative quantity in a real-world situation. *For example, for an account balance of* -30 *dollars, write* $\|-30\| = 30$ *to describe the size of the debt in dollars.*	Lesson 3.5
	d. Distinguish comparisons of absolute value from statements about *order. For example, recognize that an account balance less than* -30 *dollars represents a debt greater than 30 dollars.*	Lesson 3.6
6.NS.8	Solve real-world and mathematical problems by graphing points in all four quadrants of the coordinate plane. Include use of coordinates and absolute value to find distances between points with the same first coordinate or the same second coordinate.	Lessons 3.9, 3.10

Standards You Will Learn

Standards You Will Learn		Student Edition Lessons
Domain: Expressions and Equations		
Apply and extend previous understandings of arithmetic to algebraic expressions.		
6.EE.1	Write and evaluate numerical expressions involving whole-number exponents.	Lessons 7.1, 7.2
6.EE.2	Write, read, and evaluate expressions in which letters stand for numbers.	
	a. Write expressions that record operations with numbers and with letters standing for numbers. *For example, express the calculation "Subtract y from 5" as 5 − y.*	Lesson 7.3
	b. Identify parts of an expression using mathematical terms (sum, term, product, factor, quotient, coefficient); view one or more parts of an expression as a single entity. *For example, describe the expression 2(8 + 7) as a product of two factors; view (8 + 7) as both a single entity and a sum of two terms.*	Lesson 7.4
	c. Evaluate expressions at specific values of their variables. Include expressions that arise from formulas used in real-world problems. Perform arithmetic operations, including those involving whole-number exponents, in the conventional order when there are no parentheses to specify a particular order (Order of Operations). *For example, use the formulas $V = s^3$ and $A = 6s^2$ to find the volume and surface area of a cube with sides of length s = 1/2.*	Lessons 7.5, 10.1, 10.3, 10.5, 10.6, 10.7, 11.3, 11.4, 11.6
6.EE.3	Apply the properties of operations to generate equivalent expressions. For example, apply the distributive property to the expression $3(2 + x)$ to produce the equivalent expression $6 + 3x$; apply the distributive property to the expression $24x + 18y$ to produce the equivalent expression $6(4x + 3y)$; apply properties of operations to $y + y + y$ to produce the equivalent expression $3y$.	Lessons 7.7, 7.8

Standards You Will Learn		Student Edition Lessons
Apply and extend previous understandings of arithmetic to algebraic expressions. *(Contiuned)*		
6.EE.4	Identify when two expressions are equivalent (i.e., when the two expressions name the same number regardless of which value is substituted into them). For example, the expressions $y + y + y$ and $3y$ are equivalent because they name the same number regardless of which number y stands for.	Lesson 7.9
Reason about and solve one-variable equations and inequalities.		
6.EE.5	Understand solving an equation or inequality as a process of answering a question: which values from a specified set, if any, make the equation or inequality true? Use substitution to determine whether a given number in a specified set makes an equation or inequality true.	Lessons 8.1, 8.8
6.EE.6	Use variables to represent numbers and write expressions when solving a real-world or mathematical problem; understand that a variable can represent an unknown number, or, depending on the purpose at hand, any number in a specified set.	Lesson 7.6
6.EE.7	Solve real-world and mathematical problems by writing and solving equations of the form $x + p = q$ and $px = q$ for cases in which p, q and x are all nonnegative rational numbers.	Lessons 8.2, 8.3, 8.4, 8.5, 8.6, 8.7, 10.1
6.EE.8	Write an inequality of the form $x > c$ or $x < c$ to represent a constraint or condition in a real-world or mathematical problem. Recognize that inequalities of the form $x > c$ or $x < c$ have infinitely many solutions; represent solutions of such inequalities on number line diagrams.	Lessons 8.9, 8.10

Standards You Will Learn		Student Edition Lessons
Represent and analyze quantitative relationships between dependent and independent variables.		
6.EE.9	Use variables to represent two quantities in a real-world problem that change in relationship to one another; write an equation to express one quantity, thought of as the dependent variable, in terms of the other quantity, thought of as the independent variable..Analyze the relationship between the dependent and independent variables using graphs and tables, and relate these to the equation. *For example, in a problem involving motion at constant speed, list and graph ordered pairs of distances and times, and write the equation* $d - 65t$ *to represent the relationship between distance and time.*	Lessons 9.1, 9.2, 9.3, 9.4, 9.5
Domain: Geometry		
Solve real-world and mathematical problems involving area, surface area, and volume.		
6.G.1	Find the area of right triangles, other triangles, special quadrilaterals, and polygons by composing into rectangles or decomposing into triangles and other shapes; apply these techniques in the context of solving real-world and mathematical problems.	Lessons 10.1, 10.2, 10.3, 10.4, 10.5, 10.6, 10.7, 10.8, 11.7
6.G.2	Find the volume of a right rectangular prism with fractional edge lengths by packing it with unit cubes of the appropriate unit fraction edge lengths, and show that the volume is the same as would be found by multiplying the edge lengths of the prism. Apply the formulas $V = lwh$ and $V = bh$ to find volumes of right rectangular prisms with fractional edge lengths in the context of solving real-world and mathematical problems.	Lessons 11.5, 11.6, 11.7

Standards You Will Learn

Standards You Will Learn		Student Edition Lessons
Solve real-world and mathematical problems involving area, surface area, and volume. *(Continued)*		
6.G.3	Draw polygons in the coordinate plane given coordinates for the vertices; use coordinates to find the length of a side joining points with the same first coordinate or the same second coordinate. Apply these techniques in the context of solving real-world and mathematical problems.	Lesson 10.9
6.G.4	Represent three-dimensional figures using nets made up of rectangles and triangles, and use the nets to find the surface area of these figures. Apply these techniques in the context of solving real-world and mathematical problems.	Lessons 11.1, 11.2, 11.3, 11.4, 11.7
Domain: Statistics and Probability		
Develop understanding of statistical variability.		
6.SP.1	Recognize a statistical question as one that anticipates variability in the data related to the question and accounts for it in the answers. *For example, "How old am I?" is not a statistical question, but "How old are the students in my school?" is a statistical question because one anticipates variability in students' ages.*	Lesson 12.1
6.SP.2	Understand that a set of data collected to answer a statistical question has a distribution which can be described by its center, spread, and overall shape.	Lessons 12.6, 13.1, 13.4, 13.6, 13.7, 13.8
6.SP.3	Recognize that a measure of center for a numerical data set summarizes all of its values with a single number, while a measure of variation describes how its values vary with a single number.	Lessons 12.6, 13.4, 13.6

Standards You Will Learn

Student Edition Lessons

Summarize and describe distributions.		
6.SP.4	Display numerical data in plots on a number line, including dot plots, histograms, and box plots.	Lessons 12.3, 12.4, 12.8, 13.2
6.SP.5	Summarize numerical data sets in relation to their context, such as by:	
	a. Reporting the number of observations.	Lesson 12.2
	b. Describing the nature of the attribute under investigation, including how it was measured and its units of measurement.	Lesson 12.2
	c. Giving quantitative measures of center (median and/or mean) and variability (interquartile range and/or mean absolute deviation), as well as describing any overall pattern and any striking deviations from the overall pattern with reference to the context in which the data were gathered.	Lessons 12.5, 12.6, 13.1, 13.3, 13.4
	d. Relating the choice of measures of center and variability to the shape of the data distribution and the context in which the data were gathered.	Lessons 12.7, 13.5

Index

A

D

E

F

G